# STRESS RELIEF

## Through Holistic and Alternative Therapies

**Dr. P.K. Dutta**

M.D., Ph.D., D.Sc., N.D.

**First Edition : 2011**

Himalaya Publishing House

MUMBAI • NEW DELHI • NAGPUR • BENGALURU • HYDERABAD • CHENNAI • PUNE
LUCKNOW • AHMEDABAD • ERNAKULAM • BHUBANESWAR • INDORE • KOLKATA • GUWAHATI

**Edition : 2011**

**Published by** : Mrs. Meena Pandey
for **HIMALAYA PUBLISHING HOUSE PVT. LTD.,**
"Ramdoot", Dr. Bhalerao Marg, Girgaon, **Mumbai - 400 004.**
Phones: 2386 01 70/2386 38 63, Fax: 022-2387 71 78
**Email: himpub@vsnl.com**
**Website: www.himpub.com**

**Branch Offices:**

**New Delhi** : "Pooja Apartments", 4-B, Murari Lal Street, Ansari Road, Darya Ganj, **New Delhi - 110 002.** Phone: 23270392, 23278631 Fax: 011-23256286

**Nagpur** : Kundanlal Chandak Industrial Estate, Ghat Road, **Nagpur - 440 018.** Phone: 2738731, 3296733 Telefax : 0712-2721215

**Bengaluru** : No. 16/1 (Old 12/1), 1st Floor, Next to Hotel Highlands, Madhava Nagar, Race Course Road, **Bengaluru - 560 001.** Phone : 22281541, 22385461, Telefax: 080-22286611

**Hyderabad** : No. 3-4-184, Lingampally, Besides Raghavendra Swamy Matham, Kachiguda, **Hyderabad - 500 027.** Phone: 040-27560041, 27550139, Mobile:- 09848130433 Telefax: 040-27560041

**Chennai** : No. 85/50, Bazullah Road, T. Nagar, **Chennai - 600 017.** Phone: 044-28344020, 32463737, 42124860

**Pune** : No. 527, "Laksha" Apartment, First Floor, Mehunpura, Shaniwarpeth, (Near Prabhat Theatre), **Pune - 411 030.** Phone: 020-24496323/24496333/32326733

**Lucknow** : Jai Baba Bhawan, Near Manas Complex, Church Road, Aliganj, **Lucknow - 226 024.** Phone: 0522-2339329, 9305302158, 9415349385

**Ahmedabad** : No. 114, "SHAIL", 1st Floor, Opp. Madhu Sudan House, C.G.Road, Navrang Pura, **Ahmedabad – 380 009.** Phone: 079-26560126, Mobiles: 09327324149,09314679413

**Ernakulam** : No. 39/104 A, Lakshmi Apartment, Karikkamuri Cross Rd., Ernakulam, **Cochin – 682011**, Kerala. Phone: 0484-2378012, 2378016, Mob.: 09344199799

**Bhubaneswar** : 5 Station Square, **Bhubaneswar (Orissa) - 751 001.** Mobile: 9861046007, E-mail:- orissa@himpub.com

**Indore** : Kesardeep Avenue Extension, 73, Narayan Bagh.Flat No. 302, IIIrd Floor, Near Humpty Dumpty School, Narayan Bagh, **Indore (M.P.) 452 007** Mobile: 09301386468

**Kolkata** : 108/4, Beliaghata, Main Road, Near ID Hospital, Opp. SBI Bank **Kolkata - 700 010.** Mobile: 09910440956, E-mail:- nkmitra@himpub.com

**Guwahati** : House No. 15, Behind Prajjyotish College, Near Sharma Printing Press, P.O. Bharalumukh, Guwahati - 781009 (Assam Mobile: 07439040301; 07439040302

**Printed by** : Shri Krishna offset Press Delhi-93

# Dedication

*This book is dedicated to*

*my Loving wife, Dolly Dutta and my two daughters, Aditi Dutta and Anuradha Dutta, who have helped me to lead a Stress Free life. They were a source of Joy and Happiness – A Gift of God.*

***Prof.(Dr.) P.K.Dutta***

# FOREWORD

The world is becoming a more stressful place for many reasons. It is more complex, and the pace of change seems faster. Increasingly, we find ourselves taking on roles for which we feel unprepared. Developments in technology which were supposed to make our lives better, sometimes, just seem to overwhelm us, or else pass us by completely and leave us feeling lost.

We carry our stress with us for a lifetime. Our bodies have biological systems that respond to life-threatening danger, acting like fear alarm systems that are critical for survival. When faced with a threatening situation, such as being attacked by a tiger, a flood of hormones and chemical messengers is released into our brains and bloodstream almost instantly. These hormones rapidly shift our energy resources away from non-critical tasks, and towards more critical tasks that are required for survival. Energy is shunted to the brain and the muscles to help us think fast and run quick, and away from the stomach and digestive track as well as the reproductive system, since we are not now under a time pressure to eat lunch or reproduce. This stress-responsive activation of biological systems helps us to shift our priorities in use of resources and energy, and to focus the body in a variety of ways on doing whatever it takes to survive. If we later encounter a similar threatening situation, specific fear-related areas in the brain turn on more quickly and activate the fear areas with grater efficiency, because the stress hormones more strongly engrave the circumstances surrounding the life-threatening event in memory, by acting on brain areas that are involved in memory.

The short-term survival response can be at the expense of long-term function. For instance, release of stress hormones can cause thinning of the bones, ulcers and damage to a part of the brain involved in memory. Surprisingly, the same biological systems that help us survive life-threats can also damage the brain and body.

Human life is full of situations. Situation which appears unmanageable is normally referred to as a problem. Problem is not the situation itself but its consequences in your imagination. The negative feeling building up in imagination in high magnitude is understood as fear, is popularly known as worry. Worry which builds up pressure on body and mind is stress. The effect of stress on body is strain and on mind is tension.

When you manage the prevailing situation — the need to mange stress is irrelevant and stress stands eradicated.

In this book, 'STESS RELIFE FOR ALL' — Dr. P. K. Dutta, demonstrates the importance of identifying exactly what stress you have both due to external factors in the environment and factors within yourself. By developing appropriate coping strategies, both at professional and at personal levels, you can maintain your optimal level of stress. Using non-technical language throughout, and with an emphasis upon practical and easily-mastered strategies, Dr. P. K. Dutta takes the reader step-by-step through the things that can be done to enhance stress resistance and to increase professional efficiency.

The approach is unique, as it provides insights into our ancient methods of understanding and handling stress, as well as new methods based on scientific research.

The book is a health guide for managers and executives in industries.

It will also help people from all walks of life.

**Dr. H.N. Gupta**, M.A., Ph.D., DMS.

Professor. Department of Applied Psychology,

Calcutta University, Kolkata.

Dated: 20-1-2010

# PREFACE

We all experience stress on a daily basis. Although stress is caused by many factors, researchers conclude that stress triggers one of the two basic reactions-active fighting or passive flight ( running away or acceptance), the so — called fight — or flight response. Physiologically, this stress response is a biochemical " Passing gear" involving hormonal changes that mobilise the body for extraordinary demands. Imagine how our prehistoric ancestors responded to the stress associated with a charging saber-toothed tiger. To avoid being eaten, they could stand their ground and fight their beast or run away. In either case, their bodies would have been organised by an identical hormonal change, involving the release of adrenaline into the bloodstream.

In today's hectic urbanised and industrialised society, changing beasts have been replaced by problems such as deadlines, role conflict and ambiguity, financial responsibilities, traffic congestion, noise and air pollution, family problems, and work overload. As with our ancestors, our response to stress may or may not trigger negative side-effects, including headaches, ulcers, insomnia, heart attacks, high blood pressure and strokes. The same stress response that helped our prehistoric ancestors survive has, too often, become factors that seriously impair, our daily lives.

Since stress and its consequences are manageable, it is important for managers to learn as much as they can about occupational stress The focus is on some approaches which specialise in helping with stress management directly.

This book is made up of three parts.

**Part I** – Introduction - Stress, Emotion, Brain and Alternative Therapies. Review of Literature

**Part II** – Research - Research Findings.

**Part III** – Western and Eastern Healing Methods.

My presentation is as simple as possible for the common people to make it useful to all readers. In this book, I have written about many Western and Eastern therapies for healing and leading a happy and long life. Finally, I hope by adopting some of the remedial measures, managers will be able to create a stress-free office and the efficiency of the organisation will be elevated and the morale of the employees will be high with better performance.

The students, research scholars and other professionals will be benefited by going through the various chapters of the book and get stress relief.

Any suggestion is welcome which will be incorporated in the next edition of the book for the welfare of the readers.

**Finally**

Remember, that the Stress Management Plan is meant to act as a guide to help you focus on particular aspects of your circumstances that you may not have otherwise considered. We must point out that most of our distress results from our interactions with others and that in this book, we cannot prescribe individual tailor-made solutions. Each of us has to work on our own stress management plan, according to our own individual situation. We wish you success in managing stress by being wise about your stress.

First of all, you must consult a physician or a Doctor before you start the treatment. As they can guide you to a better life and they know which therapy is suitable for you and can solve your specific problems. Wish you all a long and happy life.

**Dr. P.K. Dutta**

Author

**Mailing Address:-askpkd@yahoo.co.in**

Dutta Nivas

House No. 82,

J.C. Chakroborty Road,

P.O. & Vill. Duillya (ANDUL) - 711302

Dist. Howrah (W.B.) India.

# ACKNOWLEDGEMENTS

I express my deep sense of gratitude to Prof. Dr. Sir Anton Jayasurya, Dean of Clinical Studies and Chairman Medicina Alternative, Colombo, Sri Lanka under whose supervision and guidance I could accomplish the research work. But for his care, without scholarly guidance and encouragement, this task would not have become possible. All chapters of this thesis bear the stamp of his scholarly guidance.

I am indebted to Shri S.K. Roy, Peerless Group, Managing Director and Professor Shyamal Banerjee, Chief Executive (Finance) of the Peerless General Finance and Investment Company Ltd. for their encouragement, kind assistance and co-operation extended to me to complete the research work.

I am grateful to Dr. N.S. Adhikari, Secretary, International Foundation of Natural Health and Yoga, New Delhi; Dr. C.P. Bhasin, Consultant and Head, Department of Anaesthesia, Dr. R.M.L. Hospital, New Delhi; Dr. T.S. Jayalakshmi, Additional Professor, Department of Anaesthesiology, All India Institute of Medical Sciences, New Delhi and also to Dr. D. Bakshi, Head of the Department of Acupuncture, Ranjit Memorial Acupuncture College and Hospital, Andul, Howrah, for their guidance and assistance related to the subject of research.

I duly acknowledge the services of the British Council Library and American Library, New Delhi,

I express my sincere thanks to Dr. D. Ray, ex-Scientist, Defence Research and Development Organisation, New Delhi for going through the whole manuscript critically and giving valuable suggestions.

I owe special thanks to my family members, relatives, official colleagues, well-wishers and others who motivated and helped me in completing the research work, as well as writing this book.

Finally, I thank Shri S. Mukherjee for typing the manuscript so nicely and Miss. Rajani Tambe for DTP.

**Prof. Dr. P.K. Dutta. (Gold Medalist)**

**B.Com., B.Mus., M.Com., M.D., Ph.D., D.Sc.**
**FABPP, FCQI-CQP, FFA, FIMM, FRAMI, FRGS, MCIM, MBIM, MHSM, MIAM, AMIEXA, AIHE, ACI**
**NDDY., Dip/Certs. in Industrial & Business Management Studies, (SISI-Govt of India).**
**Registered Marketer (C.I.M.)**
**Incorporated Administrator (I.A.M.)**
**Incorporated Financial Accountant (I.F.A.)**
**Fellow, American Institute of Stress, USA.**
**Life Member Acupuncture Association of India.**
**Life Member Medicina Alternativa Institute (Sri Lanka).**
**Life Member Indian Society for Pain Research Theraphy (India).**
**Life Member Indian Nature Cure Practitioners Association (Delhi).**
**Life Member Indian Research Institute for Integrated Medicine (Cal).**

# CONTENTS

## PART I



## PART II



## PART III

The explosion of knowledge during the Twenty-first Century has made medicine more complex and the medical treatment even more costly. The modern medical systems like Allopathy are more advanced but their theories are quite alien to human nature. Thus, the modern medicine gives instant relief but very often it induces adverse side effects which are even worse that the disease itself. Ayurveda, in ancient times a wonderful and effective balance of medicines, has lost its glory because of modernisation and commercialisation. Homoeopathy, more or less has done the same thing and it tries to silence the symptoms without removing the causes of the disease.

Medicine or drugs neither sustain the human system nor can they cure the body, otherwise nobody would have died in this world. These inorganic matters only suppress the symptoms, give temporary relief but cannot become the part and parcel of the human body. They remain in the body as foreign matters, lower the vitality of the body and in the long run, they inflict unpredictable harm in converting the acute diseases into chronic ones and chronic into fatal diseases. These foreign matters are required to be eliminated from the system involving unnecessary misuse of "Vital Force" and thereby, interfering in the vital functioning of the inherent "Healing Power" of the body. Our efforts should always be to enhance our vital force to fight destructive forces.

Health cannot be purchased by spending money on medicines and drugs. It has made the entire mankind confirmed addicts and wedded to medicine. As we are living in the instant civilisation, we expect instant service, instant results and instant relief. It has made us to think that the medicines and the drugs are easily the best short cut to perfect health, thereby, putting ourselves in deep miseries surrounded by the deadly diseases, anger, frustration, jealousy, selfishness, distress and despair, fear, tension, anguish, lust, greed, torture, etc. At present the modern man is finding himself at the cross-roads, becoming more and more restless, agitated and his miseries are compounding. In utter desperation, he is groping in the dark in search of light, comfort, solace and peace. In fact, he is more and more drifting away from the 'Mother Nature'. The only solution to his present state seems to be 'Return to Nature', adopt Nature and follow the sacred principles of Nature. Only then, we will be able to remain physically, mentally, socially and spiritually healthy.

Surprisingly, disease is our greatest friend and is the warning signal from Nature to indicate the accumulation of toxic and foreign substances within the human body which has resulted due to wrong way of living, faulty food habits, polluted surroundings and impure thinking. Right food is the greatest single factor for the promotion of health and wrong food is the greatest single factor for the promotion of diseases. Good health can be acquired, sustained, restored and conserved by healthy food which plays an active, significant, powerful and decisive role as far as the health is concerned. The perfect health means when a person is physically, mentally, socially and spiritually healthy. World Health Organisation's dream project, "Health For All by 2000 A.D." is possible, especially, in India if Naturopathy is followed truly and religiously since it is a way of life, very simple to follow, much cheaper than the other paths. It is in complete harmony with our culture, heritage and civilisation, complete unification with the pure consciousness – the ultimate objective of human existence.

## HEALTH-RELATED PROBLEMS OF EXECUTIVES

The rise of industrialisation and technology has exerted an enormous impact on our lives, has produced a number of serious risk factors to our health. The application of technology in food production and industry has helped to produce a diet high in animal fat (including cholesterol), processed sugar and salt, and the changes in our home and working environments have meant that we have become a highly sedentary population. These trends, in turn, are associated with an over-reliance on medicine and an unrealistic expectation of its power to heal. The present disease epidemics in the society – coronary heart disease, hypertension, obesity, constipation, backache, cancer, depression and many other problems – are a reflection of our present lifestyles. They will not go away of their own accord. It is no use hoping that someone will produce a magic drug or surgical procedure that will lift this burden. Prevention is the best possible area for our attention from this point onwards.

The Twentieth Century heralded the technological revolution, which was to have even greater social and environmental consequences that the industrial revolution which proceeded it. During the 40 years in particular, we have witnessed a quite staggering increase in scientific and technological expertise, which has left scarcely any part of our lives untouched. Space technology has allowed man to begin the exploration of our solar system and computers have become part and parcel of our everyday life.

## THE "ORGANISATION" AS STRESSOR

Companies and Corporate Organisations are in a constant state of flux, of evolution, and because of this they can be a source of stress. The rate of change which characterises modern corporate life is particularly stressful. Mergers and takeovers, asset stripping and changes in leadership of senior management are going on all around us. We live with the threats, euphemistically talked about, of 'downsizing' (means sacking people), 'decentralising' (means sacking people at head office), 'delayering' (means sacking selected members of management), and cost containment and reducing overheads (which may well amount to more sackings). With virtually all sources of occupational stress, the first step is the simple recognition and clear definition of the source and type of stressors. This is the essential step since each individual and organisations has unique stressors which interact in a unique fashion. For this reason there is no single intervention or solution. Once the sources of stress are identified, a committed individual or organisation can unquestionably rectify many of them in an appropriate manner.

## CONSEQUENCES OF OCCUPATIONAL STRESS

The majority of health impairments which results from stress are not dramatic instances such as heart attack. According to a recent data, the most common symptoms in order of decreasing frequency are:

(1) Anxiety and/or neurosis (25%)

(2) Depression (20%)

(3) Stress-related, psychosomatic disorders (headache, low back pain, hypertension, gastro-intestinal tract) (15%)

(4) Alcohol and other drug abuse (15%)

(5) Situational adjustment problems (e.g. divorce, finances, death in the family).(10%); and

(6) Other disorders (e.g. serve mental and/or physical morbidity or mortality) (15%)

From the organisation point of view, symptoms result in the statistics of absenteeism, reduced productivity and disruption in the workplace.

It would not be possible to make a totally comprehensive list of all the symptoms resulting from stress. Here are some of the common health-related problems of executives/managers from occupational stress.

## Physical Symptoms Include

**Table 1**

| | |
|---|---|
| Allergies | Eczema |
| Alopecia | Fainting |
| Appetite | Gastritis |
| Arthritis | Hay fever |
| Asthma | Headaches |
| Backache | Heart disease |
| Bedwetting | Heart-burn |
| Blood Pressure | Indigestion |
| Colitis | Impotence |
| Constipation | Itching |
| Cough | Menstrual problems |
| Dermatitis | Migraine |
| Diarrhoea | Nausea |
| Digestive problems | Obesity |
| Dizziness | Palpitations |
| Duodenal Ulceration | Tremors |
| | Ulcers |
| | Vomiting |

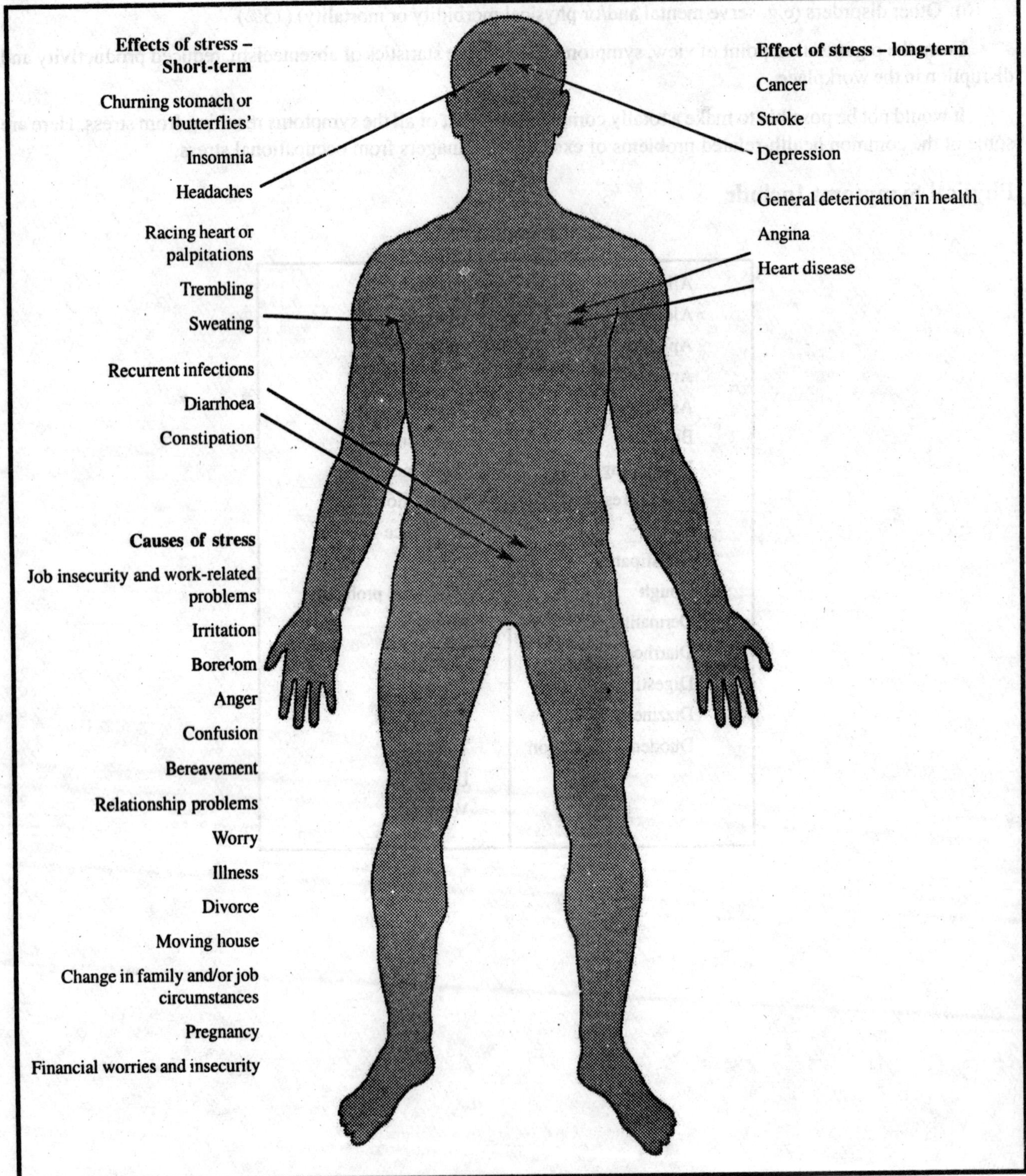


**Fig. 1 : The Causes of stress and its effects**

## Mental Symptoms Include

**Table 2**

| | |
|---|---|
| Duodenal Ulceration | Wheezing |
| Anxiety | Obsessions |
| Crying | Personality disorders |
| Depression | Phobias |
| Fear | Stuttering |
| Hysteria | Tension |
| Insomnia | |
| Irritability | |
| Memory failure | |
| Nervous breakdown | |
| Nightmare | |

## What Stress Really Means?

Stress is an adaptive response, mediated by individual characteristics and/or psychological processes, that is a consequence of any external action, situation or event that places special physical and/or psychological demands upon a person and the non-specific response of the body to any demand made upon it (Selye, 1956).

## Sources of Stress

**Table 3**

| Stressors | Causes |
|---|---|
| Macro/Global | Major socio-economic change, New Government legislations, Political development and trends Environmental threats |
| Organisational/Corporate | Poor communications Changes in technology Mergers, takeovers, Company restructuring Threat of unemployment, Redundancy, Company liquidation, Unrealistic demands, Expectation, Lack of adequate resources/training, Insensitivity to employees, Opinion, Lack of direction and leadership, Lack of managerial support, |

| Stressors | Causes |
|---|---|
| Individual | Poorly-defined goals/<br>Responsibilities<br>Family problems, pressures<br>Financial problems<br>Ageing/Illness/Self-doubts<br>Perceived lack of skills<br>Change of career |

Occupational Stress as a field of inquiry, examining job conditions and their health and performance consequences is a relatively new research domain that crystallised in the early animal research of Hans Selye (1936), discovered a wide variety of noxious stimuli (which he later referred to as stressors) evoked an identical pattern of physiological changes in his laboratory animals. Stressors included exposure to temperature extremes, physical injury and the injection of toxic substances. In each case, the cortex of the adrenal gland became enlarged, the thymus and other lymphatic structures became involuted, and deep bleeding ulcers developed in the stomach and intestines. These effects were 'non-specific' in that they occurred regardless of the nature of the insult and were superimposed on any specific effects associated with the individual agents. Some years later, Selye (1946), described this somatic response as the General Adaptation Syndrome (G A S), and defined stress as the non-specific response of the body to any demand made on it. His mention of 'nervous stimuli' among the stressor agents capable of eliciting the G A S had an energising effect on those working in the field of psychosomatic medicine.

More recently, Richard Lazarus and his colleagues added immensely to the study of stress by describing in specific terms how one's perceptions of objective events determine their health valence (Lazarus and Folkman, 1984). Cognitive appraisal is described by Lazarus as an intrapsychic process translating objective events into stressful experiences. The importance of these formulation lies in its recognition that subjective factors can play a much larger role in the experience of stress than objective conditions. Indeed, any given objective can even at once be perceived positively by one person and negatively by another-one person's meat is another person's poison.

## THE DISTRESS CYCLE

Employees are exposed to many stressors. Those who have coping deficiencies rather than coping skills become distressed. Chronic distress, in turn, leads to social and financial costs – more accidents, injuries, poor productivity and low turnovers. But it does not stop there. These symptoms of distress become, themselves, stressors, and the distress cycle develops.

### Stress Syndrome (Pressure Vs Stress)

Most executives are under pressure. Too much to do – too little time and too few resources to do it with. Up to a point, they can tolerate such pressure, even thrive on it. It keeps them on their toes, gives them a challenge and adds to the zest of their work.

When the pressure becomes too intense and/or goes on too long, their energy gives out. They lose heat. They get anxious and begin to doubt their ability to win through. They start making errors of judgment. The pressure has turned into stress.

Individuals differ in how they react. The point at which pressure becomes stress will vary from one to another. But they all have their breaking point. And once they start experiencing regular stress, they risk losing their effectiveness as managers. They also risk ulcers, high blood pressures, strokes and heart attacks. As we say, death is only Nature's way of telling them to slow down. Best they tell themselves first.

So it is important for managers to recognise the early signs of stress and to learn ways of coping with it. Our primitive ancestors knew just two ways of responding to a threat – fight or flight. Neither of these is very helpful to the more subtle threats that can make life stressful for the modern manager. One's unduly demanding boss cannot be dealt within quite the same way as a charging bull. We need to discuss various ways of dealing with stress – minimising it or, preferably, avoiding it and get rid of health-related problems.

## Factors Leading To The Need of Alternative Treatments/Healings – (Complementary Medicines)

Mental and emotional health is an area where alternative medicine has a tremendous amount to offer. The concept of treating the whole person, which is central to natural therapies, obviously involves the mental aspects of any disorder and these are inseparable from the physical side of health. Indeed, virtually all physical problems are in some way related to the mind. On the other hand, fluctuations in hormone production will lead to problems of mood, for instance, in post-natal depression or pre-menstrual tension. Inadequate absorption of nutrients can affect the nervous system, as can a lack of oxygen through shallow breathing patterns or respiratory disorder.

It is thus not possible or appropriate to separate out mental problems from the rest of the person's health and it is the very holistic nature of alternative medical systems which is their strength in assessing and treating the mind as a part of, or indeed the cause of, illness. There are a number of such approaches, which look at the mind and disturbances in occasionally differing ways, although often with many complementary treatments, for example, manipulative treatments for a back problem may well be supported by counselling for the emotional causes producing the physical discomfort.

Mental and emotional disorders, and physical problems which directly and obviously stem from the mind, are conditions where alternative approaches have often had major benefit – due in part to the importance they attach to looking at the whole person in any illness – and there are accordingly a number of treatments which are available. Therapists may also advise self-help measures, such as relaxation classes, in conjunction with their treatment.

## Coping With Stress

The effects of undue stress, and ways to cope with it when it is excessive or prolonged, are one of the major challenges to health-care today. Alternative medicine is well placed to meet this challenge, with its insistence on treating each person as an unique individual, with all levels of activity from physical to mental being taken into account. Some of the most influential work on stress mechanisms and our capacity to withstand pressures was done some years ago by Selye and others, and a feature that is emphasised by therapists in one way or another is our ability to maintain normal functioning as far as possible through a series of controls and feedback mechanisms – often called the principle of homeostasis. This self-balancing principle should be encouraged by all therapies and will be discussed in this research work that they have a physical, mental or energy-based approach.

In general, the alternative therapies see much of modern lifestyle as creating an unnecessary burden of stress on our system. The recent increased concern with the environment and the interaction between us and the natural world is one that has occupied the therapists' attention for some time. For instance, herbalism is green medicine in more ways than one – and most of the treatments will involve advice on how to adapt our lifestyle to achieve greater harmony and reduction of stress factors.

## An Integrated Approach

India as a Signatory to the Alma Ata Declaration. The Government is trying to provide primary health care to all sections of the society, especially in rural and remote areas by opening chains of hospitals and dispensaries. But to open a new dispensary requires doctors, nurses, other para-medical staff and of course, medicines, laboratory facilities, etc. Hence, tremendous cost is involved and this is more so, as ours is the modern western medicine-oriented system. In fact, even after trying to reach the target, health care in our country is till now, far below the expectation as is evident from the prevalence of different diseases. It is alone cannot help us to reach the target. We have to integrate western medicine with traditional medicines. Because of integration, the cost of the treatment will come down considerably, the treatment itself will be accessible to the rich and poor alike, it will reach the remotest parts of the country and will be based on modern scientific technology. Then the integrated medicine will rapidly spread through primary health centres, dispensaries and hospitals to the whole of the country with the help of the government agencies as well as private organisations.

To judge the feasibility of integration between the western medicine and traditional medicine, we have to analyse the merits and demerits of both the systems in the light of their application to the socio-economically weaker sections of the society as are prevalent in the Third World Countries. Ultimately, we have to integrate the merits of the two systems to get the best and the cheapest.

> World Health Organisation in 1978 observed: "Traditional medicine has intrinsic utility, it should be promoted and its potential developed for their wider use and benefit of mankind. It needs to be given due recognition and developed so as to improve its efficacy, safety, availability and wider application at low cost. It is already the people's own health care system and is well accepted by them."

Thus it is cheap, safe and accessible in the rural and remote areas. Moreover, as this system is an integral part of our culture, it can easily be popularised among the masses. Besides Ayurveda, Indian traditional system also includes Unani, Siddha, Naturopathy and Yoga medicine which are variants of Ayurveda medicine.

Now the question is how to integrate these two systems. This can be accomplished by exchanges of information between the two systems and by extensive research to explore the potentiality of the traditional medicine including Acupuncture with the help of modern technology of the western medicine.

One of the ideal examples of the effort of integration is Acupuncture Anaesthesia (A. A) for surgical operations, which came into practice in 1058 in Shanghai. Anaesthetic drugs are administered quite often intravenously and they are, in general, cardio-respiratory depressants. Drugs and their doses are carefully selected depending upon the state and age of patients. These drugs are dangerous, especially, to the acutely ill patients. Now, if Acupuncture Anaesthesia is applied along with sedatives and analgesic drugs to keep the patient free from anxiety, minimum or no anaesthetic drugs will be required and as a result toxic effects of the Anaesthesia drugs could be avoided. Hence, now we see that the traditional medicine needs intensive research to remove its stagnation and to make it worthy of modern medicine, in fact, initiation on this approach has already been started. It has already been stated that Acupuncture is moving on this direction. Following the research, newer techniques of Acupuncture like Ear Acupuncture, Electro Acupuncture, Micro Wave i.e. Laser Acupuncture and Acupuncture Anaesthesia have enriched the science of Acupuncture. Sincere efforts, is going on to modernise the Ayurvedic medicine.

These techniques can be revived after extensive research and can be incorporated in the Integral Medicine, as these techniques of surgery, which are part of our own culture inherited from ancient times may be cheaper, easier to perform than western technique and available easily to the village folk. Similarly, exponents of Homoeopathic system are also attempting to modernise their science by incorporating western system in their curriculum of teaching the art. Successful integration requires free exchanges of ideas and thoughts between practitioners of these two systems. It will provide the future physicians with increased understandings and superior tools to fight the disease. In fact, if traditional medicine combined with western medicine produces the better results, the patients have every right to demand this type of integrated medicine for their treatments in treating the patients, if physician acquires and applies the knowledge of both the systems, he will be a superior physician to others, trained only in one out of these two systems.

In China, there are efforts in integration between the traditional and western systems in the recent past. Doctors trained in traditional medicine are posted in the hospitals, clinics and Primary Health Care. Similarly, health workers called 'Barefoot doctors' work in rural areas. 'Redmedics' trained in Acupuncture for limited common diseases like common cold, influenza, common skin diseases, neuralgias and sciatica work in urban areas.

Ayurvedic, Homoeopathic or Acupuncture is simple and there is no scope of side effects or iatrogenic effect. When the physician of modern medicine gets acquainted with all these systems or rather atleast one of the traditional systems, he himself, will be the best judge to get the best out of these medicines and thus, the said communication gap due to ignorance will be narrowed down. Traditional medicine with its background of long experience along with cultural heritage and western medicine with its sophisticated technology, will have mutual respect for each other and will have complete understanding to share the responsibility of taking the health care programme to every house.

## Need of The Study

Research on human performance has made considerable progress during the past forty years, reaching a respectable depth of analysis in several areas while, at the same time becoming broader in scope. As a result, there have emerged a number of theoretical ideas which impinge on the general development of experimental psychology and, moreover, a great deal of knowledge has been obtained in ways which encourage direct, practical application. The series of studies in Human performance will be presented in our research work and is intended to explain these ideas and their applications in adequate detail.

## Coping With Stress

For the last twenty years or so, we have seen the emergence of stress as a central concept in psychological thinking. From being a topic which was originally conceived in relation to disease and illness, through a period of being considered only of relevance to the problems of industrial and military operations, stress has now become the most generally accepted term for those aspects of behaviour which relate to bodily states, environmental changes, and the like. There is even a marked tendency to use the term stress to cover all types of motivational state, at least within the context of human behaviour; this usage of stress often coincides with the use of the concepts of arousal and activation. There have been many attempts to clarify terminology in this area. Should stress be reserved for marked departures from some typical state or set of body parameters, on the one hand, or environmental conditions on the other. Alternatively, we could consider all environmental and bodily changes to result in a graded form of the stress response. Again, if there are clear cut criteria for the physiological and biochemical concomitants of stress, or these are only typical for certain kinds of state, particularly extreme ones. We shall discuss them in the next chapter.

## Stress And Anxiety

"Stress" according to Hans Selye (1956), a foremost researcher in this area, is 'the non-specific response of body to any demand'. You want your brain and body to respond in ways that help you meet the demands made by disease or by even such as a final exam, or an important job interview. Stress, in other words, is not always bad; it is an important part of everyone's life. Challenges and changes, which often engender stress, provide the opportunities for adaptation to new life circumstances.

The aim of this research is to inspire people to practice alternative medicines and to raise themselves out of their unhealthy conditions which seems to surround them like an impenetrable and inescapable wall. Our aim is to inform people that a way out exists. It is this very information which is so important, for it carries energy and becomes the idea in the mind which, when put into practice, becomes the vehicle for the cessation of their suffering. It is also intended as a guide to doctors and therapists seeking new alternatives and indicates to them the broad range of other practices applicable for conditions which have, until now, non-proven amenable to conventional medical therapies.

The impact of science and technology in the home and working environment has been as great as that in medicine and agriculture. Since the turn of this Century, we have witnessed the transformation of a physically active and essentially rural society into a population of town and city dwellers whose lifestyles have changed dramatically from that of their forefathers. Modern technology has now made it possible for us to live comfortably with the absolute minimum of physical efforts. The development of the motor car is the most obvious example of such change, but there are countless other areas in which technology has left its mark.

There is substantial evidence to suggest that exercises, music therapies, massages, etc., can make a major contribution to health. We believe there are other methods/therapies which have a major part to play in disease prevention and in health enhancement. That is not to say that it is the panacea for all our health problems, but we could not do better than make it a foundation for future action. We shall discuss various methods to deal with the occupational health problems of executives/managers.

Since the mid-seventies, a growing number of studies have evaluated the merits of prescriptive, relaxation-based stress control methods applied in work settings. Collectively labelled stress management methods such as muscle relaxation meditation, biofeedback, and cognitive strategies have been taught to workers as a means of reducing psycho-physiological and subjective distress. Such strategies have focused exclusively on providing individual workers with skills for recognising and coping with stress in a health promotion context. Accordingly, stress management is usually offered to healthy, symptomatic workers as a preventive measure. Workers exhibiting acute stress reactions or organisations where apparent stress problems exist have not been the usual targets for stress management.

The purpose of this research is to summarise evidence and to review conceptual and practical issues relating to common health problems of executive and worksite stress management. Our study will address current issues and problems in the field. The chapters will discuss stress management programmes which could be developed, implemented, evaluated and maintained in work settings. As such, our works seek to offer guidance and assistance to cope up with stress and common health problems of executives in their daily life.

In view of the aspects discussed above, an effort will be made to study the problems, developments related to health care management of executives/professionals, especially stress management. The research work will provide support to social/medical welfare issues in the field of stress management, common health problems of the working executives/professionals. The result will be of immense help to all; the results can be used by various medical institutions, universities and social organisations connected with health care management in India and abroad.

## Specific Objectives

1. To trace and document the historical development concerning health problems of executives with emphasis on stress management.
2. To study and review the various research findings in India and abroad on alternative/complementary medicines available for coping up with health problems of professionals and counteracting occupational stress.
3. To analyse the executives/patients opinion regarding their health problems specially stress management.
4. To analyse the various methods applied by different health professionals in coping up with health problems of executives/managers concerning stress management.

To draw an action plan for coping with stress for working executives.

**Stressful conditions**

## STRESS AND STRAIN SYNDROME

Stress has been with us since the beginning of time. Part of our response to any challenge or stimulus, it has proved a positive force, aiding our continued survival and providing a dynamic that distinguishes between the active 'business' of living and mere passive 'existence'. Shaping our lifestyle, setting the tempo, and determining the rhythm at which we live, stress can generate the impetus necessary to convert thought into action, whether that action is making love, conducting an orchestra, running a race, escaping from fire or flood, or meeting a deadline.

But today life's challenge are far more complex than they used to be, while life itself is altogether a harsher, less natural process than it used to be. Living in an age of immense and increasingly rapid change, we are subjected to greater, more insistent and inescapable pressure to adapt, keep up, and compete – in short to survive – than at any other time. Achieving the right balance between too much and too little stress has become an integral challenge of life in the 1980s. This is a particular problem for people who find themselves living a highly pressurised jobs, and top-level managers and directors. They usually find that the benefits of this type of existence are inseparable from its drawbacks. In fact, some stress researchers suspect that many of us are becoming addicted to our own increased levels of stress hormones, depending on constant challenge as a self-prescribed antidote to the intolerable prospect of boredom.

The human cost is severe. In America, the estimated annual cost to industry of combined absence from work, health charges, increased insurance, and diminished productivity, is thought to run close to $75 billion. The cost of stress-related coronary heart disease alone is about $30 billion. In Britain, at least 40 million working days are lost each year due to the effects of stress, and it is estimated that stress-related illness costs the medical and social services an average of Pound 55 million per year, accounting for a loss of 2-3 per cent in the gross national product. The term "stress burnout" is clearly no longer a meaningless cliché. It has become an established medical entity.

But stress is not only a problem for people living in the fast track. Those who suffer excessive monotony, boredom, or frustration because of insufficient stimulus or challenge also become ill frequently. This can be through lack of arousal or as a result of the anger or anxiety they feel at having little control over how they live and work. The boredom, envy, and loss of self-esteem that result from unemployment are also common sources of stress today.

So, for most of us it is difficult to find the perfect balance between too much challenge and too little. Coping is made all the more difficult because we are often unconscious of the stress we are suffering. We have become adept at sublimating the effects of stress through motives such as ambition, perfectionism, and dedication to work. Yet the effects of "marked stress" are all the more pervasive for being hard to identify.

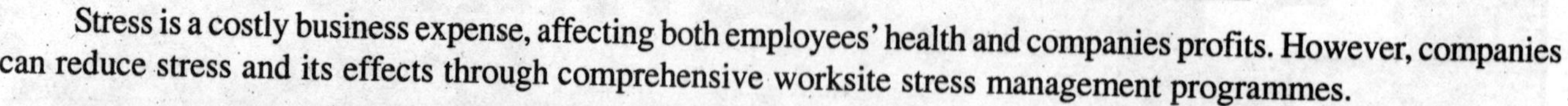

## COST OF OCCUPATIONAL STRESS

Stress is a costly business expense, affecting both employees' health and companies profits. However, companies can reduce stress and its effects through comprehensive worksite stress management programmes.

Consider these stress facts gleaned from various safety and insurance industry research (Jones, 1985):

- In 1982, the total cost of work-related accidents in the United States alone was $32 billion.
- The cause of 75 to 85 per cent of all industrial accidents are accident susceptibility factors (e.g., fatigue, poor concentration, inattentiveness).
- Psychological or psychosomatic problems contribute to over 60 per cent of long term employee disability cases.
- About 11 per cent of all occupational disease claims are for workplace stress (Jones and Dubois, 1989).

### Stress – Definition

It may be defined as follows:

An adaptive response, mediated by individual characteristics and/or psychological processes, that is a consequence of any external action, situation or event that places special physical and/or psychological demands upon a person.

## CONCEPT – PSYCHODYNAMIC APPROACH

Hans Selye's General Adaptation Syndrome (G A S), has been widely held as a comprehensive model to explain the stress phenomenon. This three-stage model states that when an organism is confronted with a threat, the general physiological response occurs in three stages.

Selye gave the name 'Alarm reaction' as it represented the bodily expression of a generalised call to arms of the defensive forces in the organism. The next phase he called the 'Stage of Resistance' as in this, the animal adapted itself to the stress producing environments. The last phase, he called the 'Stage of Exhaustion' as in this, the animal showed signs of premature wear and tear.

The entire syndrome, including its pattern of development in time, was called the General Adaptation Syndrome. Alarm Reaction is the body's response when it is suddenly exposed to stimuli to which it is not adapted. This reaction has two phases:

### Shock Phase

It is the initial and immediate reaction to the noxious stimulus. Various signs of injury such as rapid pulse rate, decreased temperature, lower blood pressure and loss of muscle tone, are typical symptoms.

### Counter Phase

This is a rebound reaction marked by the mobilisation of defensive forces of the body, during which the adrenal cortex is enlarged.

The State of Resistance is when the person's full adaptation to the stress and the consequent improvement or disappearance of the symptoms occur. At this stage, however, there is a concurrent decrease in resistance to fresh noxious stimuli and stress.

The State of Exhaustion sets in if the stress is sufficiently severe and prolonged because body's adaptability to stress is limited and exhaustion inexorably follows. Various symptoms or diseases appear and if stress is unabated, death follows.

Selye's researches showed that stress or tension, particularly if it is prolonged, is very harmful to the body.

## Indian Concept

The concept of stress in the modern sense is not easily found in the traditional texts of Indian culture and tradition such as Charak Samhita , Patanjali's Yogasutras and Bhagwad Gita. However, a number of concepts developed by Indian scholars relate to or appear similar to the phenomenon of stress. Some of these, for example, are dukha (pain, misery or suffering), Klesa (afflictions), kama or trisna (desires), atman and ahamkara (self and ego), adhi (mental aberrations) and prajnaparadha (failure or lapse of consciousness). It is interesting to note that the body-mind, relationship, characteristic of modern stress studies, is emphasised in the Ayurvedic (Indian) systems of medicine.

Palsane, Bhavsar, Goswami and Evans (1986), have discussed this issue in detail. They noted that the Indian tradition is characterised by a holistic approach to human phenomena. Behaviour is interpreted in terms of the totality of an individual's life styles and total body-mind relationship. This synthetic/electric approach can be contrasted with the predominantly annalistic approach of the western social sciences that describe behavioural phenomena according to their constituent parts. The mind-body level of self, atman or soul, which in turn is equaled with Brahman – the ultimate reality. The authors have further observed that modern psychological literature focusing on ideas related to the strength of motives and frustration and their behavioural consequences, the frustration-aggression hypothesis, ego involvement, mind-body interactions (psychosomatics) and locus of control have their parallels in ancient Indian thought.

## Role of Stress

Present-day researchers and practioners raise the phenomenon of stress in a new perspective. Each individuals needs a moderate amount of stress to be alert and capable of functioning effectively in an organisation. Indian scholars like Pestonjee (1987a) and Mathew (1995), in their conceptual papers agreed with this contention. Mathew has gone to the extent of advocating that particular types of stresses are essential for being a creative manager. However, no empirical work has been done on these lines. An exception is Pestonjee and Singh's (1987) study. While studying stresses and job satisfaction, in the case of managers and system analysts in private organisations scored higher on both stress and satisfaction as compared to their counterparts in public organisations. They explained their findings in the light of the characteristics of private organisations which generate greater stress and, in turn, lead to higher job satisfaction.

Mathew further raised queries pertaining to the relationship between creativity and stressors. He noted that such queries are relevant for two reasons: first, creativity and innovation in organisations have become a top priority for organisational practitioners. Therefore, a creative manager can be better equipped to cope with particular stressors which are identified as associated with creative activities. Second, creativity involves performance of unconventional tasks in the organisational setting by individuals. On the other hand, interaction among various subsystems of organisations such as person, task, role, behaviour setting, physical and social environments are seen as causal factors of stress. It is likely therefore that some kinds of stresses are associated with creative work. Pestonjee (1992), reviewed the concept and theory of job stress and examined the stress potential with reference to the creative owner/non-owner managers occupying creative/non-creative roles in creative/non-creative organisations.

# STRESS AND PERSONALITY

Psychologists have identified two broad personality types, one of which is more prone to stress than the other. "Type A" is the notorious stress-prone personality whose typical behaviour and lifestyle constantly elicit physical arousal. Type A's are impatient, ambitious, competitive, aggressive, and hard-working; they set high goals and demands of themselves and others; and they are particularly prone to stress including anticipatory emotions such as anxiety. "Type B's", on the other hand, have a reverse profile. They are equable, calm, relaxed, not overtly ambitious and less at risk from stress and heart disease. Few of us possess all the characteristics of either type. In general our personality is made up of a preponderance of one or other patterns of behaviour, or, in rare cases, a perfect balance of both.

## OCCUPATIONAL STRESS

Investigations have also been conducted as regards various occupations and the stress level which they generate.

Some of the professions or occupations that generate a high to moderate degree of mental tension include that of the executive (business, managerial), sales-manager, salesman, accountant. Under the condition of worry, over-work fatigue, some people pull on for some time, and then they break down with different diseases either singly or in combination. Some get high blood-pressure, others hardening of the blood vessels and coronary heart disease, other still, rheumatoid arthritis (Jaggi, 1974).

Table 4 below give various environmental factors which give rise to stress.

**Table 4: Environmental Factors and Stress***

| *Factor or Condition* | *Stress Response* |
|---|---|
| Diet | Poor diet means poor resistance to stressors. |
| Drugs | Alcoholism means impaired response. |
| Occupation | Accountants get high blood pressure during tax time, business executives are prone to ulcers. |
| Location | City living is more stressful. |
| Family situation | Single people have higher incidence of stress-related diseases and disorders. |
| Social situation | Socially isolated persons are more prone to diseases and tend to die prematurely. |
| Religious affiliation | Deeply religious persons seem to manage severe stresses well. |
| Emotional stability | Stable people react well to stress. |
| Ability to relax | Negative effects of stress may be overcome by those who can relax. |

* Morse and Furst (1979)

Occupational Stress, by definition, is the adverse emotional and physical reactions employees have to any source of pressure in their environment.

These stress reactions negatively affect personal health and organisational effectiveness and often create losses (Table 5). Employees continually confront various pressures or stressors. They experience stress if unable to effectively cope with such stressors as poor management, lack of job security, work overload, unclear communications, excessive deadline pressure, unrealistic expectations, insufficient pay, and uncertainty about job duties and responsibilities.

**Table 5: Personal and Organisational Effects of Occupational Stress**

| PERSONAL | |
|---|---|
| Alcohol abuse | Anxiety |
| Drug abuse | Psychosomatic diseases |
| Emotional instability | Eating disorders |
| Lack of self-control | Boredom |
| Fatigue | Mental illness |
| Marital problems | Suicide |
| Depression | Health breakdowns |
| Insomnia | (Cardiovascular) |

| | |
|---|---|
| Insecurity | Irresponsibility |
| Frustration | Violence |
| **ORGANISATIONAL** | |
| Accidents | Inflated health-care costs |
| Thefts | Unpreparedness |
| Reduced productivity | Lack of creativity |
| High turnover | Increased sick leave |
| Increased errors | Premature retirement |
| Absenteeism | Organisational breakdown |
| Disability payments | Disloyalty |
| Sabotage | Job dissatisfaction |
| Damage and waste | Poor decisions |
| Replacement costs | Antagonistic group action |

## CONSEQUENCES OF STRESS

We need to consider the symptoms and signs in terms of acute and chronic effects. The acute 'fight and flight' reaction was mentioned earlier. Symptoms include sweating, rapid heart rate, dilated pupils and increased blood pressue. For short periods high level of stress may be associated with increased productivity, greater personal achievement and even a sense of exhilaration. However, if the stress continues for long periods, productivity and efficiency begin to fall off rapidly and signs and symptoms of overload may begin to appear. Symptoms vary greatly, and occur in different combinations in different people. The more important are as follows:

1. Tiredness and lethargy commonly associated with changes in sleeping patterns, particularly early morning wakening and difficulty in getting off to sleep.
2. Loss of interest, apathy, boredom and depression.
3. A feeling of anxiety, tension and fear.
4. Physical symptoms: sweating, palpitations, indigestion, disturbed bowel function, breathlessness and headaches.
5. Rapid and unexplained mood changes, with aggressiveness and outbursts.
6. Poor concentration and memory,
7. Reduced sex drive,
8. Indecision,
9. Increased alcohol, cigarette or drug consumption.

As often as not, an individual will deny any such symptoms exist even when the signs of undue stress are glaringly obvious to family, friends and colleagues. These signs may include the following:

Reduced performance

Increased absenteeism

Excess irritability and rapid mood changes

Emotional instability

Indecisiveness

A look of extreme fatigue, nervousness and/or depression.

## Long-term Consequences

In the long-term, the individual who suffers chronic, unremitting stress, may be placing himself at risk of serious disease or even death. In recent years, there has been increasing recognition of the relationship between stress and a variety of diseases. Experimental evidence suggests that under prolonged stress the body's ability to fend off diseases may be seriously impaired because its immune system is damaged. Part of this evidence is the discovery that the immune function of widowers is depressed for a year after the death of their wives. Most of us notice that we are more prone to get cold sores and other minor infections during periods of increased stress.

# STRESS AND DISEASES

Stress can disrupt the normal working of the body in two ways: (1) by being beyond our power of adaptability, or (2) by causing disease because there is a particular weakness in the structure of our body. Think of a chain placed under tension – that is, physical stress. No matter what pulls on the chain and no matter in which direction, the result is the same. Just as in the chain the weakest link is most likely to break down, so in the human body there is always one organ or system, which owing to heredity or external influences, is the weakest and most likely to break down under general biological stress. In some people the heart, in others, the nervous system or the gastro-intestinal tract, may represent this weakest link. That is why people develop different types of diseases under the influence of the same kind of stress. This is also why, strictly sneaking, the pure stage of exhaustion is never reached. Before all adaptation energy is depleted, the weakest link breaks down, causing an immediate general collapse.

True physiologic ageing is not determined by the time elapsed since birth, but by the total amount of wear and tear to which the body has been exposed. There is indeed a great difference between physiologic and chronologic age. One man may be much more senile in body and mind at forty than other person at sixty.

Accordingly to Hans Selye: "Many people believe that, after they have exposed themselves to very stressful activities, a rest can restore them to where they were before. This is false. Experiments on animals have clearly shown that each exposure leaves an indelible scar, in that it used up reserves of adaptability which cannot be replaced. It is true that immediately after some harassing experience, rest can restore us almost to the original level of fitness by eliminating acute fatigue. But the emphasis is on the word almost. Since we constantly go through periods of stress and rest during life, just a little deficit of adaptation energy every day adds up – it adds up to what we call ageing."

## Stress And Health

In USA, the study of occupational stress (as opposed to other sources of stress) was given tremendous impetus by the establishment of the National Institute for Occupational Safety and Health (NIOSH) by Public Law 91-596, the Occupational Safety and Health Act of 1970 (OSH Act). The stated goal of this agency is to assure safe and healthful working conditions for America's working men and women. NIOSH is the principal U.S. Government agency engaged in research to recognise the control job-related hazards. That behavioural and motivational factors had an important bearing on the attainment of this objective was clearly acknowledged in certain research provisions of OSH Act (1970). For example, sections 20(a)(1) and 20(a)(4) explicitly directed NIOSH to include psychological, behavioural and motivational factors in researching problems of workers' safety and heath, and in developing remedial approaches for offsetting such problems. Job conditions were broadly interpreted to include those of a psychological nature, consisting of undue task demands and work conditions or work regimens which apart from, or combined with, exposures to physical and chemical hazards may degrade workers' physical or mental health (Cohen and Margolis, 1973). Since its conducted a large number of research studies that have helped to shape the course of job stress research in the United States.

Over the past 12 years, a paradigm of stress was developed by research psychologists at NIOSH to guide efforts to examine the relationship between working conditions and health consequences (Fig. 6).

This model builds on frameworks proposed by Caplan, Cobb, French, Harrison, and Pinneau (1975), Cooper and Marshall (1976), and House (1974). In it, job stress is viewed as a situation in which some working condition (called a stressor) or combination of conditions interacts with the worker and results in an acute disruption of psychological or behavioural homeostasis. These acute reactions or disruptions, if prolonged, are thought to lead to a variety of illness. As shown in Fig. 6, the most commonly researched of these job stress-related illness have been hypertension, coronary heart disease, alcoholism and mental illness.

**Table 6: Model Of Job Stress And Health**

**JOB STRESSORS**

**Job/Track demand**
- work load
- control

**Organisatoinal Factors**
- Role demands
- Management styles
- Career/ Security Issues
- Interpersonal relations

**Physical Conditions**
- Noise
- Heat/Cold

**INDIVIDUAL FACTORS**

Personality Traits
Stage of Career Development

**ACUTE REACTORS**

Psychological affect Job dissatisfaction
PHYSIOLOGICAL
Heart Rate
Blood Pressure
BEHAVIOURAL
Sleep problems
Substance use/abuse

**ILLNESS**

Hypertension CHD
Alcoholism Mental Illness

**NON-WORK FACTORS**

Financial Status
Family Situation

**BUFFER FACTORS**

Social support
Coping

## STRESS AND CANCER

While a great deal of research has been undertaken linking stress with heart disease (Cooper, 1984), particularly emphasising the importance of psychosocial factors, similar research work in the field of cancer is only just beginning. As in various fields in the medical sciences, the first research work linking stress and cancer took place in the laboratory, in animal research. Sophisticated controlled research in animals has indicated some link between stress and the formation and development of carcinoma.

More recent research on humans indicates that various life events, personality predispositions, immunological and central nervous system interactions, etc., may trigger the cancer process, or at the very latest, accelerate its development.

### Stress – Body/Mind

During the last decade the subtle internal processes by which stressful events can affect health have been mapped with increasing precision. There are extraordinary breakthroughs taking place in understanding stress affects individual health. This fascinating field has been called psychoneuroendocrine influences by Vernon Riley of the Pacific Northwest Research Foundation in Seattle and Psychoneuroimmunology by Robert Ader of the University of Rochester School of Medicine. It is not the purpose of this chapter to explore this research except to note that it is providing clear links between mind (psycho), the brain and nervous system (neuro), and the body's ability to defend against infection and tumours (immunology).

These studies clearly indicate that minor stress, major life-events, disruptions in social support systems, and difficulties at work can dramatically affect the body's system of defenses so that a person becomes more susceptible to a number of conditions. The particular disorder is influenced by many other factors including genetics, smoking, viruses, and environmental pollution, but unrelenting, inescapable Type 2 stress appears to be the most frequent precipitating cause. Among the discoveries to date is research by psychiatrist, George Solomon at the University of California School of Medicine in San Francisco, which found that "baby rats handled during the first weeks of life had a more vigorous immunological response (that is, they made more antibodies) as adults than their uncuddled cohorts." Throughout life, social supports, as scientists refer to friends and family, provide strong preventive and therapeutic aids. A recent Johns Hopkins study found that widowed men who remarried lived longer than those who did not. In a study of pregnant women undergoing numerous life stresses, 90 per cent of those who faced these changes and developed complications before or during delivery, as compared with 33 per cent of those who had "good social support" (Hales, 1981). Other studies have noted links between 'sudden death' and events which were overwhelmingly negative or positive. On a positive note, it is becoming increasingly clear that laughter and humour may indeed be the best medicines. From the writings of Norman Cousins to the research of Harvard psychiatrist George Vaillant, it is evident that healthier individuals rely upon humour and stable, enduring relationships at home and in their work to maintain and enhance health. All this research underscores the importance of the psychological climate in the workplace.

Central to the study of psychological health in the workplace is a worker's relative sense of empowerment versus helplessness. In contrast to conditions left over from the Industrial Revolution, a new work ethic is developing which seeks a sense of power, efficacy, freedom, and resptonsibility. The effects of this upon an individual's health are beginning to be understood. In his excellent book 'Helplessness', psychologist, Martin E. Seligman (1975) at the University of Pennsylvania documented the extraordinarily debilitating effects of helplessness and the equally potent, positive effects of choice and responsibility. Although most of this research has been based upon animal studies, the physical effects of "inescapable stress" have been clearly demonstrated to include: "Severe deficits learning to escape from other aversive stimuli, become submissive in competition for food, fail to escape from frustrating situations, and show less aggression when subjected to additional shock. Physiologically, inescapable shock leads to catecholamine depletion in the central nervous system, activation of the hypothalamic-pituitary-adrenal axis, weight loss, and gastric ulceration. Finally, uncontrollable aversive events increase psychological distress in humans" (Visintainer, Volpicelli and Seligman, 1982). Most recently, Seligman and his colleagues have demonstrated explicit links in the immune system, between inescapable stress and whether or not laboratory animals reject or succumb to cancer. Their research, and that of many others, indicates that uncontrollable stress does suppress or diminish the normal activity of the immune system and increases susceptibility to cancer. Summarising their experiments, the researchers concluded, "inescapable shock decreased tumour rejection (i.e., tumour rejection decreased by experience of inescapable shock) was not a function of shock perse but resulted from the animals' lack of control over shock. The psychological experience somehow interfered with the ability of the organism to resist tumour development..... This demonstrates that a psychological variable can decrease an animal's ability to reject a tumour" (Visintainer, Volpicelli and Seligman, 1982).

There is a growing body of evidence beginning to link these findings from animal research conducted by Stephen E. Locke (1982) of Harvard Medical School. Many of the links are not yet clear; it is certain that helplessness on the negative side versus a sense of individual efficacy or empowerment on the positive side is a major determinant in swinging the balance between health and illness, life and death. Psycho-neuroimmunology constitutes a major breakthrough area in the research of the 1980s. Results of these studies will be of particular pertinence to the work environment and health promotion programmes since the workplace tends to foster powerlessness and helplessness. In fact, there already appears to be enough evidence to advocate that an essential, underlying goal of any health promotion programme should be to enhance an individual's sense of efficacy, involvement, and influence (Pelletier, 1984).

## Stress And Emotion

The chemical and physical changes that are produced in the body as a result of emotionist that are brought about by the brain, through: (1) the autonomic nervous system, and (2) the endocrine glands.

## Autonomic Nervous System

The autonomic nervous system, also known as the involuntary nervous system, is outside the control of the will. It regulates the activities of the heart, blood vessels, glands and smooth muscle movements throughout the body. Normally, we are not aware that the heart is beating or that there are contractions in the intestinal tract. The autonomic nervous system is connected with the central nervous system by various pathways.

The centre in the brain of the autonomic nervous system is the thalamus, which is also the centre for the stimulation of the pituitary gland.

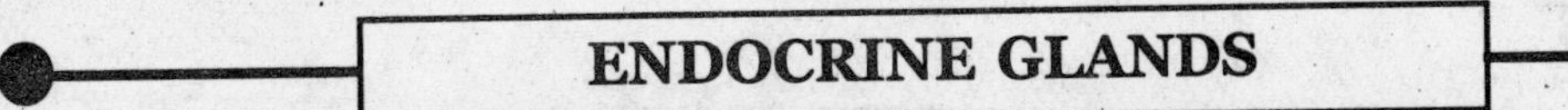

# ENDOCRINE GLANDS

The endocrine or ductless glands (they have no ducts) secrete hormines directly into the blood stream, and control a variety of body mechanisms. There are other glands like the salivary, which are not ductless glands as they secrete saliva which is transported through a duct during mastication of food. The endocrine glands in the body are: (1) Anterior and posterior pituitary, (2) Adrenal, (3) Islets of Langerhans in the pancreas, (4) Ovary and testes, (5) Thyroid, and (6) Parathyroid.

## The Pituitary And Adrenals

The pituitary-adrenal axis is responsible for the non-specific response of the body during stress, including the emotional manifestations. The pituitary is a tiny gland, about the size of a large pea, situated at the base of the brain and located inside the skull. The pituitary is the most important gland in our body and is rightly termed the leader of the "endocrine orchestra". It is the master regulator of our entire body. The pituitary factory is on the job, day and night, working swiftly and efficiently, producing hormones or chemical messengers which are necessary for the welfare of the body. The pituitary is also the key-armaments factory of our body, and, whenever there is any external or internal threat, it goes into action immediately, sending out the armaments (hormones) necessary to mobilise the body defences against the invader (various stressors). The two important hormones produced by the pituitary are somatotrophic hormone (STH) and adrenocorti-cotrophic hormone (ACTH).

**STH:** STH acts directly on the body but it also stimulates the adrenal glands, which are situated above the kidney to produce DOCA (desoxycorticosterone), which is similar in action to STH. STH mobilises the body's defences against an infection. It was formerly believed that the general non-specific signs of an infection, such as fever, headache and bodyaches, malaise, loss of appetite and "feeling ill", were due to bacterial toxins or virus infections. Dr. Selye has conclusively proved that STH is responsible for this syndrome of being sick; whether it is typhoid or infectious hepatitis or pneumonia, STH mobilises the body defences to fight the infection, though it produces the symptoms of being sick, depending upon the severity of the infection. But for STH, an individual would succumb at the slightest infection. STH is also liberated by constant depressing thoughts which will be described later.

**ACTH:** The ACTH (adrenocorticotrophic hormone) produces its effects on the body by stimulating the adrenal gland to produce cortisone. Cortisone is like an asbestos sheet which protects an individual against a fire, without extinguishing it.

ATCH opposes and neutralises the action of STH. ACTH or cortisone reverses the picture of an ill patient, dramatically. In a patient with high fever, malaise or body-aches, the temperature drops, the pains disappear and the patient who was seriously ill and depressed, is cheerful, comfortable and relaxed. But also, the infection, deprived of STH sustence, spreeds like a wild fire and the patient ultimately succumbs. ACTH has therefore to be very judiciously used in cases of infections. In STH stress disease not as a result of infection, ACTH is a great boon and very useful in its treatment.

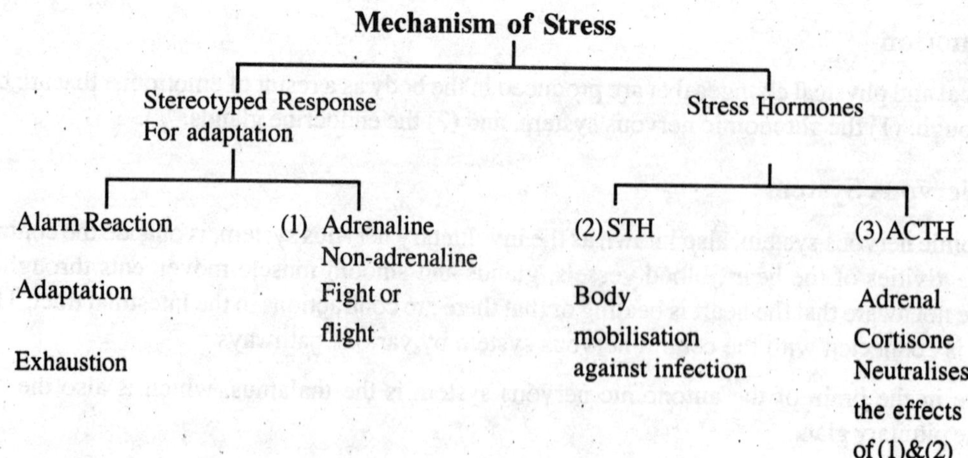


## Emotions And ACTH

Prolonged unpleasant aggressive emotions produce ACTH stress disease.

## Type of Emotions

By and large, all emotions can be classified into two groups. The first group of emotions produce the optimal stimulation of the endocrine glands. The individual feels fit and fine. The pleasant emotions are live, tenderness, hope, joy, courage and equanimity. The other large group which produces over stimulation of the endocrine glands are called the unpleasant emotions. They are anger, rage, hatred, frustration, failure and aggressiveness.

## Illness Produced By Unpleasant Emotions

We have stated earlier that infections as well as prolonged, unhealthy emotions trigger STH stress disorders. In the early stages, the individual feels tired, lethargic and has muscular aches and pains all over the body. If the STH stress is prolonged, numerous STH disorders become manifested. Bronchial asthma, rheumatoid arthritis and high blood pressure are common examples.

## ACTH Stress Disorders

ACTH stress disorders are commonly seen in persons with aggressive, unpleasant emotions. They step on the gas constantly: they are subconsciously hostile to other fellow human beings. Duodenal ulcers and heart attacks are frequently found in these disorders.

These individuals closely resemble the Type A personality. They are time-conscious, easily upset or hurt, always struggling to do or achieve something, without a definite goal in sight.

# CONTROLLING STRESS THROUGH COMPLEMENTARY MEDICINE

Mental and emotional health is an area where complementary medicine has a tremendous amount to offer. The concept of treating the whole person, which is central to natural therapies, obviously involves the mental aspects of any disorder and these are inseparable from the physical side of health. Indeed, virtually all physical problems are in some way related to the mind. On the other hand, fluctuations in hormone production will lead to problems of mood, for instance in post- Mental and emotional disorders, and physical problems which directly and obviously stem from the mind, are conditions where alternative approaches have often had major benefit – due in part to the importance they attach to looking at the whole person in any illness and accordingly there are a number of treatments which are available. Therapists may also advise self-help measures, such as relaxation classes, in conjunction with their treatment (Toon, Tripp and Evans, 1991).

Medical practitioners of any persuasion, whether they are working in conventional or complementary fields, acknowledge that cardiovascular problems are often easier to prevent than they are to cure. So how might you supplement professionals? And if you do experience some form of disease, how might they be able to help?

Practitioners of 'complementary' medicine all believe in treating the whole person rather than just a collection of symptoms. They encourage individuals to take responsibility for their own health, and stress the importance of preventive medicine. By treating our bodies and minds with respect, they argue, and caring for them properly, we can do much to help prevent problems arising.

These therapists work by looking at an individual's whole lifestyle and personality for clues to any malfunctions. Then they address the causes, rather than just the symptoms, of problems. They can also identify ways of living that may lead to problems in the future.

Treatment may include skeletal or muscular manipulation, dietary adjustments, exercise programmes and relaxation techniques as well as medication. Some practitioners work closely with 'orthodox' doctors, recognising that mainstream medicine has much to offer, especially when it comes to accurate diagnosis. Others regard their disciplines as incompatible with those of the orthodox medical professions. (Toon, Brown and Jarrett, 1991).

## Indian Medicine And Stress

Ayurvedic drugs known as 'Madhya Rasayanas' are popularly used as nervine tonics and as remedies for the treatment of mental disorders. Similarly, Amalaki Rasayanas and Amalk Rasayana are reported to be the best indigenous drugs for the treatment of peptic ulcer and traumatic stress.

Singh, Sinha, Mehta, Malviya, Singh, Sarkar and Udupa (1977) tested the anti-anxiety effect of four Indian indigenous drugs such as 'Sankhapuspi' (Convolvulus pluricaulis), 'Brahmi' (Bacopamounieri) and 'Mandukaparni' (Hydrocotyle asciatica) and 'Asvagandha' (Withania somnifera). The findings of the study revealed that these drugs reduced the level of anxiety, neuroticism and mental fatigue. Second, these drugs improved memory and performance pattern in patients suffering from anxiety neurosis. Third, a significant clinical relief from insomnia, nervousness, palpitation, tremors and irritability was noted in patients following treatment with these 'Madhya Rasayana' drugs.

Varma, Singh, Gupta and Udupa (1977), studied stress factors in peptic ulcers and its treatment with an Indian indigenous drug 'Amalaki Rasayana' (concentrated powder of the pericarp of dried Amalaki fruits – Emblica officinalis linn). Peptic ulcer is among the common stress disorders which shows an increased blood level of acetylcholine, catecholamine, histamine and plasma cortisol. The authors found that the treatment of peptic ulcer patients with Amaliki Rasayana accounted for a significant symptomatic improvement in some of the patients. For example, it decreased gastric acid secretion. Second, the blood level of plasma cortisol, urinary corticoids, catecholamines, acetylcholine and histamine decreased indicating a less stressful state in these patients. Last, a number of beneficial systemic affects such as increase in body weight, increase in haemoglobin percentage, correction of erythrocyte sedimentation rate and a significant decrease in the rate of urinary excretion (nitrogen) were seen. These characteristic improvements confirm the effect of this drug on stress-induced ulcers.

Another study was conducted by Rai, Deshpande and Udupa (1977), to test the effect of the Ayurvedic drug, 'Amalaki Rasayana' in combating stress caused trauma. Trauma was studied in terms of various bio-chemical changes such as circulating levels of acetylcholine, histamine, catecholamine, serotonin and associated metabolic alterations in serum protein, blood glucose and fat before and after various surgical operations in dogs. The findings of the study revealed that the neurohumoral and metabolic responses in operated dogs were beneficially influenced by treatment with Amalaki Rasayana prior to surgery (Pestonjee, 1992).

## Stress And Yoga

Among several relaxation practices, yoga seems to have potentiality to influence the mechanism in various ways. Udupa, Singh and Dwivedi (1977),in their study on two groups of volunteers who practiced Vipassana meditation for 19 days, had noted a significant increase in the levels of acetylcholine, cholinesterase, catecholamines and histaminase activities in the blood. On the other hand, there appeared to be a reduction in the level of plasma cortisol, urinary corticoids and urinary nitrogen. These findings suggest that volunteers were neurophysiologically more active following yogic meditation and yet, were physically and metabolically stable. However, rather than functional disturbances, where structural changes have taken place, yogic practices can be used for pollination along with routine medical procedures.

According to Bhole (1977), hatha-yoga practices like asanas (i.e., posture), pranayamas (i.e., breatnhing practices intended to influence vital forces), kriyas attitudes and bandhas (i.e., neuro-muscular locks) are mostly taught as physical practices. While various meditational techniques work at the mental level, all these practices are intended to develop a certain type of awareness within oneself. This in turn is expected to bring about a change in the emotional and visceral functions and through them, a change in the intellectual and somatic functions of the individual.

There are several studies by Indian scholars which ascertain the importance of yogic practices in producing a series of significant psychological, physiological, endocrinal and metabolic changes in the body. Singh and Udupa (1977) conducted a series of comparative psychobiological studies on apparently normal educated male volunteers who were practicing certain meditative and cultural asanas and pranayama one hour every day for six months. They found that six months of yogic practices induced a feeling of well-being, a reduction in body weight and increased vital capacity. It was also observed that blood sugar and serum cholesterol levels on fasting were lowered, and certain endocrine functions, especially adrenocortical, thyroid and testicular functions were accelerated. On the other hand, psychological studies revealed an improvement in memory and performance, lowered mental fatigue rate, a reduction in neuroticism index and a lowered incidence of physiological and psychological complaints assessed according to the Cornell Medical Index.

In another study, Podder, Gangwal, Vinod and Palsane (1984), investigated a variation of yoga and meditation called savasana meditation in a group of 32 patients of hypertension. 'No thought awareness' characteristic of all meditational techniques was combined with the yogic technique of savasana to maximise physical and mental relaxation. Subjects were trained for 20 minutes in savasana meditation for 20 days during which a regular record of their blood pressure was maintained. This was followed by 12 weeks of continued practice and the blood pressure of each subject was recorded after savasana for the entire period. A control group of 32 subjects was also given the same treatment. Analysis of findings revealed that there was a significant reduction in blood pressure levels of the experimental group also reported significant reduction in drug dosages and enhanced 'sense of well-being'. The authors concluded that psychological stress is a major cause of essential hypertension, and that savasana-meditation which emphasises physical and mental relaxation is effective in controlling blood pressure.

Sahasi, Mohan and Kacker (1989), conducted a study to measure the effectiveness of yogic teachings in the management of anxiety. A group of 91 patients suffering from anxiety neurosis were taken up for treatment. Patients were randomly assigned to yoga therapy (Group-I) or drug therapy (Group-II), subject to their willingness to participate in the yogic practices. There were 38 patients in the former group and 53 patients were administered drug therapy. Patients were assessed clinically and administered psychological tests prior to the commencement of the treatment schedule and after the completion of the treatment schedule. The anxiety level in Group I decreased, the Locus of Control Scale revealed increased inner control and the Knox Cube Imitation Test scores showed increased attention/concentration though it was not statistically significant. In the drug therapy group, pre and post-treatment scores were not statistically significant on any test except the Locus of Control Scale.

Nagendra and Nagarathna (1988) have dealt with stress management in their book entitled, "New Perspectives in Stress Management". According to them, the ancient Indian Science of yoga holds the key to combat this modern menace of stress.

## Spiritual Considerations

Naidu and Pande (1988), presented an interim research report on non-attachment and health. It was hypothesised that non-attachment would be implicated in the stress process. It would have main effects on stress and strain, and also moderate the relationship between stress and strain. It was predicted that non-attached persons, compared to less non-attached subjects, would perceive a lesser degree of stress, exhibit fewer symptoms of strain and show a smaller correlation between stress and strain.

## Acupuncture And Stress

Stress leads to psychosomatic disorders, since emotional states are often expressed in terms of bodily reactions. The common manifestations resulting from distress are depression, anxiety, cardio-vascular accidents, muscular aches and pains, insomnia, gastro-intestinal ulcers, sexual dysfunction, allergies and mental derangements.

A study conducted to assess the scope of acupuncture as a relaxation response in coping with stress and also to establish its therapeutic efficacy in the management of functional diseases revealed that Acupuncture does help in tranquillisation and psychic elation and allows one to relax (Table 7). Acupuncture does not depend on drugs, it is a safe, simple, economical and yet effective therapy with hardly any side-effects, its clinical success has demonstrated that it has a definite role to play in coping with stress.

**Table 7: Tabular Representation of the Results of Acupuncture in Stress-Related Diseases**

| ***Stress-Related Diseases*** | | ***Cure Rate (per cent)*** | ***Failure Rate (per cent)*** |
|---|---|---|---|
| Depression | Endogenous | 100 | nil |
| | Exogenous | 20 | 60 |
| Anxiety | | 64 | 36 |
| Backache | | 100 | nil |
| Insomnia | Getting up in the middle of the night | 100 | nil |
| | Difficulty in falling off to sleep | nil | 100 |
| Epigastric pain and discomfort | | 50 | 50 |
| Sexual dysfunction and Functional impotency | | 50 | 50 (Partial) |

***Source:*** Bativala, Acupuncture as a Relaxation Response for Coping with Stress, in S. Batlivala (ed.), "Stress Your Friend or Foe, 1985."

## Stress – Alternative Treatments

The effects of undue stress, and ways to cope with it when it is excessive or prolonged, are one of the major challenges to health-care today. Alternative medicine is well-placed to meet this challenge, with its insistence on treating each person as a unique individual, with all levels of activity from physical to mental being taken into account.

In general, the alternative therapies see much of modern lifestyle as creating aqn unnecessary burden of stress on our systems. The recent increased concern with the environment and the interaction between us and the natural world is one that has occupied the therapists' attention for some time, for instance herbalism is green medicine in more ways than one – and most of the treatments will involve advice on how to adapt our lifestyle to achieve greater harmony and reduction of stress factors.

Acupuncture, the flow and distribution of Chi is paramount, and treatment will be aimed at strengthening weakness in energy lines, or meridians. The functioning of the mind is linked to the functioning of our internal organs, and the acupuncturist balances these through the meridian pathways which energise our body. Massage, whether used as a part of aromatherapy or on its own, is intended primarily to achieve greater relaxation and so lesson the effects of stress. By becoming more relaxed in general, people often adopt a more easy-going attitude to the problems and so learn to manage stress levels better.

Herbal medicine has a range of remedies which can be of benefit. Many herbs have a calming effect, from the gentle relaxants to those with more sedating properties; a different class of remedies are those which are nervous restoratives, helping to nourish and build up the nervous system after prolonged stress; and a third important group are the adaptogens, which act in a complex way to help the body adapt to stress, improve stamina and so on – Ginseng is the most well-known example of this type of medicine. Homeopathy is most concerned with the individual's reactions and response to the stress, since it is the emotional stage and behaviour which determines the appropriate remedy. When homoeopathic medicines were first being tested, or 'proved', it was these mental and emotional differences that were the most noticeable symptoms that led to the remedy picure. Therefore, though they will be concerned with reducing the stresses themselves, homoeopaths concentrate more on the way in which the person is reacting to them.

Naturopathy – one of the main aims is to strengthen the ability of the individual to withstand external pressures, whilst ensuring that the nervous system is adequately nourished and supplied with blood and oxygen to function as well as possible. Through the diet or with supplements, the correct amounts of vitamins and minerals are given, and also advice on exercise and relaxation to keep the mind and body in peak condition.

Hypnotherapy and psychotherapy use a variety of techniques to help the person bring out underlying worries that are contributing to the stress levels, and also use relaxation exercises, tapes and so forth in order to calm the mind and aid the person to sort out the problems and so deal with the stress better. Often therapists nowadays run stress management courses or packages for this very purpose, recognising that for many people high levels of stress are an everyday part of their lives.

Some find that prolonged stress leads to increased strain on the body, with muscular or even structural problems developing, and it is with these latter that the manipulative therapies will be helpful. Osteopaths and chiropractors recognise the psychological component in the majority of skeletal disorders, and will often give advice or refer for additional help with this, but they can give tremendous relief from the physical discomfort itself. This in turn release energy, which improves mobility and creates better physical conditions for coping with the stress. In addition to the treatments themselves, many of the above therapists will also advocate that people look at ways to help themselves. For instance, relaxing exercise such as yoga or t'ai chi can be very beneficial – indeed, increasing exercise and physical stamina generally often helps to increase ability to cope with mental stress. The regular practice of meditation has been shown to have a marked effect on stress symptoms like high blood pressure. Postural and occupational strains on the body can also be alleviated, for example by lessons in the Alexander Techniques to learn more efficient ways to use our bodies. All these approaches can fit in very well with alternative treatments, and are often incorporated into the overall programme by the therapist (Toon, Tripp and Evans, 1991).

For all these therapies, the importance of assessing the individual lifestyle is included in treatment. For instance, the use of the contraceptive pill is almost always an aggravating factor; diet, exercise and posture are equally significant areas for evaluation. The role of stress, especially sudden stress release, has already been mentioned and counselling or hypnotherapy skills can help here. The major thing to note is that there are good choices for positive help from natural medicine.

The anxiety and stress that contributes to alcohol dependence, and certainly will accompany withdrawal, is an aspect that the counsellors will address. Of great benefit here also is massage, particularly of the abdomen and back, which stimulates circulation and internal organ function as well as aiding relaxation. For the aromatherapist, the use of oils which increases elimination and detoxification, such as juniper and fennel, is added to the massage effects. For the person dependent on alcohol or other drugs the best policy is probably to adopt a range of strategies, both conventional and alternative, that will give the greatest support to attempts to come off and stay off the drug.

## Behavioural Medicine

Some theoretical constructs and terminology used widely in behavioural medicine are useful from a therapeutic strategy point of view, and some ideas have found their way into the everyday conversation of laypeople – words such as coping and stress. Admittedly some words may be more useful therapeutically than scientifically.

In the 1970's, there was increasing dissatisfaction with the older and unwidely concepts of "psychosomatic disorder" that had grown largely out of psychodynamic theory and practice. The psychodynamic-based psychosomatic models were esoteric and did not translate well into short-term clinical solutions. Treatment based on such models was practicable only by a few therapists with the minority of patients who were sophisticated enough to be suitable. The approaches did not lend themselves easily to assessment and measurement of outcome in a medico-cultural milieu increasingly sensitive to cost efficiency. A new rationale arose, drawing largely from behavioural psychology, from studies of biofeedback, cognition, and concepts about the 'sick role'. There were new developments in the field of pain studies that allowed for alternate psychological models. There was the demonstrated efficacy of focused behavioural approaches, the palatability to psychologically unsophisticated patients of approaches that were less psychodynamic, and the simpler rationale that made behavioural concepts appeal to non-psychologists and psychologists alike. Techniques of measurement that were built into the behavioural approaches were an incentive for research in the field. The fact that these techniques addressed health problems of major public and economic concern, and not just neuroses, assured behavioural medicine a greater health-care prominence.

The dimension of thought or cognition is often emphasised, with the idea that maladaptive behaviour often correlates with maladaptive patterns of thinking and with erroneous assumptions about the sickness and symptoms. These cognitions can be corrected through analysis of the incorrect assumptions, awareness of the self-defeating thinking patterns, and education regarding the true nature of the problems. The focus on thought is paralleled by a focus on actions that the patient should take to relieve the stress or improve coping skills. A change in action can be facilitated by the patient's taking an active part in self-monitoring in order to build self-awareness, learning or applying methods for self-control of stress-induced symptoms, and achieving a sense of self-efficacy through use of effective coping strategies.

**Table 8: Comparison of Methods for Inducing the Relaxation Response**

| *Techniques* | *Psysiologtic Measurement* | | | | | |
|---|---|---|---|---|---|---|
| | *Oxygen consumption* | *Respiratory rate* | *Heart rate* | *Alpha Waves* | *Blood pressure* | *Mental tension* |
| Transcendental Meditation | D | D | D | I | D | NM |
| Zen and Yoga | D | D | D | I | NC | NM |
| Autogenic Training | NM | D | D | I | IR | D |
| Progressive Relaxation | NM | NM | NM | NM | IR | D |
| Hypnosis with Suggested Deep Relaxation | D | D | D | NM | IR | NM |
| Sentic Cycle | D | D | D | NM | NM | NM |

***Source:*** H. Benson, "Your Innate Asset for Combating Stress", Harvard Business Review, July-August 1974.

D = Decrease; I = Increase; N M = Measured;

I R = Inconclusive Results; N C = No Change

The relaxation response is an innate, integrated set of physiological changes opposite to that of the fight-or-flight response. It can be elicited by psychological means. Until recently, this relaxation response had been elicited primarily by meditational techniques. The effects of some of these techniques are given in Table 8.

## Relaxation Exercises

Relaxation procedures are the most commonly used specific treatment techniques in behavioural medicine. They are used either as the main treatment or as an adjunct to other procedures. A state of relaxation or low arousal, usually referred to as the relaxation response, in contrast to the fight-or-flight response, can be achieved using a variety of training procedures. The most frequently used relaxation training methods in clinical practice are as follows:

1. Physical relaxation techniques
   - Progressive muscle relaxation
   - Physical exercise (as in t'al chi for example)
2. Imaginal exercises
   - Autogenic training
   - Imagery
   - Sensory awareness
   - Passive progressive muscle relaxation
   - Conditioned cue relaxation
   - Meditation
3. Hypnosis
   - Therapist-directed
   - Self-directed
4. Feedback-assisted methods
   - Electromyography (EMG)
   - Temperature
   - Pulse volume
   - Electroencephalography (EEG)
   - Galvanic skin response (GSR)
   - Visceral monitoring

## Biofeedback Techniques

What the various biofeedback techniques have in common is the self-regulation of bodily processes. This is achieved by detecting, amplifying, and displaying specific physiological processes in such a way that the patient can be trained to voluntarily modify these processes. Generally, electrical amplification and visual and auditory displays are used. The most common modalities are listed as follows:

1. EMG, monitoring muscle tension.
2. Skin temperature, generally monitoring cutaneous temperature of the finger.
3. Pulse Volume, sometimes used over cranial arteries in headache management.
4. GSR, measuring skin conductance/resistance changes as a function of anxiety.

5. Electrocardiogram (ECG)
6. EEG rhythms
7. Visceral function, as for example, pressure measurement of the gut.

There is some indication that in headache cases biofeedback has about the same efficacy as relaxation. On the other hand, there is the clinical impression that biofeedback may often offer something clinically that is not obtained from the more nonspecific relaxation or cognitive therapies.The added element may be a greater facility to acquire control if there is an opportunity to come to terms actively with both physical and mental reactions. Biofeedback may be a better placebo. It may be that biofeedback promotes cognitive change, especially beliefs in self-control, because it gives a concrete illustration of self-control over a function that previously seemed unconscious.

## Cognitive Coping Techniques

We state some of the coping techniques that may be used to maximise the self-control of problems as already discussed. The basic concepts are as follows:

(1) Thinking and mental images (cognitions) are a factor in determining how we feel and behave. That is, our thoughts often determine our actions.

(2) Therapeutic change can be brought about by re-examining and altering thoughts, images, beliefs, and evaluations. This is an important step in altering psychological distress and adjusting maladaptive behaviour. This is the main focus of cognitive coping strategies.

(3) How we behave also influences how we interpret events; that is, our actions also determine our thoughts.

(4) Change also is facilitated if behaviour is prescribed in such a way that dysfunctional thought patterns and images are re-evaluated. This is the main focus of strategies such as desensitisation, assertiveness training, role-playing, and self-monitoring.

Thus, the cognitive coping approaches attempt to alter maladaptive images, inappropriate beliefs, and expectations, including what has been identified as catastrophic thinking and negative self-talk. The research and clinical literature suggest the following steps for putting this into practice.

(a) Use self-monitoring to discover your thoughts and images during distressing situations.

(b) Collect further information to re-evaluate these images and cognitions in order to see if they accurately represent the situation or whether they represent unjustified apprehensions.'

(c) Try using alternative ways of interpreting and imagining.

(d) Create new coping opportunities by trying out these alternatives in everyday stress situations.

(e) Combine the cognitive strategies with relaxation procedures.

## Alternative Therapies

Now follows a review – in chronological order, the alternative therapies, which in our opinion are of relevance to medical practice and for stress management. There is a wide variety of reasons for their importance, ranging from scientific validity manipulation to simple application.

The most prevalent of all human diseases, headaches strike 70 to 80 per cent of the world" population at least once a month. Over 15 million people in the U.S. alone are believed to suffer from migraine, while another 25 million are afflicted with chronic "tension" headaches. Tollison and Tollison (1982), have combined traditional remedies. Such as medication, with new, innovative and non-addictive techniques of pain relief, most of which can be done at home. The techniques which have received much professional attention are:

1. Biofeedback
2. Massage and acupressure

3. Diet Control
4. Hypnosia
5. Physical Conditioning
6. Relaxation exercises

The authors have discussed the detailed procedure and application in the book. Designing the pain management programme, the doctor gets the headache sufferer actively involved, and that involvement itself is an essential part of the headache treatment. They are of the opinion that pain relief is possible.

Santwani (1982), has written an authoritative book, "Magneto Therapy for Common Diseases". He has given simple step-by-step guidance on the theory and treatment of different diseases by magnets. In his opinion, magnet healing is simple, rapid, inexpensive, efficacious and free from any adverse side or after effects. It is based on natural laws and has basically a scientific approach.

Magnets are easy to apply and give rapid relief specifically in cases of inflammation, stiffness, cervical spondylosis, sciatica and arthritis. He has suggested use of magneto therapy for:

- common colds and coughs
- backache, spondylosis
- tootache, earache, headache
- conjunctivitis
- asthma
- obesity
- paralysis
- tonsillitis
- high blood pressure

## Meditations from the Tantras

Swami Satyananda Saraswati (1983), feels that the majority of mankind is searching for happiness, yet very few seem to find anything that approaches contentment in their lives. People look to television, cinema, sports and so on for happiness, but though it might come for a short time, any lasting happiness seems to elude them. People seek power, status, material possessions. In return most people suffer from fear, hated, insecurity, ulcers, heart attacks, mental disturbances, etc.

There is a striking balance between theory and practice in this excellent treatise. The theory of meditation expounded in the Upanishads, Tantras and in the several systems of yoga that have come to be developed in the East.

Swamiji elucidates the 'why' and 'what for' of meditation, in the regions of the mind associated with one's consciousness (awareness), the psychological aspects and repercussions on a scientific basis, clarifying the relationship of the brain (beta, alpha, theta and delta) waves and the state of the individual, the effects on health and the psychic physiology with clarification of the charkas (centres), psychic passages and respective bija mantras, etc. The writer also explains all the basic techniques of yoga and tantra, many of which have perhaps never been published.

"The Effects of Yoga on Hypertension" written by Dr. Swami Shankardevananda Saraswati (1984), is a manual of the principles and application of yogic techniques developed by Swami Satyananda Saraswati. Hypertension is only one of the many psychosomatic diseases which can be easily treated through a combination of yoga with modern and ancient medicines. This disease is only a symbol of all the other maladies from which mankind is suffering at the moment and which cause seemingly endless suffering. Externals may vary in each individual case and seem to produce a multitude of differing and separate diseases, but this multitude forms a single spectrum into which each illness fits as one part. The root cause of all disease is the same: ignorance of our true nature and lack of awareness of who we really are.

Our body-mind complex is a marvel of creation both intricate and subtle in design. Man, who inhabits it, is finding out new and astounding facts about his inner workings, facts which are helping to open up his awareness, understanding and knowledge of himself. This knowledge is leading him out of the mire of disease and suffering to better health and longevity.

The author feels that the science of yoga offers a theoretical construct for the working of the body and mind and their malfunction in disease, as well as the actual practices designed to correct imbalance and help us gain better health and realisation. Yoga provides a path to the cure of high blood pressure but it is you, the seeker of health, who must tread it. With increased knowledge of the body, its energy systems, the mind, the soul, and their inter-relationships, we can learn to live more harmonious, better integrated lives, and health is a natural consequence of this. He points out that to be healthy, mentally and physically, one must know the body-mind complex, its needs and requirements just as a car requires a good driver as well as servicing, oiling, petrol, grease, tyre adjustment and so on. People are sick because they do not know their bodies and minds, what they need and how to keep them properly. Yoga is designed to help us maintain this body-mind vehicle in top running condition for as long as possible so that life can be joyful, free and fulfilling.

The author is of the opinion that through the combination of medicine and yoga, both doctor and patient can come to a better understanding of the disease process involved in hypertension and so learn from experience, growing and maturing within. In this way, we become not only physically healthy, but gain a dynamic personality, mental and emotional stability, and deeper wisdom and insight. This is real healing which fulfils the function of the doctor (from the Latin 'docere' to teach) and lifts the patient into the higher spheres, towards union with higher consciousness.

"Yoga and Cardiovascular Management" (1984), a book published by Bihar School of Yoga, Munger which was the result of discussions with Swami Satyananda Saraswati and research correlated by Swami Karmannda Saraswati tells that heart disease is by far the number one killer in the technological, industrialised societies today. Its rising incidence has been truly phenomenal. Consider the statistics: in 1905, 25% of all deaths in USA were due to coronary heart disease or its complications; by 1955 the figure had risen to 55%, and today 70% of all deaths occurring there are due to cardiovascular disease. In 1969, the Executive Board of the World Health Organisation (WHO), described heart disease as, 'the greatest epidemic mankind has faced'. Even in India, heart disease has become the third largest killer amongst the city – dwellers who adhere to the modern lifestyle, but fortunately, it remains a rarity in the villages, where 85% of the population lives, following a simple, natural and stress-free lifestyle. The research are of the opinion that the death rate from heart diseases could be decreased through:

1. Changes in lifestyle, including more natural diet containing less animal fats and cholesterol, decrease in cigarette smoking, etc.
2. Improved medical care, especially in the acute coronary case.

The belief that there has been definitely an awakening of spiritual awareness on our planet in the last decade, and in this, yoga has been at the forefront. The impact of yoga upon a culture is as subtle as it is profound. A gradual transformation of consciousness is occurring. People everywhere are more health conscious, more diet conscious and more conscious of yoga. Whether they practice or not, definitely a very high proportion of people today are now aware of yoga asanas, relaxation, meditation, dietary and living habits, and the physical and mental benefits they bestow. Almost everyone is making some effort to improve in a practical, spiritual way, even if they are not, they definitely want to. Yoga is also a preventive medicine. Yoga has an enormous role to play in the preventive medicine of the future. By preventive medicine they mean that we can do now by way of personal and social actions to ensure that our family members and friends do not suffer and die prematurely as so many do today, facing heart attacks even in the fourth or fifth decade of life.

The remarkable achievements of modern medical science in managing acute heart disease must be acknowledged. Nevertheless, as doctors, you yourselves have sought to incorporate yoga into this sphere of medical management, and most of your questions reflect this. They concern management or cure of major cardiac conditions using yoga. Yoga definitely has a role to play here.

Thompson J an eminent Physician and Consultant Psychiatrist with wide experience in the medical profession, in her book, "Spiritual Considerations in the Prevention, Treatment and Cure of Disease", is of the opinion that spiritual medicine could be an ambiguous term, unlike 'orthopaedic" medicine, or 'psychiatric' medicine, or neurological medicine, all of them names for specialisms within the body of medical practice. It is, however, a valid term, and extremely necessary for this day and generation, when so much of the physical has crept into all our thinking about almost everything, and perhaps very specially, into medical and human thinking and practice. She feels that the human being is a tripartite creation of spirit, mind and body and these interact upon each other in health and in sickness. At present there is far too much emphasis placed on the purely physical, be this of body or mind, and commonly no consideration at all is given to the fundamental spiritual being. Each cell of the whole human being is a tripartite creation of spirit, mind and body; and a breach in the spiritual part can cause serious mental and/or physical illness; but all too often it has not, up-to-date, been forthcoming.

In the preview of her book, "Spiritual Considerations in the Prevention, Treatment and Cure of Disease", she has shown the need for an advocated development in spiritual considerations in illness and in the healing of illness. This book deals with the neglected but important matter. The writer's intention is to further the relationship between the medical practice and the healing potential of religion for the good of the individual, and of the society, as well as for the right scientific practice of medicine in all its branches.

Keller J (1984), had written a book on, "Healing with Water: Special Applications and Uses of Water in Home Remedies for Everyday Ailments". The author has discussed the various forms of water applications as a means of healing to those in need of health, in securing better health. She has explained in her book the various methods of application for treating various ailments which help the patient giving great relief and in turn brings happiness to them. The author has given the guidelines which could be used by people who wish to retain their health and the functioning of a specific organ. They will find that water not only cleaneses the body on the outside but also purifies it internally and creates a radiance of gloriously good health, strength and youth in inner feeling that anyone can't miss noticing about you. She is of the view that many ailments cleanses can be cured with water treatment such as:

(1) Healing external infections and inflammations

(2) Strengthening and improving bladder and kidneys

(3) Relieving Hemorrhoids

(4) Insomnia

(5) Relieving Constipation

(6) Getting rid of Lumbago

(7) Stopping Diarrhoea and Vomiting

(8) Eliminating gas pains

(9) Overcoming depression

(10) Getting rid of sciatica

(11) Getting rid of Rheumatism

(12) Reducing fever

(13) Help for stomach ulcers and heartburn

(14) Strengthening nerves

Cerney (1985), has written a book, "Acupuncture Without Needles" to show how to apply finger-pressure acupuncture to any part of the body for the speedy relief of pain and discomforts. With crystal-clear illustrations, he explains where pain begins, how it may show up in other parts of the body, and how it may disappear to treat a wide variety of ailments such as fatigue, migraine, colds, tension, loss of hearing, eye problems, blood pressure problems, asthma, arthritis, heart ailments and muscle pains.

Coleman (1985), has written a book, "Life Without Tranquillizers". He pointed out that the benodiazepines are addictive. In 'Life without Tranquillizers' he describes why and how Valium (and the many similar drugs now available), has become so popular; he deals with the history of the drug, the known side-effects associated with its use and the reasons why he thinks the benzodiazepines should be withdrawn. Most important of all he tells readers how to get off the drug and how to live without it.

Kirsta (1986), has written books on health and well-being. Her book, "The Book of Stress Survival – How to relax and live positively" is the most useful and comprehensive reference available on stress management. Not only does it examine the causes and effects of stress, it also shows how to pinpoint and reduce the stress in your life. With beautiful illustrations and clear, step-by-step instructions, the book takes you through meditation and relaxation exercises to yoga and massage – essential skills for developing a stress-free lifestyle. Her book is a comprehensive guide to understanding, living with, and coping with stress.

Ashton and Davies (1996), have written a book "Why Exercise ?". They have given expert medical advice to help people enjoy healthier life. They have explained how moderate, regular exercise can be of overwhelming benefit to people of both senses and all ages and occupations – if approached properly. Detailed guidelines are given on how to assess the state of fitness and then on how to improve it; how to judge the importance of personality type and how to eat sensibly to establish a reasonable weight level. They had given just hard medical fact, lucid explanation and sound advice – and the inspiring truth that for a modest amount of effort, dramatic and long-lasting improvements in the real standard of living are within everyone's reach.

Dr. Montgomery (1987), a consultant psychologist in his book "Coping With Stress" explains the difference between enough stress which causes us to act at peak levels of efficiency, and too much stress, which causes unpleasant feelings, physical damage and fatigue. He offers a self-help programme for stress management giving proven techniques to reduce stress overload. He is of the opinion that stress is often seen as a dreadful consequences of modern life that could be avoided if we returned to a simpler lifestyle. The book is a brief self-help manual for stress management.

Poppen (1988), in his book, "Behavioral Relaxation Training and Assessment" presented a behaviour analytic approach to relaxation training and application. Behaviour analysis is a useful system for organising current knowledge of complex human behaviour, and for guiding research into the many areas yet unknown. He has provided a general framework to organise and guide research and application of relaxation training procedure. The other thing he presented is new training and assessment procedures based on the behavioral tradition.

Fudler (1989), has written a book, "The Handbook of Complementary Medicine" which is a definitive reference work on alternative medicine. He has presented in his book all aspects of complementary medicines from scientific to the social. The book also includes an up-to-date list of organisations providing the facilities. Dr. Fulder has produced a fascinating, stimulating, and critical account of complementary medicine. He has given most abled and authoritative medicine which includes all the later development in a very fast growing area. He has given answers to the question. Murphy and Schoenborn (1989), the editors of "Stress Management in Work Settings", have presented in this publication a summarised scientific evidence and reviewed conceptual and practical issues relating to worksite stress management. Their collection of original papers addresses current issues and problems in the fiend. Their discussions provide a context within which stress management programmes can be developed, implemented, evaluated and maintained in the work settings. They have provided guidance for stress management programmes. They are of the opinion that a more appropriate application of stress management would be as a complement to job redesign or organisational change interventions. Secondly, considerable efforts should be given at the outset to define the purpose of the programme, delineate organisational and individual goals, acquire organisational support and co-ordinate the programme with existing occupational safety and health efforts. The foundation is to be laid for a more stable and holistic programme for controlling organisational stress.

Weikang (1986), had written a book, "The Story of Chinese Acupuncture and Moxibustion". He is of the opinion that acupuncture and moxibustion are an important branch of China's traditional medicine and pharmacology, with a recorded history of more than two thousand years. The book also elucidates vividly and concisely the beginnings and development of these therapeutic methods as well as recent achievements.

Ashton (1989), has written a book, "The Corporate Healthcare Revolution – Strategies for Preventive Medicine at Work". The writer has discussed the origins and scale of our current health problems – both from a medical and an economic point of view. He had provided some basic but essential background information about the principal risk factors to our health and how these can interact to produce the modern Western diseases. He has provided a brief overview of the United States experience during the past eight to ten years. Workplace 'wellness' programmes have flourished there during this period; clearly there are some important lessons for us to learn and some mistakes we can avoid. Finally, he has provided some practical suggestions as to how companies may establish their own worksite health promotion programmes with specific reference to the major diseases, faced by the executives. The book provides the corporate organisation with the information necessary to construct and maintain a medically sound and cost-effective health programme. The author takes a critical look at the evidence available from the companies who have introduced such schemes. The book contains comprehensive and practical guidance of company culture and attitudes towards health.

Fontana (1989), has written a book, "Managing Stress", a practical handbook – a precise perception of personal stresses together with practical suggestions for meeting them. Stress is a normal and universal phenomenon, neither good nor bad in itself. Clearly people under too much stress (or too little) do not work at their best and may suffer symptoms such as poor concentration, backaches, sleeplessness and a general feeling of hopelessness. The author using non-technical language throughout, and with an emphasis on practical and easily mastered strategies, takes the reader step-by-step through the things that can be done to enhance stress resistance and to increase professional efficiency. Relevant case studies illustrate just how stress can be managed in practice.

Turner (1990), has written a book "Naturopathic Medicine – Treating the whole Person: The Principles and Practice of Naturopathy". The writer is a naturopathic practitioner, osteopath and acupuncturist. He describes the principles of naturopathic medicine in his book which are:

1. the recognition of the body's own ability to heal.
2. the restoration of the body's equilibrium or homoeostasis.
3. the recognition that emotional, physical and biochemical factors all play a part in governing health.
4. the treatment of the whole patient not just a specific symptom.
5. the integration of orthodox (analytical) diagnosis with complementary (holistic and qualitative) diagnosis.

He has presented clear explanations of the procedures derived from these principles, and their subsequent use in diagnosis and treatment which are combined to give a thorough and informed overview of what is finally being recognised as a legitimate – indeed vital approach to health-care. The author has argued an excellent case for the naturopathic approach in health without being dogmatic. He clearly recognises the attributes of conventional general practice but also makes a strong case for a more comprehensive and philosophical understanding of health and disease.

Dr. Jaggi (1990), in his book "Mental Tension and Its Cure", describes the result in the grab and push of daily life, mental tension has become as inevitable as the rush hour traffic jam. Though not a disease in itself, mental tension leads to a number of ailments, amongst them seriousness like heart attack, stomach ulcers, ne us break-down and even insanity. In this book, the author examines the various causes and effects of mental tension, based on extensive research over a number of years. His ideas will help conquer everyday worries and achieve calm and happiness.

Toon, Tripp and Evans (1991) in their book "Your Mind" discussed the term 'mental health' and phobias. Again, the more serious psychoses were explained and dealt with. The authors gave practical and positive advice on how to define and recognise problem areas in order to keep stress within manageable limits. They were of the opinion that many of the problems associated with the mind can be helped by alternative therapies: a number of people have experienced tremendous relief from conditions such as migraine by using herbalistic and homeopathic approaches.

Whiteside (1991), has published a well-researched book, "Good Nutrition for long life" with trends in food production, which gives fascinating information on the basic principles of good nutrition, stressing the importance of planning our diets to include a good variety of whole foods that provide us with a sufficient intake of minerals, vitamins and fibre. Covering such subjects as organic farming, vegetarianism and slimming diets, the book proves to be an invaluable guide to all students of nutrition and a useful reference book for all those who like to take good care of their health.

Saks (1991), editor of "Alternative Medicine in Britain", has cited collection of readings on alternative medicine in Britain which is intended to fill a major gap in the social scientific literature on alternative medicine. As a social scientist, the book draws together both previously published and original commissioned work relevant to social scientists on the past, present and future of alternative medicine in Britain, covering areas such as acupuncture, homoeopathy, osteopathy, and spiritual healing. He has given a special reference to the professionalisation of medicine, which is seen as having a crucial influence on the conceptual boundaries and destiny of alternative medicine in British society. His writings will have an impact on the social scientists, as well as the practicing health professionals.

Pestonjee (1992), in his book, "Stress & Coping – The Indian Experience" expresses stress as occurring when demands on an individual exceed his adjustment resources. While stress is generally believed to have a deleterious effect on health and performance, recent research has revealed that a minimal level of stress is essential for effective functioning. It is the individual's reaction to stress which makes all the difference and may prove to be harmful.

Bhagwan Dash (1992), has written a book entitled, "Massage Therapy in Ayurveda". An effort has been made in his publication to acquaint the reader about the specialised therapy of ayurveda. He has tried through his untiring efforts of practice, the knowledge of ayurveda in general and ayurvedic massage therapy in particular through his writings. He feels that Ayurveda is the rich store house of time-tested and effective recipes for the treatment of several obstinate and otherwise incurable diseases. More important than these recipes are the specialised therapies which, while curing such diseases strengthen the immunity system in the body and thus, help in the prevention of diseases and preservation as well as promotion of positive health. These specialised therapies in ayurvedic parlance, are called 'Panchakarma'. The term 'Panchakarma' literally means five (Pancha) specialised therapies (karma). The therapies which are included under this collective term are as follows:

(1) Yamana Karma or Emetic therapy

(2) Virecana Karma or Purgation therapy

(3) Niruha Karma or a therapy administered through medicated enaema containing decoction of drugs, among others.

(4) Anuvasana Karma or a therapy administered through medicated enaema containing medicated oils, among others.

(5) Nasya Karma or Inhalation therapy.

He has classified the therapies into two categories, namely (1) Apatarpana or Depleting Therapy and (2) Santarpana or Nourishing Therapy. The latter category i.e. Nourishing Therapy is further sub-divided into three groups namely:

(1) Brmhana (which promotes corpulence of the body)

(2) Snahana (Oleation Therapy); and

(3) Stambhana (which inhibits unnatural secretions and excretions from the body).

Dr. Sahoo (1992), in his book "Handbook of Recent Acupuncture Treatment and Research" has given an excellent kind of the practice and scientific basis of acupuncture and ancillary methods. In his writings their traditional aspects have never been neglected or undermined.

Being an acupuncture therapist with wide experience he has thus published a well-balanced literature, critical and comprehensive book with a clinical therapeutic basis. The newer modalities used in acupuncture find a mention in his book. The chapter on therapeutic management of the various conditions amenable to acupuncture is an exhaustive one. The book, according to Chinese traditional medicines, has also mentioned the description of all standard acupuncture points.

## EMOTION, STRESS, AND HEALTH

**The Universal Nature of Emotions:** Various theorists argue that emotions result from our attempts to adapt to the environment. Evidence suggests that all humans experience a common set of emotions. Lazarus (1991), has suggested that these emotions can be described by their *core relational themes.* By adopting this term, Lazarus emphasises that our emotional responses grow out of our interactions with the environment (are relational); are highly cognitive; and are often complex, frequently involving two or more emotions operating simultaneously. Identifying the various core themes in an emotional response would obviously help us to reduce its complexity.

**Core relational themes for various emotions**

| *Emotion* | *Core Relational Theme* |
|---|---|
| **Anger** | A demeaning offense against me and mine. |
| **Anxiety** | Facing uncertain, existential threat. |
| **Fright** | Facing immediate, concrete, and over-whelming physical danger. |
| **Guilt** | Having transgressed a moral imperative. |
| **Shame** | Having failed to live up to an ego-ideal. |
| **Sadness** | Having experienced an irrevocable loss. |
| **Envy** | Wanting what someone else has. |
| **Jealousy** | Resenting a third party for loss of or threat to another's affection. |
| **Disgust** | Taking in or being too close to an indigestible object or idea (metaphorically speaking). |
| **Happiness** | Making reasonable progress towards the realisation of a goal. |
| **Pride** | Enhancement of one's ego-identity by taking credit for a valued object or achievement. |
| **Relief** | A distressing goal-incongruent condition that has changed for the better or gone away. |
| **Hope** | Fearing the worst but yearning for better. |
| **Love** | Desiring or participating in affection, usually but not necessarily reciprocated. |
| **Compassion** | Being moved by another's suffering and wanting to help. |

The first studies of the stress response focused on the role of stress in adapting to disease. However, Selye discovered that stress is not only involved in adapting to injury and diseases but has other health implications, which he referred to as diseases of adaptation.

There is considerable evidence that here are bi-directional effects between stress and disease. For example, cancer triggers stress, and stress itself plays a central role in the progression of cancer. One application of this is that anything we can do to reduce stress will slow the progression of a disease such as cancer.

The immune system is affected both directly and indirectly by a number of systems and behaviours. Stress has a direct effect. Thus, lowering stress through relaxation, for example, can have a direct effect. Diet, exercise, and alcohol seem to have a more indirect effect.

There is some evidence of a direct effect between certain patterns of thought – for example, optimism – and the immune system, but more research is needed on this topic.

However, even if there is no direct effect, it is clear that optimistic thinking has positive health benefits.

## Basic Points

1. Emotions arise out of our interactions with the environment and represent out attempts to adapt to the environment.
2. According to the Kleinginnas' definition emotions give rise to affective experiences, stimulate us to generate cognitive explanations, trigger a variety of internal responses, and elicit behaviours that are expressive, goal-directed, and adaptive.
3. It has been suggested that emotions are universal in nature and can be described by certain core relational themes.
4. Evidence for the universal nature of emotions comes from the study of facial expressions.
5. Lazarus has suggested that appraisal plays a critical role in determining the emotions we experience.
6. Stress is frequently conceptualised as the fight-or-flight response.
7. Stress can be elicited by a variety of physical and psychological stimuli called stressors.
8. Two separate systems – the sympathetic/adrenal and the pituitary/adrenal – are involved in the stress response.
9. The sympathetic system acts quickly and produces, among other things, a general increase in arousal.
10. In the case of the pituitary/adrenal response, the hypothalamus initiates actively in the endocrine system by stimulating the pituitary, which secretes ACTH (adrenocorticotropic hormone).
11. Endorphins are mobilised from the pituitary and are important for their analgesic and euphoric properties. The stress response triggers the release of endorphins.
12. Considerable research indicates that the stress response changes certain aspects of the immune response.
13. There are two immune systems – the innate (non-specific) and acquired (specific) systems.
14. There is clear evidence that immunity cannot be explained simply in physical terms.
15. The brain participates in the immunity cannot be explained simply in physical terms.
16. The brain participates in the immune response, which originates in the periphery of the body, by activating the stress response.
17. It has been argued that the existence of bi-directional effects between stress and the immune system is highly functional.
18. It seems that one of the main reasons immunity is downgraded during stress is to free up energy for the flight-or-fight response.
19. It has been suggested that the suppressed immune response came to be controlled by the stress response at some point in our evolutionary past.
20. Generally, the stress response is more likely to be triggered by unpredictable events than by predictable events.
21. Being able to discriminate (predict) the onset of stress can reduce the magnitude of the stress response.
22. Coping responses can reduce stress.
23. Under certain conditions, it is possible to habituate the stress response.
24. We can learn to respond appropriately under stress by learning a prescribed set of rules. Sometimes, it is important to learn not to respond.
25. It has been suggested that some organizations are more conflict-prone than others and that more conflict-prone organizations are likely to lead to health problems.

26. In primary appraisal, we assess three categories: harm/loss, threat, and challenge.
27. Secondary appraisal involves the evaluation of coping resources and options and may be either problem-focused or motion-focused.
28. Whether we use a problem-focused or an emotion-focused approach depends on whether we perceive the situation to be controllable and on whether we perceive that we have the ability to control it.
29. Perhaps the most important biological moderator of stress is social support. People with a repressive temperament who are resistant to biological support, tend to experience more stress.
30. One good way to manage stress is to break information down into manageable units.
31. Epstein has identified constructive thinking as one of the universal coping styles that can lead to a reduction in the stress reaction.
32. Emotion-focused strategies for coping with stress include meditation, relaxation, exercise, and biofeedback.
33. Studies have confirmed that talking or writing about a trauma can lead to health benefits.
34. The personality profile of people who remain healthy after experiencing high degrees of life stress – known as the hardy personality – is distinguished by three main characteristics: control, commitment, and challenge.
35. Other moderators of stress include optimism, instrumentality, sensation seeking, and a sense of humor.
36. The immune system is affected both directly and indirectly by various behaviors.
37. Since stress has been found to control the immune system, relaxation can directly affect the immune system.
38. Diet, exercise, drugs, social support, coping strategies, and compliance are thought to have an indirect effect on the immune system.
39. There is considerable evidence that thinking may have a direct effect on the immune system.
40. It may well be that how we think about the world – in particular, whether we view it positively or negatively – has a direct effect on the magnitude of the stress response.

## WORKPLACE DIMENSIONS, STRESS AND JOB SATISFACTION

(By Kerry Fairbrother and James Warn, School of Economics and Management, ADFA, Canada, Australia on July 2002).

Keyboards Occupational health, Stress, Job satisfaction, Working conditions, Navy, Training.

Applied research indicates strong connections between dimensions of the work place, stress and job satisfaction. Yet, there is an absence of theory to provide conceptual understanding of these relationships. In 1999, Sparks and Cooper advocated using job-specific models of stress as a way of developing a better understanding of the relationships. The current study adopted this recommendations and investigated a specific job context, specifically, naval officer trainees undergoing their sea training. The results indicate that a general model of stress is unhelpful in identifying the predictors of stress and job satisfaction in specific job contexts. Instead, the authors recommend identifying salient workplace dimensions rather than a broad brush approach when seeking workplace associations with stress.

The authors recommend that workplace surveys measuring job satisfaction and occupational stress incorporate distinct measures of workplace dimensions in order to avoid confounding the two sets of measures. Relevant workplace dimensions can be identified by comparison with workplaces that share salient characteristics. This approach identifies important similarities that provide the basis for generalisations that can be tested to evolve theoretical understanding.

## Eustress, distress, and interpretation in occupational stress

(By Mark Le Fevre, Jonathan Matheny and Gregory S. Kolt, (Auckland University of Technology, Auckland, New Zealand on June 2003)

Keyboards stress, Control theory, Individual perception.

We examine the concepts of stress, distress, and eustress and develop three tenets that are used to relate these concepts to three major theories or models of occupational stress. Selye's concept of eustress or "good stress" appears to be largely ignored in the literature, while the Yerkes Dodson Law is eustress as a model for management practice. We suggest that the meaning assigned to the word stress has shifted from Selye's original formulation, and that this shift, in conjunction with the use of the Yerkes Dobson Law leads to inappropriate management of stress in organisations. We conclude that the concept that some stress is good and enhances performance should be rejected in favour of most useful and accurate concepts.

## The constructs of eustresses and distress today

Eustress receives very little treatment in the literature. As Mesler (1996), stated there are "relatively few studies, and no adequate models, proposing the concept of eustress and its associated regenerative qualities". Moreover, it is interesting to note that three major reviews of occupational stress and management interventions (De Frank and Cooper, 1987; van der Hek and Plomp, 1997; van der Klink *et. Al,* 2001) made no mention of any possible positive aspect or effort of stress. Finally, a search of PsycINFO for the years 1960 to 2003 using stress as a keyword yielded 72,689 citations. A search using eustress as a keyword yielded 26 citations nine of which were unpublished dissertations. The concept of eustress appears to be outside the realm of consideration in scholarly literature.

However, quite to the contrary, the concept of eustress gains significant coverage in the popular press. Unfortunately, the popular treatment of eustress appears to rest on a limited view of the "Yerkes Dodson Law" (Yerkes and Dodson, 1908) and does not reflect a distinction between distress and eustress. Rather, it is frequently covered in basic management texts (e.g. Certo, 2003; Lussier, 2002; Schemerhorn, 2003) as that amount of stress that increases performance. Popularly speaking, eustress has taken "for-granted" status among managers as the optimum amount of stress.

Distress receives some treatment in the popular and scholarly literature. However, there would seem to be no systematic treatment of distress as contrasted with eustress. Thus, as usually employed in research or in common parlance, the broader construct of stress has become synonymous with distress.

With stress and distress operating as synonyms, the distinction Selye intended between distress and eustress is lost. In this light, stress and distress are used interchangeably and eustress is another entity altogether. Continuing this line of thought the idea of "good stress" can be re-stated as the oxymoron "good distress". The semantic shift away from rigorous consideration of eustress and distress leads to popular lessons about managing stress to optimum levels and providing "good distress to employees.

## A new model of occupational stress

Of the three models reviewed, the control theory of occupational stress holds the most promise for inclusion of the three tenets. It provides adequate scope for characterising stressors beyond "amount". It provides adequate scope for interpreters of stress to identify distress and/or eustress rather than simply stress. Also, control theory is the only approach reviewed that places individuals in the key role as interpreters of stressors. With its emphasis on perceptions, Spector's (1998) model could easily be revised to explicitly address all three tenets.

The model emphasises the interface of environmental stimuli and individual perception of those stimuli. Control is included as one characteristic of the individual, amount many, that may impact his or her interpretation of stressors. Thus, the revised model in Figure 10 integrates our three tenets with control theory in a parsimonious and powerful model.

This is a simple model. The model doesn't differentiate moderating and mediating variables. It doesn't provide an exhaustive list of what self-perceptions may influence an individual's interpretation of a stressor nor does it provide an exhaustive list of what characteristics of that stressor may influence the perception. Rather, we are suggesting a re-consideration, a stepping back if you will, of what we know about occupational stress. The model simply provides a powerful foundation of core elements, sum of which have not received the attention they deserved in the research on stress.

**Table 9**

| | |
|---|---|
| **The Individual**<br>Characterised by perceptions of one's locus of control, efficacy, and affective disposition<br>**The Perception of Stressors**<br>The interface of environmental Stimuli and the individual's Way of understanding<br>**The Stressor**<br>An environmental stimulus characterised by the perceived source, timing, and desirability | **The Experience of Stress:**<br>The eustress or distress experienced by the individual leading to behavioural, physical, and/or psychological outcomes |

This chapter provides a fresh look at some of the seminal sources of stress literature. From that and more recent research, we have derived three tenets of stress. We believe these tenets reflect elemental components of early and contemporary thought about stress. However, through an analysis of leading models of occupational stress, we found that these tenets are not well-represented.

We provided a discussion regarding the use of eustress and distress in the literature and suggested that a semantic shift has occurred which may explain their lack of representation in the models of occupational stress. To re-introduce the tenets, we provided a revised model based on Spector's (1998) control theory and discussed the implications of our work for research and practice.

Finally, there would appear to be little or no evidence in the occupational stress literature to support the assertion that a reasonable amount of stress, pressure, or anxiety in the workplace leads to high performance as suggested by the Yerkes Dodson Law. We suggest, therefore, that it may be time to explicitly reject this stance.

## Pull the Plug on Stress

(By Bruce Cryer; HeartMath, Rollin McCraty; HearMath, Doc Childre; Quantum Inch, Harward Business Review on July 2003 reports)

Stress is rampant, stress is growing, and stress hurts the bottom line. A 1999 study of 46,000 workers revealed that health care costs are 147% higher for those who are stressed or depressed, independent of other health issues. But what exactly is stress? It usually refers to our internal reaction to negative, threatening, or worrisome situations – a looming performance report, say, or interactions with a dismissive colleague.

Accumulated over time, negative stress can depress you, burn you out, make you sick or even kill you – because it's both an emotional and a physiological habit. Of course, many companies understand the negative impact of cumulative stress and offer programmes to help employees counteract it. The problem is that employees in the greatest need of help often don't seek it. Since 1991, the authors have studied the physiological impact of stress on performance, at both the individual and organisational levels. Their goal largely has been to decode the underlying mechanics of stress. After working with more than 50,000 workers and managers in more than 100 organisations, the authors have found that learning to manage stress is easier than most people think. They have devised a scientifically based system of tools, techniques, and technologies that organisations can use to reduce employee stress and boost overall health and performance.

**Body:** These days, stress is even more rampant than it was in 1983, when Time magazine declared it to be "the epidemic of the eighties." Stress is growing: According to a survey by CareerBuilder, an on-line recruitment site, the overall percentage of worker stress increased by 10% between August 2001 and May 2002. And Stress hurts the bottom line: In 1999, a study of 46,000 workers published by the Health Enhancement Research Organisation, or HERO, revealed that health care costs are 147% higher for those individuals who are stressed or depressed, independent of other health issues. The study, which included employees from Chevron, Hoffman-La Roche, Health Trust, Marriott, and the states of Michigan and Tennessee, also found that health care costs generated by stress and depression exceeded those stemming from diabetes and heart disease – both stress-related illnesses.

Of course, many companies understand the negative impact of cumulative stress and do their best to help employees counteract it. Some offer on-site yoga classes and massage; others provide stress management seminars; still others require workers to take a vacation every year. The problem is that the overall company culture, exacerbated by the stress in people's private lives, works against such approaches. Stressed-out employees are unwilling to take precious time away from work, even for an hour, to partake of amenities that they – and their bosses – generally regard as optional. Moreover, those who use the employee wellness programmes are the ones already most willing to confront their stress head-on. Those in the greatest need often don't show up.

Since 1991, we have studied the mind-body-emotion relationship – specifically, the physiological impact of stress on performance, both at the individual and organisational levels. (Thoughts and emotions have different types of physiological responses, so we distinguish between thoughts, which are generated by the mind, and emotions, which are produced throughout the body.)

Our goal, in large part, has been to decode the underlying mechanics of stress. We've sought to understand not only how stress works on a person's mind, heart, and other body systems but also to discover the precise emotional, mental, and physiological levers that can counteract it. Having worked with more than 50,000 workers and managers in more than 100 organisations, including Boeing, BP, Cisco, Unilever, Bank of Montreal, and Shell, we've found that learning to manage stress is easier than most people think. And stress reversal can do a lot of good for your organisation.

## Five Strategies for Turning Stress into Productive Energy

Nelson, author of *1001 Rewards & Recognitions: The Field Book,* offers five concepts that you and your firm's supervising partners can incorporate into your management style – at no cost – to help transform law firm stress into productive energy. *It pays to consider the access your firm provides to:*

1. **Interesting work:** Not every job is interesting all the time. The key is to offer associates and staff opportunities to work on matters and other tasks that they enjoy, especially when there's a need to redistribute workloads.
2. **Information:** Many law firms adhere to the premise that "no news is good news." *Remember:* People want to feel empowered. Inform them regularly about how the firm is doing overall and how they are performing individually. "Open channels of communication are critical during times of high stress. Keep your people informed about the developments that affect their lives and encourage them to ask questions about the new tasks they are being asked to assume."
3. **Involvement:** Partners who feel they've best suited to handle important issues and client-related matters may resist involving others, even in decisions that directly affect these. Yet Nelson says that engaging others is practical – since those closest to a situation often have the best insight – as well as respectful. The more involved members of your law firm feel and actually are in the work process, the more committed they will be

to achieving its goals. This is especially important for associates, *CBLO* believes, since most are looking to gain a sense of "belonging" to your firm.

4. **Independence:** Micromanagement is a true demotivator; few like to have their every action closely monitored. "Most people want to do a good job – in a way that works best for them," Nelson explains. Offer more latitude to boost the chances of everyone producing the desired – or better than desired – results.

5. **Increase visibility:** Give credit and give it publicly when a member of your law firm does something well. Sending a congratulatory thank you e-mail for a job well done is simple and effective, and copying it to others in positions of authority is a powerful way to reinforce the idea that people are appreciated and that their efforts make a difference.

**Surviving Stress In The Workplace**

(By John A Uzzi, August 2004)

Stress in the workplace continues to be a major concern and it can be brought on through several factors. The major ones include: lack of communication; ineffective supervisors; inadequate training systems; lack of recognition for on the job performance; increasingly workloads; antiquated promotion systems; mistrust of senior management and/or co-workers; personality conflicts; being kept to the dark about forthcoming changes; and favouritism, and what some employees conceive to be a double-standard – all leading to a general feeling of frustration, discontent and irritability among some or many employees. Often, because of stress, is a sense that an employee has little or no control of his/her work life.

However, relief from stress in the workplace is within sight of any organisation by recognising generational and other differences found within any workplace and taking appropriate actions tailor-made to alleviating employees' concerns. Recommended steps to follow include:

- Constant communication with employees and maintaining a relaxed, informal atmosphere.
- Re-evaluating and updating, when deemed necessary, training systems and procedures.
- Enhancing the sense of employee control through job design, clear accountability and participative management.
- Mining all the talent that's available and focusing on the needs and interests of each generation.
- Developing staff-driven personal development plans.
- Facilitating discussion about generational and other differences on a regularly scheduled basis.
- Openly addressing challenges and plans to overcome them.
- Having regularly scheduled meetings with each employee to get their suggestions, ascertain their ambitions and focus on their career path.
- Making policies and procedures as clear as possible and designed to meet, as much as possible individual needs.
- Assuring that all employees take their paid vacation.
- In addition, it's necessary to work for developing various perks for employees' performance that can bolster their morale. This could include periodic days off for a job well done, bonuses for excellent service above and beyond on an assigned and involves project, flexible working hours, and luncheons, dinners and other planned get togethers honouring one or more employees.

## Managing Work-related Stress

(UK experience, Business News Update, March 2005)

- The UK Health and Safety Executive has launched a new approach to help employers work with their employees to manage the risks from work-related stress.

- Minister for Work Jane Kennedy said: "This is a practical example of what can be done to demonstrate how easy it can be to reduce the causes of work-related stress.

  "The Management Standards for Work-related Stress provide clear advice for employers to follow".
- More than 13 million days a year are lost through work-related stress. It is the biggest occupational cause of working days lost through injury or ill-health.

  With an average of 29 days lost per case, it costs the society about £3.7 billion a year.
- In 2001/02, more than half a million individuals in Britain experienced work-related stress at levels that made them ill.
- With input from a range of businesses, professional bodies, unions, and other Government agencies such as ACAS, the HSF has developed an approach based on a continuous improvement model featuring a benchmarking tool to help managers gauge stress levels, compare themselves with other organisations, and work with employees to identify solutions.
- The Management Standards are not new regulations. Along with the toolkit, the standards help large organisations meet their existing duty of care and their duty to assess the risk of work-related stress.

  The standards define the characteristics of an organisation where stress is managed effectively.
- Janet Asherson of the CBI said: "This is an authoritative set of principle and a framework to help employers and employees tackle stress at work".

## The Right Relief

(By Chang, Julia Rauch, Maggie, USA, May 2005)

Stress is an inevitable consequence of today's pressure-laden work environment. But before passing it off as per for the course, consider this: Stressed-out staffers are often unproductive. According to ComPsych Corporation, a human-resource firm based in Chicago, 40 per cent of workers blame their stress on work. Forty-four per cent say they lose at least an hour of daily productivity due to stress, while 47 per cent have worked one to four days a year when they were too stressed out to be effective.

Despite these statistics, dealing with the problem is often left to the employee. Companies should consider offering strategies to relieve stress the same way they offer skills training, says Jim Bird, CEO of WorldLifeBalance.com, a work/life consultancy based in Atlanta Bird's stress-relief training includes everything from the management tactics to teaching workers how to keep separate states of mind during work and leisure activities. His programmes make stress relief an analytical and tactic-driven process. "Too much so-called stress relief training talks about a general awareness," he says. "But salespeople are aware of what's causing them stress. What they need is a tool that helps."

Peter Callaghan, Vice President of sales and marketing for Maximizer Software Inc., a provider of customer relationship management software based in Vancouver, Canada, prefers an informal approach.

"Management agrees there are principles we should be helping our staff with," he says, adding that salespeople are often stressed when they don't have the proper support. "When I started in high-tech sales, I was given a thirty-six page product guide, and was them told, 'Good luck".

Callaghan likes to stay on top of his salespeople's individual challenges. For instance, if a team member is having a hard time with a prospect, he may offer coaching that reinforces skills from the company's training course on understanding the customer's mindset. If a rep is stressed out about his career, Callaghan may provide guidance through a one-on-one discussion. The company also conducts employees surveys that managers use to identify areas in which they need improvement.

## Coping With Workplace Stress

(Clínica Mayo Libro de la Salud familiar, Mexican experience)

To celebrate the release of the Mayo Clinic's news book, the Spanish translation of the "Family Health Book". De Scott Littin, professor of medicine at Mayo Medical School, took some time to chat with Business Mexico, Dr. Littin discussed the effects of stress on a person's health and some of the more practical ways to cope with stress in the workplace.

Apparently, that annoying headache is not the only thing that stress can do to the body. Littin estimates that 50 per cent or more of medical complications have a background in stress. But stress does not necessarily have to be bad.

"For all of us to function to our best we have to have a little bit of stress". Littin said: In general, when a person experiences stress, the body reacts in order to prepare a person for the fight-or-fight response. When the stress is removed, the body goes back to normal. Under a situation of constant stress the body does not have time to recover which leads to health problems.

Prolonged stress affects the digestive system, the immune system, the nervous system, and the cardiovascular system. And this can lead to problems like atheroselerosis and heart disease.

So learning how to manage stress can do a lot more than just shorten the "to do" list. It could lengthen a life. And managing workplace stress could save employers the pain of sick days and the cost of high insurance.

In the U.S. workplace, the most common causes of stress are work overload, a lack of control over how work is done, job ţit and relationships in the workplace, said Dr. Timothy Craunmins, M.D. and Vice President of General Mills. He suggested employees could avoid unnecessary stress by setting priorities, allowing employees to control the way in which they do their jobs, assuring the individual employed is a good match for the position and seeing that people are always treated with respect.

## Is your Boss Good For Your Health?

In addition to advice about stress, the new book provides a wealth of information about specific medical terms available treatments and general well-being. Both Crimunis and Littin agreed employers play an important role in their employees health.

"The most important thing a business can do is to get their employees to stop smoking," said Crimunis. He recommends that companies reduce indoor smoking and encourage their employees to quit the habit.

Some companies in the United States, realising the health of their employees benefits their business, have put gymnasiums in the workplace, Littin noted. Others have focused on incentive programmes to encourage health among employees.

"The book is not meant to take the place of a doctor, but it better educate the patient". Littin said, Instead of encouraging people to self-medicate he hopes the book will give people the opportunity to learn more about their symptoms in order to be more active participants in their own healthcare.

### Mind, Body, Spirit

(Times of India, January 2007)

**Relieving stress:** To have a clean mind, change it frequently, one would be busy condemning great ideas of transformation, says Swami Sukhabodhananda.

Understanding the mind, transforming it and transcending the mind are the mantra for enlightenment. Understand the mind: This is awareness of how the mind functions. Mind only exists in thoughts. It can create a lot of illusions. Most of us don't experience the world as it is, but rather through our minds. The world can be beautiful or ugly, depending on how our minds look at it. Also we have not one mind, but many. The mind of a father in us is different from the mind of a son, husband or businessman in us. We have different, "I's". So too we have different minds. Understanding how the mind operates gives us a better leverage to handle it. Transform the mind: The next step is changing negative words to positives words, negative pictures to positive pictures. Mind is a series of thoughts, thoughts are words and pictures. They emanate from our values. If we have a negative value, we get a negative thought or picture; if you have a positive value you get a positive thought or picture. So transforming our values is in essence transforming the mind. Transcend the mind: Between two thoughts, there exists silence.

Learn to see the gaps between thoughts. The observer of silence is nothing but silence. Then, one learns to enjoy silence.

Sit on the bed with a deep awareness of your body, a deep sense of gratitude of the miracle of the body. Breathe deeply three times as though you are inhaling God's blessings. Exhale all tensions. Visualise that a great secret is hidden in a stressful incident. Relieve your tense mind and see it as a great lesson existence is teaching you. Now re-live this tense moment as though you are a Buddha... an enlightened being. Visualise how you are not affected by that tension. You are as calm as a Buddha. You are just a witness. Then, lie down and sleep.

### Stress takes toll on tech toddlers

(The Telegraph, January 2007)

BPOs may be the surest way to financial freedom for freshers, but the path is paved with pitfalls.

For, the cost of pressure to perform, strict quality norms, irregular work hours and night shifts at times out-weighs the benefits.

"Around 70 per cent of BPO employees, in their early and mid-twenties, who come for a check-up suffer from various stress-related disorders," says Milan Chetri, consultant physician of Internal Medicine at Apollo Gleneagles Hospitals.

Insomnia, fatigue, disorientation, gastrointestinal problems, back pain and visual disorders are some of the common complaints among BPO employees. According to Chetri, the problems arise due to job-related stress and late-night shifts, affecting normal sleep-cycle and causing hormonal changes, daytime sleepiness and irritability.

"Stress is a big issue, because we are supposed to perform and meet targets constantly. Inability to live up to expectations is a major concern," says a call centre employee.

The situation is a shade better in high-end, non-voice BPOs, but a majority of companies do not have adequate arrangements or training modules to ensure a healthy work-life for employees.

"If we have a sore throat we are asked to have a cup of coffee... In Delhi, employees are given massages and sent to yoga workshops," says a BPO employee, complaining of lack of care.

GenY. iPod-flashing and Coke-sipping, often gets into the BPO lifestyle without realising the potential health hazards.

"The sedentary nature of the job, compounded with wrong choice of food and irregular eating habits, leads to obesity among executives," points out Sushila Sharangdhar, dietician at Saffola Healthy Heart Foundation.

Doctors also warn that a stressful life and erratic eating habits make BPO workers more prone to cardiovascular diseases and high blood pressure.

But BPO companies claims employee problems are treated with care through medical allowance, regular health check-ups and counseling.

"It is an employees' market... With such high attrition levels, we cannot afford to be negligent about their needs." Agrues the head of a BPO firm.

## Suggestions

- Drink at least two litres of water at work
- Eat small but frequent meals
- Increase fibre in diet, use cereal-pulse combination
- Avoid red meat, fried food and heavy meals
- Do not depend on antacids, tranquilizers
- Get proper sleep
- Change shifts, from mornings to afternoons to nights
- Exercise regularly and take breaks
- Maintain a distance from the monitor, with the computer screen at eye level

**The Impact from Pressures on Your Face.**

When you get angry, your face will drive every guest away, no matter who he or she is, because of your brutal face. The feelings of anger which have been accumulated in your mind for a long time can also harm your physical body tremendously. Anger is likened to fire; when it increasingly gets accumulated, it will turn destructive and will first burn your body and mind directly. In particular, it can cause physical illness to your body. The following diseases occur apparently when the mind is continuously burnt by anger.

**Fig. 2**

## ENVIRONMENTAL FACTORS THAT PRODUCE STRESS- IMPACT ON HUMAN HEALTH

*"Nothing gives one person so much advantage over another as to remain always cool and unruffled under all circumstances."*

—Thomas Jefferson

As the pace at which our society operates increases, the pressures for every member of society to keep up with this pace also increases. Many of these pressures affect people through their jobs. Stress has become the "buzzword" that many people use to describe the impact that these pressures cause. In the short-term, stress can enable individuals to meet high levels of demand or pending deadlines. Prolonged stress, however, has been shown to cause illness and other conditions that can have detrimental effects on an employer's workforce.

Stress has existed throughout the evolution. About 4 billion years ago, violent collision of rock and ice along with dust and gas, led to the formation of a new planet. The planet survived more than 100 million years of meltdown to give birth to microscopic life. These first organisms endured the harshest of conditions—lack of oxygen, exposure to sun's UV rays and other inhospitable elements, to hang on to their dear life. Roughly 300,000 years ago, the Neanderthals learnt to use fire in a controlled way, to survive the Glacial Age. And around 30,000 years, Homo sapiens with their dominant gene constitutions and better coping skills, won the game of survival. Each step of evolution a test of survival, and survival, a matter of coping with the stress of changing conditions.

Millions of trials and errors in the life process have brought men to this stage. Coping with events to survive has led men to invent extraordinary technologies, beginning with a piece of sharpened stone.

From the viewpoint of micro-evolution, stress induction of transpositions is a powerful factor, generating new genetic variations in populations under stressful environmental conditions. Passing through a 'bottleneck', a population can rapidly and significantly alter its population norm and become the founder of new, evolved forms.

Gene transposition through Transposable Elements (TE)—'jumping genes', is a major source of genetic change, including the creations of novel genes, the alteration of gene expression in development, and the genesis of major genomic rearrangements. In a research on 'the significance of responses of the genome to challenges,' the Noble Prize winning scientist, Barbara McClintock, characterised these genetic phenomena as 'genomic shock'. This occurs due to recombinational events between TE insertions (high and low insertion polymorphism) and host genome. But, as a rule TEs remain immobilised until some stress factor (temperature, irradiation, KNA damage, the introduction of foreign chromatin, viruses, etc.) activates their elements.

The moral remains that we can work a stress condition to our advantage or protect ourselves from its untoward follow-throughs subject to how we handle a stress situation. The choice is between becoming a slave to the stressful situations of life or using them to our advantage.

In a challenging situation the brain prepares the body for defensive action—the fight or flight response by releasing stress hormones, namely, cortisone and adrenaline. These hormones raise the blood pressure and the body prepares to react to the situation. With a concrete defensive action (fight response) the stress hormones in the blood get used up, entailing reduced stress effects and symptoms of anxiety.

When we fail to counter a stress situation (flight response) the hormones and chemicals remain unreleased in the blood stream for a long period of time. It results in stress related physical symptoms such as tense muscles, unfocused anxiety, dizziness and rapid heartbeats. We all encounter various stressors (causes of stress) in everyday life, which can accumulate, if not released. Subsequently, it compels the mind and body to be in an almost constant alarm-state in preparation to fight or flee. This state of accumulated stress can increase the risk of both acute and chronic psychosomatic illnesses and weaken the immune system of the human body.

Stress can cause headaches, irritable bowel syndrome, eating disorders, allergies, insomnia, backaches, frequent cold and fatigue to diseases such as hypertension, asthma, diabetes, heart ailments and even cancer. In fact, Sanjay Chugh, a leading Indian psychologist, says that 70 per cent to 90 per cent of adults visit primary care physicians for stress-related problems. Scary enough. But where do we err?

Just about everybody—men, women, children and even foetuses—suffer from stress. Relationship demands, chronic health problems, pressure at workplaces, traffic snarls, meeting deadlines, growing-up tensions or a sudden bearish trend in the bourse can trigger stress conditions. People react to it in their own ways. In some people, stress-induced adverse feelings and anxieties tend to persist and intensify. Learning to understand and manage stress can prevent the counter effects of stress.

Methods of coping with stress are aplenty. The most significant or sensible way out is a change in lifestyle. Relaxation techniques such as meditation, physical exercises, listening to soothing music, deep breathing, various natural and alternative methods, effective of the known non-invasive stress busters.

**STRESS** is a word that can be used to describe both the cause and the results of pressure building up in the body and mind. Commonly, bullying, job insecurity, relationship difficulties, and many other situations associated with the home or work place generate stress internally and externally. At its root, stress is caused by the difference between expectation and reality. The health and safety executive's definition is that stress occurs "When the demands placed upon a person exceed the capacity to cope with them". If the factors causing stress build up for too long, we can experience 'symptoms'— usually at the physical and emotional level.

Although these signs are called symptoms, stress is not an illness: stress is a psychological condition which has unpleasant physical side effects-but it is a condition which can be addressed by learning about it and changing behaviour associated with pressure to work hard, it can also arise from boredom, procrastination, perfectionism.

## Model of Occupational Stress

OB researchers Michael Matteson and John Ivancevich developed an instructive model of occupational stress. As illustrated in Table 10 stressors lead to stress, which in turn produces a variety of outcomes. The model also specifies several individual differences that moderate the stressor-stress-outcome relationship. A moderator is a variable that causes the relationship between two variables—such as stress and outcomes—to be stronger for some people and weaker for others.

For example, a recent field study of 102 clinical staff in a hospital revealed that employees with high organizational commitment reported less stress and job displeasure than did people with low organisational commitment. Organizational monument moderated the effects of stress. Let us consider the major components of this stress model.

## STRESSORS: ENVIRONMENTAL FACTORS THAT PRODUCE STRESS

Stressors are environmental factors that produce stress. Stated differently, stressors are a prerequisite to experiencing the stress response. Fig. shows the four major types of stressors: individual, group, organisational, and extra-organisational. Individual-level stressors are those directly associated with a person's job duties; for example, emergency room nurses experience stress uniquely associated with treating patients who are high on drugs and alcohol. The most common examples of stressors are role overload, role conflict, and role ambiguity: these role characteristics create stress because they make people feel both overworked and uncertain about what they should be doing. Managers can reduce these stressors by providing direction and support for their employees.

Group-level stressors are caused by group dynamics and managerial behaviour. Managers create stress for employees by (1) exhibiting inconsistent behaviour, (2) failing to provide support, (3) showing lack of concern, (4) providing inadequate direction, (5) creating a high productivity environment, and (6) focussing on negatives while ignoring good performance.

Organisational stressors affect large numbers of employees. Organisational climate or culture is a prime example. For instance, a high-pressure environment that places chronic work demands on employees fuels the stress response. In contrast, research provides preliminary support for the idea that participative management can reduce organisational stress. Finally, the office design and general office environment are important organisational-level stressors. Research demonstrates that poor lighting, loud noise, improper placement of furniture, and a dirty or smelly environment creates stress. Managers are advised to monitor and eliminate these stressors Extra-organisational stressors are those caused by factors outside the organisation. For instance, conflicts associated with balancing one's career and family life are stressful; so is an individual's socio-economic status. Stress is higher for people with lower socio-economic status, which represents a combination of (1) economic status, as measured by income, (2) social status, assessed by educational level, and (3) work status, as indexed by occupation. These stressors are likely to become more important in the future. Outcomes: Theorists contend that stress has behavioural, cognitive, and physiological consequences, or outcomes.

### Stressors on the Job

Following are the main stressors that have been identified as those causing the most stress for most people:

1. "Politics" in general and organisational politics in particular.
2. Too much/too little independence in performance and decision-making.
3. Responsibilities without adequate power to fulfill them.
4. Lack of adequate knowledge to fulfill assignments or make plans for self within the organisational structure
5. Lack of motivators for performance.
6. Too much or too little responsibility.
7. Too much or too little work.
8. Interruptions and conflicting demands.
9. Role conflict.
10. Managing time on the job.

Job stress comes in many different forms and affects our bodies in various ways. Minor sources of stress may include equipment that won't work or phones that won't quit ringing. Major stress comes from having too much work, fearing a job layoff, or not getting along with your boss.Usually it is the major sources of stress that lead to burnout, causing people to become unhappy and less productive in their work. Job stress can affect health and home life as well. Low levels of stress may not be noticeable; slightly higher levels can be positive and challenge us to act in creative and resourceful ways; and high levels can be harmful, contributing to chronic disease.

**Table 10**

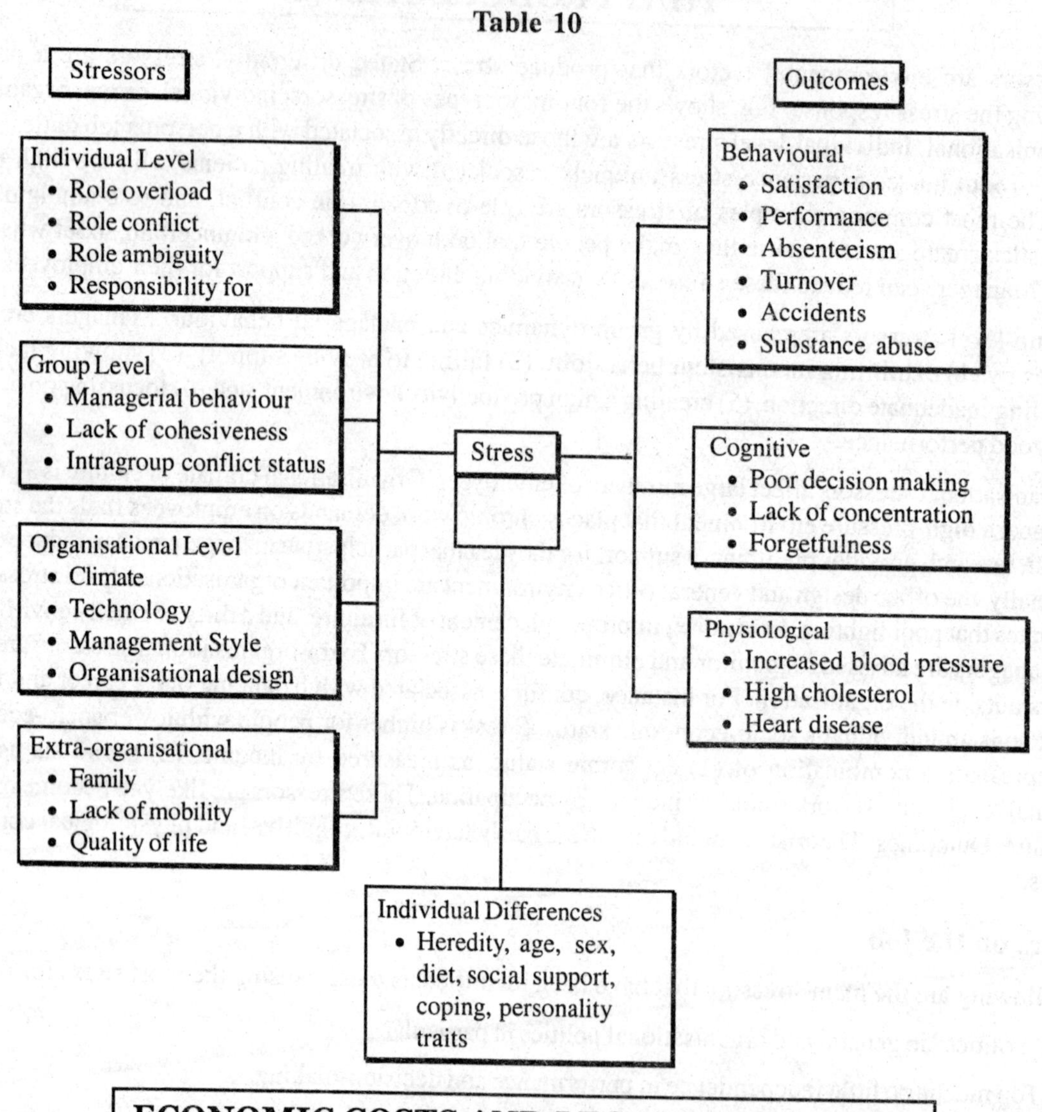


## ECONOMIC COSTS AND LEGAL LIABILITIES

Managers need to understand the causes and consequences of stress for at least four compelling reasons. First, from a quality-of-work-life perspective, workers are more satisfied when they have a safe and comfortable work environment. Second, a moral imperative suggests that managers should reduce occupational stress because it leads to negative outcomes. For example, mental health experts estimate that 10 per cent of the workforce suffers from depression or high level of stress that may ultimately affect job performance. A third reason centres on the staggering economic costs of stress. Experts estimate that stress-related illnesses cost American business approximately $68 billion a year. The fourth reason revolves around recent court cases where employees sued their employers for workers' compensation for stress- related problems.

In a nutshell, managers cannot afford to ignore the many implications of occupational stress.

The stress can be classified into four groups.

**1. Distress** **2. Euphoric stress** **3. Hyper stress** **4. Hypo stress**

The term **distress** is the most commonly accepted interpretation of the term stress. It account for all the happenings and resultant feelings of unpleasantness, losses. The opposite of distress is **eu-stress** or stress caused by experiences of over joy, over pleasantness or a windfall or sudden gain. The **hyper** stress is the situation characterised by over activities, pressure of meeting the deadlines, etc. Opposite to this is **hypo** stress, indicated by lack of activity, absence of challenge and pressure for performance. Generally, executives complain about hyper stress but if possible avoid the situation of hypo stress or hyper stress. In fact, many organisations create legitimate tasks and regular systematic work routine of responsibilities. The stress is essential to reach the definite performance. In fact, excellence in any sphere of life is essentially accompanied by stress. It is a bad master, but a good servant.

## Effects of Stress on the Body

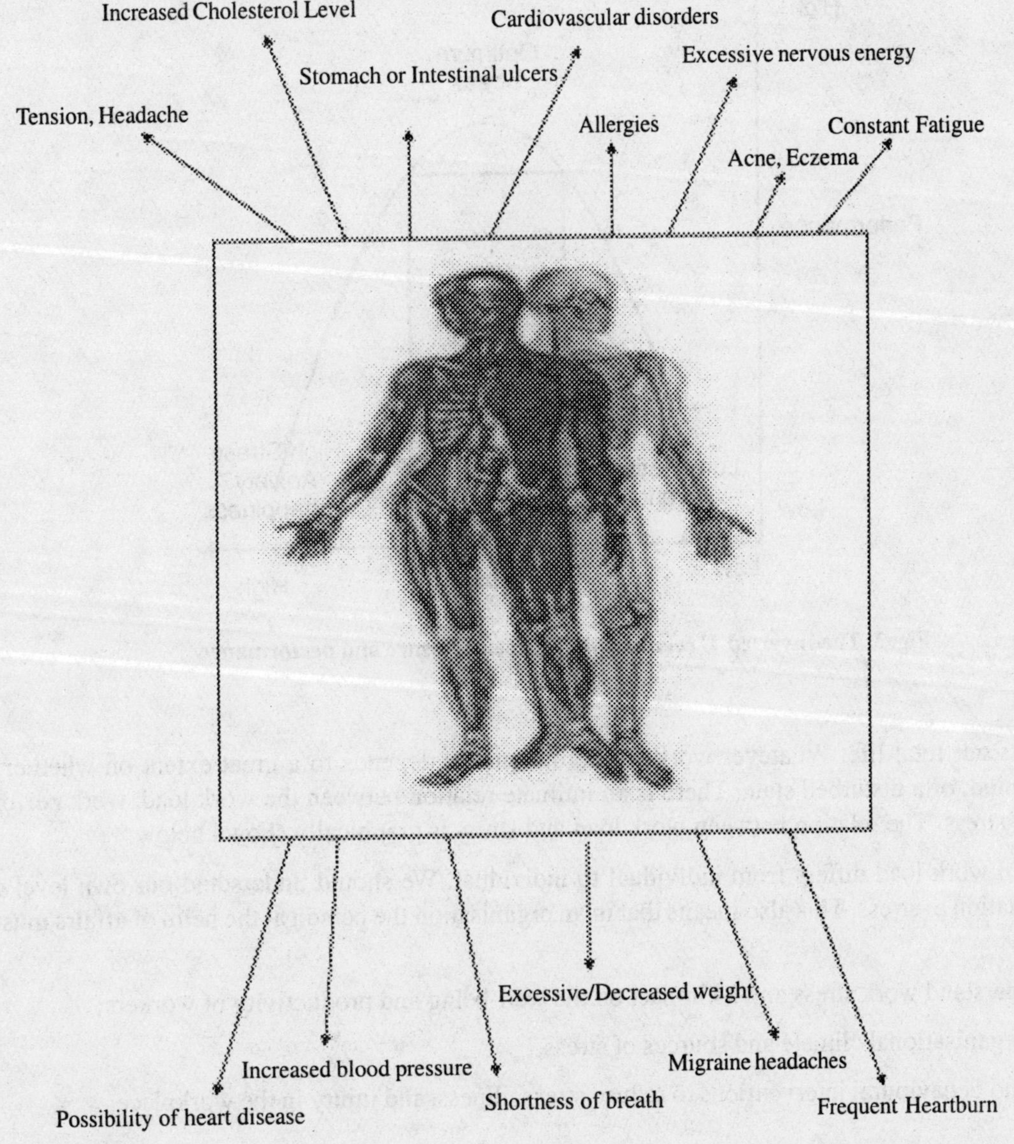

## STRESS AND WORK PERFORMANCE

Relationship between occupational stress and job performance! The amount of money workplace stress is extracting from the economy is estimated to be billions of dollars. Such estimates are based on the assumption that workplace stress leads to increased healthcare costs, higher rates of absenteeism and turnover, accidents, and lower levels of performance and organisational productivity. A comprehensive, research-based examination of the relationship between occupational stress and job performance presents a concise overview of the field, a clear explanation of terms and concepts, and a summary of relevant theoretical models of the stress process. the relationship between major job-related stressors (such as workload, interpersonal conflict and lack of control) and a variety of performance indices explores a number of other factors that may affect the relationship between occupational stress and job performance, including gender differences, age, personality, and job experience.

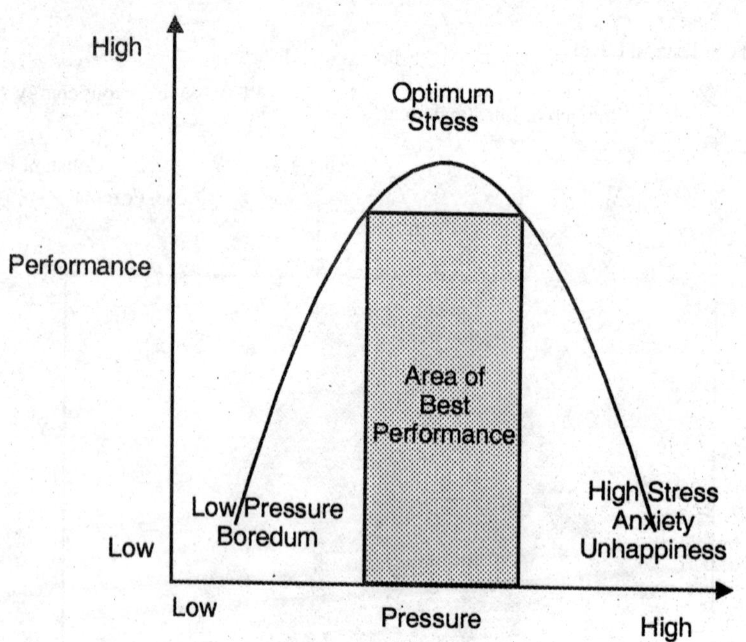


**Fig. 3: The Inverted-U relationship between pressure and performance**

### Work & Stress

Stress affects our total life. Whatever work we do, its quality depends to a great extent on whether we are having peace of mind, or a disturbed state. There is an intimate relation between the work load, work performance and experience of stress. The relation between work load and stress is graphically shown below:

The optimum work load differs from individual to individual. We should understand our own level of peak performance in relation to stress. This also means that in an organisation the person at the helm of affairs must do the following:

- Try to understand work stress and its impact on the well-being and productivity of workers;
- Explore organisational climate and sources of stress,
- Seek to find behavioural interventions to reduce stress, illness, and injury in the workplace.

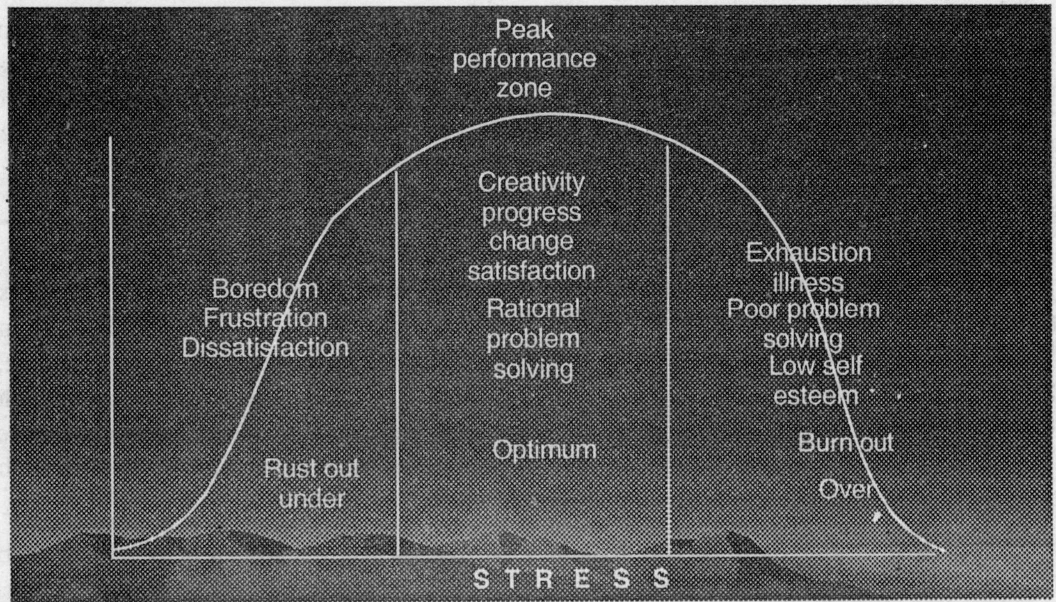


Fig. 4

## STRESS PERFORMANCE AND ACHIEVEMENT

Many people, especially executives, regard stress as a bad word and they prefer to use a word such as "challenge" for positive stress. Hans selye, the physician who such popularised the stress concept, chose the word *eustress*, which may be defined as the health, positive, constructive outcome of stressful events and the stress response. The relationship between stress and performance has been known since 1908, when Robert Yerkes and James Dodson demonstrated increased performance under conditions of arousal up to an optional point, as shown in Figure ( The Yerkes – Dodson Law).

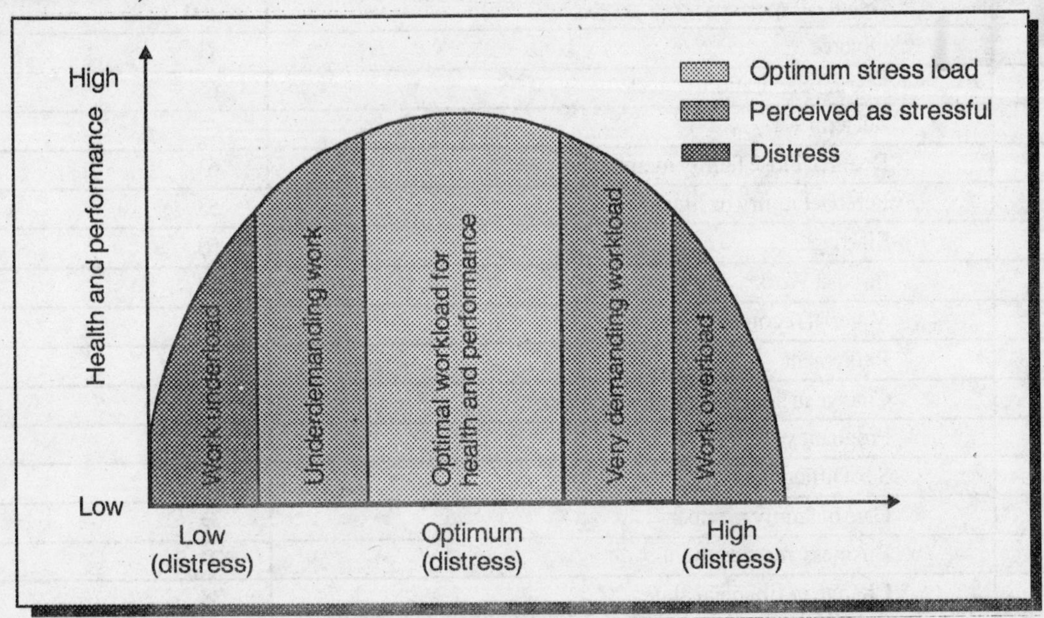


Fig. 5

As the figure shows, performance increases with increasing stress loads up to an optimum point, and then the stress load becomes too great, resulting in depressed performance. The optimum stress load that maximises performance varies by individual and by task, based on several considerations; Individual considerations include susceptibility to stress, fatigue, psychological and cognitive skills and physical capacity. Task considerations include the complexity, difficulty, duration, and intensity of the work. The interaction, as reflected in the person's familiarity with the task, also affects the shape and size of the particular Yerkes-Dodson curve. Too little stress and arousal often fail to stimulate performance, just as too much stress and arousal can interfere with performance, especially on complex tasks.

## STRESS IN ORGANISATIONS

As Leon Warshaw noted in 1979 in his book on dealing with stress in the workplace: "Stress affects personality, modifying our perceptions, feelings, attitudes and behaviour." There are many factors that contribute to making a workplace stressful. Research clearly indicates that certain jobs are more stressful than others. For example, people who work as police officers, fire fighters, air traffic controllers, and elected officials are exposed to higher levels of stress. The factors that contribute to making some jobs more stressful include: level of decision-making required; level of monitoring workers must endure; unpleasant or dangerous physical or emotional conditions; repeated exchange of information with others; and whether job tasks are generally structured or unstructured.

Understanding the factors that contribute to creating stress in the workplace can help employers begin to manage stress among the workforce.

Organisations cutting across industries are gearing up to provide employees with a stress-free healthy environment. The efforts to address this issue were more pronounced in some industries than others. Experts felt that, though stress at the workplace is a global phenomenon, professionals in some industries were more susceptible to stress than others.

### Holmes Scale of Stress Value

**Table 11**

**Social Readjustment Rating Scale**

| *Rank* | *Life Event* | *Mean Value* |
|---|---|---|
| 1. | Death of spouse | 100 |
| 2. | Divorce | 73 |
| 3. | Marital Separation | 65 |
| 4. | Jail term | 63 |
| 5. | Death of close family member | 63 |
| 6. | Personal injury or illness | 53 |
| 7. | Marriage | 50 |
| 8. | Fired at Work | 47 |
| 9. | Material reconciliation | 45 |
| 10. | Retirement | 45 |
| 11. | Change in health of family member | 44 |
| 12. | Pregnancy | 40 |
| 13. | Sex Difficulties | 39 |
| 14. | Gain of family member | 39 |
| 15. | Business readjustment | 39 |
| 16. | Change in financial state | 38 |
| 17. | Death of close friend | 37 |
| 18. | Change to different line of work | 36 |
| 19. | Change in number of arguments with spouse | 35 |

| | | |
|---|---|---|
| 20. | Mortgage over $10,000 | 31 |
| 21. | Foreclosure of mortgage or loan | 30 |
| 22. | Change in responsibilities at work | 29 |
| 23. | Son or daughter leaving home | 29 |
| 24. | Trouble with in-law | 29 |
| 25. | Outstanding personal achievement | 28 |
| 26. | Spouse beginning or stopping work | 26 |
| 27. | Beginning or ending school | 26 |
| 28. | Change in living conditions | 25 |
| 29. | Revision of personal habits | 24 |
| 30. | Trouble with boss | 23 |
| 31. | Change in work hours or conditions | 20 |
| 32. | Change in residence | 20 |
| 33. | Change in schools | 20 |
| 34. | Change in recreation | 19 |
| 35. | Change in Church activities | 19 |
| 36. | Change in social activities | 18 |
| 37. | Mortgage or loan less than $10,000 | 17 |
| 38. | Change in sleeping habits | 16 |
| 39. | Change in number of family get-togethers | 15 |
| 40. | Change in eating habits | 15 |
| 41. | Vacation | 13 |
| 42. | Christmas | 12 |
| 43. | Minor violations of the law | 11 |

## Life Events Stress Scale: Indian case

Dr. Aam Batlivals, a consultant physician administered the Holmes and Rahe Life Events Scale to a mixed group of 330 senior exeeutives in order to find out the typical role stresses faced by the Indian executives.

The most common event producing stress for the group was 'pressure to work harder'. The next common stressful event found was the festivals like Diwali, Pongal, Onam, Christmas. The commonly felt stressor was 'change in health of family members', and 'change in responsibilities at work'. Arguing with spouse was the next commonly experienced stressor. Items like noise pollution in the neighborhood, wife constantly comparing with others, poor performance of children in examinations, arranging dowry for daughter's marriage, getting children admitted to schools were some of the important stressors for Indian executives.

## The General Adaptation Syndrome (GAS)

Selye considered stress a non-specific response to any demand made upon an organism. He called the three phases of the defense reaction that a person establishes when stressed as the General Adaptation Syndrome (GAS). Selye called the defense reaction, general because stressors had effects on several parts of the body, adaptation refers to a stimulation of defenses intended to help the body adjust to or deal with the stressors, and syndrome shows that individual pieces of the reaction take place more or less together. The three distinct phases are known as: alarm, resistance and exhaustion.

The alarm stage is the initial mobilisation by which the body meets the challenge posed by the stressor. When a stressor is identified, the brain sends forth biochemical messages to all of the body's systems. Respiration increases, blood pressure rises, pupils dilate, muscles tense up and so forth.

If the stressor continues, the GAS proceeds to the resistance stage. The signs of resistance stage include: tension anxiety and fatigue. The person is now fighting the stressor. While resistance to a specific stressor may be high during this period, resistance to other stressors may be low. A person has only finite sources of energy, concentration, and ability to resist stressors. Individuals are often more illness-prone during periods of stress than at other times.

Exhaustion occurs if the stressor continues and the body exhausts its ability to adapt. The symptoms of this stage are similar to the alarm reaction. If the stress persists unduly, severe wear and tear will occur, resulting in damage to a local area or death to the organism as a whole. This is, more or less, a 'fight or flight' response. Here, the autonomic nervous system makes dozens of immediate responses to prepare the body for physical action. When pedestrians are crossing the street and suddenly see a car speeding toward them, the alarm reaction prepares their bodies to quickly get out of the way. Some of the major responses that the body makes during the alarm reaction may be listed thus: (Table 1), Triggered off by the 'emergency' hormone adrenaline shooting into the bloodstream.

The figure below shows the course of syndrome.

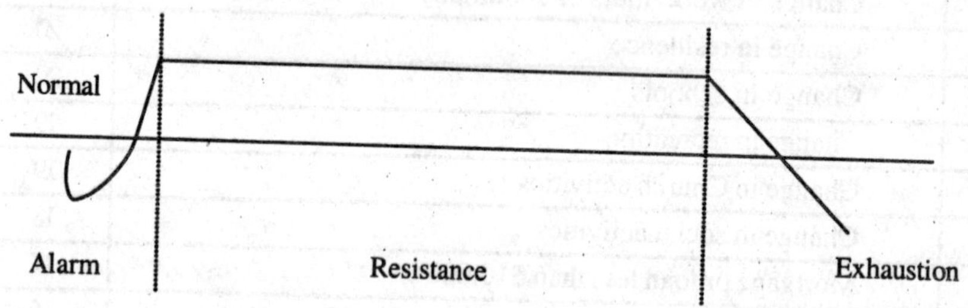


**Fig. 6**

## Physiological Responses to an Alarm Reaction

- The respiration rate to provide more oxygen
- Red blood cells flood the bloodstream to carry more oxygen to the muscles
- The heart beats faster and blood pressure soars to provide blood to needed areas
- Stored sugar and fats are converted to blood glucose to provide fuel for quick energy
- Blood-clotting mechanisms are activated to protect against possible bleeding
- Digestion ceases so that blood may be diverted to muscles and brain
- Perspiration and saliva increase
- Bowel and bladder muscles loosen
- Muscles tense in preparation for strenuous activity
- The pupils dilate, allowing more light to enter the eye

**Table 12: Twelve Jobs with Most Stress as per research findings**

1. Labourer
2. Secretary
3. Inspector
4. Chief laboratory technician
5. Office manager
6. Foreman
7. Manager/administrator
8. Waitress/waiter
9. Machine operator
10. Farm owner
11. Miner
12. Painter

## Discussion through a case study

A major corporation like Nynex goes through downsizing. Thousands of people are affected. But the complete picture includes both the employees who were laid off and those who survived the cutbacks. Both suffer from conflict and stress.

Nynex had already been through a series of downsizing efforts when the last big one was instituted (intended to reduce the number of employees by more than 20,000). Thus, the morale of survivors was already low. "Two months ago, I would have said that morale of survivors was so low that it couldn't go any lower", declared one executive. "But I'd have to say it's even lower today". When word of the new firings and buyouts was received, many reacted with fear and anger. "The officers all have golden parachutes," says Pat, a middle manager. "They're in charge of their own fates. We're just affected."

Although the organisation tried to reduce stress by offering accelerated pensions, which executive vice president Robert. Thrasher claimed, would remove "the anxiety and angst in the work force," the buyouts simply weren't enough. "Even if people won't be fired this time, they're still frightened of the future," observes Pat. "It affects their self-esteem and their pocketbook. And most people aren't going from something to something. They have no place to go."

Survivors also had to adjust to a new working environment, one in which there was no security, no matter how hard or long they worked. With a reduced work force, they had to put in longer, harder hours anyway. "Now we'll have to learn to work smarter and completely change the way we do things," explains Nancy P Karen, director of Nynex's personal-computer network. "It's a different mentality. My weekends and holidays are not reserved."

Pat believes the cost of this stress to the organisation will ultimately be very high-perhaps not on the bottom line right away. But in the long run. If the organisation is not committed to its employees, she reasons, how long-and how well-will surviving employees be committed to Nynex? She cites an instance in which she walked for hours through a blizzard to get to work one day but wonders whether future Nynex employees would be compelled to do that. And she wonders if emergency repair teams will be as quick and as responsive in the future if they could lose their jobs at any moment.

Downsizing has two sides, but both sides experience conflict and stress. Only time will reveal the true cost to organisations like Nynex.

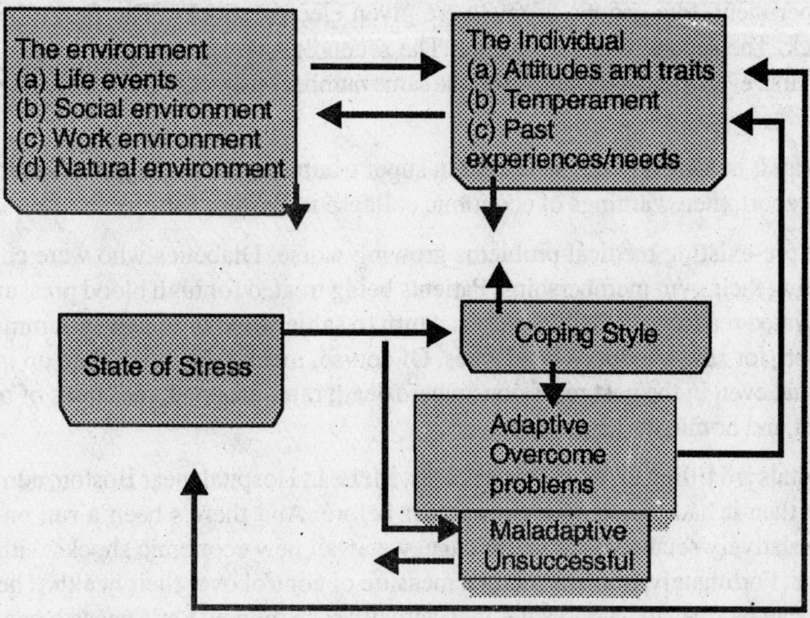


**Fig. 7: A working Model of Stress**

# THE STRESS FACTOR

## Recession Stress

Do recessions make people sicker? Some studies say yes, some say no. The better question might be, "How is *this* recession affecting health?" Not in a good way, comes the answer. This recession — depression — seems different. This recession is messing with our heads.

When the economic arrows first turned downward, a crop of silver-lining stories contended that health-habits improve in down economies. During boom times, the upwardly mobile drink too much and dine often at fatty-food restaurants. Working long hours, they skip exercise and put off visits to the doctor. Some of these unhealthy tendencies reverse themselves in a recession.

For example, Shelley McGuire, a nutritionist at Washington State University in Pullman, recently predicted that a return to home cooking would helpfully add whole grains and subtract salt from the American table. She called this new regime the "back-to-basics bailout diet."

Professor Christopher Ruhm, an economist at the University of North Carolina at Greensboro, studied death rates during the 1974 and 1982 recessions, and found that they dropped significantly. Less heart disease and fewer car accidents seemed to be the biggest factors.

I asked Ruhm whether he anticipates the same trends in this recession. "It's hard to predict what will happen this time," he responded. "This is a different kind of downturn — longer and more severe than we have seen in recent years."

We believers in the mind-body connection know that stress and anxiety, painful in themselves, can make other conditions worse. And stress is coming at us in battalions. In this crazy economy, we can't plot the extent to which things will get worse before they start getting better. We face the big black box of the unknown.

Those who owe little or no money and have jobs are also anxious. They see their real-estate values shrinking and neighbours' work disappearing. Their investment safety net lies in the gutter. There seems to be no safe harbour anymore.

In a famous experiment, two groups of rats were given electric shocks. The first group received a warning signal before the shock. The second had no warning. The second group showed much more stomach ulceration (a sign of stress) than the first, even though they received the same number of shocks. The conclusion: Lack of predictability increases stress.

And that's the way it is. One day the banks are in super trouble; the next day, it's General Motors. Out comes a horrid employment report, then warnings of economic collapse in Eastern Europe.

Hospitals report pre-existing medical problems growing worse. Diabetics who were controlling their disease with exercise are quitting their gym memberships. Patients being treated for high blood pressure and still taking their medications show elevated readings. Possible causes: a turn to saltier food or to anti-inflammatory remedies, which increase water retention, for stress-induced headaches. Of course, mental disorders flare up in these circumstances. Ruhm's study found that even in the past recessions where death rates dropped, measures of mental health suffered. Suicide rose 2 per cent and homicide 12 per cent.

Psychiatric hospitals are filling up with serious cases. McLean Hospital, near Boston, admitted 31 per cent more patients in December than it had the same month a year before. And there's been a run on anti-depression pills, including among the relatively secure. Back in our cage, we await new economic shocks without knowing when or whence they will come. Fortunately, humans retain a measure of control over their health. There are proven ways to lower stress. Exercise can be free, and a good diet may actually save money. Let's unearth one of those silver linings and tell ourselves: We're still in charge of many things.

The full-blown recession has hit behavioral health hard. More people need help. Fewer can afford it.

It has become virtually impossible to ignore bad news about the economy. Every day, Americans are bombarded with reports of slumping stock markets, massive layoffs, and dismal business forecasts. Many are experiencing these phenomena firsthand.

And it's increasingly apparent that the constant onslaught of economic gloom and doom is not only impacting people's wallets—it's also affecting their psyches. Social workers and other professionals around the country report that the slowdown has put an enormous amount of pressure on their clients. For many clients, the stress is too much to handle. They are falling victim to anxiety and depression and trying to ease their fears with alcohol and other drugs.

Such responses are not uncommon during times of economic turmoil, but the situation may be more dire this time around. There are signs that people are already cutting back or foregoing services in an attempt to save money or because they no longer have insurance coverage. Observers say they fear that if this skimping continues for an extended period, it will result in an eventual influx of people with major problems—an influx the system may not be able to handle.

"As time goes on, people's problems just fester. They get worse," says Jill Wiedemann-West, senior Vice President and chief operating officer of clinical and recovery services for Minnesota-based Hazelden, which operates a national network of treatment facilities. "I'm not sure the system is going to be able to meet the needs as successfully as we think it can. I think [the economy] is going to drive demand for services to a point where we can't meet it."

## Struggling Financially and Mentally – Stressful Conditions in USA

Anecdotal evidence suggests that the recession is becoming a top reason why people are seeking mental health services. For example, several national insurance companies report that more people are using their employee assistance programmes (EAPs). These programmes offer employees a confidential way to access short-term counselling and connect with services such as child and elder care.

Philadelphia-based CIGNA Corporation has seen calls to its EAP climb 60 per cent during the months following the financial collapse in the fall of 2008, says Doug Nemecek, MD, the insurer's national medical director. Representatives of Hartford, CT-based Aetna Inc. and Indianapolis-based WellPoint, Inc. say their companies also have seen increases.

Not only is the number of calls to EAPs going up, the topics of conversation have shifted away from traditional issues such as marital stress and family discord to job troubles, struggles with mortgages, and financial stress, Nemecek says.

"Clearly, there are people who have struggled with anxiety, depression, or substance abuse, and the economic crisis has made their problems worse," he says.

More people also are reaching out to providers of community-based mental health services. Members of the New Jersey Association of Mental Health Agencies, Inc. have seen a roughly 20 per cent increase in demand for services since the late summer of 2008, says Debra Wentz, PhD, the association's CEO. Crisis calls are going up, and more people are reporting stress-related physical symptoms such as stomach ulcers and headaches.

It's been busier for the staff of the Family Involvement Centre, a nonprofit organisation in Arizona that helps families with children who have behavioural health needs. Many of the children the centre serves sense their caregivers' increased stress and are exhibiting more anxiety and frustration at home and in school, says Jane Kallal, the centre's executive director. At the same time, Boys & Girls Clubs of America and other nonprofits that traditionally provide recreational and educational outlets for youth have to cope with reduced donations, Kallal says.

"All of this compounds and does create more stress for the families," she says. "It's a vicious cycle that we're in right now."

Changes have been felt in the world of substance abuse treatment as well. Until a few months ago, the majority of people seeking help at Townsend, a chain of outpatient facilities in the Southeast, had a primary diagnosis of prescription drug addiction. Now, the majority of new clients are addicted to alcohol. Alcohol is the current drug of choice because it's cheaper than other addictive substances, says Michael Handley, CEO of Destin, FL-based Townsend.

Jodi Conway, LCADC, who runs a private practice in Dumont, NJ, says many of her clients are having trouble kicking their addictions or are relapsing because of financial stress. The effects aren't limited to patients with alcohol or drug addictions.

"One of my specialties is sexual addictions, and that is running rampant right now," Conway says. "People have lost their jobs and are spending more time looking for pornography online. They're reacting by acting out sexually."

The downturn has renewed interest in research related to the psychological effects of financial stressors, particularly unemployment. Recent reports have linked job displacement and unemployment to lower rates of participation in social activities (Brand & Burgard, 2008), lower levels of mental health (Cassidy & Wright, 2008; Scutella & Wooden, 2008), and heavy drinking (Mossakowski, 2008).

The psychological impact of unemployment can be deep and long lasting, says Arthur Goldsmith, PhD, the Jackson T. Stephens professor of economics at Washington and Lee University in Lexington, VA. Even though many people initially see unemployment as a chance for a new start, research done by Goldsmith (Goldsmith, Veum & Darity, 1997; Goldsmith, Veum & Darity, 1996) shows that optimism is often replaced by hopelessness, depression, anxiety, and low self-esteem as unemployment lingers.

"Employment is important to people psychologically because it gives us status, organises our day, puts us in connection with other people, and gives us a purpose," Goldsmith says. "When you take away work, it really jostles someone. You can really go into a deeper sense of psychological anguish."

University of Chicago research shows that as the nation continues in a period of economic uncertainty, many of the 50 million Americans living near or below the poverty line are more vulnerable than at any time in recent years. Yet, the help they need to get a job, locate housing, access healthcare, or provide for their children is less likely to be found in their neighbourhoods as agencies serving the poor face potential financial problems of their own.

## GLOBAL CREDIT CRUNCH AFFECTS EMPLOYEE HEALTH

### The Economic Slowdown is Causing Stress and Unhealthy Life Choices

As well as affecting the ability of businesses to be profitable, the global credit crunch is affecting health. Employers can work to lessen the personal health cost.

Reports out of the United Kingdom have found that, as the global credit crisis and economic slowdown takes hold, employees are spending less money on healthy food items such as fruits, vegetables and lean cuts of meat. Expenditure on items such as gym memberships and visits to healthcare practitioners has also decreased.

Anxiety and stress levels are also increasing due to fear about job losses and the tightening labour market. Other physical health problems that may potentially increase as a result of stress include blood pressure levels, coronary artery disease and certain cancers.

In the past, some employees have taken to self-medicating their anxiety during an economic downturn by using excessive amounts of alcohol, tobacco and other recreational drugs.

The emotional health of employees has also been affected as a result of the Global Credit Crunch. The emotional effects of ongoing stress on a person can result in mental health issues, burnout and relationship difficulties with family and colleagues.

Employers have a duty of care to ensure that the health of their employees is not decreased as a result of their working environment. Although the economic slowdown is not the fault of any one particular employer, it can create an unhealthy level of stress and lead to potential physical health issues. Some simple tips to help employers care for the mental and physical health of their employees are set out below.

## STRESS AND CONFLICT

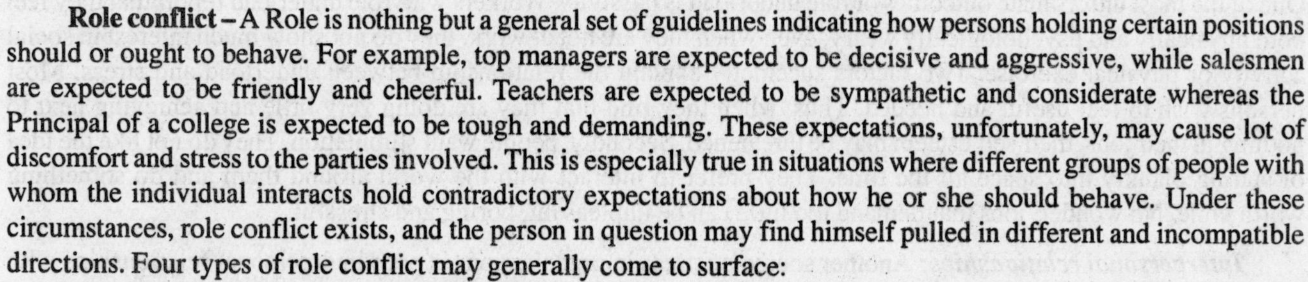

**Role conflict** – A Role is nothing but a general set of guidelines indicating how persons holding certain positions should or ought to behave. For example, top managers are expected to be decisive and aggressive, while salesmen are expected to be friendly and cheerful. Teachers are expected to be sympathetic and considerate whereas the Principal of a college is expected to be tough and demanding. These expectations, unfortunately, may cause lot of discomfort and stress to the parties involved. This is especially true in situations where different groups of people with whom the individual interacts hold contradictory expectations about how he or she should behave. Under these circumstances, role conflict exists, and the person in question may find himself pulled in different and incompatible directions. Four types of role conflict may generally come to surface:

- *Intrasender conflict* occurs when one person asks you to accomplish two objectives that are in apparent conflict. If your boss asks you to hurry up and finish your work but also decrease your pay for your mistakes, you would experience this type of conflict.
- *Intersender conflict* occurs when two or more senders give you incompatible directions. Your boss may want you to complete a crash project on time, but company policy temporarily prohibits authorising overtime payments to clerical assistance.
- *Interrole conflict* results when two different roles you play are in conflict; Your company may want you to travel 50 per cent of the time (to be promoted) while your spouse threatens a divorce if you travel more than 25 per cent of the time.
- *Person-role conflict* occurs when the role(s) that your organisation expects you to occupy are in conflict with your basic values. Your company may ask you to fire substandard performers, but this could be in conflict with your humanistic values.

Consider the following examples:

| *Workers want the manager.* | *The manager may look at his job as one demanding the following:* |
|---|---|
| To be friendly and helpful | • Keep employees under check |
| To take care of their interests | • Achieve targets |
| To reward superior effort | • See that the policies of the company are strictly *adhered* to |
| To advise and counsel when they go off | • Allow no room for lethargy, mistakes, complacency, etc. |

As you can readily see, the person facing such a situation probably cannot easily satisfy these contrasting expectations at the same time. The result: stress arising out of role conflict.

***Role ambiguity:*** Role ambiguity occurs when position holders are uncertain about limits of their authority and that of others, company rules, job security and the methods used to evaluate their work. Research studies have indicated that the more ambiguity a person reported, the lower the person's utilisation of intellectual skills, knowledge and leadership skills. It was also found that role ambiguity was significantly related to low job satisfaction and to feelings of job related threats to mental and physical well-being.

***Role overload:*** Imagine for a moment about an executive who is attempting to dictate a letter, talk on three phones, conducting an interview and writing a report all at the same time. There is no use trying to do too much in too little time. Constant interruptions, changing hats every minute, a constant stream of visitors, a mountain of files and papers to process and a number of subordinates looking up to his valuable advice and guidance- all increase the quantitative and qualitative overload. Persons who experience such conditions show clear signs of stress and report health problems.

***Role underload:*** At the other extreme, having nothing to do or being asked to do too little in one's work can also be quite stressful. Sales people in a store with no customers, standing around all day with nothing to do could be said to experience role underload. Assembly line workers also generally experience role underload; rarely do they perform more than one or two tasks day-after-day. Ironically, role underload can lead to many of the same problems as role overload; low self esteem, increased frequency of nervous symptoms and complaints, increased health problems. One of the most unfortunate outcomes of role underload is passivity. Workers with role underload report that they feel both physically and psychologically weary; even when they are not at work, they do not show much interest in social activity or physical exercise. Two factors succinctly explain the relationship between underload and stress. Most persons wish to feel useful and needed. Thus, when they find that they are doing very little and achieving next to nothing in their jobs, their self esteem may be threatened. Secondly, people want stimulation. They do not like the idea of staring blankly into space all the time. They prefer to interact with the world around them and do something worthwhile. No wonder, jobs that demand too little can be unpleasant, boring and stressful.

***Interpersonal relationships:*** Another source of stress in organisations is poor interpersonal relationships with others, be they supervisors, co-workers, subordinates or clients. When interpersonal relationships at work are not pleasant, employees develop a generalised anxiety, a feeling of fear about upcoming meetings and interactions. Three aspects of interpersonal relationships at work, in particular, have a negative influence on job stress: amount of contact with others, amount of contact with people in other departments and organisational climate.

***Ineffective communication:*** Stress can result from a lack of communication or from a lack of the right kind of communication at the right time. We begin to see the world differently and we tend to interpret communication efforts differently. For example, there is nothing more stressful than finding that you have arrived at an appointment with your boss at the wrong time. You misunderstood the appointed time, your boss is upset and you are edgy.

***Responsibility:*** Any type of responsibility can be burdensome for some people. Different types of responsibility function differently as stressors. One way of classifying this variable is in terms of responsibility for people versus responsibility for things. The more responsibility for people reported, according to one research study, the more likely the person was to smoke heavily, have high blood pressure and show higher cholesterol levels. On the contrary, the more responsibility for things the employee reported, the lower these indicators were.

***Job change:*** Individuals and work undergo constant changes as organisations try to become more competitive and aggressive in the marketplace. These changes can cause stress for the job holder. For example, a bank may computerise its accounting function. As a result, a job that did require certain decisions and calculations may become merely a data collection and entry position for the computer. As with most changes, job change entails a certain amount of uncertainty that may ultimately lead to stress. Change can be especially stressful for individuals afraid of losing their jobs.

***Climate within a company:*** Employees can also experience stress when they feel that they should get more money for their work, of if company restrains them from doing things they feel they must do to be effective in their job. For example, a manager wishes to assign a few extra duties to an individual for a special project but union regulations do not permit it. Stress can also result from prohibitive physical settings such as heat, cold, safety hazards, air pollution, uncomfortable spatial arrangements, shift work, etc. Apart from the physical surroundings, the psychological

## Organisational Stressors: A Snapshot

| ADMINISTRATIVE POLICIES AND STRATEGIES |
|---|
| Downsizing |
| Competitive pressures |
| Merit pay plans |
| Rotating work shifts |
| Bureaucratic rules |
| Advanced technology |

| ORGANISATIONAL STRUCTURE AND DESIGN |
|---|
| Centralisation and formalisation |
| Line-staff conflicts |
| Specialisation |
| Role ambiguity and conflict |
| No opportunity for promotion |
| Restrictive, untrusting culture |
| **ORGANISATIONAL PROCESSES** |
| Tight controls |
| Only downward communication |
| Little performance feedback |
| Centralised decision-making |
| Lack of participation in decisions |
| Punitive appraisal systems |
| **WORK CONDITIONS** |
| Crowded work area |
| Noise, heat, or cold |
| Polluted air |
| Strong odour |
| Unsafe, dangerous conditions |
| Poor lighting |
| Physical or mental strain |
| Toxic chemicals or radiation |

climate within a company is also important. When day-to-day life in an organisation is characterised by unfriendly, hostile exchanges, employees feel the tension, all around. They do not trust each other and do not express their concerns openly. They are unsupportive of each other and spend little time helping each other with problems. Likewise, if employees are not encouraged to participate actively in organisational activities, stressful situations may develop. Employees may feel 'left out' and neglected, because they have no opportunity to influence important events relating to their jobs. Additionally, factors like insufficient authority (where a manager does not receive the backing needed from management to carry out its directives) pressures toward conformity (where members are expected to follow established norms whether they like them or not); faulty job designs also produce lot of stress for people working within a company.

When the negative reactions to life's situations become repetitively intense and frequent we develop symptoms of depression. Life throws up innumerable situations, which we greet with both negative and positive emotions such as excitement, frustration, fear, happiness, anger, sadness, joy, et al. Depression is prevalent among all age groups, in almost all walks of life.

Persons of any age—children or adults, may develop depression symptoms. Even minor stress events can stir up depression symptoms depending on the personality type. Symptoms such as intense sadness, loss of interest or pleasure in normal activities, sleep disturbances or oversleeping, change in appetite and decreased energy level; feelings of helplessness and thoughts of suicide are sequels to stress induced depression.

## The Juvenile Angle

According to Dr. Sharad Chandra, a practicing psychiatrist in India, depression is an abstract feeling and cannot be recognised as such by children below the age of eight. As in adults various stress factors create depression in children. The most critical period is that of puberty where a child undergoes many hormonal changes and is especially prone to mood fluctuations and social withdrawal. Inabilty to understand the problem and immaturity often lead them to suicides. In New Delhi, India, alone there were 15 cases of exam-related suicide cases in 1997. Sarthak, a NGO in New Delhi, had set up a 24-hour hotline called Operation Hope for students to cope with exam results in the same year. It received almost 2,000 calls from all over India. Five hundred of these came from teenagers with suicidal tendencies.

According to Arpita, a member of the NGO, "in such situations, parents need to understand their children instead of criticising them for not being up to the mark".

## The Feminine Angle

Dr. Sadhana Vohra, a psychologist in India, feels that by nature women might not be prone to depression, but the society makes them so. Women, in these days, have a lot of balancing to do between home and workplace, including balancing between social and personal requirements. It has the ingredients to create a lot of stress in women that can easily lead them to depression.

"A working women has to do better than men to be noticed and appreciated. And if that wasn`t tiring enough, a woman is still expected to look after the household by the in-laws as well as the husband," says Maya Srinivasan, an executive in a multinational firm. "This continuous tension of having to balance the two aspects of my life makes me feel useless and exploited. I am not normally prone to depression, but lately, I have begun to feel a certain amount of frustration."

## Men are Equally Prone to it

It has often been stated that women are more prone to depression than men. But Dr. R.K. Singh, professor and head of the department of psychiatry in Lady Hardinge Medical College, New Delhi, India, feels that this might be a wrong assumption. "Men are conditioned to deny their feelings whereas a woman feeling slightly upset is more likely to say that she is depressed. A man may express the same feeling either through anger or alcoholism. This doesn't mean that men feel any less depressed than women," he argues.

Many factors such as job stress, strained family relationships or sometimes stress from 'midlife transitions' plunge men into depression.

Then exactly what causes depression? Researchers and medical practitioners are of the opinion that there is no one cause to the condition of depression. As depression is closely linked with one's mental disposition or inner personality, the road to this condition is complex and subtle.

Often, the physiological constitution of an individual decides the tendency towards depression. The co-ordinated working of brain and various neurotransmitters prompts all decisions for action and reaction. Neurotransmitters are chemicals that help different areas of the brain to communicate with each other. If these chemicals are low then miscommunication can occur and one may show signs of depression. This type of depression may run in the family. Additional factors, possibly stresses at home, work, or school, precipitate its onset.

## Stress and Depression

There appears to be a complex relationship among stressful situations, our mind and body's reaction to stress, and the onset of clinical depression. It is clear that some people develop depression after a stressful event in their lives. Events such as the death of a loved one, the loss of a job, or the end of a relationship are often negative and traumatic and cause great stress for many people. Stress can also occur as the result of a more positive event such as getting married, moving to a new city, or starting a new job. It is not uncommon for either positive or negative events to become a crisis that precedes the development of clinical depression.

Whether a stressful event itself can actually cause a person to become depressed is not fully known. There are times when we all must struggle with very painful situations in our lives. More times than not these changes do not result in a person becoming clinically depressed. In fact, sometimes people become depressed even when there is little or no stress in their lives and everything seems to be going very well. And, no single stressful event will cause depression to develop in every person. The same type of stressor may lead to depression in one person, but not another.

If a stressful experience causes a person to become depressed, it may happen indirectly. In other words, if a young woman with a family history of major depression suffers the death of a loved one, she may become clinically depressed. In this situation it is not necessarily the traumatic loss itself that caused the development of depression, but the combination of a genetic predisposition with the stressful event that made her vulnerable to becoming depressed.

For those who struggle with more chronic depression, the effects of stress may be more complicated. A stressful event such as a job loss or the death of a loved one is more likely to come before a first or second depressive episode. After that, further depressive episodes may develop spontaneously. It is not certain why stress may lead to depression in this way. However, researchers have theorised an explanation called the "kindling effect," or "kindling-sensitisation hypothesis." This theory surmises that initial depressive episodes spark changes in the brain's chemistry and limbic system that make it more prone to developing future episodes of depression. This may be compared to the use of kindling wood to spark the flames of a campfire. Since early episodes of depression make a person more sensitive to developing depression, even small stressors can lead to later depressive episodes.

Some people may become depressed as a result of having to struggle with chronic stress. These constant difficulties may come in the form of having to juggle multiple roles at home and work, making major changes in lifestyle, being in an abusive environment, etc. They may also come with important and normal transitions in life such as late adolescence and early adulthood when many people separate from their families to establish their own independence. Middle age may require adjustment to changes in fertility and virility, children leaving the home, concern about job advancement, and a re-evaluation of accomplishments in life. Retirement is another time of major change as some people struggle with a reduction of position and finances. If a person is under continuous stress, a single difficult event may be more likely to induce a depressive episode. For instance, if a middle-aged woman is in an unhappy marriage, she may be more likely to become depressed after her youngest child leaves home for college. The event of her child leaving home may not by itself have been enough to lead to depression, but the constant stress of an unhappy marriage combined with this event may be enough to trigger clinical depression.

In studying how stressful events may lead to depression, researchers have developed a theory called, "learned helplessness." This theory states that when people experience chronic or repeated stressful events, they learn to feel helpless. This feeling of helplessness is strengthened when a person believes he or she has no control over the stressful situation. Although the research to support this theory was initially done with animals, the effects of learned helplessness may be seen in depressed humans. People who are depressed very often have negative beliefs about their ability to manage aspects of their lives based on perceived failures in the past. For example, imagine an adolescent girl living in a home with verbally abusive parents who tell her that she is stupid and cannot do anything right. Over time the young girl may believe her parents and come to doubt her abilities and self-worth. She may begin to feel helpless and believe that most things are beyond her control. This feeling of helplessness may make her vulnerable to developing clinical depression at some point in her life.

## Featured Articles

### Stress Relief

Stress is all around us. It's become a normal part of daily life. But over time, its effects can become taxing, both mentally and physically. Stress becomes a problem when you feel overwhelmed by its challenges. And though it may be difficult to define, that doesn't mean it's all in your head. Researchers have found that significant biological changes take place in the body during periods of stress. And extended periods of stress can cause destructive changes in the body, such as depression and a suppressed immune system, which can eventually lead to heart disease, cancer, and stroke. So if you are feeling stressed out, its time to get some relief. Learn about stress: how to identify it, and how to find relief.

## Anxiety

Some degree of anxiety is perfectly normal. We all experience situations that make us fearful and apprehensive. However, there are some people who feel anxious even when there is no discernible cause. In these cases, the anxiety usually becomes overwhelming and may interfere with day-to-day functioning. People who regularly have a debilitating level of anxiety are suffering from an anxiety disorder.

## Depression

Some people have described depression as a heavy black curtain of despair that envelops their lives. Depression affects your life, and the lives of those around you. It can severely disrupt how you function, eat, sleep, and get along with others. Although most people who suffer from depression feel as though they are suffering alone, roughly 20 per cent of the American population suffers from depression. Depression is a disease, and like any other disease, it can be treated and managed.

## Antidepressant Drug Information

Once you've been diagnosed with depression, your doctor may prescribe a specific drug regimen. Every person is different, so your treatment will be tailored to your needs. Below you'll find a list of antidepressants that may be prescribed to treat depression.

Celexa Oral

Effexor Oral

Effexor Withdrawal

Lexapro Oral

Paxil CR Oral

Prozac Oral

Remeron Oral

Wellbutrin Oral

Xanax XR Oral

Zoloft Oral

Zyban Oral

**Featured**

**Celexa Oral:** Citalopram is an antidepressant (selective serotonin reuptake inhibitor-SSRI) used to treat depression. It works by restoring the balance of certain natural substances (neurotransmitters such as serotonin) in the brain. Citalopram may improve your feelings of well-being and energy level.

**Lexapro Oral:** Escitalopram is an antidepressant (selective serotonin reuptake inhibitor-SSRI) used to treat depression and anxiety. It works by restoring the balance of certain natural substances (neurotransmitters such as serotonin) in the brain. Escitalopram may improve your feelings of well-being and energy level and decrease nervousness.

**Paxil CR Oral:** Paroxetine is a selective serotonin reuptake inhibitor (SSRI) used to treat depression, panic attacks, obsessive-compulsive disorder (OCD), anxiety disorders, post-traumatic stress disorder, and a severe form of premenstrual syndrome (premenstrual dysphoric disorder).

**Effexor Oral:** Venlafaxine is an antidepressant (serotonin-norepinephrine reuptake inhibitor type-SNRI) used in the treatment of depression and anxiety. It works by restoring the balance of natural substances (neurotransmitters such as serotonin and norepinephrine) in the brain. Venlafaxine may decrease nervousness and improve your mood, feelings of well-being, and energy level.

**Effexor Withdrawal:** Learn more about Effexor's side effects and the withdrawal symptoms you may be experiencing.

**Prozac Oral:** Fluoxetine is a selective serotonin reuptake inhibitor (SSRI) used to treat depression, anxiety disorders (panic attacks), obsessive-compulsive disorder (OCD), a certain eating disorder (bulimia), and a severe form of premenstrual syndrome (premenstrual dysphoric disorder).

**Wellbutrin Oral:** Bupropion is used to treat depression. It can improve your mood and feelings of well-being. It may work by helping to restore the balance of certain natural chemicals (neurotransmitters) in your brain.

**Xanax XR Oral:** This medication is used to treat the panic and anxiety symptoms associated with panic disorder. Alprazolam belongs to a class of medications called benzodiazepines which act on the brain and nerves (central nervous system) to produce a calming effect. It works by enhancing the effects of a certain natural chemical in the body (GABA).

**Remeron Oral:** Mirtazapine is used to treat depression. It improves mood and feelings of well-being. Mirtazapine is an antidepressant that works by restoring the balance of natural chemicals (neurotransmitters) in the brain.

**Zoloft Oral:** Sertraline is used to treat depression, panic attacks, obsessive compulsive disorders, post-traumatic stress disorder, social anxiety disorder (social phobia), and a severe form of premenstrual syndrome (premenstrual dysphoric disorder). It is known as a selective serotonin reuptake inhibitor (SSRI).

**Zyban Oral:** This medication is used in combination with a stop-smoking programme (e.g., support group, counselling) to help you quit smoking. Bupropion can decrease your nicotine withdrawal symptoms (e.g., irritability, anxiety, restlessness) and your urge to smoke. Quitting smoking decreases your risk of heart and lung disease, as well as cancer.

## JOB STRESS AND ITS MANAGEMENT TECHNIQUES

- "Job stress can be defined as the harmful physical and emotional responses that occur when the requirements of the job do not match the capabilities, resources, or needs of the worker. Job stress can lead to poor health and even injury."

  [Stress at Work, United States National Institute of Occupational Safety and Health, Cincinnati, 1999.]

- "The emotional, cognitive, behavioural and physiological reaction to aversive and noxious aspects of work, work environments and work organisations. It is a state characterised by high levels of arousal and distress and often by feelings of not coping."

  [Guidance on work-related stress: Spice of life - or kiss of death,European Commission, Directorate-General for Employment and Social Affairs]

- "Stress is the reaction people have to excessive pressures or other types of demands placed on them."

  [Managing stress at work: Discussion document, United Kingdom Health and Safety Commission, London, 1999.]

STRESS is a word that can be used to describe both the cause and the results of pressure building up in the body and mind. Commonly, bullying, job insecurity, relationship difficulties and many other situations associated with the home or work place generated internally and externally. At its root, stress is caused by the difference between expectation and reality. The health and safety executive's definition is that stress occurs "When the demands placed upon a person exceeds the capacity to cope with them". Each of us has an optimum level at which we work for our satisfaction and achievements and when that is out of balance we often achieve, less and are dissatisfied, no matter how hard we work or how much we try to relax. If the factors causing stress build up for too long, we can all experience 'symptoms'- usually at a physical and emotional level.

Although these signs are called symptoms, stress is not an illness: stress is a psychological condition which has unpleasant physical side effects- but it is a condition which can be addressed by learning about it and changing the behaviour associated with pressure to work hard, it can also arise from boredom, procrastination, perfectionism.

## Stress, Health, and Productivity

Some employers assume that stressful working conditions are a necessary evil-that companies must turn up the pressure on workers and set aside health concerns to remain productive and profitable in today's economy. But research findings challenge this belief. Studies show that stressful working conditions are actually associated with increased absenteeism, tardiness, and intentions by workers to quit their jobs-all of which have negative effects on the bottom line.

Recent studies of so-called healthy organisations suggest that policies benefiting worker health also benefit the bottom line. A healthy organisation is defined as one that has low rates of illness, injury, and disability in its workforce and is also competitive in the marketplace.

## Stress at Work or Job stress

Job stress can be defined as the harmful physical and emotional responses that occur when the requirements of the job do not match the capabilities, resources, or needs of the worker. Job stress can lead to poor health and even injury.

The concept of job stress is often confused with challenge, but these concepts are not the same. Challenge energises us psychologically and physically and motivates us to learn new skills and master our jobs. When a challenge is met, we feel relaxed and satisfied. Thus **"a little bit of stress is good for you"**.

## NIOSH Approach to Job Stress

On the basis of experience and research, NIOSH (National Institute for Occupational Safety and Health), favours the view that working conditions play a primary role in causing job stress. However, the role of individual factors is not ignored. According to the NIOSH view, exposure to stressful working conditions (called job stressors), can have a direct influence on worker safety and health. But as shown below, individual and other situational factors can intervene to strengthen or weaken this influence.

Examples of individual and situational factors that can help to reduce the effects of stressful working conditions include the following:

- Balance between work and family or personal life
- A support network of friends and coworkers
- A relaxed and positive outlook.

**NIOSH research** has identified organisational characteristics associated with both healthy, low-stress work and high levels of productivity. Examples of these characteristics include the following:

- Recognition of employees for good work performance

NIOSH Model of Job Stress

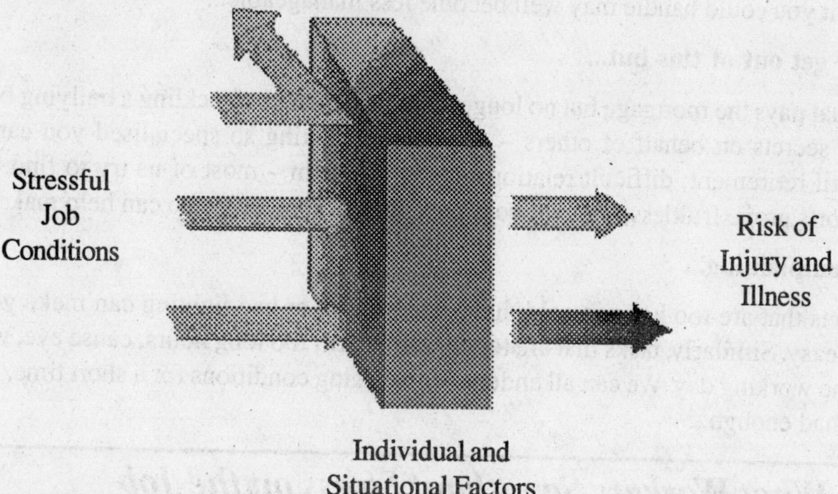


Fig. 8

- Opportunities for career development
- An organisational culture that values the individual worker
- Management actions that are consistent with organisational values

## KNOWN CAUSES OF STRESS

Nearly everyone agrees that job stress results from the interaction of the worker and the conditions of work. Views differ, however, on the importance of worker characteristics versus working conditions as the primary cause of job stress. These differing viewpoints are important because they suggest different ways to prevent stress at work.

According to one school of thought, differences in individual characteristics such as personality and coping style are most important in predicting whether certain job conditions will result in stress-in other words, what is stressful for one person may not be a problem for someone else. This viewpoint leads to prevention strategies that focus on workers and ways to help them cope with demanding job conditions.

Although the importance of individual differences cannot be ignored, scientific evidence suggests that certain working conditions are stressful to most people. The excessive workload demands and conflicting expectations describe good examples of stress. Such evidence argues for a greater emphasis on working conditions as the key source of job stress, and for job redesign as a primary prevention strategy.

Apart from extreme mental or physical hardships, it is difficult to categorise about what will cause stress. We have attempted to list those sources of stress that we most frequently hear about:

### Job Conditions That May Lead to Individual Stress

➤ **Unfair Treatment...**

None of us likes to work in situations where we, or others, are aggrieved by a sense of Unfairness. Not being able to remedy situations where people are taken advantage of, manipulated or discriminated against can be a prime source of stress building up…

➤ **Exhaustion...**

Feeling pushed to perform, to be perfect, to take on more responsibility, to please everyone, to compete, to attract more money, to stay ahead of others, to work all hours – all are conditions which can be brought on by others or by our own demands of ourselves. Over time, and with two or three things coming to a head at the same time, feelings that you thought you could handle may well become less manageable...

➤ **I wish I could get out of this but...**

Trapped in a job that pays the mortgage but no longer satisfies; fearful of tackling a bullying boss because of the consequences; holding secrets on behalf of others – or yourself; getting so specialised you can't see any career options; holding on until retirement; difficult relationships in the team – most of us try to find ways out of these situations but if our efforts prove fruitless, it might be time to talk to someone who can help make changes...

➤ **My body is complaining...**

Working conditions that are too hot, too cold, have bad seating or bad lighting can make you feel tense even when the work itself is easy. Similarly, tasks that are too repetitive, for too long hours, cause eye, wrist or back strain take all the joy out of the working day. We can all endure bad working conditions for a short time, but the body starts to tell you when it has had enough...

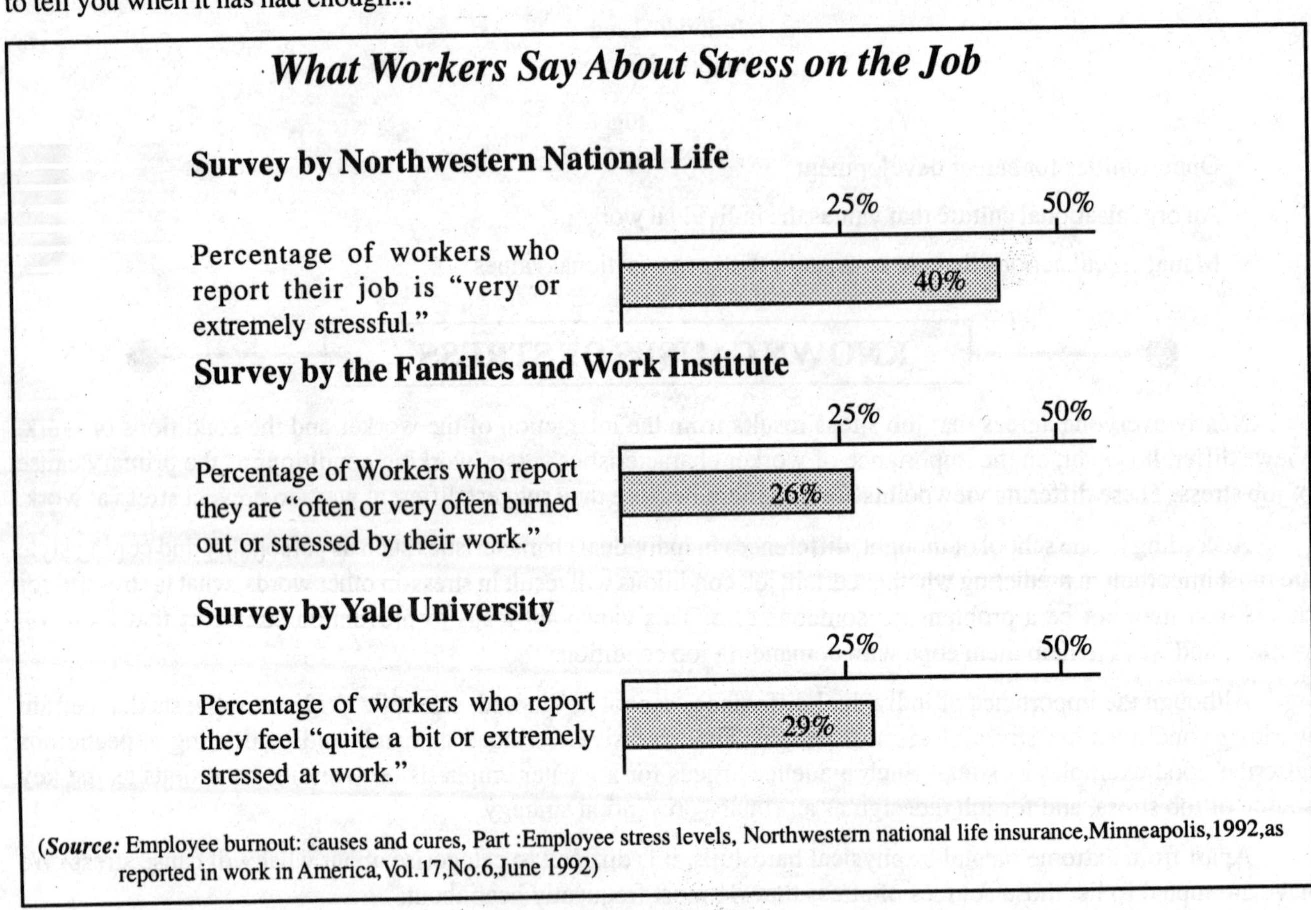


**Fig. 9**

## Job Conditions that May Lead to Organisational Stress

- **The Design of Tasks:** Heavy workload, infrequent rest breaks, long works hours and shift work; hectic and routine tasks that have little inherent meaning, do not utilise workers' skills, and provide little sense of control.
- **Management Style:** Lack of participation by workers in decision- making, poor communication in the organisation, lack of family-friendly policies, company's insensitivity to employees' family needs.
- **Interpersonal Relationships:** Poor social environment and lack of support or help from co-workers and supervisors e.g. Employees physical isolation reduces her opportunities to interact with other workers or receive help from them.

- **Work Roles:** Conflicting or uncertain job expectations, too much responsibility, **too many "hats to wear."**
- **Career Concerns:** Job insecurity and lack of opportunity for growth, advancement, or promotion; rapid changes for which workers are unprepared.
- **Environmental Conditions:** Unpleasant or dangerous physical conditions such as crowding, noise, air pollution, or ergonomic problems.

## Victims of stress

All of us are affected at one time or another by work-related stress. Although occupational stress is by no means a new phenomenon, it is becoming increasingly globalised and affects all countries, all professions and all categories of workers, including both blue and white-collar workers, as well as families and society in general. While stress at work is most frequently considered in the context of the industrialised countries, workers in developing countries are also undoubtedly affected.

The evidence also indicates that a broad and growing range of occupations are prone to work-related stress. The following table lists those occupations which equal or exceed the rate of 6 on a stress rating scale of 0 to 10 elaborated by the University of Manchester Institute of Science and Technology, (U.K.)

**Table 13**

| Occupations with high stress levels | |
|---|---|
| ***Occupation*** | ***Rating scale*** |
| Miner | 8.3 |
| Police officer | 7.7 |
| Prison officer | 7.5 |
| Construction worker | 7.5 |
| Airline pilot | 7.5 |
| Journalist | 7.5 |
| Advertising executive | 7.3 |
| Dentist | 7.3 |
| Actor | 7.2 |
| Doctor | 6.8 |
| Broadcasting personnel | 6.8 |
| Nurse | 6.5 |
| Film production crew | 6.5 |
| Ambulance personnel | 6.3 |
| Musician | 6.3 |
| Firefighter | 6.3 |
| Teacher | 6.2 |
| Social worker | 6.0 |
| Personnel manager | 6.0 |

(***Source:*** Conditions of work digest: Preventing stress at work)

## Gender Responses to Stress

One of the most basic behavioural differences between men and women is how they respond to stress. Researchers found that men often react to stress with a **"fight-or-flight"** response, but women are more likely to manage their stress with a **"tend-and-befriend" response.**

Psychology professor and lead researcher, Shelley E. Taylor points out that this stress response is seen in many species. Females respond to stressful conditions by protecting and nurturing their young (the **"tend"** response), and by seeking social contact and support from others – especially other females (the **"befriend"** response).

This pattern is in sharp contrast to the fight-or-flight behaviour, long considered the principal method both sexes used to cope with stress. Until Government grant policies changed in 1995, "women were largely excluded in stress research," says Taylor, "because many researchers believed that monthly fluctuations in hormones created stress responses that varied too widely to be considered statistically valid."

## Gender, work and stress

The relationship between gender, work and stress is complex. Several factors appear to magnify the impact of stress on women, chief among them being the preponderant role that women still play in the provision of family care. It is well-established that the total workload of women who are employed full-time is higher than that of full-time male workers, particularly where they have family responsibilities.

> Research carried out in Sweden found that the total workload of women employed full time is much higher than that of men employed full time, and that the total workload for women employed part time is as much as that of men employed full time. Sweden is a country in which 86 per cent of women are in the workforce, but the division of labour between spouses at home has remained much the same.

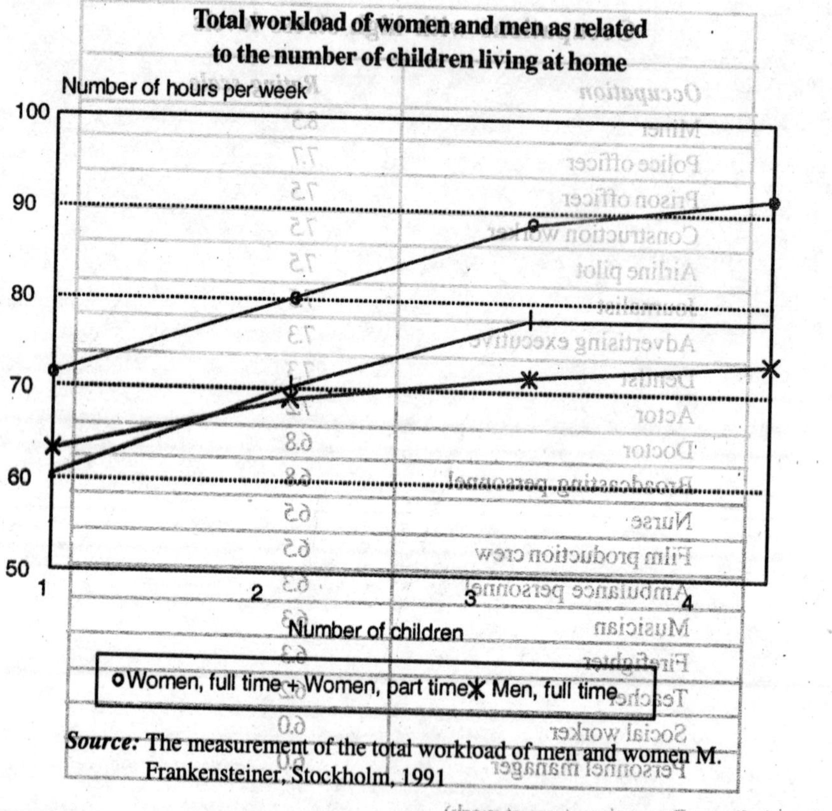


***Source:*** The measurement of the total workload of men and women M. Frankensteiner, Stockholm, 1991

In addition to their family responsibilities, other factors also tend to make women more vulnerable to work-related stress. These include:

- Lower levels of control in their jobs, since the great majority of women still tend to occupy less senior jobs than men.
- The higher proportion of women who work in *precarious* forms of employment;
- The proliferation of women in high-stress occupations, such as nursing, teaching and work with visual display units (VDUs); and the prejudice and discrimination suffered by many women who are in more senior positions,

such as managerial jobs, both as a result of organizational and corporate policy and from their collegues at work.

## The Sex Divide: How Men and Women React under Pressure

India has had a woman prime minister, a woman as head of the Police service and a woman in space. We may believe we are all equal now. But when it comes to stress – think again.

Most studies show equal numbers of men and women complain of stress. But that's where equality ends. Experts in the science of stress say that men and women are stressed by different things and they react in different ways.

It's not just that traditional roles persist – so that most working women have more responsibility for the family and home while men are more likely to be focussed on breadwinning. We also think differently too.

## Reaction of Men and Women under pressure

- **Women and stress**

Women have always been more up front in talking about the strains of everyday life. Around twice as many women as men see their doctors about anxiety and depression.

But do women really suffer more from stress? Experts in stress-related illness believe that modern life does place more strains on women than men. However, as women often cope better with stress, this tends to even out the stress toll.

- **Why women get stressed?**

Most women today work. In fact, over the last few decades, the British work force has become increasingly female. Women, therefore, face all the stresses which the modern workplace brings. Yet at the same time, many working women also do the lion's share of childcare, housework and caring for older relatives. This means women are coping with strains from several fronts at once.

In some ways women have greater experience of having to deal with stress, says Carole Spiers, an occupational stress counsellor. 'Women feel more pressures because they have to be all things to all people.'

### A woman's work...

Yet women often cope with lots of demands because they are naturally more 'multi-tasked' – meaning they can manage to do more than one thing at a time, she says. Men often prefer to concentrate on the task in hand.

This difference dates back to prehistoric times, when men had to be single-minded about going out to find food for the family while women coped with more varied tasks, according to Dr Tina Ambury, a GP (General Practitioner) in Manchester (U.K.).

As a busy doctor, with young children herself, she can speak from experience. 'My husband finds looking after the children a completely stressful experience. When he does look after them he can't do anything else. It is not that women don't find that stressful but we find ways of coping. We are very good at juggling.'

There are several **other reasons** women specifically face stress.

➢ **Pregnancy:** Pregnancy can be stressful as women face a barrage of tests, financial worries and uncertainties about what childbirth and motherhood will bring. Research has shown that babies of very anxious mothers tend to be smaller or born earlier and may even suffer development delays. A recent study at one London hospital found the stress hormone cortisol passes from anxious mothers to their unborn babies and may cause these babies to be more prone to stress themselves in later life.

➢ **Having a new baby:** Looking after a new baby is stressful for anyone but more so if you are alone, or have relationship problems with your partner, or are short of money. These pressures can lead to postnatal depression, which one in five mothers suffer.

➢ **Looking after children:** Being a full-time mum is no opt-out. Indeed, one recent survey, cited in a parenting magazine, found that 51% of full-time mothers felt regularly stressed, compared to 29% of women working full-time.

➢ **Caring for relatives:** Caring for elderly or sick relatives – a job which frequently falls to women – can be very stressful. Carers may feel exhausted by a constant stream of repetitive jobs and demands and frustrated at being tied to the home.

There are 6.8 million people in Britain caring for disabled or frail elderly friends and relatives and most of them are women.

➢ **Bereavement:** Any loss can lead to stress, and losing a loved one is especially stressful. Women are more likely to suffer bereavement as they generally live longer than men. A recent US study also found that widows suffer more stress and depression after bereavement than widowers. These symptoms were likely to lead to medical problems such as cancer or heart attack and thoughts of suicide.

### Women coping with stress

Yet while women may face multiple pressures, they are often better than men at seeking help when it all gets too much. Women are happy to talk over their feelings with friends or partners, and are more likely to see their GP (General Practioner) when they feel anxious or stressed, rather than waiting for a physical problem to develop.

### Men and stress

One battle for a seat on the early morning train, you are up against deadlines all day, you leave the office late and get home too tired to talk to your partner or the kids. Or maybe you are out of work and spend the day worrying over how the next bill will get paid.

Whether you are in work or out, it is often the traditional role of breadwinner which is the source of stress for most men. And over the last few decades – as society has changed – men seem to have become increasingly vulnerable to stress and other mental health problems.

In most families men are still the main providers. But recent years have brought dramatic changes to the workplace which pile on the pressure.

➢ **Unemployment:** In the 1980s and early 1990s huge numbers of traditionally male jobs were lost, as heavy industries shut down. There was a 17% drop in numbers of men in work and although employment figures have since gone up, many men still face long-term unemployment.

Although lots of jobs are stressful, studies have found that being without a job is the most stressful role of all. Men are more likely than women to experience long-term unemployment.

One in seven men who lose their job develops depression within six months, according to mental health charity Mind. Being unemployed for long periods has also been shown to harm your physical health.

➢ **Changing roles:** Just as men's jobs declined, there was a 12% rise in women in work, as traditionally female jobs increased. For some families this has meant a reversal in the role of breadwinner – bringing tensions and feelings of confusion for many men.

'Stress is not just about having a hyperactive lifestyle,' says Peter Baker, editor of the men's health website, malehealth.co.uk. 'Having no role and being hard-up is very stressful too.'

➢ **Men at work:** Alongside the decline in 'male' industries, work practices in Britain have changed enormously. Many companies have 'downsized' – shedding large numbers of staff – while others have gone in for 'outsourcing' – putting permanent jobs on temporary contracts.

Both these trends have created widespread insecurity at work, both for those directly affected and those who fear they may be next in line. This is even true in the Indian context.

➢ **Working longer:** Meanwhile, work itself has become more stressful, experts in stress management believe, with the constant attack of technology in the form of e-mails, mobile phone calls and faxes, and the growth of a culture of long hours.

In Europe, specifically in Britain, men in full-time employment work an average 42 hours compared to 38 for women – although obviously many people work far beyond these averages. *Taking the Strain (2000),* a survey published by the Chartered Management Institute, revealed that 91% of managers regularly exceeded their contracted hours.

## Men coping with stress

Men also react under stress very differently to women. They are less likely to talk about how they feel and less likely to seek help from a doctor or anyone else. Most men only visit their GP when medical symptoms of stress emerge, such as chest pains, headaches and stomach upsets, but some don't even bother to go then.

It all goes back to the way boys are conditioned not to show emotion, says Peter Baker. 'Men have difficulties admitting stress even to themselves.'

➢ **Escape routes:** Rather than try to resolve their stress, he says, they are more likely than women to try to escape by drinking to excess, smoking too much, driving aggressively or resorting to violence.

Although the latest research suggests men are equally likely to suffer from depression as women, they are less likely to be diagnosed by a doctor. And over the last two decades, men have also turned increasingly to suicide. Three-quarters of suicides in the UK are by men, according to Mind.

➢ **Express yourself :** The solution is not easy, says Peter Baker. But it will mean men becoming more willing to acknowledge their stress, to talk about it with friends and family, to express their emotions generally and – importantly – to seek help from a doctor or other professional.

## The Effects of Stress

Because stress is so widespread, it has a very high cost for individuals, companies and organisations, and for society.

For the individual, in addition to the devastating impact of the serious health impairments referred to above, the loss of capacity to cope with working and social situations can lead to less success at work, including loss of career opportunities and even employment. It can give rise to greater strain in family relationships and with friends. It may even ultimately result in depression, death or suicide.

For the company or organisation, the costs of stress takes many forms. These include absenteeism, higher medical costs and staff turnover, with the associated cost of recruiting and training new workers. It has also been shown in recent years that stress takes a heavy toll in terms of reduced productivity and efficiency.

## What can be done about Job Stress?

The *two different approaches* for dealing with stress at work are explained as:

**Stress Management:** The companies can provide stress management training and an employee assistance program (EAP) to improve the ability of workers to cope with difficult work situations. Nearly one-half of large companies in the United States provide some type of stress management training for their workforces. Stress management programmes teach workers about the nature and sources of stress, the effects of stress on health, and personal skills to reduce stress-for example, *time management or relaxation exercises.* EAPs provide individual counselling for employees with both work and personal problems. Stress management training may rapidly reduce stress symptoms such as anxiety and sleep disturbances; it also has the advantage of being inexpensive and easy to implement. However, stress management programmes have two major disadvantages:

## Confident! Go-getter! Leader!

## Power of Attitude

"Our loves are not determined by what happens to us, but how we react to what happens; not by what life brings to us, but by the attitude we bring to life. A positive attitude causes a chain reaction of positive thoughts, events, and outcomes. It is a catalyst…A speak that creates extraordinary results."

- The beneficial effects on stress symptoms are often short-lived.
- They often ignore important root causes of stress because they focus on the worker and not the environment.

**Organisational Change:** In contrast to stress management training and EAP programmes, the companies can try to reduce job stress by bringing in a consultant to recommend ways to improve working conditions. This approach is the most direct way to reduce stress at work. It involves the identification of stressful aspects of work (e.g., excessive workload, conflicting expectations) and the design of strategies to reduce or eliminate the identified stressors. The advantage of this approach is that it deals directly with the root causes of stress at work. However, managers are sometimes uncomfortable with this approach because it can involve changes in work routines or production schedules, or changes in the organisational structure.

## EFFECT OF JOB INVOLVEMENT ON THE BURNOUT

Study was carried out to determine the level of Job Involvement and extent of Burnout among managers. The results revealed that managers scored high on Job Involvement, to on Depersonalization and Emotional Exhaustion and moderate on Personal Accomplishment. The study also found the correlation between Job Involvement and Burnout measured on three dimensions two negative dimensions-De-personalization and Emotional Exhaustion and one positive dimension Personal Accomplishment. It was found that Job Involvement had a negative correlation with Depersonalisation and Emotional Exhaustion and positive correlation with Personal Accomplishment. The correlation result indicate that Burnout can be minimised avoided if individuals develop a high level of involvement in their jobs and they are able to identify themselves psychologically with their jobs.

## Introduction

High levels of stress can ultimately cause exhaustion and break down. Excess stress can lead to Burnout, the fall out being low levels of Job Involvement or other low levels of Job Involvement leading to Burnout. Like the proverbial chicken and egg story, it is difficult to establish a cause effect relationship between Burnout and Job Involvement. Burnout can have serious implications for the managers as it can lead to chequered promotion avenues and slow career progression. It could also affect their productivity and thereby, affect the organisations adversely. It is not the complacent, easy going individual who runs the highest risk of Burnout. Instead, it is those with high expectations and a sense of purpose who are the greatest victims, people with high standards for themselves and for others.

## Concept of Burnout

Substantial research work is being done to study Burnout. Individual Burnout has received considerable attention (Adams 1978, Lauderdale 1982). Kim (1990) calls Burnout an index of organisational quality of life. According to Leatz and Stolar (1993), Burnout is a physical, emotional and mental exhaustion caused by long-term involvement in stressful and emotionally demanding situations, combined with high personal expectations for one's performance. It happens when work looses its meaning, and the ratio of stress to rewards leans heavily towards stress, Burnout is a severe psychological and physical outcome of prolonged and high levels of stress at work. It commonly occurs among employees who are unable to cope with extensive work pressures which demand on their energy, time and resources and among employees whose work requires dealing with people, Researchers have found that Burnout bring enormous costs to both organisations and individuals because it negatively impacts employees job attitudes and leads to undesirable behaviours such as lower job involvement, reduced task performance, and increased turnover intentions (Jackson & Maslach 1982, Leier & Maslach 1988, Motowidlo & Packard 1986, Shirom 1989, Wrright & Bonett 1997, Wright & Cropanzano 1998). Several studies (Etzion 7984 Maslach & Jackson 7984), have raised the question of vagueness of the term Burnout as well as of job stress. However, several definitions and models have emerged to serve as a basis for further research attempts. Maslach and Jackson (1982), and Etzion (1984), have defined Burnout as a syndrome or a state of physical, emotional, and mental exhaustion, and cynicism, towards one's work in response to chronic organisational stressors.

Maslach and Jackson (1981), conceptualised. Burnout as consisting of the following three components (1) Emotional Exhaustion refers to mental and physical tension and strain resulting from job-related stressors; (2) De-personalisation refers to distancing of, oneself from others and viewing others impersonally, and (3) Diminished Personal Accomplishment is a feeling of negative self-evaluation. Emotional Exhaustion, one of the most extreme varieties of work-related strain, manifests itself in employees as a general loss of feeling, concern trust, interest, and spirit. (Maslach 1982) Etzion (1984) relates the Emotional Exhaustion dimension, one of the most Burnout to feeling depressed trapped, hopeless. "Etzion (1988), further emphasised on Burnout syndrome's dynamic aspects as a process of energy depletion and deterioration of performance caused by continuous daily pressures rather than, discrete critical life events. In this, process, enthusiasm wanes while previous involvement, initiative seriousness, and sense of responsibility are gradually replaced by patterns of routine and indifference. Clearly, this definition goes beyond the early research Maslach (1976, 1982) and Maslach and Jackson (1982), which was based mainly on people employed in care or service professions."

## Burnout Stages

Burnout is the culmination of a long-term process and occurs over a long period of time and passes though different stages (Matteson & Ivancevich 1987).

1. The first stage is characterised by 'stagnation' in which signs of fatigue and depression appear. They are hardly noticeable to the outsiders.
2. The second stage takes the form of "detachment" when signs of Burnout becomes apparent, characterised by psychological and physical withdrawal, apathy, and below average performance.

3. The final stage is where an individual is completely "burnout and emotionally exhausted". He is de-personalised, apathetic, doubtful about his self-efficacy, devoid of a sense of accomplishment, and becomes a poor performer.

## Burnout Symptoms

Leatz and Stolar (1993), have explained Burnout in term, of physical emotional and mental exhaustion.

i. *Physical exhaustion* is characterised by fatigue, nausea, muscle tension, changes in eating and sleeping habits, and generally a low energy level probably the first symptom, most suffers notice, is a general malaise with no apparent cause. Sometimes people say "I don't know. I just get tired by lunch or early afternoon," (Leatz & Stolar 1993).

ii. *Emotional exhaustion* is characterised by a number of negative feelings. These are expressed as feeling frustrated, hopeless, trapped, helpless, depressed, sad, and apathetic towards work. People say they feel that their "soul is dying" or report frequently feeling irritated or angry for no specific reasons. The scariest part is when they just don't care any more about parts of their hob that were really important to them earlier in the cycle (Leatz & Stolar 1993).

iii. *Mental exhaustion* Leatz & Stolar (1993), claim that mentally exhausted people are found to be dissatisfied with themselves, their jobs, and life in general, while feeling incompetent or inferior even thought they are not any of those. Over time, mental exhaustion causes people to see customers, clients, or colleagues as sources of irritation and problems rather than as challenges or opportunities. They also tend to believe that there is something wrong with themselves because the work that once gave them such pleasure has become boring and burdensome. This negative self image gets further eroded as they tend to blame themselves for their present state. Managers who reach this state often no longer care about their goals or the people they manage. The demands of family and friends are perceived to be taxing on them in terms of time, patience and they feel obliged to fulfill their demands.

## Factors Leading to Managerial Burnout

A variety of individual and organisational factors contribute to "Managerial Burnout", which manifests itself in terms of lack of initiative, rapid, employee turnover and low motivation, and low productivity. Seven major organisational factors have been identified which lead to Burnout among managers: lack of autonomy, high stress level, ineffective communication, organisation-person misfit, job-person misfit, alcoholism, authoritarian leadership and lack of participation in the decision making. Broadly burnout could be two type of factors i.e., relating to the environment organisation and other to the person himself. Some of these factors are detailed below:

## Environmental/Organisational Factors

i. *Organisational Climate:* According to Leatz & Stolar (1993). It is important to understand two things about Burnout First; the root cause does not lie within the person suffering from it. The biggest cause is a dysfunctional work environment that permits unrelenting level of stress, frustration, and pressure for long periods of time, yet offers few rewards to people for putting up with all of that. Second, if we subscribe to the learn do teach cycle theory, there is the potential that Burnout can occur several times during our working lives as we master each new job function we are given. Work environment can significantly affect the Burnout rates of highly motivated people by helping or preventing them from utilising their potential for peak performance for achieving organisational/personal goals. Given the high costs of lost of motivation turnover, tardiness absenteeism, poor delivery of services, and so on, organisations have a high stake in trying to prevent Burnout (Pines & Aronson 1981).

ii. *Management Support:* Drory and Shamir (1988), found management support to be a major correlate of Burnout. Other variables that have been found to have an effect on Burnout include role ambiguity, the task dimension of autonomy, variety task significance and extra organisational variables of community support and family role conflict. Golembiewski, Munzenrider and Stevenson (1986), suggested that poor work conditions modified by work group and personal characteristics lead to Burnout and other outcomes, such as physical symptoms, poor performance, and low productivity. Moreover, supervisory style and practices are inversely related to Burnout (Seltzer & Number of 1988).

iii. *Organisational Commitments Jackson, Turner and Brief (1987), and Leiter and Maslach (1988),* found Burnout to be associated with low organisational, commitment. As such, Burnout serves a trigger for job turnover. Clearly, from an organisational perspective, the outcomes of Burnout are costly, either from the negative attitudinal aspects or from the behavioural aspects of job performance and eventual turnover.

iv. *Non-communicate*: Verges and Spradley (1981), found that a tension-producing bosses is the one we does not communicate. In some ways is easier to work for an openly hostile boss; at least you know where you stand. The silent boss creates tension in three ways. First, silence places you squarely in a situation of "role conflict" and lack of clarity on expectations. Second most silent bosses produce "Occasional ponies." Since they are non-communicative they seldom let subordinates know about future plans and corresponding work-flow patterns. Consequently, subordinates find themselves having to deal with new demands unexpectedly. A third point of tension comes from the fact that excepts for your salary, the silent boss does not provide rewards for working.

## Person Related Factors

i. **Stress:** While some tend to view Burnout and stress as identical concepts that can be used interchangeably, recent studies have distinguished between the two, emphasising their differences and in some cases, their causal relationship. Maslach and Jackson (1982), view work pressure as one of the determinants of Burnout. Friesen and Sarris (1989), have found that only one Burnout dimension, i.e. emotional exhaustion, was closely related to work stress. Etzion (1988), argues that the accumulation of empirical data calls for a redefinition of the Burnout concept as a separate entity, different from, but related to stress. Unlike explicit stressors on the job, Burnout is caused by vague and elusive stressors, has more of a psychological orientation and difficult to identify and record, creating psychological erosion in a slow and subtle manner. This process of erosion can continue for a long time without being detected. Consequently, a person may arrive at exhaustion without going through the stage and therefore, may fail to develop resistance to or mechanism for dealing with stress.

ii. **Job Involvement:** is defined as the degree to which one identifies with one's present job (Kanungo 1982, Lawler & Hall 1970). Despite the importance of the concept, relatively little attention has been paid to the question of how job involvement is related to physical and mental well-being. Well-being is a multi-faceted and value-laden concept (Campbell 1976, Jahoda 1958), but its primary indicator is its affective level and quality, in terms of positive affecting, feelings of happiness, satisfaction, high self-esteem and feeling of distress (e.g., anxiety, depression, sense of hope less ness) (Warr 1987). Burnout affects the well-being of an individual adversely. The relation between job involvement and well-being may also be confounded by job satisfaction, a "positive emotional state resulting from the appraisal of one's job experiences" (Locke 1976). Job satisfaction may contribute to well-being (war 1987), but a high level of satisfaction does not necessarily signify level of involvement (Rabinowitz & Hall 1977).

Job Involvement has been conceptualised as a personal characteristic and has been perceived as a response to organisational conditions (Dangwal 1995). A person identifies psychologically with his job or the importance of work in his total self-image to the degree. In a study by Hackman & Lawler, (1971) job involvement was to be significantly correlated with five job dimensions viz, task variety, autonomy, task identity, feedback and friendship opportunities.

Codes and Dougherty (1993), proposed that Burnout would lend to negative employee attitudes or behaviour towards customers, work and the organisation (e.g., diminished service quality, reduced degree of job involvement, or increased absenteeism, turnover, and decreased task performance). Wright and Burnout investigated 44 professional employees of a public human services department and found that emotional exhaustion was related negatively to task performance, whereas depersonalisation and diminished personal accomplishment had no effect on task performance. Job involvement is the extent to which employees psychologically identify with their job or the degree of importance of the job in employees self image (Lodahl & Kejner 1965). Burnout may have negative effect on employee hob attitudes e.g. reduction in job involvement, organisational commitment and job satisfaction (Burke & Richardson 1993, Kahili 1988). Euoyet all (1991) surveyed 387 non-union re-processing plant employees and demonstrated a negative relationship between Burnout and involvement.

## Burnout

A phenomenon that is receiving great attention in recent times is the problem of burnout. Generally speaking, everyone is a potential candidate for burnout. But the most likely candidate to face this serious problem is the over-achiever. In the words of Herbert J. Freudenberger, burnout is a state of fatigue or frustration brought about by devotion to a cause, way of life or relationship that failed to produce the expected reward. *It may be defined as the total depletion of physical and mental resources caused by excessive striving to reach an unrealistic work-related goal.* In his book, Burnout, Dr. Freudenberger poses a set of questions designed to be a self-test to help us find out if we are in danger of burnout. The test includes the following questions (Table 14):

**Table 14**

| | *Yes* | *No* |
|---|---|---|
| • Are you working more now and enjoying it less? | | |
| • Do you find it more difficult to confide in others? | | |
| • Must you force yourself to do routine things? | | |
| • Are you listless, bored, constantly seeking excitement? | | |
| • Would you rather be somewhere else? | | |
| • Have you lost the joy of sex? | | |
| • Do you drink more than you used to? | | |
| • Do you need a tranquiliser to face the day...........a sleeping pill to get through the night? | | |
| • Are you resigned about your future? | | |
| • Is your need for a particular crutch increasing? (smoking, nail biting, etc.) | | |

## Burnout self-test

Burnout is frequently associated with people whose jobs demand close relationships with others under tension-filled circumstances. The dangerous part of burnout is that it is contagious. A highly cynical and pessimistic burnout victim can quickly transform an entire group into burnouts. It is, therefore, important to put out the fires early.

## Symptoms of Burnout

Some of the symptoms of burnout include: chronic fatigue, anger at those making demands, self-criticism for putting up with demands; negativism and irritability; a sense of being besieged; and hair-trigger display of emotions. Other symptoms include recurring health problems, such as ulcers, back pain or frequent headaches. The burnout victim is generally unable to maintain an even keel emotionally. The victim may burst out often and express his rage and hostility in totally inappropriate circumstances. Let's look into the checklist provided by Andrew J. Dubrin in this regard:

**Table 15**

| | *Mostly true* | *Mostly false* |
|---|---|---|
| 1. I feel tired more frequently than I used to | | |
| 2. I snap at people too often | | |
| 3. Trying to help other people often seems hopeless | | |
| 4. I seem to be working harder but accomplishing less | | |
| 5. I get down on myself too often | | |
| 6. My job is beginning to depress me | | |
| 7. I often feel I am headed nowhere | | |

| | | |
|---|---|---|
| 8. I have reached (or am fast approaching) a dead end in my job | | |
| 9. I have lost a lot of my zip lately | | |
| 10. It's hard for me to laugh at a joke about myself | | |
| 11. I am not really physically ill, but I have a lot of aches and pains | | |
| 12. Lately I have kind of withdrawn from friends and family | | |
| 13. My enthusiasm for life is on the wane | | |
| 14. I am running out of things to say to people | | |
| 15. My temper is much shorter than it used to be | | |
| 16. My job makes me feel sad. | | |

## Reducing Burnout

W.S Paine suggested four techniques to reduce burnout. These are:

- ***Identification:*** This is the analysis of the incidence, prevalence and features of burnout in individuals, workgroups and subunits in an organisation.
- ***Prevention:*** Serious attempts should be made to prevent burnout process before it begins through employee wellness programmes (designed to keep employees healthy and happy). These programmes focus on such things as smoking cessation, weight control, physical fitness, high blood pressure control, nutrition education and stress management.
- ***Mediation:*** This involves procedures for slowing, halting or reversing the burnout process.
- ***Remediation:*** Techniques are designed for persons who are already burned out or are rapidly reaching the end stages of this process.

Burnout is a logical but avoidable response to prolonged stress. It can be avoided or relieved by avoiding career ruts, staying physically active, focusing on non-business relationships, stimulating the intellect, making spiritual discoveries, and consciously improving one's life-style.

**Table 16: Checklist of Temporary Escape Techniques**

| |
|---|
| — Spend time reading those books you're been promising yourself you'd read. |
| — Go to the movies. |
| — Listen to good music. |
| — Work it off by exercising. |
| — Avoid striving. Shun the Superperson urge. |
| — Give in more often. |
| — Create a quiet scene and escape for a while. |
| -- Use "not now" buttons. |
| — Plan your work. |
| — Write a letter. |
| — Take an adult education course. |
| — Take a walk. |
| — Talk it out, confide in someone you trust. |
| — Cry. |
| — Take a bubble bath. |
| — Focus on enjoyment. |
| — Avoid making too many big changes at once. |
| — Be realistic. |
| — Tackle one task at a time. |

| — Hit a tennis ball against a wall and work off your anger. |
|---|
| — Do something for others. |
| — Go easy with criticism. |
| — Establish a nutritious diet. |

## STRESS MANAGEMENT FOR LIBRARIANS

Rapid technological change has become a fact of life in the libraries of the 21st Century. While this change touches all parts of the library organisation, nowhere is it more visible, or its effects more keenly felt, than in reference departments. Consider these "snapshots"—fictional, but real enough:

- A librarian begins a mediated online search session by apologising to the user: "I hardly ever do this any more. Most people just search on the CD-ROMs." During the search, he/she mistakenly downloads too large a file, resulting in a "disk full" error.
- A user comes to the reference desk with a question that could be answered in five minutes with a "ready reference" database search. As the librarian hesitates, trying to decide whether to go online for this user, he/she sees three others waiting for help: one whose CD-ROM printer has evidently jammed, one who is waving from an online catalog terminal, and another who is carrying a volume of L'Annee Philologique.

Free time will not be taken over but these commitments can be difficult, especially for someone dedicated to their profession. The solution is to learn how to say 'NO' when you already have a full plate. Finally, remember to use some of your free time to exercise and relax. By dedicating time to rejuvenating your body and mind, recovery from the rigours of work is possible. If you do nothing else but follow these simple tips, you will attain the mastery of library stress.

Stress is an exceedingly complex concept that does not lend itself to a simple definition. It can best be understood in terms of the internal and external conditions necessary for its arousal and the symptoms by which it is identified. Its identifiable symptoms are both psychological and physiological. Stress carries a negative connotation for some people, as though it were something to be avoided. This is unfortunate, because stress is a great asset in managing legitimate emergencies and achieving peak performance. Some definitions of stress are given below:

According to J.C Quick and J.D Quick "Stress, or the stress response, is the unconscious preparation to fight or flee a person experiences when faced with any demand".

According to Mikhail A, "Stress refers to a psychological and physiological state that results when certain features of an individual's environment challenges that person, creating an actual or perceived imbalance between demand and capability to adjust that results in a non-specific response".

### Recession Stress

Redundencies and lengthening dole queues tend to grab the headlines during a recession. But growing levels of stress and other mental health problems can be just as damaging to individuals, employers and society in general.

The World Health Organisation and the mental health charity, Rethink have both warned of a surge in these problems as the economic crises worsens and people become increasingly worried about debt, home repossession and job security. Add growing work intensity, change and workplace conflict to the mix and you have the ingredients for a stress epidemic.

Work-related stress was, of course, a growing problem for employers even before the current economic downturn. According to the Health and Safety Executive (HSE), the number of people in employment experiencing ill health as a result of work-related stress rose from 820 people per 100,000 in 1974 to 1620 people per 100,000 in 2007-08.

One likely reason for this increase is that work has become more intense in recent years. Economist, Francis Green has identified a number of factors contributing to this trend, including competitive pressures being passed on to employees, the decline of union representation and power and the growing use of incentives linking efforts to pay. Technological advances have also speeded up the pace of work, and increasing reliance on the internet, emails and instant messaging have blurred the line between work and home, making ir harder for employees to switch off. Worries about job security at a time of sharply rising unemployment can only make matters worse.

The impact of rising stress levels on employers is significant. The CIPD's 2008 Absence Management Survey found that stress was the number one cause of long-tern absence for non-manual employees, and the fourth biggest cause for manual workers. However, absence is only one of the harmful consequences of high levels of stress, which is linked to lower levels of employee motivation, commitment and retention. Stress is also one of the main causes of conflict at work. In addition, research by the Sainsbury Centre for Mental Health found that mental health problems, including stress, were a major cause of presenteeism (people going to work while ill and not performing), which annually costs employers more than £600 per employee each year. The Government, which is planning to launch the first national strategy on mental health and employment later this year, has clearly recognised the need to tackle these problems. But for employers, too, there's a cast iron business case for investing in effective stress management.

The trouble is that too few employers understand what stress is, how it affects their people and organisation and how to deal with it. One of the difficulties they face is that not all the stress- related problems that affect employees' attendance and performance are rooted in the workplace. In many cases, there is a complex relationship between the work and non-work-related causes of stress. So someone with debt problems and a deteriorating personal relationship, for example, may find that the demands of their job – though perfectly manageable in normal circumstances – start to get on top of them. Employers, however, cannot afford to say, "This is not a work problem so it is not my responsibility". Because the chances are that the situation will lead to changes in the individual's behaviour, attendance or performance in the workplace.

What, then, should employers do to promote the well-being of their employees and keep stress levels down as the economic environment become tougher? The starting point for managing stress at work at any time is good people management – particularly on the part of front – line managers. They are the people who to a large extent can help to prevent and manage stress at work – or make it worse. Their behaviour can often be the reason why people become stressed in the first place.

## Occupational Stress

Occupational stress has become a topic of great interest to academic researchers, managers in organisations, and to the general public as well. The negative impact of stress is often thought to be due to increases in health care costs. It is claimed that employee stress is costly to organisations in terms of reduced productivity, decreased quality of customer service, increased accident rates, and increased employee withdrawal.

The nature of work is changing at whirlwind speeds. Perhaps now, more than ever before, job stress poses a threat to the health of workers. Stress has long been associated with the onset of significant physical and mental health problems. Stress began to be implicated in areas beyond the bounds of physical and mental health as far back as the 1980s. In the organisational environment, stress has been implicated in the deterioration of performance efficiency by both managers and subordinates. When performance efficiency suffers the quality of the overall organisational environment and productivity deteriorates. A deterioration of the organisational environment is accompanied by deterioration in organisational communication.

The primary sources of occupational stress within an organisation originate from four areas. These areas include task demands, physical demands, role demands, and interpersonal demands. "Any demand, either of a physical nature or psychological nature, encountered in the course of living is know as a 'stressor'. A stress response will occur as a result of an individual's interaction with and reaction to the stressor". Task-related stress is directly related to the specific characteristics of the job itself. This type of stress involves role ambiguity, conflicting task demands, work overload or work underload, inadequate resource support, no provision for meaningful participation in decision-making, and insecurity, among others. Physical demands of the workplace are another source to be considered. Environmental factors such as temperature variations, noise vibrations, and lighting may significantly affect individual stress. For example, "extremes in lighting can cause stress, which often results in headaches and nervous tension". Role demands are external to the tasks associated with a job.

This particular type of stress typically develops as a result of flawed organisational structures, ineffective organisational development, the inability of an individual to successfully pursue achievement goals within an organisation, or some combination of all three. The individual's stress often results when his or her work role and responsibility has not been clearly defined. The final source area of occupational stress relates to interpersonal demands. "Interpersonal stress at work is concerned with the demands that are placed on us in developing working relationships with other people in our organisations". Leadership style of managers and supervisors is often a source of stress for their employees. Stress Outcomes the result of stressors commonly associated with occupational stress tends to vary widely. Workers may simply resort to daydreaming or fantasising. Alternatively, employees may react more actively by creating interpersonal and intraorganisational conflicts involving escalating levels of communication problems. Workers may also experience effects in their psychological and physical health. Psychological consequences may include anxiety, boredom, low self-esteem, forgetfulness, depression, anger, apathy, or worry. Physical consequences may include, but are certainly not limited to, headaches, diabetes, fatigue, hypertension, chest and back pain, ulcers, or even infectious diseases. From the organisational aspect, stress has many consequences. Reductions in effectiveness, productivity, and communication are results that are not as easy to identify; however, such outcomes can be among the most debilitating for both the organisation and for the individual. Other results may include accidents in the workplace, job turnover, low morale, poor work relations, poor organisational climate, and absenteeism.

Like many areas in the organisational sciences, the study of occupational stress is relatively new. In assessing the effects of job-related stressors over the years, however, a clear pattern has developed in terms of the various outcomes that researchers have investigated. Specifically, stress outcomes (called "strains") have typically been *psychological*, *physical*, and *behavioural* in nature. Common psychological outcomes that have been studied include anxiety, depression, and general psychological well-being. Physical outcomes have been popular due to the potential link between experiencing job-related stressors and ill health. Most researchers have opted to measure physical strain through self-reported physical symptoms, although some researchers have used more objective measures such as physiological indicators (e.g., blood pressure) or even healthcare utilisation. Behavioural outcomes (e.g., job performance, absenteeism, and turnover) have been studied the least, due largely to the practical difficulties associated with obtaining these indicators.

## Stress- A "Modern Disease"

Each of these scenarios portrays a mixed blessing: the dramatic and liberating benefits of information technology, coupled with new time demands, knowledge/skill deficiencies, and the resulting psychological pressure.

One name for this kind of pressure is technostress. Craig Brod, who may have coined the term and certainly brought it into the popular consciousness, defines technostress as: "... a modern disease of adaptation caused by an inability to cope with the new computer technologies in a healthy manner. It manifests itself in two distinct and related ways: in the struggle to accept computer technology, and in the more specialised form of over identification with computer technology."

The most commonly studied aspects of technostress are machine-based stress (physical and psychological, caused by poor ergonomics, badly designed software, etc.); computer anxiety; and computer obsession. The populations most often studied in the mainstream psychological literature are clerical and office workers, professionals, executives, home computer users, hackers, students, and adolescents.

**Table 17: Model of Occupational System**

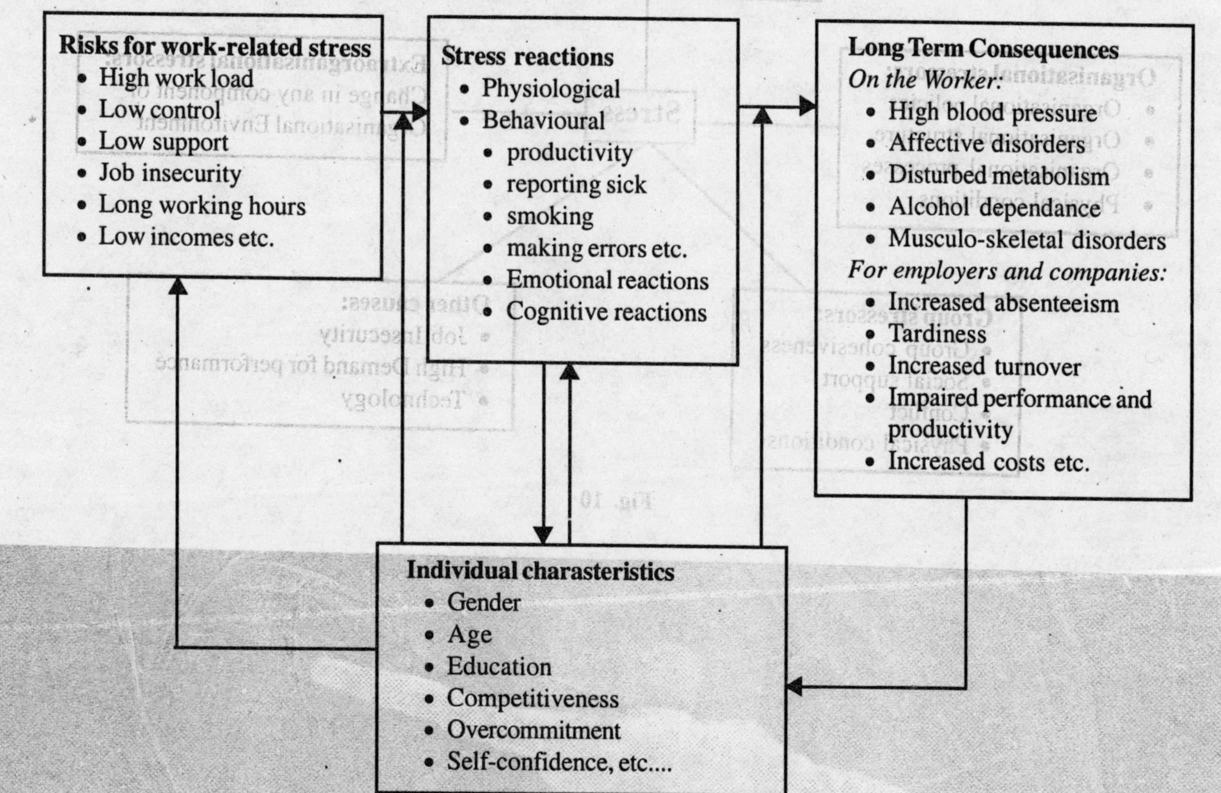


## NIOSH Approach to Job Stress

On the basis of experience and research, NIOSH (National Institute for Occupational Safety and Health), favours the view that working conditions play a primary role in causing job stress. However, the role of individual factors is not ignored. According to the NIOSH view, exposure to stressful working conditions (called job stressors) can have a direct influence on worker safety and health. But as shown below, individual and other situational factors can intervene to strengthen or weaken this influence. (For reference see page 67).

Examples of individual and situational factors that can help to reduce the effects of stressful working conditions include the following:

- Balance between work and family or personal life
- A support network of friends and co-workers
- A relaxed and positive outlook.

## Potential Sources of Stress

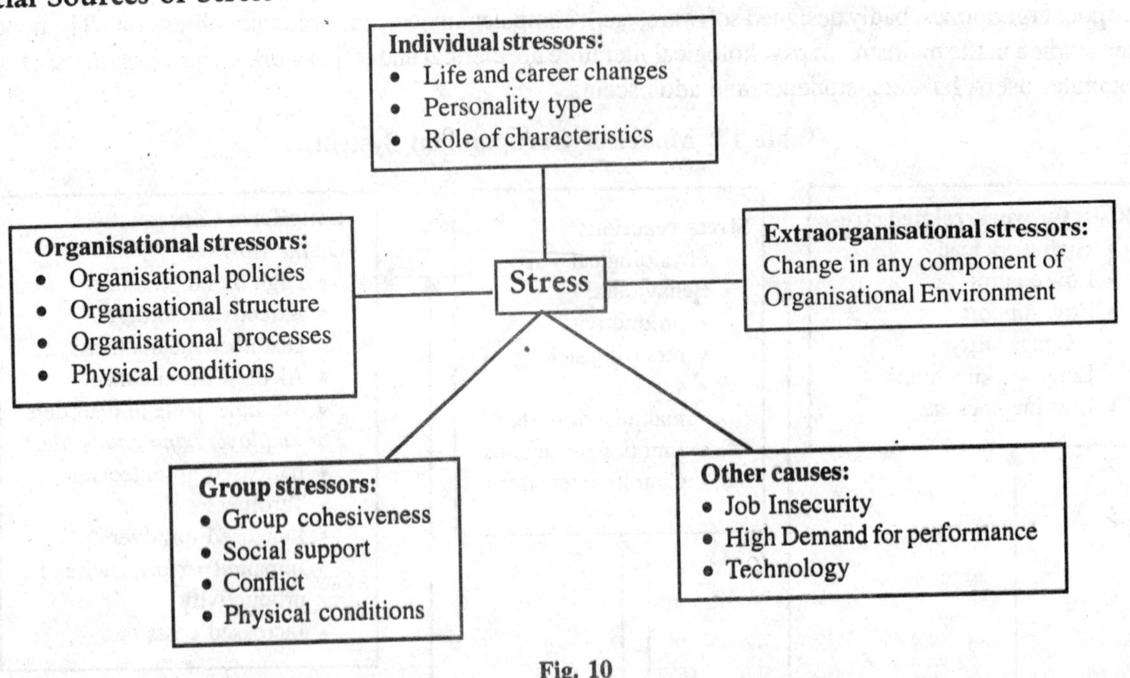


**Fig. 10**

**Fig. 11: Next time you feel life is collapsing around you, take a step back and welcome the changes, says Karen Hall**

The effects of technostress on librarians have been studied by Bichteler, Champion, Dobb, and Sievert et al. Among the many discussions of the related problem of resistance to technological change in libraries, those by Fine, Malinconico, Luguire, and Giesbrecht and McCarthy are especially relevant.

While reference librarians are as prone as anyone to suffer from poor ergonomics or badly-designed software, and while some certainly become obsessively involved in over identification with the computer, the technostress phenomenon of greatest interest here is "computer anxiety."

Brod's elaboration on this term seems to ring true for many librarians:

"The primary symptom of those who are ambivalent, reluctant, or fearful of computers is anxiety. This anxiety is expressed in many ways: irritability, headaches, nightmares, resistance to learning about the computer, or outright rejection of the technology. Techno anxiety most commonly afflicts those who feel pressured—by employer, peers, or the general culture—to accept and use computers."

While it is fortunately rare for a reference librarian to be truly computerphobic to the extent that he/she "locks up" or panics, milder symptoms of technostress are fairly common.

These include:

- feelings of isolation and frustration.
- negative attitudes toward new computer-based sources and systems.
- indifference to users' computer-related needs (as in "It's not my job to fix that printer").
- self-depreciating thoughts or statements about one'stability to cope.
- an apologetic attitude toward users.
- a definition of self as "someone who doesn't search."

## Discussion through

This page presents the results of an online survey on technostress (computer-related stress) among library staff members, taken in August 2003. This survey was posted on the web for 10 days and collected 92 responses, most coming from people who work in academic libraries.

**Highlights:**

- 59% of survey participants said their level of computer-related stress has increased in the past 5 years, 34% felt it has not changed much, and only 4% believed it has decreased.
- 65% of participants reported that this type of stress is a somewhat serious problem for them, 8% said it is very serious, while 27% felt it is not at all serious.
- Leading causes chosen from a list of possibilities were information overload, networking problems, security issues, computer hardware and ergonomics, and vendor-produced databases. Security issues may have drawn special attention because of the "Blaster" and "SoBig" attacks going on at the time. Interestingly, library catalogs and web sites ranked low on the list of causes; Participants also listed several other causes.
- The survey also collected numerous strategies for managing and coping with technostress. Prominent themes in these responses include the need for individuals to cultivate flexibility and continuous learning, and for organisations to provide training and support.

This was an informal poll, not a scientific sample. Respondents were self-selected .The survey questions elicited subjective perceptions of stress levels, not objective measures of symptoms or behaviour. Thus, we can't conclude from these results that X percentage of library staff suffer from any given level of computer-related stress. Nonetheless, since 92 people took the time to respond in the ways described below, I do think it's reasonable to conclude that substantial numbers of library staff are experiencing this type of stress. That in itself should be of concern to those who manage and study libraries. This survey was conducted by John Kupersmith (1999-2003).

## Survey results

**Table 18**

| 1. Do you work in: | Responses | Per cent |
|---|---|---|
| an academic library? | 53 | 58 % |
| a public library? | 18 | 20 % |
| another type of library? | 13 | 14 % |
| A library-related business or organization? | 5 | 5 % |
| (none of the above) | 3 | 3 % |
| Total | 92 | 100 % |
| **2. In the past 5 years, has your level of technostress:** | **Responses** | **Per cent** |
| Decreased | 4 | 4 % |
| Not changed much | 31 | 34 % |
| Increased | 54 | 59 % |
| Don't know | 2 | 2 % |
| Total | 91 | 100 % |
| **3. For you personally, is the problem of technostress:** | **Responses** | **Per cent** |
| Not at all serious | 25 | 27 % |
| Somewhat serious | 60 | 65 % |
| Very serious | 7 | 8 % |
| Don't know | 0 | 0 % |
| Total | 92 | 100 % |

| 4. **What are the main causes of technostress for you? Check the 3 most important causes below.** (Arranged in order as ranked by participants) | **Responses** | **Per cent** |
|---|---|---|
| Information overload | 54 | 59 % |
| Networking problems | 40. | 43 % |
| Security issues (viruses, authentication, etc.) | 38 | 41 % |
| Computer hardware and ergonomics | 38 | 41 % |
| Vendor-produced databases | 28 | 30% |
| Application software (word processors, etc.) | 21 | 23 % |
| Library catalogs | 9 | 10 % |
| Library web sites | 9 | 10 % |
| Other web sites | 6 | 7 % |

## Successful Coping- Strategies

Coping involves reconfiguring your life landscape. Take the time to downsize. Rearrange your priorities, tasks and activities. Use any combination of the strategies described below to create more balance and less stress in your life.

**(a) Mentoring:** Making use of mentors is a giant step towards becoming a happy, stress-free librarian. Mentoring in the library field can come in many forms. Finding a mentor is easiest when your library already has a mentoring system in place. Having a colleague as a mentor will help you find answers in a very low-key, informal manner. Look to your local, state, and national library associations as well; many of these organisations have mentoring programmes. Everyone can feel his/her stress dissipate when he/she finds solutions to the work-related problems.

**(b) Asking For Advice:** If you work as a librarian long enough, chances are you will run across unfamiliar situations that you are not sure how to handle. Try posting your questions on library-related listservs. You can receive responses from people of varying backgrounds and environments, which can give you more opinions and options. The sharing of information and stories among colleagues is a great way to make a stressed librarian feel like he or she is not alone.

**(c) Creating A Network:** Learn when and how to delegate. It's important to recognise what you have to do yourself and what you can allow others to do. Don't be afraid to ask for help when you need it. Perhaps, you can partner with someone or form a team to accomplish some tasks. Through sharing, your workload and stress load can be lightened.

**(d) Prioritising And Being Selective:** Being stressed will affect your job performance and your quality of life. Learn the power of prioritising and being selective in your commitments. Learn to say NO and you will be one step ahead of the pack. No matter how much we love our work, or want to stay on top of the growing paper piles on our desk, it is not healthy to spend all of our free time doing work, thinking about work, or worrying about work.

**(e) Making Healthy Lifestyle Choices:** Engaging in healthy habits such as eating well, getting enough sleep, and exercising helps to form a solid base upon which we can build stress-busting habits. Stress is dissipated when you do something that stimulates the mind or the body in an activity that is completely separate from work. By taking your mind off of work, you will be able to relax, your body will be less tense, and come the next workday, you will find yourself renewed, rested and ready once more to face the daily challenges of your profession.

**Remedies:** * Let it flow over you.

1. Deep breathing.
2. Roll with the flow
3. Realise that the technology changes are going to continue and that I have a choice: move with it or get stressed (and left behind). I choose to move with the technology!
4. Keep reading and learning always!
5. Vacations
6. I'm younger and a new librarian, so honestly I'm not having terrible stress. One things that helps is that I almost never use computers outside of work and keep technology low in my home (ie no games, no cell phone, no dvd player,...)
7. Go home and leave work at work; yoga/meditaion/prayer.
8. Stay up to date and stay calm
9. The best way for me to cope has been to learn more about the technologies so I can feel more empowered to troubleshoot or otherwise try to solve those inevitable technology glitches that occur when I have multiple systems talking to each other.
10. Gardening. Deep breaths. Going for walks.
11. Complete change of pace for time outside of work is essential.
12. The ability to focus on one issue at a time helps; making a list can help this.
13. Through Training
14. Focus on task goals, rather than the particular software tools/interfaces that may actually impede progress.
15. When possible, minimise time spent online. Unsubscribe to e-letters and try to avoid new ones.
16. Calm attitude
17. Relaxing breaks
18. Separate work from home life—leave stress at the office
19. Just cope, then go home and garden
20. Focus on the software needed for the job and keep current sharing solutions with others helps. Network with the techies. Laugh often; laugh hard.
21. Exercise, 'proper' diet, plenty of sleep, sailing on the lake, realise that the fast pace of tech innovation will take this moment away without a tear for the latest new thing...
22. I haven't found a "best" way yet other than chilling out. There will always be another problem tomorrow
23. Learn more, and make lots of friends in the IT department!
24. Completely remove self from the environment. Vacation.
25. Communication rather than complaining

## TEACHERS STRESS IN EDUCATION AND RELIEF STRATEGIES

Teacher stress becomes problematic, and potentially harmful, when the challenges teachers face outpace their perceived ability to cope, or when they perceive that important needs are not being met. Perhaps the most effective strategy for reducing stress is knowing one's own stress points and practicing the coping techniques that work best.

One important part of our lives, which causes a great deal of stress, is our job or our work. Work-related stress is a growing concern because it has significant economic implications for the organisations through employee dissatisfaction, lowered productivity and lowered emotional and physical health of the employees. It has been argued that organisational and extra-organisational stressors lead to stress through cognitive appraisal which, in turn, leads to poor emotional health, poor physical health, and behaviours which harm the organisations. Given the research findings that job stressors cause stress, the terms "stress" and "stressors" will be used interchangeably in the present article.

There is fair degree of agreement on the variables that act as organisational stressors. Cooper et al., have identified intrinsic job factors (e.g. poor working conditions and work overload), role in organisations (e.g. role conflict and role ambiguity), career development (e.g. lack of promotion policies and job security), poor relationships at work, and organisational culture (e.g. politics in organisations and lack of participation in decision-making) as organisational stressors. Matteson and Ivancevich have also identified similar job factors as job stressors. Not only do various stimuli at work act as stressors, various things that happen to people outside their work environment may also contribute to their work stress. These extra-organisational stressors include factors such as family problems, personal problems, and social problems. As mentioned above, job-related stressors and extra-organisational stressors cause stress, which, in turn, causes strains. The strains caused by stress are:

- Lower emotional health which is manifested as psychological distress, depression and anxiety;
- Lower physical health which is manifested as heart disease, insomnia, headaches, and infections;
- Organisational symptoms such as job dissatisfaction, absenteeism, lower productivity, and poor work quality.

A certain amount of stress in teaching is inevitable, even beneficial. Hinton and Rotheiler (1998), point out that the excitement and challenge of teaching naturally causes the raised adrenaline levels associated with stress, while Dunham (1992), illustrates that teachers work at peak efficiency when the demands placed on them are in balance with their own perceived coping ability, and that too little challenge and too much can be equally detrimental. Teacher stress becomes problematic, and potentially harmful, when the challenges teachers face outpace their perceived ability to cope, or when they perceive that important needs are not being met.

## Causes of teacher stress

Stress in teachers can be more insidious than in other professions by its "fuzzy" nature: it arises from a vague system of rules and returns; it is often self-inflicted; and unlike in the business or medical professions, the debilitating effects are not often counterbalanced by moments of exhilaration and satisfaction (Claxton, 1989, p. 49). While all the possible permutations of the causes and effects of stress have yet to be thoroughly investigated, it is probable that other things being equal, stress tends to affect younger, less experienced teachers over older, more experienced ones; those of lower academic rank over higher; single teachers over married; and women over men, although men are at greater risk of self-destructive reactions to stress (Griffith et al., 1999).

Teacher stress can be caused by a number of factors, both external and internal. External causes may include institutional conditions such as large, mixed-ability classes, lack of student discipline and motivation, lack of resources, overwork or uneven distribution of workloads, poor communication, unclear expectations, and inadequate rewards and recognition (Brown & Ralph, 1998; Gmelch, 1993; Travers & Cooper, 1998). Problematic relationships with colleagues can generate other stressors, such as personality conflicts, lack of community spirit, feelings of isolation, lack of support, and limited academic and social interaction with other teachers (ibid.). Internal causes may include an aggressive, impatient, competitive "Type A" personality; workaholism; negative attitude toward students; and in particular, unrealistic self-expectations (ibid.). Some of the causes of teacher stress mentioned above are beyond the control of individual teachers, arising from external circumstances that require co-operation from administrators and colleagues to change, while others are within the teacher's control and can be managed with the help of appropriate coping strategies. There are numerous reports in the literature on teacher stress and burnout. A nation-wide survey done in the United States indicates that there has been a considerable rise in the stress levels of teachers over the years. Burnout in teachers (described by Maslarch, 1982, as a three-dimensional phenomenon characterised by feelings of exhaustion, depersonalisation, and a lack of personal accomplishment) can not only manifest itself as various physical ailments and emotional problems, but can result in teachers actually leaving their chosen career. Administrators in the National Education Association worry that thousands of sensitive, thoughtful and dedicated teachers are abandoning the teaching profession. Canadian teachers are affected too. In a national study done by the Canadian Teachers' Federation, 55% of teachers responding to a stress scale questionnaire indicated that they were almost always exhausted at the end of a regular day. All of this research has resulted in some positive changes in the operation of the education system, however, it appears that the emphasis for change often relates directly to: (a) the physical environment the teacher works in, (b) a shift in task overload, (c) training in the area of conflict resolution and (d) training in communication skills. What is missing in the data is the importance of the personal health and well-being levels of the teachers themselves and how this important aspect can play a role in managing stress.

## Effects of teacher stress

Behaviours symptomatic of teacher stress include poor time management; inability to concentrate; job dissatisfaction; irritation and aggression; introversion and withdrawal from supportive relationships; inappropriate, cynical humour; abuse of alcohol, caffeine or tobacco; and if left untreated, absenteeism, resignation, and withdrawal from the profession. Emotional consequences include feelings of anxiety, dissatisfaction and resentment; depression; inability to relax and unwind; feelings of inadequacy and low self-esteem; and ultimately burnout. Long-term physical effects include fatigue and low energy; frequent colds; irregular sleeping patterns, insomnia and bad dreams; appetite disorders; and potentially, psychosomatic illness and heart disease (Brown and Ralph, 1998; Hinton and Rotheiler, 1998; Travers and Cooper, 1998).

## Discussion through a case study

Job stressors and their effects on physical health, emotional health, and job satisfaction in a university By Jagdish K. Dua University of New England, Armidale, New South Wales, Australia

In recent years, researchers have investigated the role of stressors and the effects of stressors in various organisations. Research reported in the present article was designed to investigate the nature and effects of stress in a university setting. The project was conducted at the University of New England. The aims of the research were to determine:

- The extent to which staff at the university experienced job-related stressors.
- If job-related stressors acted differentially as stressors in staff belonging to subgroups in a variety of categories (e.g. did male and female staff, in the sex category, experience different amounts or degrees of job-related stress?). The categories investigated in this connection were sex, age, campus (and faculty at the Armidale campus) to which the staff member belonged job-type (e.g., academic and administrative), permanent/ temporary, full-time/part-time, supervising/not-supervising, top-of-the-scale/not top-of-the-scale, ethnic background, qualifications, and disability.
- The degree of self-reported extra-organisational or non-work stressors experienced by staff at the university and to determine if staff belonging to subgroups in different categories experienced differential non-work stress.
- The relationship between job-stressors and non-work stressors, and physical health, emotional health, and job satisfaction.

The necessary infrastructure or equipment at work; 28 per cent of the respondents reported that that they were not sure how recent reorganisation would affect them; and 32 per cent of the respondents reported that that events related to amalgamation had produced too many changes in too short a time.

Analysis of job stress and stress due to job stress factors in different subgroups revealed that, in many cases, respondents belonging to different subgroups experienced differential job stress and stress due to job stress factors. It is worth remembering that job stress was the average scores over 21 stressors whereas job stress factors scores were scores averaged over a smaller number of questions. Thus, as one would expect, there were a number of instances where the overall job stress in subgroups within a category was not significant but there were significant differences in stress caused by job stress factors. For example, there was no significant difference in job stress between males and females, but males reported more workload stress than females, and females reported more stress due to work politics than males.

Results showed that, in general, younger staff reported more job stress than older staff. This may be because as people get older they become more experienced and more worldly-wise [10]. In addition, older employees have often reached a stage where career development is not their major concern, and hence a number of job characteristics, which may cause stress to younger staff, who have their career ahead of them, do not cause stress to older staff.

The result of stress in staff across different campuses and across different faculties of the Armidale campus was revealing. Generally, staff in the Faculty of Education, Nursing, and Professional Studies were more stressed than other staff. They were followed, in the level of stress, by staff, who did not belong to any of the faculties in Armidale. The latter group comprised administrative staff, support staff, and library staff. It is worth remembering that the University of New England had undergone an amalgamation about four years ago and many staff had felt the effects of amalgamation. The amalgamation involved a college at Orange, a college at Lismore, a college at Armidale, and a university at Armidale. It might be argued that amalgamation produced maximum changes for staff who had previously belonged to the college at Armidale before undergoing a complete amalgamation with the university at Armidale. Staff of Lismore and Orange had also become part of the university, but these campuses functioned as autonomous units. Most of the staff at the previous college at Armidale belonged to the Faculty of Education, Nursing and Professional Studies, and the greatest change due to amalgamation for these staff may have been the cause of their stress.

Staff below senior lecturer level, followed by support staff and staff below senior technical officer, reported more job stress than other staff. These results suggested that staff in lower jobs were more stressed than staff in higher jobs.

It is important to point out that the personal factor categories were not mutually exclusive. Thus, differences within one category may exist because of the effect of another category. For example, differences within job-type category may be due to age or vice-versa. Stepwise multiple regressions in which personal factor categories served as predictor variables for the prediction of job stress and scores on job stress factors were applied to the data. One general conclusion from these multiple regressions was that supervising/not-supervising and job-type factors were the two most common and significant predictors of stress. In addition, within the job-type category, there was a trend for staff employed at lower job level (e.g., staff below senior lecturer level and support staff) to be more stressed than staff employed at higher job levels (e.g., staff above senior lecturer level). Thus, it seems that many significant associations between personal factors and stress (for example, the correlation between age, and stress) could be explained through the supervising/not-supervising and job-type factors.

Researchers have presented evidence to show that general stress and work-related stress lead to poor physical health, poor emotional or mental health, absenteeism, low morale, and job dissatisfaction [e.g., 10,13]. Poor physical health consequences have been observed in relation to cardiovascular disease, infections, cancer headaches, and gastro-intestinal diseases. However, there is a significant amount of evidence to suggest that the stress-illness relationship may be explained through the personality dimension of negative affectively, that is, people who show negative affectivity are more likely to be ill [20]. In relation to emotional health, researchers have found increased depression and anxiety, and lower psychological well-being as a result of both the general stress and work-related stress. The results of the present study supported previous research. The present study found that both the high job stress and high non-work stress were associated with more job dissatisfaction, psychological distress, negative effect, manifest anxiety, absence from work due to illness, doctor visits and illness, and worse physical health.

The research reported in the article identifies many higher-educational job characteristics which acted as stressors for staff employed at the University of New England. The research also found that staff belonging to different subgroups experienced different stressors. I believe that many job characteristics identified as stressors at the University of New England would also be found to act as stressors in other higher education institutions in Australia and perhaps, other countries. University authorities should be encouraged to determine the stressors for different subgroups of staff in their university and then take action to remove the sources of stress from the work environment. In the medium to long-term such action would produce benefits for the institution in terms of improved physical and emotional health, increased job satisfaction, and improved morale of the employees. These benefits would be followed by increased productivity in terms of quality and quantity of work.

The next sections will explore ways in which teacher stress can be treated at each of these three levels: administrative, collegial, and individual.

Three ways administrations can help create a more positive working environment for faculty are:

1. ***Treat faculty as an investment:*** An important first step in improving the overall quality of education is for administrations to view faculty members as valuable investments rather than expendable assets. Many universities neglect an important resource by assuming faculty to be self-sufficient with no further need for training or support (Gmelch, 1993, p. 35). This situation can be remedied in part by administrative faculty staying current in the field, and encouraging, supporting and rewarding teaching faculty who do the same. Providing support for research, in-service training and other professional development activities, at all levels, is also important. As Brown (2002) memorably observed, "Treat [teachers] like professionals and they will be professionals; treat them like part- time scum and they will be part-time scum!" Furthermore, institutions that invest their resources in helping faculty do the best possible job are more likely to feel inclined to protect their investments, resulting in greater job security for faculty.

2. ***Provide clear expectations, feedback, and rewards:*** A clear statement of expectations and rewards in all areas of responsibility (teaching, research, and service) helps faculty perform at their best (Gmelch, 1993, p. 26). Regular feedback in each of these areas is also essential. In many institutions, feedback on teaching comes only in the form of a series of yes/no or multiple-choice questions on surveys administered to students at the end of the semester. Whether such instruments are capable of including all the subtleties of good teaching is highly questionable (Palmer, 1998, p. 143; Simmons, 1996, pp. 12-16). In addition, administrators may not even see the results at all (Naoumi & Fujimaki, 2002); or if they do, the results can easily be ignored or selectively invoked (Palmer, op. cit.). While the number of students and volume of questionnaires may make it logistically difficult at larger institutions, administrators could profitably pay attention to qualitative as well as quantitative feedback from students. In addition, while classroom observations tend to inspire a sense of dread in many teachers, who equate them with judgment rather than support (Claxton, 1989, p. 34), they can be a source of constructive feedback if used well, and when a trusting relationship exists between the observer and teacher (Woodward, 2001). One American university obtained good results by training education majors to be participant-observers in classes, giving feedback to the teacher from the perspective of an informed student. Feedback from faculty indicated that they found the system so valuable that they often actively sought the participant- observers' advice: "What do you think happened yesterday when we had that conflict in class?" or "Any suggestions about how I can make the transition to the next topic without losing the students who still don't understand the last one?" (Palmer, 1998, p. 160)

3. ***Establish support systems for teachers:*** A simple and important first step in supporting teachers is keeping two-way lines of communication open between teaching and administrative faculty. Teachers need to know that they can safely consult a respected senior colleague when they have questions or concerns; one way of providing this has been to establish a "consulting teacher" among the senior faculty, who teaches a reduced load and is available for consultation with newer teachers (Palmer, 1998, p. 159).

Also, as an alternative to the exchanges of advice that "typically take place in the context of busy staff rooms in a very short space of time and rarely with any possibility of reviewing the effects of the advice" (Daniels et al., 1998, p. 132), support groups in which teachers who teach similar courses can meet on a regular basis to share concerns and ideas (possibly including senior colleagues as guiding members) are also helpful (Claxton, 1989; Daniels et al., op. cit.).

## Managing Stress

**(a) Teacher caring for each other:** Supportive relationships with co-workers are a teacher's best protection against the sense of isolation that is a major cause of teacher stress (Griffith et al., 1999). A harmonious atmosphere among the staff, characterised by interdependence and togetherness, helps create an optimal working environment (ibid.). Development of such an environment is hindered, however, by an academic culture that builds barriers between colleagues and discourages professional interaction and shared knowledge (Palmer, 1998; Daniels et al., 1998).

Every teacher can benefit from an informal support network of trusted colleagues who can discuss concerns and share failure stories without fear (Kyriacou, 1998, p. 10). A particularly valuable skill in members of such a network is the ability to listen. Asking colleagues for help is a risk and an admission of vulnerability (Troman, 2000), and teachers who overcome their anxieties and lay bare their concerns often find themselves surrounded by colleagues who ply them with advice, thereby (consciously or unconsciously) casting themselves in the role of sempai (senior) passing down knowledge to their kouhai (juniors) and thus increasing the latter's feelings of inadequacy and reinforcing fears of lowering defenses (Claxton, 1989, p. 81).

As an alternative, Palmer (1998, pp. 151ff) describes a "clearness committee" as practiced in Quaker communities since the 17th century, in which one "focus person" describes the problem and the other members respond only in the form of an honest, open question, offering no advice either during or after the session, but rather helping the focus person to discover his or her own solution. Even without convening a formal "committee", individual teachers can resist the temptation to play the sempai-kohai game when a colleague shares a problem, and instead help that person find clearness. Palmer (op. cit.) describes how the process of seeking clearness can bring revelations not only to the focus person, but to other participants as well.

Pairs or small groups of teachers can provide valuable support for each other, including helping each other keep "new semester's resolutions", giving "wake-up calls" to partners who seem to be succumbing to stress (Claxton, 1989, p. 83), and practicing what Claxton (op. cit., p. 78) calls "creative ranting and raving", in which one partner complains as much as possible (preferably in a self-consciously exaggerated and irrational way) for ten minutes strictly measured by the other, after which the two turn their attention to seeking constructive solutions.

Finally, small gestures such as words of appreciation, sweets, and back pat can help foster a sense of camaraderie among faculty. And in times of stress, as Claxton (1989, p. 75) notes: "Cuddles and hugs, preferably accompanied by deep sighs, are highly recommended – although they can be risky in staffrooms."

**(b) Teacher caring for themselves:** Many of the internal causes of teacher stress can be reduced by appropriate coping strategies (the definition of which, of course, depends on what each individual finds most effective). One important step is to recognise and avoid counterproductive coping strategies; these include disengagement (giving up, withdrawal, pretended or real indifference); suppression of conflicting activities (putting hobbies, personal commitments or rest on hold when there is work to be done); alcohol, tobacco and drugs; and defensiveness (Griffith et al., 1999; Claxton, 1989). Good organisation and time management, including concentrating on one task at a time, are keys to reducing stress, as is a sense of humour and perspective, as well as realistic self-expectations, which may mean aiming for excellence in one area of faculty responsibility and competence in others, rather than excellence in all (Gmelch, 1993).

Other effective strategies for reducing stress include physical activity (working out, individual or team sports); entertainment (movies, dining out, TV, concerts, reading for pleasure); and personal interests (hobbies, musical instruments, or cultural activities). While drawing a clear line of demarcation between work and personal time is difficult for teachers, setting aside some personal time off limits to work (which may consist simply of idleness or unstructured leisure) is recommended (Gmelch, 1993). There are also many who find meditation, progressive relaxation, and deep breathing helpful. Finally, perhaps the most effective strategy for reducing stress is knowing one's own stress points and practicing the coping techniques that work best.

## Teacher Wellness Programme

Health and wellness experts such as Ardell (1986), Travis (1981), and Pelltier (1996), suggest that attention to personal lifestyle can improve well-being; that making healthy lifestyle choices can increase our levels of joy, satisfaction and zest for living. Healthy and well employees are also more productive employees. Teacher wellness might be the missing link in the strategic planning process of education reform and could assist in the transformation and revitalisation of both the institution system and individual teachers.

There are many definitions of wellness: an integration of body, mind and spirit; a way of life which we design to enjoy the highest level of health and well-being possible; or a link between our physical, social, spiritual, intellectual, occupational and emotional selves. What we have discovered as we attempt to balance our roles of teacher, student, consultant, wife and mom, is that it doesn't really matter what definition we choose to work with - what does matter is how we choose to put our 'teacher wellness plan into action'.

There are many different wellness models teachers can follow. A model developed by Dr. Donald Ardell - a guru of sorts in the wellness field,it is simple, easy for us to follow, and is the only wellness model we have found that reminds us that "We" are ultimately in charge of our own well-being.

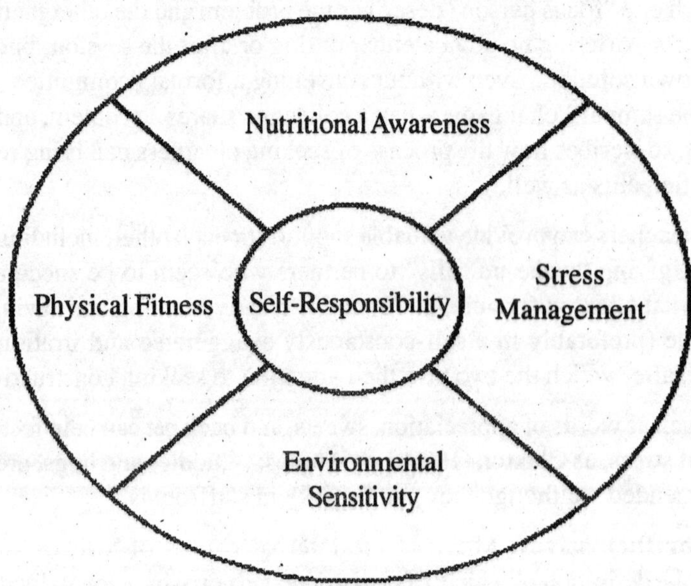


*Source: Dimensions of Wellness Dr. Donald Ardell (1977)*

## Practical Application– DE- Stressing

## Some Rules for Dealing with Stress

A wide variety of organizations and educational institutions are offering courses designed to help people deal with unwanted stress. Some teach methods for reducing the magnititude of the stress reaction, including meditation, relaxation, exercise, and biofeedback. Others help people plan their lives so that they encounter fewer stressors or the stressors come at times when they are physically and psychologically prepared to deal with them. Here are seven rules for dealing with unwanted stress.

**1. Plan activities to reduce or eliminate stressors:** Our daily routine exposes many of us to a wide variety of stressful events, such as traffic snarls on the way to and from work, periodic interruptions, noise, the need to make quick decisions, requests for assistance in areas that are not our responsibility, criticisms of the quality or quantity of our work, and involvement in hostile exchanges. Although some of the events are unavoidable, it is often possible to reduce the number or magnititude of such stressors. For example, arranging to go to work earlier and leaving earlier could allow us to avoid traffic jams, to work at least for a time without interruptions, and to experience less noise and would also limit the opportunity for people to make unwarranted requests, and reduce hostile exchanges. If we can do at least part of our job before the other employees arrive, we may have more time to make decisions and to respond tactfully to criticisms and requests. The resulting reduction in stress may decrease irritability and arousal and thus make us less sensitive to other potential stressors. It could also lead to improved performance, with further reduction in criticisms and the possibility of rewards and promotions.

**2. Plan activities so that stressors come at times when they are easier to handle or tolerate:** The same event may induce a more intense stress reaction at certain times than at others. For example, a common source of stress results from interruptions that occur when we are trying to complete a task – a ringing telephone, a person dropping by to ask questions or simply to chat, or certain distracting noises. It is often possible to reduce or eliminate this source of stress by systematic planning. Turning off the telephone ringer, telling the secretary to hold all calls, putting up a "Do not Disturb" sign, or moving to a location where such interruptions are unlikely are some possible solutions. People often find that after an important task is completed, distracting events are less stressful or not stressful at all. Alternatively, we might take care of details early in the day, so that a block of time is available later in the day to work at certain tasks.

**3. Learning to relax between activities:** Some people tend to experience less stress than others do in the course of a demanding or rigorous schedule. Although constitutional differences may play a role here, another contributory factor is the way people pace themselves. Shutting down the stress reaction periodically by relaxing appears to keep stress under control. Research from a variety of sources suggests that stress becomes distressful when it is allowed to become intense. Unless we shut down the stress reaction periodically, the stress of one activity tends to add to the stress of another. At some point, stress becomes our enemy. It is likely to have an adverse affect not only on our health but on our performance. We can reduce these effects by learning to relax between activities. It may also be easier to reduce low stress than high stress. When the stress reaction becomes very intense, it frequently provokes a psychological state of helplessness; we feel that we no longer have control over events. Such a feeling can, of course, act as a primary source of stress. Because stress can interfere with our ability to cope, we are caught in a vicious circle, in which the experience of stress becomes a stimulus for further stress.

**4. Learn to recognise the early signs of stress:** Because humans are dynamic, their reactions to events are always affected by previous activities. This means that are certain times an event may cause only mild stress, while at other times it may cause intense stress. If we are to gain control of the stress reaction before it becomes too intense, we must be able to recognise when stress is starting to exceed some *safe limit.* This is not an easy task for many people, who can recognise stress only when it has reached a high intensity. Biofeedback training can help such people understand the stress reaction and teach them how to intervene when it starts to exceed some safe limit.

**5. Learn to treat stress as a challenge:** Stressful events often demand that we react. We can react with fear and helplessness, or we can rise to the challenge. If we treat a stressor as a challenge, we will trigger a norepinephrine response, which not only helps supply us with energy but provides us with positive affect. In other words, it appears that norepinephrine has evolved to help us cope with stress. To tap that adaptive chemical, we must rise to the challenge. We must view stress as an opportunity to exercise our adaptive responses or to develop such responses. Failure to rise to the challenge will only undermine our self-concept and our natural tendency to control stressful events in our environment.

**6. Learn to prevail by becoming problem-focused:** Considerable research emphasises that people need to learn how to manage self-doubt because it is an important aspect of learning to prevail. As Bandura, (1991), points out, everybody experiences self-doubt from time to time, especially when faced with a negative life-event. What differentiates those who prevail from those who give up is how they deal with such self-doubt. People who fail typically ruminate on their self-doubts, rehearse all their past failures, and count all their inadequacies. Those who succeed, in contrast, learn to rehearse their past successes and to enumerate their strengths.

The key to managing self-doubt is learning to become problem-focused. When attention is focused on the problem, some change may happen; that is the basis for hope and optimism. When people become self-focused, by contrast, they tend to focus on the negative and to accept that nothing can change because the source of their difficulty lies in their personal inadequacies. The more they ruminate, the more distressed they become, and the harder it is for them to think about a solution to their problem (e.g., Wood, Saltzberg, Neale, Stone, & Rachmiel, 1990).

In order to become more problem-focused, start by thinking of how you succeeded in the past under similar circumstances. In other words, give yourself a pep talk. Next, look for ways that other people succeeded under similar circumstances. This will get your thinking off yourself. Finally, ask people to help you find a solution. This is a good way to establish social relations and make use of the considerable skills that other people have.

**7. Actively develop those personality characteristics that will ward off stress:** Your personality is largely a matter of your attitude towards the world and yourself. People who are healthy are positive and optimistic, accept themselves, take charge of their lives, have a sense of humour, and have good social relations. Most people cannot change their personality overnight. But people do change; personality is not carved in stone. One of the most powerful reasons I can think of for wanting to change is to be physically healthier and as a result live longer. Stress is not inevitable. We can keep it to a minimum if we are willing to create an environment that is conductive to harmony, co-operation, and support.

## MANAGING TECHNOSTRESS IN LIBRARIES: A REALISTIC GUIDE

### Stress

"Stress" has become the defining malaise of modernity. Until around twenty years ago, the term was used exclusively to refer to the "fight or flight" mechanism in a specific medical context. Today, however, the word has undergone a radical semantic widening. Like "nerves" in the nineteenth century, "stress" is now used by individuals to explain a huge number of maladies and by journalists, advertisers and cultural pundits as a convenient hook upon which to hang any number of social ills. In short, the enemy is everywhere. The social ubiquity of stress is reflected in our everyday parlance: "stress" is now commonly used as a verb as well as a noun, as in the popular injunction: "don't stress."

Yet the proliferation of discussions of stress in the popular culture of today often hinders, rather than helps, serious discussion of the phenomenon. In Angela Patmore's view (1998-99), the popular wresting of "stress" from its original medical meaning has allowed a cynical stress management industry to exploit a "culture of helplessness" for financial gain. Patmore's is a salutary and in many ways insightful analysis: unscrupulous "stress managers" doubtless exist; and their definitions of stress may not always withstand close scrutiny (in particular, the "causes" and "symptoms" of stress are often inadequately distinguished). Nevertheless, there is nothing radical about denying the existence of problems that are commonly experienced by workers in library and information services. Responsible managers must develop an awareness of the specific medical and legal consequences of a rapidly changing working environment, whether or not these are regarded as manifestations of stress.

In view of the semantic problems raised above, two points must be made clear before stress – or indeed technostress - can be discussed without confusion. First, stress in the most general sense can be a force for good or ill. While most commentators make a distinction between adaptive and maladaptive stress, some appear to confuse the two. Having correctly recognised the positive, as well as the negative, potential of stress, Atherley (1996: 20), goes on to describe "anticipatory interview nerves" as a negative form of stress. In fact, stress in such situations may have a useful, galvanising effect; for the purposes of this article, however, stress is taken to mean unproductive stress. Second, it is important to distinguish stress from pressure. The former is subjective, the latter objective; and there is not necessary a causal relationship between the two. Many busy employees do not suffer stress; others become stressed apparently without reason; individual circumstances must therefore be considered. Nevertheless, common sense says that stress, in many employees, increases in relation to pressure, whether from variations in workload, physical environment, or even from travelling to work.

In conclusion, stress is not an illness in itself, but rather the term given to a maladaptive response to pressure. Thus, the word 'stress' may be used as an umbrella term covering all of an employee's physical and emotional problems. Despite their steadfastly conservative image, there is no reason to suppose that librarians are less susceptible to such problems than other professionals. Of course all librarians and information workers suffer temporary frustrations at work; in order to take stress - or technostress - seriously, therefore, these problems must have been encountered over a period of time.

## Technostress: definition

Like the term "stress", "technostress" has been defined in so many ways – sometimes by the same authors - that its utility as a concept is in doubt (Fisher 1996). The original and still popular definition is that of Craig Brod, who describes technostress as "a modern disease of adaptation caused by an inability to cope with new technologies in a healthy manner" (Brod 1984:16). Brod's definition certainly requires closer scrutiny than it has often received. While it may be spurious to call technostress a disease, the second clause provides a working definition: "technostress" covers that range of chronic human psychological and physiological problems that may result from the use of automation. This sounds a broad enough definition; yet an even wider definition is possible if we understand "techne" in its original Greek sense of "skill". While Brod talks of "new technologies" (the phrase already sounds dated), what of a librarian struggling to adopt the procedures involved, for example, in the use of a library circulation system that uses cards and tickets, such as the Browne system? For such an employee, even a manual issuing system might be a new technology – new, that is, to the employee.

Although the word itself is a neologism, "technostress" is hardly a new concept. On the contrary, the belief that Westerners are subject to a psychologically devastating rate of technological change may have its origins nineteenth-century responses to the Industrial Revolution (for a survey of these see Rosen 1968). But how does technostress affect modern librarians and information workers? The increasing body of literature on the subject certainly presents no firm evidence of an "epidemic" of librarian technostress. As Fisher, in one of the best articles on the subject, writes: "there are sufficient problems with Brod's original definition of the term as to render it unreliable… Most commentators within the library and information field have built unwisely upon these unsteady foundations and asserted rather than proved the existence of technostress" (1996:13-14). Nevertheless, common sense and a growing body of anecdotal evidence suggest that the explosion of automation in libraries poses some particular problems for librarians – these, for our purposes, may be said to fall under the rubric of technostress. While various in nature, these problems – physical, psychological and organisational - are a little easier to identify than the those caused by stress generally.

## Physical Forms of Technostress

Heavy use of computer technology, in particular, may result in eyestrain, headaches and backaches as well as:

- **Repetitive Strain Injuries:** Carpal Tunnel Syndrome, whose symptoms include pain, tingling and numbness in the hand, wrist and arm, can be caused by continuous rapid use of the fingers, and is common among those whose use keyboards frequently.
- **Overexposure to Visual Display Units (VDUs):** Headaches and muscular dysfunctions may result from overexposure to computer terminals, while electromagnetic radiation produced by VDUs has been linked to miscarriages and to serious medical conditions including cancer (Coghill 1990: 123-40). The heat and static electricity produced by terminals may also lead to fatigue and general debility (Graham and Bennett 1974:89). Older VDUs are likely to radiate more than newer ones.

## Psychological Forms of Technostress

Psychological forms of technostress – which may have physical consequences – are rather more complex in nature. Technostress may be environmental in origin: poor ergonomics at computer workstations, for example, may leave staff feeling drained. Employees may also struggle to cope with the skills demanded by new technology, as in the case of many rural public libraries which are only now becoming automated; on the other hand, many staff overidentify with technology. Other factors include:

- "Information Overload": In large libraries, the introduction of automated circulation, networked catalogue systems, online and CD-ROM information retrieval systems and telecommunications technologies (e-mail, telefaxing, teleconferencing and interactive television) can lead to a situation where employees feel overwhelmed by information (Bartlett 1995).
- Underwork and Routine Jobs: Many staff become frustrated when underemployed or when the work they are doing involves only routine operations; this can happen when employees spend long hours with automated systems. While a certain amount of routine work is to be expected by librarians, managers must be aware of the proportion of time employees spend performing a single task.
- Job Insecurity and Demotivation: Recent massive investments in automation in the UK ILS sector may contribute to a fear that computers are usurping human roles. Job insecurity may be compounded by jealousy among co-workers when levels of technological competency differ. Over a prolonged period, this may lead to loss of motivation and team spirit. More specifically, it may also lead to an erosion of trust among staff, as more "technologically aware" employees become reluctant to share their skills and knowledge, in the paranoid belief that by so doing they are making themselves more indispensable than technical novices. This kind of "skills hoarding" prevents effective communication within an organisation.
- Uncertainty about Job Role: Where automation is introduced to replace other technologies, the job roles of employees may be unaffected. Sometimes, however, staff may find that they are spending increasing time working with new technology; this may lead to uncertainty about job role. A librarian working more and more with computer technology, for example, may soon find herself doing the job of a systems librarian.

## Consequences for Organisations

Workplace technostress may have consequences for organisations as well as individuals. Certainly, organisations failing to tackle the problems of technostress can expect to experience high levels of absenteeism and staff turnover. Managers who suggest that employees must simply cope or leave the organisation may not realise the potential costs of retraining new staff in the technology skills required. At the same time, far-sighted UK library managers must look to the United States, where employees have increasingly been litigating against organisations on the grounds of work-related stress (Goss 1994:134-35). At the same time, European Union law is increasingly affecting UK managers' demands on staff; a recent example is the EU Directive on maximum working hours, whose introduction may have a bearing on work-related stress litigation.

Bartlett (1995:229), suggests that increased use of automation has led to a flattening out of the pyramidal organisational structure "allowing people to self-manage in smaller groups". Certainly, library managers must accept that employees typically favour participatory management style in the implementation of automation, as Winstead (1997:19) has shown in her study of three academic libraries in the US. Managers may find that top-down communications are less well received, if not less effective, when automation is being introduced.

## Successful Coping Strategy

**The Employee Responsibility** – Before considering senior management solutions for technostress, it should be emphasised that employees have a responsibility for managing their own reaction to technological change. Employees must remember that it is not necessary to "know it all": few librarians can be expected to be familiar with every feature of the ever-increasing number of databases or computer applications. Nevertheless, responsible librarians must attempt to adapt to new technologies. In doing so they fulfil a duty both to the library and to themselves, since technological skills are an important part of most library and information jobs today.

There is undoubtedly a two-way relationship between employees' attitudes towards technology and physical or psychological damage technology is said to cause. Thus, Staufer's study of older first-time technology users found that those who regarded technology as a threat, rather than a challenge, showed "the highest amount of health-related complaints" such as visual strain, headaches, and lack of concentration (Staufer 1992:49).

**The Management Responsibility** – It will be important for UK managers to come up to speed on the problems that can accompany the introduction of new technology in libraries. Osif and Harwood's review of the literature on the subject (1996) is a useful starting point.

To reduce employee technostress, library managers must lead by example, showing an enthusiastic commitment to learning new technologies, as well as giving adequate warning to staff about planned technological changes: involving employees at the planning stage is always a good idea. In the short term, it may be necessary simply to increase management presence where appropriate. It will also be necessary to emphasise the importance of technological adaptability to job candidates at the recruitment stage (Clark and Kalin 1996:31).

The speed with which automation programmes are implemented is also crucial; Bartlett (1996:228), describes how her school library introduces new technology at a slow enough rate to allow mastery of each element as it is introduced. It is also the job of managers in networked libraries to ensure that there is a sufficient number of employees and competent staff to install, manage, troubleshoot and repair equipment (Clark and Kalin 1996:32). All of this must be included in comprehensive policies for the implementation of technology.

To protect employees, managers should be aware of the hazards of VDUs, especially older models, and consider employee safety when ordering new equipment. Many suppliers produce low-radiation screens which use a high refresh rate; amongst others benefits, this may help to keep extra low frequencies (ELFs) from interfering with brain functions (Coghill 1990:134-35). Older VDUs might be made safer by any of the anti-radiation devices now on the market. VDU operators, meanwhile, should be given practical advice on ways of minimising their exposure to EMRs, such as positioning themselves at safe distances from computer terminals.

Some UK library managers might dismiss staff fears about the safety of automation as excessive or hypochondriacal. This would be both unfortunate and foolhardy, since employers are obliged to follow the EU Directive incorporated as amendments into the Health and Safety at Work Act, 1974. This includes responsibilities to analyse such things as workstations and keyboard designs and remedy any health and safety problems discovered, to ensure that employees working with VDUs receive adequate rest and a varied role and even to provide employees with regular eye and eyesight tests (Graham and Bennett 1974:320).

On the other hand, managers who concentrate only on the ruinous effects of technology may overlook the advantages of new technologies to increase the wellbeing of employees. While technostress may be *caused* by the introduction of computer technology, it may be *reduced* by further technological developments. Many libraries, even in the cash-starved public sector, are beginning to introduce self-issue terminals. Clearly, the major advantage of introducing self-issue terminals is to reduce the amount of time staff need to devote to the routine task of issuing books and other materials; but a side benefit is the reduced risk of repetitive strain injuries among staff.

**Redesigning Jobs and Organisational Structure** – Staff who are spending an increasing amount of time working with new technology may feel that the nature of their work is changing. An important point for management to establish is whether job roles have been altered significantly by automation; if so, there will be need to draw up new job descriptions and possibly to review salaries and wages.

Where staff experience serious difficulties in adapting to new technology, there may be a reason to redesign jobs. Organisational restructuring at the Western Kentucky University's Helms-Cravens Library resulted in the centralisation of several service points into one Reference Centre (Etkin 1995-96). This led to "information overload" among many reference librarians, who may be the most prone of all librarians to technostress (Kupersmith 1992). The solution was to provide a new training programme stressing core knowledge for electronic information services among all reference desk personnel. There may be lessons here for public libraries in the newly formed UK local authorities, as they struggle to provide adequate standardised computer training for their staff.

**Complementary Medicine and Ergonomics** – Technostress might be included in management development programmes. As well as training both managers and employees to acknowledge technostress (which is still a relative newcomer in the UK vocabulary), advice might be offered on means of combating it through meditation or ergonomics. Solutions might include those posited for stress in general, such as the workshops run by organisations such as

Mindstore, relaxation techniques, reflexology, aromatherapy, kinesiology, colour and nutrition therapy. Such solutions, which are increasingly discussed in library and information circles, would obviously have to be provided by trained practioners. Even so, the health benefits of some of them have not been demonstrated conclusively and much more scientific research into these areas is required. For these reasons budgets for such solutions must be carefully justified. This might be done by keeping records of stress-related absenteeism.

It might be wiser, one feels, for library managers to concentrate on offering more rational, "targetted" solutions to technostress problems. Specific remedies for technostress would be aimed at reducing the physical discomfort associated with the use of automation. Recent research suggests that Carpal Tunnel Syndrome, for example, may be reduced through the use of a lowered keyboard holder on a preset tilt away from the user. This keeps the operator's wrists in a low-risk, "neutral" position (Lang 1995:10).

**Technology-based Training** – Identifying the training needs of employees suffering from the psychological forms of technostress may be difficult, since employees may be embarrassed about their lack of confidence or ability to cope and seek to hide their deficiencies. This will be particularly common where staff have had no contact whatsoever with computer technology, such as those working in the many rural public libraries still not automated. It is therefore important to cultivate an open atmosphere in the workplace, so that staff are willing to discuss their difficulties. Moreover, training should never be made compulsory.

Technology-based training is now common in libraries of all types, with most libraries keeping costs low by using staff members as instructors. A disadvantage of in-house training is that the trainer must reschedule her duties for a given period of time. Moreover, external courses offer the advantages of better technological facilities and the opportunity for staff to learn away from the distractions of the library. Even using outside instructors, however, training may not always be easy to organise. For example, low staffing levels, especially in rural libraries, may reduce employee availability for training (Jones and Sprague 1999:97). In such cases training may have to be "on the job". Nevertheless, training clearly reduces anxiety about technology.

While highly specific IT training may be desirable in some cases, it is not always necessary. UK academic libraries might wish to follow the example of Pennsylvania State University in the United States, which runs a mandatory 12-hour Automation Skills Training course, designed to reduce the anxiety of new employees around technology rather than provide training in specific applications. Flexibility is the key. In environments where relationships among employees have suffered as a result of variations in technological competence, it may be important to introduce elements of group work. As well as offering training in those areas central to the organisation, it will be useful to stress the opportunities for personal and professional development offered by services such as library discussion groups on the Internet.

Moreland (1993), advocates the use of the psychometric Myers-Briggs Type Indicator to determine the most suitable style of technology training for individuals. Without scientific corroboration, however, not all managers or employees will be willing to accept the Myers-Briggs premise of sixteen possible personality types. What *is* clear from Moreland's article is that managers must be sensitive to different styles of learning: some staff will learn better from formal and traditional instruction, others from a more hands-on or self-starting approach. One-to-one training may be best for those with very little technological confidence or skill. Library managers must consider the most appropriate form of technology training for each of their staff. In all cases, however, adequate time should be allocated for practice and reinforcement of skills (Clark and Kalin 1996:32).

The effectiveness of any training scheme may be assessed through oral feedback, group conversation or questionnaires; managers should also monitor the employees' job behaviour level before and after training.

## Summary

Rather than worrying excessively about the definition of stress, managers must be aware that UK libraries are undergoing increasingly rapid technological change and that this change will have consequences at every level of an organisation, all of which must be managed. Just as the symptoms of technostress reach beyond the individual and extend to the organisation as a whole, so the solutions managers must adopt wide range from addressing technical and health issues to being prepared to review job descriptions and roles.

If the professional literature is any guide, solutions such as stress management may become more common in the treatment of technostress, especially as managers realise the potentially enormous losses to an organisation in terms of lost working hours resulting from stress-related absenteeism. Specific remedies for technostress are now being developed, however, which seem to offer more quantifiable results. Technology-based training, for example, is still probably the most useful way of making employees more comfortable with new technology and more aware of its dangers.

**Physiological aspect of stress:** Hans Selye first introduced the term stress to medicine in 1926, as a result of conducting medical research to develop a new ovarian hormone. He and his colleagues noted that the research animals used (rats) in the study experienced changes to various glands and the stomach that were not related to effects of the hormone injections received. Similar changes in glands and the stomach resulted when other animals were exposed to various stimuli (cold, heat, infection, trauma, hemorrhage, nervous irritation, etc.). He induced the "syndrome of just being sick" which resulted in adrenal enlargement, gastro-intestinal ulcers, shrinkage of the thymus and lymph nodes. He termed this the "general adaptation syndrome or biologic stress syndrome". According to Selye, "stress is the nonspecific [common] response of the body to any demand made upon it". This definition views stress as a physiological response and stressor as the demand that evokes the response.

Selye was primarily concerned with what is going on inside the skin when a person is stressed.

With this in mind, I will give a brief description of what types of internal changes might take place in a person while using computers.

Research has shown that persons experience higher levels of adrenaline and noradrenaline during work periods with computers (Arnetz & Berg, 1993). Adrenaline and noradrenaline are catecholamines secreted by the adrenal gland. Increased excretion rates of adrenaline and noradrenaline are associated with both underload and overload (stress) stimulation and emotional arousal (Frankenhaeuser, 1978). Other effects of the increased catecholamines levels, as part of sympathetic nervous responses, are increased heart rate and blood pressure. Increased heart rate and blood pressure have been observed in persons performing a computer task (Muter, Furedy, Vincent, & Pelcowitz, 1993). Other research has shown that there is increased skin conductance level (SCL), while performing a computer task (Muter, et al., 1993). Skin conductance level is an indicator of increased sympathetic nervous reaction (the more you sweat the better the conductance). Another indirect indicator of being "stressed" by computer use, is an increased jaw muscle electromyograph (like clenching your teeth an index of the user's 'anger') while performing a computer task (Emurian, 1991;1993).

This brief account suggests that using computers and dealing with computer technology may in principle cause stress reactions in individuals as evidenced by physiological changes.

**Psychological stress:** Although many can identify possible physical stress reactions, stress for many persons is a "state of mind". Next we will consider psychological stress perspectives. Richard Lazarus (1966), in his book, 'Psychological Stress and the Coping Process, has focused on the cognitive processes of evaluation of stimuli (stressors) from the environment and the selection of appropriate responses (coping) based on this evaluation.

Lazarus and Folkman (1984), have defined psychological stress as, "a particular relationship between the person and the environment that is appraised by the person as taxing or exceeding his or her resources and endangering his or her well-being."

Lazarus points out that people go through primary and secondary appraisal processes.

The primary appraisal process determines whether the environment is perceived as psychologically threatening, harmful, or challenging. This primary process will determine whether the environment is perceived as a stressor. The secondary appraisal process is a complex evaluative process in which a person considers resources available to cope with the primarily appraised stressor. The secondary appraisal process allows the person to select coping strategies to cope with the stressor. During the secondary appraisal process a person may not have the resources to cope, which would result in stress reactions such as somatisation (physical/body complaints), and negative emotions (such as anger, fright, anxiety, shame, guilt, sadness, envy, jealousy and disgust).

**Technostress — how to measure it:** Considering the opening scenario, Brod's description of technostress, and the general background on the concept of stress, I would now like to discuss my research on technostress. When humans interact with computers there may be several potentially negative outcomes. Various terms have been employed to describe these outcomes: computer stress, computer anxiety, negative computer attitudes, computerphobia, and computer aversion. These terms have appeared in the research literature of human-computer interactions.

Are these terms describing different reactions? From a descriptive (ideographic) perspective they seem to describe the same symptoms that Brod described in his book. The systematic approach of research in psychology is to define what it is you are measuring, develop a way to measure it, and validate the measure by relating it to other types of similar reactions and differentiating it from dissimilar reactions. This is the systematic empirical approach.

In the early stages of my research on technostress, I tried to make a clear distinction between measuring stressors and stress reactions. My approach to measuring technostress has concentrated on measuring computer stressors and determining what relationship exists with potential stress reactions. My initial research efforts (Hudiburg, 1989a, 1989b) focused on the development of the Computer Technology Hassles Scale. The scale was modeled after Richard Lazarus and his colleagues' Daily Hassles Scale. The Daily Hassles Scale measured stressors a person experienced using a checklist of 118 "daily hassles".

"[Daily] hassles are the irritating, frustrating, distressing demands that to some degree characterise the everyday transactions with the environment." Examples of "daily hassles" are: trouble relaxing, trouble making decisions, job dissatifactions, etc. The level of stress assessed by the Daily Hassles Scale was empirically related (correlated) to somatic complaints (stress reactions) and health-related problems.

Since my research focused on transactions within a computer technology environment, I compiled a list of "computer hassles" "using instances of contact with common computer technology, use of computers, computer-generated information, and the impact of computers on society" (Hudiburg, 1989a, p. 768). Using the computer hassles, I developed two research scales: the Computer Technology Hassles Scale and the Computer Hassles Scale. The Computer Hassles Scale is a shortened version of the first scale and is composed of only "computer hassles" that might result from actual use of microcomputers or mainframe computers. This is the scale you completed at the beginning of this talk.

The Computer Hassles Scale yields three scores, a total severity of hassles score, and two scores on the subscales: Computer Runtime Problems and Computer Information Problems. Based on a normative sample of 1199 college student computer users (Hudiburg, 1995), the following were the eight most frequently endorsed hassles from each of the subscales:

Computer Runtime Problems hassles:

# 10 slow programme speed (61.6%),

# 11 slow computer speed (60.8%),

# 1 computer system is down (54.1%),

# 2 lost in the computer (46.0%),

# 6 programming errors (45.1%),

# 7 illegal input message (44.2%)

# 9 poor user/computer interface (44.1%)

# 3 poorly documented software (43.5%)

Computer Information Problems hassles:

# 34 lack of computer expertise (68.3%),

# 25 need to learn new software (65.6%),

# 24 keyboard typing errors (63.1%),

# 33 lack of help with a computer problem (60.1%)

# 23 need to update skills (59.5%)

# 16 increased time demands (55.8%)

# 35 increased computer use expectations (53.6%)

# 14 incomprehensible computer instructions (48.7%)

The three severity of hassles scores from the Computer Hassles Scale have been shown to correlate with reports of somatic complaints and anxiety reactions (e.g., headaches, nausea or upset stomach, trembling, feeling fearful, feeling pushed to get things done). Therefore, those who report high severity of hassles tend to report high levels of somatic complaints and anxiety reactions. It might be concluded that the person is experiencing a high level of technostress.

The Computer Information Problems Hassles gives some indications of those who might experience technostress, from the point of view of a librarian.

The use of the Computer Hassles Scale is but one of the ways to identify a person who is experiencing technostress. It has the advantage of being objectively derived and objectively measured. Many persons who experience stress are reflecting on their personal experience and may have little use for an objectively derived measure. The benefits of using the Computer Hassles Scale is that a collective assessment of technostress could be determined for an individual or group. My research focuses on the experiences of the individual dealing with computer technology and does not focus on issues related to occupational or job stress. Detailed treatment of that topic is beyond the scope of this talk but I will mention some brief points.

The research literature has identified many potential "job stressors" that can contribute to occupational stress. One way to characterise occupational stress is as the result of a lack of fit between the person and his or her work environment. One way to portray this lack of fit is in job role problems: role overload, role insufficiency, role ambiguity, and role conflict. Role overload is when job demands get too great the person feels he or she has too much to do and too little time. For example, new equipment, new software, and new information sources (the Internet) place increased work demands on the librarian and time constraints might not allow for proper implementation. Role insufficiency occurs when the person feels the lack of training, education, skills or experience to accomplish the job. This might occur when person is asked to learn a new computer system or CD-ROM software that has been purchased from a vendor who does not provide training, but the price was right! Role ambiguity occurs when the person does not know clearly what the priorities of the organisation are and what is generally expected of him or her. This could occur, especially in the university setting, when the administration of the university views a library as just a place to hold books! Role conflict is the classic "damned if you do, damned if you don't" dilemma. As a librarian you have the role demanded by your patrons and your supervisors. The patrons might expect "librarians should know everything" about information sources while the supervisor knows staff limitations and seeks new personnel.

**Negative effects of technostress and coping:** Most persons might experience mild forms of technostress but for those who experience extreme levels of technostress there may be some dire negative effects. Extreme stress may result in health related problems, like cardiac problems, hypertension, migraine headaches, etc., A possible negative outcome is "job burnout". Job burnout has been defined as "...a syndrome of emotional exhaustion, depersonalisation, and reduced personal accomplishment that can occur among individuals who do 'people work' of some kind" (Maslach, 1982). There are many symptoms that characterise job burnout. For example, the person may feel emotionally drained, be unable to "express a sense of humour; they might skip rest periods and food breaks, and they may report increased physical complaints". The burned out worker may began pulling away from co-workers, and he/she might adopt an "I-don't-give-a-damn" attitude which may be associated with decreased job performance. The worker may experience increased frustration, low self-esteem, and have the "trapped" feeling.

If one determines that a person or group of people are experiencing a high level of technostress, the next step would be to determine how to cope with the technostress.

## DEALING WITH TECHNOSTRESS

### Coping Strategies

In Richard Lazarus' psychological theory of stress, people are appraising potential stressors. The appraisal process includes primary and secondary appraisal. The secondary appraisal process will determine whether the person has the necessary resources to cope with the primarily appraised stressor. Coping is the process of managing external and internal demands that are perceived as taxing or exceeding a person's resources.

Coping may consist of behaviour or cognitive responses that are designed to reduce, overcome, or tolerate the demands placed on the individual, known as coping strategies. Coping strategies have been classified into two major categories: emotion-focused strategies and problem-focused strategies.

According to Monat and Lazarus (1991), "Problem-focused coping refers to efforts to improve the troubled person-environment relationship by changing things, for example, by seeking information about what to do, by holding back from impulsive and premature actions, and by confronting the person or persons responsible for one's difficulty.

Emotion-focused (or palliative) coping refers to thoughts or actions whose goal is to relieve the emotional impact of stress. These are apt to be mainly palliative in the sense that such strategies of coping do not actually alter the threatening or damaging conditions but make the person feel better. Examples are avoiding thinking about the trouble, denying that anything is wrong, distancing or detaching oneself as in joking about what makes one feel distressed, or taking tranquilizers or attempting to relax." (Monat & Lazarus, 1991, p. 6)

Problem-focused coping strategies have sometimes been referred to as direct approaches, while emotion-focused coping strategies are indirect approaches. Another issue concerns the general effectiveness of these two general types of coping strategies. This is a difficult question to answer, since what may be an optimal strategy is highly dependent upon the individual's situation and perception. Generally, emotion-focused strategies have been viewed as maladaptive (and less effective) when they prevent essential direct actions (problem-focused). Conversely, emotion-focused strategies maybe useful in maintaining psychological well-being when conditions precipitate possible psychological disintegration.

Let me introduce a second scenario, applicable to librarians, and discuss some coping strategies for dealing with the technostress revealed. First, the stressors will be identified and possible coping strategies will be suggested.

Scenario #2 (this scenario was provided by Mimi King, Univ. of Toledo Library)

You have been at the reference desk going on twenty years. You are proud that you helped shape the original online catalog system. It was an integrated system giving you all the access points and data you needed for both searching and for managing the collection. True, after you had used it a while you had ideas on ways to make it more "friendly" to your patrons; still, you designed it and knew its ins and outs. But, after the renovation (jack hammers, etc.), the vendor for the original system announced they were getting out of that line and would not support that system any longer. Within 6 months, your library had to install another system (from another vendor). That new system was a collection of components, not all of them working just yet — "but any day now." All the folks you had so carefully trained on the old system see no redeeming value to the new system, though you see that it is magnitudes more powerful than the old one. The CD-ROMs you had carefully selected to have the same search platform first became available on the LAN right then as well. You've gotten several new CD's by popular demand, but they have all different command structures and little or no documentation—the online "help" screens only help you know who's to blame for the thing. Now your original terminals, dumb and dating circa 1980-something, are being replaced by Pentiums. There are now several "icons" for your patrons—excuse me—users (sounds sort of dysfunctional, doesn't it?) to select:

(1) one for a vastly augmented online catalog (with attached periodical indexes and your holdings linked to the journals—so that the old question "but you don't have this, do you?" is now automatically answered, but users never seem to know how to find this information on the screen);

(2) one for the off-site vendor who's giving you a "deal," free access until just before all the student papers are due;

(3) one for some (not all) of the CD-ROM's from your LAN (some of the faculty think it's for political reasons);

(4) one for Netscape (version 1.2, 2.0, 3.0 or futureware)—you have used Yahoo pretty well and have tried some of the web search engines, but you don't want to have to patrol the equipment to bounce users of various ages who just happen to find pornography on the Web...; and finally,

(5) an icon for the nifty little notepad which allows downloading instead of printing—which is getting mixed reviews from your users who want to know why the Mac version isn't available and why there are no printers attached.

The automation staff have to wait until everyone is off the system to back it up. They said "hopefully, the server won't die or you'll be in a world of hurt." The server locks up—has it crashed or is this just "a networking problem?"

All in all it's been a pretty busy two years, but this morning at the department heads meeting the director broke the news that you need to begin planning for the shift into the new online system which is imminent—the only stumbling block is they don't yet know which system it will be. But it will be here in the next biennium and you'll be ready with handouts and guides to it the week after they tell you—that's the day after it's installed...

## Analysis

The perspective of "technostressors" is from the librarian. The first "technostressors" are outdated computer skills or software, the switch from off-site "librarian mediated" online databases to on-site "user mediated" online and CD-ROM based databases. This "technostressor" may have the effect that ones skills as a database searcher are less of a critical need to the function of the library (deskilled) (Bichteler, 1987; Champion, 1988; Kupersmith, 1992). The introduction of the CD-ROM database presents a new problem in that each system has different interfaces (e.g., DOS, Windows, proprietary) and may employ different search protocols (Stone, 1993). The new CD-ROM systems come with little or no documentation except internally based documentation —like an F1 help screen or hypertext help menu.

Another "technostressor" is the outdated computer equipment. The old 286 base IBM-AT systems have been replaced by 486 or Pentium systems and the double speed CD-ROMS with 4X, 6X, 8X or 10X speed CD-ROMs. There is an increment of speed with each new hardware upgrade. Computer users seem to want computers to run faster and faster (note the two most common computer hassles were "slow programme speed" and "slow computer speed"). Institutions are slow to discard old computer equipment or get new faster computers due to the cost of the equipment and the fact that some computers will run and run (I had an old IBM-XT clone machine that I gave to a niece who uses it to write papers for college).

Integrating the CD-ROMs as part of a larger LAN makes them less dependent on one dedicated computer or smaller single purpose LANs. Being part of a larger "network" system increases the chances that the "technostressor" of the "computer system is down" when the network server has crashed or needs a "system upgrade" will occur. You now might be expected to know more about networks than you expected before. Microcomputers were probably easier to understand as a single machine that could be turned on and off and booted up with the single machine dedicated software.

The Internet is probably becoming the numero uno "technostressor". The Internet is a massively available off-site source of information. A concern with the Internet is how to find the information; since there is a proliferation of Web search tools (Lycos, Infoseek, Altavista, Webcrawler, just to name a few) and graphic browsers to use. The Internet seems to add hundreds of new information sites daily with no standard to how they are designed maintained and updated. Dealing with the "information overload" (Kupersmith, 1992) is a real problem. Learning the nuances of the graphic and text-based Internet browsers presents its challenges (Gaff, 1994). Now users have to learn what to download and to save to those "floppies" due to limitations of hard disk space and the cost of paper; not to mention what they can and cannot email to themselves and others.

Planning for change when it will come is a common technostressor portrayed by the announcement of a new online system, will be implemented but which one is not known. When the system is installed and up and running, you are expected to "know" how to use and teach everything about the new technology already (Moreland, 1993).

**Coping with these technostressors:** There are four excellent articles written on how to deal or cope with "Technostress" from a librarian's perspective. Sandra Champion's 1988 article, "Technostress: Technology's Toll"; John Kupersmith's 1992 article, "Technostress and the reference librarian"; Steven Stone's 1993 article, "Technostress: taking some steps to cope" and Katie Clark and Sally Kalin's, "Technostressed Out? How to cope in the digital age: that apperared in the August 1996 issue of *Library Journal.* These writers suggest several "coping" strategies in dealing with "technostress". I would like to relate what they have to say with the Richard Lazarus' framework of problem-focused and emotion-focused coping strategies.

The first and foremost way to cope is through education and training (a problem-focused coping strategy). Educating oneself to new developments is an ongoing process. Part of the educating process is accepting the fact that computer technology will always be changing, with some periods of slower change than others. Not resisting change (Champion, 1988; Clark & Kalin, 1996; Hanson, 1994; Malinconico, 1991) is important, because resistance is more emotion-focused and less effective in reducing the stressor. One of the problems in using training and education is the element of time, there never is enough of it. The training methods used for the staff, which in turn will provide training to users, might have to be individualised (Moreland, 1993).

**When coping doesn't work and you become "stressed out":** People may judge for themselves that they cannot cope and are "stressed out". This could be indicative of feeling "helpless" in the face of stressors or they might report high levels of somatic complaints (body/physical) and anxiety. These typical stress reactions would indicate the person is "stressed out". The person is unable to cope with the "technostressors" on his/her own volition and needs assistance in learning coping strategies. To put it another way, the person is judged and is unable to change the way he or she perceives and manages his or her interactions with the immediate environment. At this stage of dealing with "technostress" a person might need to employ one of the several stress management techniques.

Ethel Roskies suggests that "stress has become the fashionable disease of our time, and the treatment of stress is a popular and profitable activity." (Roskies, 1991; p. 411) There are several types of stress management used today. They may be placed in the following broad categories (adapted from Monat & Lazarus, 1991):

**Environment/Lifestyle:** time management, proper nutrition, exercise, finding alternatives to frustrated goals, stopping bad habit (smoking, drinking, excessive eating, etc.)

**Personality/Perception:** assertiveness training, thought stopping, refuting irrational ideas, stress inoculation, modifying type A behaviour

**Biological responses:** progressive relaxation, relaxation response, meditation, breathing exercises, biofeedback. autogenics

## Stress-management Techniques

As you can see there are many techniques that could be used to manage stress with varying claims of effectiveness, of which very few have been empirically documented. It is important to note that a single technique might not be effective for everyone and one technique can be combined with another. An important issue related to stress management is whether one should utilise an individual intervention or an organisational stress-management intervention (Everly, 1989). My presentation focuses on "individual" interventions which could be used concurrently in an organisational stress management programme. My presentation only scratches the surface in this growing field. For further interest in stress management techniques, books like Jerrold S. Greenberg's (1990) Comprehensive Stress Management, 3rd edition or George S. Everly, Jr.'s (1989) A Clinical Guide to the Treatment of the Human Stress Response are useful sources of information. Let us look at two stress management techniques. Kuppersmith (1992), mentioned several of these techniques in his article on technostress for reference librarians.

**1. Stress Inoculation:** Donald Meichenbaum (1977), developed the stress-management technique called stress inoculation training (SIT). Stress inoculation is a three stage process:

(1) education (2) rehearsal and (3) application.

During the first stage (education), the person is given a framework for understanding her or his response to stressful events. During this phase data is collected by the individual; these data could be collected in the form of a diary as suggested by Greenberg (1990). The person should pay more attention to the "internal dialogue" that accompanies responses to stressors. This will hopefully "educate" people by making them more aware of their responses to stress.

During second stage (rehearsal), the person learns how to make cognitive self-statements as a form of coping and problem solving skills. Examples of coping self-statements can be placed into the following categories with sample self-statements (from Greenberg, 1990):

Preparing for a stressor—You can develop a plan to deal with it;

Confronting and handling a stressor—One step at a time: You can handle the situation;

Coping with the feeling of being overwhelmed—Keep the focus on the present; what is it you have to do?;

Reinforcing self-statements—It worked; you did it!

Other skills can be taught during this stage as well to enhance the stress management.

The third stage (application), has the individual use the information and skills learned during the first two stages (education and rehearsal) in actual stressful situations. It is appropriate to evaluate the use of the skills in low stress situations and then move on to higher stress situations. During the evaluation of the these new skills, changes can be made so the person can develop a set of self-statements to effectively respond to most stressful situations.

Stress inoculation training has been shown to be an effective stress management technique in a variety of circumstances (e.g., control of anger, test anxiety, phobias, pain, etc.) and could be effective in treating techonstress.

**2. Relaxation Response:** One component of the stress response is the increased arousal of the individual. This is evident in physical changes in: heart rate, blood pressure, the central nervous system, the autonomic nervous system, and the endocrine system. It is also evident in the psychological (cognitive) changes experienced by the individual; increased awareness of being "stressed". The opposite of arousal or hyperarousal is elicitation of the "relaxation response". The elicitation of the relaxation response in the presence of a stressor has been shown to be an effective treatment. "The relaxation response is perhaps best understood as a psycho-physiological state of hypoarousal engendered by a multitude of diverse technologies (e.g., meditation, neuromuscular relaxation)" (Everly, 1989, p. 149). Thus, one could think of being relaxed as quite opposite from being stressed and that the two states have different psychological and physiological mediators. As suggested there are a variety of techniques [technologies] that can engender the relaxation response. No one such technique would be effective for everyone.

One of the techniques used to induce the relaxation response is meditation. Briefly, meditation is "...a mental exercise that affects body processes... The purpose of meditation is to gain control over your attention so that you can choose what to focus upon rather than being subject to the unpredictable ebb and flow of environmental circumstances" (Greenberg, 1990, p. 157).

Neuromuscular relaxation, known as progressive relaxation, was developed by Dr. Edmund Jacobson in the 1930s. Using this technique the person learns to progressively relax selected muscles by first tensing then relaxing the muscles. The progressive relaxation could concentrate on the whole body or one part of the body. The therapeutic effect of this technique is the person's learned awareness of the difference between tense muscles and relaxed muscles. Neuromuscular relaxation has been shown to be effective in treating a variety of stress-related reactions: insomnia, tension headaches, subjective reports of anxiety, general autonomic arousal, and development of a calmer attitude to possibly combat excessive stress arousal (McGuigan, Sime, & Wallace, 1984).

## STRESS AT WORKPLACE AND WELLNESS PROGRAMMES

In the first years of the twenty-first century, the health of employees was a major concern for many companies due to the escalating costs of occupational (work-related) and non-occupational health care. In 2004, national health expenditures rose 7.9 per cent over the previous year in USA, more than three times the rate of inflation. In 2004 total spending on health expenditures was $1.9 trillion, or $6,280 per person in the United States. Health care expenditures in 2004 represented 16 per cent of the gross domestic product (GDP). Health care expenditures are projected to reach $4 trillion in 2015, or a 20 per cent share of the GDP. This is up from only 8.8 per cent in 1980. Such escalating costs reduce companies' profits and inflate the prices of goods and services. Government regulations have also influenced health in the workplace. Since 1970, federal regulations have required companies to maintain accurate records of work-related illnesses and injuries, institute medical surveillance programmes, provide safety equipment, and control the use of hazardous chemicals. As a result, the number of serious occupational injuries and illnesses has been greatly reduced. Companies must continue to monitor the health of their workers to keep insurance spending and premiums to a minimum.

Today's occupational health care professional is not only responsible for the health of the employee but also may be involved with company medical policies and benefits, disability and workers' compensation evaluations, health promotion, wellness and fitness programs, industrial safety, and compliance with State Government regulations. Employee health services vary widely from company to company. Employers may provide any or all of the programmes outlined below to their employees.

### Concept of Stress

- There is an intuitive and familiar sense of "stress" that anyone can explain. Beyond this popular conception, however, there is wide disagreement over a more exact definition and over how it should be measured.
- Before stress was used in a scientific context, it meant hardship, adversity or affliction.
- Osler's writings on angina early this century, equated stress with hard work, and strain with worry.
- Adolf Meyer studied the role of stressful events in causing physical and psychological disorders. This later led to the study of "life-events" - sudden changes that may trigger sickness.
- Research after Meyer has identified a consistent relationship between a variety of stressful events and physical and psychological disorders. The general view is that such events create a temporary state of disequilibrium, which requires adjustments aimed at establishing a new homeostasis. The extra effort required in the adaptation process is viewed as potentially draining, and thus, contributes to the deterioration of one's general well-being (Cronkite & Moos, p. 373).
- Hinkle noted: "It is now generally agreed that diseases may be as much the result of the adaptive reactions of the host as they are of the damaging effects of pathogenic agents, and it is widely accepted that the relation of people to the other people around them and to the society in which they live are important causes of disease." (Hinkle, 1973:31)

- Research into the link between stress and disease is heuristic, not phenomenal. It is different from isolating a particular enzyme and studying its effect - stress is not an objective phenomenon that we can study under various circumstances and interpret.
- Lazarus suggested that stress should be looked upon as a rubric (rather like motivation, or cognition), rather than as a simple variable. The research task is to select from among alternative concepts of stress that which offers the most explanatory power, and then to find ways to measure it in empirical studies.

**Below:** The Moment of Anxiety

## The wellness concept

Some are uncertain of what corporate wellness even means. Mok Lan Ho, Director of Benefits of the Total Compensation Group at Scotiabank, admits that employers often struggle with the concept of wellness. "Many companies face the challenge of determining what wellness means to the organisation and within its cultural environment. Most define wellness in the form of activities and events."

Given that corporate wellness has been conventionally viewed as a soft item or issue, many employers are dubious about making such a large commitment and investment of their resources.

Rob Weingust, a former events and meeting planner and founder of Spa Party Events agrees that, historically, most companies have done some nice things for their employees, be it an annual holiday party, barbeque, or bonus; however, employers see these gestures and events as money thrown away. "They do these events because they have to, but there's no result, no return for them," he says.

A corporate wellness programme, though, consists of more than a steak dinner and an office picnic. "'Wellness' whether at the personal or organisational level is a long-term response and commitment, not a one-time event," explains Ho. "Intuitively, we know that 'wellness' and a healthy workforce make good business sense, but certain fundamentals are crucial first steps. For example, identifying key wellness needs relevant to the organisation; defining a framework including metrics to guide supporting activities, policies and practices that align consistently toward targeted objectives."

## Understanding workplace wellness

Health at work is aimed at fostering wellness. Organisations are beginning to be held accountable for ensuring that the environment in which people work fosters health not disease.

To foster wellness, organisations need to understand the precursors to disease, particularly those related to stress.

Wellness is the personal experience of physical and mental health. Home stress and job stress affect wellness - and the measure of wellness is usually self-reported health status.

There are three major contributors to wellness:

1. *Health practices* – the voluntary activities of individuals that affect their health
2. *Personal resources* – the psychological and social means by which people cope with environmental stress
3. *The environment* – in which they are trying to cope, which includes: their surroundings, the conditions in which they work, their circumstances, as well as the supports and opportunities available to them to maintain or improve their health.

The work environment can help or hinder an individual's efforts to reduce stressors in his/her life. Workplace Wellness Programmes Provide Benefits to Individuals and Organisations.

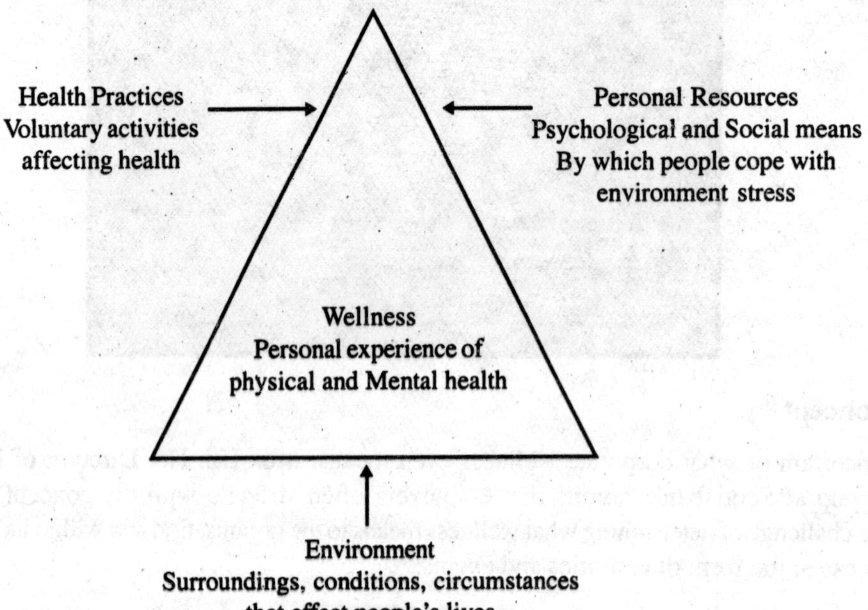


Workplace stress or job-related stress can be attributed to employers if:

- The workplace defeats the employees' sense of control over their work and their health which, in turn, reduces motivation to pursue positive health practices; and
- The workplace makes it difficult to maintain a healthy lifestyle and pursue positive health practices.

Personal health practices include:

- Physical activity;
- Eating;
- Smoking;
- Sleeping; and
- Drinking alcohol.

Siting correctly whilst using a computer can prevent physical problems/damage such a carpal tunnel syndrome and backache. This picture shows how to keep the back supported and the body aligned.

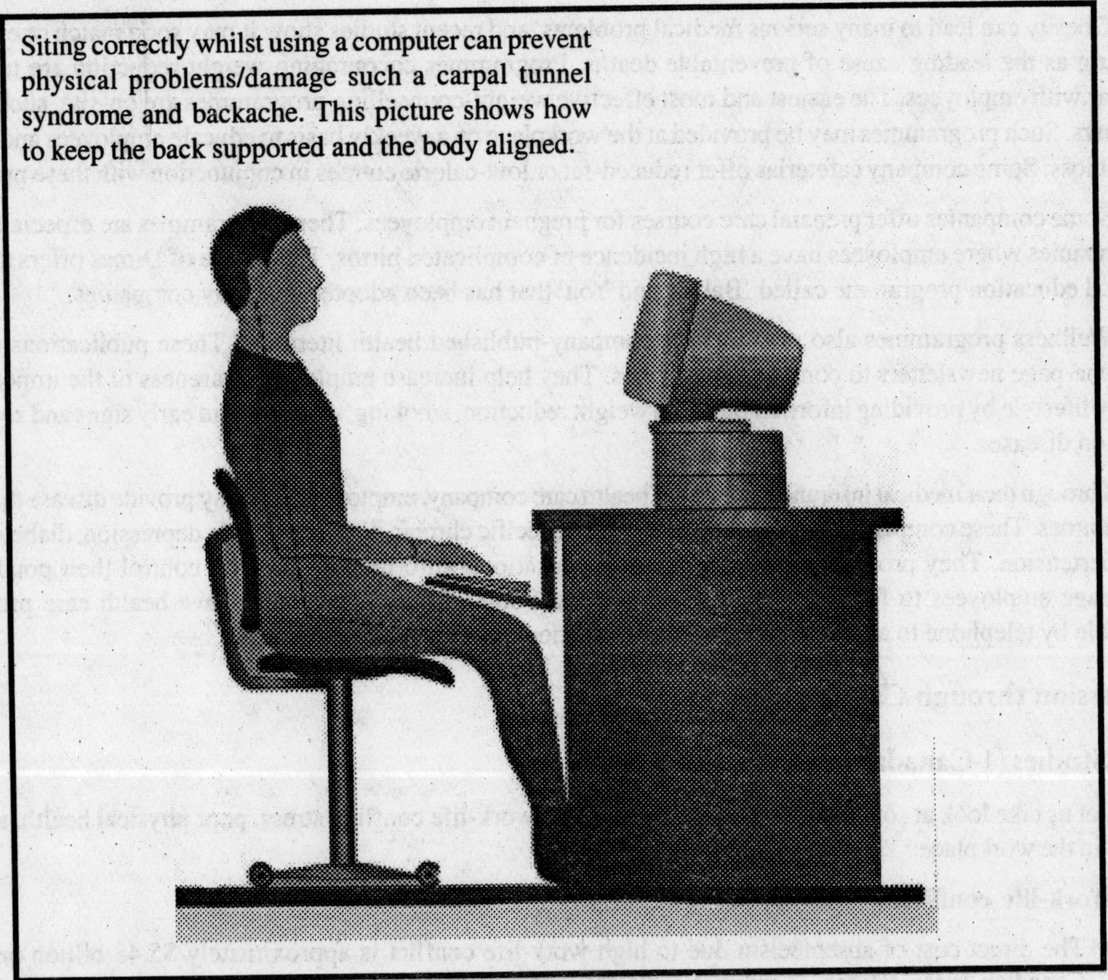

Fig. 12 : Pain and Stress

## Wellness Programs

Many companies have introduced wellness programmes or disease management programs to promote good health. Companies subsidise such programmes, which can be implemented onsite or in the community, in order to reduce future health care costs and losses in productivity from workers' preventable illnesses. While these programmes vary greatly from company to company, they usually include courses on smoking cessation, general nutrition, low-salt diets, cholesterol reduction, weight loss, hypertension, diabetes, asthma, prenatal care, stress management, and depression.

Smoking is the leading cause of preventable diseases in the United States today. The Centres for Disease Control and Prevention estimates that cigarette smoking causes 440,000 deaths, or 20 per cent of all deaths, each year. Adults who smoke will die, on average, thirteen or fourteen years earlier than nonsmokers. Cigarette smoking is a primary cause of many diseases, such as lung cancer, heart disease, emphysema, and chronic bronchitis. Because of these statistics, many companies have instituted smoking cessation programmes, such as the American Cancer Society's Fresh Start Programme or Smokenders, to help employees stop smoking. In addition, most companies have established strict policies to create smoke-free workplaces.

Elevated cholesterol is also a significant risk factor in the development of heart disease, the leading cause of death in the United States today. Programmes that educate employees about cholesterol and good nutrition are the most effective methods for long-term reduction of cholesterol.

Obesity can lead to many serious medical problems, and recent studies show it may soon match or even replace smoking as the leading cause of preventable deaths. Programmes encouraging weight reduction are usually very popular with employees. The easiest and most effective weight-counselling programmes are on-site, such as Weight Watchers. Such programmes may be provided at the workplace on a weekly basis to educate employees and encourage weight loss. Some company cafeterias offer reduced-fat or low-calorie entrees in conjunction with these programmes.

Some companies offer prenatal care courses for pregnant employees. These programmes are especially valuable in companies where employees have a high incidence of complicated births. The March of Dimes offers an effective prenatal education programme called 'Babies and You' that has been adopted by many companies.

Wellness programmes also may include company-published health literature. These publications may range from one-page newsletters to complete magazines. They help increase employee awareness of the importance of a healthy lifestyle by providing information about weight reduction, smoking, exercise, and early signs and symptoms of common diseases.

Through their medical insurance or another health care company, employers also may provide disease management programmes. These companies identify employees with specific chronic diseases such as depression, diabetes, asthma, or hypertension. They provide the employees with educational information to better control their conditions and encourage employees to follow physician instructions. Some of these companies have health care professionals available by telephone to answer general medical questions employees may have.

## Discussion through Case Studies

### Case Studies (1-Canada)

Let us take look at some of the costs associated with work-life conflict, stress, poor physical health, and mental illness in the workplace:

**Work-life conflict:**

- The direct cost of absenteeism due to high work-life conflict is approximately $5.48 billion per year for Canadian organisations. If indirect costs are included, this number rises to as much $10 billion per year. (Duxbury & Higgins)

**Stress:**

- Stress-related absences cost Canadian employers about $3.5 billion each year. (Statscan)
- Health care expenditures are nearly 50 per cent greater for workers who report high levels of stress. (Statscan)
- 20 per cent of Canadian workers experience a stress-related illness each year. (Canadian Mental Health Association)
- 83.1 per cent of Canadian workers identified stress as the major health concern within their organisation. (Canadian Mental Health Association)

**Health:**

- Every smoker costs a company $2,500 per year in increased absenteeism, lost productivity, increased group benefit insurance costs, and increased facility maintenance. (Conference Board of Canada)
- Employers pay an extra $597 per year for each employee who consumes excessive amounts of alcohol. (Lowe "Dollars and Cents")
- Employers pay an extra $488 per year for every sedentary employee. (Lowe)

Mental Illness:

- Direct costs of productivity loss from clinically diagnosed mental illness is in excess of $11 billion per year in Canada; this number triples to $33 billion when indirect costs of health and social services are counted. (Martin Shain et al. "Mental Health and Substance Abuse at Work")

Employers can significantly reduce these figures. As Mok Lan Ho points out, many chronic health conditions are lifestyle-related, and therefore preventable. "For an organisation, advocating 'wellness' and healthy lifestyles is a common-sense approach to mitigating the compounding impact of poor health," she explains. "Health cost is the end result of a health profile. A corporate wellness strategy focusing on prevention and raising awareness offers cost avoidance opportunity, one case at a time."

## Case Studies (2)

## Health Care Trends in the United States

A serious health care crisis exists in the United States today. It is an economic crisis as well as a medical one. According to the National Coalition on Health Care, insurance premiums increased by 10 per cent in 2005. This increase was nearly three times the rate of inflation. The annual family health plan premium averaged $10,800 in 2005, which is more than the earnings of a full-time, minimum wage worker.

National health expenditures are expected to continue to outpace inflation. Inflation, the aging of the population, and major technological innovations have contributed to the increase in the cost of health care. To make matters even worse, according to an April 2005 article in the *Hamden Journal*, the U.S. health care industry is losing $100 billion a year due to payment errors. This means even higher premiums for employers and employees.

In the past, many employees and their families had health benefits paid entirely by their companies. Employees were enrolled in indemnity programmes, which provided the freedom to see any physician and go to any hospital. Rising health care costs have caused many companies to switch to managed care plans, which include health maintenance organisations (HMOs), preferred provider organisations (PPOs), and point-of-service (POS) plans. Under managed care, employees are limited to network physicians and hospitals and are required to get referrals to see specialists. In addition, employees may be asked to pay a larger percentage of their health insurance premiums while receiving less coverage and having higher deductibles. Coverage for new employees may not start for one to six months from the date of employment. This trend of rising costs and declining coverage is projected to continue.

Some companies have even tried to eliminate or reduce the medical benefits of retirees. With escalating costs for their medical benefits and longer life expectancies, many medical plans for retirees were underfunded. As a result, many companies are reducing and eliminating medical benefits for future retirees.

In 2004, 45.5 million Americans under age sixty-five were uninsured. More than 80 per cent of these uninsured people come from families with workers, and 70 per cent of them from families with at least one full-time worker. Two-thirds of uninsured people come from low-income families. Uninsured people rarely receive primary care, generally waiting until their condition reaches the emergency stage before seeking medical attention. The results are higher costs and poorer prognoses (predictions of the probable course of a disease and the chances of recovery).

Companies have looked to insurers to better manage their health care costs. As a result, insurance companies developed physician networks, such as managed care systems and HMOs, to reduce health care costs. These networks of hospitals and doctors provide medical services at discounted fees. Companies did not, however, realise the savings they anticipated because they incurred increased administrative costs from the programmes. Instead, companies have reduced costs primarily by shifting premium increases to employees for the same or less coverage than they had before. Unfortunately, this trend will continue as companies try to remain competitive in an increasingly changing business environment.

## Developing Leadership Roles

Leadership support is vital to successful culture change efforts. One strategy for working with leaders is to help define their role. The following four leadership support roles can be of tremendous value.

### Sharing the Wellness Programme Vision

- Explaining how wellness contributes to the overall goals of the organisation (such as improving morale, increasing productive capabilities, valuing employees and reducing costs).

- Explaining the directions, purposes, structure and philosophy of the wellness programme.
- Asking questions useful for aligning the wellness programme with overall organisational direction and mission.

**Serving as a Role Model**

- Sharing your enthusiasm for adopting a health and wellness philosophy in your own life.
- Telling about personal efforts to adopt healthier lifestyle practices.
- Participating in organisational health and wellness activities.

**Gaining Resource Commitment**

- Assisting with planning an adequate health promotion budget.
- Helping to modify institutional/organisational policies and procedures so that they better support wellness (such as assistance with smoking policies and release time for wellness activities).
- Working to reduce internal political barriers (such as ensuring that department heads support the programme by providing appropriate resources in their areas).

**Rewarding Success**

- Recognising employee progress in achieving healthier lifestyle practices.
- Tracking outcomes and celebrating positive results.
- Honouring those involved in the delivery of the health promotion programme

## Corporate philosophy as a foundation for employee health

The following principles and values lay a foundation for a corporate culture that embraces intervention programmes like wellness and active living programmes:

- People are an organisation's most important resource, and each has a unique, value-adding contribution to make.
- Concern and care for the health of people is essential to achieve business success.
- Healthy employees enhance an organisation's competitive position.
- A company with healthy employees has a positive impact on its community and customers.
- A change in individual employee health metrics can be an early indicator of changes in other aspects of business performance.
- Optimal employee health is compatible with and supportive of excellence in other aspects of business activity.
- Health, like other aspects of business, can be managed and self-managed.
- People adopt values that are emphasised by their organisational leaders.
- Employee health is an integral part of the business and is built on the belief that all injuries — and most illnesses — are preventable.
- Every employee at every level has responsibility for creating a healthy work environment and promoting healthy lifestyles.

## Motivating staff to participate

One of the major challenges organisations face is motivating and sustaining staff commitment to active living interventions. The same can be said for health clubs who have many more members than regular participants.

Ultimately, the organisation can only educate and provide the opportunity - it is the employee that must choose a more active lifestyle. However, the organisation can undertake many activities that help make *active* choices *easy* choices.

Sustained communications/education, encouragement, corporate philosophy and behaviour are the critical factors that influence motivation and sustained participation.

Many of the studies on workplace active living and wellness programmes and strategies have small sample sizes and/or low participation rates in the programmes.

Most of these studies indicate a need for ways to increase employee participation, and therefore have more impact on employee health, organisational effectiveness and the quality of any research conducted.

Dishman, et al (1998) report from their meta-analysis of published literature that participation rates in workplace active living programmes *are at best 20-30 per cent* of the workplace population.

Other studies have looked specifically at the determinants of high participation rates in programmes, determining the barriers, and the factors contributing to increased participation.

Their findings can be summarised as follows:

- The determinants that affect participation rates are:
    - ➢ Attitude toward the programme;
    - ➢ Self-efficacy expectation; and
    - ➢ Social support.
- Promotion for programmes should focus first on health benefits and second on overcoming barriers.
- Sustained promotion/marketing of programmes is critical to participation rates.
- Barriers that can be addressed when structuring the programme include:
    - ➢ Convenient times and locations;
    - ➢ Flex-time to allow employees to participate;
    - ➢ Onsite facilities; and
    - ➢ Management support/marketing.
- Participation is dependent on organisational context, therefore staff must participate in development.
- Targeted stage-of-change based messages are effective, which means that organisations need benchmark information about their audiences.

## Teacher Wellness Programme

Health and wellness experts such as Ardell (1986), Travis (1981), and Pelltier (1996), suggest that attention to personal lifestyle can improve well-being; that making healthy lifestyle choices can increase our levels of joy, satisfaction and zest for living. Healthy and well employees are also more productive employees. Teacher wellness might be the missing link in the strategic planning process of education reforms and could assist in the transformation and revitalisation of both the institution system and individual teachers.

There are many definitions of wellness: an integration of body, mind and spirit; a way of life which we design to enjoy the highest level of health and well-being possible; or a link between our physical, social, spiritual, intellectual, occupational and emotional selves. What we have discovered as we attempt to balance our roles of teacher, student, consultant, wife and mom, is that it doesn't really matter what definition we choose to work with - what does matter is how we choose to put our 'teacher wellness plan into action'.

There are many different wellness models teachers can follow. A model developed by Dr. Donald Ardell - a guru of sorts in the wellness field,it is simple, easy for us to follow, and is the only wellness model we have found that reminds us that "We" are ultimately in charge of our own well-being.

**What causes stress at the workplace**

- Unrelenting and unreasonable pressure to perform
- Lack of communication
- Conflict between workers or employers
- Lack of job security
- Long hours
- Excessive time spent away from home and family
- Office politics
- Salary not equal to one's levels of responsibility

**How to reduce work-related stress**

- Establish a network of friends at work and home
- Focus on the positive aspects of your work. But if the job is unendurable, seek a change inside or outside the company
- Schedule pleasant activities frequently, including some physical or mental exercises during lunch
- Work out what you want to do with your life. Identify the activities you love
- Stress caused by job dissatisfaction will not go away unless you get a job you love or like

## Stress-Management Techniques

A national survey conducted by Louis Harris Associates revealed that Americans are fatter, do less strenuous exercise, eat less healthful foods, experience more and sleep less than they did in the 1980s. All told, the American Medical Association estimated that lifestyle and social problems contribute more than $171 billion annually to our nation's health care costs. It is, therefore, not surprising that organisations are increasingly implementing a variety of stress-reduction programmes to help employees cope with modern-day stress.

There are many different stress-reduction techniques available. The four most frequently used approaches are muscle relaxation, biofeedback, meditation, and cognitive restructuring. Each method involves somewhat different ways of coping with stress (see Table )

**Table 19**

| *Technique* | *Description* | *Assessment* |
|---|---|---|
| Muscle relaxation | Uses slow deep breathing, systematic muscle tension reduction, and an altered state of consciousness to reduce stress. | Inexpensive and easy to use, may require trained professional to implement. |
| Biofeedback | A machine is used to train people to detect muscular tension; muscle relaxation is then used to alleviate this symptom of stress. | Expensive due to costs of equipment, however, equipment can be used to evaluate effectiveness of other stress reduction programmes. |
| Meditation | The relaxation response is activated by redirecting one's thoughts away from oneself, a four-step procedure is used. | Least expensive, simple to implement, and can be practiced almost anywhere. |
| Cognitive restructuring | Irrational maladaptive thoughts are identified and replaced with those that are rational or logical. | Expensive because it requires a trained psychologist or counsellor. |
| Holistic wellness | A broad, interdisciplinary approach that goes beyond stress reduction by advocating that people strive for personal wellness | Involves inexpensive but often behaviourally Difficult lifestyle changes. |

## WORKPLACE STRESS, JOB SATISFACTION AND STRESS PREVENTION

With the advent of globalisation, constantly evolving business models, progress in Information Technology, changing environment and lifestyles, the term 'stress' is so very often used in our lives today and is yet enshrouded by a thick veil of conceptual confusion and divergence of opinion. Stress is viewed as a crucial and pervasive component of both personal as well as contemporary work life. An increasing concern about stress appears to be well founded. Cost arising out of occupational stress to business enterprises and industry has been well-documented in the recent past. Mounting research evidence proves beyond dispute that stress has a dysfunctional impact on both individual and organisational outcomes. The emergence of computer and information systems has been perhaps the single biggest factor impacting organisations and their functioning in the last few decades. The proliferation of computers and information systems in organisations has generated an increased demand for information systems professionals to support technology-intensive transformations needed to compete successfully in a dynamic business environment.

**Introduction:** Stress is what you feel when you have to handle more than you are used to. When you are stressed, your body responds as though you are in danger. It makes hormones that speed up your heart, make you breathe faster, and give you a burst of energy. This is called the "fight-or-flight" stress response. Some stress is normal and even useful. It can help if you need to work hard or react quickly. For example, it can help you win a race or finish an important job on time. But if stress happens too often or lasts too long, it can have bad effects. It can give you headaches, an upset stomach, back pain, or trouble sleeping. It can weaken your immune system, making it harder to fight off disease. If you already have a health problem, stress may make it worse. It can make you moody, tense, or depressed. Your relationships may suffer, and you may not do well at work or school.

**Job Stress:** Stress—the responses our bodies and minds have to the demands placed on them—is a normal part of life and a normal part of any job. Without stress, we wouldn't meet deadlines, strive to hit sales or production targets, or line up new clients. Meeting the demands and challenges of a job is part of what makes work interesting and satisfying, and it's often what allows people to develop new skills and advance in their careers. In the workplace, we regularly experience stress-causing situations, react to them with heightened tension, and then return to a more relaxed state when the crisis, big or small, is resolved. However, problems occur when stress is so overwhelming or constant that the tension never abates and we never get to relax.

What we think of as "job stress" is what happens when:

- The challenges and demands of work become excessive.
- The pressures of the workplace surpass workers' abilities to handle them.
- Satisfaction becomes frustration and exhaustion.

When stress crosses the line from normal to excessive, it can trigger physical and emotional responses that are harmful to employees and businesses alike. And unfortunately, for many people "stress" has become synonymous with "work."

**Causes of Stress at Job place:** Some jobs are stressful by definition because they're physically dangerous (such as firefighting or criminal justice), involve matters of life and death (emergency functions), or are psychologically demanding (social work, teaching). But people who stamp metal or crunch numbers can also be subject to stress on the job. Workplace stress is usually the result of high demands on the job, real or perceived lack of control concerning those demands, poor day-to-day organisation and communication, and an unsupportive work environment. The following chart lays out many of the factors that lead to job stress:

| | |
|---|---|
| **Specific work factors** | • Excessive workload.<br>• Tedious or meaningless tasks.<br>• Long hours and low pay.<br>• Infrequent rest breaks.<br>• Unreasonable performance demands |
| **Physical environment** | • Noise and overcrowding.<br>• Poor air quality.<br>• Ergonomic problems.<br>• Health and safety risks. |
| **Organisational practices** | • Unclear responsibilities or expectations.<br>• Conflicting job demands.<br>• Multiple supervisors.<br>• Lack of autonomy or participation in decision-making.<br>• Inefficient communication patterns. |
| **Workplace change** | • Fear of layoff.<br>• Frequent personnel turnover.<br>• Lack of preparation for technological changes.<br>• Poor chances for advancement or promotion.<br>• Tensions brought about by greater workplace diversity. |
| **Interpersonal relationships** | • Distant, uncommunicative supervisors.<br>• Poor performance from subordinates.<br>• Office politics, competition, and other conflicts among staff.<br>• Bullying or harassment.<br>• Problems caused by excessive time away from family. |

## Wellbeing at work

What is the most effective way to reduce sickness absence and improve the health and wellbeing of your workforce? If the sheer volume of coverage is anything to go by, it's a challenge facing many organisations today. Most offer counseling and absence services to staff, yet figures remain too high.

First Assist, a leading provider of health and wellbeing (U.K), services, including Employee Assistance Programmes (EAP) and Absence Management Solutions, believes the key to success in achieving health and wellbeing objectives lies in the engagement between service providers and the customer.

"In our experience, it's the development of a solid partnership and ongoing communication between HR, and even line managers, which generates greater value from the services – with the end result impacting positively on absence figures and the overall performance of employees," says Kevin Dewhurst, Health and Wellbeing Sales Director at First Assist England.

### Occupational Stress

Survey of the literature on occupational stress reveals that there are a number of factors related to job which affect the behaviour of the employees and as a result of it, normal life is disturbed (McLean, 1974; Brief, Schular and Vansell, 1981).

Cooper and Marshal (1976), stated that occupational stress includes the environmental factors or stressors such as work overload, role ambiguity, role conflict and poor working conditions associated with a particular job. Orpen (1991), observed that major source of stress is derived from the occupational environment; proponents of this view tend to argue that role holders in certain occupation, irrespective of individual differences, are much more likely to experience stress. Here, the emphasis is on the individual demands of various jobs that have the capacity over a period of time to exhaust the physical and psychological resource of employees in the organisation. Upadhyay and Singh (1999), found that the executive as well as the teachers experienced a moderate level of stress, the executives experienced more stress than the teachers did. The results revealed a significant difference between these two groups on the experience of stress due to factors such as role overload, intrinsic impoverishment and status variable. Emsley (2003), in their research study, 'multiple goals and managers' job-related tension and performance, suggested that job-related tension and performance deteriorate as managers pursue multiple goals although the relationship seems to be non-linear. The relative importance of goals does not appear to be important. Manshor, Fontaine and Chong Siong Choy (2003), in their study examined the sources of occupational stress among Malaysian managers Jain, Jabeen, Mishra & Gupta working in multi-national companies(MNCs).It was found that workloads, working conditions, and relationship at work were the main concern of the managers that lead to stress at the work place. The results also indicated that certain demographic variables do influence the level of stress among managers.

**Now we will discuss two case studies**

(1) Hong Kong (2) India

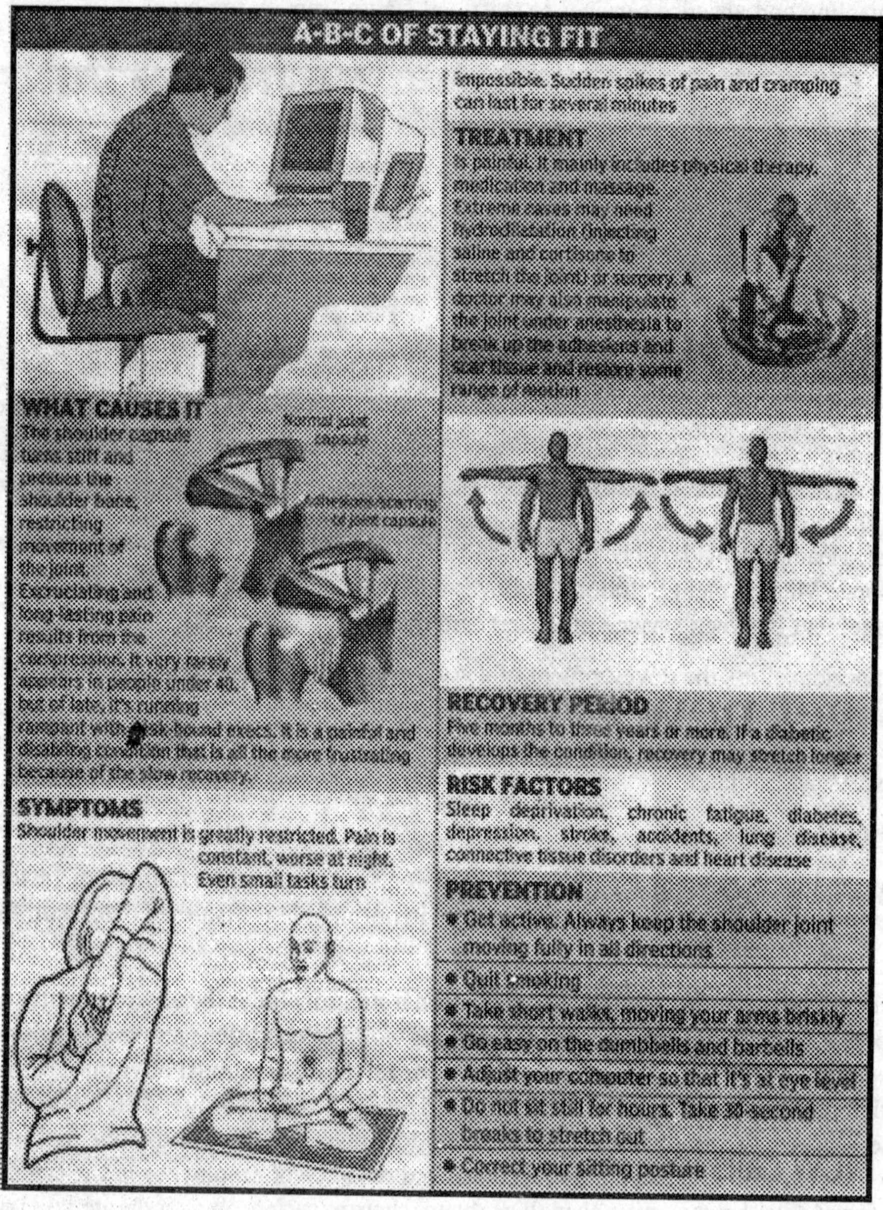

A-B-C OF STAYING FIT

**WHAT CAUSES IT**

The shoulder capsule turns stiff and presses the shoulder bone, restricting movement of the joint. Excruciating and long-lasting pain results from the compression. It very rarely appears in people under 40, but of late, it's running rampant with desk-bound execs. It is a painful and disabling condition that is all the more frustrating because of the slow recovery.

**SYMPTOMS**

Shoulder movement is greatly restricted. Pain is constant, worse at night. Even small tasks turn impossible. Sudden spikes of pain and cramping can last for several minutes

**TREATMENT**

is painful. It mainly includes physical therapy, medication and massage. Extreme cases may need hydrodilatation (injecting saline and cortisone to stretch the joint) or surgery. A doctor may also manipulate the joint under anesthesia to break up the adhesions and scar tissue and restore some range of motion

**RECOVERY PERIOD**

Five months to three years or more. If a diabetic develops the condition, recovery may stretch longer

**RISK FACTORS**

Sleep deprivation, chronic fatigue, diabetes, depression, stroke, accidents, lung disease, connective tissue disorders and heart disease

**PREVENTION**

- Get active. Always keep the shoulder joint moving fully in all directions
- Quit smoking
- Take short walks, moving your arms briskly
- Go easy on the dumbbells and barbells
- Adjust your computer so that it's at eye level
- Do not sit still for hours. Take 30-second breaks to stretch out
- Correct your sitting posture

**Fig. 13: IT shoulder syndrome**

## Case study -1

## Job Satisfaction and Occupational Stress among General Practitioners

**Results:** A questionnaire was sent to members and fellows of the Hong Kong College of General Practitioners only and not to all GPs. in Hong Kong. The results, therefore, may not be truly representative of the whole profession. This possible bias might be increased by the fact that the response rate was relatively low (38.06 per cent). It is speculated that people who are satisfied with their work are more likely to respond to a survey like this. Moreover, people tend to give socially acceptable answers.

**Table 20: Percentage Distribution of Respondents by Various Characteristics (N=189)**

| Characteristic | Category | Percentage |
|---|---|---|
| Sex | Male | 87.3% |
| | Female | 12.7% |
| Age | 25 to 44 years | 50.3% |
| | 45 to 64 years | 49.7% |
| | 65 and over | O |
| Place of Training | Hong Kong | 61.9% |
| | Overseas | 38.1% |
| Years of Experience | Less than 5 years | 20.1% |
| | 5 to 15 years | 40.2% |
| | More than 15 years | 39.7% |
| Location of Practice | Public Housing Estate | 20.1% |
| | Private Building | 69.8% |
| | Government Clinic | 6.9% |
| | Hospital | 3.2% |
| Mode of Practice | Solo | 73.5% |
| | Group | 20.2% |
| | General Outpatients | 6.3% |
| Predominantly in General Practice | Yes | 93.7% |
| | No | 6.3% |

**Table 21: Mean Scores for the Dimensions of Job Satisfaction (in order of importance)**

| Dimension | Mean Score | (Standard Deviation) |
|---|---|---|
| 1. Amount of clinical responsibility | 3.79 | (0.94) |
| 2. Opportunity to use clinical skill | 3.77 | (0.91) |
| 3. Knowing the patients and their families | 3.74 | (1.14) |
| 4. Recognition and praise from patients | 3.68 | (0.86) |
| 5. Degree to which you can help people | 3.66 | (0.91) |
| 6. Freedom to choose methods of working | 3.61 | (1.48) |
| 7. Amount of variety of clinical conditions encountered | 3.57 | (1.01) |
| 8. Getting patients to understand their own problems | 3.51 | (0.97) |
| 9. Physical working condition (of clinic) | 3.44 | (1.05) |
| 10. Income/pay | 3.38 | (0.96) |
| 11. Hours of work | 3.06 | (1.22) |
| 12. Overall job satisfaction | 3.57 | (0.98) |

**Table 22: Mean Scores Satisfaction for Sources of Job**

| *Source of Satisfaction and its Dimensions* | *Mean Score* |
|---|---|
| **Clinical aspect** | 3.71 |
| - amount of clinical responsibility | |
| - amount of variety of clinical conditions encountered | |
| - opportunity to use clinical skill | |
| **Psychosocial aspect** | 3.65 |
| - knowing the patients and their families | |
| - getting patients to understand their problems | |
| - degree to which you are able to help people | |
| - recognition and praise from patients | |
| **Managerial aspect** | 3.37 |
| - freedom to choose methods of working | |
| - physical working condition (of clinic) | |
| - income/pay | |
| - hours of work | |

**Table 23: Mean Scores for the Sources of Stress**

| Sources of Stress | Mean Score (Standard Deviation) |
|---|---|
| 1. Dealing with problem patients | 3.74 (1.15) |
| 2. Demand of job on family and social life | 3.37 (1.31) |
| 3. Dealing with friends and relatives as patients | 3.28 (1.28) |
| 4. Uncertainty and insecurity | 3.28 (1.12) |
| 5. Worrying about patient's complaints against you or your clinic | 3.21 (1.22) |
| 6. The stress and strain of general practice | 3.11 (1.22) |
| 7. Concerned that you are not up-to-date in medical knowledge | 3.04 (1.18) |
| **Summary Stress Score (For Items 1 To 7)** | 3.29 (0.73) |
| 8. 24-hour responsibility for patients | 2.95 (1.89) |
| 9. Home visits/night calls | 2.94 (1.84) |
| 10. Poor status in the eyes of specialists | 2.92 (1.22) |
| 11. Emergency calls during surgery hours | 2.85 (1.86) |
| 12. It is a burden to deal more and more with patient's psychosocial problems | 2.83 (1.21) |
| 13. Dealing with terminally ill patients and their relatives | 2.85 (1.41) |
| 14. Competition from other G.P.s | 2.84 (1.52) |
| 15. Interruption of family life by telephone | 2.77 (1.60) |
| 16. Feeling of isolation | 2.78 (1.39) |
| 17. Increased patient demand for second opinion from specialist | 2.76 (1.18) |
| 18. Managing the practice | 2.78 (1.29) |
| 19. Adverse press publicity | 2.75 (1.63) |
| 20. Feel inadequately trained to manage patient's social and personal problems | 2.74 (1.16) |
| 21. Regular contact with chronically ill patients | 2.72 (1.25) |
| 22. Paperwork and arranging referrals | 2.66 (1.20) |
| 23. Occupational hazards such as exposure to infectious diseases | 2.59 (1.22) |
| 24. Lack of emotional support at home | 2.27 (1.21) |
| 25. Examining patients of the opposite sex | 2.08 (1.01) |

The survey results showed that the majority of respondents were generally satisfied with their work (88.1 per cent had overall job satisfaction score of 3 or above). This was echoed in the satisfaction scores of the clinical, psychosocial and managerial aspects of work. These findings are in agreement with the results of the two studies by Makin et al and Branthwaite & Ross which showed that G.P.s' satisfaction with the different aspects of their work was relatively high.

It is noteworthy that doctors in group practice were more satisfied with their work than those in solo practice. It is equally significant that doctors in general outpatient clinics were the least satisfied with their work. This warrants a thorough review of the various aspects of general outpatient clinics, such as organisation, salary structure and vocational training for the doctors.

It appeared from this study that the main sources of stress were related to emotional involvement. Of the seven items that were considered stressful (mean score greater than 3), four items were related to emotional involvement (items 1,3,4,5 in Table 19). Pressure in the work/home interface (i.e., 'demand of job on family and social life') was rated second, and inability to keep pace with recent advances ('concerned that you are not up-to-date in medical knowledge') was rated seventh in the sources of stress. These findings differed from the study of Makin et al which showed that four out of six sources of stress were interruptions of one kind or another. This may be due to the fact that G.P.s in the United Kingdom (UK) provided more after-hour service and home visits than their counterparts in Hong Kong.

The remaining 18 items in Table 4 included interruptions of various kinds, other emotional involvement and routine medical work. Although these items scored below the midpoint score of 3, most of them were close to 3, and should probably be regarded as lesser sources of stress. It is interesting to note that 'managing the practice' and 'paperwork and arranging referrals' were rated low in the stress score, probably because such activities involve less bureaucratic red tapes in HK than in UK. 'Lack of emotional support at home' was considered the second least stressful in this study. This may be due to the fact that the traditional Chinese culture encourages a close family relationship in which members are willing to give care and support.

## Case study- 2

Job Satisfaction as Related to Organisational Climate and Occupational Stress: A Case Study of Indian Oil

**Table 24: Influence of High and Low Occupational Stress on Job Satisfaction among Managers**

| Groups Compared | N | Mean | S.D | SE.d | T | Level of Significance |
|---|---|---|---|---|---|---|
| JS of High OS group | 35 | 66.86 | 9.13 | | | |
| | | | | 1.85 | 5.57 | 0.01 |
| JS of Low OS | 43 | 77.16 | 6.74 | | | |

**Table 25: Influence of High and Low Occupational Stress on Job Satisfaction among Engineers**

| Groups Compared | N | Mean | S.D | SE.d | T | Level of Significance |
|---|---|---|---|---|---|---|
| JS of High OS group | 31 | 67.58 | 8.50 | | | |
| | | | | 1.99 | 2.96 | 0.01 |
| JS of Low OS | 43 | 73.49 | 8.47 | | | |

**Table 26: Influence of High and Low Organizational Climate on Job Satisfaction among Managers**

| Groups Compared | N | Mean | S.D | SE.d | T | Level of Significance |
|---|---|---|---|---|---|---|
| JS of PerceivedHigh OC | 41 | 73.83 | 8.03 | | | |
| | | | | 2.11 | 1.90 | NS |
| JS of Perceive Low OC | 39 | 69.82 | 10.58 | | | |

**Table 27: Influence of Organisational Climate on Job Satisfaction among Engineers**

| Groups Compared | N | Mean | S.D | SE.d | T | Level of Significance |
|---|---|---|---|---|---|---|
| JS of Perceived High OC | 35 | 75.54 | 8.07 | | | |
| | | | | 1.99 | 4.53 | 0.01 |
| JS of Perceived Low OC | 41 | 66.32 | 9.36 | | | |

**Discussion:** The results of this study confirmed the assumption that there is no significant difference between managers and engineers in terms of their job satisfaction and both the groups appeared almost equally satisfied with their jobs. When the managers and engineers were compared on organisational climate, it was found that both the groups differed significantly. Managers scored significantly high on organisational climate scale than the engineers indicating that the managers are more satisfied due to the empowerment given to them. On the basis of calculated data, marked and significant differences were observed between managers and engineers of IOCL in terms of occupational stress which led to the conclusion that engineers experienced higher degree of stress as compared to managers.

When job satisfaction of high income group managers were compared with low income group managers, the results revealed that both the groups differed significantly. On the other hand, comparison of job satisfaction of high income group engineers with low income group engineers showed non-significant results.

However, the trend of the results shows that the high income group of managers and engineers are more satisfied with their jobs when compared to the low income group. The reason to this trend can be attributed to the universal truth that the monetary compensation is one of the important motivators for the employees that largely affects their performance and satisfaction level.

The results of the study also confirmed the assumption that high-age group managers as well as high-age group engineers were equally satisfied with their jobs and the study revealed the same findings when low-age group managers and low-age group engineers were compared on their job satisfaction level. The results also revealed that the managers who scored high on occupational stress were less satisfied with their jobs while the managers who scored low on occupational stress had higher job satisfaction level. On the basis of the result obtained, it may be interpreted that the presence of higher degree of occupational stress adversely affected the level of job satisfaction. Similarly, the high occupational stress group of engineers scored less and thus, had low job satisfaction level as compared to low occupational stress group of engineers. The influence of high and low organisational climate on job satisfaction of managers was studied and it was found that high organisational climate group scored more on job satisfaction scale, though the difference was non-significant.

Thus, the findings confirmed the assumption that managers who perceived organisational climate high and conducive were found more satisfied with their jobs than those who perceived organisational climate as low. However, when the high and low organisational climate group of engineers were compared, it was found that high organisational climate group of engineers were more satisfied.

The following strategies are helpful for reducing job stress:

1. **Organise your time.** Use a schedule planner and schedule tasks. Stick to the schedule! Be sure to schedule in time you need to meet deadlines, make phone calls, and send correspondence, write reports, and so on.
2. **Follow your bio-clock.** Try to schedule the hardest tasks during your hours of peak performance and concentration.
3. **Make "TO DO" lists.** List everything you need to do in order of priority. As you finish a task, check it off and go to the next one.
4. **Throw it away.** Don't let things accumulate! Sort mail and toss what you don't need. Sort e-mails and delete what you don't need to read. Sort files and toss what's out-of-date.
5. **Organise your work space.** Organise papers, files, or items so that you know where everything is, and things can be found quickly.
6. **Don't procrastinate.** Don't wait. Do it now. You'll be happy you got it done!
7. **Think in steps.** Take a large project and break it down into small steps. Then do the project one small step at a time.
8. **Take breaks.** Avoid working around the clock. Go get a cup a coffee. Eat lunch away from your desk or work area. Try to go home on time.
9. **Share a problem.** If you encounter an unusually challenging work problem, talk with co-workers. They may not have a solution, but it helps to talk through issues. Sometimes just by talking through a problem, you can recognise a solution.
10. **Sleep.** Make sure you get enough sleep. Lack of sleep impairs concentration which can add pressure and anxiety.
11. **Target ideas.** Each time you feel stress, write down a list of targeted things you need to do to reduce the stress for that event.

12. **Take a real vacation.** When you take time off, avoid thinking about work. Focus on things you enjoy. This applies to your time off on weekends as well.
13. **Transition.** Between work and home, do something to get your mind off work. Listen to the car radio, stop for a coffee, drop by the library, and stop at the store.
14. **Leave work at work.** Take home as little work as possible.
15. **Practice relaxation techniques.** During times of stress, try:
    (a) deep breathing;
    (b) muscle relaxation techniques;
    (c) exercising;
    (d) taking a walk;
    (e) mentally rehearsing by mentally walking through an upcoming event;
    (f) talking with a friend;
    (g) listening to relaxing music;

**Enjoy your freedom**

...✎...✎...✎

## NATURE OF EMOTIONS

Various theorists argue that emotions result from our attempts to adapt to the environment. Evidence suggests that all humans experience a common set of emotions. Lazarus (1991), has suggested that these emotions can be described by their care relational themes. By adopting this term, Lazarus emphasises that our emotional responses grow out of our interactions with the environment (are relational); are highly cognitive; and are often complex, frequently involving two or more emotions operating simultaneously, Lazarus (1991) states:

*The fundamental premise is that in order to survive and flourish, animals (humans in particular), are constantly evaluating and appraising their relationships with the environment with respect to significance for well-being.*

## FACIAL EXPRESSIONS

Studies of facial expressions reveal that certain basic emotions, such as happiness, anger, distress, and disgust, can be identified in a wide range of cultures. Some researchers have even argued that most – if not all – emotions are a product of heredity. Researchers view emotions as largely the product of learning and culture (Ekman, 1994; Russell, 1995).

It is a fact that when people experience an emotion, they are inclined to wear that emotion on their face. Further, there is evidence that, when people deliberately put on a happy or a sad face, they tend to trigger the emotion that corresponds to the facial expression (e.g., Izard, 1990). Noting the close link between emotions and facial expression, Izard has suggested that people can learn to regulate their subjective feelings by learning to control their facial expressions (Izard, 1990). The bottom line is that, if you want to be happy, you put on a happy face.

### Using Emotions to Identify Goals, Motives, and Concerns

We can use our emotions to help identify our goals, motives, and concerns (Frijda, 1988). At first, this may second like an odd exercise. As humans, we have goals, motives, and concerns of which we are largely unaware (Epstein, 1991) – in particular, those that our parents gave us early in life. We like to analyse reactions that do not fit with our perceptions of about ourselves or the image that we like to project about ourselves.

As an exercise, identify an emotional response to a situation, either positive or negative, and see if you can explain it. Why did you feel so proud or so mortified? One reason why people experience rage is that they have failed to clearly differentiate their emotions. You may not be able to totally explain your reactions the first time, but you will improve with practice. When you can explain why, then you have discovered the meaning structure for that emotion in that situation. Because emotions are situation-specific, you need to keep track of the situation in order to discover your meaning structure for a certain emotion.

## What is Stress?

### The Definition of Stress

In our daily lives, we speak of stress in connection with negative feelings for instance, taking examinations, the breakup of a marriage or relationship, struggling to pay our bills, commuting on congested roads, and dealing with people we dislike. Notice that stress has come to describe a diverse set of negative feelings. Failing an examination produces feelings of humiliation and shame; the breakup of a relationship may lead to a deep sense of loss and remorse; not being able to reach our goal can be frustrating and irritating;; conflicts in interpersonal relationships may lead to contempt and disgust.

Scientist thinks of stress somewhat differently – as a set of neurological and physiological reactions that serve some ultimate adaptive purpose. How the individual responds to those reactions determines whether they produce feelings of *distress* (a negative feeling) or *eustress* (a positive feeling). In general, when people view an event as threatening, they experience distress; when they view it as challenging, they experience eustress.

Current research indicates that, when people interpret an event as challenging, their health is not adversely affected; however, when they interpret it as threatening, their health can be adversely affected. Learning appropriate coping responses will lead to improved health (Cohen & Williamson, 1991; Friedman, 1991). We will consider the links between stress and health, later in the chapter.

### Stress as a Fight-or-Flight Response

Stress is frequently referred to as the fight-or-flight response. This label grows out of an evolutionary analysis. Animals have two basis ways of dealing with threats: they fight or they flee. A rabbit will flee in order to stay alive. A lion, in contrast, depends on its ability to fights to stay alive and to obtain the food supply that it requires. Whether we fight or flee, certain basic requirements must be met. First, we need to expend a great deal of energy. Second, we have to keep our head. Third, we frequently have to deal with injury. The stress reaction clearly meets these requirements. To maximise energy needs, blood rushes to the sites where it is needed (the muscles and brain); fats are released into the bloodstream; we perspire to cool ourselves; and so forth. To keep our head, the high level of arousal that we experience helps us to focus our attention on survival cues. To help us deal with injury, our blood thickens, and chemicals are released to enable our body to deal with injury, should it occur.

In our lives today, we do not have to expend as much physical energy as our foraging ancestors did, nor are we normally threatened with injury, when we experience stress. We no longer need to have so much fat released in our blood; we do not need to perspire; our blood pressure need not skyrocket; our blood need not thicken to guard against an injury; we do not need chemicals circulating in our blood to attack some foreign body that might enter our system. Nevertheless, each time we experience stress, our body prepares itself as though we were still living as our ancestors lived.

## THE BIOLOGICAL COMPONENT OF STRESS

### The Sympathetic/Adrenal and Pituitary/Adrenal Responses

When people are challenged, or when people lose control, they may try to reassert control. Under these conditions, the body makes a sympathetic/adrenal response. The sympathetic system allows us to respond to the immediate demands of the situation by activating the body; our heart rate accelerates, our blood pressure rises, and we become more alert. In short, we become aroused.

To provide a longer-term chemical backup to the immediate action of the sympathetic system, the adrenal glands – specifically, the adrenal medulla (the inner part of the gland) – releases epinephrine and norepinephrine.

Whereas, the sympathetic/adrenal system takes care of arousal, the pituitary/adrenal system is more closely associated with what is traditionally called the stress reaction – our fight-or-flight responses. The adrenal cortex (the outer part of the gland) secretes two main types of hormones; the mineral corticoids and the glucocorticoids (including cortisol and corticosterone). The release of these hormones is linked to the release of other chemicals, so we will see shortly. Note that, under stress, the sympathetic/adrenal and the pituitary/adrenal responses typically occur together. However, these two systems operate separately in some circumstances – generally when we attempt to gain control over stress by engaging in some kind of adaptive behaviour. As we gain control, the cortisol level frequently drops, while the epinephrine level remains high (Frankenhaeuser, Lundberg, & Forsman, 1980). Cortisol is frequently used as a measure of the action of the pituitary/adrenal system, whereas urinary epinephrine is a measure of the activity of the sympathetic/adrenal system. The endocrine glands and hormones associated with stress responses are summarised. We explored the sympathetic/adrenal system. Let's now turn to the pituitary/adrenal system.

*Epinephrine and norepinephrine are also referred to as adrenaline and noradrenaline respectively, especially when they are released to the periphery of the system rather than to the brain. This distinction is often ignored, however.*

## THE PITUITARY/ADRENAL RESPONSE

The hypothalamus initiates activity in the pituitary/adrenal system by secreting corticotrophin-releasing factor (CRF), which stimulates the pituitary. The pituitary, in turn, secretes adrenocorticotropic hormone (ACTH).

Animal research indicates that ACTH is released approximately 10 seconds after a stressful event. The slowness of this reaction – relative to the central nervous system, which acts immediately – suggests that the endocrine system is probably involved in longer-term survival reactions, rather than the immediate survival responses of fight-or-flight. For example, ACTH stimulates fatty acid release and glucose utilisation, thereby providing the energy to deal with a threat (White, Handler, & Smith, 1964). It takes between 15 minutes and 1 hour for the glucocorticoids to reach a level sufficient to terminate ACTH secretion (Vernikos-Danellis & Heybach, 1980). Thus, once set in motion, the stress reaction continues for a time. The glucocorticoids remain active much longer than ACTH.The continued presence of glucocorticoids in the blood may account for some post-stress reactions, such as weight loss, changes in body temperature, and increased secretion of stomach acid (Weiss, 1968).

It appears that prolonged stress results in a breakdown of the adrenal system, accompanied by susceptibility to a wide variety of diseases. We'll return to this topic shortly.

### Endorphins and Stress

Laboratory studies of endorphins indicate that the endorphin response can be triggered not only by physical stressors, such as shock, but by fear (Bolles & Fanselow, 1982). This may explain why people expose themselves to situations that elicit fear, such as parachuting and mountain-climbing.

### Stress and the Immune System

Over the past 30 years, numerous studies have demonstrated how stressors cause changes in the immune system (Maier, Watkins, & Fleshner, 1994). Specifically, stressors seem to turn off the immune response. For example, it has been demonstrated that stress makes us more susceptible to infections and common colds (Cohen, Tyrrell, & Smith, 1991). There is still some question about the role of stress in cancer, but a number of researchers assert, mainly on the basis of correlational studies, that there is a link. These findings need to be replicated using designs that can establish a casual link (Andersen, Kiecolt-Glaser, & Glaser, 1994).

This research has wide-ranging implications for our health. Why would the immune system not work at maximum efficiency when we need it most? To answer that question, let us look at how the immune system operates.

**Table 28: Endocrine glands involved in stress, distress, and coping**

| *Gland* | *Hormone* | *Action/Function* |
|---|---|---|
| Hypothalamus | Corticotropin-releasing hormone | Stimulates the pituitary to release ACTH. The hypothalamus is initially triggered by the thalamus, but that action can be inhibited by the cortex. |
| Pituitary | ACTH (adrenocorticotropic hormone) | Stimulates adrenal cortex to release glucocorticoids. |
| Adrenal Cortex | Glucocorticoids | The glucocorticoids are also important in energy metabolism. |
| | Cortisol | Anti-inflammatory, anti-allergy (important in the fight-or-flight response). |
| | Corticosterone | Suppresses the immune system (important for keeping the immune response in check). |
| Adrenal Medulla | Epinephrine | Released following environmental extremes (for example), physical exertion, fear. Increases heart rate, oxygen consumption, and glycogen mobilisation. |
| | Norepinephrine | Released during coping, especially when coping response is vigorous. Increases blood pressure and constricts blood vessels. |

## Two Immune Systems

The immune system is very complex. In fact, it is divided into two systems, non-specific (innate) and specific (acquired). The non-specific immune system is present from birth and, as its name suggests, operates in a non-specific way, without regard to particular pathogens (for example, bacteria). The specific immune system is an acquired system; it learns to recognise foreign substances. T and B lymphocytes play a critical role in this system, which is involved in fighting such things as cancer and AIDS. The specific system has evolved more recently and involves some of the same mechanisms as the non-specific system.

Let us begin by examining the bi-directional effects between stress and non-specific immunity and non-specific immunity on stress. Understanding bi-directional effects allows us to understand such things as how and why such coping serves to not only improve our mental health but our physical health as well. Following that discussion, I will discuss some of the current thinking on how and why stress affects the specific system. My purpose is to show that there is, indeed, good reason to argue, that if we want to be physically healthy, we need to develop certain health-enabling behaviours, including coping.

## STRESS AND THE NON-SPECIFIC IMMUNE SYSTEM

In humans, both *acute stressors*, such as final examinations, battle task vigilance and sleep deprivation, and *chronic stressors*, such as divorce and bereavement, have been shown to affect the immune response. Additionally, it has been shown that depression, anger, and anxiety affect the immune system (Maier et al., 1994). Note, however, that different stressors cause different mixes of autonomic activation and hormone activity. Thus, it is necessary to study each stressor to determine how it affects us. As we will see shortly, many things moderate the effects of stressors.

It appears that an activated immune response triggers circuitry in the central nervous system to increase our sensitivity to pain. Sensitivity to pain is thought to have adaptive value during the recuperative process; for example, it helps us to avoid re-injuring ourselves. Further, research is needed to determine how mood, emotional reactivity, and attention are affected by the immune response.

The acute phase response involves processes such as the production of agents to fight pathogens; the removal of the nutrients necessary for pathogens to grow; the synthesis of proteins involved in scavenging and removing cellular debris; and fever. Fever is highly adaptive. Elevated body temperature enhances a number of enzymatic reactions important for repairs and the proliferation of immune cells but suppresses the relocation of unwanted microbes (Maier et al., 1994). The acute phase also involves reduced activity; being lethargic has benefits for recuperation. Since, the hypothalamus is responsible for the regulation of temperature, the involvement of the central nervous system is important in the acute phase response.

## STRESS, ENERGY, AND IMMUNITY

Under stress, the body's energy is redistributed. When we perceive that we are threatened, cardiac output is increased, blood from the digestive tract is shunted to the muscles, the muscles become more receptive to blood, the brain becomes active, pupils dilate for better distance vision, and so forth.

Moreover, when dealing with a threat, to reduce the feeling of pain, fever, and reduced activity, analgesic effects is produced under stress.

Theorists have suggested that, when the fight-or-flight response emerged, it simply made use of the inflammation system (Maier et al., 1994). All that was required was to insure that the system reacted immediately, and not 8-12 hours later, when the acute phase of the inflammatory process normally begins.

What this means is that our immune response is now under the control of the stress response. There are links between not only behaviours and the immune system but thinking and the immune system, So, if we learn how to think and act when stressed.Our immune system will continue to do what it was designed to do.

### Brief Stress and Disease

Researchers often distinguish between acute stress, such as bereavement and divorce. In both cases, the response occurs over a period of time – hours, days, months, or even years – and seems to take its toll on health. Brief periods of stress, such as an encounter with hostile person or a visit to the dentist do not have much effect on health. The stress response and its associated health problems are provoked by stressors that last many hours or days. Many people learn to deal successfully with brief stressors on a regular basis and show no long-term effects.

### The Learned Component of Stress

In this section, we focus on how people deal with brief periods of stress. Briefs stresses are often associated with threats to our survival and/or sensory overload. This form of stress is hard to distinguish from anxiety. Anxiety, however, has typically more to do with our perceptions about the future. Stress is here and now; it has to do with what is impacting us at the moment.

### Unpredictability and Stress

Whether we experience stress depends on a number of psychological factors. In particular, it has been shown repeatedly that exposure to aversive events is much more likely to produce stress and disease if the events are unpredictable than if they can be foreseen. In comparison, with predictable stress, unpredictable stress produces higher levels of corticonterone (Weiss, 1970, 1971a), more seven stomach ulceration (Caul, Buchanan, & Hays, 1972; Weiss, 1971a), greater weight loss (Weiss, 1970), alterations in the levels of glucose and free fatty acids (Quirce, Odio, & Solano, 1981), and myocardial dysfunction (Miller, Grossman, Richardson, Wistow, & Thomas, 1978).

In exploring the role of unpredictability, researchers have examined three main factors that influence whether an aversive event will lead to stress: discrimination of stress cues; availability of a coping response; and repeated experience with the aversive stimulus. Let us look at these factors.

## Discrimination of Stress Cues

Research has shown that, if an organism experiences intermittent stress, knowing when that stress will come, helps the organism to prepare for the stress, just before onset and to relax after the stress has ended. The problem for the organism, therefore, is to learn to discriminate the cues that predict the onset of stress. Laboratory research has confirmed that this is an important factor. In one study (Weiss, 1970), rats were given a warning signal that they were about to receive a tail shock. A yoked control group received the same duration and pattern of shocks but without a warning signal. Intermittent shocks produce not only a reliable stress reaction but also lesions in the stomach (thought to be a precursor to ulcers). The question was whether signaled or unsignaled shock would produce more lesions. As we see unsignaled shocks are more stressful than signaled shocks. The analogy with humans is obvious. For instance, scheduled tests are difficult enough; unscheduled tests are even more stressful, because they do not allow the student to relax. In the office, knowing when the boss is scheduled to arrive or when things normally go wrong can have important implications of learning to deal with stress.

Several studies have failed to show that signaled shock leads to less stress (Averill, 1973). Commenting on these studies, Averill notes that signaled shock seems to work only if the signal tells the subject not only when the shock will come but also when the subject can relax. The key, in other words, is knowing when to reflex.

## Availability of a Coping Response

Monkeys in a shock-avoidance situation show somewhat different patterns of catecholamine output when they can and cannot avoid shock (Brady, 1975). Weiss (1968, 1971a) found that animals that learn an avoidance response not only experience less lessning of the stomach but show less stress (as measured by level of plasma corticosterone), than do yoked control subjects with no opportunity to make an avoidance response. Exactly why coping responses reduce stress is not altogether clear. Studies have ruled out the possibility that their effectiveness is due to the greater activity (exercise) that accompanies active avoidance (Weiss, Glazer, & Pohorecky, 1976). As we'll see in the next section, there is good evidence that the effect is cognitively mediated, at least in part.

If it is to be effective, the coping response must be fairly easy, as well as free of conflict. In one study, rats had to perform either an easy coping response (a single bar press) or a more difficult response (several bar presses) to avoid shock. Animals with an easy response had fewer stomach lesions than did their yoked partners (Tsuda & Hirai, 1975). In another experiment, rats had to experience a brief shock while making an avoidance response that prevented a longer train of shocks. In this situation, the coping group developed more stomach lesions than did the yoked control subjects.

In everyday life, we learn to experience less stress if we know what to do. Say, for example, that your job is to deal with customer complaints. How can you learn to deal with constant exposure to customers' anger? Many training programmes have been designed to deal with such situations. After training, most people experience very little stress. What these programmes teach is how to diffuse the anger and solve the problem. This involves two steps. First, they need to accept that the customer has been inconvenienced and so has a right to be angry, but that such anger is not directed at them personally. In accepting the anger, they communicate to the customer that they understand how the customer feels and are sympathetic. Second, they need to turn their attention to solving the problem. Once people see that someone is willing to help them, their anger often subsides and they too become involved in helping to solve the problem. People who learn this technique well can often turn a bad situation into a positive one for both themselves and the customer.

We will return to the role of coping when we discuss moderators of stress.

## Repeated Experience with the Aversive Stimulus

Studies have shown that an acute stress reaction depletes norepinephrine (Miller, 1980). Animals are slow to learn after an acute stress reaction, and it has been suggested that the failure to learn is due to the norepinephrine depletion.

In a study to determine if the stress response can be habituated, rats were exposed to acute stress for 15 consecutive days. Control rats were exposed to acute stress on only one day, with no prior exposure. After exposure, indices of norepinephrine metabolism in the rats' brains were examined. The prior-exposure animals had higher levels of enzymes involved in norepinephrine synthesis than did the no-exposure animals (Weiss, Glazer, Pohorecky, Brick, & Miller, 1975).

Marianne Frankenhauuser (1980), has argued that repeated exposure to a stressor will reduce the stress reaction (particularly the activity of the adrenal medulla), only if there is a decrease in psychological involvement. For example, she notes that parachute-jumping never becomes routine. Catecholamine secretion during jump periods tends to remain high even after several jumps (Bloom, von Euler, & Frankenhaeuser, 1963). Probably the reason is that parachute-jumping demands constant attention and concentration. In other words, when a high degree of psychological readiness is required, the stress reaction remains high.

Prior exposure is often used as a training procedure to help people in a variety of situations deal more effectively with stressful stimulation. Training soldiers for combat duty typically involves exposing them to acute stress over a period of time. Mountain climbers train extensively, by exposing themselves to the conditions that they may expect to encounter in an important climb, such as cold, rain, wind, and prolonged physical exertion. Pilots are trained in simulators to react to a wide range of emergencies. In all these situations, the goal is not only to train the stress reaction but to teach the person to correctly evaluate the nature of the stimulus that is a potential stressor. Certain patterns of stimulation should elicit the stress reaction and others should not.

## Learning How to Respond to Stress

As a general rule of thumb, it is not a good idea to make decisions or engage in a wide variety of behaviours when under stress. Here are two suggestions for functioning under stress.

1. Learn a prescribed set of rules for making decisions under stress. Why do people tend to take bad decisions under stress? Research indicates that it is largely due to their failure to fulfill an elementary requirement of the decision-making process, which is to systematically consider all the relevant alternatives (Keinan, 1987). To ensure sound decision-making – for example, when controllers are guiding planes into an airport for a landing – people are carefully trained to make sure they follow a prescribed set of rules. Sometimes, they are required to actually check off each function as they complete it.
2. Learn not to react. It is not just poor decision-making that leads to poor performance under stress. Stress has been shown to disrupt behaviour that we consider automatic or habitual. After being told that his wife has cancer, a man drives through a stop sign on his way home; after being refused a loan by her banker, a woman forgets to pick up her purse. The reasoning behind learning not to react immediately is that humans tend to process information with two systems; one a quick and dirty system that does not fully process all the information and another a more thorough system that involves rational thought processes (LeDoux, 1993). If an individual feels pressured to respond quickly, such as when threatened, they are inclined to make use of the quick and dirty system, a system that evolved to help us deal with emergencies, however, a system that is based on incomplete information processing.

One way to help people deal with emergencies is to teach them a pattern of response that they can automatically use in an emergency situation. Airplane pilots are given special training in simulators to insure that in the event of an emergency, they will know what to do without having to think. Astronauts are trained not to respond personally and consult ground control. Because of the complexity of a spaceship, it is necessary to use a computer to analyse all the implications of a particular response before it is executed. In our daily lives, we would do well to resist the temptation to respond to stress with a hasty action and instead allow our more thorough information processing system to help us decide a proper course of action.

## Social Factors and Stress: The Workplace Example

The stress reaction is elicited by a wide variety of psycho-social stimuli – stimuli associated with our jobs, our residences, our social interactions, and the activities we engage in. Because they are part of our daily lives, they can elicit a prolonged stress reaction, which may precipitate a variety of adaptive diseases. To illustrate social factors, let us look at stress in the workplace.

## Conflict-Prone and Conflict-Resistant Organisations

Stokols (1993a), suggests that the physical arrangements and the social conditions of an organisation can predispose their members towards chronic conflict and resultant health problems. The qualities of conflict-prone and conflict-resistant organisations, under three general categories: (1) the social-psychological qualities of groups; (2) organisational structure; and (3) environmental conditions. Stokols argues that the conflict-prone organisation is often a major source of stress and illness in people.

## The Individual-Environment Interaction

In his work on organisations, Stokols (1992a), argues that more attention needs to be paid to the physical environment and the socio-cultural environment. In the past, researchers have focused on the individual's ability to adapt as the main source of difficulty and have put the blame more or less on the individual for his or her stress. While an individual with a disposition towards optimism, hardiness, and high self-esteem, for example, will tend to be less affected by stress, these factors alone may not be sufficient to eliminate work-related stress. If the environment plays havoc with people who have relatively positive dispositions, then how much more impact will it have on people with more negative dispositions (towards hostility, anger, and low self-esteem). As yet, we do not have any direct estimates, but indirect evidence gives cause for concern. Indeed, some people's jobs are killing them, and it is worse for those who have more negative dispositions.

## Qualities of conflict-prone and conflict-resistant organisations

| *Levels of Organisational Analysis* | *Tendencies toward conflict or Cohesion* | |
|---|---|---|
| | *Conflict-prone Organisations* | *Conflict-Resistant Organisations* |
| **Social-psychological qualities** *(norms, goals, and role expectations)* | Absence of shared goals among group members. Incompatible styles and role assignments among group members. Presence of rigid ideologies; low tolerance for diverse points of view. | Presence of and commitment to shared goals among group members. Compatible style and role assignments among group members. Absence of rigid ideologies, high tolerance for diverse points of view. |
| **Organisational structure** *(interrelations among roles and resources)* | Existence of competitive coalitions. Non-participatory organisational processes. Overstaffed organisation Pervasive competition among members for scare roles and resources. Ambiguous organisation of space and territory among group members. Relatively unstable role structure and membership. Absence of formal and informal dispute-resolution mechanisms. | Absence of competitive coalitions. Participatory organisational processes. Adequately staffed organisation. Minimal competition among members for roles and resources. Clear-cut territorial organisation and use of space among group members. Relatively stable role structure and membership. Availability of formal and informal dispute-resolution mechanisms. |
| Environmental conditions | Local and remote environmental resources for meeting organisational goals are inadequate Environment external to the organisation is anomic and turbulent. | Ample environmental resources for meeting organisational goals are available. Environment external to the organition is cohesive and non-turbulent. |

***Source:*** From "Conflict-Prone and Conflict-Resistant Organisations," by D. Stokols. In H.S. Friedman (Ed.), Hostility, Coping and Health. Copyright © 1992 by the American Psychological Association. Reprinted with permission of the author.

Note that people who have a competitive orientation tend to react poorly to stress. Among other things, they tend to engage in denial and to behaviourally and mentally disengage; show poor active coping skills, do not seek out social support, which is important in dealing with stress; and tend not to accept or interpret events in an adaptive manner (Franken & Brown, (1996). Since all of these characteristics have negative health implications, it is not surprising that organisations that promote a competitive atmosphere are typically characterised by poor employee health. By contrast, people who hold an exchange orientation (the general expectation of reciprocity) and a communal orientation (a positive regard for the needs and feelings of others) tend to experience less stress in organisational settings (Buunk, Doosje, Jans, & Hopstaken, 1993).

These principles apply not only to the workplace but to marital relationships, family functioning, interactions with friends, and casual interactions. It would be a useful exercise to analyse such everyday situations in terms of the principles.

## THE COGNITIVE COMPONENT OF STRESS

One of the most comprehensive theories about the role of cognitive factors in stress has been developed by Richard Lazarus and his colleagues (Coyne & Lazarus, 1980; Folkman, 1984; Folkman, Lazarus, Dunkel-Schetter, Delongis, & Gruen, 1986; Folkman, Schaefer, & Lazarus, 1979; Lazarus, 1981, 1991; Lazarus & Launier, 1978). According to this theory, how an individual appraises an event plays a fundamental role in determining not only the magnitude of the stress response but the kind of coping strategies that the individual may employ to deal with the stress. Appraisal occurs in two stages.

1. Primary appraisal. At this stage, we determine whether a stressful event represents harm/loss, threat, or challenge. *Harm/loss* refers to injury or damage that has already taken place, such as loss of a limb, loss of a job, or simply loss of self-harm or loss. *Challenge* refers to the potential for growth, mastery, or some form of gain. As we will see, numerous factors, both personal and situational, are involved in an individual's appraisal of a situation. From this perspective, the origins of stress cannot be assessed by looking solely at the nature of the environmental event that precipitates it. Rather, stress involves the interaction of the individual with the environment.

2. Secondary appraisal. After determining whether a stressful event represents harm/loss, threat, or challenge, we evaluate our coping resources and options; we ask what we can do. Generally, we have access to physical, social, psychological, and material coping resources. Physical resources include health and energy; social resources include family and friends; psychological resources include self-esteem and problem-solving abilities; and material resources include money and equipment.

### Problem-focused and Emotion-Focused Coping

According to Lazarus's theory, coping refers to cognitive and behavioural efforts to master, reduce, or tolerate the internal and/or external demands created by the stressful transaction (Folkman, 1984). Note that, by this definition, coping refers to efforts to manage rather than to the outcome of those efforts. In other words, having or developing a positive attitude is a form of coping, even if that positive attitude ultimately fails to resolve the situation.

The theory makes an important distinction between two ways of reducing stress. In *problem-focused coping*, we engage in some kind of problem-solving behaviour designed to resolve the stressful transaction. If I am experiencing stress on the job because of another person, for example, I may be able to reduce that stress by asking to be transferred to another department, arranging some strategy to change the other person's behaviour. In *emotion-focused coping*, by contrast, we focus on controlling the symptoms of stress. If it is impossible to avoid the other person, for example, I might deliberately take time out after every encounter to relax and think about the positive who might provide sympathy.

## Situational Factors and Personal Control

Whether an individual tends to focus on the problems or on the emotions in dealing with stress depends very largely on whether the individual appraises the situation as controllable and on whether the situation is, in fact, controllable. Some stressful situations are basically uncontrollable, such as living near a nuclear reactor, perhaps, or working as a police officer, or having a friend who is dying of cancer. Other situations are subject to control (controllable), such as having an examination scheduled next week, perhaps, or having a tyre on your car that has a slow leak, or having no money but having a job that permits you to work overtime. Note that circumstances may make what appears to be an uncontrollable situation controllable and vice-versa. More importantly, people sometimes appraise as uncontrollable a situation that is really under their control and, conversely, may perceive themselves to have control when they do not.

## Potentially Controllable Situations

When people are faced with a forthcoming examination, they tend to appraise that event as both challenging and threatening (Folkman & Lazarus, 1985). When people appraise an event as challenging, two things typically happen. First, they engage to problem-solving behaviour. Second, they develop a positive emotion (excitement, eagerness, hopefulness) that acts as a motivational support for their problem-solving. In other words, two complementary processes lead to effort. When people appraise an event as threatening, however, something quite different happens; they experience negative emotions. Negative emotions are an indicator that something is wrong – at least that is our traditional way of viewing negative emotions. Whatever the exact reason, humans experiencing a negative emotion tend to focus on that emotion, and the time and effort devoted to coping with it distract the individual from activities better calculated to solve the problem. Note that people tend to appraise a situation as threatening when they perceive that it may not be altogether controllable.

Getting a promotion or simply having a high-level job can be perceived as both challenging and threatening. What makes a promotion threatening is the possibility that we may not succeed in the job. As long as the job is perceived as challenging, we are likely to handle it effectively. When feelings of threat arise, however, we will tend to waste time and effort in coping with those feelings. Management systems that use threats to motivate people obviously undermine the employees' motivation.

## Controllability and Longevity

Apparently, perceived controllability even promotes longevity. In a long-term study, two groups of older people in institutions with different levels of opportunity for control and responsibility were compared. Those given more control not only became more active but reported being, happier. Their reduced levels of corticosteroids suggested that these subjects were experiencing loss stress. After two years, this group was significantly healthier than the comparison group. Moreover, in that period, half as many people died in this group as in the comparison group (Rodin & Langer, 1977).

## Moderators of Stress

A moderator of stress tends to reduce the stress response. Stress moderators can be broken down roughly into biological, learned, and cognitive factors. While the fit is not perfect, these categories emphasise the idea that moderators work in different ways to achieve their final common goal, which is to reduce stress.

## The Biological Component - Social Support and Stress

Social support has consistently emerged as a moderator of life stress (Vaux, 1992; Baumann, 1992). Three dimensions of social support have been identified (Schwarzer, Dunkel-Schetter, & Kemeny, 1994; Vaux, 1992).

1. Emotional support (intimacy and reassurance), which can come from family, friends, spouses or partners, volunteers, and community groups such as churches.

2. Tangible support (the provision of aid and service), which involves receiving such necessities as clothing, foods, and shelter, as well as help with daily chores, such as cleaning, shoveling snow, raking leaves, and banking.
3. Informational support (advice and feedback), which involves receiving information and advice on how to take care of ourselves, on the one hand, and having someone who will listen in an empathetic manner, on the other.

Whether social contacts are beneficial depends on whether they are discretionary or obligatory (Bolger & Eckenrode, 1991). If it is apparent that someone is only helping out of a sense of duty, we are not likely to experience a reduction in stress.

## The Repressive Personality Type and Social Support

It appears that certain people who resist seeking out social support are susceptible to a number of physical diseases, particularly cancer (Eysenck, 1988). These people, who are said to have a *repressive* personality, are characterised by their tendency to chronically defend themselves against negative effects, particularly anger and anxiety, and to deny that they are distressed (Emmons, 1992). Of particular interest is evidence that repressors tend to experience difficulties in interpersonal functioning. They seem to be preoccupied with issues of relatedness and are troubled by feelings of dependency and ambivalence in their relations with others (Bonanno & Singer, 1990).

Several mechanisms have been offered to explain how repressive individuals are more susceptible to diseases (Weingberger, 1990). The bottom line, it appears, is that people tend to be healthier when they have good social support systems and feel connected.

## Social Support and Bereavement

Can social support help us to cope with the considerable stress associated with the death of a loved one? Some theorists contend that bereavement can be compensated by a strong social support network (e.g. Stroebe & Stroebe, 1987), but attachment theory suggests that no amount of social support can make up for such losses (Bowlby, 1979). Tests of these two opposing views indicate that attachment theory is a better explanation of the research findings (Strobe, strobe, Abakoumkin, Schut, 1996). When a loved one dies, we experience emotional loneliness, which cannot readily be compensated by reducing social loneliness.

## The Learned Component - Managing Stressful Information

Once of the main theoretical explanations of stress due to serious life-events is based on the idea that we need to be in control of events in our lives (Geer, Davison, & Gatchel, 1970; Krantz & Schulz, 1980). Horowitz (1979), argues that in order to deal with life stressors, we must avoid becoming overwhelmed. To do this, we engage in a variety of control operations that allow us to keep the stress within bounds. For example, we might use denial in order to regain composure or we might focus on only one aspect of the event. Horowitz speaks of breaking the stressful information down into a series of micro-intervals, so that it is within our ability to deal with it. In this way, we master a stressful event by sequentially attacking each of its units. Failure to put the stressful information under tight control. Horowitz says, might lead to information overload, which could precipitate a total breakdown. In computer language, we might say that the system would crash.

## Epstein's Theory

Epstein's theory is largely cognitive, but the way people think is habitual. As we will see in this section, it is because we learn to think about things in certain ways that we experience stress. By learning to think differently, we gain control over stress.

In a nutshell, Epstein's theory is that people who are effective in dealing with stress tend to think more *constructively* when faced with problems, whereas those who tend to experience stress think more *destructively* (Epstein & Meier, 1989).

Specifically, academic intelligence does not predict mental health, physical health, good family relations, satisfactory romantic relations, or success at work. According to Epstein's cognitive-experiential self-theory (CEST), people have three semi-independent systems that help them deal with daily life; a rational system, roughly corresponding to academic intelligence; an experiential system, which we will consider shortly; and an associationistic system, observed in altered states of consciousness system, observed in altered states of consciousness. Epstein believes that the experiential system gives rise to good mental and physical health, good relationships, and success at work. Note that, while academic intelligence predicts grades and is therefore indirectly related to success at work, many people who are successful at work do not have high academic intelligence. Academic intelligence does not predict who makes the most money, who gets promoted, and other indicators of success at work (Epstein, 1990).

To test this theory, Epstein and Meier (1989), created an inventory to measure experiential abilities – the Constructive Thinking Inventory (CTI). This inventory provides an index of the degree to which people tend to be constructive thinkers rather than destructive thinkers when dealing with daily problems. It contains a global measure of coping, plus six specific measures or scales; emotional coping, behavioural coping, categorical thinking, superstitious thinking, naïve optimism, and negative thinking. The first two scales – emotional coping and behavioural coping – are not only the best predictors of coping but correspond to Lazarus's emotion-focused coping and problem-focused coping. Often, the best way to understand what a scale measures is to examine some of the items. Scales such as this typically contain positively and negatively worded items, and subjects are asked to indicate, using a five-point scale, the degree to which they think the item is like them or not like them. A minus sign (–) beside the item indicates that the item is reverse-scored; that is, if a person scores the item as 1, it will be recorded as 5 when computing the final score.

*Differences between constructive and destructive thinkers.* Work with the CTI scales (especially the global scale) has provided some indication of how people who are good constructive thinkers differ from poor constructive thinkers. The main difference, it appears, relates to dealing with negative outcomes. While both good and poor constructive thinkers tend to respond favourably to good outcomes (they remain positive and optimistic about future performance), poor constructive thinkers tend to over generalise about the self after negative outcomes. Among other things, their self-esteem plummets, they feel depressed, and they assume a helpless attitude about future performance. Interestingly, these are some of the symptoms that characterise depressed individuals.

*Origins of destructing thinking.* Why do some people develop such a profound negative self-view following poor performance, while others do not? Epstein (1992), speculates that this may be linked to self-schemata within the implicit self theory that we developed as children. Like any others before him, he suggests that, when love is withdrawn for poor performance or when love is made conditional on good performance, we tend to develop, as part of our implicit self theory, the idea or belief that making mistakes or performing poorly will result in the withdrawal of love. Since the withdrawal of love is one of the most profound and devastating experiences that a child can experience, making mistakes or performing poorly takes on much greater significance than it should. Even though, as adults, we may come to the conclusion that our reactions are inappropriate, we often have difficulty learning how to respond more appropriately. Why we have difficulty unlearning this belief and replacing it with a more rational or reasonable one is not altogether clear. Among other things, it has been suggested that the experimental system does not work by rules of reason or logic and, therefore, to change requires something more than just understanding the source of our problem (Epstein & Meier, 1989).

*Poor constructive thinking and stress.* (Katz & Epstein, 1991). Physiological measures of poor constructive thinkers also indicated that they experienced greater stress than did good constructive thinkers. It was concluded that poor constructive thinkers contribute to the stress they experience by spontaneously generating negative thoughts in the absence of external stressors and that they appraise external stressors as more threatening.

## PRACTICAL APPLICATION

### Becoming a Constructive Thinker

From the work of Epstein, it appears that those who think destructively focus their negative thinking not only on the self but also on the outside world. As a result, they see themselves as inadequate and the world as threatening. Research suggests these two tendencies are different but highly related and probably have a common origin in the implicit theories that people have constructed about their ability to deal with the external world. All behaviour involves, at least to some degree, an attempt to interact with the environment. To interact successfully involves an assessment of our abilities (the self) and the challenge offered by the environment.

We need to believe that we can succeed and then we need to learn the skills that will enable us to succeed. Many people never make the effort to develop the skills they need, because they do not believe they can succeed. The first step, therefore, is to develop a more positive attitude about our ability to deal with the environment. The second thing, of course, is to see the world in terms of opportunity – as a source of pleasure as opposed to pain.

I often have difficulty changing the way I think. Even when I know, at a rational level, that I need to think differently, I find myself falling back into my previous mode of thinking. It seems easier and more natural – more me. Eventually, however, I feel very comfortable with my new way of thinking.

It has been my experience that, when I do change the way I think – often after repeated attempts – the world looks very different to me; it is a better world.

*Constructive thinking and success in life.* Epstein's theory is relevant not only to managing stress but to achieving success.

### Emotion-Focused Coping Strategies

Strategies that have been advocated to deal with stress include exercise, relaxation, meditation, and even biofeedback training.

*Meditation.* Transcendental Meditation (TM), was introduced to North America by Maharishi Mahesh Yogi in the 1960s.

The various techniques for meditation seem to be equally effective in lowering anxiety and countering the effects of stress.

### Activity

Find a quiet place with a straight-back chair. Sit in any comfortable position with your back straight. Close your eyes. Bring your full attention to the movement of your breath as it enters and leaves your nostrils. Do not follow the breath into your lungs or out into the air. Keep your focus at the nostrils, noting the full passage of each in and out breath, from its beginning to its end. Each time background noises, bring your attention back to the easy, natural rhythm of your breathing. Do not try to control the breath; simply, be aware of it. Fast or slow, shallow or deep, the nature of the breath does not matter; your total attention to it is what counts. If you have trouble keeping your mind on your breath, count each inhalation and exhalation up to 10, and then start over again. Mediate for 20 minutes; set a timer, or peek at your watch occasionally. Doing so will not break your concentration. For the best results, meditate regularly, twice a day, in the same time and place.

The evidence showing that meditation does reduce the stress reaction is fairly impressive. It has been shown, for example, that meditation will reduce high blood pressure (Benson & Wallace, 1972) and the frequency of headaches, colds, and insomnia (Wallace, Benson, & Wilson, 1971). One series of studies showed that transcendental meditation practiced by volunteer subjects produced a decrease in oxygen consumption (Wallace & Benson, 1972). These results are particularly impressive oxygen consumption reflects metabolic rate, a physiological response that cannot be altered through voluntary efforts. We might ask whether meditators can reduce the activity of the adrenal cortex. It appears that meditation does reduce adrenocortical activity, as indicated by reduced cortisol level (Jevning, Wilson & Davidson, 1978).

Goleman (1976), has noted that meditators typically recover rapidly from stress and suggests that fact is the key to understanding why meditators successfully resist the effects of stress. If a person can relax after each stressful-event, the aversive effects associated with stress are kept to a minimum, and the person has greater reserves of energy to deal with future stressful events. Rather than letting each stressful event add to the previous one, the person treats each event more or less separately. As we have noted, stress seems to have a damaging effect only if it is prolonged. It appears that, because meditators recovery so rapidly, they do not experience prolonged stress.

*Relaxation.* If the beneficial effects of meditation are due to the increased relaxation that it produces, then other forms of relaxation might be just as effective. Indeed, several lines of research have shown that to be the case (Beary, Benson, & Klemchuk, 1974; Cauthen & Prymak, 1977; Fenwick et al., 1977; Holmes, 1984; Morse, Martin, Furst, & Dubin 1977). Relaxation is found to be effective in reducing both systolic and diastolic blood pressure (e.g. Fey & Lindholm, 1978; Mount, Walters, Rowland, Barnes, & Payton, 1978). In *The Relaxation Response,* Herbert Benson (1975), tells how relaxation can be readily learned and used.

*Exercise.* Research data on exercise relate mainly to anxiety, which is often associated with stress. A study comparing the effects of exercise and meditation found that, although exercise reduced certain somatic aspects of anxiety, it did not necessarily reduce the cognitive aspects (Schwartz, Davidson, & Goleman, 1978). These researchers argue that exercise, if combined with relaxation could enhance the beneficial effects of relaxation, but exercise cannot be substituted for relaxation. Nonetheless, there is considerable evidence that physical fitness does moderate the negative health effects of life stress (Brown, 1991).

*Biofeedback.* Since the discovery that involuntary responses mediated by the autonomic nervous system can be altered through operant conditioning procedures, there has been considerable interest in using these procedures to reduce the stress reaction. After reviewing the relevant research, Tarler-Benlolo (1978), found no evidence that biofeedback is better than relaxation for dealing with a variety of stress-induced disorders, including migraine headaches and elevated blood pressure. Each technique may be particularly suited to certain people or certain disorders, but more data are required before specific conclusions can be drawn. There may be reason to use both techniques at once (Cuthbert, Kristeller, Simons, Hodes, & Lang, 1981; Fey & Lindholm, 1978).

## The Cognitive Component

**Inhibition and Trauma:** Individuals who have suffered from a variety of traumas in childhood are far more likely to become ill if they never talk about the traumas (Pennebaker, 1992). Several studies have confirmed that talking or writing about a trauma leads to health benefits. Among other things, people who wrote about their traumas visited the doctor less and had an improved immune response (Pennebaker, 1990). Pennebaker argues that while inhibition is normally highly adaptive, because inhibition allows us to control our thinking and behaviour (as in goal-directed behaviour), inhibition of traumatic events is very harmful. Over time, he argues, the constant injunction to not think about the trauma creates stress. In order for people to reduce this stress, they need to deal with the trauma and put it to rest. Various theorists have argued that, when people actually translate an experience into language, they can *assimilate* it (Horowitz, 1976). Whatever the actual process, talking and writing seem, to reduce the tension associated with constantly repressing something that affected us deeply.

**The Hardy Personality:** People who remain healthy after experiencing high degrees of life stress often exhibit a distinctive personality profile – the *hardy personality*, with three main characteristic (Kobasa, 1979a, b, 1982; Kobasa, Maddi, & Kahn, 1982):

1. Control – the belief that it is possible to influence the course of life-events.
2. Commitment – the belief that life is meaningful and has a purpose.

3. Challenge – the attitude that difficult or onerous events are normal and can provide an opportunity for mastery and development.

The concept of hardiness may account for other moderators of stress, such as the locus of control and sensation seeking, which we will discuss shortly (Kobasa & Puccetti, 1983). Suzanne Kobasa has shown that people with a hardy personality profile are less likely to become ill after experiencing stress. The work of Hull, Van Treuren, and Virnelli (1987), suggests that hardiness should be treated as three separate phenomena. They found that only commitment and control were significantly related to health outcome.

The concept of a hardy personality has generated a great deal of interest. A number of studies have been designed to determine exactly how and why the hardy personality leads to lower rates of illness. The bulk of the evidence seems to indicate that hardy people not only see the world as less threatening but see themselves as more capable of dealing with stressful events by means of problem-solving and support-seeking strategies (Florian, Mikulincer, & Taubman, 1995). When confronted with stress, hardy people show less frustration (Wiebe, 1989), and offer more positive self-statements and fewer negative self-statements (Allred & Smith, 1989).

**Internal and External Locus of Control:** According to the locus-control theory, as we know, some individuals (internals) believe that the ultimate source of control is within themselves, whereas others (externals) believe that control rests outside themselves, in the environment. Internals' belief that the environment contributes to stress reduction (Lefcort, Miller, Ware, & Sherk, 1981). But what happens in a situation that is not controllable? Lundberg, and Frankenhaeuser (1978), have shown that internals give evidence of greater stress in such situations than in situations that are controllable, whereas externals show less stress when the situation is uncontrollable than when it is controllable. Thus, in both cases, the stress was greater when their cognitive orientation was inconsistent with the outcome of their efforts to control the stressor.

One particularly interesting finding is that, compared to externals, internals derive greater benefits from social support (Lefcourt, Martin, & Saleh, 1984). This may help to explain the variability in research data on internal orientation and stress. Apparently, the internal orientation interacts with variables such as social support and cognitive appraisal. One study demonstrated that internals appraise situations in a more adaptive fashion than do externals (Parkes, 1984).

**Optimism and Health:** There is considerable evidence that optimists – people who adopt a positive and hopeful outlook – are healthier than pessimists. Shelly Taylor (1989), makes the case that people who see the world from an-optimistic point of view tend to show better recovery from a wide range of illnesses, including cancer. The current evidence suggests that, when pessimists are under stress, their catecholamines become depleted; this triggers the endorphin response, which, in turn, shuts down the immune system (Seligman, 1990).

**Instrumentality and Stress:** Both cross-sectional and longitudinal studies show that instrumentality is a significant stress buffer (Shaw, 1982; Roos & Cohen, 1987). Instrumentality is a measure, among other things, of problem-solving behaviour, which has been implicated in adjustment. Confirming previous work, Roos and Cohen (1987), found that instrumentality was negatively related to psychological distress. Interestingly, androgynous individuals – those who scored high on both instrumentality and expressiveness on Spence and Helmreich's (1978) Scale – showed the greater resilience to recent life stress.

The positive link between instrumentality and health is consistent with the idea that active coping is important for good health. When people take charge of their lives, they are less likely to fall prey to the debilitating effects of stress.

**Sensation Seeking and Stress:** Sensation seeking has also been found to be a moderator of stress (Cohen, 1982; Smith, Ptacek, & Smoll, 1992). Like hardy individuals, sensation seekers tend to view the world as less threatening (Franken, Gibson, & Rowland, 1992) and to engage in more active coping (Smith, Ptacek, & Smoll, 1992). Like optimists they tend to view the world in positive terms, and they tend to be highly instrumental (Franken, 1992).

As we will discuss, sensation seekers see the world as benevolent. They take the view that life is to be embraced and enjoyed and are ready to disclose their feelings to others (Franken, Gibson, & Mohan, 1990). They are able to accept imperfection, and they like people and have a great deal of tolerance for different values and points of view. They also, have a good sense of humour. In short, they have many qualities that make them resistant to the effects of stress.

**Humour and Stress:** Initial work on humour showed that humour helps to reduce stress (Martin & Lefcourt, 1983). In a follow-up study, it was shown that humour reduces stress but only for depressed individuals and not for individuals with anxiety symptomology (Nezu, Nezu, & Blissett, 1988). Why does humour reduce stress? One possible interpretation is that people with a sense of humour appraise stressful situations differently than a sense of humour leads to responses that are incompatible with the stress reaction. It has been shown, for example, that putting on a happy face is sufficient to produce the changes in heart rate and other physiological reactions associated with happiness. Ekman, Levenson, and Friesen (1983), established that even thinking about an emotion produces the reactions that generally accompany the emotion and concluded that some sort of feedback mechanism helps to reduce stress.

What ever the exact mechanism, we would expect intuitively that humour would reduce stress. It remains to be seen why humour fails to reduce feelings of anxiety.

## PRACTICAL APPLICATION

### Some Rules for Dealing with Stress

A wide variety of organisations and educational institutions are offering courses designed to help people deal with unwanted stress. Some teach methods for reducing the magnitude of the stress reaction, including meditation, relaxation, exercise, and biofeedback. Others help people plan their lives so that they encounter fewer stressors or the stressors come at times when they are physically and psychologically prepared to deal with them. Here are seven rules for dealing with unwanted stress.

1. Plan activities to reduce or eliminate stressors. Our daily routine exposes many of us to a wide variety of stressful events, such as traffic snarls on the way to and from work, periodic interruptions, noise, the need to make quick decisions, requests for assistance in areas that are not our responsibility, criticisms of the quality or quantity of our work, and involvement in hostile exchanges. Although some of these events are unavoidable, it is often possible to reduce the number or magnititude of such stressors. For example, arranging to go to work earlier and leaving earlier could allow us to avoid traffic jams, to work at least for a time without interruption, and to experience less noise and would also limit the opportunity for people to make unwarranted requests, and reduce hostile exchanges. If we can do at least part of our job before the other employees arrive, we may have more time to make decisions and to respond tactfully to criticisms to make decisions and to respond tactfully to criticisms and requests. The resulting reduction in stress may decrease irritability and arousal and thus, make us less sensitive to other potential stressors. It could also lead to improved performance, with further reduction in criticisms and the possibility of rewards and promotions.

2. Plan activities so that stressors come at times when they are easier to handle or tolerate. The same event may induce a more intense stress reaction at certain times than at others. For example, a common source of stress results from interruptions that occur when we are trying to complete a task – a ringing telephone, a person dropping by to ask questions or simply to chat, or certain distracting noises. It is often possible to reduce or eliminate this source of stress by systematic planning. Turning off the telephone ringer, telling the secretary to hold all calls, putting up a "Do Not Disturb" sign, or moving to a location where such interruptions are unlikely are some possible solutions. People often find that after an important task is completed, distracting events are less stressful or not stressful at all. Alternatively, we might take care of details early in the day, so that a block of time is available later in the day to work at certain tasks.

3. Learn to relax between activities. Some people tend to experience less stress than others do in the course of a demanding or rigorous schedule. Although constitutional differences may play a role here, another contributory factor is the way people pace themselves. Shutting down the stress reaction periodically by relaxing appears to keep stress under control. Research from a variety of sources suggests that stress becomes distressful when it is allowed

to become intense. Unless we shut down the stress reaction periodically, the stress of one activity tends to add to the stress of another. At some point, stress becomes our enemy. It is likely to have an adverse affect not only on our health but on our performance. We can reduce these effects by learning to relax between activities. It may also be easier to reduce low stress than high stress. When the stress reaction becomes very intense, it frequently provokes a psychological state of helplessness; we feel that we no longer have control over events. Such a feeling can, of course, act as a primary source of stress. Because stress can interfere with our ability to cope, we are caught in a vicious circle, in which the experience of stress becomes a stimulus for further stress.

4. Learn to recognise the early signs of stress. Because humans are dynamic their reactions to events are always affected by previous activities. This means that at certain times an event may cause only mild stress. While at other times it may cause intense stress. If we are to gain control of the stress reaction before it becomes too intense, we must be able to recognise when stress is starting to exceed some safe limit. This is not an easy task for many people, who can recognise stress only when it has reached a high intensity. Biofeedback training can help such people understand the stress reaction and teach them how to intervene when it starts to exceed some safe limit.

5. Learn to treat stress as a challenge. Stressful events often demand that we react. We can react with fear and helplessness, or we can rise to the challenge. If we treat a stressor as a challenge, we will trigger a norepinephrine response, which not only helps supply us with energy but provides us with positive affect. In other words, it appears that norepinephrine has evolved to help us cope with stress. To tap that adaptive chemical, we must rise to the challenge. We must view stress as an opportunity to exercise our adaptive response or to develop such responses. Failure to rise to the challenge will only undermine our self-concept and our natural tendency to control stressful events in our environment.

6. Learn to prevail by becoming problem-focused. Considerable research emphasises that people need to learn how to manage self-doubt because it is an important aspect of learning to prevail. As Bandura (1991), points out, everybody experiences self-doubt from time to time, especially when faced with a negative live-event. What differentiates those who prevail from those who give up is how they deal with such self-doubt. People who fail typically ruminate on their self-doubts, rehearse all their past failures, and count all their inadequacies. Those who succeed, in contrast, learn to rehearse their past successes and to enumerate their strengths.

The key to managing self-doubt is learning to become problem-focused. When attention is focused on the problem, some change may happen; that is the basis for hope and optimism. When people become self-focused, by contrast, they tend to focus on the negative and to accept that nothing can change because the source of their difficulty lies in their personal inadequacies. The more they ruminate, the more distressed they become, and the harder it is for them to think about a solution to their problem (e.g., Wood, Saltzberg, Neale, Stone, & Rachmiel, 1990).

In order to become more problem-focused, start by thinking of how you succeeded in the past under similar circumstances. In other words, give yourself a pep talk. Next, look for ways that other people succeeded under similar circumstances. This will get your thinking off yourself. Finally, ask people to help you find a solution. This is a good way to establish social relations and make use of the considerable skills that other people have.

7. Actively develop those personality characteristics that will ward off stress. Your personality is largely a matter of your attitude towards the world and yourself. People who are healthy are positive and optimistic, accept themselves, take charge of their lives, have a sense of humour, and have good social relations. Most people cannot change their personality overnight. But people do change; personality is not carved in stone. One of the most powerful reasons I can think of for wanting to change is to be physically healthier and as a result live longer. Stress is not inevitable. We can keep it to a minimum if we are willing to create an environment that is conducive to harmony, co-operation, and support.

# ECONOMIC INCENTIVES

Typically, organisations respond to statutory legislation by implementing and maintaining requirements to conform to the law. Rather than merely punishing "bad practice", the more effective way of encouraging "good practice" is to reward it. This could take the form of providing tax incentives for validated health and safety expenditure incurred by organisations as discusses in the recent European Founding Publication (Bailey, Jorgensen, Kruger & Litske, 1994).

Another option is to more directly link risk-assessment and stress-prevention strategies to insurance premiums. Currently, the cost of employee accident and compensation for injuries and illness and negligence is met by a variety of insurance bodies in both the public and the private sector. Insurance premiums may be levied as a flat rate or vary according to the claims experience of the industry sector or the individual organisations. When premiums are linked to the claims experience or past accident history of the individual organisation, employers become more aware of the true cost of their actions. If an employer is penalised by an increased premium as a result of a high accident rate, they are likely to take steps to address and improve the situation. However, there are drawbacks to such arrangements. For example, employers may put pressure on employees not to pursue claims on report accidents. Claims experience shows data-based cost scan give a distorted picture when there is a large payment made for a long-term disability or fatality. Similarly, experience-based solely on accident frequency rates may unfairly penalise an organization which has a lot of relatively inexpensive minor accidents compared to an organisation with fewer, but which result in a more severe and costly outcome. These issues are particularly relevant to small and medium-sized enterprises. Most importantly, experienced based insurance rating focus on historical record, and so do not take into account the efforts an organisation may be making to reduce future risk. However, there would perhaps be some benefit in insurance providers pooling their collective experiences and statistics on an industry basis to help identify particular business sectors which might benefit from more specifically targeted health and safety initiatives.

A more effective and fairer way in which organisations could be rewarded for the efforts in creating more healthy working environments would be to link incentives to stress audits and the presence of stress intervention programmes. A rather similar scheme, the Work Injury Reduction Programme (WIRP), is currently being trially in Alberta, Canada. Employers which have voluntarily opted to join the scheme are required to undergo an annual audit of their management systems. This audit focuses on six areas: corporate leadership operations, human resources, facilities and services, administration and health, and safety information and promotion.

## Definition of Emotions

Probably because emotions are so complex, many different definitions have been proposed over the years. Paul Kleinginna and Anne Kleinginna (1981a), have proposed a definition that incorporates the key elements of previous definitions. According to this consensual definition, emotions occur as a result of an interaction between subjective factors, environmental factors, and neural and hormonal processes. In support of this definition, they make the following points:

1. Emotions give rise to affective experiences, such as pleasure or displeasure.
2. Emotions stimulate us to generate cognitive explanations – to attribute the cause to ourselves or to the environment, for example.
3. Emotions trigger a variety of internal adjustments, such as increased heart rate.
4. Emotions elicit behaviours that are often, but not always, expressive (laughing or crying), goal-directed (helping or avoiding), and adaptive (removal of a potential threat to our survival).

As we see, this definition acknowledged that emotions result from the interaction of biological, learned, and cognitive processes.

Another very important function of emotions is to reward and punish behaviour. When people experience a very positive emotion, they are likely to engage in behaviours that will produce that emotion again. Similarly, when people experience a very negative emotion, they will avoid behaviours that will cause them to feel that emotion again. In other words, emotions act as reinforcers of behaviour (Thorndike's Law of effect; Thorndike, 1913).

## Nature of Emotions

*Core Relational Themes:* Various theorists argue that emotions result from our attempts to adapt to the environment. Evidence suggests that all humans experience a common set of emotions. Lazarus (1991), has suggested that these emotions can be described by their *core relational themes.* By adopting this term, Lazarus emphasises that our emotional responses grow out of our interactions with the environment (are relational); are highly cognitive; and are often complex, frequently involving two or more emotions operating simultaneously. Identifying the various core themes in an emotional response would obviously help us to reduce its complexity.

Summing up his approach, Lazarus (1991) states: The fundamental premise is that in order to survive and flourish, animals (humans in particular), are constructed biologically to be constantly evaluating (appraising) their relationships with the environment with respect to significance for well-being.

*Facial Expressions:* Studies of facial expressions reveal that certain basic emotions such as happiness, anger, distress, and disgust, can be identified in a wide range of cultures. This supports the idea that there are core relational themes underlying emotions. On the basis of data on facial expressions, some researchers have even argued that most – if not all – emotions are a product of heredity. Whether this is true is still being hotly debated, since other researchers view emotions as largely the product of learning and culture (Ekman, 1994, Russell, 1995).

What seems quite clear is that, when people experience an emotion, they are inclined to wear that emotion on their face. Further, there is evidence that, when people deliberately put on a happy or a sad face, they tend to trigger the emotion that corresponds to the facial expression (e.g., Izard, 1990). Noting the close link between emotions and facial expression, Izard has suggested that people can learn to regulate their subjective feelings by learning to control their facial expressions (Izard, 1990). The bottom line is that, if you want to be happy, you put on a happy face.

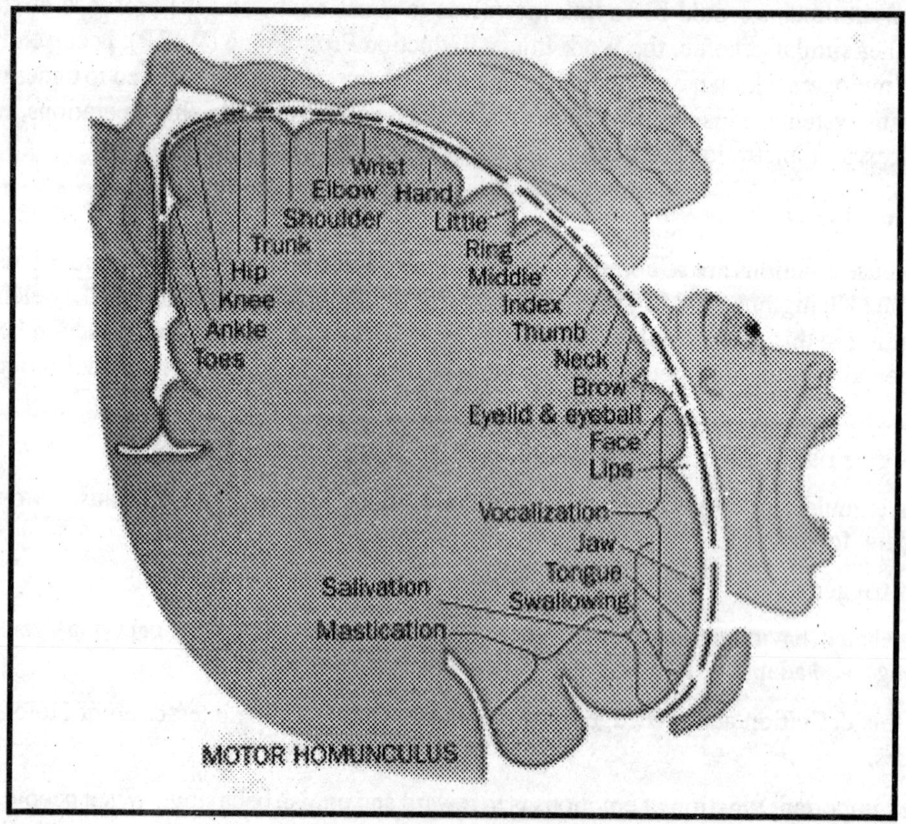


**Fig. 14 : The Brain and Motor Homunculus**

**The Role of Appraisal in Emotions:** According to Lazarus (1991), whether we experience a certain emotion depends on how we appraise a situation. For example, we might ask ourselves, "what emotion is appropriate for this situation, given my goals, my motives, and my concerns?" The idea that appraisal plays an important role in our emotions suggests, of course, that cognitions are central to emotions. If cognitions (ways of thinking) are important, then the implicit theories that people hold are also important. For example, people who tend to be optimistic and those who tend to pessimism will experience very different patterns of emotions; people are happier if they think optimistically. As we will see, how much stress people experience depends very largely on whether they appraise a situation as a threat or a challenge. Because people are inclined to appraise situations differently, large individual differences in emotions often occur.

## Patterns of bodily response in Emotion

Activity occurs in the body's hormonal system and in both the autonomic and somatic parts of the peripheral nervous system during emotional states. We have just described the autonomic nervous system. The *somatic nervous system* is that part of the peripheral nervous system which activates the striped muscles of the body – the arm, leg, and breathing muscles, for instance. Thus, the changes in breathing, muscle tension, and posture seen in emotion are brought about by the activity of the somatic nervous system.

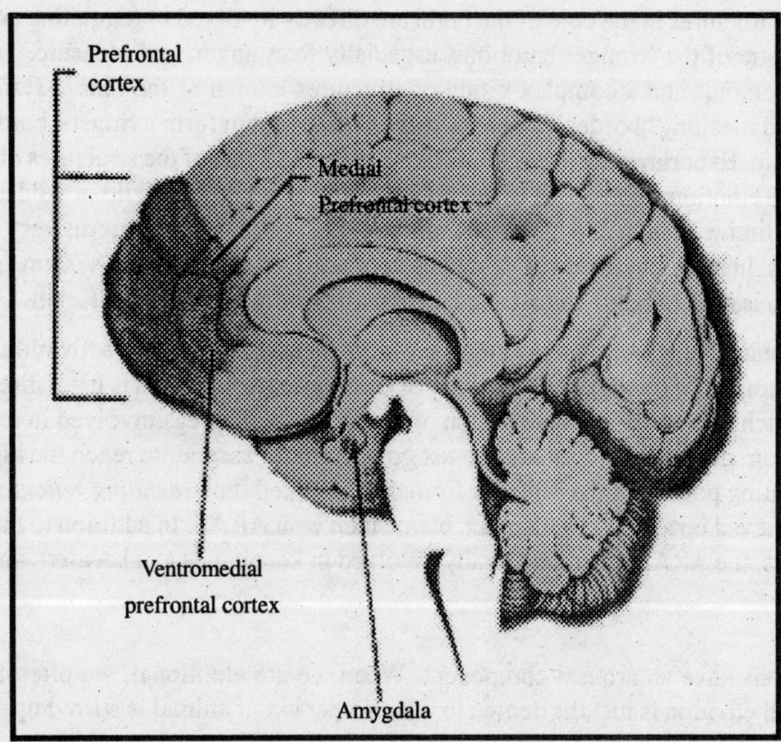


**Fig. 15 : Brain Structures involved in dealing with Fear and Stress**

To illustrate the patterns of bodily changes which accompany emotion, consider the emotions of fear and anger. The bodily changes that accompany these emotions are largely due to increased activity in the sympathetic nervous system; this activity helps the body deal with threatening situations, and therefore the pattern of activity in these emotions is known as the *emergency reaction,* or the *flight-or-fight response.* For example, in both anger and fear, the heart rate usually increases, blood vessels in the muscles dilate so that the body is more prepared for action, blood sugar is mobilised from the liver, the hormones epinephrine and norepinephrine are released from the adrenal gland, the pupils of the eyes dilate, and the peripheral blood vessels of the skin are constricted, thus reducing the possibility of bleeding and making more blood available to the muscles. Muscle tension and breathing rate, which are mediated by the somatic nervous system, tend to increase in both fear and anger.

In contrast to the emergency reaction in fear and anger are the bodily reactions in calm, meditative, emotional states. These reactions make up what is called the *relaxation response.* The pattern of bodily responses during relaxation includes decreased activity in both the sympathetic and somatic nervous systems, together with increased parasympathetic activity. As far as sympathetic and somatic activity are concerned, the relaxation response is almost the opposite of the emergency reaction.

The body changes just described are part of the general emergency and relaxation responses. But are there specific patterns of bodily responses which are different in the various emotions? Early studies (Ax, 1953; Funkenstein, 1955) indicated that fear and anger are characterised by somewhat different response patterns. Now it seems that different bodily-response patterns may be present in a number of emotions and that these patterns are related to the facial expressions of emotions (Ekman et al., 1983).

## The Brain and Emotion

The brain is involved in the perception and evaluation of situations that give rise to emotion. If a situation results in an emotional state, the brain controls the somatic and autonomic patterns of activity characteristic of the emotion; in other word, it controls the physiological expression of the emotion. Of course, the brain is also involved in directing the behaviour driven by the emotional state and is necessary for the emotional feelings we have.

A number of structures in the core of the brain are directly involved in regulating and co-ordinating the activity patterns characteristic of the stronger emotions, especially fear, anger, and pleasure. These core parts of the brain include the hypothalamus and a complex group of structures known as the *limbic system.* The term *limbic* comes from the Latin word meaning "border." The structures of this system form a ring, or border, around the brain stem as it enters the forebrain. Experimenters have found that damage to some of the structures of the limbic system produces great changes in the emotional behaviour of animals, making tame animals wild or wild animals tame. Stimulation of certain parts of the limbic system and hypothalamus produces behavioural patterns very much like those in naturally occurring emotions. In addition, electrical stimulation of portions of the limbic system and hypothalamus, as well as other brain regions, is rewarding to animals and pleasurable for human beings (Heath, 1964).

The aroused state that is part of many emotions is due in part to increased activation of brain cells in the cerebral cortex, limbic system, and hypothalamus. Activity of cells in these brain area is itself directly or indirectly influenced by nerve fibres which fan out from a core region of the higher brain areas involved in regulating emotion. Since the activating fibres from the reticular formation must go upward, or ascend, to reach the higher brain areas involved in emotion, the activating portion of the reticular formation is called the *ascending reticular activating system (ARAS).* Next time you are keyed up and unable to relax, blame it on your ARAS. In addition to the tinge of arousal it provides for emotional states, the ARAS is fundamentally involved in keeping us awake, alert, and conscious.

## Arousal

Many emotions have an arousal component. When we are emotional, we often feel excited. Some theorists have argued that all emotion is just the degree to which a person of animal is stirred up. Although not all students of emotion agree with this idea, the degree of arousal is an important part of emotionality. For instance, high levels of arousal are present in anger, fear and joy, while low levels may accompany sadness and depression.

*Indicators of Arousal:* The *electroncephalogram (EEG),* tells us something about the state of arousal. The EEG is a record of the changing electrical activity of million of nerve cells, all functioning at the same time in the brain. With suitable amplification, this electrical activity of the celebral cortex of the brain waxes and wanes spontaneously to give a wavelike record, and this is why the EEG is popularly said to "record brain waves." The waves of the EEG are really very small voltage changes, in the range of several millionths of a volt. The number of alternations of voltage, or the frequency of the electrical changes, varies from 1 or 2 alternations per second in deep sleep to 50 or more in highly aroused states. The waves of the EEG also vary in amplitude, or height. Brain waves are thus characterised by their frequency and amplitude. When a person is aroused or excited, the EEG consists of high-frequency, low-voltage (amplitude) waves. As an individual becomes more relaxed, the frequency of the EEG tends to decrease, while the voltage (amplitude) of the waves tends to increase.

To make somewhat finer distinctions among degrees of arousal, a number of other measures might be used: heart rate, blood pressure, breathing rate and depth, pupil size, and skin and skin conductance, for instance. (Four of these arousal indicators – heart rate, blood pressure, breathing patterns, and skin conductance – are used in lie-detector tests. Skin conductance is a measure that might not be familiar to you. If a small amount of electricity – so small that it cannot be felt – is passed across an area of the skin (usually the palm of the hand), the resistance to the flow decreases (conductance increases) as a person becomes more aroused and alert. This is called the *galvanic skin response (GSR).*

Another indication of arousal in both humans and lower animals is the *orienting reaction* – an organism's orientation to a new stimulus or to a stimulus change. The *orientation* consists of tensing muscles and changing the position of the body and the head in order to maximise the effectiveness of the stimulus. The exact nature of the orienting reaction depends on the stimulus, the species of the organism, its age, its present state of arousal, and other factors. A cat seeing the slightest movement may make itself ready to prounce. A dog hearing the faintest sound of another dog may perk up its ears, stand at attention, and get ready to defend its territory. Infants turn their heads and eyes toward novel stimuli, such as new toys or strange faces.

## Stress

The term stress has many definitions (Lazarus & Folkman, 1984). We will define *stress* as an internal state which can be caused by physical demands on the body (disease conditions, exercise, extremes of temperature, and the like) or by environmental and social situations which are evaluated as potentially harmful, uncontrollable, or exceeding our resources for coping. The physical, environmental, and social causes of the stress state are termed *stressors*. Once induced by stressors, the internal stress state can then lead to various responses. On the one hand, it can result in a number of physical, bodily responses. On the other hand, psychological responses such as anxiety, hopelessness, depression, irritability, and a general feeling of not being able to cope with the world can result from stress state.

Stress is a big problem in our society (Allen, 1983). Some 75 per cent of bodily disease is said to be stress-related. For example, stress is often a factor in heart disease and cancer, two of the leading causes of death. Furthermore, stress-related diseases cost American industry billions of dollars a year; several billion tranquiliser pills are prescribed in the United States each year; and, although it cannot be quantified, stress seems to be involved in much of our unhappiness, irritability, and dissatisfaction.

## Stressors

Almost any change in the environment – even a pleasant change, such as a vacation – demands some coping; and a little stress is useful in helping us a adapt. But beyond the some point, "stress" becomes "*dis*tress." What acts to produce distress varies greatly from person to person, but some events seem to be stressors for many of us. Chief among these are injuries or infections of the body; annoying or dangerous events in our environments; major changes, or transitions, in life which force us to cope in new ways; and anticipated or actual threats to our self-esteem.

Changes in one's life are important stressors (T. H. Holmes, 1984). A sampling of the life changes – not all of them unpleasant – that can act as stressors is given in Table 1. A rough indication of stressor strength, based on the judgments of adults (Holmes & Rahe, 1967), adolescents (Ruch & Holmes, 1971), and elderly people (Muhlenkamp et al., 1975) is given under the headings "Life Change Units." Note how the importance of certain stressors varies throughout life; compare, for example, the elderly with adults on the bottom life-events. By adding the life-change units during a year, a life-crisis score can be obtained for that year. As the severity of life crises increases from *mild* (150-199 life change units), to *moderate* (200-299) life-change units), to *major* (over 300 life-change units), susceptibility to illness rises progressively (Holmes & Masuda, 1974).

Not only changes, but many ongoing situations are stressors. These include physical stressors, such as injury, infection, exercise, noise, and climate. In addition, the hassles of everyday life centering around work, family, social activities, health, and finances are important stressors which have been found to be related to bodily illness (DeLongis et al., 1982). Frustration and the conflicts which cause frustration are also major stressors.

**Table 29: The Social Readjustment Rating Scale, with life-change units for adults, adolescents, and elderly people**

| LIFEEVENT | LIFE-CHANGE UNITS (ADULTS) | LIFE-CHANGE UNITS (ADOLESCENTS) | LIFE-CHANGE UNITS (ELDERLYPEOPLE) |
|---|---|---|---|
| Death of spouse | 100 | 69 | 73 |
| Divorce | 73 | 60 | 72 |
| Marital separation from mate | 65 | 55 | 63 |
| Detention in jail or other institution | 63 | 50 | 73 |
| Death of a close family member | 63 | 54 | 60 |
| Major personal injury or illness | 53 | 50 | 65 |
| Marriage | 50 | 50 | 50 |
| Being fired at work | 47 | 50 | 62 |
| Marital reconciliation with mate | 45 | 47 | 35 |
| Retirement from work | 45 | 46 | 33 |
| Major change in the health or behaviour of a family member | 44 | 44 | 59 |
| Pregnancy | 40 | 45 | 47 |
| Sex difficulties | 39 | 51 | 36 |
| Gaining a new family member (e.g., through birth, adoption, oldster moving in, etc.) | 39 | 43 | 36 |
| Major business readjustment (e.g., Merger, re-organisation, bankruptcy, etc.) | 39 | 44 | 61 |
| Major change in financial state (e.g., a lot better off than usual) | 38 | 44 | 43 |
| Death of close friend | 37 | 46 | 52 |
| Changing to different line of work | 36 | 38 | 42 |
| Major change in the number of arguments with spouse (e.g., either a lot more or a lot less than usual regarding child-rearing, personal habits, etc.) | 35 | 41 | 45 |
| Taking out a mortage or loan for a major purchase (e.g., for a home, business, etc) | 31 | 41 | 61 |
| Foreclosure on a mortage or loan | 30 | 36 | 61 |
| Major change in responsibilities at work (e.g., promotion, demotion, lateral transfer) | 29 | 38 | 40 |
| Son or daughter leaving home (e.g., marriage, attending college, etc.) | 29 | 34 | 43 |
| Trouble with in-laws | 29 | 36 | 31 |
| Outstanding personal achievement | 28 | 31 | 34 |
| Wife beginning or ceasing work outside the home | 26 | 32 | 35 |
| Beginning or ceasing formal schooling | 26 | 34 | 34 |
| Major change in living condition (e.g., building a new home, remodeling deterioration of home or neighborhood) | 25 | 35 | 48 |
| Revision of personal habits (dress, manners, associations, etc.) | 24 | 26 | 39 |
| Trouble with the boss | 23 | 26 | 28 |
| Major change in working hours or conditions | 20 | 30 | 27 |
| Change in residence | 20 | 28 | 39 |
| Change to a new school | 20 | 26 | 34 |
| Major change in usual type and/or amount of recreation | 19 | 26 | 35 |
| Major change in church activities (e.g., a lot more or a lot less than usual) | 19 | 21 | 40 |

| | | | |
|---|---|---|---|
| Major change in social activities (e.g., clubs, dancing, movies, visiting, etc.) | 18 | 28 | 35 |
| Taking out a mortage or loan for a lesser purchase (e.g., for a car, TV, freezer, etc.) | 17 | 28 | 52 |
| Major change in sleeping habits (a lot more or a lot less sleep, or change in part of day when asleep) | 16 | 18 | 36 |
| Major change in number of family get-togethers (e.g., a lot more or a lot less than usual) | 15 | 22 | 37 |
| Major change in eating habits (a lot more or a lot less food intake, or very different meal hours or surrounderings) | 15 | 18 | 45 |
| Vacation | 13 | 19 | 30 |
| Christmas | 12 | 16 | 34 |
| Minor violations of the law (e.g., traffic tickets, jaywalking, disturbing the peace, etc.) | 11 | 12 | 47 |

(***Sources:*** Holmes & Rahe, 1967; Ruch & Holmes, 1971; Muhlenkamp et al., 1975)

## What stressors do to the body

Hans Selye (1956, 1976) termed the body's response to stressors the *general adaptation syndrome.* The general adaptation syndrome consists of three stages: (1) the alarm reaction, (2) the stage of resistance, and (3) the stage of exhaustion.

***Alarm Reaction:*** The *alarm reaction* is essentially the emergency response of the body already described in an earlier section of this chapter. In this stage, prompt responses of the body, many of them mediated by the sympathetic nervous system prepare us to cope with the stressor here and now.

***State of Resistance:*** If the stressor continues to be present, the *stage of resistance* begins, wherein the body resists the effects of the continuous stressor. However, resistance to new stressors is impaired during this stage. During the state, certain hormonal responses of the body are an important line of defense in resisting the effects of stressors. Especially important among these hormonal responses is increased activity in what is known as the *adrenocorticotropic (ACTH)* axis.

*Adrenocorticotropic hormone (ACTH),* is secreted into the bloodstream by certain cells in the pituitary gland. The rate of ACTH secretion is, in part, controlled by another hormone-like chemical substance – *corticotropin-releasing factor (CRF)* – that is made by certain cells in the brain structure known as the *hypothalamus.* The corticotropin-releasing factor flows from the hypothalamus to the pituitary gland through a specialised system of blood vessels. Stressors are able to activate the nerve cells of the hypothalamus so that more corticotropin-releasing factor is sent to the pituitary gland, thus increasing secretion of ACTH into the blood. In this way brain activity triggered by stressors influences hormone release; thus this is a major link between environmental events – stressors – and the bodily state of stress.

ACTH stimulates cells in the *outer* layers, or cortex, of the adrenal glands so that corticoid hormones such as *cortisol* are secreted into the bloodstream. [Remember that is the *inner* tissue of the adrenal glands that is activated as part of the emergency response to give us an activating "shot of adrenalin."]

Cortisol and other similar hormones have many actions which allow the body to deal adaptively with stressors for long periods of time during the stage of resistance. But maintained high levels of these hormones can be harmful. For instance, cortisol promotes the formation of glucose (blood sugar) – a fuel needed for nerve and muscle activity – by breaking down fats and proteins. In the short run, this is adaptive; the body has more fuel available. In the long run, though, the increased use of protein to make fuel may be serious because proteins are needed in the manufacture of new cells. For example, white blood cells, which are crucial for fighting infection, have a short lifetime and must be continuously replaced. If the proteins needed to make new white blood cells are in short supply because they are being used to make fuel, fewer white blood cells can be produced and the body will be less able to fight infection. Add to this the inhibitory action of cortisol on the formation of the infection-fighting proteins called antibodies, together with shrinkage of the tissues which manufacture white blood cells, and it is clear that high levels of cortisol can, in the long run, seriously impair the body's defenses to infection. Prolonged elevation of cortisol levels can also have other harmful effects, such as raising blood pressure. In addition to cortisol, other hormones which, in excess, may have their own harmful actions are involved in the body's response to stressors during the stage of resistance. But what has been said about cortisol should be enough to give the idea of the role played by hormones in stress.

*Stage of Exhaustion:* The final stage of the general adaptation syndrome is the *stage of exhaustion.* In the stage, the body's capacity to respond to both continuous and new stressors has been seriously compromised. For instance, due to the actions of cortisol described above, a person may no longer be able to ward off infection and may become sick and perhaps die. Or, because of other stressor-induced hormonal effects, stomach ulcers, diabetes, skin disorders, asthma, high blood pressures, increased susceptibility to cancer (Bammer & Newberry, 1983), or a host of other diseases may occur at this stage or late in the stage of resistance (Selve, 1976; Allen, 1983).

The term *psychosomatic* ("mind-body") *disorders* is used when perceived stressors – mental events – increase the susceptibility of the body to disease. Of course not all instances of the diseases listed above are psychosomatic, but many are, and thus the control of stress has become a major problem for medicine. Treatment fo psychosomatic disorders involves medical help for the physical problems and, at the same time attention to the psychological factors producing the stress.

**Coping with stressors:** As we have seen, stress can have serious consequences. Fortunately there are methods for coping with stress. Several of these methods are described. Among them are relaxation, training, biofeedback and systematic desensitisation.

The impact of stressors can sometimes be reduced if a person has control over the stressor (Cohen, 1980). The effect of control has also been shown in animal studies (Weiss, 1972).

Rats were subjected to stress produced by an electric shock to the tail. In the experiment illustrated in Figure 26, groups of rats, matched for weight and age, were studied in sets of three.

The rat in the left-hand chamber could shut off the programmed shocks by turning a wheel. The rat in middle chamber was yoked to the left-hand rat, meaning that it received shocks of the same intensity and duration as the left-hand rat. However – and this is the important point – the yoked animal could do nothing about the shocks. The rat in the right-hand box got no shocks at all but was hooked up like the others.

After this procedure had gone on for some time, stomach ulceration in the rats subjected to the three conditions was studied. The rats which could do something about the shocks showed much less ulceration than did the helpless, yoked animals. The non-shocked animals showed little or no ulceration.

## Stressful Life Events

Death of a spouse, injury to one's child, war, failure in school or at work, an unplanned pregnancy – unless we lead truly charmed lives, most of us experience traumatic events and changes at some time or other. What are their effects on us? This question was first investigated by Holmes and Rahe (1967), who asked a large group of persons to assign arbitrary points (to a maximum of one hundred) to various life-events according to how much readjustment each had required. It was reasoned that the greater the number of points assigned to a given even, the more stressful it was for the persons experiencing it.

Participants in Holmes and Rahe's study assigned the greatest number of points to such serious events as death of a spouse, divorce, and marital separation. In contrast, they assigned much smaller values to such events as change in residence, vacation, and minor violations of the law, such as a parking ticket.

Holmes and Rahe (1967), then related the total number of points accumulated by individuals during a single year to changes in their personal health. The results were dramatic – and did much to stir psychologists' interest in the effects of stress. The greater the number of "stress points" people accumulated, the greater was their likelihood of becoming seriously ill.

Newer research has put a finer point on the relationship between stress and illness. For example, in one recent study, Cohen and his colleagues (1998), asked a group of volunteers to describe stressful events they had experienced during the previous year and to indicate the temporal course (the onset and cessation) of each were brief in duration (e.g., a severe reprimand at work or a fight with a spouse) to more choice ones that typically lasted a month or more and involved significant disruption of everyday routines (e.g., ongoing marital problems or unemployment). Then the researchers gave these persons nose drops containing a low dose of a virus that causes the common cold. The results showed that volunteers who reported chronic stressors (those lasting longer than a month) were more likely to develop a cold than volunteers who had experienced only acute stressors. Moreover, the longer the duration of the stressor, the greater was the risk for developing a cold. These results suggest that chronic stressors may be a more important determinant of disease risk than are short-term stressful events.

This picture is complicated, however, by the existence of large differences in individuals' ability to withstand the impact of stress (Oulette-Kobasa & Puccetti, 1983). While some pesons suffer ill effects after exposure to a few mildly stressful events, others remain healthy even after prolonged exposure to high levels of stress; these individuals are described as being *stress-resistant* or *hardy*. I will return to such differences later in the chapter. For the moment, I wish merely to exphasise the fact that in general, the greater the number of stressful life-events experienced by an individual, and the longer these events are in duration, the greater the likelihood that the person's subsequent health will be adversely affected. When individuals experience stressful life events, such as those near the top of this list, their health often suffers. The greater the number of points for each event, the more stressful it is perceived as being.

**Table 30: Life Events, Stress, and Personal Health**

| No. | Event | Points | No. | Event | Points |
|---|---|---|---|---|---|
| 1. | Death of spouse | 100 | 22. | Change in responsibilities | 29 |
| 2. | Divorce | 73 | 23. | Son or daughter leaving home | 29 |
| 3. | Marital separation | 65 | 24. | Trouble with inlaws | 29 |
| 4. | Jail term | 63 | 25. | Outstanding personal achievement | 28 |
| 5. | Death of close family member | 63 | 26. | Wife beginning or stopping work | 26 |
| 6. | Personal injury or illness | 53 | 27. | Beginning or ending school | 26 |
| 7. | Marriage | 50 | 28. | Change in living conditions | 25 |
| 8. | Getting fired at work | 47 | 29. | Revision of personal habits | 24 |
| 9. | Marital reconciliation | 45 | 30. | Trouble with boss | 23 |
| 10. | Retirement | 45 | 31. | Change in work hours or conditions | 20 |
| 11. | Change in health of family member | 44 | 32. | Change in residence | 20 |
| 12. | Pregnancy | 40 | 33. | Change in school | 20 |
| 13. | Sex difficulties | 39 | 34. | Change in recreation | 19 |
| 14. | Gain for new family member | 39 | 35. | Change in church activities | 19 |
| 15. | Business readjustment | 39 | 36. | Change in social activities | 18 |
| 16. | Change in financial stage | 38 | 37. | Taking out a loan for a lesser purchase (e.g., car or TV) | 17 |
| 17. | Death of close friend | 37 | 38. | Change in sleeping habits | 16 |
| 18. | Change in different line of work | 36 | 39. | Change in number of family get-together | 15 |
| 19. | Change in number of arguments with spouse | 35 | 40. | Change in eating habits | 15 |
| 20. | Taking out mortgage for major purchase (e.g., home) | 31 | 41. | Vacation | 13 |
| 21. | Foreclosure of mortgage or loan | 30 | 42. | Christmas | 12 |
| | | | 43. | Minor violation of the law | 11 |

***(Sources: Based on data from Holmes & Masuda, 1974)***

**The hassles of daily life:** While certain events, such as the death of someone close to us, are clearly stressful, they occur relatively infrequently. Does this mean that people's lives are mostly a serene lake of tranquility? Hardly. As you know, daily life is filled with countless minor annoying sources of stress – termed **hassles** – that seem to make up for their relatively low intensity by their much higher frequency. That such daily hassles are an important cause of stress is suggested by the findings of several studies by Lazarus and his colleagues (DeLongis, Folkman, & Lazarus, 1988; Kanner et al., 1981; Lazarus et al., 1985). These researchers developed a Hassles Scale on which individuals indicate the extent to which they have been "hassled" by common events during the past month. The items included in this scale deal with a wide range of everyday events, such as having too many things to do at once, shopping, and concerns over money. Although such events may seem relatively minor when compared with the life changes studied by Holmes and Rahe (1967), they appear to have important effects. When scores on the Hassles Scale are related to reports of psychological symptoms, stress positive correlations are obtained (Lazarus et al., 1985). In short, the more stress people report as a result of daily hassles, the poorer their psychological well-being. Let's turn now to a discussion of the effects of work-related stress.

**Work-related stress:** Most adults spend more time at work than in any other single activity. It is not surprising, then, that jobs or careers are a central source of stress. Some of the factors producing stress in work settings are obvious; for example, blatant sexual harassment, discrimination, or extreme *overload* – being asked to do too much in too short a time. Interestingly, being asked to do too little can also cause stress. Such *underload* produces intense feelings of boredom, and these, in turn, can be very stressful.

Several other factors that play a role in work-related stress may be less apparent. One of these is role *conflict* – being the target of conflicting demands or expectations from different groups of people. For example, consider the plight of many beginning managers. Their subordinates often expect such persons to go to bat for them with the company to improve their work assignments, pay, and conditions. In contrast, the managers' own bosses often expect them to do the opposite: somehow to induce the employees to work harder for fewer rewards. The result: a stressful situation for the managers.

Another work-related factor that can sometimes generate intense levels of stress involves *performance appraisals,* procedures used for evaluating employees' performance. If employees perceive these as fair, employee stress tends to be low; if employees view them as arbitrary or unfair, it is almost certain to be high. After all, no one wants to feel that rewards such as raises, promotions, or bonuses are being distributed in an unjust manner (Vredenburgh, McLeod, & Nebeker, 1999). Additional factors that have been found to contribute to stress at work are summarised.

Can anything be done to reduce such effects? Fortunately, several lines of research suggest that the answer is yes. First, employers can reduce workplace stress by considering the **person-environment (P-E) fit** (Edward & Harrison, 1993). Mismatches between characteristics of workers and characteristics of their jobs or work environment are associated with increases in stress-related illnesses (Harrison, 1985). Second, sources of social support, both on and off the job, can serve as a buffer against stressful events that occur at work (Frese, 1999; Uchino, Cacioppo, & Kiecolt-Glaser, 1996). Finally, companies can help reduce the potential negative effects of workplace stress by implementing interventions that improve their employees' ability to cope with workplace stress and change unhealthy practice that can intensify the effects of stress (Maturi, 1992).

**Stress and Health: The silent killer:** The link between stress and personal health, according to medical experts, is very strong (Kiecolt-Glaser & Glaser, 1992). Some authorities estimate that stress plays some role in 50 to 70 per cent of all physical illness (Frese, 1985). Moreover, included in these percentages are some of the most serious and life-threatening ailments known to medical science. To list just a few, stress has been implicated in the occurrence of heart disease, high blood pressure, hardening of the arteries, ulcers, and even diabetes.

How does stress produce such effects? The precise mechanisms involved remain to be determined, but growing evidence suggests that the process goes something like this: By draining our resources and keeping us off balance physiologically, stress upsets our complex internal chemistry. In particular, it may interfere with efficient operation of our *immune system* – the mechanism through which our bodies are known as *antigens.* When they appear, certain types of white blood cells (lymphocytes) begin to multiply. These attack the antigens, often destroying them by engulfing them. Other white blood cells produce antibodies, chemical substances that combine with antigens and so neutralise them. When functioning normally, the immune system is nothing short of amazing. Each day it removes or destroys many potential to our health.

Unfortunately, prolonged exposure to stress seems to disrupt this system. In studies with animals, subjects exposed to inescapable shocks demonstrate reduced production of lymphocytes relative to subjects exposed to shocks from which they could escape (Ader & Cohen, 1984). Additional research on the effects of stress on animals and humans suggests that a variety of stressors, including disruptions in interpersonal relationships, loneliness, academic pressure, daily hassles, and the lack of social support, can interfere with our immune systems (Cohen et. al., 1992; Miller et. al., 1999).

For example, in one study, Cohen and his colleagues (1992), asserted the effects of social stability on the immune systems of monkeys. During the year preceding the study, a group of monkeys lived in stable (unchanging) social conditions. When the study began, however, they were randomly assigned to live in either a stable group lived, or in the same environment through the entire study period. In the unstable condition, however, social groups were reorganized frequently. The researchers then observed and assessed the amount of time the monkeys in each group spent in various forms of social interaction, including affiliative behaviours such as engaging in passive physical contact and grooming with other group members. Why were the researchers interested in observing affiliative behaviours? They reasoned that if social support serves as a stress buffer, then the monkeys in the unstable group that engaged in the least amount of affiliative behaviours would experience the greatest negative impact on measures of immune functions. The results of the experiment confirmed these predictions. In short, social support may be an important buffer against the adverse effects of chronic stress.

These results are relevant to people, too. Persons who are divorced or separated from their spouses often experience reduced functioning in certain aspects of their immune system, compared to individuals who are happily married (Kiecolt-Glaser et al., 1987, 1988). Additionally, some recent evidence suggests that the effects of stress on the immune system may be less potent for people who have effective ways of dealing with their stressors than for those who do not. Some research shows that optimism, regular exercise, and feelings of control over stressful events are associated with reduced suppression of the immune system under stress (Taylor, 1999). Such findings are both unsetting and encouraging. On the one hand, they suggest that our complex, high-stress lifestyles may be undermining, at least to a degree, our ability to resist many serious forms of illness. On the other hand, these findings indicate that reductions in such stress may be beneficial to our health.

**Stress and Task Performance:** Psychologists once believed that stress actually improves performance on a wide range of tasks. They held that the relationship between stress and task performance takes the form of an upside-down U: at first, performance improves as stress increases, presumably because the stress is arousing or energising. Beyond some point, though, stress becomes distracting, and performance actually drops.

While this relationship may held true under some conditions, growing evidence suggests that even low or moderte levels of stress can interfere with task performance (Motowidlo, Packard, & Manning, 1986; Steers, 1984). There are several reasons why this is so. First, even relatively mild stress can be distracting. People experiencing stress may focus on the unpleasant feelings and emotions it involves, rather than on the task at hand. Second, prolonged or repeated exposure to even mild levels of stress may exert harmful effects on health, and health problems may interfere with effective performance. Finally, a large body of research indicates that as arousal increases, task performance may rise at first, but that at some point it falls (Berlyne, 1967). The precise location of this turning, or *inflection,* point seems to depend to an important extent on the complexity of the task performed. The greater the complexity, the lower the level of arousal at which the downturn in performance occurs. Many observers believe that the tasks performed by today's working people are more complex than those in the past. For this reason, even relatively low levels of stress may interfere with performance in today's complex work world.

Together, these factors help explain why even moderate levels of stress may interfere with many types of performance. However, stress does not always produce adverse effects. For example, people sometimes do seem to rise to the occasion and turn in sterling performances at times when stress is intense. Perhaps the most reasonable conclusion, then, is that although stress can interfere with task performance in many situations, its precise effects depend on many different factors, such as the complexity of the task being performed and personal characteristics of the individuals involved. As a result, generalisations about the impact of stress on work effectiveness should be made with considerable caution.

**Individual differences in resistance to stress: optimism and pessimism:** As I noted earlier, it is clear that individuals differ in their resistance to stress. Some people seem to be disease-prone – they suffer ill-effects from even mild levels of stress. Other people, sometimes referred to as *self-healers,* are able to function effectively even in the face of intense ongoing stress (Friedman, Hawley, Tucker, 1994). How do such persons differ?

One answer involves the dimension of *optimism-pessimism.* Optimists are people who see the glass as half full; pessimists are those who see it as half empty. Some evidence indicates that optimists – people who have general expectancies for good outcomes (Scheier & Carver, 1988) – are much more stress-resistant than pessimists – people who have general expectancies for poor outcomes. Research seems to indicate that this resistance stems from beneficial changes that occur in their immune system. For example, in one recent study. Segerstrom and her colleagues (1998) examined the effects of optimism on mood and immune changes among law students in their first semester of study. The results showed that optimism was associated with better mood, higher numbers of helper T cells (involved in immune reactions to infections), and higher natural killer cell activity (thought to be important in fighting viral infections and some types of cancers). Additional evidence helps explain why this is case. Briefly, optimists and pessimists seem to adopt different tactics for coping with stress (Scheier & Carver, 1992). Optimists focus on problem-focused coping: making and enacting specific plans for dealing with sources of stress. They also seek to obtain social support – the advice and help of others (Carver et al., 1993). In contrast, pessimists tend to adopt different strategies such as giving up the goal with which stress is interfering or denying that the stress exists (Scheier, Weintraub, & Carver, 1986). Needless to say, the former strategies are often more effective than the latter, although *flexibility* seems to be the key: Problem-focused coping is associated with positive outcomes when the source of the stress is controllable, but with poorer outcomes when it is not (Lester, Smart, & Baum, 1994). In short, success in dealing with stress is best accomplished through the use of a wide variety of coping strategies. The Table presents a summary of strategies adopted by optimists and pessimists.

Some evidence also indicates that men and women differ in terms of their choice of coping strategies. Studies have reported that men tend to engage in more problem-focused coping and that females tend to seek social support from friends or to engage in emotion-focused strategies. These findings have been attributed to the different ways men and women are taught to cope with stress (Ptacek, Smith, & Dodge, 1994). A study by Porter and Stone (1995), however, seems to cast doubt on these conclusions. Their results instead indicate that men and women differ very little in the amount of stress they report or in the coping strategies they use to cope with the stress. They do differ, however, in terms of the content of their respective problems – men are more likely to report work-related problems, whereas women tend to report problems relevant to themselves, parenting, and interactions with others.

People from different cultures may also differ in this regard. In one study, Chang (1996) examined whether Asian students and students of European descent differed in terms of optimism, pessimism, and their preferences for coping strategies. The results indicated that the Asian students were more pessimistic and tended to use more problem avoidance and social withdrawal as coping strategies.

These and other findings indicate that individuals differ greatly in terms of their ability to deal with stress. Understanding the reasons for such differences can be of considerable practical value.

Optimists and pessimists employ different strategies in coping with stress. The strategies used by optimists seem to be more effective than those adopted by pessimists.

**Table 31: Optimists and Pessimists: Contrasting Strategies for Coping with Stress**

| *Strategies Preferred* | *Description* |
|---|---|
| **By Optimists** | |
| Problem-focused coping | Making specific plans for dealing with the source of stress; implementing such plans |
| Supressing competing activities | Suppressing from other activities until the problem is solved and stress is reduced |
| Seeking social support | Obtaining the advice of others; talking the problem over with others |
| **By Pessimists** | |
| Denial/distancing | Ignoring the problem or source of stress; refusing to believe that it exists or is important |
| Disengaging from the goal | Giving up on reaching the goal that is being blocked by the stressor |
| Focusing on the expression of feelings | Letting off steam instead of working on the problem directly |

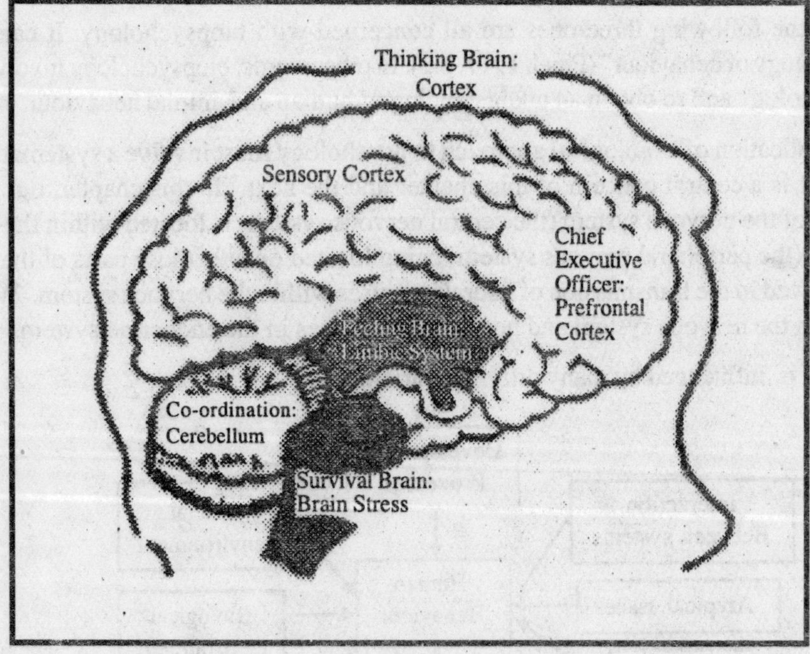


**Fig. 16 : Thinking Brain Cortex**

...✎...✎...✎

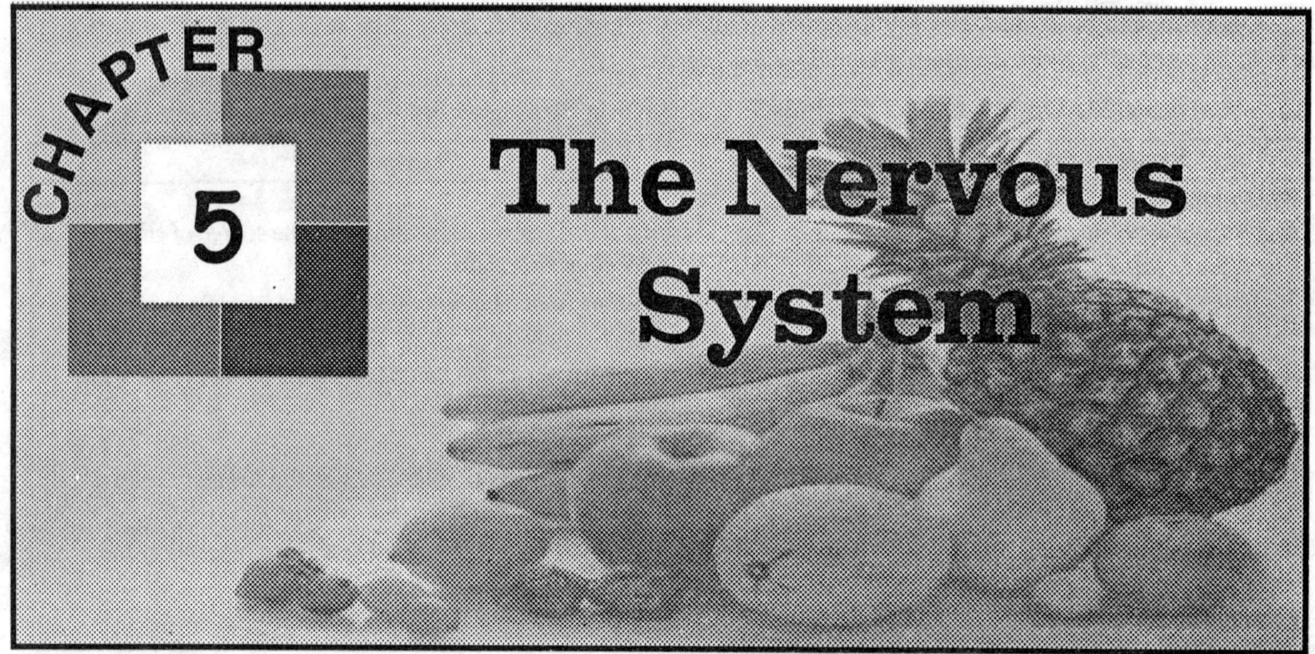


This chapter and the following three ones are all concerned with biopsychology. It can be defined as "the scientific study of the biology of behaviour" (Pinel, 1977, p.3). In other words, biopsychology involves using a biological approach to study psychology and to obtain an understanding of human and animal hebaviour.

Any serious application of a biological approach to psychology must involve a systematic focus on the brain and how it works. That is a central concern of this chapter and the next. In this chapter, our starting point is the nervous system. Some of the nervous system (the central nervous system) is located within the brain and the spinal cord, with the rest of it (the peripheral nervous system) being located outside those parts of the body. We will deal with the processes involved in the transmission of neural impulses within the nervous system. We will also discuss the relationship between the nervous system and hormonal processes in the endocrine system.

Human behaviour is influenced by many different variables:

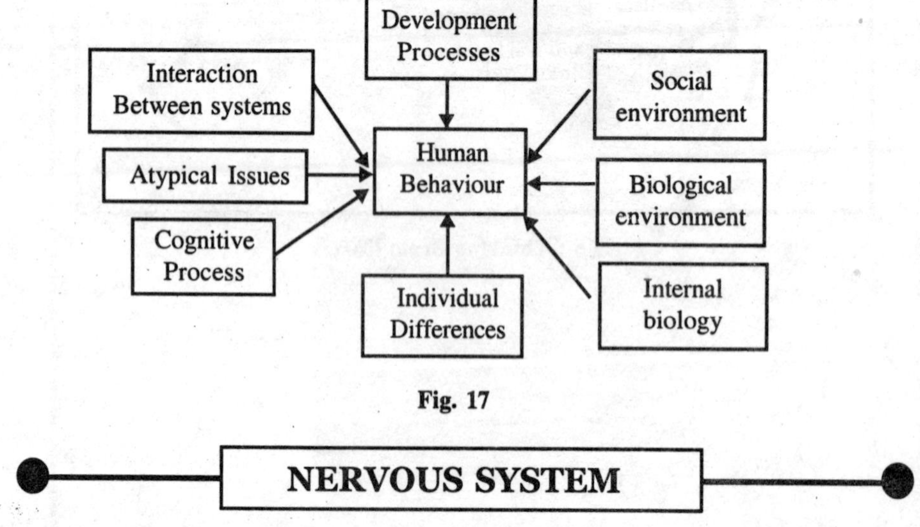


**Fig. 17**

## NERVOUS SYSTEM

The nervous system contains all of the nerve cells in the body. It is made up of between 15 and 20 billion neurons. Neurons are cells that are specialised to conduct electrical impulses, and they form the basic units of the nervous system. There are various kinds of neurons, but they all process certain key features.

- All cell body or soma which contains a nucleus.
- At one end of the cell body are dendrites, which conduct nerve impulses towards the soma.
- At the other end of the cell body is the avon, which conducts nerve impulses away from the soma and towards the terminal buttons.
- There is an outer layer or cell membrane, which allows electrically charged particles or ions to enter or to leave the neuron.
- Receptors, which are cells that respond to specific types of stimuli.

The nervous system is divided into two main sub-systems:

- Central nervous system: this consists of the brain and the spinal cord; it is protected by bone and by fluid circulating around it.
- Peripheral nervous system: this consists of all the other nerve cells in the body. It is divided into the somatic nervous system, which is concerned with voluntary movements of skeletal muscles (those attached to our bones), and the autonomic nervous system, which is concerned with involuntary movements of non-skeletal muscles (e.g. those of the heart).

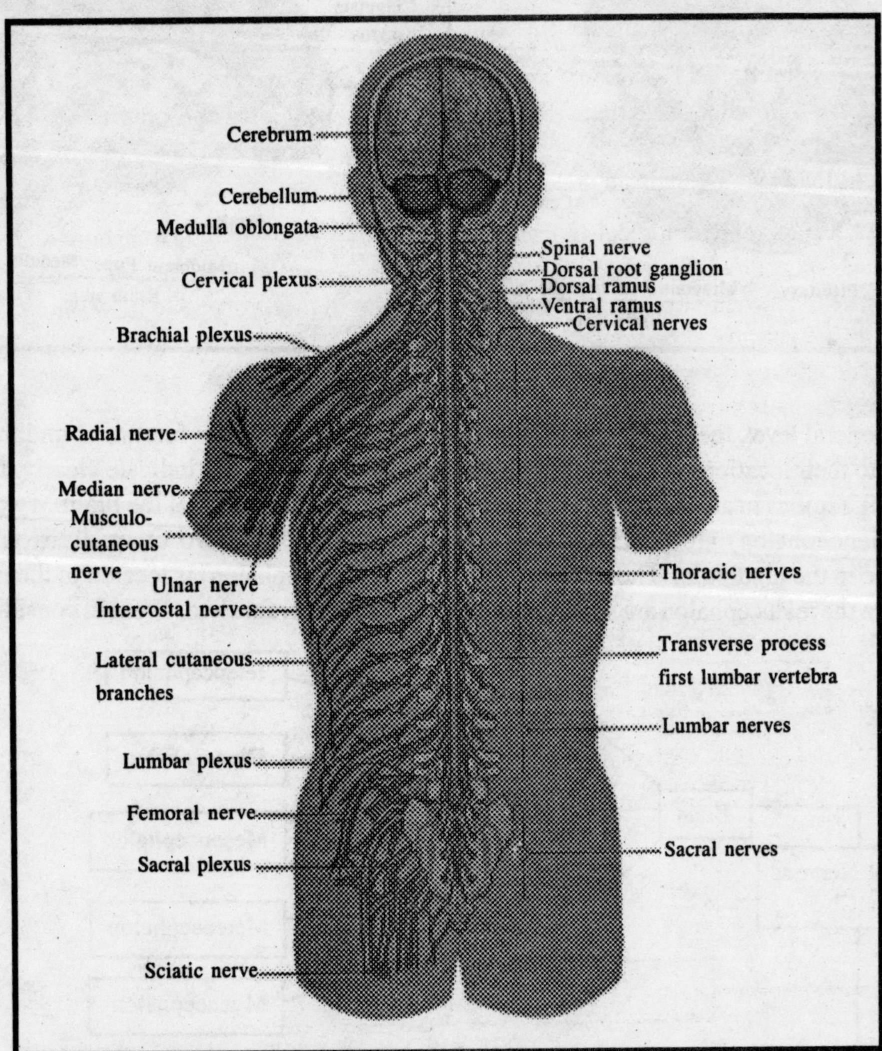


**Fig. 18 : The Human Body and Central and Peripheral Nervous System**

## Central Nervous System

We will start our coverage of the central nervous system with brain, and the then consider the spinal cord. The first point that needs to be made about the brain is its complexity. In order to understand the brain, we must learn about its structure and about the functions of the various parts. It has proved rather easier to study structure than function. Only recently have technological advances allowed us to identify the functions of different brain areas by observing the brain in action.

In view of the importance of the brain, it is not surprising that it is the most protected part of the body. Both the brain and the spinal cord are encased in bone and covered by protective membranes. In addition, there is what is known as the blood brain barrier. The blood cells in the brain are designed in such a way that they prevent several toxic or poisonous substances in the blood from gaining access to the brain.

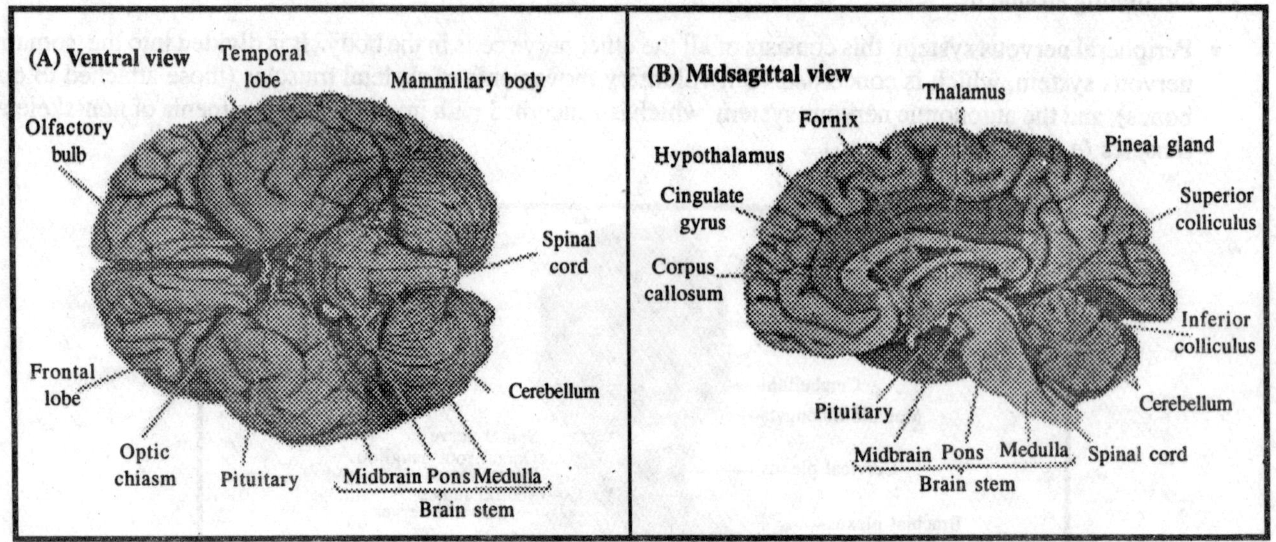


**Fig. 19 : The Brain (Two views)**

At the most general level, the brain can be divided into three main regions: forebrain; midbrain, and hindbrain. These terms refer to their locations in the employ's nervous system, and do not indicate clearly the relative position of the different brain regions in an adult. There are actually five major divisions of the brain. Two of these divisions (telencephalon; diencephalon) are contained within the forebrain, and two other divisions (myencephalon, myencepthalon) are in the hindbrain. The remaining division (mesencephalon) is located in the midbrain. The four divisions apart from the telencephalon are sometimes described as the brain stem. We will consider all five divisions of the brain in turn.

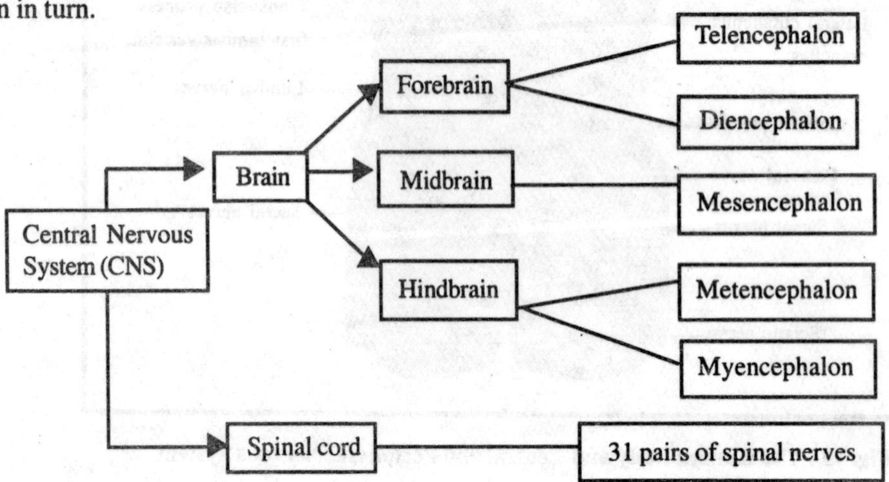


**Fig. 20 : The five divisions of the brain**

**Telencephalon:** This is easily the largest and the most important division of the human brain. It plays a crucial role in thinking, the use of language, perception and numerous other cognitive abilities. The two cerebral hemispheres are covered by a layer of tissue known as the cerebral cortex. The cerebral is deeply furrowed or grooved. The ridges between these furrow are known as gyri. By far the largest furrow is the longitudinal fissure that runs between the cerebral hemispheres. The two hemispheres are almost separate from each other, but are connected by the corpus callosum and a few other structures.

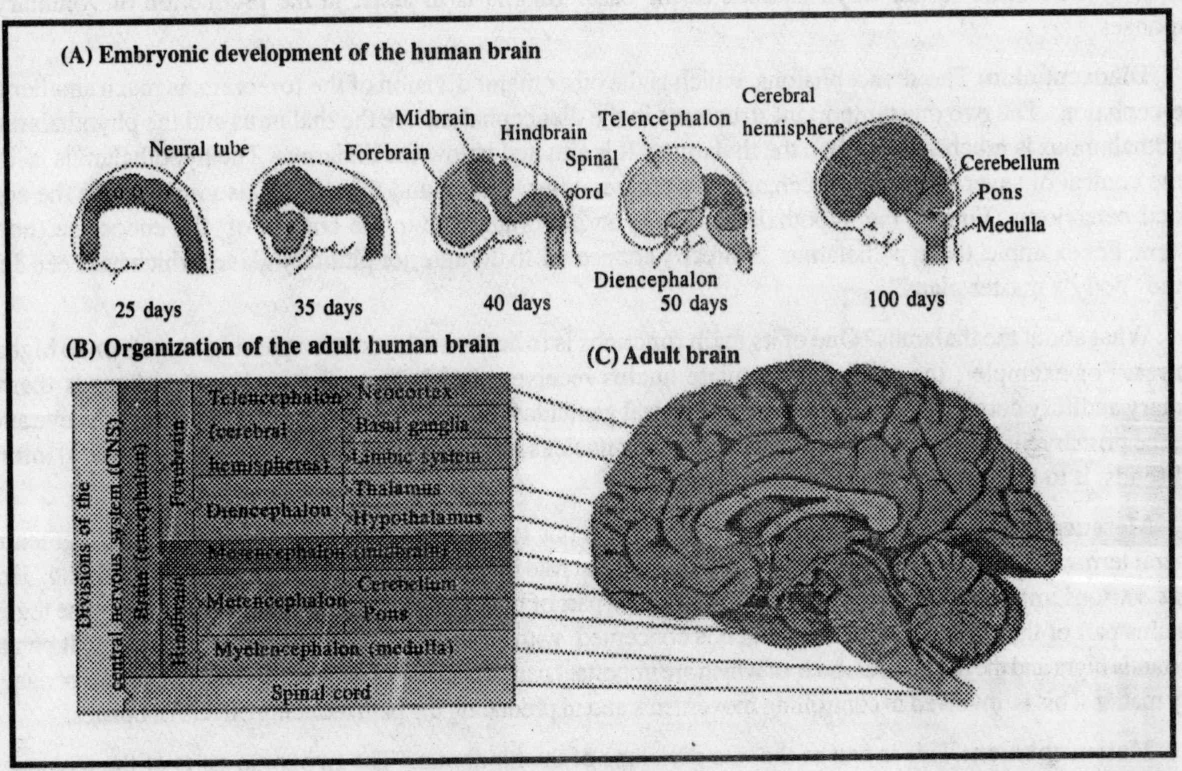


**Fig. 21 : Development of Human Brain**

**(A) Beginning with the primtive neural tube in the human embryo, the CNS develops rapidly and by day 50 of gestation, the six divisions of the CNS were apparent in the foetus.**

**(B) The organisation of the CNS (brain and spinal cord) is presented in the table and coded to match the divisions.**

Two of the most obvious features of each hemisphere are the central fissure or furrow and the lateral fissure. These fissures help to define the four lobes or areas of each hemisphere. The frontal lobes are at the front of each hemisphere, and their boundary is formed by the central and lateral fissures. The precentral gyri, which contain the motor cortex, are located in the frontal lobes. Behind the frontal lobe at the top of each hemisphere is the partietal lobe. The parietal lobes contain the postcentral gyri, which in turn contain the somatosensory cortex concerned with bodily sensations.

The other two lobes are the temporal lobe and the occipital lobe. The temporal lobes are behind the frontal lobes and underneath the parietal lobes. The superior temporal gyri, which contain the auditory cortex, are located in the temporal lobes. The occipital lobes are at the back of the cortex, and they are involved in visual processing.

About 90 per cent of the human cerebral cortex is neocortex (literally nex cortex), which consists of six layers. The neurons in the neocortex are mainly linked to other neurons within the same layer or within an adjacent layer. As a result, neocortex is organised in columns, with each column running vertically through the six layers. One part of the cortex that is not neocortex is the hippocampus, which is located in the temporal lobes. According to Pinel (1977, p.374), it is involved in the consolidation of long – term memories for spatal location, not their storage".

Some parts of the telencephalon are located mostly or entirely in the subcortical areas; they include the limbic system and the basal ganglia motor system. The limbic system consists of a number of structures including the amygdale, the septum, the hippocampus, the cingulated cortex, the fornix, and the mammiliary body. The main functions of the limbic systems are to regulate several kinds of motivated behaviour, including eating, aggression, avoidance behavour, and sexual behaviour and associated emotions such as anger and anxiety. The basal ganglia consist of the striatum, globus pillidus, and the amygdale (which is often regarded as part of this system as well as the limbuc system). One of the key functions of the basal ganglia is to assist in the production of voluntary motor responses.

**Diencephalon:** The diencephalons, which is the other major division of the forebrain, is much smaller than the tele-cephalon. The two most important structures in the diencephalons are the thalamus and the phyothalamus. The hypothalamous is much smaller than the thalamus. It is situated below the thalamus. The hypothalamus is involved in the control of several functions such as body temperature, hunger, and thirst. It is also involved in the control of sexual behaviours. Finally, the hypothalamus plays an important role in the control of the endocrine (hormonal) system. For example, the hypothalamus is directly connected to the anterior pituitary gland, which has been described as the "body's master gland".

What about the thalamus? One of its main functions is to act as a relay station passing signals on to higher brain centres. For example , the medical geniculate nuclus receives signals from the inner ear and sends them to the primary auditory cortex. In similar fashion, the lateral geniculate nucleus receives information from the eye and sends it to the primary visual cortex, and the ventral posterior nucleus receives somatosensory (bodily sensation) information and sends it to the primary somatosensory cortex.

**Mesencephalon:** The mesencephalon or midbrain has two major parts : the tectum and the tegmentum. In general terms, the mesencephalon plays a much less central role in human behaviour than does the forebrain. However, it has various important functions. The tectum forms a part of both the visual and auditory systems. The tegmentum contains part of the reticular formation, which is concerned with arousal and other functions (see later). It contains the substantia nigra and the red nucleus, both of which are important parts of the motor system. It also contains the periaqueductal grey matter. This is involved in controlling movements and in producing the pain reducing effects of opiates.

**Metencephalon:** This is one of the two divisions of the hindbrain. The two main parts of the metencephalon are the pons and the cerebellum. The pons contains part of the reticular formation concerned with consciousness, and the cerebellum is concerned with precise control of movements.

**Myencephalon:** The myencephalon is the other division of the hindbrain. It contains one important structure known as the medulla. Parts of the reticular formation are located in the medulla oblongata, and are involved in the control of respiration and regulation of the cardiovascular system. Most of the myencephalon is devoted to the function of relaying signals between the other divisions of the brain and the body.

**Spinal Cord:** The only part of the central nervous system we have not discussed is the spinal cord. It is a thin structure going from the base of the brain all the say down to the coccyx bone at the lower end of the back. The spinal cord is protected by 24 vertebrae or bony segments running from the neck to the lower back regions. There are holes in these vertebrae and the spinal cord passes through these holes.

The spinal cord consists of an inner area of grey matter and an outer area of white matter. White matter consists mainly of myelinated or sheathed axons, whereas grey matter consists of cell bodies and unmyelinated axons. The spinal cord contains 31 pairs of spinal nerves, with each nerve dividing into two roots as it approaches the spinal cord. The dorsal root, which is at the back, contains sensory neurons that assists in the transmission of sensory signals to the brain. The ventral root, which is at the front, contains motor neurons. These neurons are involved in the transmission of motor signals to the skeletal muscles and to the internal organs (e.g., stomach; heart).

**Peripheral nervous system:** The peripheral nervous system comprises all the nerve cells in the body that are not contained within the central nervous system. It consists of two parts : the somatic nervous system and the autonomic nervous system. The somatic nervous system is concerned with interactions with the external environment, whereas the autonomic nervous system is concerned with the body's internal environment.

The first issue to be discussed is the relationship between the peripheral nervous system and the central nervous system. Most of the nerves of the peripheral nervous system project from the spinal cord. Some spinal nerves are involved in receiving signals.

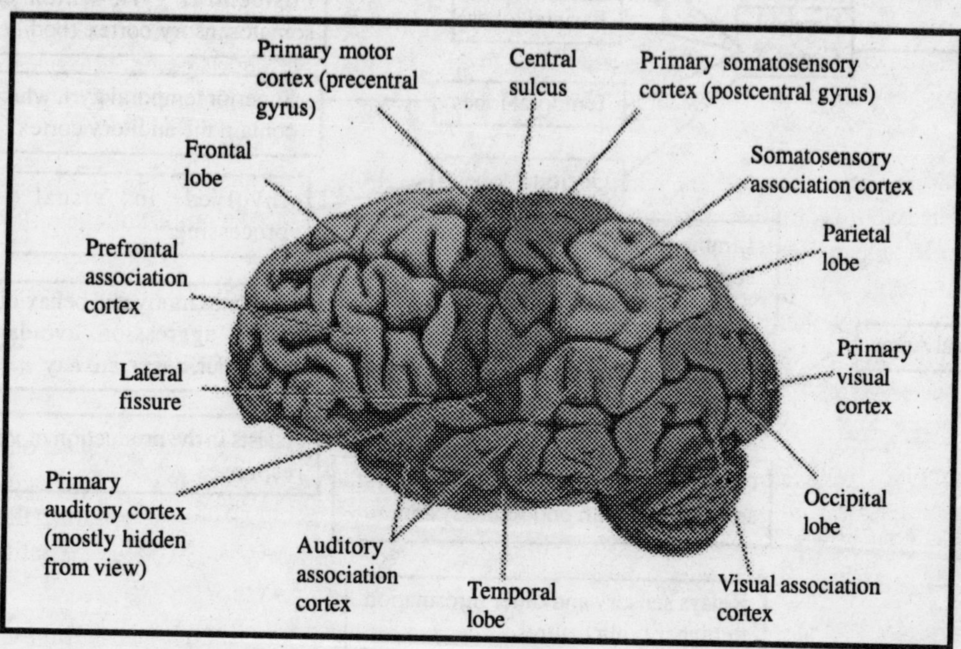


Fig. 22 : Parts of Brains

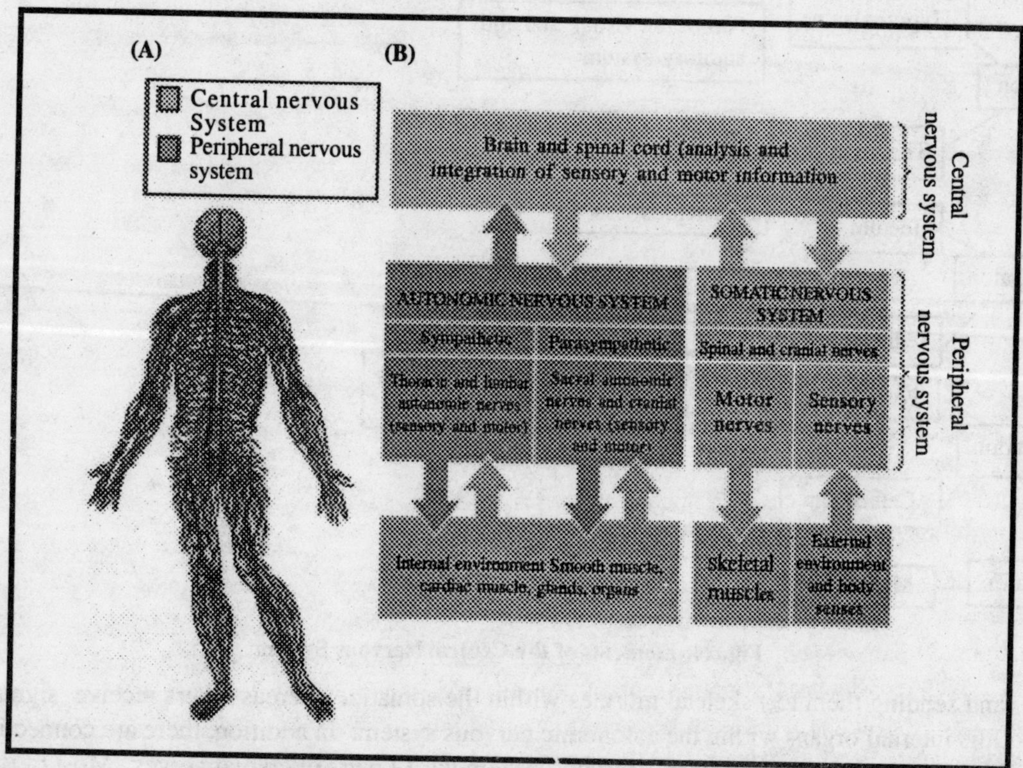


Fig. 23 : The central and peripheral nervous systems

(A) The brain and spinal cord, shown in the figure, comprise the central nervous system. The peripheral nervous system, connects all parts of the body to the central nervous system. (B) Organisation of the nervous system. The internal and external environments send sensory information by way of peripheral nerves to the CNS, the where neural circuits analyse and integrate the information before sending signals to regulate the muscles.

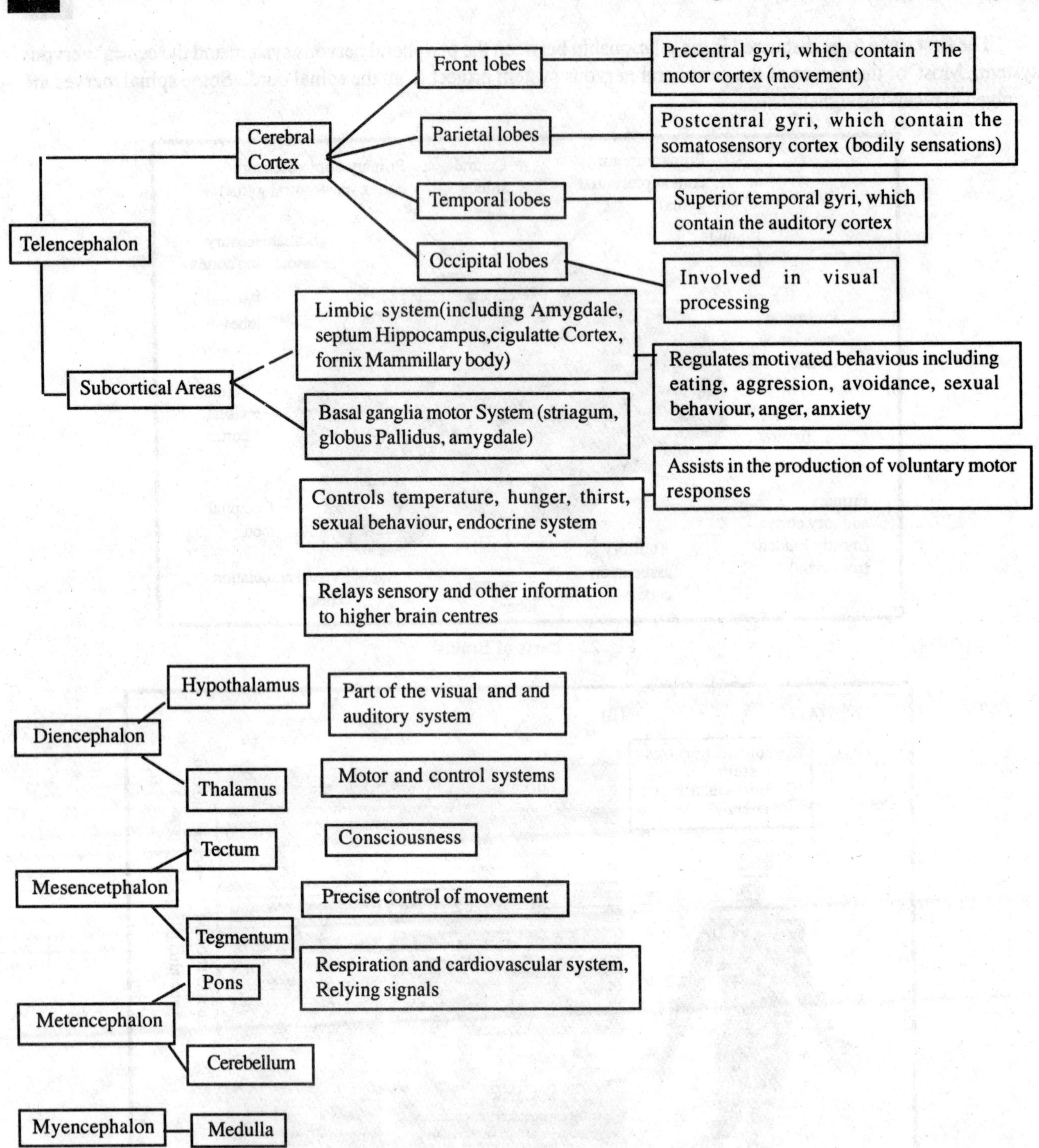


**Fig. 24: Elements of the Central Nervous System**

From (and sending them to ) skeletal muscles within the somatic, whereas others receive signals from (and send them to )the internal organs within the autonomic nervous system. In addition, there are connections between the central nervous system and the peripheral nervous system via 12 pairs of cranial nerves. Most of them contain both sensory and motor fibres and nearly all transmit signals to and from the head or neck. The major exception is the tenth or vagus nerve, which regulates the functioning of the abdominal and thoracic organs.

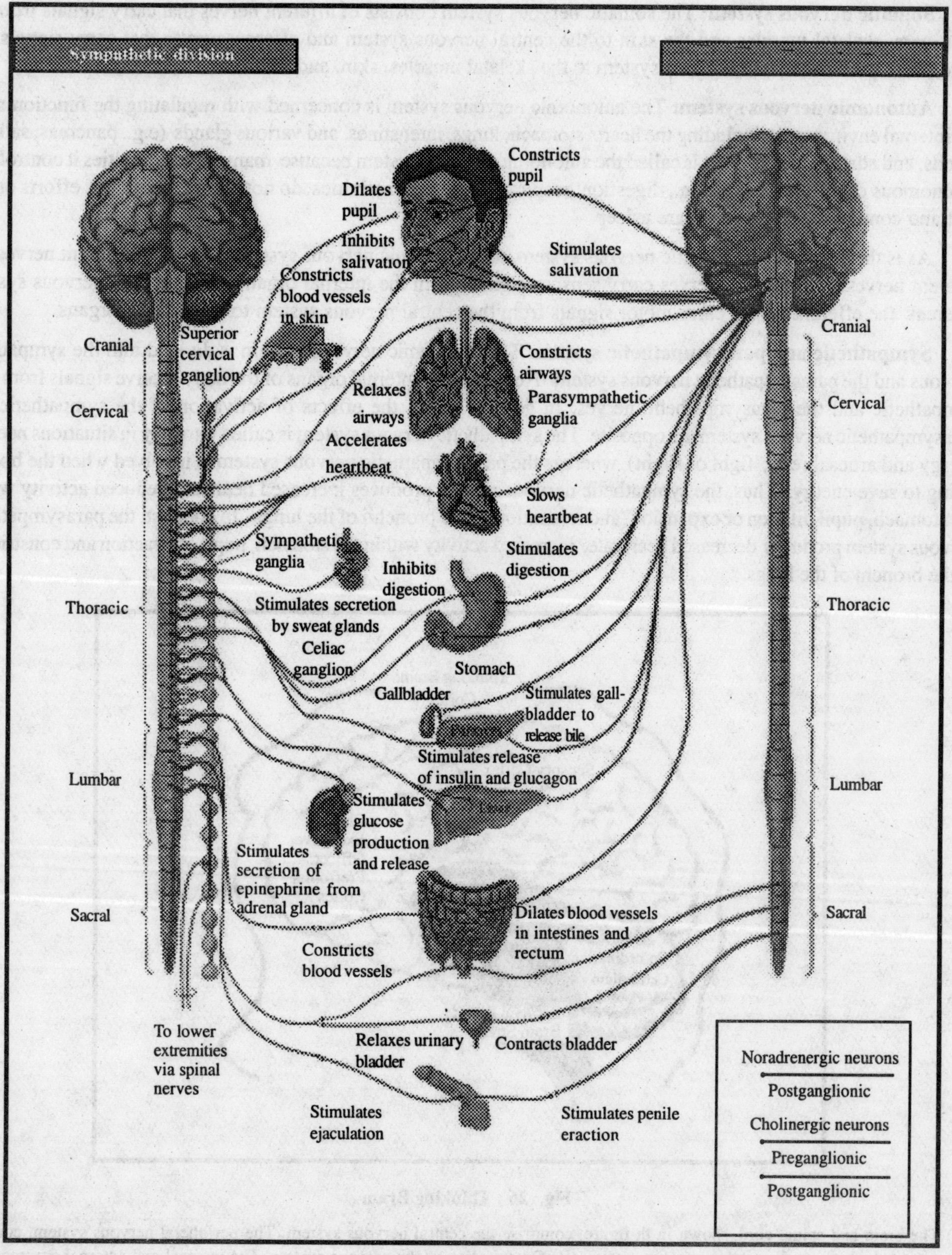


Fig. 25 : Nervous System

**Somatic nervous system:** The somatic nervous system consists of afferent nerves that carry signals from the eyes, ears, skeletal muscles and the skin to the central nervous system and efferent nerves that carry signals that have come from the central nervous system to the skeletal muscles, skin, and so on.

**Autonomic nervous system:** The autonomic nervous system is concerned with regulating the functioning of the internal environment, including the hearts stomach, lungs, intenstines, and various glands (e.g., pancreas; salivary glands, and adrenal medulla). It is called the autonomic nervous system because many of the activities it controls are autonomous or self regulating (e.g., digestion; respiration). These activities do not require conscious efforts on our part and continue even when we are asleep.

As is the case with the somatic nervous system, the autonomic nervous system consists of afferent nerves and efferent nerves. The afferent nerves carry sensory signals from the internal organs to the central nervous system, whereas the efferent nerves carry motor signals from the central nervous system to the internal organs.

**Sympathetic and parasympathetic system:** The autonomic nervous system is divided into the sympathetic nervous and the parasympathetic nervous system. Nearly all the internal organs of the body receive signals from both sympathetic and the parasympathetic nerves. In general terms, the effects of activation of the sympathetic and parasympathetic nervous system are opposite. The sympathetic nervous system is called into play in situations needing energy and arousal (e.g., fight or flight) whereas the parasympathetic nervous system is involved when the body is trying to save energy. Thus, the sympathetic nervous system produces increased heartrate, reduced activity within the stomach, pupil dilation or expansion, and relaxation of the bronchii of the lungs. In contrast, the parasympathetic nervous system produces decreased heart rate, increased activity within the stomach, pupil contraction and constriction of the bronchi of the lungs.

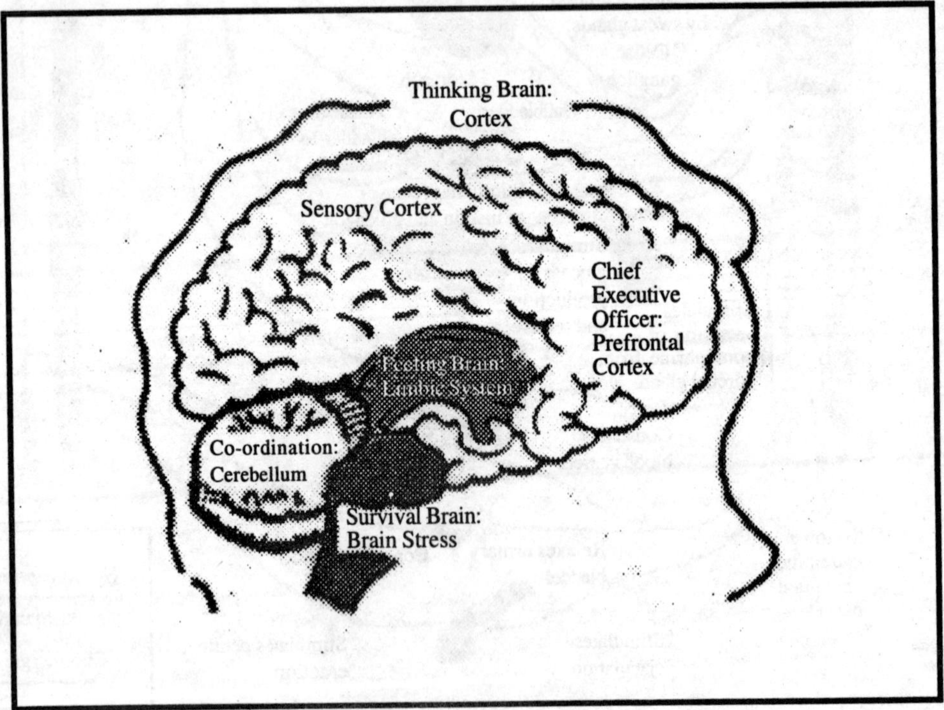


**Fig. 26 : Thinking Brain**

(A) The brain and spinal cord, shown in th figure, comprise the central nervous system. The peripheral nervous system, connects all parts of the body to the central nervous system. (B) Organisation of the nervous system. The internal and external environments send sensory information by way of peripheral nerves to the CNS, where neural circuits analyse and integrate the information before sending signals to regulate muscle.

In general terms the sympathetic nervous system tends to act as a whole, whereas the parasympathetic nervous system often affects only one organ at a time.

The level of activity in any of the internal organs depends on the relative level of activity within the sympathetic and parasympathetic nervous system. For example, heart rate will tend to be high if there is more sympathetic than parasympathetic nervous system activity, whereas, it will be low if parasympathetic activity is greater.

The sympathetic and parasympathetic nervous systems often operate in opposition to each other. However, as Atkinson et. al(1993) pointed, out there are some exceptions. For example, the sympathetic nervous system is very active in states of fear or excitement,

**Functions of the peripheral nervous system**

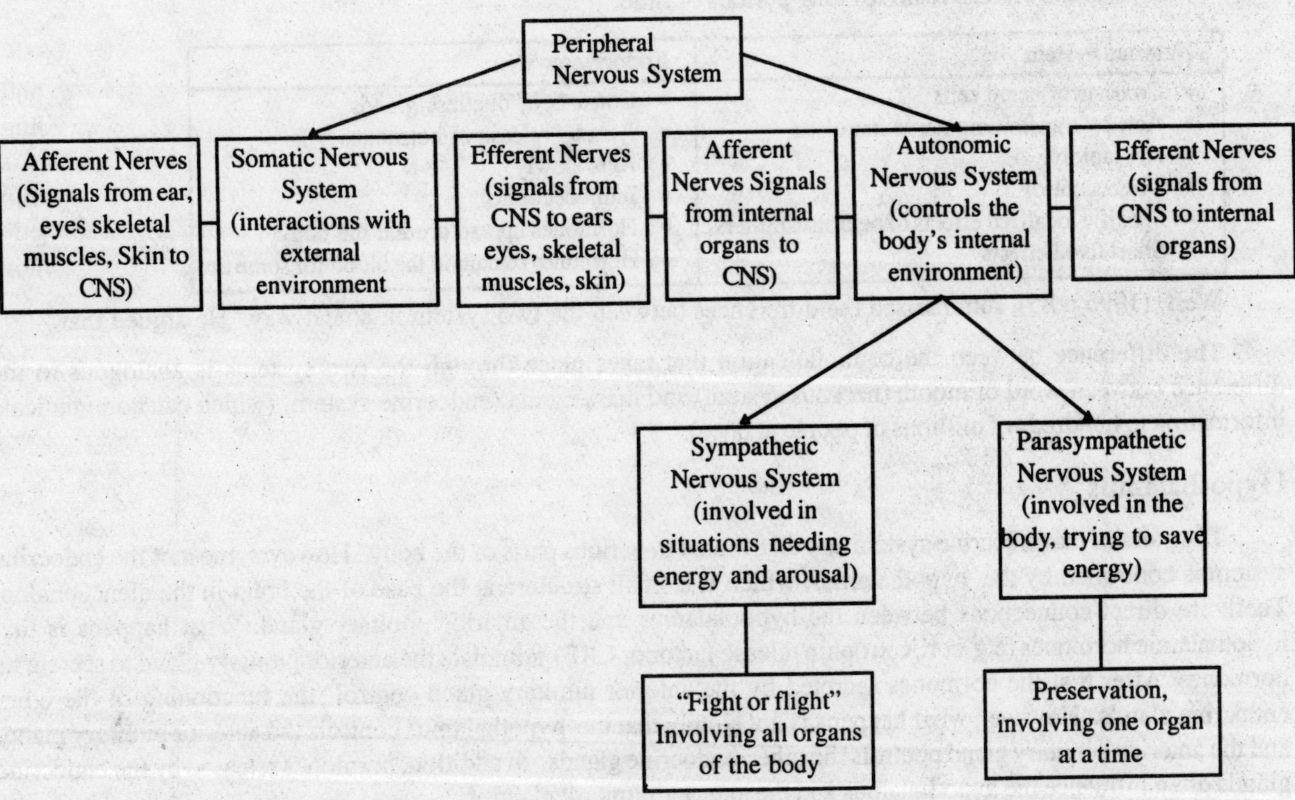


And yet parasympathetic activity can cause people who are fearful or excited to have an involuntary discharge of their bladder or bowels. Another example is sex in the male. Parasympathetic activity is required to obtain an erection, whereas sympathetic activity is needed for ejaculation.

## Endocrine System

The endocrine system consists of a number of glands, including the following, the pituitary gland, the thyroid glands the parathyroid gland, the adrenal gland, the pancrease, and the gonads. The endocrine system is not a part of the nervous system, but there are numerous interactions between the endocrine system and the peripheral nervous system. More specifically, the endocrine glands secrete hormones, which are chemical substances released into the bloodstream. The are so important that they have sometimes been described as "The messengers of life".

Hormones can have dramatic effects on our feelings and behaviour. However, they take some time to produce their effects because they are transmitted fairly slowly by the bloodstream. Endocrine glands are ductless glands. They can be contrasted with glands having ducts or passage along which substances such as sweat or tears travel to the surface of the body.

What are the main differences between the endocrine system and the nervous system ? Some of the key ones are as follows:

- The nervous system generally acts rapidly, whereas the endocrine system acts fairly slowly,.
- The nervous, control, the activities of the body directly by activating muscles and glands whereas the endocrine system exerts control indirectly via hormones circulating in the blood stream.
- Neurotransmitters (chemicals see later) in the nervous system have specific and highly localised effect, whereas hormones typical spread amount the body.
- Neurotransmitters in the nervous system generally have short lived effects.
- Neuroransmitters in the nervous system generally have have shrot – lived effects, whereas hormones can remain in the blood stream for long periods of time.

| Nervous System | Endocrine system |
|---|---|
| • Consists of nerve cells<br>• Acts by transmitting nerve impulses<br>• Act rapidly<br>• Direct control<br>• Specific localized effects of neurotrnsmitters<br>• Short lived effects | • Consists of ductless glands<br>• Acts by release of hormones<br>• Acts slowly<br>• Indirect control<br>• Hormones spread around the body<br>• Hormones remain in the blood for some time |

West (1996 p.85), summarised the differences between the two system in a neat way. He argued that –

The difference between the communication that takes place through the two systems is analogous to the difference between word of mouth (nervous system) and mass media (endocrine system) (which can communicate information to hundreds of millions of people at once).

## Hypothalamus

The parts of the endocrine system are distributed in various parts of the body. However, most of the endocrine system is controlled by the hypothalamus, which is a small structure at the base of the brain in the diencephalon. There are direct connections between the hypothalamus and the anterior pituitary gland. What happens is that hypothalamic hormones (e.g corticotrophin release factor or CRF) stimulate the anterior pituitary gland to secrete its hormones. After that the hormones secreted by the anterior pituitary gland control the functioning of the other endocrine glands. However, what happens is not simply that the hypothalamus controls the anterior pituitary gland, and the anterior pituitary gland controls the other endocrine glands. In addition, hormones released by the endocrine glands often influence the hypothalamus and the anterior pituitary gland.

## Pituitary Gland

In view of its importance, the pituitary gland, anterior and posterior, is often referred to as the "master gland" of the body. The anterior pituitary gland release several hormones, including the following : somatotrophic hormone, which stimulates the panc[illegible]s, adrenocortiotrophic hormone (ACTH), which stimulates the adrenal cortex, gonadotrophic hormones, which stimulate the sex glands, and thyrotrophic hormone, which stimulates the thyroid gland. The posterior pituitary gland is an outgrowth of the hypothalamus, and releases the following hormones: antidiuretic hormone, which stimulates the kidney to retain wat[illegible] in the body; and oxytocin hormone, which produces contractions of the smooth tissues of the uterus during labour.

Action of the pituitary gland

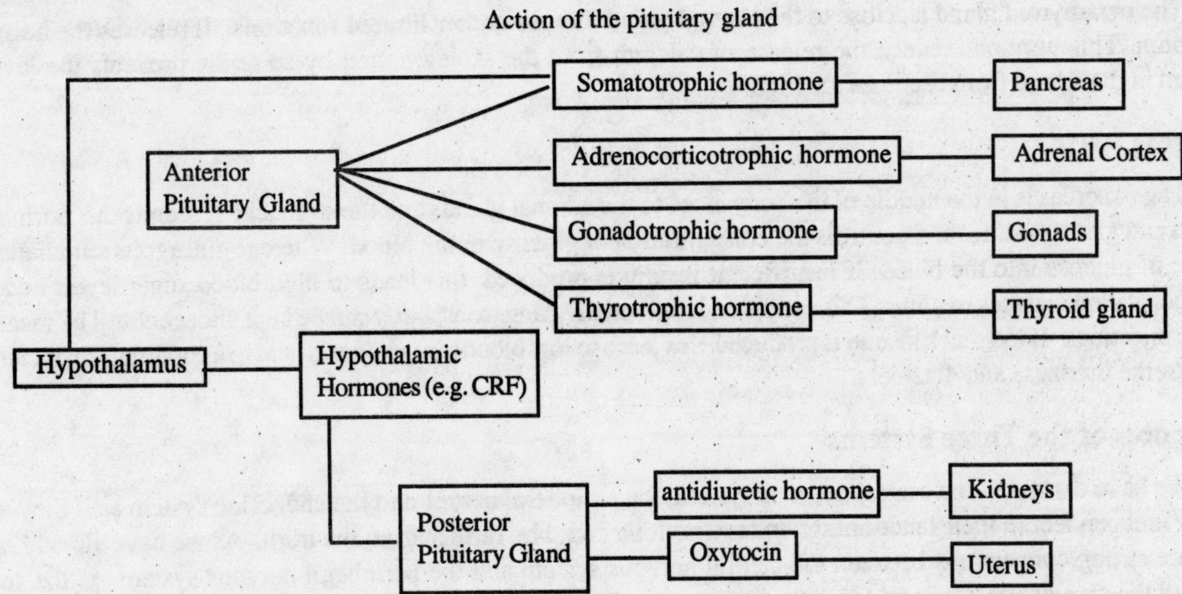


**Gonads:** The gonads are the sexual glands of the body. The male gonads are known as testes and the females gonads as ovaries. Activity in the gonads is stimulated by the luteinsing hormone from the anterior pituitary gland. The male gonads produce sperms, and the female gonads produce ova or eggs. The gonads also secrete various hormones.

**Androgens:** These are male sex steroid hormones, and are found in greater quantities in male gonads; the main androgen is testosterone, which affects sex drive.

**Estrogens:** a range of sex hormones produced mainly in the ovaries, the main one being estradiol; they influence the growth of breast, the development of the female genitals, and may affect sex drive.

**Gestagens:** a range of hormones produced by the ovaries, these hormones (of which progesterone is the main one) helps to facilitate and to maintain pregnancy.

Female primates have a reproductive cycle known as the menstrual cycle, whereas the females of other mammalian species have estrous cycles. Both kinds or reproductive cycle start with the anterior pituitary gland secreting gonadotrophic hormones. These hormones stimulate the growth of ovarian follicles which surround the ovum or egg. Estradiol is secreted as the ovarian follicles develop producing growth in the lining of the uterus.

**Adrenal Glands:** There are two adrenal glands, which are located just above the kidneys. Each gland consists of a central part known as the adrenal medulla, and an outer covering known as the adrenal cortex. The corticosteroids released by the adrenal medulla include adrenaline and noradrenaline, both of which produce increased arousal (e.g. increased heart rate and blood pressure). Their effects resemble those of the sympathetic nervous system. Indeed according to Green (1994 p. 107), adrenaline and noradreanaline "can almost be seen as part of the ANS (autonomic nervous system)".

The adrenal cortex releases the glucocorticoids including cortisone, hydrocortisone, and corticosterone. The glucocorticoids help to store protein and fat into more usable forms of energy. They also serve to suppress the immune system.

## Thyriod and Parathyroid Glands

The thyroid gland is situated just underneath the larynx, which contains the vocal cords. The thyroid gland produces the hormone thyroxin, which increase the body's metabolic rate. Someone whose thyroid gland produces too much thyroxin suffers weight loss and insomnia, whereas under production of that hormone causes obesity and general sluggishness.

The parathyroid gland is close to the thyroid gland. It has rathther limited functions. It releases the hormone calcitonin. This hormone reduce the release of calcium from the skeleton, and by so doing prevents the level of calcium in the blood from becomes too high.

## Pancreas

The pancreas is in the middle of the body close to the adrenal glands and the stomach. It secrets the hormones: insulin and glucagons. Insulin controls the concentration of glucose in the blood. Whereas glucagons stimulates the release of glucose into the blood. If insufficient insulin is produced, this leads to high blood sugar levels and to a condition called diabetes mellitus. This condition is potentially dangerous, but it can be kept under control by means of insulin injections. If too much insulin is produced, this leads to low blood – sugar levels, and to a condition characterised by extreme tiredness and dizziness.

## Influences of the Three Systems

We have discussed the central nervous system, the peripheral nerves and the endocrine system as if they were largely independent in their functioning. In fact, nothing could be further from the truth. As we have already seen there are strong connections between the central nervous system and the peripheral nervous system via the spinal cord and the cranial nerves. In addition there are neuronal pathways from the hypothalamous in the central nervous system to parts of the autonomic nervous system within the brain stem. The hypothalamus also plays a central role in determining activity within the endocrine system.

It is probably correct to say that all three systems are nearly always involved in determining our behaviour. The involvement of all three systems is especially clear with respect to motivation, emotion and stress, all of which are discussed in Chapter 6, In this chapter we will consider combined influences of the three systems in connection with the important phenomenon of homeostatasis. This refers to the body's tendency to maintain a fairly constant internal state that permits cells to function and to live.

## Homeostasis

The French physiologist, Claude Bernard noticed that the body's internal environment generally remains almost constant in spite of large changes in the external environment. This observation led to much work into the phenomenon of homeostasis. One of the most obvious examples of homeostasis is body temperature, which in humans is normally very close to 98.6°F or 37°C This is the case is spite of the fact that the external temperature in the United Kingdom can vary by as much as about 54°F or 30°C between winter and summer.

There are numerous other forms of homeostasis. Including the body's water supply, its oxygen concentration and its concentration of nutrient substances of glucose in the blood steam needs to be between 60 and 90 milligrams per 100 cubic centimetres of blood. If it falls below this range, then coma and death can result. If it consistently, exceeds this range then diabetes or some other disease is likely to follow. In a similar fashion, death can occur if our body temperature remains considerably above or below its normal level for several hours, or if it was totally deprived of water for four or five days.

As Carlson (1994), pointed out the regular mechanisms within the body that allow homeostasis to occur all involve four key features.

1. A system variable : this is the characteristic (e.g., temperature) that needs to be regulated
2. A set point : the ideal or most appropriate value of the system variable.
3. A detector : the actual or current value of the system variable needs to be assessed.
4. A correctional mechanism : the serves to reduce or eliminate the discrepancy between the actual value and the ideal value.

Homeostatic mechanism for regulating body temperature

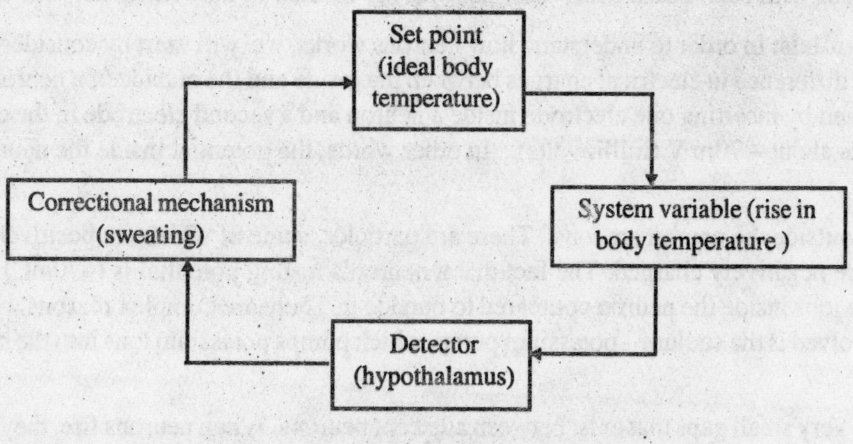


Fig. 27

All these regulatory mechanisms are present in the central heating systems, which are designed to regulate temperature. The thermostat is set to the chosen temperature and it detects deviations between the actual and chosen temperatures,. When the temperature falls too low, the boiler of the central heating system is activated to restore the chosen temperature.

Here we will focus mainly on the ways in which regulating mechanism produce homeostasis for body temperature. This is achieved in different ways in different species, and we will focus mainly on warm blooded animals including the human. Specific parts of the hypothalamus (which is in the central nervous system) seem to be involved in detecting the current value of blood temperature, which is usually closely related to body temperature. The hypothalamus is also involved in initiating corrective action.

## Body Temperature

How does the hypothalamus regulate body temperature ? It contains receptor cells responding to the temperature of the fluids surrounding the brain. Evidence for this was obtained by Magoun et.al(1938) Cats whose anterior hypothalamus was heated artificially reacted as if they were too hot by panting and by vasodilation (widening of the skin's capillaries) even though the rest of their bodies were below normal temperature.

Detailed research suggests that the anterior hypothalamus plays a role in cooling the body down, whereas the posterior hypothalmaus is involved in heating the body up. For example, Andersson, Grant and Larsson (1956), found in goats that electrical stimulation of the anterior hypothalamus caused vasodilation and panting. In contrast, destruction of that area caused death by overheating.

The hypothalamus influences the autonomic nervous system in the regulation of body temperature. The parasympathetic nervous system is activated when the body temperature is too high. It is involved in producing sweating or panting which causes heat loss by evaporation. It also produces vasodilation which sends warm blood to the skin and causes heat loss by radiation. The sympathetic nervous system is activated when the body temperature is too low. There is vasoconstriction, in which there is narrowing of the skin's capillaries. This conserves heat by removing blood from the cold periphery of the body. The sympathetic nervous system is also involved in producing shivering, in some species, it also causes the fur to stand and so creates additional protection against the cold. The goose pimples were experienced in cold weather are the human equivalent, but are of no use to us because members of the human species are no longer covered in fur!

Regulation of body temperature can include deciding to take various actions, and this involves parts of the central nervous system within the telencephalon. If we are too cold, we often put on extra clothes such as a sweater or coat, or we become more active. On the other hand, if we are too hot, we may take off some clothes, have a cold drunk, or go for a swim. Afferent neurons transmit signals from receptors that detect events inside or outside the body. Motor or efferent neurons transmit signals from the brain to the body's musculature or glands. Finally, inter-neurons connect neurons with each other. Most inter-neurons are located in the central nervous system.

**Membrane potentials:** In order to understand how neurons works, we will start by considering the membrane potential, which is the difference in electrical charges between the inside and the outside of a neuron. The membrane potential can be assessed by inserting one electrode inside a neuron and a second electrode in the extracellular fluid. The resting potential is about – 70m V (milliovolts). In other words, the potential inside the neurons is 70m V less than outside it.

Both inside and outside the neuron are ions. These are particles, some of which are positively charged and the remainder of which are negatively charged. The fact that a neuron's resting potential is (–70mC) is due to a higher proportion of negative ions inside the neuron compared to outside it. There are complex reasons why this should be so. Part of what is involved is the sodium – potassium pump, which pumps potassium ions into the neuron and sodium ions out.

Synapses are the very small gaps that exist between adjacent neurons. When neurons fire, they release chemicals or neurotransmitters which cross the synapses and affect the receptors on the adjacent neurons. These neurotransmitters either increase or decrease the membrane potential of the adjacent . If they increase the membrane potential, they reduce the likelihood of the receptive neuron firing.

So far we have been talking as if the receptor area of each neuron only has a single synapse. In fact, there are generally thousands of synapses associated with the receptor area of each neuron. What determines whether or not any given neuron fires. According to Pinel (1977, p.86), it depends "on the balance between the excitatory and inhibitory signals reaching its axon hillock – the conical (cone-shaped) structure at the junction between the cell body and the axon". If the membrane potential is reduced to – 65m V or less, then the neuron fires. This consists of an action ptential which is generated at the axon hillock. It is a brief electrical and chemical event, and it is always the same size and duration. More specifically, an action potential lasts for about 1 millisecond, and it reverses the membrane potential from about – 65m V to about +50m V.

Pinel (1997), compared the firing of a neuron to the firing of a gun. In both cases, there is a threshold that has to be reached, sufficient stimulation by other neurons or sufficient pressure on the trigger. In both cases, exceeding the threshold does not increase the size between a strong and a weak stimulus. When a strong stimulus is presented, far more neurons fire, and they fire more frequently, than is the case when weak stimulus is presented.

We will now discuss in a little more detail some of the process that occur during an action potential. What happens initially is that the sodium and potassium ion channels open. This causes sodium ions to enter the neuron, followed very shortly by potassium ions being driven out of the neuron. After about 1 millisecond , the sodium ion channels close, followed by the potassium channels. The closure of these channels causes the action potential to come to an end. However there is a period of 1 or 2 millisecond after the start of an action potential before a neuron can fire again , this is known as the absolute refractory period.

Many neurons in the nervous system have axons that are covered in a fatty sheath known as myelin, whereas other neurons do not. In addition, there are numerous neurons that do not have axons and so do not produce action potentials. Myelinated axons have gasps in the myelin sheath known as the Nodes of Ranvier, and action potentials jump from node to node along the axon. Action potential travels much faster along myelinated axons than along unmyelinated axons, with respective speeds of 80 – 100 metres per second versus only 2 or 3 metres per second.

**Synaptic transmission:** Most synapses are directed synapses, meaning that the site of the neurotransmitter release from one neuron is very close to the site of neurotransmitter reception at another neuron. Neurotransmitters initiate reactions in the postsynaptic neuron by binding to its receptors. Most neurotransmitters are able to bind to various types of receptors, but the nature of receptor response varies from one type to another. It is possible to think of neurotransmitters as keys and of receptors as locks, there has to be a fit between the two for anything to happen.

There are two basic types of receptor (Pinel, 1997).

1. Ion channel linked receptors; neurotransmitters often have the effect of opening sodium channels ( producing excitatory postsynaptic inhibitory postsynaptic potentials); other neurotransmitters close ion channels.
2. G-protein linked receptors, the effects of neurotransmitters on these receptors (compared to ion-channel linked receptors) are "slower to develop, longer-lasting more diffuse, and move varied" (Pinel 1977, p.95). In some G-protein linked receptors, neurotransmitters produce excitory or inhibitory postsynaptic potentials. In others, they produce a chemical known as a second messenger that can affect the postsynaptic neuron in various ways.

There are two mechanisms that prevent neurotransmitters from having as long – lasting effect on synapses. First, there is re-uptake, in which neurotransmitters are drawn back into the presynaptic neuron. Second, there is enzymatic degradation. What happens here is that the neurotransmitter is degraded or broken apart in the synapses by the action of chemicals known as enzymes.

**Neurotransmitters:** There are five classes of neurotransmitters, one of which is a large-molecule and four of which are small-molecules. The class of large-molecule transmitters consists of neuropeptides. Some neuropeptides are neuromodulators, meaning that they affect the sensitivity of neurons to signals but do not themselves send signals to other neurons. Endorphins are among the most important neuropeptides. They play a significant role in activating the systems involved in pain suppression and in pleasure. Drugs such as heroin, morphine, and opium affect the same receptors as the endorphins.

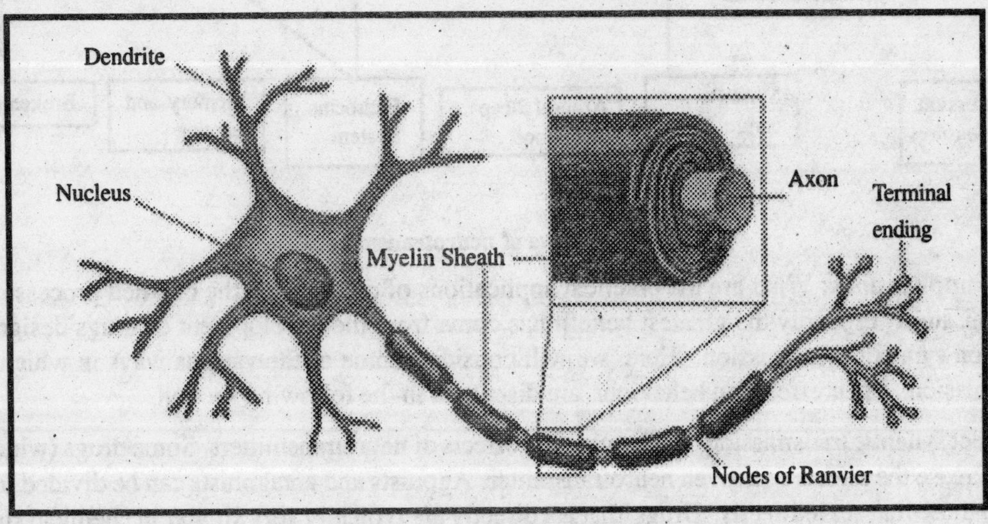


**Fig. 28 : Brain and Nervous System**

The four classes of small molecule neurotransmitters are as follows : the amino acids, the monoamines; acetycholine and the soluble gases.

**Amino acids:** Two of the most commonly found amino acids in the central nervous systems of mammals are gamma aminobutyric acid (GABA) and glutamate. GABA acts as an inhibitory neurotransmitter, whereas glutamate acts as an excitatory neurotransmitter.

**Monoamines:** There are four monoamine neurotransmitters : dopamine; serotonin; adrenaline; and noradrenaline. All these neurotransmitters are important. It has been argued that dopamine and serotonin are both involved in schizophrenia. Degeneration of the dopamine – releasing neurons in the substantia nigra plays a part in causing Parkinson's disease, a disorder involving poor muscular control. Serotonin is involved in the regulation of arousal, sleep, and mood. Adrenaline and noradrenaline are involved in emotion and in the workings of the Endocrine System.

**Acetylcholine:** Acetylcholine is the only neurotransmitter in its class. It is found at numerous synapses within the nervous system, including those in the central nervous system and the autonomic nervous system. Acetylchloline is involved in learning and memory. Old rats who received neural transplants containing acetylchlone showed great improvements in learning ability (Bjorklund & Lindvall, 1986).

**Soluble gases:** The soluble gas transmitters were discovered more recently than most of the other neurotransmitters. They include carbon monoxide and nitric oxide. These neurotransmitters work for a very short period of time, because they are rapidly broken down and produce other chemicals or second messengers.

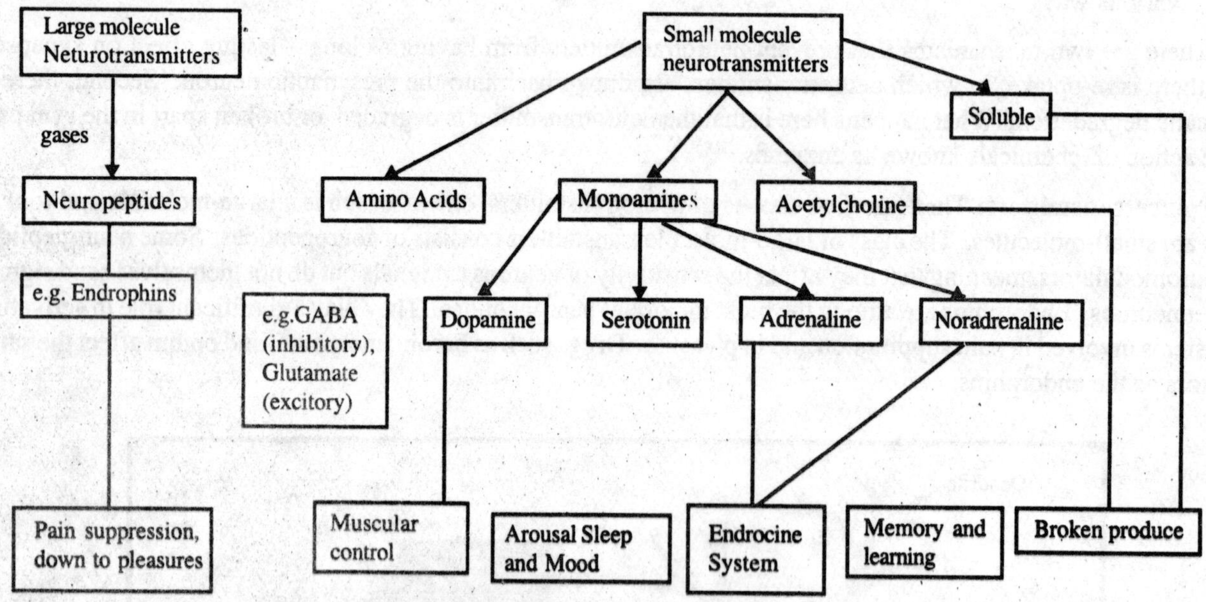


**Fig. 29 : The five of neurotransmitters**

**Practical applications:** What are the practical applications of discovering the detailed processes involved in synaptic transmission? Probably the greatest benefit has come from the development of drugs designated to have certain effects on synaptic transmission. Here, we will consider some of the various ways in which drugs affect synaptic transmission. Their effects on behaviour are discussed in the following section.

Drugs affect synaptic transmission by changing the effects of neurotransmitters. Some drugs (which are known as agonists), increase the effects of a given neurotransmitter. Agonists and antagonists can be divided into those that act directly and those that act indirectly. Drugs that act directly are typically very similar in chemical structure to the neurotransmitter, and like the neurotransmitters they affect synaptic receptors. Direct acting agonists stimulate synaptic receptors, whereas direct acting antagonists prevent the neurotransmitter from stimulating synaptic receptors. Heroin is an example of a direct acting agonist, and the depressant drug, chlorpromazine is an example of a direct-acting antagonist (Cardwell et.al., 1996).

Indirectly acting drugs also change the effects of neurotransmitters, but they do not do so by affecting synaptic receptors. Cardwell et. al, gives examples of indirect-acting drugs. The stimulant drug amphetamine is an indirect acting agonist that increases the release of neurotransmitter substance from the presynaptic terminal. Parachlorophenylalanine (PCP) is an indirect antagonist. It produces a large reduction in the product of the neurotransmitters serotonin by inhibiting one of the enzymes needed to synthesise serotonin.

The effects of neurotransmitters and drugs on synaptic transmission are much more complex in some ways than has been indicated so far. Pinel (1997), argued that neurotransmitter action often involves seven distinct stages or processes (some of which we have discussed already):

1. Neurotransmitter molecules are synthesised under enzymal control.
2. Neurotransmitter molecules are stored in vesicles (cavities).
3. Any molecules that leak from vesicles are destroyed by enzymes.
4. Action potentials cause vesicles to release the neurotransmitter molecules into the synapse.
5. Neurotransmitter molecules bind with presynaptic receptors and inhibit additional neurotransmitter release.
6. Neurotransmitter molecules bind to postsynaptic receptors.
7. Neurotransmitters molecules cease to affect postsynaptic receptors via re-uptake or enzymatic degradation.

As you can imagine, the fact that several processes are involved in neurotransmitter action means that there are several ways in which drugs can change neurotransmitter action. Pinel (1997), identified six mechanism of agonistic drug action and five mechanisms of antagonistic drug action. Some agonists increase the synthesis of neurotransmitter molecules (Stage 3), or block the inhibition of neurotransmitter release (Stage 5), or block the processes of re-uptake or enzymatic degradation (Stage 7). Some antagonists destroy synthesising enzymes (Stage 1), and others increase the leakage of neurotransmitter molecules from vesicles or cavities (Stage 3), or increase the inhibition of neurotransmitters release (Stage 5) or block the binding of neurotransmitter molecules to postsynaptic receptors (Stage 6).

**Pinel's seven stages of neurotransmitter action**

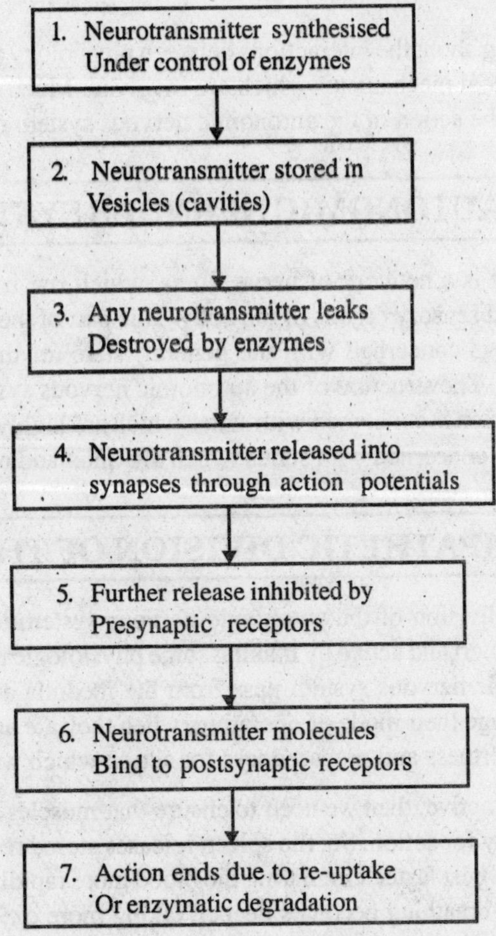

CHAPTER 6

# Arousal and Stress

In order to understand something about the interactions between physiology and emotional experience, we need to begin by looking at the physiological mechanisms which are involved. Much of our experience of stress, and of negative emotions, is influenced by the action of the autonomic nervous system referred to as arousal.

## THE AUTONOMIC NERVOUS SYSTEM

The autonomic nervous system is a network of nerve fibres, which run from the spinal cord and the lower regions of the brain to the internal and sensory organs of the body. This part of the nervous system is rather different from the central nervous system. It is concerned with the general 'state' of the body, rather than with specific behaviours like talking or movement. The structure of the áutonomic nervous system, or ANS, reflects two distinct types of 'state'. The sympathetic division is concerned with states which are highly activated and prepared for action, while the parasympathetic division is concerned with states which are quiet and restorative.

## THE SYMPATHETIC DIVISION OF THE ANS

Activation of the sympathetic division of the autonomic nervous system is often given the general term of arousal. It makes the individual more alert and active by making some physiological changes in the body. Fibres of the sympathetic division of the autonomic nervous system pass from the medulla and spinal cord to the viscera (the internal organs of the body), and change their mode of operating, when they are activated in this way. Each of these changes contributes to the state of alertness and preparedness for action which we loosely call 'arousal'.

If we are preparing to be highly active, then we need to ensure that muscles are strong and well-supplied with the blood sugars and oxygen necessary for action. So, the spleen releases stored red blood cells so that the blood can carry more oxygen; the heart begins to best faster, circulating the blood more rapidly round the body and replenishing the oxygen supply more rapidly; and breathing becomes deeper, taking more oxygen into the lungs. The digestive system also changes its mode of operation, so that sugar is metabolised much more quickly, to provide an instant energy supply, but foods which require longer-term digestion, like proteins and fats, take longer.

These changes are sometimes described as the *fight or flight response.* In evolutionary terms, it is a response which maximises an animal's chances of survival when danger threatens, by allowing the animal to produce as much energy as possible, to help it either fight or to run away. In that section, the body would need, to be prepared for tissue damage, so additional blood platelets, which help the blood to clot, are produced and distributed throughout the bloodstream, and the brain produces endorphins: neurotransmitters which block out immediate feelings of pain resulting from injuries.

There are number of other features of the fight or flight response, including an increase in the rate of sweating – one of the body's cooling mechanisms – helping to deal with the heat produced by active muscles. In a state of arousal, we also become more alert, the pupils of the eyes dilate, and perceptual thresholds are lowered, producing increased receptivity to external stimuli. Each of these changes helps the body to produce, and utilise, physical energy. Arousal responses are not always as dramatic as the fight or flight reaction, though – we can become mildly, as well as extremely, aroused.

*The physiological changes involved in arousal are stimulated by neural impulses from the sympathetic division of the autonomic nervous system, but they are maintained by the action of the endocrine system.* This is a series of glands which release hormones into the blood-stream, thereby helping to maintain consistent states within the body. *The hormones which are concerned with stress arousal are released from the pituitary and adrenal glands, following stimulation from the sympathetic nerve fibres of the ANS.*

The pituitary gland releases *glucocorticoids*, which are concerned with the digestive and tissue repair functions – converting fat stores to glucose and suppressing the immune response – so physiological studies of stress reactions often involve measuring the amount of glucocorticoids in the blood or urine. *Acting on chemical instructions from the hypothalamus, the pituitary gland also releases a 'messenger hormone', called adrenocorticotrophic hormone (ACTH), which stimulates the adrenal gland to release adrenaline, into the bloodstream. Adrenaline is mainly concerned with maintaining levels of muscular activity and an adequate blood supply, so an injection of adrenaline will produce an almost instant increase in heart rate, blood pressure and sweating.*

## The Parasympathetic Division of the ANS

The activities of the parasympathetic division of the ANS are much less dramatic than those of the sympathetic divisions. Perhaps, as an inevitable consequence, they have received less attention from researchers. *Parasympathetic nerve fibres run from the medulla and the brain stem to the internal organs,* and stimulation from many of them has an effect which seems to counteract that of the sympathetic division, although it is not an exact mirror-image.

For many practical purposes, though, the two responses can be seen as opposing actions. For example: where sympathetic action dilates the pupil of the eye, parasympathetic action constricts it; where heart rate increases by sympathetic action, it decreases by parasympathetic action, where effective long-term digestion is inhibited by sympathetic action, parasympathetic action stimulates it, and so on. Essentially, *the parasympathetic division of the ANS is concerned with restoring the body's resources: stimulating tissue repair and storing sugars as fats for future energy needs.*

Although, the two divisions are in operation at different times, *it seems that the parasympathetic division automatically becomes activated as intense activity in the sympathetic division dies down.* So, for example, an intensive, exercising session would produce activation of the sympathetic division, but this would then be followed by a quiescent period which involves parasympathetic activity. But the parasympathetic division of the ANS is active at other times too: during the relaxed period which many people experience after eating a full meal.

## Arousal

*The concept of arousal relates to the activities of the ANS and its effects on human behaviour. As we have seen, the two divisions of the ANS – the sympathetic and parasympathetic divisions – have different effects. The function of the sympathetic division (generally speaking), is to prepare the body for action, whereas the parasympathetic division (generally speaking), is concerned with resting, and storing energy for future use.*

Psychological interest in arousal has tended to centre on the relationship between a physiologically aroused condition, and the experience of emotion. *Periods of high physiological activity, such as that which happens when we take vigorous exercise, are accompanied by high levels of adrenaline and by all the other symptoms of the generalised arousal state. But aroused states also accompany the emotional states of fear and anger.* Some evidence suggests that the sensation of arousal appears to interact reflexively with these emotions, with each enhancing the other. We will look at some of this in more detail later in this chapter, when we explore some of the theories of emotion which have been put forward by psychologists.

## Measuring Arousal

As we have seen, changes in autonomic arousal levels produce a number of physiological changes. These are readily detectable and can be measured in several different ways. The most visible changes, of course, concern the changes in facial colour, which occurs as a result of emotion –.pallor, particularly in the ease of fear, or flushine, in the case of anger or annoyance. There are other visible signs of arousal too, which are familiar to most people, such as muscle trembling and changes in the breathing rate.

*Signs of arousal, though, are highly variable: some people seem to show emotion more readily than others.* A more reliable indicator of arousal is that of *galvanic skin resistance* (GSR), which is a measure of how much the skin conducts electricity. *When we are anxious or aroused in some other way, we sweat, and this changes the conductivity of skin.* Even a very slight anxiety-producing stimulus, like a worrying thought, produces a change in skin conductivity, and this can be detected by electrodes attached to the skin.

Another system for measuring stress or arousal is by using a *voice stress analyser.* Minute tremors of the vocal cords occur naturally, but *when we are worried, anxious, and angry or frightened, our vocal muscles become tenser, which changes the sound of the voice.* Although, with practice people can learn to hide most of the effects of that tension, so that their voice sounds virtually normal because the natural tremors have been suppressed by the effort of maintaining control. This shows up clearly in an analysis of the voiceprint on a *sound spectrograph* – a visual image of a sound.

Normal speech shows a general waveform, super-imposed on the changes in pitch and tone of what is being said. Stressed speech does not – the pattern simply reflects the changes in speech and tone without any regular rhythmic variation.

*The most practical instrument for gaining overall measurements of levels of arousal is known as a polygraph.* 'Poly' means 'many', and this instrument is called a polygraph, because it combines measures of several difficult indicators of arousal, such as GSR, pulse rate, heartbeat and blood pressure. It then combines the information to give a general estimate of the level of arousal. *"Lie detectors' are polygraphs which detect arousal level. They work on the principle that people are more anxious, when they are telling a lie than when they are telling the truth.* Since, anxiety produces arousal in the same way that other sources of stress do, the polygraph detects the difference in arousal level between the lie and more ordinary truthful statements that the person has made. But you will probably already have detected a problem with this since, it is only physiological arousal which is being measured; it is not possible to tell the difference between an anxiety-producing true statement and a lie.

## THE YERKES-DODSON LAW OF AROUSAL

There are degrees of arousal – we can be only mildly aroused, or extremely so. And the overall level of arousal which we experience can affect our performance. This relates to a principle known as the *Yerkes-Dodson Law of arousal, is concerned with describing the relationship between the states of arousal of a given individual, and how well that individual will perform on a given task.* According to the Yerkes-Dodson law, *this relationship can be expressed on a graph as an inverted-U curve.* In other words, *arousal improves performance only upto a point, but beyond that point, level of arousal will help us to do things better; an extreme level will impair how well we do. So, the best state to be in – the optional state – is one in which the level of arousal is not too high or too low.*

*The optimal level of arousal varies for different tasks, with complex tasks showing an earlier performance decrement than simple tasks, for the same level of arousal. If we are performing a relatively simple task, then we can cope with a much larger range of arousal levels – the curve is flatter. So, for example, if you are doing the washing*, you would not do it very well if your state of arousal was very low indeed, and you were half-asleep; but equally, you would have to be very upset indeed before you started to break things (accidentally, that is). *But if you were engaged in a complex task, like trying to write an essay, you might need to be a bit more aroused – or at least, alert – before you could get started. Equally, however, getting upset would interfere with your ability to write the essay much more than it would interfere with your ability to wash up.*

An illustration of the Yerkes-Dodson Law was provided by Stroh (1971), when investigating sustained attention using the alpha rhythms which occur spontaneously in electro-encephalograms to provide a measure of relaxation – people who are relaxed produce EEGs with more alpha rhythms than people who are aroused. Stroh found that, when research participants were undertaking a very boring vigilance task, some of them would show more alpha activity, while others would show less, before a missed signal.

It was understandable that those who showed more might miss the signal, since it indicated that they were more relaxed, and so they might not have been concentrating. But the other finding was puzzling. On investigation, Stroh found that those who showed lower alpha activity before a missed signal tended to be younger and more neurotic than the other group. Stroh summarised that what had happened was that their arousal levels had become too high for them to perform effectively. They had gone past the optional arousal level on the inverted-U curve.

Hardy (1988), suggested a modification of the Yerkes-Dodson principle of arousal. Hardy suggested that work with athletes implied that the inverted-U shape is not a realistic reflection of the relationship between arousal and performance. *An inverted-U implies that if you become so upset or angry that it interferes with your performance, then just calming down a little bit, will restore you to the high level that you had before. But in high-powered athletic performance, Hardy argued, it does not work like that. If athletes become too upset that it interferes with their performance, they need to calm down a lot, not just a little, before they can gradually work their way back to performing to the peak of their ability.*

*Hardy suggested that the catastrophe theory provided a better model for describing the relationship between performance and arousal. In this model, a curve changes smoothly to a point but then there is discontinuity – a sudden and rapid change. This model, according to Hardy, reflects more accurately the sudden decline in performance produced by extremes of arousal during intensive competition, and it might also explain why it is often so hard for high-powered athletes to get back to peak performance once they have been upset.*

## Problems with the Concept of Arousal

A number of questions have arisen to do with how useful the concept of arousal really is. These have come about as a result of some of the detailed investigations of arousal conducted by researchers, which have shown that, although they may seem superficially similar, arousal states produced by different types of stimuli or emotions can in fact involve quite different physiological effects.

In discussing these problems, Gale (1981), pointed out that, *'The term 'arousal' has been used in so many different contexts, and to describe so many different types of response, that it becomes almost impossible to state exactly what is being measured, and what the different forms of arousal that researchers have studied actually have got in common.'*

Green (1987), argued, however, that the general concept of arousal is one which is useful in many respects, particularly when we are trying to look at broad patterns rather than specific reactions, or when we are trying to understand everyday experience. We need to bear in mind, though, that *the idea of autonomic arousal is a generalisation which encompasses a number of different types of response when examined at the level of fine-detailed research, and not an extremely precise concept.*

Some critics have also queried just how closely an experimentally-induced arousal state can replicate arousal which occurs in real life. For example, one of the main problems which psychologists studying anger have faced is, defining what we actually mean by 'anger'. Rose, Kamin and Lewontin (1984), pointed out that when researchers use the term 'aggression' they are often referring to several very different concepts, and the same thing applies to the way that we use the term 'anger'.

We can see this more clearly if we look at how other communities define the different experiences which we call 'anger'. Lutz (1990), in an anthropological study of the Ifaluk people of Micronesia, found that their language includes words for at least five different types of anger, each of which is differentiated very sharply from the others. Each refers to a different type of anger, and we can recognise the different experiences which they are describing. But in our language, each of these experiences would be lumped together under the same name, 'anger', whereas in the Ifaluk language, they are quite different.

This has implications for research, since the fact that we do not distinguish them clearly in our own language means that they can often become confused, to that researchers all investigate 'anger' but in reality examine experiences which are very different from one another. Alternatively, it can result in researchers investigating only one specific type of anger, and using those investigations to draw conclusions about 'anger' in general.

## Stress

Immediate response to stressful or anxiety-provoking events, as we have seen, generates a rapid high level of physiological arousal. But what happens when the threat simply does not go away? The 'fight or flight' response is very costly in terms of energy, and not the sort of thing that the body can keep up for very long. Yet, in modern living, perceived threats are rarely responded to by physical action. Moreover, they are often continuous and non-specific – a constant anxiety that financial problems will result in homelessness, for instance, represents an acute but ongoing perceived threat, which does not take a direct physical form.

## Type of Anger

| | |
|---|---|
| *tipmochmoch* | The feeling of irritability which is often experienced by people who are ill. |
| *nguch* | The irritability which occurs when relatives have not fulfilled their obligations. |
| *tang* | The kind of anger which arises from frustration or helplessness in the face of personal misfortune, or some other unfairness which cannot be tackled. |
| *lingeringer* | The anger which builds up gradually when a whole series of little unpleasant events occur. |
| *song* | A sense of 'justifiable anger', or righteous indignation. |

## The General Adaptation Syndrome

*In 1956, Selye identified what became known as the general adaptation syndrome (GAS), a model which described how people and animals respond to long-term stress.* Selye was particularly interested in the effects that prolonged exposure to stressful situations has on the body's resistance to disease and illness. From studies with animals, Selye identified three phases to the general adaptation syndrome. *The first of these is the alarm stage, involving 'fight or flight' reactions, and therefore the activation of the sympathetic division of the ANS. In animals, this stage has been shown to produce enlargement of the adrenal glands, shrinking of the thymus gland and lymph nodes, and sometimes ulceration of the stomach walls.*

*As the stress continues, however, the body attempts to revert to normal functioning,* which at the same time coping with the additional adrenaline in the bloodstream and the effects which it produces. *This is the second phase, which Selye described as the resistance stage. Rats which were exposed to long-term cold stress for long enough to have entered this stage, survived much lower temperature, than rats which had not been exposed to this type of long-term experience.*

## Stress Performance and Achievement

Many people, especially executives, regard stress as a bad word and they prefer to use a word such as "challenge" for positive stress. Hans Selye, the physician who such popularised the stress concept, chose the word *eustress*, which may be defined as the healthy, positive, constructive outcome of stressful events and the stress response. The relationship between stress and performance has been known since 1908, when Robert Yerkes and James Dodson demonstrated increased performance under conditions of arousal up to an optional point, as shown in Figure ( The Yerkes – Dodson Law)

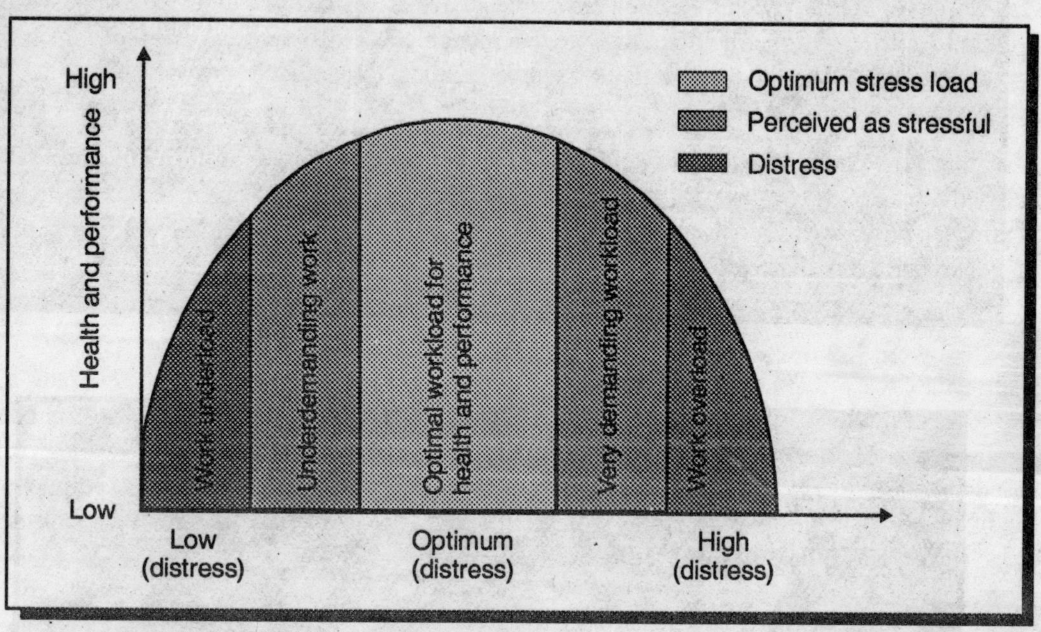


**Fig. 30**

As the figure shows, performance increases with increasing stress loads up to an optimum point, and then the stress load becomes too great, resulting in depressed performance. The optimum stress load that maximises performance varies by individual and by task, based on several considerations; individual considerations include susceptibility to stress, fatigue, psychological and cognitive skills and physical capacity. Task considerations include the complexity, difficulty, duration, and intensity of the work. The interaction, as reflected in the person's familiarity with the task, also affects the shape and size of the particular Yerkes-Dodson curve. Too little stress and arousal often fail to stimulate performance, just as too much stress and arousal can interfere with performance, especially on complex tasks.

## Work & Stress

Stress affects our total life. Whatever work we do, its quality depends to a great extent on whether we are having peace of mind, or a disturbed state. There is an intimate relation between the work load, work performance and experience of stress. The relation between work load and stress is graphically shown.

The optimum work load differs from individual to individual. We should understand our own level of peak performance in relation to stress. This also means that in an organisation the person at the helm of affairs must do the following:

1. Try to understand work stress and its impact on the well-being and productivity of workers;
2. Explore organisational climate and sources of stress,
3. Seek to find behavioural interventions to reduce stress, illness, and injury in the workplace.

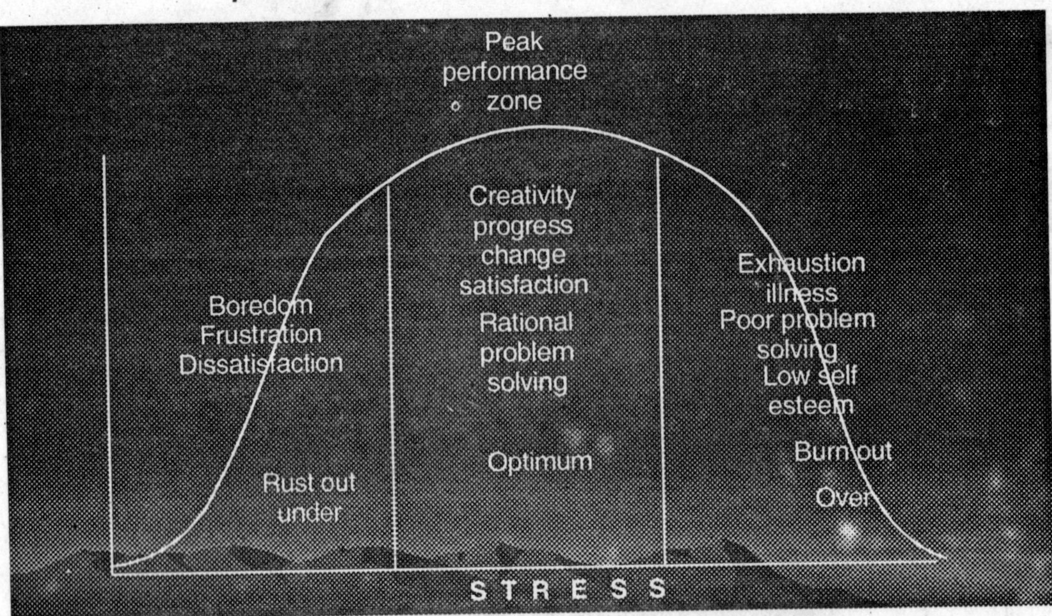


Fig. 31

Well, I would suggest making the best physical fitness for yourself should be among your top resolutions.

It has been proved beyond doubt that physical fitness directly affects human behaviour such as self esteem, anxiety, depression and attention span.

Realizing that better physical fitness can significantly affect an individual by way of improvement in his personality and behaviour, a number of organizations have started fitness programs for their employees and managers.

Physical fitness increases self-confidence, which is the hallmark of great individuals. The health of an individual to a large extent determines his success of failure in his life.

Look around you'll easily identify people with self confidence who influence others with ease. You will observe that those who are physically fit radiate poise and assurance and have a strong aura, which undoubtedly helps them to succeed in life, whereas those who lack self-confidence repel others rather than attracting them.

Remember these words: "Ultimately, I am what I choose to be; my self-esteem follows the same path." Anonymous.

## STRESS AND PAIN

The relationship between stress and pain is complex and more likely circular than linear. Chronic pain promotes an extend and destructive stress response that produce, neuroendocrine deregulation, fatigue, dysphasia, myalgia and impaired mental and physical performance (Chapman & Gavrin 1999).

Depression, fatigue, limitations in one's activities and belief that the pain is uncontrollable leads to increased stress in daily life. Excessive stress in life may disrupt sleep, appetite and posture and may cause underlying muscle tension, all of which may contribute to ongoing chronic pain. Further, excessive stress affects psychological well-being and reduces the ability of the person to cope effectively with chronic pain.

Stress management strategies, particularly relaxation strategies and modification or resolution of psychological, social or physical factors that contribute to stress at home or work, may be very helpful to enable the person to cope better with chronic pain. They may also reduce acute exacerbations of chronic pain.

## ANXIETY AND FEAR

In the initial onset of a chronic non-malignant pain an individual may be highly anxious because the pain is thought to be associated with underlying damage that will need assessment and intervention. If no evidence of substantive pathology can be found then anxiety may be replaced by frustration, hostility and discouragement.

Anxiety about pain can be due to many factors. Exposure to repeated acute episodes of unrelieved pain increases anxiety about pain. The uncertainty of pain occurrence, especially if the pain is difficult to manage, may generate anxiety. Pain anxiety is also increased by painful medical or health procedures, if these environments do not provide adequate relief from pain. If these procedures are carried out in an atmosphere of indifference about pain, and then they also increase the client's anxiety about pain. For example, many adults have fears about dental pain or pain due to needles, in part due to negative childhood experiences with such pain exposure.

The disbelief of others about the legitimacy of the pain complaint also contributes to pain anxiety. Greg Lum who developed chronic pain following a motor vehicle accident wrote:

*What I don't need (beside the physical pains) is to have to deal with someone else's 'attitude' or feel guilty and anxious about something I don't seem to be able to do anything about (Lum 1997 p.68).*

Chronic pain may be associated with fear about further pain, fear about re-injury or fear about underlying disease progression. Often chronic pain is increased by activity, and if the pain is already severe, further pain will be feared and avoided. Clients often associate with tissue damage and they may become fearful that persistent pain signifies more or continued damage. If there is known disease that is causing the pain, then the pain may be forced as an in disorder of the progression of the disease. Fear of pain may be more disabling than the pain itself (Waddell et al. 1993).

Anxiety or fear of pain may produce crisis reactions to the pain that interferes with coping and may lead to pain disability beyond what may be expected by the severity of the pain (Cipher & Fernandez 1997). When anxiety or fear is present, careful assessment of possible physical, psychological and social factors is very important.

## Impact of persistent pain in performance and quality of life

I simply want to stop. I can't stand being out of control. I'm so tired of being in pain. I'm pained from being in pain (Lum 1997, p. 64).

As noted in Chapter 1, occupation refers to clusters of tasks and activities that give meaning to everyday life (Law et al. 1997). Daily life consists of self-care occupations, leisure occupations and productivity occupations. The quality of a person's engagement in occupations can be understood by considering the volition, habituation and performance aspects of human occupation, also referred to as the 'Model of Human Occupation' (Kielhofner 1985, 1995). This model of human occupation is utilised extensively in occupational therapy as an analysis of the inter-relationship between the individual and the environment in relationship to occupations of daily life.

Another approach is the 'Canadian Model of Occupational Performance' (Law et al. 1997). In this model, occupational performance is considered as the outcome of the international relationship between person, environment and occupation.

Volitional factors include awareness of oneself as a factor, and perception of control over ones' own behaviour. Interests and values influence choice of activities. Our values also affect our sense of obligation and conviction of what is important in life and how we experience and interpret life situations.

Habituation refers to the routines, habits and roles that organise daily activities into a time structure that gives regularity and identity. Performance is the integrated function of physical and mental factors that in a dynamic process form the capacity for planned and goal-directed actors.

People with chronic muscular pain usually experience limitations to performanance of daily involving static or repetitive eccentric movements such as carrying bags, climbing stairs, vacuum cleaning, peeling vegetables, stirring and holding tools are more difficult to perform. Also, certain movements and positions not normally thought of as tiring or difficult can be impossible to manage for clients in pain. Not only lifting and carrying small children but also dressing and undressing and feeding small children can be unmanageable. Holding a mug or a spoon when feeding involves state muscular work and is often reported as difficult.

Clients with chronic muscular pain need to learn to work in a dynamic fashion, avoiding static positions and repetitive tasks. Frequent pauses and relaxation techniques may be helpful and may decrease the level of pain during activity (Henriksson 1995). The majority of clients with chronic muscular pain, regional or generalised, report that they need rest periods of half and hour or more in the afternoon, in order to be able to continue their scheduled activities in the late afternoon and evening (Henriksson et al., 1996, Henriksson & Burckhard 1996).

For many clients, pain will fluctuate from day to day or during the day, and on certain days may be more problematic than on others (Henriksson & Liedberg 2001). These variations in pain may be large. It is not unusual for clients to report that on 'a bad day' they may have problems getting out of bed and moving around, whereas, on 'a good day' the symptoms can be may less pronounced and most activities can be performed without problems.

## Habits

Habits are the habitual ways in which we perform different tasks and activities of everyday occupations. Habits are the result of previous repetitions of certain behaviour and they allow us to perform ordinary well-known tasks without having to concentrate on the performance or decide how the actions should be performed. Habits help us to organise our daily activities into stable patterns of behaviour and to regulate time.

When pain or injury occurs, habits are often disrupted (Henriksson 1995a). Some movements cannot be performed in the usual way but have to be changed to lessen pain and fatigue provoking procedures. Clients apply different strategies to cope with everyday life (Henriksson 1995b). All tasks take longer to perform and more attention has to be focused on the performance.

## Quality of life

Quality of life is usually rated as low by clients with acute pain. However, individual clients may also report a high and sometimes increased quality of life. When the first critical period has passed and clients have adjusted their life situation to new limitations and feel more in control of their life, quality of life may increase.

Some clients revalue their life tasks and find new meaning and new arenas for developing social contacts and personal interests. Certain aspects of life may however be rated as low. Professional career, economic situations, physical activities and sexual satisfaction may represent areas of loss and limitations.

Linda Martinson, who is a poet and also lives with chronic pain, has expressed some of the feelings of happiness, grief, anger and sadness that may be experienced by people with chronic pain (Martinson 1996). Her poetry about the ferociousness of pain eloquently illustrates the difficulty in maintaining quality of life that may be experienced.

## Wading through the words

Throbbing

Burning

Pounding

Shooting

Stabbing

Ceaseless

These words are flat

Compared to the pain feel.

## Anxiety and stress reduction

Beecher (1960) and Wickramasekers (1985), proposed that reduction of anxiety and stress was the principle mechanism of placebo analgesia. Anxiety (regarding the cause and consequences of a pain) is the most common psychological symptom accompanying a new pain. Anxiety and pain each result in a general activation of sympathetic arousal and excessive motor behaviour (Gross & Collins 1981).

Pain-induced anxiety drives us to seek medical assistance and a diagnosis for the pain. It causes us to cancel our most urgent appointments and to obey our physician's or therapist's advice to rest the injured part and take medications so that pain can subside and healing can occur (Sterobach 1968). Pain-induced anxiety is therefore a principal mechanism of survival, by which we remove ourselves from the painful stimulus, seek appropriate medical advice and behave in a manner which is consistent with pain reduction, healing and the earliest possible resumption of normal activity (Wall 1979).

Nevertheless, significant stress results from pain and the accompanying anxiety. It seems entirely rational, therefore, to propose that placebo analgesia may be strongly linked to a desire to reduce anxiety. Nevertheless, the proposition that lowered anxiety has the direct effect of inducing placebo analgesia has not been well supported (White et al. 1985); the relationship in likely to be more complex.

Although there is no solid evidence that reduced anxiety directly affects placebo analgesia, the concept is not without merit. Conditioning, expectation (of pain relief) and anxiety reduction are not mutually exclusive (Richardson 1994). Manipulations of cognitive dissonance that are said to have a placebo effect (Totman 1989), could instead be affecting anxiety.

The study of specific psychological theories adds to our knowledge of the depth and complexity of mechanisms surrounding placebo analgesia. It is, however, accepted that several interrelated mechanisms account for the effect. No single model accounts fully for placebo phenomenon (Price 2000).

## Psycho-immunology

A number of researchers began to investigate how psychological factors such as long-term stress can make people (and animals) more susceptible to illness. One of the most important findings which emerged as a result of this interest was the mapping out of the physiological effects of long-term stress – which, as we have seen, turned out to be very different from the body's response to emergencies.

The immune system is one of the most complex systems of the body. It consists of a number of defences which the body has, to protect itself against disease. As the first line of defence, white blood cells patrol the body and lymphatic system, seeking out foreign organisms such as bacteria, fungi and viruses, while natural killer cells roam through body tissue, destroying cells which have become infected by a virus or transformed into cancer cells.

There are two types of immune reactions which the body produces. **Non-specific immune reactions** are general ones, which can deal with a range of different problems. One of them is the inflammatory reaction, in which damaged tissue becomes red and inflamed because the blood and lymph supplies to the area are increased. These secretions also attract white blood cells, which get rid of the debris produced by the body's own cells, and any invading strange cells. Another non-specific reaction occurs when cells have become infected with some viruses. This causes the cells to release a chemical known as interferon, which prevents the virus from reproducing and infecting other cells. These general defences are the body's way of dealing with minor infection, such as from cuts and abrasions.

**Specific immune reactions** are targeted against particular invaders, such as the organisms which cause illnesses like measles, smallpox, or poliomyelitis. Many of these are chemically mediated: the immune system learns to recognize proteins known as antigens, on the surface of invading bacteria, and manufactures a set of antibodies, known as immunoglobulins, which seek out and destroy those particular bacteria.

Immunisation works on that principle: by giving the body a mild and harmless exposure to polio or smallpox bacteria, the immune system is 'taught' to recognise those bacteria, so that if they enter the body again, they are sought out and destroyed.

Some specific immune reactions are mediated by the cells themselves. Special cells, known as T-lymphocytes, are produced by the thymus gland. These also produce antibodies, but instead of floating freely through the system, those anti-bodies remain stuck to the surface of the cell. When an invader, such as fungus, virus, or parasite, comes into the area of the cell, the antigens on their surface stick to the antibodies on the surface of the T-lymphocyte cell, and the cell responds either by killing the invader directly, or by sending out a message which attracts other white blood cells to come and kill it.

The problem is that stress increases the secretion of glucocorticoids in the blood, and over a long period of time these glucocorticoids attach themselves to the white blood cells, and lower their effectiveness. Solomon (1963), showed that a significant outcome of the general adaptation syndrome seems to be lowered resistance to illness, and a tendency to feelings of fatigue and general weakness. Long-term psychological effects have also been identified;

taking form of increased irritability and a tendency to a pessimistic outlook. Over time, too, this can lead to seriously negative thinking styles which can actually prolong the stress which the individual is under.

It is thought that many of the characteristics of the syndrome known as burnout, which affects people in helping professions like social work, teaching or nursing, can be attributed to a combination of these factors. The long-term stress which these people are under produces the general adaptation syndrome, which reduces their mental and physical resilience, and their experiences mean that they feel powerless in the working situation, augmenting and exaggerating their stress.

Several studies have suggested a link between long-term stress and minor illnesses; although it is always difficult to be certain that it is the stress itself which is producing the effect. For example, in a study by Glaser et al. (1987), medical students showed distinct changes in their immune systems during exam times. They also reported that they were more likely to contract coughs and colds during exam times than at other times, but this aspect of the study was not really fully controlled, as Watson and Pennebaker (1989), point out, it is possible that the students expected to be ill at such times, or noticed it more because they found the experience of illness even more unpleasant when they had other stressors.

Other studies also showed changes in the immune system as a result of stress. For example, Irwin et al. (1988), took blood samples from women whose husbands had recently died, and found that they showed significantly less natural killer cell activity during the six months after their bereavement than at other times.

Treatments for illness in non-technological societies often show recognition of how long-term stress can lower resistance to disease. Horton (1967), discussed how traditional African medicine practioners, sometimes derogatively called 'witch doctors', go about treating infectious illnesses. Typically, they will talk with the patient abut what has been going on in their lives, looking for sources of social stress like quarrels or arguments with friends or relatives. To Western ears, this does not make any sense, because we 'know' that these diseases are caused by infection. But Horton points out that, in a country with a high infant morality rate, the people who survive to adulthood are likely to have a high natural immunity.

So the real question is not whether the infection is around, but why the person has become susceptible to it – in other words, why their immune system is less efficient than usual. In this context, and given what we are finding out about physiological factors in illness, the idea that social stress might be an important factor makes much more sense. Since much of the traditional medicine practioner's approach is to deal with the source of this stress, by appeasing or reconciling the two parties, then taking such an approach to the treatment of illness, far from being primitive, is actually far more sophisticated than it appears on the surface.

Long-term stress has also been linked with coronary heart disease – an illness which has been observed to be common among certain kinds of patients, but rare for others. In 1959, Friedman and Rosenman drew up a summary of those patient characteristics which seemed to correlate with an increased likelihood of coronary heart disease. Their list included high compositeness, a high level of achievement motivation, restlessness and hyperalertness, and tendency to feel as though they were continually under pressure from time, and from their own responsibilities. As we saw the researchers concluded that they were, typically, two very different personality styles, manifested by these traits.

Friedman and Rosenman (1974), reported a longitudinal study of over 3500 healthy men aged between 39 and 59, which lasted for over twelve year. The men were assessed by means of structured interviews, which involved about 25 questions, like 'would your partner or a close friend describe you as a hard-driving person?' or 'how would you be likely to react if you were stuck towards the end of slow queue?' The research participants were also observed as they answered the questions, and assessed in terms of how impatient or restless they seemed to be. Certain questions were deliberately asked very slowly, to see if the individual interrupted.

As the study progressed, more than twice as many men as developed coronary heart disease, 178 out of 257. Even when the figures were adjusted for factors such as whether they smoked more, or had higher blood pressure, the risk for Type A's was 197 times as high as the risk for Type B's.

In a more detailed analysis, Jenkins et al., (1978), found that there were different kinds of Type A behaviour which correlated with different forms of heart disease, angina sufferers tended to be impatient with other people and very conscious of work pressure, but those with heart failure or likely heart failure tended to have hasty personal habits and schedules, inflicting the pressures on themselves rather than on others.

Long-term stress has been linked with a number of other illnesses too. One of these is cancer, although it is unclear just what the relationship actually it. Unfortunately, many of the studies which seemed to show a direct relationship between stress and cancer did not really control for other kinds of factors, like smoking, diet or alcohol intake, and it is also very difficult to sort out how far the stress people are under, may be an effect of the disease, rather than a cause. Nowadays, more researchers working in this field tend to take the view that stress is unlikely actually to cause cancer, but that it may well influence the rate of growth of cancerous tumours, once the cancer has begun.

There are a couple of studies, thought, which do seems to provide us with some good evidence on this question. One of them was reported by Spiegel et al., (1989), who were originally investigating whether psychotherapy would help women to cope with the experience of having a fatal illness – advanced breast cancer. They selected 86 women, all of whom were receiving the standard medical treatment for their illness, and offered an additional psychotherapy treatment to half of them. He found that the psychotherapy did seem to help the women, they became less anxious, and less depressed, and also learned to reduce their pain through self-hypnosis.

Originally, that was all that was planned for the study. However, about thirteen years later, the researchers decided to follow up the medical records of those patients, just to see if there had been any difference to the medical progress of the illness, but when they consulted the records, they found that those women who had received psychotherapy had lived on for an average of 37 months after the treatment, b y comparison with only 10 months for the others. And three of them were even still alive.

We do have to be careful, though, about jumping to the conclusion that it was the reduction of stress which prolonged the patients' illnesses, even though the study does seem to suggest that kind of link. It is always possible that, because the women became a little more relaxed, they complied better with medical instructions, or might have been able to get more exercise because they were in less pain. But even though it many not be absolute proof, the study does suggest quite strongly that stress reduction might be able to ameliorate the disease, at least a little bit.

Another illness which has been linked with long-term stress is that of **gastric ulcers**. This research began with some early studies on animals. In 1958, Brady conducted an experiment involving four pairs of monkeys, linked together as 'yoked controls' (in other words, each monkey received the same experiences as the animal that was paired with it). The monkeys were given regular electric shocks to the feet, but one of each pair was provided with a lover which allowed it to turn the shocks off for 20 seconds at a time (the shocks were given at 20 second intervals). The second monkey in each pair could do nothing but receive the shock passively. Brady argued that, in this set-up, both animals were subjected to the same physical stress but only the 'executive' monkey – the one which could press the lever – was subjected to the psychological stress of having to maintain the response.

The experimental sessions continued for six hours at a time, with an intervening six-hour rest period. Brady found that many of the 'executive' monkeys died of duodenal ulcers. Their yoked controls, on the other hand, did not show any gastro-intestinal abnormalities. Following a series of investigations of different schedules, in which the experimental conditions were maintained for one-hour, three-hour and six-hour periods. Brady found that only the six-hours on, six-hours off schedule was sufficient to produce ulcers. He related this to the changes in stomach acidity brought about by long-term stress; there were fewer changes in acidity resulting from the shorter sessions.

In a different study, Weiss (1972), performed a similar study with laboratory rats. This time, the 'executive' rats were able to postpone an electric shock by turning an exercise wheel, while they also had a yoked control who experienced exactly the same shocks. Interestingly, though, Weiss found that it was the helpless rats which developed gastric ulcers, rather than the ones which had been able to take action – a finding exactly opposite to Brady's. Weiss explained this by arguing that what was important was not so much whether the animal had control over the stressor, but two other factors. The first was the sheer amount of stressor – the degree of stress the animal experienced. The second was whether there was any feedback, indicating to the animal that its actions were having an effect.

For Brady's monkeys, the rapid rate of the stimulus had meant that the rate of stressors was extremely high. In fact, when the pairs were being set up, the monkey which could respond most quickly was the one from each pair which was assigned as the 'executive' rather than at the control. So this high degree of stress meant that they were more prone to ulcers. But in addition, they had relatively little feedback about the effectiveness of their actions – just that the shock did not arrive on schedule. Weiss's rats, on the other hand, had heard a warning tone to signal each shock, and so also became aware that the shock had been averted.

Another possible interpretation of these differences is to do with the degree of body movement involved in the animals' responses. As we have seen, the alarm response prepares the body for action. But Brady's monkeys were only required to perform molecular actions (action involving a small part of the body), in the sense that all they had to do was to press a lever. Weiss's rats on the other hand, performed molar actions to avert their shock – movements which involved the whole body, like running in the wheel or, in one condition, jumping into a little box. These molar responses would utilise the bodily energy generated by the alarm response, so the animal was responding in a way that was appropriate to its physical state. But Brady's monkeys would have experienced the alarm response with no way of utilising that energy, and it is possible that this is why their stress was so much more.

## Therapies for reducing long-term stress

Levonkeon et al. (1983), investigated how useful therapy was for modifying Type A behaviour, and found that it often had quite a high degree of success. Some of the most successful therapies were based on behaviour therapy, training the client to develop coping strategies so that they could deal effectively with training as well. A five-year intervention programme of such training for 1935 post–heart attack patients showed that the recurrence rate for both fatal and non-fatal heart attacks was reduced to half that of the control group. The control group was equal on other factors but received just the normal cardiological treatment and not the additional therapy.

There is some evidence that Type A may be a cultural factor. Although it seems to be a reliable phenomenon in America, a study in Britain by Bass and Wade (1982), found that among patients complaining of heart pain, those with Type A personality matters tended to have normal coronary arteries – although they were also the most psychiatrically disturbed. Some other researchers though, argue that Type A is not really a characteristic in itself. Instead, it is made up of whole series of sub-characteristics like ambition and activity levels, so to treat it as if it were a single, complete character trait is misleading. What seems to be more important is the stress which the person is experiencing as part of their way of going about their life, rather than the style of activity itself.

## Biofeedback

Some of the relaxation techniques which are used in programmes of stress reduction involve biofeedback. This is a method for teaching people to have some control over their autonomic responses. It used to be believed that autonomic activity was not susceptible to learning, until HHa series of studies by Miller and DiCara (1967), showed that rats which had been paralysed using curate cold learn to lower or raise their heartbeat, if they received an incentive in the form of direct electrical brain stimulation. Since then, a number of studies have shown that human being, too, can gain some control over autonomic functioning like blood pressure or heart rate. To do that, though, we need to have immediate feedback as to what our current heart rate or blood pressure is.

Typically, someone who is using biofeedback to learn to control stress responses will use some kind of equipment which gives them information about their physiological state. In its simplest form, this might simply be a GSR-sensitive pad which wraps around the finger, which is connected to a box which produces a tone. The higher the tone, the higher the level of autonomic activity. There are, of course, many more sophisticated biofeedback machines in the market, but the type described is fairly typical, and commonly available. By practicing relaxation exercises, the person finds that they can lower the tone of the feedback signal, or that, alternatively, they can raise it by allowing themselves to become more agitated. This provides the feedback for learning how to relax effectively and reduce their level of autonomic arousal.

## Attributional therapy

Solomon (1969), found that there were considerable variations between people in what constitutes 'stress'. An experience which is highly stressful for one person might be taken in their stride by someone else. Part of that seems to come from how people explain what is happening to themselves. Maier and Seligman (1976), found that depressive people tend to have a consistent attributional style, which means that they tend to feel that they have no control over what is happening. This in turn increases their stress levels and so contributes to maintaining their depression.

As we have seen, locus of control – whether one perceives oneself as a victim, or as an agent in one's own life – appears to be a major factor in stress reduction. People who see themselves as being more in control of what happens to them experience far less stress than those who feel themselves as being victims of circumstances, even when their objective conditions are exactly the same. The cognitive therapies which we looked at aim to help people to develop new types of attributional style, which will help them to take more control over their lives and so reduce their stress levels.

Biofeedback and atrributional therapies are two different ways of combating the effects of long-term stress. Another approach aims to utilise the relationship between arousal and physical exertion, by drawing on the high levels of adrenaline found in the body as part of the general adaptation syndrome.

## Emotion

Until relatively recently, almost all psychological research into emotion concentrated on negative emotions, and in particular on fear and anger. This is partly because these emotions appear to link much more closely with physiological arousal, but psychological, research also reflects the values of the society in which it is located, and modern society also neglects or undervalues the positive emotions. So we will begin our exploration of the psychology of emotion by looking at some of the theories of emotion which psychologists proposed on the basis of studies of fear and anger, before going on to look at some of the positive emotions.

## Humour

Another of the positive emotions, and one which is easily overlooked, is that of humour. As with many of the positive emotions (and possibly the other emotions too, as we have seen) social factors are a very important face of the experience. With humour, particularly, social factors are more than important, since humour is by definition a social phenomenon.

Emerson (1960) pointed out that humour, in the form of jokes or asides, is judged differently from other forms of social interaction, in that it officially does not 'count' as part of a serious exchange. This means that people find themselves able to take risks with humour which they would not feel able to take if they were required to make the comment or observation in a loss protected way. As such, humour is an important social tool, for defusing tense situation or encouraging a fresh perspective on a problem.

Kahn (1980) identified five primary functions that humour serves for individuals and groups. The first is that of coping. Humour helps people to become detached from potentially threatening aspects of their situation, so that they can cope with it a bit better. So, for example, people who work in the emergency services often use humour in a way that appears to outsiders to be callous, but which in reality allows them to cope better with things that are happening. The second function is reframing – humour allows people to see things that they have previously taken for granted, in a new light or to restructure their experience in such a way that it conveys different implications. Kahn also pointed out that communicating is an important role for humour. It allows people to deliver messages that they would otherwise not be able to say, particularly with reference to socially 'taboo' experience like death or bereavement.

The fourth function of humour which Kalm identified is expressing hostility – it is not uncommon for hostile racist or sexist feelings, for example, to be expressed using a joking medium. Framing the comment like this makes it difficult for a recipient to protest, but such humour can sometimes be extremely vicious. Aggressive humour between different groups often reflects the existing group tensions. It may also, more innocuously, serve to ridicule or derogate members of the other group, or substitute for more blatant confrontation.

The fifth function of humour that Kahn identified has to do with constructing identities. 'In jokes' are often used to maintain or establish group cohesion, and to provide evidence that the person speaking is a member of that social group. As such they are often used to help members of a group to draw the boundaries between their group and other people.

There are, of course, many more positive emotions than this, and some of them have even been the subject of research – for instance, the studies of love and loving which we will be looking. So far, though, researchers are only just beginning to explore the range of positive emotions in our lives. As Argyle's study showed, positive emotions are many, and complex. But, sadly, many of them are still regarded as relatively unimportant, at least when it comes to gaining research grants, and as a result, our understanding of them is still relatively limited.

The study of emotion, then, has taken many different forms, ranging from investigations or physiological mechanisms to explorations of the personal and social dimensions of experience. The same complexity applies to the psychological investigation of motivation. While early research into motivation emphasised the physiological dimensions, more recent investigations have spanned social, cognitive and cultural dimensions as well.

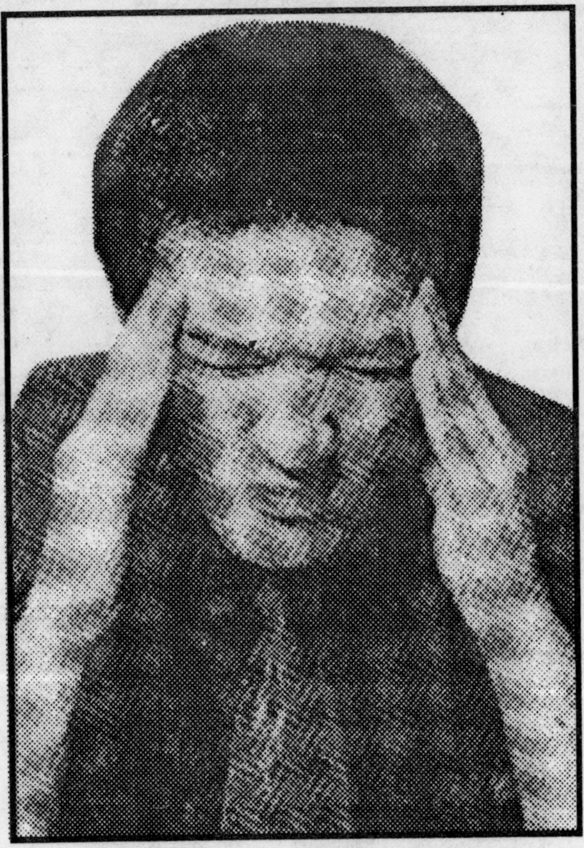

**Fig. 32 : Painful Condition Stress**

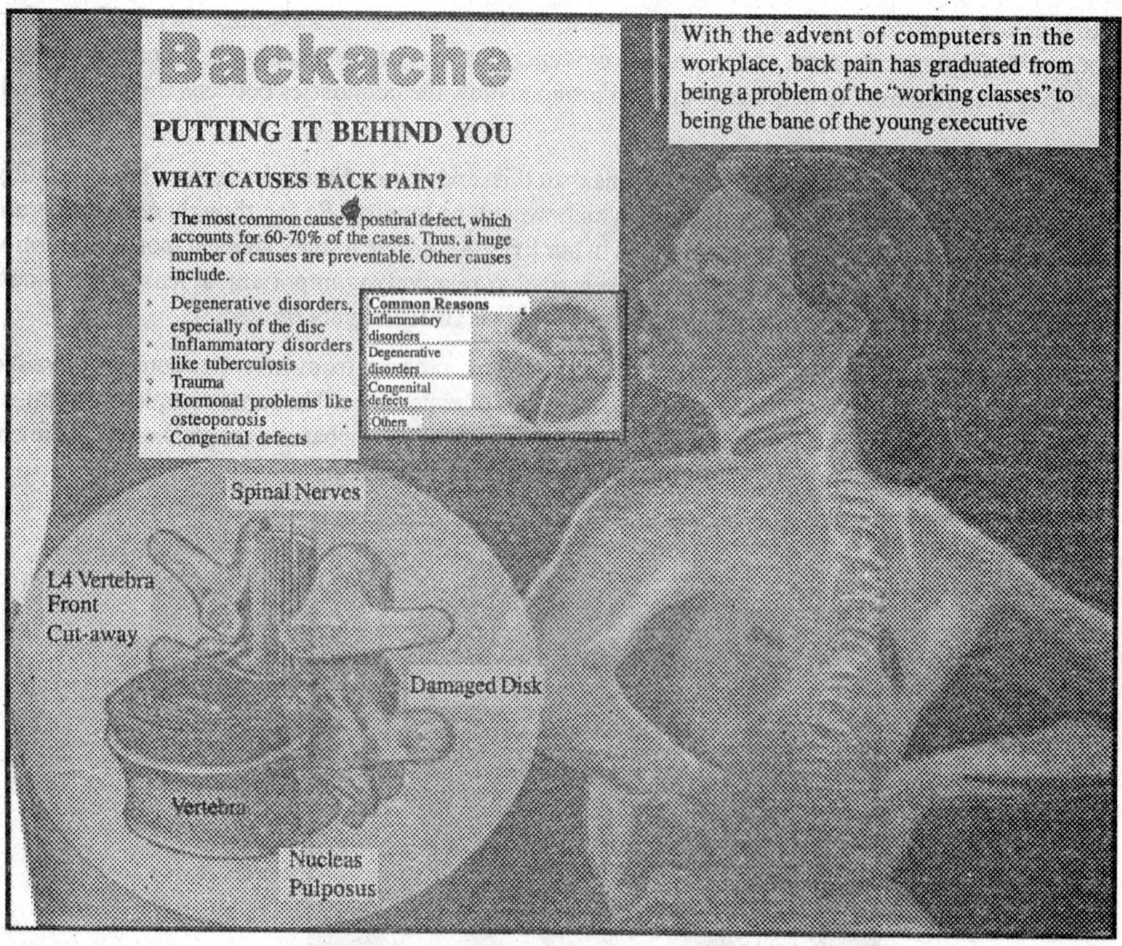


## Healing Process

1. Exercise regularly, according to your health care provider's recommendation.
2. Limit the amount of alcohol you drink because it can cause neuropathy too.
3. Eat a healthy diet with fruits and vegetables (some vitamin deficiencies can cause neuropathy).
4. Keep your checkup appointments with your health care provider.
5. Practice yoga.

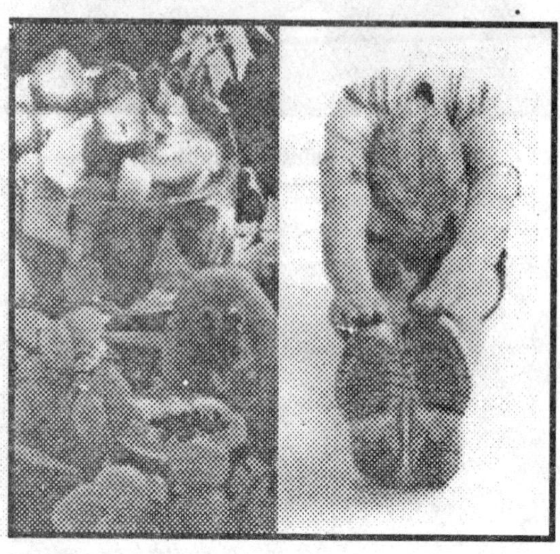

## Less pain, more gain

Until recently, Massage Therapist Bruria Ginton told Newsweek, "Massage has been slow to catch on in this country because people cannot believe that some thing which feels so good can be good for them." That misbegotten and harmful belief has long been a part our cultural heritage along with the "no pain, no gain philosophy of present-day fitness fanatics. The signal and sensations we get from the body are valuable messages to be heeded; the pain is telling you something. So is the pleasure.

We're beginning to listen. You know that "less pain, more gain" is taking hold when *Time Magazine* can report that in places like Murfreesboro, Tennesse "it seems as if the whole town is beating a path to (Michele Balliet's) table. Not just the doctors, lawyer and bankers, but the factory workers, farmers and handicrafters. "Massage," Balliet says, "has become necessary part of their lives."

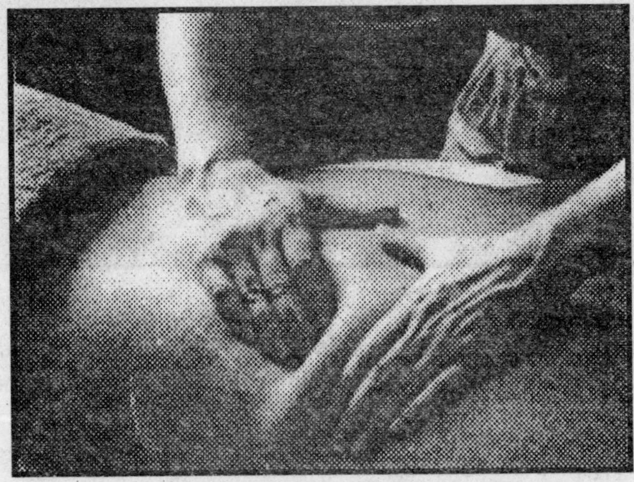

**Massage Therapy**

The present study is an attempt to examine the role of alternative/complementary systems of medicine in treating the stress and strain related health problems of working executives. Two categories of population have been considered for this study.

1. Working executives/managers/professionals
2. Health professionals (Doctors/Specialists)

Separate opinion surveys have been conducted for each of the two categories. Questionnaires have been developed and pretested on few respondents. Pretesting has helped in making improvements in the questionnaire. Necessary data have been collected in the revised questionnaire. The methodologies adopted for these surveys are discussed below:

### A. AN OPINION SURVEY OF WORKING EXECUTIVES/MANAGERS/PROFESSIONALS

#### Universe

The universe of the survey consists of executives/managers/professionals working in various companies, private/ government organisations and public sector undertakings in Delhi.

#### Sample and Sample Design

The domain of the survey has been restricted to Delhi Metropolitan City. Selection of executives/managers/ professionals was made from the consolidated list of such individuals working in various types of organisations. A sample of 150 working executives was selected at random with the help of random numbers tables ensuring that all the executives have equal chance of their inclusion in the sample.

#### Data Collection

As already mentioned, data were collected by interviewing the selected individual with the help of a pretested questionnaire. The questionnaire was of a structured and non-disguised type. To develop the list of information items for framing the questionnaire, a comprehensive review of existing literature on causes of stress and strain and various alternative/complementary systems of medicines was made. The preliminary draft of the questionnaire was pretested on 25 individuals. This helped in improving upon the questionnaire and also gave an indication as to the kind of responses that will be forthcoming. With a few deletions, additions and alterations, final questionnaire was developed which has been given in Appendix-I.

## Data Analysis

The response of the individuals have been given in all the tables in terms of both the numbers and percentages. Figures in tables within parantheses represent percentages while those without parantheses are simple frequencies.

The weighted average scores were calculated at the appropriate place where the respondents were asked to rank, rate different statements according to the level of stress. Five types of responses were envisaged to devote the level of stress viz. (i) Always stress, (ii) Frequent stress, (iii) Occasional stress, (iv) Rarely any stress and (v) No stress at all. These being qualitative in nature, a scoring of 4,3,2,1 and 0 was allotted to (i) to (u).

The weighted average score W is given by

$$W = \frac{1}{\Sigma fw} \frac{4}{\Sigma_0 wfw}$$

Where W is the weight/score given to the type of response and fw is the number of respondents for the type of response for which the weight/score W is given. Thereafter, the statements have been ranked on the basis of their weighted average scores.

## B. AN OPINION SURVEY OF HEALTH PROFESSIONALS

The universe of the survey consists of doctors practicing various systems of medicine in the city of Delhi. A random sample of 100 doctors was selected.

## Data Collection

To collect the data, a preliminary draft of a questionnaire was prepared. It was then revised on the basis of the results of pretesting on few individuals. The data was collected in the revised questionnaire which has been shown in Appendix-II.

## Data Analysis

The responses of the doctors have been tabulated in terms of both the numbers and percentages. Figures in tables within parantheses represent percentages while those without parantheses are simple frequencies.

In this case also the weighted average scores were calculated at places where the doctors were asked to rank, rate different statements either according to the extent they agree with the statements or according to degree of their importance as the case may. Again five types of responses were envisaged to devote the degree of agreement/ degree of importance viz. (i) Strongly agree/Most important, (ii) Agree/Important, (iii) Neither agree nor disagree/ Neither important nor unimportant, (iv) Disagree/Unimportant and (v) Strongly disagree/Most unimportant. Scores of –2, –1, 0, 1 and 2 were allotted to (i) to (v) respectively. The weighted average scores are calculated in the same manner given earlier except that in this case summation is from –2 to 2.

## Limitations of the Study

Any survey conducted through pre-designed questionnaire suffers from the basic limitation of the possibility of difference between what is recorded and what is the truth, no matter how carefully the questionnaire has been designed and field investigation has been conducted. However, in order to minimise the error, respondents were interviewed personally and through persuasions and helpful discussions it has been possible to a large extent to elicit reliable information from them. But there is no foolproof method of making it completely free.

Besides this, the conclusions drawn may have some limitation due to the fact that the samples are drawn only from the city of Delhi. Although it is felt that opinions of executives and doctors from elsewhere in India will not vary to an extent as to make the present conclusions unrealistic.

## Stress Management of Executives by Complementary Medicines – An Opinion Survey of Executives/Managers/Professionals

This chapter deals with the findings of the survey conducted to know the opinions of executives/managers/ professionals towards managing their stress and strain problems by complementary medicines. The data have been collected with the help of a comprehensive questionnaire (Appendix-I) prepared for this purpose from a sample of one hundred fifty executives. Section I of this chapter gives the general description of the respondents. Detailed analysis of opinions of the respondents is presented in Section 2.

**Section 1:** This section related to general information about sex, age, marital status, size of the family, number of dependents in family, working position of both husband and wife, educational qualifications, average monthly income, types of organisations in which working and housing facilities available and are given in Tables 33 to 38.

**Table 32: Sexwise Distribution**

| Sex | Respondent |
|---|---|
| Male | 126 (84.00) |
| Female | 24 (16.00) |
| N | 150 |

The above table shows that majority of the sample (84.00 per cent) is male and only 16.00 per cent comprise females.

The next table 33 shows a two-way classification of individuals by sex and age groups. Four age groups have been considered namely, '30 years & below', '31-40 years', '41-50 years' and '51 years and above'.

**Table 33: Distribution of individuals by sex and age group**

| *Age Group* | *Sex* | | |
|---|---|---|---|
| | *Male* | *Female* | *Total* |
| 30 years & below | 21 (16.67) | 4 (16.67) | 25 (16.67) |
| 31-40 years | 57 (45.24) | 12 (50.00) | 69 (46.00) |
| 41.50 years | 22 (17.46) | 4 (16.67) | 26 (17.35) |
| 51 years & above | 25 (19.84) | 1 (4.17) | 26 (17.33) |
| Non response | 1 (0.79) | 3 (12.50) | 4 (2.67) |
| N | 126 | 24 | 150 |

For the total population we find that the highest percentage (46.00 per cent) of individuals belongs to age group '31-40 years' whereas each of the other three age groups consists of only about 17 per cent. Similarly 50.00 per cent of females and 45.24 of males belong to second age group i.e. '31-40 years'. For the age group, '51 years & above', the percentage (19.84 per cent) of males is quite high compared to females (4.17 per cent) Table 34 shows the marital status of the executives.

**Table 34: Marital Status**

| *Marital Status* | *Sex* | | |
|---|---|---|---|
| | *Male* | *Female* | *Total* |
| Married | 110 (87.30) | 22 (91.67) | 132 (88.00) |
| Unmarried | 16 (12.70) | 2 (8.33) | 18 (12.00) |
| N | 126 | 24 | 150 |

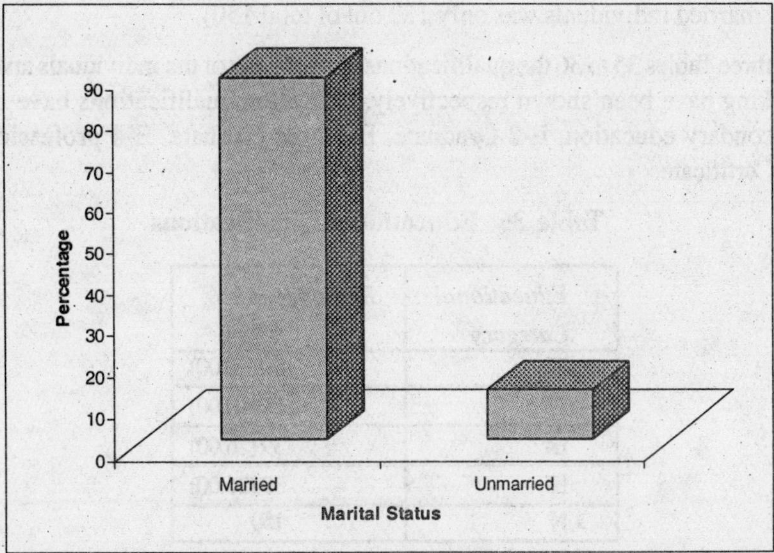


It is clear that married executives (88.00 per cent) out number the unmarried ones (12.00 per cent). In fact, ratio of married and unmarried in case of males and females taken separately are approximately of the order 7:1 and 11:1 respectively.

Now, 132 married individuals (Table 35) were then asked as to whether both husband and wife are working and their responses given in Table 35 shows that 44.70 per cent of them are working couples.

**Table 35: Employment Status of Married**

| *Employment Status* | *Respondent* |
|---|---|
| Both Working | 59 (44.70) |
| Both not Working | 73 (55.30) |
| N | 132* |

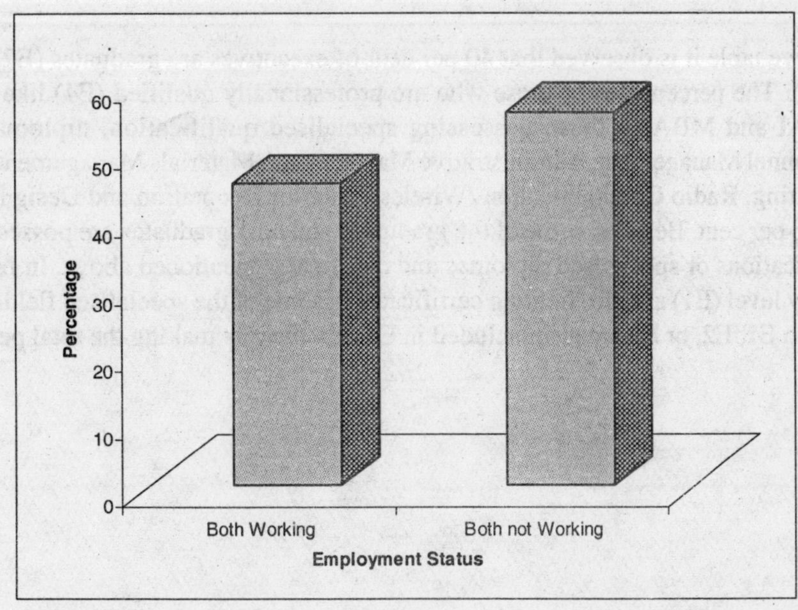

(* The number of married individuals was only 132 out of total 150).

In the subsequent three Tables 35 to 36 the qualifications, professions of the individuals and the types of organization in which they are working have been shown respectively. Education qualifications have been grouped under five categories iz. E-1 secondary education, E-2 Graduate, E-3 Post graduate, E-4 professional and E-5 specialised qualification Diploma/Certificate.

**Table 36: Educational Qualifications**

| *Educational Category* | *Respondent* |
|---|---|
| | 8(5.33) |
| E2 | 60 (40.00) |
| E3 | 60 (40.00) |
| E4 | 39 (26.00) |
| E5 | 39 (26.00) |
| N | 150 |

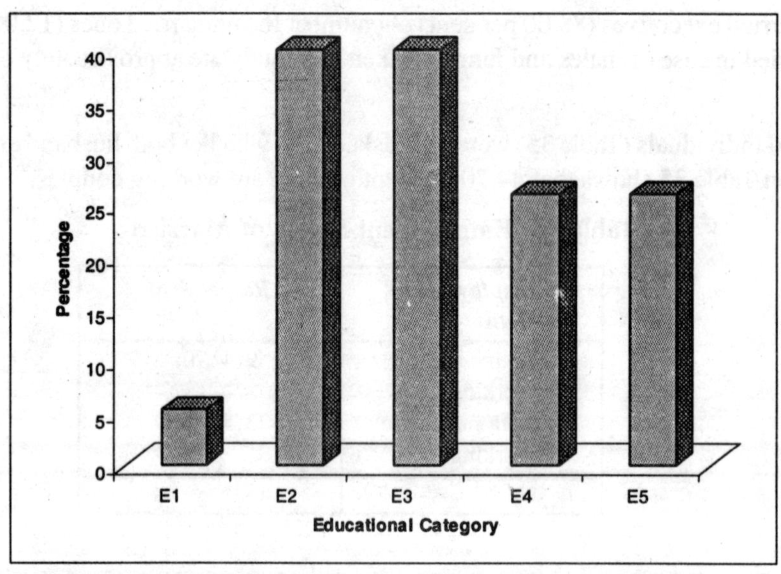


From the above table it is observed that 40 per cent of executives are graduates (E2) and another 40 per cent post graduates (E3). The percentages of those who are professionally qualified (E4) like B.Ed., LLB/LLM, B.E., MBBS/MD, ICWAI and MBA or those possessing specialised qualification, diploma/certificate in Business Management, Personnel Management, Administrative Management, Materials Management, Journalism, Computers, Pharmacy, Engineering, Radio Communication /Wireless, Interior Decoration and Design and Company Secretary are same namely 26 per cent. Besides, some of the graduates and post-graduates are possessing, in addition, various professional qualifications or specialised diplomas and certificates mentioned above. In fact few who are educated only upto secondary level (E1) are also holding certificates in some of the specialised fields. Thus, these individuals who belong either to E1, E2, or E3 are also included in E4, E5, thereby making the total percentage exceeding 100.

**Table 37: Profession**

| Profession | Sex: Male | Female | Total |
|---|---|---|---|
| Doctor | 6(4.76) | - | 6(4.00) |
| Teacher | 2(1.59) | 2(8.33) | 4(2.67) |
| Engineer | 3(2.38) | 1(4.17) | 4(2.67) |
| Administrator/ Manager/Mg. Director | 106(84.12) | 14(58.33) | 120(80.00) |
| Businessman | 7(5.56) | 1(4.17) | 8(5.33) |
| Computer Professional | - | 2(8.33) | 2(1.33) |
| Research Worker | 2(1.59) | - | 2(1.33) |
| Nursing Service | - | 2(8.33) | * |
| Social Service | - | 1(4.17) | 1(1.67) |
| Beautician | - | 1(4.17) | |
| N | 126 | 24 | 150 |

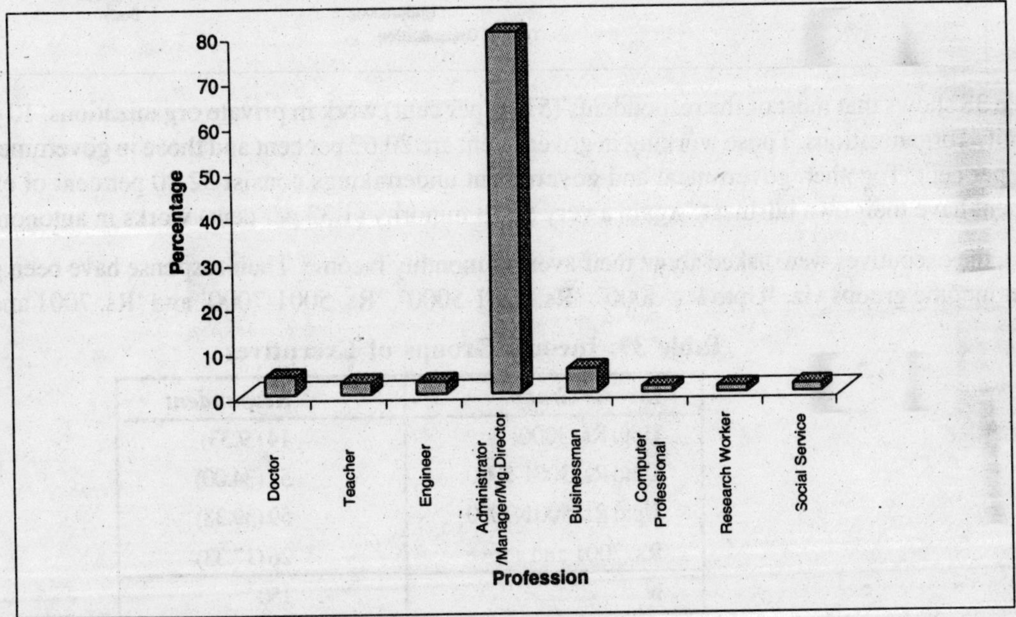


(* These professions are exclusively for females and as such percentages for total have not been given).

It is clear from the table that majority (80.00 per cent) of the executives are administrators. Sexwise this percentage is 84.12 for males and 58.33 for females. For the rest of the profession, 4.76 per cent of males are doctors, and another 5.56 per cent businessman. In case of females, 8.33 per cent are in each of the three professions viz. teaching, computers and nursing.

**Table 38: Types of Organisation In Which Executives Worked**

| Type of Organisation | Respondent |
|---|---|
| Private | 77(51.33) |
| Public/Limited | 15(10.00) |
| Government | 31(20.67) |
| Government Undertaking | 17(11.33) |
| Own Business | 8(5.33) |
| Autonomous Body | 2(1.33) |
| N | 150 |

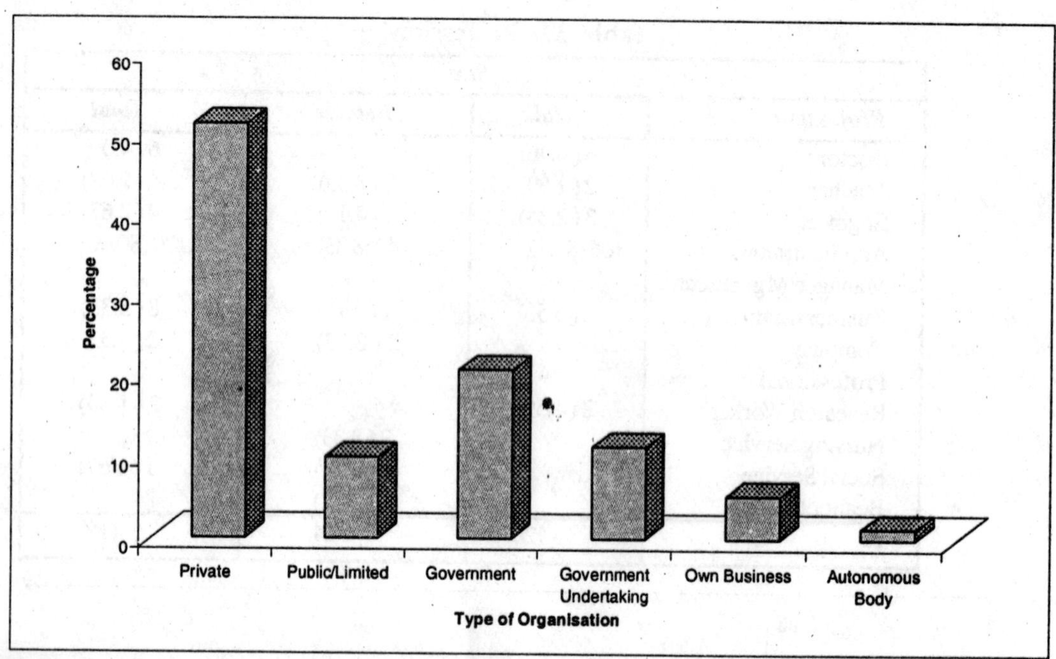


Table 38 shows that most of the respondents (51.33 per cent) work in private organizations. 10 per cent work is public/limited organizations. Those working in government are 20.67 per cent and those in government undertakings are 11.33 per cent. Together, government and government undertakings consist 32.00 per cent of executives. Only 5.33 per cent have their own business. Again a very small minority (1.33 per cent) works in autonomous bodies.

Next, the executives were asked about their average monthly income. Their response have been give in Table 39 under four income groups viz. 'Upto Rs. 3000', 'Rs. 3001-5000', 'Rs. 5001-7000' and 'Rs. 7001 and above'.

**Table 39: Income Groups of Executives**

| *Income Group* | *Respondent* |
|---|---|
| Upto Rs. 3000 | 14 (9.33) |
| Upto Rs. 3001-5000 | 51 (34.00) |
| Upto Rs. 5001-7000 | 59 (39.33) |
| Rs. 7001 and above | 26 (17.33) |
| N | 150 |

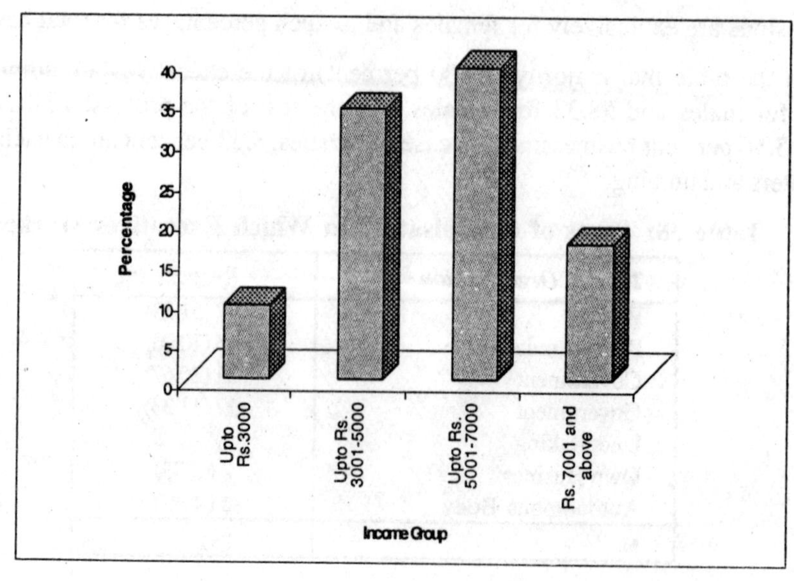

From the above table we find the maximum number of executives (39.33%) belongs to high income range of 'Rs. 50001-7000' followed by 34.00 per cent in the middle income group 'Rs. 3001-5000'. The very high income group of 'Rs. 7001 and above' consists about 17 per cent and only 9.33 per cent belong to low income group viz. 'Upto Rs. 3000'. (These are basic pay – perks DA etc. not tak n into account).

The information as to whether the executives are staying in their own houses or rented houses was ascertained and shown in Table 40.

**Table 40: Housing Facility**

| *Type of House Occupied* | *Number of Respondents* |
|---|---|
| Own | 62 (41.33) |
| Rented | 88 (58.67) |
| N | 150 |

We observe from the table that 41.33 per cent are having their own houses and while the rest 58.67 per cent are staying in rented houses.

Finally, Table 41 gives the distribution of families by number of adults, number of children and number of dependents in the family.

**Table 41: Distribution Of Family Size And Number Of Dependents**

| *Number Of Adults* | *Number Of Children* 0 | 1-2 | *More Than* 2 | *Number Of Dependents (Parents etc.)* 0 | 1-2 | *More Than* 2 |
|---|---|---|---|---|---|---|
| 1-2 | 16 (10.67) | 63 (42.00) | 18 (12.00) | 58 (38.67) | 31 (20.67) | 8 (5.33) |
| More Than | 18 2(12.00) | 27 (18.00) | 8 (5.33) | 11 (7.33) | 30 (20.00) | 12 (8.00) |
| N | | | 150 | | 150 | |

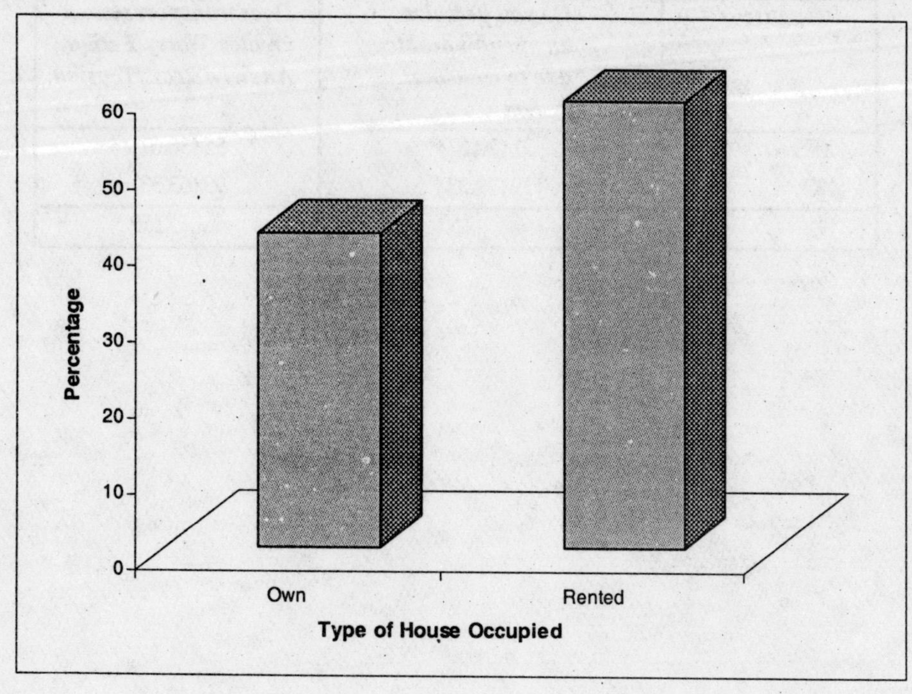

The table reveals that irrespective of number of adults in the family, a large number of families 60.00% is having either one child or two children. Only 22.67 per cent of families are not having any children whereas 17.33 per cent are having more than 2 children. Similarly in case of number of dependents, the families either having no dependent or having dependents between 1 and 2 are more or less of the same order i.e. 46.00 & 40.67 per cents respectively. Very few families (13.33%) have more than 2 dependents.

**Section 2:** This section contains detailed analysis of the opinions of executives on various stress related health problems and their management through complementary medicines.

## (A) Job Details

At the outset, responses of the executives as to whether they are satisfied with their present job or looking for a change in job or location are tabulated in Table 42.

**Table 42: Job Satisfaction**

| *Response* | *Happy with the Job* | *Looking for change in Job/Location* |
|---|---|---|
| YES | 131 (87.33) | 43 (28.67) |
| NO | 19 (12.67) | 107 (71.33) |
| N | 150 | 150 |

It is evident from the table that a very large number of respondents (87.33 per cent) are satisfied with their present jobs and only 12.67 per cent indicated their dissatisfaction about the job. The reasons for their dissatisfaction can be listed as lack of discipline in company, mismanagement, position not commensurate with qualifications, work atmosphere/office environment not suitable, work load not sufficient and no promotional avenues. Again 28.67 per cent want change in job or location and reasons they attribute for a change are lack of job satisfaction, better opportunity/better position and family settlement and housing problems.

Table 43 gives an idea of the health problems perceived by the executives due to transport system. They were also asked to give their opinions whether transport system creates any worry, fatique, anxiety, stress and tension problems.

**Table 43: Health Problems Faced Due to Transport System**

| *Response* | *Do you perceive any health problems due to transport system* | *Does transport system creates Worry/Fatique Anxiety/Stress/Tension* |
|---|---|---|
| YES | 31 (20.67) | 55 (36.67) |
| NO | 119 (79.33) | 95 (63.33) |
| N | 150 | 150 |

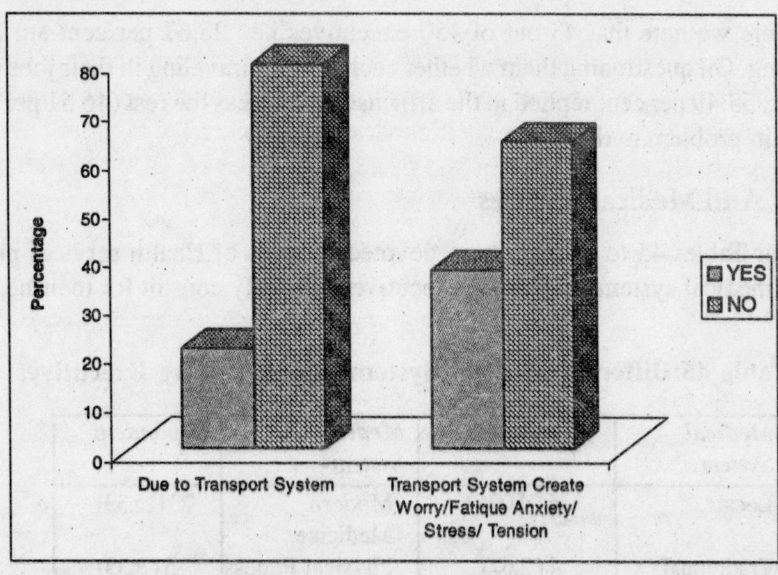


About 21 per cent felt that transport system does create various health problems like, headache, eye diseases, weakness, etc. A large majority of 36.67 per cent agreed that transport system causes worry, fatigue, anxiety, stress and tension.

Next, information on jobs involving touring/travelling was obtained and shown in Table 44.

**Table 44: Jobs Involving Touring/Travelling**

| *Response* | *Does your job Require touring/ Traveling* | *Does touring/traveling jobs cause you stress/strain* |
|---|---|---|
| YES | 43 (28.67) | 23 (53.49) |
| NO | 107 (71.33) | 20 (46.51) |
| N | 150 | 43 |

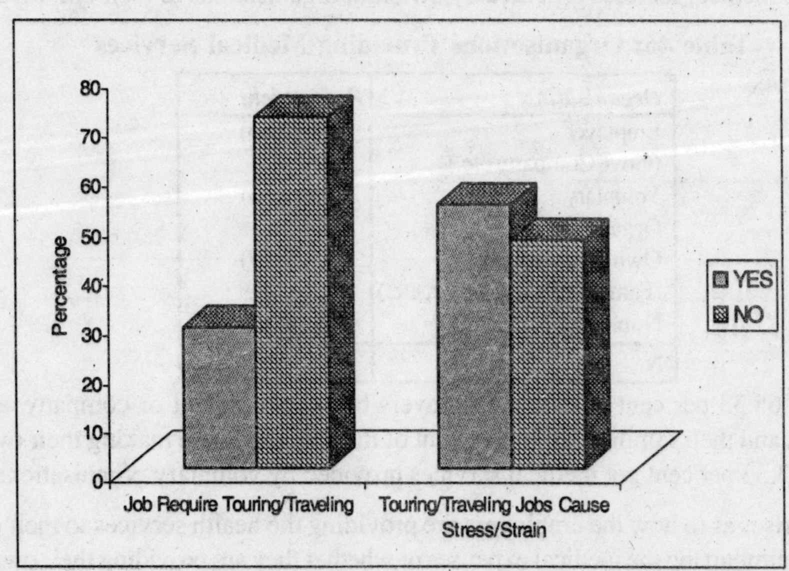

From the above table we note that 43 out of 150 executives i.e., 28.67 per cent are having jobs involving extensive touring/traveling. On questioning them whether such touring/traveling in their jobs cause any stress/strain problem, 23 out of 43 i.e., 53.49 per cent replied in the affirmative whereas the rest (46.51 per cent) felt such jobs do not create any stress/strain problem to them.

## (B) Medical Systems And Medical Services

The subsequent four Tables 45 to 46 have been devoted to types of Health services provided to executives. Table 45 gives different medical systems which the executives normally consult for their health problem specially stress and strain problem.

**Table 45:Different Medical Systems Consulted by Executives**

| *Medical System* | *Respondent* | *Medical System* | *Respondent* |
|---|---|---|---|
| Local | 6 (4.00) | Modern Medicine | 23 (15.33) |
| Traditional | 4 (2.67) | Physical Fitness Exercises | 5 (3.33) |
| Ayurveda | 12 (8.00) | Acupuncture / Massage | 2 (2.67) |
| Unani | 2 (1.33) | Psychotherapy | 1 (0.67) |
| Homoeopathy | 28 (18.67) | Yoga Therapy | 16 (10.67) |
| Allopathy | 81 (54.00) | | |
| Naturopathy | 24 (16.00) | | |
| N | 150 | | |

As expected, most of them (54.00 per cent) consult Allopathy. Homoeopathy and Naturopathy account for 18.67 per cent and 16.00 per cent of respondents. Modern medicine is consulted by 15.33 per cent whereas Yoga and Ayurveda by 10.67 per cent and 8.00 per cent respectively. The rest of the systems are consulted only by a small minority, ranging from about 1 per cent to 4 per cent.

Table 46 shows medical services provided by different organisations to their employee and their families.

**Table 46: Organisations Providing Medical Services**

| *Organisation* | *Respondent* |
|---|---|
| Employer (Govt/Company etc.) | 98 (65.33) |
| Voluntary Organisation | 5 (3.33) |
| Own Arrangement (Family/Private Doctor, etc.) | 31 (20.67) |
| Non-response | 16 (10.67) |
| N | 150 |

We observe that in 65.33 per cent of cases, employers be it government or company, are providing health services to the employees and their families. 20.67 per cent of the executives are making their own arrangements for medical treatment. Mere 3.33 per cent got medical services provided by voluntary organisations.

The question now arises as to how the employers are providing the health services to their executives, whether they are fully or partially reimbursing the medical expenses or whether they are providing their own doctors, medicines and other facilities e.g. Central Government Health Scheme (CGHS), and Health Services Schemes for defence personnel. The information under these breakdowns for individuals for whom employers are providing medical services (Table 46) has been given in Table 47.

**Table 47: Type of Medical Services Provided**

| *Type of Medical Service* | *Respondent* |
|---|---|
| Full reimbursement of medical expenses | 26 (26.53) |
| Partial reimbursement of medical expenses | 67 (68.37) |
| Free medical treatment provided by organisations by their own doctors, medicines, etc. | 5 (5.10) |
| N | 98 |

From the table, we find that 26.53 per cent got full reimbursement of the medical expenses by their employers and another 68.37 per cent got partial reimbursement. About 5 per cent of these are provided free medical treatment by their employers. Further, from Table 48 we have seen that 31 executives out of 150 (20.67 per cent) are making their own arrangement for medical treatment. It has been found that 16 among them (10.67 per cent) are covered under medical insurance.

Table 48 gives an idea of the monthly medical expenses incurred by the respondents.

**Table 48: Medical Expenses Incurred**

| *Monthly Amount Spent* | *Respondent* |
|---|---|
| Upto Rs. 250 | 61 (40.67) |
| Rs. 251-500 | 52 (34.67) |
| Rs. 501 and above | 8 (5.33) |
| No expenses/ Non-response | 29 (19.33) |
| N | 150 |

It is observed that 40.67 per cent spent 'Upto Rs. 250' and another 34.67 per cent between 'Rs. 251-500' i.e. together 75.34 per cent of them spent up to Rs. 500 on medical expenses. Only 5.33 per cent spent more than Rs. 500.

## (C) Nutrition

All the executive except two who did not respond i.e., 98.67 per cent of them agreed that good health is related to natural food.

The replies to the query 'whether vegetarian or non-vegetarian food causes any discomfort' have been given in Table 49.

**Table 49:Discomfort Due To Food**

| *Discomfort due to* | *Respondent* |
|---|---|
| Vegetarian Food | 25 (16.67) |
| Non-Vegeratian Food | 91 (60.67) |
| Non response/ No discomfort | 34 (22.67) |
| N | 150 |

Non-vegetarian food caused discomfort to large number of individuals (60.67 per cent). Only 16.77 per cent felt discomfort due to vegetarian food specially those having excess oil and spice or fried items. About 23 per cent either did not respond or they did not feel any discomfort.

It is felt that by changing food habits, it may be possible to control stress and strain. The opinion on this was sought from the respondents which has been shown in Table 50.

**Table 50:Controlling Stress/Strain By Changing Food Habits**

| *Response* | *Respondent* |
|---|---|
| YES | 51 (34.00) |
| NO | 84 (56.00) |
| Not Applicable/ Non-response | 15 (10.00) |
| N | 150 |

From above, we find 56.00 per cent did not believe that stress/strain can be controlled by changing food habits. But another 34.00 per cent felt that by switching over to less spicy vegetable food and balanced diet, by taking seasonal vegetable and fruits, by changing over to soups, juices and dry fruits, by reducing intake of food or by fasting, it has been possible for them to control stress and strain to a reasonable extent.

The executives were next asked as to whether they would like to gain weight, loose weight or stay same. Table 51 tabulates their opinions.

**Table 51:Opinion On Body Weight**

| *Like To* | *Respondent* |
|---|---|
| Loose Weight | 55 (36.67) |
| Stay Same | 61 (40.67) |
| Non Response | 24 (16.00) |
| N | 150 |

Most of them (40.67 per cent) would like to stay same since their weight is under permissible limit and they feel quite fit and no discomfort in their day-to-day activities. In order to keep themselves fit, active and disease–free, 36.67 per cent of the executives wanted to reduce there weight, thereby, keeping it under prescribed limits. They felt, loosing weight would not only help them look smart but also in controlling health at later age. Very few viz. 6.67 per cent wanted to gain weight. Under weight, making the body more healthy and strong were some of the reasons put forward by them for gaining weight.

It is quite common that pattern of consumption of each of the various food items in a family is not same e.g., some items are consumed daily, some monthly, etc. Table 52 shows the intake of food items like milk, bread, rice, cereal, green vegetables, fish, meat, etc. under five types of periodicity viz., daily, occasionally, monthly, seasonal and never.

**Table 52: Food Intake**

| | *Period of Intake* | | | | |
|---|---|---|---|---|---|
| *Item* | *Daily* | *Occasionally* | *Monthly* | *Seasonal* | *Never* |
| Milk | 112 (74.67) | 2 (1.33) | 7 (4.67) | 5 (3.33) | 3 (2.00) |
| Cheese | 22 (14.67) | 4 (2.67) | 39 (26.00) | 42 (28.00) | 9 (6.00) |
| Yogurt | 39 (26.00) | 2 (1.33) | 17 (11.33) | 22 (14.67) | 28 (18.67) |
| Ice Cream | 2 (1.33) | 4 (2.67) | 22 (14.67) | 76 (50.67) | 9 (6.00) |
| Bread | 83 (53.33) | 9 (6.60) | 23 (15.33) | 16 (10.67) | 2 (1.33) |
| Rice | 94 (62.67) | 7 (4.67) | 27 (18.00) | 7 (4.67) | 1 (0.67) |
| Cereal | 94 (63.33) | 2 (1.33) | 11 (7.33) | 5 (3.33) | 5 (3.33) |

| | | | | | |
|---|---|---|---|---|---|
| Potatoes | 113 (75.33) | 5 (3.33) | 16 (10.67) | 8 (5.33) | – |
| Eggs | 37 (24.67) | 5 (3.33) | 25 (16.67) | 31 (20.67) | 15 (10.00) |
| Fruit | 101 (67.33) | 2 (1.33) | 15 (10.00) | 22 (14.67) | – |
| Fruit Juice | 23 (15.33) | 6 (4.00) | 36 (24.00) | 51 (34.00) | – |
| Fried Beans | 9 (6.00) | 3 (2.00) | 23 (15.33) | 43 (28.67) | 17 (11.33) |
| Peas | 25 (16.67) | 3 (2.00) | 21 (14.00) | 66 (44.00) | 3 (2.00) |
| Peanut | 10 (6.67) | 4 (2.67) | 23 (15.33) | 59 (39.33) | 3 (2.00) |
| Green Vegetable | 134 (89.33) | – (2.00) | 3 (6.67) | 10 | – |

***Period of Intake***

| *Item* | *Daily* | *Occasionally* | *Monthly* | *Seasonal* | *Never* |
|---|---|---|---|---|---|
| Salads | 114 (76.00) | 3 (2.00) | 10 (6.67) | 15 (10.00) | 1 (0.67) |
| Red Meat | 3 (2.00) | 2 (1.33) | 36 (24.00) | 11 (7.33) | 53 (35.33) |
| Fish | 13 (8.67) | 5 (3.33) | 26 (17.33) | 22 (14.67) | 43 (28.67) |
| Poultry | – (2.67) | 4 (22.00) | 33 (12.00) | 18 (28.67) | 43 |
| Candy/ Sweet | 16 (10.67) | 7 (4.67) | 45 (30.00) | 28 (18.67) | 10 (6.67) |
| Soda | 1 (0.67) | 5 (3.33) | 24 (16.00) | 39 (26.00) | 28 (18.67) |
| Cookies | 11 (7.33) | 3 (2.00) | 41 (27.33) | 24 (16.00) | 14 (9.33) |
| Cake | 3 (2.00) | 8 (5.33) | 43 (28.67) | 36 (24.00) | 10 (6.67) |
| Pulses | 110 (73.33) | 2 (1.33) | 11 (7.33) | 8 (5.33) | – |
| Ghee | 104 (69.33) | 3 (2.00) | 13 (8.67) | 11 (7.33) | 3 (2.00) |
| Others | 3 (2.00) | 1 (0.67) | – | – | – |
| N | 150 | | | | |

Let us now look into some of the salient features of the table. Incidentally, green vegetables are consumed daily by a very large number of individuals (89.33 per cent). Other items like salads, potatoes, milk, pulses and fruits are consumed daily by 76.00 per cent to 67.33 per cent of executives. Similarly, daily consumption of cereal, rice and bread are by 63.33 per cent, 62.67 per cent and 55.33 per cent of them. Regarding the occasional intake of all these items, there are very few people ranging only from 0.67 per cent to 6.60 per cent who make such consumption. In case of monthly consumption, candy/sweets, cake, cookies, cheese and fruit juices are consumed by 30 per cent, 28.67 per cent, 27.33 per cent, 26 per cent, 24 per cent of executives respectively. Further, we know that there are certain items which are consumed by more number of people in any particular season e.g. ice-cream in summer. Such seasonal variations in consumption have been reflected in the table. It is interesting to know that many executives have never eaten any non-vegetarian products like red meat (35.33 per cent), fish (28.67 per cent) and poultry (28.67 per cent). Similarly, 18.67 per cent and 11.33 per cent have not taken soda and fried beans respectively. Only 10.00 per cent have not tasted eggs.

Table 53 gives an idea of daily consumption of tea, coffee and soda in terms of number of cups/glasses which have been grouped into '1-2', '3-4', '5-6', '7-9' and '10-13'.

**Table 53: Daily Intake of Tea, Coffee and Soda**

| | *Number of Cups/Glasses* | | | | |
|---|---|---|---|---|---|
| ***Type of Drink*** | ***1-2*** | ***3-4*** | ***5-6*** | ***7-9*** | ***10-13*** |
| Tea | 41<br>(27.33) | 62<br>(41.33) | 30<br>(20.00) | 3<br>(2.00) | 6<br>(4.00) |
| Coffee | 28<br>(18.67) | 7<br>(4.67) | 1<br>(0.67) | 1<br>(0.67) | – |
| Soda | 3<br>(2.00) | – | – | – | – |
| N | 150 | | | | |

From the above, it is clear that most executive prefer tea in comparison to coffee and soda. 41.33 per cent of them take 3 to 4 cups of tea daily followed by 27.33 and 20.00 per cent who consume 1-2 cups and 5-6 cups respectively. Only 4.00 per cent drink tea between 10-13 cups daily. The average daily consumption of tea per head works out to be about 3.5 cups. In case of coffee, 18.67 per cent drink 1-2 cups and 4.67 per cent between 3 to 4 cups. Soda is taken by a negligible minority. In fact, only 2.00 per cent take soda between 1 to 2 glasses.

The executives were then asked as to whether they are on any specialised diet, whether they frequently add salt to their diet or whether they supplement their diet by taking iron, vitamin, etc. and the reasons the in. Table 54 contains all these information.

**Table 54: Special Diet, Intake of Salt, Iron, Vitamins, etc.**

| ***Response*** | ***Are you on Special diet Salt to your food?*** | ***Do you add frequently and other diet supplement?*** | ***Do you take iron, Vitamins?*** |
|---|---|---|---|
| YES | 9<br>(6.00) | 36<br>(24.00) | 34<br>(22.67) |
| NO | 141<br>(94.00) | 114<br>(76.00) | 116<br>(77.33) |
| N | 150 | 150 | 150 |

Only 6.00 per cent are on a specialised diet and reasons given for this are heart trouble, diabetes, over weight and stone problem. Again 24.00 per cent add salt to the food for enhancing the taste. But the majority (76.00 per cent) do not add salt frequently to their food due to various reasons viz. it is harmful for body and health, it puts strain or heart, it is necessary for controlling blood pressure, likes to take food without salt and it is not allowed by physician. About 23 per cent supplement their food with iron, vitamins, etc. The type of supplements are green vegetables, fruit, fruit juices, salad, milk, vitamin B Complex tablets, Chavanprash, codliver oil and Waterbury's Compound and these are necessarily taken to make oneself healthy and fit, to remove deficiencies, to make the diet balanced, to overcome

bronchial troubles, to provide natural vitamins and iron, to prevent weakness or on doctor's advice. Of course 77.33 per cent do not need any type of diet supplement in their food intake.

Table 55 gives an idea of outside food habits of executives.

**Table 55: Fast food and food from outside**

| | *Do you take* | |
|---|---|---|
| ***Response*** | ***Fast Food*** | ***Snacks from outside*** |
| YES | 66<br>(44.00) | 84<br>(56.00) |
| NO | 84<br>(56.0) | 66<br>(44.00) |
| N | 150 | 150 |

So far as the consumption of fast food is concerned, it is observed that the response to those who take and to those who do not take are more or less of the same order viz. 44.00 per cent and 56.00 per cent respectively. Similarly, in case of taking snacks from restaurants, hotels, etc., these percentages have been reversed i.e., 56.00 per cent of those who eat snacks outside, 44.00 per cent of those who do not.

Two subsequent tables are devoted to ascertain the smoking and drinking habits of the individuals.

**Table 56: Smoking Habits**

| *Type of Smoking* | *Respondents* |
|---|---|
| Cigarettes | 23<br>(15.33) |
| Cigar | 1<br>(0.67) |
| Chewing Tobacco<br>(Pan Masala) | 5<br>(3.33) |
| N | 150 |

It appears majority (80.67 per cent) of the executives are non-smokers. Among smokers (19.33 per cent), the highest percentage is for those who smoke cigarettes only viz. 15.33 per cent. Most smokers say they smoke to relieve tension, stress and worry and feel relaxed.

The information on daily/weekly consumption of wine/beer/others as asked for in the questionnaire could not be ascertained. However, an estimate of the number of individuals who take once in day/once in a week/occasionally have been obtained and shown in Table 57.

**Table 57: Drinking Habits**

| *Periodicity* | *Respondents* |
|---|---|
| Daily | 4<br>(2.67) |
| Weekly | 21<br>(14.00) |
| Occasionally | 6<br>(4.00) |
| N | 150 |

Again it can be seen that very few people, in fact only 20.67 per cent are having drinking habits out of which 14.00 per cent consume once in a week, 4.00 per cent occasionally and 2.67 per cent once in day.

## (D) Stress

We now come to one of the important aspect of the analysis namely causes of stress. A working executive/ manager/professional has to face various problems in his day-to-day duties causing stress. 37 statements on problems which may cause stress have been listed and executives were asked to give their opinions as to what extent these contribute to stress under 5 levels of stress viz. (i) Always stress, (ii) Frequent stress, (iii) Occasional stress, (iv) Rarely any stress and (v) No stress at all. Opinions of the executives have been tabulated in Table 58. The last two columns of the table also show the weighted average score (W.A.S.) for each of the statement and rating based on the weighted average score respectively.

**Table 58: Stress Problems Of Executives**

| | *Levels of Stress* | | | | | | *Weighted average* | |
|---|---|---|---|---|---|---|---|---|
| *Statement* | *Always stress* | *Frequent stress* | *Occasional stress* | *Rarely and stress* | *No stress at all* | *average* | *Rating* | *Score* |
| Planning your career | 19 (12.67) | 18 (12.00) | 47 (31.33) | 29 (19.33) | 37 (24.67) | 1.69 | 7 | V1 |
| Getting on in your job | 16 (10.67) | 20 (13.33) | 43 (28.67) | 28 (18.67) | 43 (28.67) | 1.59 | 13 | V2 |
| Managing Boss | 7 (4.67) | 10 (6.67) | 48 (32.00) | 41 (27.33) | 44 (29.33) | 1.30 | 25 | V3 |
| Keeping upto job (knowledge) | 16 (10.67) | 22 (14.67) | 32 (21.33) | 34 (22.67) | 46 (30.67) | 1.52 | 16 | V4 |
| Maintaining your integrity | 14 (9.33) | 13 (8.67) | 24 (16.00) | 34 22.67) | 65 (43.33) | 1.18 | 27 | V5 |
| Your monthly Check-up (medical) | 3 (2.00) | 4 (2.67) | 29 (19.33) | 34 (22.67) | 80 (53.33) | 0.76 | 30 | V6 |
| Analysis of your job | 14 (9.33) | 23 (15.33) | 39 (26.00) | 32 (21.33) | 42 (28.00) | 1.57 | 14 | V7 |
| Managing Operations (all types) | 18 (12.00) | 21 (14.00) | 48 (32.00) | 27 (18.00) | 36 (24.00) | 1.72 | 6 | V8 |
| Planning | 17 (11.33) | 36 (24.00) | 33 (15.33) | 25 (16.67) | 39 (26.00) | 1.78 | 3 | V9 |
| Managing with objectives | 18 (12.00) | 27 (18.00) | 42 (28.00) | 27 (18.00) | 36 (24.00) | 1.76 | 4 | V10 |
| Controlling Staff | 25 (16.67) | 20 (13.33) | 44 (29.33) | 30 (20.00) | 31 (20.67) | 1.85 | 1 | V11 |
| Decision Making | 15 (10.00) | 19 (12.67) | 43 (28.67) | 38 (25.33) | 35 (23.33) | 1.61 | 11 | V12 |
| Communicating at all levels | 16 (10.67) | 20 (13.33) | 30 (20.00) | 41 (27.33) | 43 (28.67) | 1.47 | 19 | V13 |
| Managing your time | 19 (12.67) | 29 (19.33) | 34 (22.67) | 22 (14.67) | 46 (30.67) | 1.69 | 7 | V14 |
| Co-ordinating with various department | 17 (11.33) | 24 (16.00) | 34 (22.67) | 35 (23.33) | 40 (26.67) | 1.62 | 10 | V15 |
| Working with your team | 16 (16.67) | 15 (10.00) | 34 (22.67) | 38 (25.33) | 47 (31.33) | 1.43 | 20 | V16 |
| Human Resources Development | 10 (6.67) | 16 (10.67) | 26 (17.33) | 37 (24.67) | 61 (40.67) | 1.18 | 27 | V17 |

| | | | | | | | | |
|---|---|---|---|---|---|---|---|---|
| Selection/ Interviewing | 11 (7.33) | 8 (5.33) | 45 (30.00) | 38 (25.33) | 48 (32.00) | 1.31 | 24 | V18 |
| Training | 9 (6.00) | 12 (8.00) | 35 (23.33) | 35 23.33) | 59 (39.33) | 1.18 | 27 | V19 |
| Deligating | 5 (3.33) | 15 (10.00) | 38 (25.33) | 40 (26.67) | 52 (34.67) | 1.21 | 26 | V20 |
| Motivating your staff | 13 (8.67) | 24 (16.00) | 31 (20.67) | 38 (25.33) | 44 (29.33) | 1.49 | 18 | V21 |
| Improving People's job | 10 (6.67) | 28 (18.67) | 46 (30.67) | 29 (19.33) | 37 (24.67) | 1.63 | 9 | V22 |
| Developing Leadership | 13 (8.67) | 23 (15.33) | 35 (23.33) | 39 (26.00) | 40 (26.67) | 1.53 | 15 | V23 |
| Counselling your staff | 13 (8.67) | 20 (13.33) | 39 (26.00) | 37 (24.67) | 41 (27.33) | 1.51 | 17 | V24 |
| Running a staff appraisal system | 9 (16.00) | 15 (10.00) | 42 (28.00) | 40 (26.67) | 44 (29.33) | 1.37 | 22 | V25 |
| Discipling Staff | 22 (14.67) | 29 (19.33) | 35 (23.33) | 29 (19.33) | 35 (23.33) | 1.83 | 2 | V26 |
| Controlling your organisation | 23 (15.33) | 18 (12.00) | 42 (28.00) | 28 (18.67) | 39 (26.00) | 1.72 | 6 | V27 |
| Handling your organization | 20 (13.33) | 16 (10.67) | 44 (29.33) | 24 (16.00) | 46 (30.67) | 1.60 | 12 | V28 |
| Managing Meetings | 11 (7.33) | 7 (4.67) | 56 (36.67) | 34 (22.67) | 43 (28.67) | 1.39 | 21 | V29 |
| Writing Reports etc. | 9 (6.00) | 15 (10.00) | 43 (28.67) | 35 (23.33) | 48 (32.00) | 1.35 | 23 | V30 |
| Reading Research Findings etc. | 5 (3.33) | 13 (8.67) | 34 (22.67) | 42 (28.00) | 56 (37.33) | 1.13 | 29 | V31 |
| Listening to Employees | 15 (10.00) | 19 (12.67) | 24 (16.00) | 37 (24.67) | 55 (36.67) | 1.35 | 23 | V32 |
| Speaking in Public/Seminar | 13 (8.67) | 16 (10.67) | 40 (26.67) | 35 (25.33) | 46 (30.67) | 1.43 | 20 | V33 |
| Telephoning | 8 (5.33) | 17 (11.33) | 29 (19.33) | 34 (22.67) | 62 (41.33) | 1.17 | 28 | V34 |
| Negotiating Labour | 21 (14.00) | 16 (10.67) | 39 (26.00) | 34 (22.67) | 40 (26.67) | 1.63 | 9 | V35 |
| Managing Conflict | 17 (11.33) | 26 (17.33) | 43 (28.67) | 30 (20.00) | 34 (22.67) | 1.75 | 5 | V36 |
| Managing Change | 13 (8.67) | 20 (13.33) | 52 (34.67) | 30 (20.00) | 35 (23.33) | 1.64 | 8 | V37 |
| N | 150 | | | | | | | |

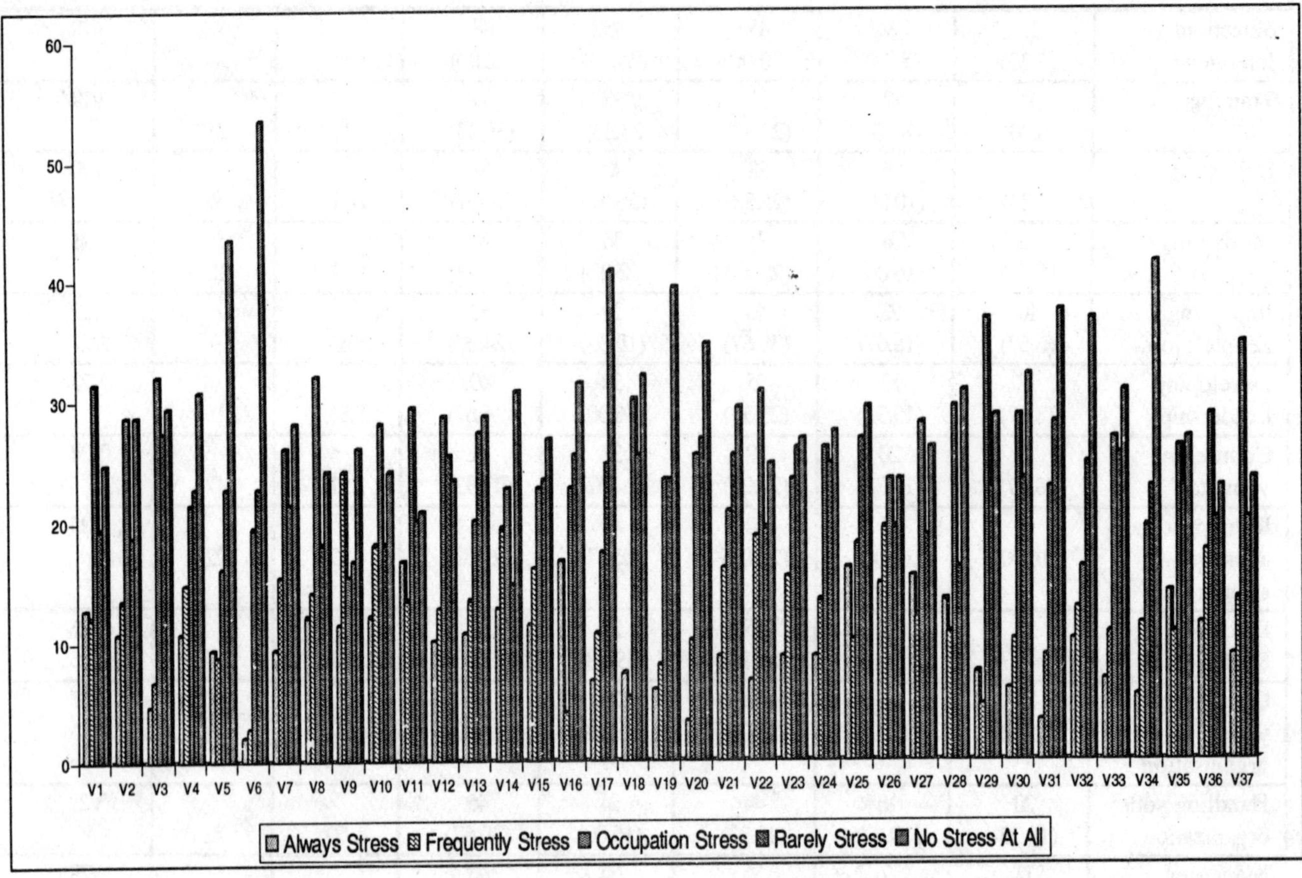


Let us now examine few salient features of the table. It is clear that almost all the statements do cause stress to executives ranging between 60 to 75 per cent only in case of the statement 'Your monthly check up (medical)', however, 53.33 per cent feel no stress i.e., 46.67 per cent feel stress. Coming next to ratings, we find that highest rating has been given to the statement 'Controlling the staff' (W. A. S. – 1.85) followed by 'Disciplining the staff' (W.A.S.-1.83). Significantly it is in dealing with the staff, an executive feels the maximum stress. The ratings of some of the statements are identical e.g., statements 'Planning your career' and 'Managing your time' are both rated as 7 since weighted average scores for both are 1.69. Few statements like 'Human Resources development' (W.A.S.-1.18), 'Managing your integrity' (W.A.S.-1.18), 'Telephoning' (W.A.S.-1.17) have been given lower rating of 27, 27 & 28. Obviously the lowest rating of 30 has been given to 'Your monthly check up (medical)' (W.A.S.-0.76).

## (E) Health Problems

In this sub-section various health problems faced by the executives in the past one year have been considered. First, their responses to the problems like appetite, change of body weight, fever and sweat are given in Table 59.

**Table 59: Problems Of Appetite, Body Weight, Fever And Sweat**

| | *Do you have* | | | |
|---|---|---|---|---|
| ***Response*** | ***Any problem with appetite*** | ***Change of weight more than 10 kg*** | ***Fever*** | ***Sweat*** |
| YES | 28 (18.67) | 12 (8.00) | 32 (21.33) | 33 (22.00) |
| NO | 122 (81.33) | 138 (92.00) | 118 (78.67) | 117 (78.00) |
| N | 150 | 150 | 150 | 150 |

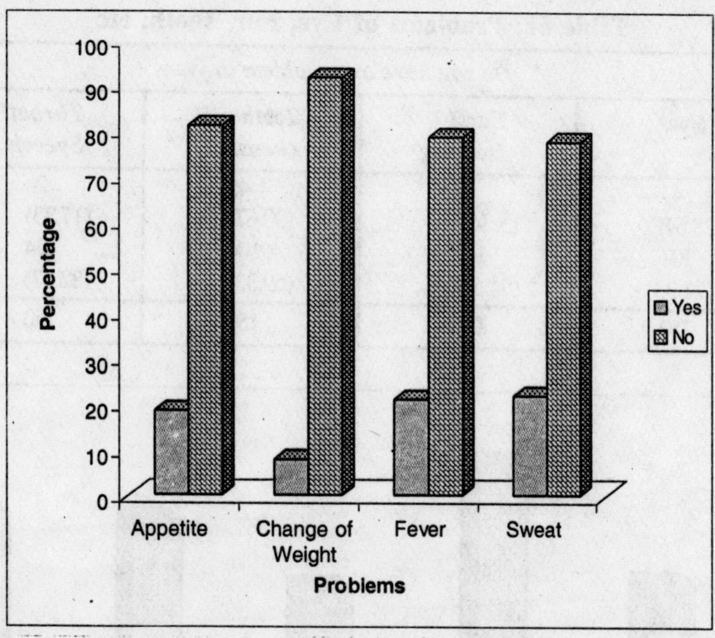


Only 18.67 per cent have appetite problem which is caused due to various reasons like gastric trouble, over eating, stress, indigestion, change of routine and touring, pollution in environment, cereals, pulses and vegetables, diarrhoea, constipation and acidity. Very few (8.00 per cent) have undergone changes in body weight and they feel this may be due to age, reduced activity, etc. Similarly 21.33 per cent and 22.00 per cent have fevers and sweats respectively. Possibly tonsils, environment changes are some of the reasons for fever whereas heat in body during summer is responsible for sweats.

Next, the executives were asked as to whether they have any skin problems like skin rashes, sores and itching or whether they are allergic to penicillin, other drugs and any food. Their responses are shown in Table 60.

**Table 60: Skin Problems/Allergies**

| | *Do you have any* | | | *Are you allergic to* | | |
|---|---|---|---|---|---|---|
| ***Response*** | ***Skin Rashes*** | ***Sores*** | ***Itching*** | ***Penicillin*** | ***Other drugs*** | ***Any food*** |
| YES | 11<br>(7.33) | 3<br>(2.00) | 12<br>(8.00) | 7<br>(4.67) | 13<br>(8.67) | 3<br>(2.00) |
| NO | 139<br>(92.67) | 147<br>(98.00) | 138<br>(92.00) | 143<br>(95.33) | 137<br>(91.33) | 147<br>(98.00) |
| N | 150 | 150 | 150 | 150 | 150 | 150 |

It is evident from above that majority of the executives have neither any skin problem nor allergy. In fact, only 7.33 per cent, 2.00 and 8.00 per cent suffer from skin rashes, sores and itching, respectively. Similarly, about 5 per cent are allergic to penicillin, 8.67 per cent to other drugs like brufen, sulphur drugs, aspirin and analgin and 2.00 per cent to some foods like black pepper, guava, etc.

Three subsequent tables 60, 61 and 62 relate to problems of Eye, Ear, Tooth, etc., Respiratory problems and Cardiac problems of the individuals respectively.

**Table 61: Problems of Eye, Ear, Tooth, etc**

| | *Do you have any problem in* | | | | |
|---|---|---|---|---|---|
| ***Response*** | ***Eye*** | ***Ears/ Hearing*** | ***Teeth Gums*** | ***Throat/ Speech*** | ***Sinus*** |
| YES | 43 (28.67) | 8 (5.343) | 46 (30.67) | 26 (17.33) | 24 (16.00) |
| NO | 107 (71.33) | 142 (94.67) | 104 (69.33) | 124 (82.67) | 126 (84.00) |
| N | 150 | 150 | 150 | 150 | 150 |

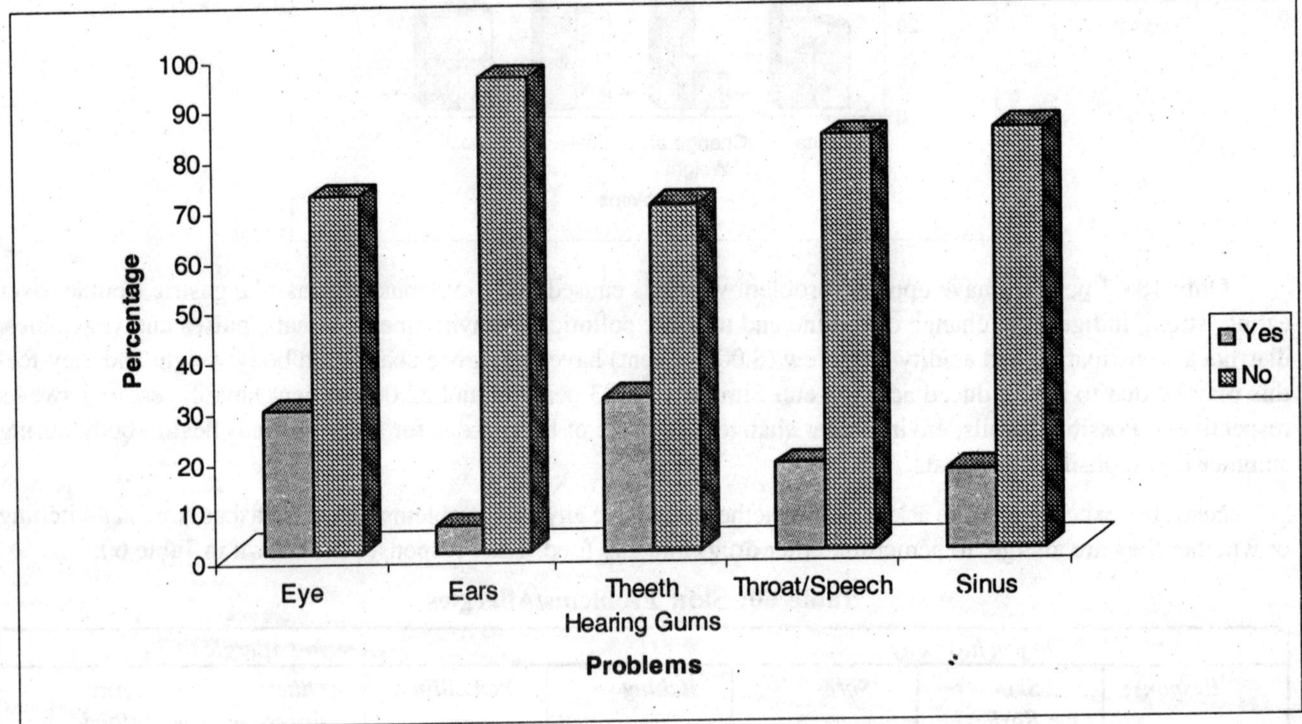


The above table shows that 30.67 per cent are affected by teeth/gums trouble followed by 28.67 having throat/ speech problem and 16.00 per cent sinus. A very small minority (5.33 per cent) has trouble in their ears and in hearing. Thus, it appears all these troubles do not pose any serious threat to the health of the executives.

**Table 62: Respiratory Problems**

| ***Response*** | ***Do you have Persistent cough or phlegm production*** | ***Wheezing*** | ***Do you ever Cough up Blood*** |
|---|---|---|---|
| YES | 22 (14.67) | 9 (6.00) | 6 (4.00) |
| NO | 128 (85.33) | 141 (94.00) | 144 (96.00) |
| N | 150 | 150 | 150 |

We find from Table 63 that respiratory troubles do not bother most of the executives. In fact, only 14.67 per cent are having persistent cough, 6.00 per cent wheezing, only 4.00 per cent have coughed up blood.

**Table 63: Cardiac Problems**

| Response | *Do you have* Breathing trouble | Pain or tightness in chest | Do your ankles swell |
|---|---|---|---|
| YES | 12 (8.00) | 20 (13.33) | 11 (7.33) |
| NO | 138 (92.00) | 130 (86.67) | 139 (92.67) |
| N | 150 | 150 | 150 |

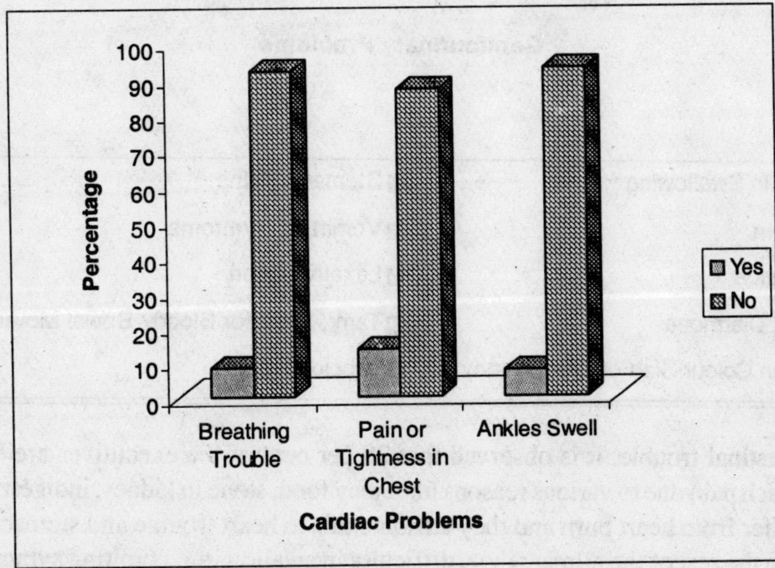


It is noteworthy that 92.00 per cent are not having any breathing trouble, only 8.00 per cent have. Similarly, about 13 per cent have pain or tightness in chest. Only 7.33 per cent suffer from ankle swelling.

Next two tables 63 and 64 are devoted to the responses of the executives about their gastro-intestinal and genito-urinary problems respectively.

**Table 64: Gastro-intestinal Problems**

| Response | *Do you have* Difficulty in swallowing | Stomach Pains | Heart Burn | Vomitting symptoms | Constipation | Do you use a laxative often | Do you have frequent diarrhoea | Have you had any tarry, black, or bloody bowel movements | Is there any change in colour, size or consistency in your bowel movements | Do you have orhoids |
|---|---|---|---|---|---|---|---|---|---|---|
| YES | 2 (1.33) | 34 (22.67) | 15 (10.00) | 13 (8.67) | 42 (28.00) | 6 (4.00) | 9 (6.00) | 4 (2.67) | 3 (2.00) | 5 (3.33) |
| NO | 148 (98.67) | 116 (77.33) | 135 (90.00) | 137 (91.33) | 108 (72.00) | 144 (96.00) | 141 (94.00) | 146 (97.33) | 147 (98.33) | 145 (96.67) |
| N | 150 | 150 | 150 | 150 | 150 | 150 | 150 | 150 | 150 | 150 |

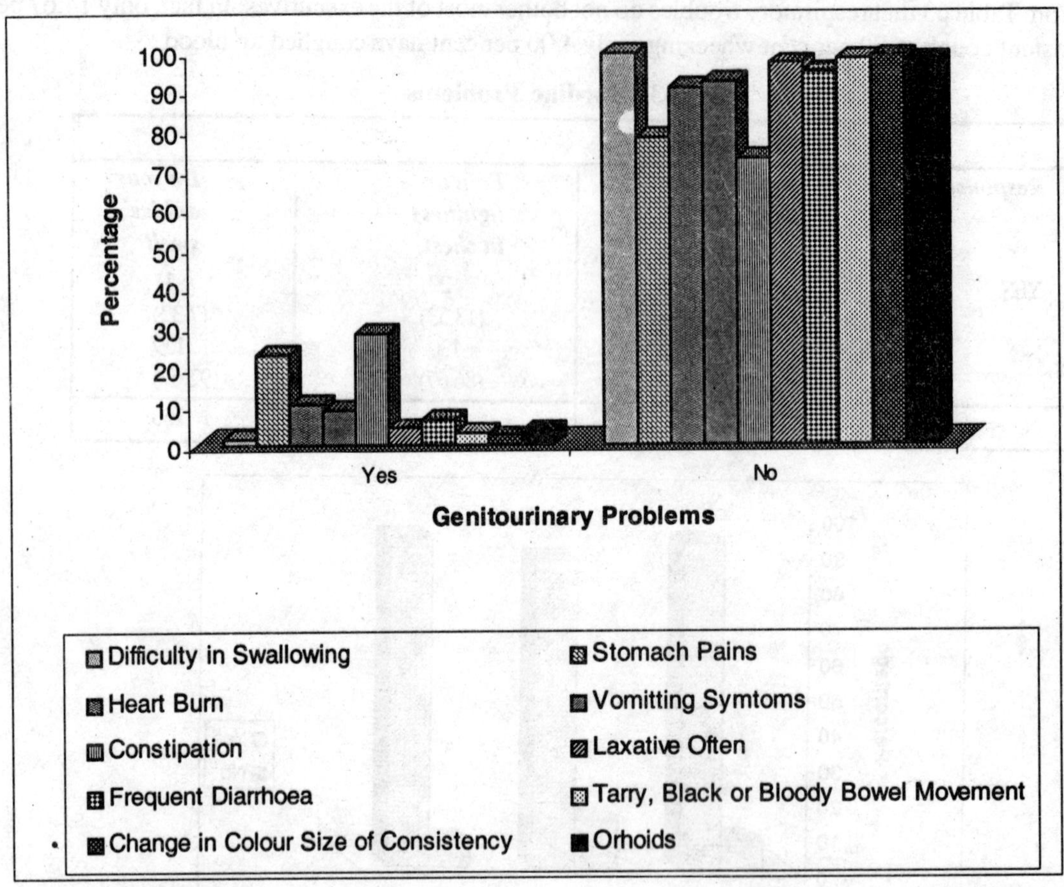


In case of gastro-intestinal trouble, it is observed that 28 per cent of the executives are having constipation. About 23 per cent get stomach pain due to various reasons like spicy food, stone in kidney, indigestion and constipation. Another 10.00 per cent suffer from heart burn and they attribute this to heart trouble and stomach trouble. Only 1.33 to 8.67 per cent suffer from the rest of the ailments viz. difficulty in swallowing, vomiting symptoms, passing black, tarry or bloody stools, rectal hemorrhoids, etc.

**Table 65: Genitourinary Problems**

| *Response* | *Get up more than once at night* | *Urinate at night* | *Feel burning sensation during urination* | *Pass red or dark urine* | *Have trouble in starting and stopping urine* | *Lose urine while coughing or sneezing* |
|---|---|---|---|---|---|---|
| YES | 39<br>(26.00) | 50<br>(33.00) | 9<br>(6.00) | 3<br>(2.00) | 5<br>(3.33) | 4<br>(2.67) |
| NO | 111<br>(74.00) | 100<br>(66.67) | 141<br>(94.00) | 147<br>(98.00) | 145<br>(96.67) | 146<br>(97.33) |
| N | 150 | 150 | 150 | 150 | 150 | 150 |

About 33 per cent urinate at night and another 26.00 per cent get up more than once at night due to noise, to drink water, etc. The percentages of individuals who feel burning sensation during urination or difficulty in starting are 6.00, 3.33 and 2.67. Those who pass red or dark urine are only 2.00 per cent.

Musculoskeletal, Neurologic, Hematologic and Emotional problems faced by the executives have been summarised in Tables 63, 64 and 65.

**Table 66: Musculoskeletal Problems**

| Response | Pain in back | Are you bothered by Pain in arms | Pain in legs or joints | Slipped disc |
|---|---|---|---|---|
| YES | 36 (24.00) | 11 (7.33) | 31 (20.67) | 5 (3.33) |
| NO | 114 (76.00) | 139 (92.67) | 119 (79.33) | 145 (96.67) |
| N | 150 | 150 | 150 | 150 |

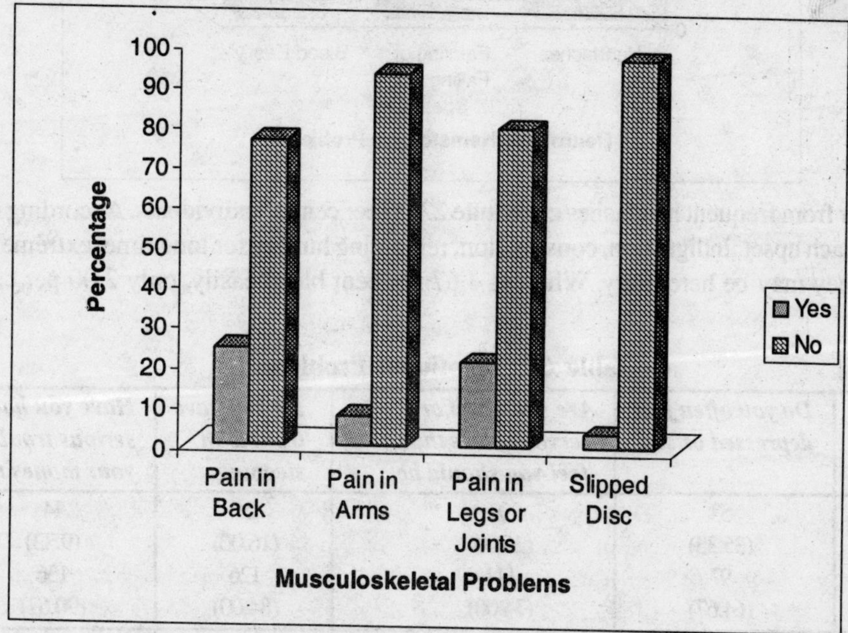


Most of the executives are not bothered by pain in arms (92.67 per cent) or slipped dissc (96.67 per cent). However, 24.00 per cent are troubled by back pain which is due to over exertion, weight lifting, etc. Similarly 20.67 per cent have pain in legs or joints caused by accident or cold.

**Table 67: Neurologic, Hematologic Problems**

| Response | Are you bothered by frequent headaches | Do you have fainting or falling out spells | Do you bleed easily |
|---|---|---|---|
| YES | 33 (22.00) | 3 (2.00) | 7 (4.67) |
| NO | 117 (78.00) | 147 (98.00) | 143 (95.33) |
| N | 150 | 150 | 150 |

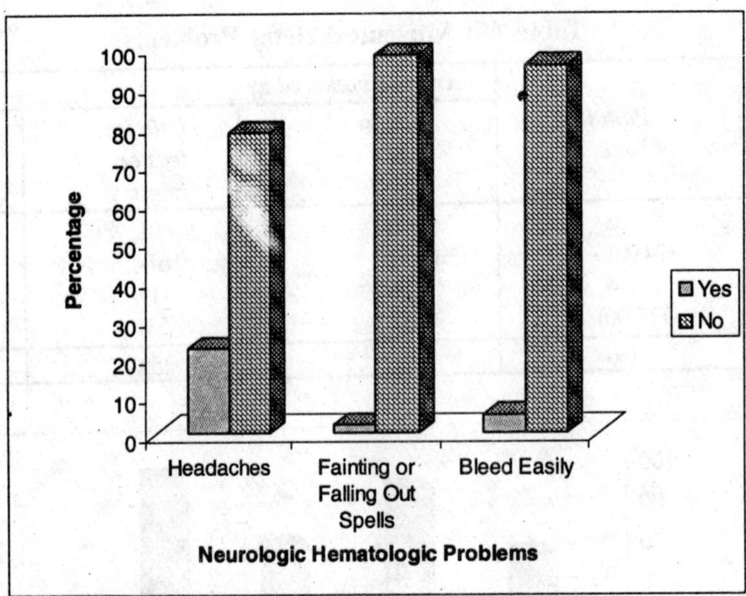


These who suffer from frequent headaches constitute 22.00 per cent of individuals. According to them, headaches are caused due to stomach upset, indigestion, constipation, remaining hungry for long time, extreme heat or cold, sinus, heavy work load or they may be hereditary. Whereas 4.67 per cent bleed easily, only 2.00 per cent feel fainting or falling out spells.

**Table 68: Emotional Problems**

| *Response* | *Do you often feel depressed or sad* | *Are you upset or nervous more than you feel you should be* | *Do You have trouble in sleeping* | *Have you had any serious trouble with your money matters* |
|---|---|---|---|---|
| YES | 53<br>(35.33) | 39<br>(26.00) | 24<br>(16.00) | 14<br>(9.33) |
| NO | 97<br>(64.67) | 111<br>(74.00) | 126<br>(84.00) | 136<br>(90.67) |
| N | 150 | 150 | 150 | 150 |

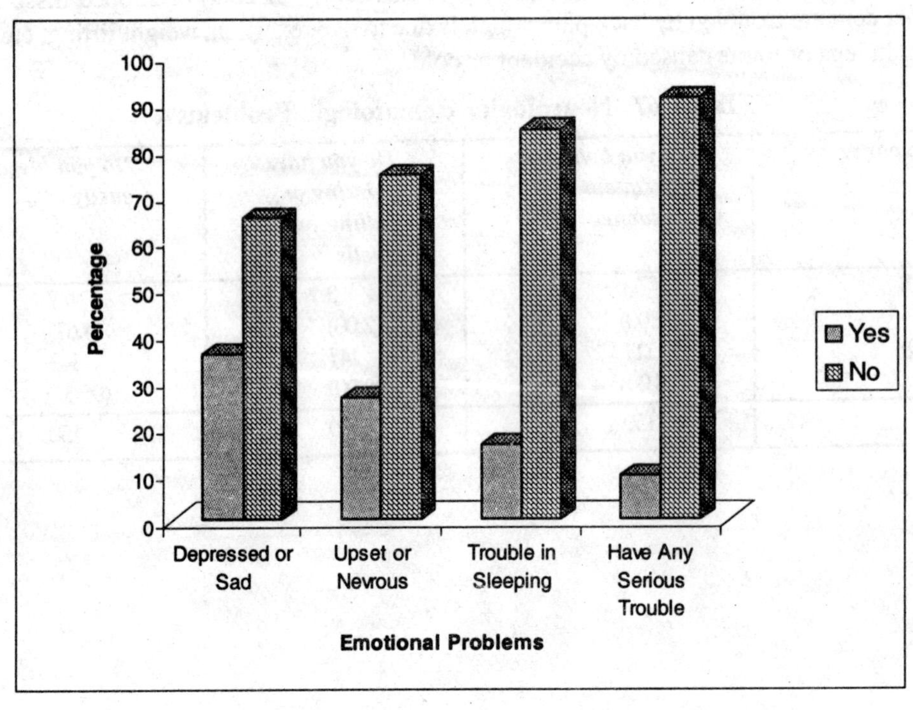

It can observed from the table that 35.33 per cent often feel depressed or sad which may be due to tension, back pain, etc. 26.00 per cent are upset or nervous, one of the reason can be excessive stress. Similarly, back pain, frequent urination in night are some of the reasons which cause trouble in sleeping to 16.00 per cent of executives. Only 9.33 per cent have said that they had some serious trouble with money matters.

Table 69 relates exclusively to male sexual problems based on 126 male executives out of total 150.

**Table 69: Male Sexual Problems**

| *Response* | *Do you have* | |
|---|---|---|
| | *Any discharge or drip From your penis* | *A sore or lump on or near your penis* |
| YES | 12 (9.52) | 6 (4.76) |
| NO | 114 (90.48) | 120 (95.24) |
| N | 126* | 126* |

* Excludes 24 female executives

Male sexual organs do not pose any problem to majority of the executives considered here. In other words few (9.52 per cent) are having discharge or drip from penisi and still fewer (4.76 per cent) a sore or lump on the penis.

We now deal with the problems of women executives divided into two categories viz. those having menstrual periods and those not having menstrual periods. However, there are certain problems which are common to both these categories and have been dealt separately. Table 70 gives the information on length of heavy and lighter bleeding and usual time between menstrual period for 22 executives belonging to first category.

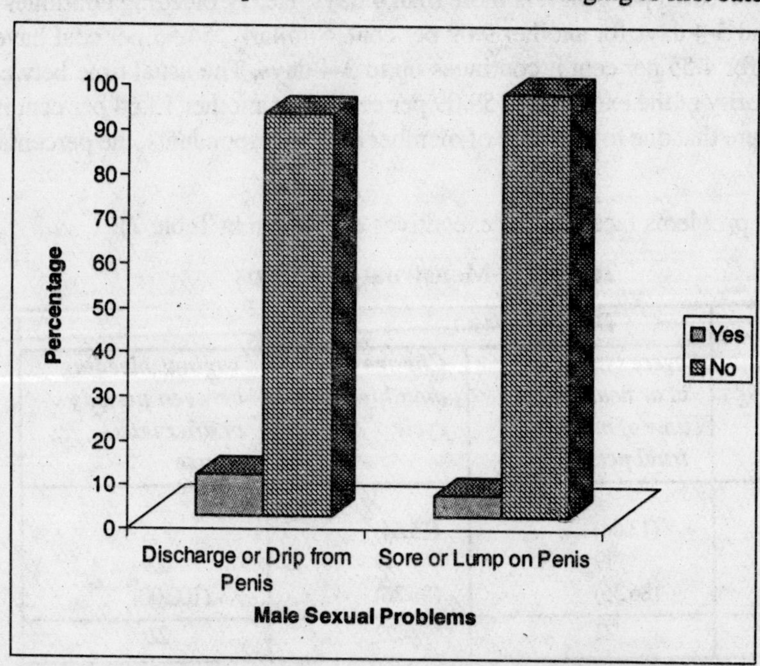


**Table 70: Menstrual period and bleeding**

| *Length of usual Menstrual period (in days)* | | *Heavy bleeding (in days)* | | *Lighter bleeding or spotting (in days)* | | *Usual time between periods (in days)* | |
|---|---|---|---|---|---|---|---|
| (3-4) | More than 4 | (1-2) | (3-4) | (1-2) | (3-4) | (26-28) | (29-32) |
| 15 | 4 | 12 | 2 | 12 | 1 | 13 | 3 |
| (68.18) | (18.18) | (54.55) | (9.09) | (54.55) | (4.55) | (59.09) | (13.64) |
| N | 22 | 22 | | 22 | | 22 | |

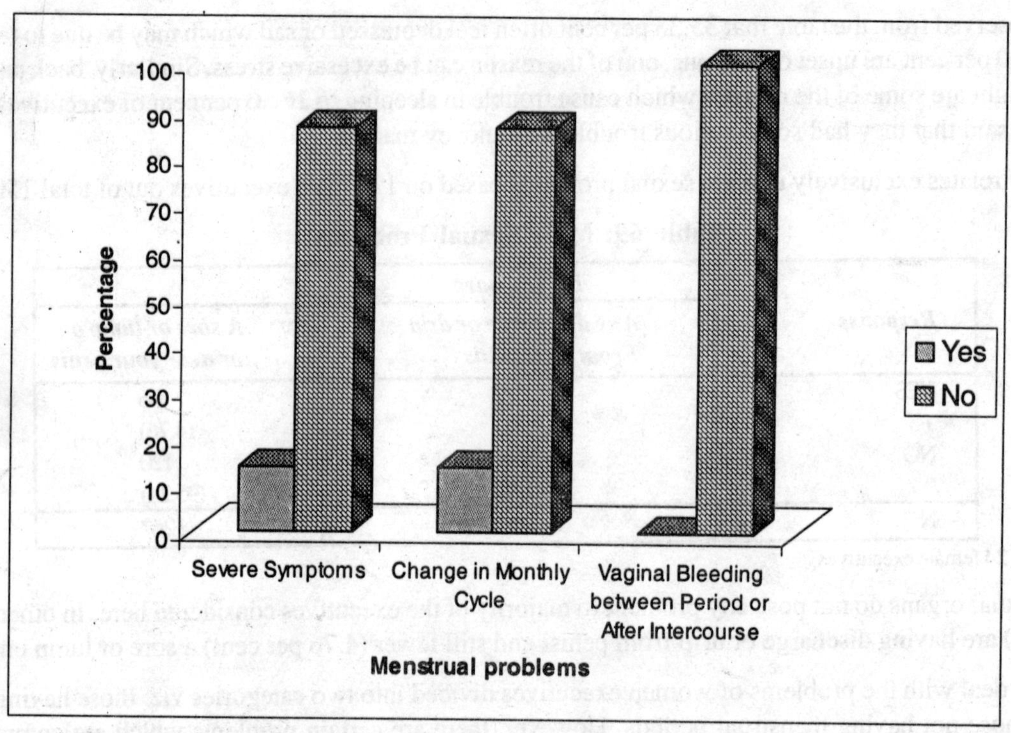


From the above table, we observe that the length of usual menstrual period is between (3-4) days for 68.18 per cent of executives whereas for 18.18 per cent it is more than 4 days. Heavy bleeding continues for 1-2 days in case of 54.55 per cent of them and 3-4 days for another 9.09 per cent. Similarly, 54.55 per cent have lighter bleeding or spotting for 1-2 days. Only for 4.55 per cent it continues up to 3-4 days. The usual time between periods has been found to 26-28 days for majority of the executives (59.09 per cent). For another 13.64 per cent it lies between 29-32 days. It may be mentioned here that due to presence of member of non-respondents, the percentages do not work out to be 100 in all such cases.

Some of the menstrual problems faced by the executives are shown in Table 71.

**Table 71: Menstrual problems**

| *Response* | *Do you have any* | | |
|---|---|---|---|
| | *Severe symptoms at or near the time of menstrual period* | *Change in monthly cycle* | *Vaginal bleeding between periods or after intercourse* |
| YES | 3 (13.64) | 3 (13.64) | - |
| NO | 19 (86.36) | 19 (86.36) | 22 (100.00) |
| N | 22 | 22 | 22 |

About 14 per cent say that they get severe symptoms like stomach ache, nausea, heaviness in abdomen and pain in legs at or near the time of menstrual period. Again only 13.64 per cent indicate change in their menstrual cycle. However, none of them (100.00 per cent) have any problem of vaginal bleeding between periods or after intercourse.

The number of female executives without menstrual period happened to be only 2 and both of them replied in negative to the queries – 'Are you bothered by Hot flashes' and 'Do you have vaginal bleeding or spotting'.

Table 72 shows some of the common problems faced by all women executives.

**Table 72: Women's Problems**

| *Response* | *Are you bothered by a vaginal discharge or vaginal itching* | *Do you have any breast lumps, discharge or pain* | *Do you examine your breasts regularly* |
|---|---|---|---|
| YES | 3<br>(12.50) | -<br>(25.00) | 6 |
| NO | 21<br>(87.50) | 24<br>(100.00) | 18<br>(75.00) |
| N | 24 | 24 | 24 |

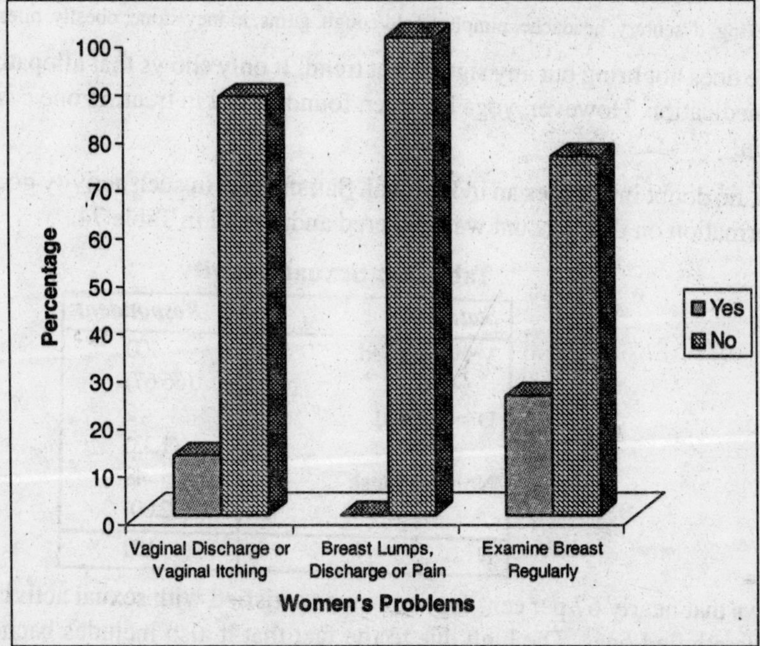


It may be noted from above that only a small minority (12.50%) suffer from a vaginal discharge or vaginal itching. Regarding any lump, discharge or pain on breasts, all of them replied that they do not have any such problem. Surprisingly only 25.00 per cent examine their breasts regularly. In fact, it is essential that all women should examine their breasts regularly so as to guard them against any serious problems like cancer tumor etc. which may arise in future.

The type of medication like allopathy, homoeopathy, ayurvedic, unani and others which include acupressure, yoga and naturopathy, used by the executives in dealing with diabetes, thyroid, high and low blood pressure, angima etc. have been summarized in Table 73.

**Table 73: Medication for Health Problems**

*Type of Medication*

| *Health Problems* | *Allopathy* | *Homeopathy* | *Ayurvedic* | *Unani* | *Others** |
|---|---|---|---|---|---|
| Diabetes | 2<br>(1.33) | – | – | – | – |
| Thyroid | – | – | – | – | 1<br>(0.67) |
| High/Low Blood Pressure | 2<br>(2.00) | – | – | – | – |
| Allergies/ Bronchial Congestion/ Asthma | 6<br>(4.00) | – | – | – | – |
| Eye | 3<br>(2.00) | – | – | – | – |

| | | | | | |
|---|---|---|---|---|---|
| Angina | 2 (1.33) | – | – | – | – |
| Pain | 9 (6.0) | – | – | – | 2 (1.33) |
| Others* | 18 (12.00) | 3 (2.00) | 1 (0.67) | – | 2 (1.33) |
| N | | | | | 150 |

* Includes Acupressure, Naturopathy and yoga.

** Includes wheezing, dysentary, headache, pimples, cold/cough, gums, kidney stone, obesity, piles and mental depression.

The above table does not bring out any significant trend. It only shows that allopathy has been used more often than other types of medication. However, yoga has been found useful in treating one case has been used for treating the other case of pain.

Sexual activity, no doubt influences an indivudual. Satisfaction in such activity goes a long way for his success in life. As such, information on this account was gathered and placed in Table 74.

**Table 74: Sexual Activity**

| *Status* | *Respondent* |
|---|---|
| Very satisfied | 100 (66.67) |
| Dissatisfied | 2 (1.33) |
| Non-response | 48 (32.00) |
| N | 150 |

The table shows that nearly 67 per cent are very much satisfied with sexual activity. Two individuals (1.33 per cent) are the only dissatisfied ones. The high due to the fact that it also includes bachelors, spinsters and very old people.

## (F) Hobbies and Leisure Activities

Seven tables 4.44 to 4.50 which follow subsequently are devoted to responses of the individuals with regard to their hobbies/recreation, exercises and leisure activities.

**Table 75: Occupation of leisure time**

| *Category* | *Respondent* |
|---|---|
| Reading | 85 (56.67) |
| Watching TV/Movies, Listening to Music | 50 (33.33) |
| Shopping/Outing | 8 (5.33) |
| Miscellaneous | 42 (28.00) |
| N | 150 |

A large majority of 56.67 per cent spend their leisure time in reading and another 33.33 per cent in watching TV/ movies and listening to music. However, 28.00 per cent are engaged in miscellaneous activities which include gossiping, doing household jobs, cooking, teaching/playing with children, meeting friends, playing cards, doing physical exercise, gardening, writing poetry, aero modeling and meditation.

**Table 76: Community/Social Activity**

| *Response* | *Respondents* |
|---|---|
| Yes | 46 (30.67) |
| NO | 67 (44.67) |
| Non-response | 37 (24.67) |
| N | 150 |

A majority of individuals (44.67 per cent) are not associated with any type of community or social activity although about 31 per cent involve themselves in some kind of social activities like social work, teaching yoga, satsang, visiting refugee camps, providing free medical services, becoming members of clubs and welfare associations and rendering nature services. A good number of them (24.67 per cent) however have not responded.

**Table 77: Vacation taken per year**

| *Duration of Vacation* | *Respondent* |
|---|---|
| Upto one week | 11 (7.33) |
| More than one week to 2 weeks | 29 (19.33) |
| More than 2 weeks to 4 weeks | 50 (33.33) |
| More than 4 weeks | 20 (13.33) |
| N | 150 |

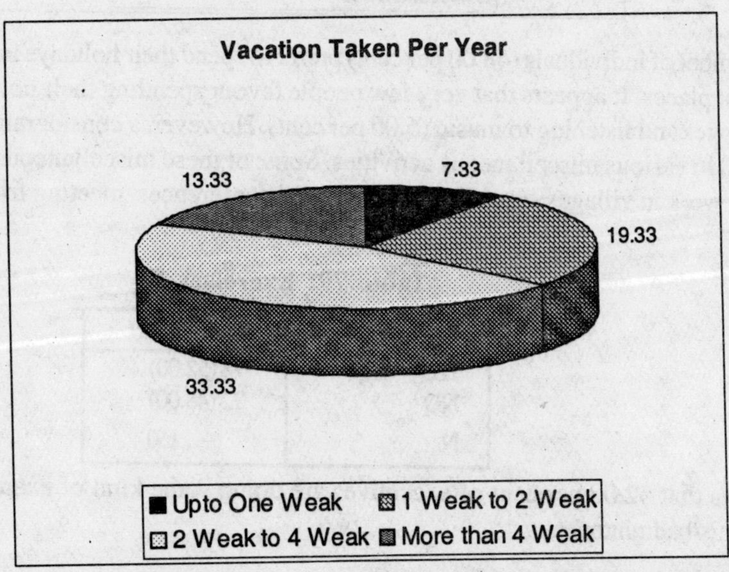


From the above table, we observe that 73.34 per cent of executives have taken vacation ranging from less than one week to more than 4 weeks. Out of this 33.33 per cent have taken vacation of duration 'more than 2 weeks to 4 weeks' followed by 19.33 per cent of those who have taken 'more than 1 week to 2 weeks'.

**Table 78: Ways of spending holidays**

| *Way* | *Respondent* |
|---|---|
| Reading | 9 (6.00) |
| Watching TV/Movies, Listening to Music | 9 (6.00) |
| Outing/Shopping | 72 (48.00) |
| Miscellaneous | 60 (40.00) |
| N | 150 |

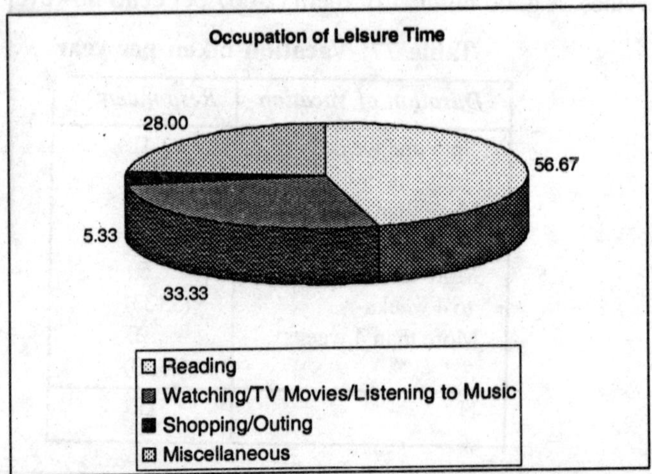


Maximum member of individuals (48.00 per cent) prefer to spend their holidays in going for shopping or traveling and visiting different places. It appears that very few people favour spending their holidays in reading (6.00 per cent) or watching TV/Movies and listening to music (6.00 per cent). However, a considerable majority (40.00 per cent) get themselves involved in various miscellaneous activities. Some of these miscellaneous activities are doing household chores, doing social work in villages, attending seminars and conferences, meeting friends and relatives and teaching children.

**Table 79: Exercises**

| *Responses* | *Respondent* |
|---|---|
| YES | 78 (52.00) |
| NO | 72 (48.00) |
| N | 150 |

Table 80 shows that 52.00 per cent of executives are doing some kind of exercises e.g., swimming, walking, jogging, playing tennis/badminton, etc.

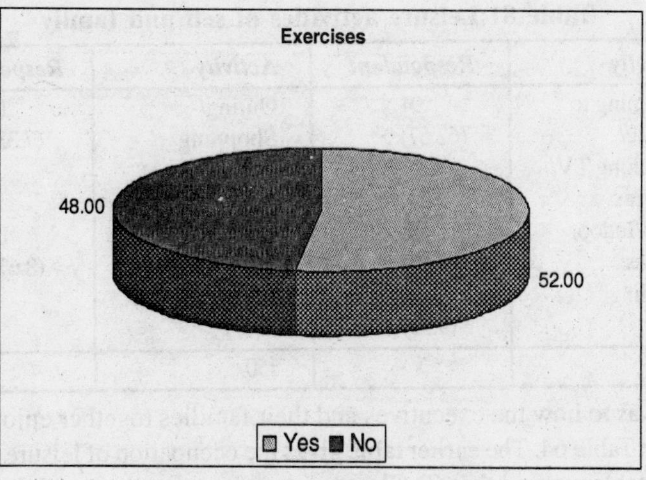


**Table 80: Type of Exercises**

| *Type* | *Respondent* | *Type* | *Respondent* |
|---|---|---|---|
| Swimming | 3 (3.85) | Playing Golf/Hockey | 2 (2.56) |
| Walking | 46 (58.97) | Cycling | 1 (1.28) |
| Jogging | 18 (23.08) | Yoga | 18 (23.08) |
| Playing Tennis/ Badminton/ Free hand | 12 (15.38) | | |
| N | 78* | | |

* Number of executives who do some kind of exercise.

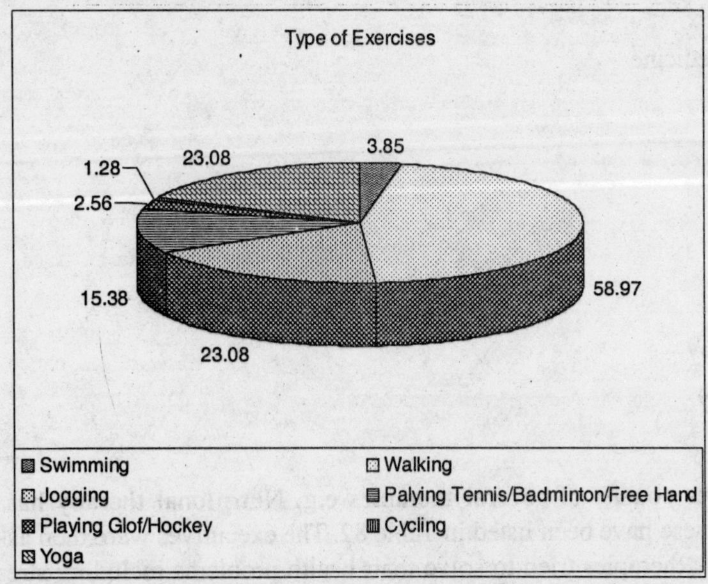


Table 80 gives the breakdown executives doing each of the various types of exercises and is obviously based on the responses of 78 executives who do some kind of exercise (Table 81. Walking seems to be the most favourite type of exercise among majority of these executives (58.97 per cent). This is followed by those who prefer jogging (23.08 per cent) and yoga (23.08 per cent). Playing tennis/badminton or doing freehand exercises is limited to 15.38 per cent individuals.

Table 81:Leisure activities of self and family

| *Activity* | *Respondent* | *Activity* | *Respondent* |
|---|---|---|---|
| Listening to Music/ Watching TV/ Movies | 94 (62.67) | Outing/ Shopping | 11 (7.33) |
| Club/Indoor Games | 22 (14.67) | Miscellaneous | 13 (8.67) |
| Reading | 14 (9.33) | | |
| N | | 150 | |

The above table shows as to how the executives and their families together enjoy their leisure activities. This table is slightly different from Table 64. The earlier table gives the occupation of leisure time by individual executives only. Examining the present table we find that 62.67 per cent of the executives and their families enjoy their leisure activities in listening to music or watching TV programmes or movies. 14.67 per cent prefer to go to a club or play indoor games, followed by 9.33 per cent who are interested in reading. Only 7.33 per cent engage themselves in various miscellaneous activities like playing outdoor games, jogging, etc. Comparing these with the observations on individual executives (Table 64), we find that in most cases they differ e.g. in case of listening to music or watching TV programmes/movies, the percentage for individuals is 33.33 as compared to 62.67 for individuals and their families together. In case of reading, the difference is much more wide viz. 56.67 for individuals and only 9.33 for the other. However, so far as outing is concerned both are almost of the same order viz. 5.33 per cent and 7.33 per cent respectively.

## (G) Role of Complementary Therapies

We now consider one of the most important aspects of the survey about the role of complementary therapies in tackling health/medical problems of the executives. These therapies have been first divided into following ten broad categories.

A. Traditional Medicine

B. Oriental/Chinese Medicine

C. Homoeopathy

D. Natural Remedies

E. Nutritional Therapy

F. Yoga

G. Spiritual Healing

H. Manipulative Therapy

I. Behavioural Therapy

J. Other Therapies

Each of these therapies consist of several therapies e.g. Nutritional therapy has Dietetics, Fasting and Vegetarianism under it. All these have been listed in Table 82. The executives were then asked to indicate the types of alternative/complementary therapies tried to solve their health problems including stress/strain problem. Their responses have been summarised in Table 82.

**Table 82: Complementary Medicines/Therapies in Solving Health/Medical Problems of Executives**

| | *Medicine/Therapy* | *Respondent* |
|---|---|---|
| **A.** | **Traditional Medicines** | |
| | Ayurveda | 49 (32.67) |
| | Unani | 8 (5.33) |
| | Folk/Primitive Medicine | 9 (6.00) |
| | Siddha | 6 (4.00) |
| | Indigenous/Herbal Medicine | 30 (20.00) |
| **B.** | **Oriental/Chinese Medicines** | |
| | Acupuncture/Bar Acupuncture | 7 (4.67) |
| | Acupressure (Shiatzu) | 7 (4.67) |
| | Electro Acupuncture | 2 (1.33) |
| | Moxibustion | 1 (0.67) |
| **C.** | **Homoeopathy** | |
| | Homoeopathic Remedies | 54 (36.00) |
| | Biochemic Remedies | 22 (14.67) |
| **D.** | **Natural Remedies** | |
| | Hydrotherapy | 21 (14.00) |
| | Massage | 45 (30.00) |
| | Reflexology | 12 (8.00) |
| | Naturopathy (Nature Cure) | 43 (28.67) |
| | Psychosomatic Therapy | 4 (2.67) |
| | Mud Therapy | 11 (7.33) |
| | Colour Therapy | 11 (7.33) |
| **E.** | **Nutritional Therapies** | |
| | Nutritional Therapy | 27 (18.00) |
| | Dietetics | 21 (14.00) |
| | Fasting | 48 (32.00) |
| | Vegetarianism | 35 (23.33) |
| **F.** | **Yoga** | |
| | Yogic Asanas | 47 (31.33) |
| | Breathing Exercises | 38 (25.33) |
| | Pranayama | 30 (20.00) |
| **G** | **Spiritual Therapies** | |
| | Faith Healing | 8 (5.33) |
| | Spiritual Healing | 18 (12.00) |
| | Mantras | 12 (8.00) |
| | Meditation | 37 (24.67) |
| | Tantras | 1 (0.67) |
| **H.** | **Manipulative Therapies** | |
| | Manipulative Therapies | 5 (3.33) |
| | Chiropractice | 1 (0.67) |
| | Osteopathy | 2 (1.33) |
| | Bone Setting | 4 (2.67) |
| | Postural Therapy/ Postural Integration | 10 (6.67) |
| **I.** | **Behavioural Therapies** | |
| | Biofeed back | 3 (2.00) |
| | Relaxation Techniques | 47 (31.33) |

| J. | Other Therapies | |
|---|---|---|
| | Physical Exercises | 46 (30.67) |
| | Electrical Therapy | 6 (4.00) |
| | Magnetic Therapy | 5 (3.33) |
| | Bach Flower Remedies | 2 (1.33) |
| | Hypnotherapy | 3 (2.00) |
| | Physiotherapy | 21 (14.00) |
| | Art Therapy | 1 (0.67) |
| | Organic Remedies | 1 (0.67) |
| | Music Therapy | 19 (12.67) |
| | Speech Therapy | 7 (4.67) |
| | N | 150 |

From the above table, we observe that in case of traditional medicines, 32.67 per cent have tried ayurveda followed by 20.00 per cent for indigenous/herbal medicines. Oriental/Chinese medicines have been tried by very few, only 4.67 per cent for acupuncture/ear acupuncture and another 4.67 per cent for acupressure. As per popular belief, homoeopathy appears to be the favourite among the executives. In fact, 36.00 perr cent and 14.67 per cent have tried homoeopathic remedies and biochemic remedies respectively. In case of natural remedies, 30.00 per cent have tried massage and 28.67 per cent nature care. For nutritional therapies, fasting has been tried by a large number of executives (32.00 per cent). It is quite well-known that fasting do help in reducing pressure in stomach, thereby allowing the human system to work more efficiently. Again 23.33 per cent have tried Vegetarianism. Yog is extremely useful in treating most of the diseases. Here we find that 31.33 per cent practice yogic asanas, 25.33 per cent do breathing exercises and 20.00 per cent do pranayana for treating their ailments. In case of spiritual therapies, meditation has been tried by a fairly large section of executives viz. 24.67 per cent. Another 12.00 per cent have attempted spiritual healing. Manipulative therapies like chiropractice, osteopathy seem to have least acceptance among the executives and only 6.67 per cent have tried postural therapy/postural integration. Relaxation techniques among the behavioural therapies have been tried by 31.33 per cent of the individuals. Regarding other therapies, physical exercises appear to be quite popular and 30.67 per cent have tried them. Only 14.00 per cent and 12.67 per cent have attempted physiotherapy and music therapy. Very few people have tried some of the other therapies like electrical therapy (4.00 per cent), bach flower remedies (1.33 per cent), art therapy (0.00 per cent), organic remedies (0.67 per cent) etc.

Next, opinions were invited from the executives as to which of the therapies mentioned in Table 82 have been found to give best results in controlling stress and strain problems and these have been given in Table 83.

**Table 83: Therapies in Controlling Stress and Strain Problems**

| *Therapy* | *Respondent* | *Therapy* | *Respondent* |
|---|---|---|---|
| Ayurdeva | 8 (5.33) | Biochemic Remedies | 1 (0.67) |
| Folk/Primitive Medicine | 3 (2.00) | Hydrotherapy | 4 (2.67) |
| Indigenous/ Herbal Medicine | 2 (1.33) | Massage | 6 (4.00) |
| Acupuncture | 1 (0.67) | Reflexology | 1 (0.67) |
| Acupressure | 2 (1.33) | Naturopathy (Nature Cure) | 19 (12.67) |
| Physical Exercises | 7 (4.67) | Fasting | 5 (3.33) |
| Yogic Asanas | 21 (14.00) | Vegetarianism | 4 (2.67) |
| Breathing Exercises | 2 (1.33) | Relaxation Techniques | 3 (2.00) |
| Pranayama | 5 (3.33) | Physiotherapy | 1 (0.67) |

| | | | |
|---|---|---|---|
| Spiritual Healing | 2 (1.33) | Mud Therapy | 2 (1.33) |
| Mantras | 2 (1.33) | Colour Therapy | 1 (0.67) |
| Meditation | 16 (10.0) | Music Therapy | 6 (4.00) |
| Homoeopathic Remedies | 9 (6.00) | Speech Therapy | 1 (0.67) |
| N | 150 | | |

It is evident from the above that to get best results in controlling stress and strain problems, 14.00 per cent of the executives practice yogic asanas, 12.67 per cent adopt naturopathy (nature cure) and 10.67 through meditation. Rest of the therapies have been tried by very few of them and their percentages range between 0.67 per cent to 6.00 per cent for such therapies. It may also be noted that some of the executives have adopted more than one type of therapies at a time.

On being asked to name any other therapies which might have been used to combat stress/strain problems, there were few responses from the individuals. These responses are shown in Table 84.

**Table 84: Other Therapies Tried To Combat Stress/Strain Problems**

| *Other Therapy* | *Respondent* | *Other Therapy* | *Respondent* |
|---|---|---|---|
| Diverting attention from normal routine work, attending lectures on naturopathy etc. | 1 (0.67) | Walking in garden | 1 (0.67) |
| Thinking life to be temporary and that we have ultimately to go to Lord for permanent abode | 1 (0.67) | Spending maximum time with family | 1 (0.67) |
| Spending time with family | 2 (1.33) | Reading books on religion and great men and women | 1 (0.67) |
| N | | 150 | |

It is clear that the therapies mentioned above are just used by one or two individuals and as such no worthwhile conclusions can be drawn about their utility in combating stress/strain problems. However, it is felt that these therapies, if practiced regularly, may help in bringing mental peace.

The major health problems which the executives have been facing presently are given in Table 85.

**Table 85: Health Problems Presently Faced By Executives**

| *Health Problem* | *Respondent* | *Health Problem* | *Respondent* |
|---|---|---|---|
| Bronchial Asthma/ Breating Trouble | 4 (2.67) | Muscular Pain | 4 (2.67) |
| Blood urea | 1 (0.67) | High Blood Pressure | 3 (2.00) |
| Backache | 7 (4.67) | Cold | 2 (1.33) |
| Headache | 7 (4.67) | Neck | 1 (0.67) |
| Heat Trouble | 1 (0.67) | Kidney Stone | 1 (0.67) |
| Stomach upsets (Acidity, indigestion gas etc.) | 5 (3.33) | Obesity | 1 (0.67) |

| | | | |
|---|---|---|---|
| Tension (Stress/Strain) | 3 (2.00) | Insomia | 1 (0.67) |
| Dental | 2 (1.33) | Allergy | 2 (1.33) |
| Eye | 2 (1.33) | Over work | 1 (0.67) |
| N | 150 | | |

Most of the executives have not been facing any major health problems at the time of investigation. Though a large number of problems have been enumerated but those suffering from them are few e.g., 4.67 per cent are suffering from a backache and another 4.67 per cent from headache. Those suffering from other ailments like Asthma, muscular pain, cold, tension, eye, obesity, etc. are as small as 2.67 per cent to 0.67 per cent.

Next, executives were asked about the results obtained in dealing with their health problems through complementary medicines. No specific comments could be obtained from them on this account. However, they have commented in general that satisfactory to good response have been obtained in combating asthma, obesity, migraine, acidity, cold, allergies, diabetes, heart trouble through therapies like walking, meditation, yogic asanas, diet control, homoeopathy and ayurveda.

Finally, the opinions of the executives as to who should be responsible for health care management have been given in Table 86.

**Table 86: Opinion on Responsibility of Health Care Management**

| *Category Responsible* | *Respondent* |
|---|---|
| Individual | 46 (30.67) |
| Government | 23 (15.33) |
| Voluntary Organisations | 3 (2.00) |
| Society | 8 (5.33) |
| Corporate Office | 6 (4.0)) |
| N | 150 |

A majority of 30.67 per cent have expressed the view that health care management should be individual's own responsibility. Another 15.33 per cent feel that it should be the government's responsibility. 5.33 per cent and 4.00 per cent have favoured to deal with health care management of individuals. Only 2.00 per cent feel that it should be the responsibility of voluntary organisations.

## (H) Problems of Ladies/Mothers

This sub-section is exclusively devoted to problems faced by female executives specially those during pregnancy and child birth. The analysis is based on 19 female executives who have children. Out of the remaining five, two have not responded, two are unmarried and one has no children.

Table 87 gives the information regarding visits to anti-natal clinics during pregnancy.

**Table 87: Visit to anti-natal clinics**

| *Response* | *Respondent* |
|---|---|
| YES | 16 (84.21) |
| No | 3 (15.79) |
| N | 19 |

A large majority (84.21 per cent) have visited anti-natal clinics for check up. The regularity of their visits have been shown in Table 88.

**Table 88: Regularity of visits to anti-natal clinics**

| *Regularity of Visit* | *Respondent* |
|---|---|
| Regularly | 11 (68.75) |
| Irregularly | 1 (6.25) |
| Occasionally | 3 (18.75) |
| Once only | 1 (6.25) |
| N | 16* |

* Excludes 3 who have never visited any clinic.

68.75 per cent of them visited the clinics regularly, whereas, 18.75 per cent visited occasionally.

From Table 88 it can also be seen that 3 out of 19 (15.79 per cent) have not visited any clinic. On being asked as to the source of their information about pregnancy, two have replied that it is through a doctor. The other said she has learnt it froı ı an elderly lady.

The categories of medical experts who have attended to the executives at the time of their child birth have been given in Table 89.

**Table 89: Categories of medical experts who attended child birth**

| *Category* | *Respondent* |
|---|---|
| Doctor | 17 (89.47) |
| Nurse | 3 (15.78) |
| Trained Dai | 1 (5.26) |
| Untrained Dai | - |
| N | 19 |

From above, we find that in 89.67 per cent of cases, doctors have attended child births. Nurses have attended the child birth for 15.78 per cent of executives. The help of trained Dai was taken for 5.26 per cent cases. It has also been observed in few cases that both doctor and nurse have attended a child birth. As such the total percentage in the table has exceeded 100.

Table 90 gives different locations at which the child birth has taken place.

**Table 90: Location of child birth**

| *Location* | *Respondent* |
|---|---|
| Home | 1 (5.26) |
| Nursing Home | 6 (31.58) |
| Government Hospital | 8 (42.10) |
| Private Hospital | 4 (21.03) |
| N | 19 |

Evidently for 94.76 per cent of cases, child births have taken place either at hospitals (government or private) or nursing homes, the maximum (42.10 per cent) being at government hospitals. Only one child (5.26 per cent) was born at home.

During child birth, 4 individuals (21.05 per cent) have experienced stress. Two of them have mentioned that the cause of their stress is working place. The other two have felt that family conditions are responsible for their stress.

The subsequent two tables viz. Table 91 and Table 92 are devoted to details about complementary medicines tried by the executives.

**Table 91: Trial Of Complementary System Of Medicines**

| *Response* | *Respondent* |
|---|---|
| YES | 9 (47.37) |
| NO | 10 (52.63) |
| N | 19 |

Nearly half of the executives (47.37 per cent) have tried complementary systems of medicines.

**Table 92:Types Of Complementary Systems Of Medicines**

| *Type* | *Respondent* |
|---|---|
| Ayurveda | 2 (2.22) |
| Naturopathy | 7 (77.78) |
| Homoeopathy | 3 (33.33) |
| Folk Medicine | 1 (11.11) |
| N | 9 |

The above table is based on the observations of nine executives who have actually tried complementary system of medicines (Table 92). Here, we observe that mostly viz. 77.78 per cent have tried naturopathy. Homoeopathy and auruveda have been tried by 33.33 per cent and 22.22 per cent respectively. Only about 11 per cent have tried folk medicine.

The concept of an ideal family and the appropriate spacing between children as conveyed by the individuals are shown in Table 92 and 93.

**Table 93: Concept Of An Ideal Family**

| | *Number of male child* | | |
|---|---|---|---|
| **Number of female child** | **0** | **1** | **2** |
| 0 | – | 1 (5.00) | – |
| 1 | – | 15 (75.00) | – |
| 2 | 2 (10.0) | 2 (10.00) | – |
| N | 20 | | |

Incidentally in this table and in the subsequent table, the number of individuals is 20 instead of 19 since the individual who has no children has also expressed her views on ideal family and spacings. It can be seen from the above table that 85.00 per cent have recommended ideal family to consist of two children, 75.00 per cent favouring one male and one female and 10.00 per cent two female children. Another 10.00 per cent feel that the ideal family should be 3 consisting of 1 male child and 2 female children. In 5.00 per cent of cases, one-child norm is recommended with only the male child.

**Table 94: Spacings Between Children**

| *Spacing (in years)* | *Respondent* |
|---|---|
| 1-2 | 2 (10.00) |
| 2-3 | 4 (20.00) |
| 3-4 | 9 (45.00) |
| 4 and above | 9 (25.00) |
| N | 20 |

A considerable majority (45.00 per cent) have suggested spacings between children to be 3 to 4 years followed by 25.00 per cent who are in favour of spacings as 4 years and above. Another 20.00 per cent have suggested 2 to 3 years whereas only 10.00 per cent recommended 1 to 2 years.

Table 95 relates to complications during pregnancy and intake of extra diet of expectant mother.

**Table 95: Complications During Pregnancy And In Take Of Extra Diet Of Expectant Mother**

| *Response* | *Did you experience Any complications During pregnancy* | *As excpectant mother did you take any extra Diet* |
|---|---|---|
| YES | 7 (36.84) | 15 (78.95) |
| NO | 12 (63.16) | 4 (21.05) |
| N | 19 | 19 |

We find that only 36.84 per cent have experienced some complications during pregnancies. On the other hand, 78.95 per cent of them have taken extra diet to supplement their normal diet. The additional diet includes milk and milk products, green vegetables, dry fruits, fruit juices, high protein food, vitamin, iron and calcium tablets.

In conclusion, we enlist below few salient features which the above analysis has brought out.

(i) The executives mostly belong to age group 30 to 50 years, which is the most active and creative period of their professional career.

(ii) Economically they are quite well-off.

(iii) They belong to various professionals giving a wide range of representation in different managerial fields.

(iv) Their families are in general small.

(v) They have healthy habits. Most of them neither smoke nor drink. They spend their leisure time and holidays in reading, watching TV/movies, in shopping, going out, spending time with family members and friends, teaching children, etc.

(vi) In their professional career, they no doubt have undergone stress and strain in varying degrees due to several reasons, the foremost cause as rated by them being 'in controlling the staff'.

(vii) Bodily and mentally they are quite healthy. Consequently they have not faced any major health problems. However, they did suffer from common ailments like headache, backache, high blood pressure, diabetes, stomach upsets, tension, fatigue, etc. Though, allopathy still remains the major therapy, there is a general awareness among the executives about the benefits of the complementary systems of medicine.

Many of them have got relief from these diseases through homoeopathy, ayurveda, yogic asanas, pranayamas, physical exercises, breathing exercises, acupuncture, massage therapy and so on by adopting the therapies singly or by combination of several of them.

(viii) The majority of female executives while speaking exclusively about women's problems have suggested that the ideal family should consist of two children, preferably one male child and one female child. Regarding their views about spacing between children, most of them seem to favour 3 to 4 years of gap. Further, most of them do not suffer from any serious menstrual problems and only very few face stress during pregnancies.

## Stress Management of Executives by Complementary Medicines Opinion Survey of Health Professionals (Doctors/Specialists)

In the previous chapter we have seen how the executives have tried to manage the stress and strain problems faced by them through complementary systems of medicines. In this connection, it was felt that the same problem of health care management can be posed to doctors practicing various systems of medicine seeking their opinion as to what are the causes of stress/strain related health problems faced by the executives and how far the complementary medicines are helpful in bringing relief to them. For this purpose, a survey on hundred doctors was conducted and data collected in a pretested questionnaire (Appendix-II) prepared for this survey. The present chapter deals with the findings of the survey. Section 1 gives the general description of the sample and Section 2 contains detailed analysis of the responses of the doctors.

### Section 1

This section gives general information about the sample namely age, sex, marital status, education and professional experiences of the doctors.

Out of the total of 100 doctors, 69,000 per cent are males and 31.00 per cent are female doctors. Table 96 gives the sex and marital status wise distribution.

**Table 96: Sex And Marital Status Wise Distribution**

| Marital | Sex | | |
|---|---|---|---|
| Status | Male | Female | Total |
| Married | 60 (86.94) | 21 (67.74) | 81 (81.00) |
| Unmarried | 9 (13.04) | 10 (32.96) | 19 (19.00) |
| N | 69 | 31 | 100 |

Examining the marital status we find 81.00 per cent of the total sample are married and the rest 19.00 per cent unmarried. Taking sexwise, 86.94 per cent of males are married and the rest (13.04%) are unmarried. In case of females it is 67.74 per cent married and 32.96 per cent unmarried.

**Table 97: Sex And Age Wise Distribution**

| | Sex | | |
|---|---|---|---|
| Age Group | Male | Female | Total |
| Upto 30 years | 12 (17.39) | 12 (38.71) | 24 (24.00) |
| 31-45 years | 39 (56.52) | 16 (51.61) | 55 (55.00) |
| Above 45 years | 18 (26.00) | 3 (9.68) | 21 (21.00) |
| N | 69 | 31 | 100 |

The above table gives the sex and age wise distribution of the doctors, For the purposes of age, three age groups viz. 'Upto 30 years', '31-45 years' and 'Above 45 years' have been chosen here. It is interesting to note that the4 maximum concentration is for the age group '31-45 years' which is 55.00 per cent on total and 56.62 and 51.62 per cents separately for males and females respectively. Again though 24.00 per cent of the total population belong to age group 'Upto 30 years', it is much higher in case of females (38.71%) than that of males (17.39%). But this trend is opposite for the age group '45 years and above' where female population is only 9.68 per cent in comparision to 26.08 per cent of males, the percentage on total being 21.00 per cent.

The three subsequent tables 96 to 97 give all information about professional qualifications and experiences of the doctors.

### Table 98: Professional Qualification

| Qualifi-Cation | System of Medicine | | | | | | | |
|---|---|---|---|---|---|---|---|---|
| | Ayurveda | Homoeo-pathy | Allopath | Naturo-path | Phsio-therapist | Electro-therapist | Yogic Therapist | Total |
| Doctorate | 11<br>(55.00) | -<br>(26.47) | 9<br>(66.67) | 8<br>(100.00) | (29.00) | 1 | - | 29 |
| Post Graduate | - | - | 4<br>(11.76) | - | - | - | - | 4<br>(4.00) |
| Graduation | 8<br>(40.00) | 16<br>(61.54) | 20<br>(58.82) | - | - | - | - | 44<br>(44.00) |
| Diploma | 1<br>(5.00) | 10<br>(38.46) | 1<br>(2.94) | 4<br>(33.33) | 5<br>(100.00) | -<br>(100.00) | 2<br>(23.00) | 23 |
| N | 20 | 26 | 34 | 12 | 5 | 1 | 2 | 100 |

Some of the notable features in the table can now be examined. Maximum number of doctors are graduates (44.00%). Among homoeopaths it is 61.54 per cent followed by 58.82 per cent and 40.00 per cent among allopaths and ayurvedic practitioners respectively. 38.46 per cent of homoeopaths and 33.33 per cent of naturopaths are having diploma. Again there are 66.67 per cent in ayurveda. Finally, from the last row of the table we can get an idea of composition of our sample e.g., there are 20 ayurvedic practitioners, 26 homoeopaths etc. in the sample.

### Table 99: Specialised Training In Complementary Medicine

| Type of Training Course | Respondent | Type of Training Course | Respondent |
|---|---|---|---|
| Acupuncture | 15<br>(10.00) | Preventive and social medicine | 1<br>(0.67) |
| Reflexology | 1<br>(0.67) | Chiropractics | 1<br>(0.67) |
| Occupational | 3<br>(2.00) | | |
| Yoga | 7<br>(4.67) | | |
| N | | 100 | |

It is evident that very few have undergone specialised training courses in complementary medicines e.g., only 10.00 per cent have specialised training in acupuncture, 4.67 per cent in Yoga and 2.00 per cent in occupational therapy.

### Table 100: Professional Experience

| Number of Years | Respondent | Number of years | Respondent |
|---|---|---|---|
| 0-5 | 22 (22.00) | 15-20 | 23 (23.00) |
| 5-10 | 27 (27.00) | More than 20 | 17 (17.00) |
| 10-15 | 11 (11.00) | | |
| N | | | 100 |

The length of professional experiences in years has been grouped into five categories viz. '0-5', '5-10', '10-15', '15'20' and 'More than 20'. We find that 27.00 per cent of them are having experiences between '5' 10' years. Those who are having experiences '0-5' years and '15-20' years are 22.00 per cent and 23.00 per cent respectively. A fair majority (17.00%) have more than 20 years experience in their professional fields.

## Section 2

This section gives the analysis of opinions of doctors about the role of complementary medicines in managing the stress related health problems of executives and results achieved thereon.

### A. General Opinion About Complementary Medicines

In the beginning, the doctors were asked as to how they feel in general about complementary medicines specially with regard to characteristics like whether they are expensive, less time consuming, having no side effects etc. The responses of the doctors on seven such characteristics are given in Table 101.

**Table 101: Opinions About Complementary Medicines**

| | Response | | Non-Response | | |
|---|---|---|---|---|---|
| **Characteristic** | **YES** | **NO** | **YES** | **NO** | **N** |
| Expensive | 32 (32.00) | 63 (63.00) | 5 (5.00) | | 100 |
| Cheaper | 63 (63.00) | 32 (32.00) | 5 (5.00) | | 100 |
| Safer | 90 (90.00) | 6 (6.00) | 4 (4.00) | | 100 |
| No side affect | 85 (85.00) | 9 (9.00) | 6 (6.00) | | 100 |
| Avoiding drugs | 82 (82.00) | 8 (8.00) | 10 (10.00) | | 100 |
| For the masses | 76 (76.00) | 9 (9.00) | 15 (15.00) | | 100 |
| Easily administered | 79 (79.00) | 13 (13.00)' | 8 (8.00) | | 100 |
| Less time consuming | 61 (61.00) | 27 (27.00) | 12 (12.00) | | 100 |
| Less Technicalities | 73 (73.00) | 13 (13.00) | 14 (14.00) | | 100 |
| Curative in nature | 74 (74.00) | 16 (16.00) | 10 (10.00) | | 100 |
| Preventive in nature | 78 (76.00) | 12 (12.00) | 10 (10.00) | | 100 |
| More time consuming For recovery | 51 (51.00) | 36 (36.00) | 13 (13.00) | | 100 |

The doctors have shown positive reactions to complementary medicines with respect to all the characteristics listed in the table e.g. 63.00 per cent feel these medicines are not expensive, they are safer (90.00%), have no side effects (85.00%), can be easily administered (79.00%), involve less technicalities (73.00%), curative in nature (74.00%) and also preventive in nature (74.00%). However, 51 per cent feel that they are more time consuming for recoveıy specially in chronic cases.

### B. Stress – Causes and Remedies

Next, 49 statements were listed as the possible causes of stress and strain for working executive/managers/ professionals and the doctors were asked as to what extent they agree with these statements under 5 levels of agreement viz. 'Strongly agree', 'Agree', 'Neither agree nor disagree', 'Disagree' and 'Strongly disagree'. Their responses have been given in Table 5.7. The table also contains the weighted average score (W.A.S.) for each of the statements and its rating on the basis of this score. Weighted average score has been calculated after assigning weights 2,1,0,-1 and –2 to five levels of agreement. (For calculation refer chapter 3).

**Table 102: Opinions On Causes Of Stress/Strain**

| Statement | Level of Agreement | | | | | | |
|---|---|---|---|---|---|---|---|
| | Strongly Agree | Agree | Neither Agree nor Disagree | Disagree | Strongly Disagree | Weighted Average Score | Rating |
| Socio-economic Changes | 40 (40.00) | 45 (45.00) | 13 (13.00) | 2 (2.00) | 0 | 1.23 | 2 |
| Political Changes | 17 (17.00) | 50 (50.00) | 26 (26.00) | 7 (7.00) | - | 0.70 | 19 |
| Military Crisis | 7 (7.00) | 27 (27.00) | 46 (46.00) | 18 (18.00) | 2 (2.00) | 0.19 | 31 |
| Environmental Threats | 16 (16.00) | 51 (51.00) | 27 (27.00) | 5 (5.00) | 1 (1.00) | 0.76 | 15 |
| New Government Legislations | 15 (15.00) | 43 (43.00) | 32 (32.00) | 8 (8.00) | 2 (2.00) | 0.61 | 25 |
| Racial Violence | 16 (16.00) | 40 (40.00) | 34 (34.00) | 9 (9.00) | 1 (1.00) | 0.61 | 25 |
| Threat of Unemployment | 35 (35.00) | 39 (39.00) | 18 (18.00) | 6 (6.00) | 1 (1.00) | 1.01 | 5 |
| Hiring Policies | 9 (9.00) | 46 (46.00) | 33 (33.00) | 11 (11.00) | 1 (1.00) | 0.51 | 29 |
| Plant Closings | 14 (14.00) | 46 (46.00) | 26 (26.00) | 11 (11.00) | 3 (3.00) | 0.57 | 27 |
| Lay Offs | 12 (12.00) | 51 (51.00) | 27 (27.00) | 9 (9.00) | 1 (1.00) | 0.64 | 24 |
| Relocation | 10 (10.00) | 49 (49.00) | 29 (29.00) | 11 (11.00) | 1 (1.00) | 0.56 | 28 |
| Automation | 12 (12.00) | 46 (46.00) | 33 (33.00) | 8 (8.00) | 1 (1.00) | 0.60 | 26 |
| Market Shifts | 11 (11.00) | 56 (56.00) | 21 (21.00) | 11 (11.00) | 1 (1.00) | 0.65 | 23 |
| Changes in Technology | 20 (20.00) | 45 (45.00) | 20 (20.00) | 14 (14.00) | 1 (1.00) | 0.69 | 20 |
| Mergers/take overs | 12 (12.00) | 51 (51.00) | 31 (31.00) | 4 (4.00) | 2 (2.00) | 0.67 | 22 |
| Task/Target | 20 (20.00) | 49 (49.00) | 22 (22.00) | 8 (8.00) | 1 (1.00) | 0.79 | 14 |
| Supervision | 25 (25.00) | 46 (46.00) | 21 (21.00) | 8 (8.00) | - | 0.88 | 9 |
| Co-workers Participation | 20 (20.00) | 52 (52.00) | 21 (21.00) | 8 (8.00) | - | 0.85 | 10 |
| Decision Making | 28 (28.00) | 50 (50.00) | 19 (19.00) | 3 (3.00) | - | 1.03 | 4 |
| Divorce | 29 (29.00) | 40 (40.00) | 20 (20.00) | 8 (8.00) | 3 (3.00) | 0.84 | 11 |
| Seperation | 27 (27.00) | 46 (46.00) | 17 (17.00) | 8 (8.00) | 2 (2.00) | 0.88 | 9 |
| Marital Dischoral | 29 (29.00) | 48 (48.00) | 15 (15.00) | 7 (7.00) | 1 (1.00) | 0.97 | 6 |
| Conflict in family | 38 (38.00) | 42 (42.00) | 11 (11.00) | 8 (8.00) | 1 (1.00) | 0.97 | 3 |
| Conflicts with friends | 18 (18.00) | 59 (59.00) | 13 (13.00) | 7 (7.00) | 3 (3.00) | 0.82 | 12 |
| Children's education | 31 (31.00) | 48 (48.00) | 15 (15.00) | 5 (5.00) | 1 (1.00) | 1.03 | 4 |
| Financial Problem | 44 (44.00) | 40 (40.00) | 14 (14.00) | 1 (1.00) | 1 (1.00) | 1.25 | 1 |
| Illness | 21 (21.00) | 59 (59.00) | 13 (13.00) | 5 (5.00) | 2 (2.00) | 0.92 | 8 |
| Housing | 23 (23.00) | 58 (58.00) | 17 (17.00) | 1 (1.00) | 1 (1.00) | 1.03 | 4 |
| Neurosis | 15 (15.00) | 51 (51.00) | 25 (25.00) | 8 (8.00) | 1 (1.00) | 0.71 | 18 |
| Mental Illness | 20 (20.00) | 49 (49.00) | 23 (23.00) | 6 (6.00) | 2 (2.00) | 0.79 | 14 |
| In Effective coping skills | 18 (18.00) | 43 (43.00) | 23 (23.00) | 6 (6.00) | 2 (2.00) | 0.68 | 21 |
| Poor Communication | 14 (14.00) | 50 (50.00) | 27 (27.00) | 7 (7.00) | 2 (2.00) | 0.67 | 22 |
| Addictive behaviour | 20 (20.00) | 41 (41.00) | 29 (29.00) | 6 (6.00) | 4 (4.00) | 0.67 | 23 |
| Disease | 20 (20.00) | 60 (60.00) | 14 (14.00) | 5 (5.00) | 1 (1.00) | 0.93 | 7 |
| Disability | 27 (27.00) | 46 (46.00) | 20 (20.00) | 6 (6.00) | 1 (1.00) | 0.92 | 8 |

| | | | | | | | |
|---|---|---|---|---|---|---|---|
| Appetite Disturbance | 12 (12.00) | 52 (52.00) | 27 (27.00) | 7 (7.00) | 2 (2.00) | 0.65 | 23 |
| Chemical dependency | 13 (13.00) | 39 (39.00) | 32 (32.00) | 16 (16.00) | - | 0.49 | 30 |
| Biochemical imbalance | 8 (8.00) | 46 (46.00) | 36 (36.00) | 9 (9.00) | 1 (1.00) | 0.51 | 29 |
| Pregnancy | 12 (12.00) | 46 (46.00) | 30 (30.00) | 11 (11.00) | 1 (1.00) | 0.57 | 27 |
| Poor Air | 18 (18.00) | 51 (51.00) | 23 (23.00) | 8 (8.00) | - | 0.79 | 14 |
| Climatic condition | 16 (16.00) | 48 (48.00) | 25 (25.00) | 11 (11.00) | - | 0.69 | 20 |
| Noise Exposure | 16 (16.00) | 55 (55.00) | 23 (23.00) | 5 (5.00) | 1 (1.00) | 0.80 | 13 |
| Toxic Substance | 20 (20.00) | 47 (47.00) | 20 (20.00) | 12 (12.00) | 1 (1.00) | 0.73 | 17 |
| Poor Lighting | 13 (13.00) | 62 (62.00) | 14 (14.00) | 8 (8.00) | 3 (3.00) | 0.74 | 16 |
| Radiation Exposure | 19 (19.00) | 49 (49.00) | 19 (19.00) | 10 (10.00) | 3 (3.00) | 0.71 | 18 |
| Poor equipment design | 14 (14.00) | 47 (47.00) | 27 (27.00) | 10 (10.00) | 2 (2.00) | 0.61 | 25 |
| Change Sleep/ Wake Habits | 24 (24.00) | 44 (44.00) | 21 (21.00) | 9 (9.00) | 2 (2.00) | 0.79 | 14 |
| Lack of Managerial support | 20 (20.00) | 58 (58.00) | 17 (17.00) | 4 (4.00) | 1 (1.00) | 0.92 | 8 |
| Poorly defined Goals/ Responsibilities | 20 (20.00) | 50 (50.00) | 21 (21.00) | 8 (8.00) | 1 (1.00) | 0.80 | 13 |
| N | | | 100 | | | | |

Combining the first two columns i.e. 'Strongly agree' and 'Agree' we observe that 85.00 per cent attribute 'Socio-economic changes' to be responsible for stress and strain problems of executives whereas 84.00 per cent to 'Financial problems'. Similarly 79.00 per cent to 'Children's education', 74.00 per cent to 'Threat of unemployment' and so on, the least being 34.00 per cent to 'Military Crisis'. The weighted average scores and the ratings more or less confirm our above conclusions arrived at on the basis of percentages of agreement. Firstly, all weighted averages being positive show there is agreement in all the statements though to varying degree. Next, examining the ratings we find highest rating 1 has been given to 'Financial problems' and the next rating 2 to 'Socio-economic changes' which is slightly different in case of percentages of agreement. The lowest rating 31 is given to 'Military Crisis'. It may be mentioned here that there are only 31 distinct ratings since for some statements the ratings are identical due to the fact that the weighted average scores for them are same e.g. statements, 'Mergers/takeover', 'Poor communication' and 'Addictive behaviour' are rated as 22, W.A.S. being 0.67 for all of them.

Table 103 gives the success achieved in combating problems specially related to stress and strain with the help of complementary system of medicines. The degree of success has been categorized as Excellent (E) Good (G) and Fair (F) and the results are given under these categories.

**Table 103 Degree Of Success Achieved In Combating Stress And Strain Related Problems Through Complementary Medicine**

| Medical Problem | Grading | System of Medicine | | | | | | | | |
|---|---|---|---|---|---|---|---|---|---|---|
| | | Ayurveda | Acupuncture | Homoeopathy | Nature Care | Dietary habits | Yoga/ Breathing exercises | Relaxation Techniques | Physical Exercises | Physiotherapy |
| Alchoholism | E (1.00) | 1 (1.00) | 1 | - | 1 (1.00) | 1 (1.00) | 1 (1.00) | 1 (1.00) | - | 1 (1.00) |
| | G | 6 (6.00) | 3 (3.00) | 13 (13.00) | 2 (2.00) | - | 1 (1.00) | 2 (2.00) | - | - |
| | F | 1 (1.00) | 3 (3.00) | 10 (10.00) | 3 (3.00) | - | 2 (2.00) | 1 (1.00) | - | - |
| | E | 5 (5.00) | 4 (4.00) | 7 (7.00) | 1 (1.00) | - | 1 (1.00) | - | 1 (1.00) | |

| | | | | | | | | | | |
|---|---|---|---|---|---|---|---|---|---|---|
| Asthma | G | 6 (6.00) | 3 (3.00) | 14 (14.00) | 7 (7.00) | - | 11 (11.00) | 1 (1.00) | - | - |
| | F | 8 (8.00) | - | 3 (3.00) | 1 (1.00) | - | - | - | - | - |
| | E | 8 (8.00) | 1 (1.00) | 6 (6.00) | - | - | - | - | - | - |
| Allergies | G | 5 (5.00) | 2 (2.00) | 13 (13.00) | 7 (7.00) | 4 (4.00) | 6 (6.00) | - | - | - |
| | F | 8 (8.00) | 1 (1.00) | 4 (4.00) | 2 (2.00) | - | - | - | - | - |
| | E | 3 (3.00) | - | 2 (2.00) | - | - | - | - | - | - |
| Cancer | G | 4 (4.00) | - | 10 (10.00) | - | - | - | - | - | - |
| | F | 6 (6.00) | 1 (1.00) | 8 (8.00) | 4 (4.00) | - | 2 (2.00) | - | - | |
| | E | 10 (10.00) | 1 (1.00) | 4 (4.00) | 1 (1.00) | - | - | - | - | - |
| Diabetes | G | 4 (4.00) | - | 9 (9.00) | 5 (5.00) | 12 (12.00) | 6 (6.00) | 1 (1.00) | 4 (4.00) | - |
| | F | 4 (4.00) | 1 (1.00) | 11 (11.00) | 5 (5.00) | 2 (2.00) | 2 (2.00) | - | 1 (1.00) | - |
| | E | 9 (9.00) | 1 (1.00) | 3 (3.00) | 1 (1.00) | 2 (2.00) | - | - | - | - |
| High Blood Pressure | G | 3 (3.00) | 1 (1.00) | 13 (13.00) | 6 (6.00) | 11 (11.00) | 11 (11.00) | 2 (2.00) | 3 (3.00) | - |
| | F | 5 (5.00) | 2 (2.00) | 7 (7.00) | 4 (4.00) | 1 (1.00) | 1 (1.00) | - | - | |
| | E | 6 (6.00) | 1 (1.00) | 1 (1.00) | 1 (1.00) | 1 (1.00) | 1 (1.00) | - | - | - |
| Angima | G | 6 (6.00) | 1 (1.00) | 13 (13.00) | 5 (5.00) | 2 (2.00) | 2 (2.00) | - | - | - |
| | F | 6 (6.00) | 1 (1.00) | 8 (8.00) | 2 (2.00) | 4 (4.00) | - | 3 (3.00) | - | |
| | E | 10 (10.00) | - | 8 (8.00) | 2 (2.00) | 4 (4.00) | - | - | - | - |
| Intestinal Disease | G | 5 (5.00) | 3 (3.00) | 13 (13.00) | 5 (5.00) | 6 (6.00) | 4 (4.00) | 1 (1.00) | 1 (1.00) | - |
| | F | 5 (5.00) | 1 (1.00) | 3 (3.00) | 6 (6.00) | - | 2 (2.00) | - | - | - |
| | E | 4 (4.00) | 1 (1.00) | 4 (4.00) | 4 (4.00) | - | 1 (1.00) | - | - | - |
| Migraine | G | 8 (8.00) | 6 (6.00) | 11 (11.00) | 7 (7.00) | 3 (3.00) | 6 (6.00) | 3 (3.00) | - | - |
| | F | 7 (7.00) | 1 (1.00) | 5 (5.00) | 2 (2.00) | - | 1 (1.00) | - | - | 1 (1.00) |
| | E | 5 (5.00) | - | 2 (2.00) | 2 (2.00) | 2 (2.00) | 2 (2.00) | - | 2 (2.00) | - |
| Obesity | G | 5 (5.00) | 1 (1.00) | 11 (11.00) | 8 (8.00) | 10 (10.00) | 6 (6.00) | 1 (1.00) | 5 (5.00) | - |
| | F | 9 (9.00) | 2 (2.00) | 8 (8.00) | 3 (3.00) | 5 (5.00) | 1 (1.00) | - | 4 (4.00) | 1 (1.00) |

| | | | | | | | | | | |
|---|---|---|---|---|---|---|---|---|---|---|
| | E | 6 (6.00) | - | 3 (3.00) | 1 (1.00) | - | 1 (1.00) | - | - | - |
| Smoking | G | 3 (3.00) | 1 (1.00) | 12 (12.00) | 5 (5.00) | 1 (1.00) | 3 (3.00) | 2 (2.00) | - | - |
| | F | 5 (5.00) | 2 (2.00) | 6 (6.00) | 2 (2.00) | - | 3 (3.00) | - | - | - |
| | E | 7 (7.00) | 1 (1.00) | 1 (1.00) | - | - | - | - | - | - |
| Stroke | G | - | 1 (1.00) | 14 (14.00) | 3 (3.00) | - | 1 (1.00) | - | - | 3 (3.00) |
| | F | 9 (9.00) | 2 (2.00) | 6 (6.00) | 3 (3.00) | 2 (2.00) | 2 (2.00) | 1 (1.00) | - | - |
| | E | 8 (8.00) | - | 10 (10.00) | - | - | - | - | - | - |
| Kidney/ Stone Disease | G | 4 (4.00) | - | 8 (8.00) | 4 (4.00) | - | 1 (1.00) | - | - | - |
| | F | 9 (9.00) | 1 (1.00) | 5 (5.00) | 3 (3.00) | 2 (2.00) | 2 (2.00) | - | - | - |
| | E | 4 (4.00) | - | 3 (3.00) | - | - | - | - | - | - |
| Gallstone | G | 5 (5.00) | - | 9 (9.00) | 2 (2.00) | - | - | - | - | - |
| | F | 7 (7.00) | - | 8 (8.00) | 3 (3.00) | - | 3 (3.00) | - | - | - |
| | E | 6 (6.00) | - | 7 (7.00) | - | - | - | - | - | - |
| Urinery Infection | G | 5 (5.00) | - | 13 (13.00) | 1 (1.00) | - | - | - | - | - |
| | F | 10 (10.00) | 3 (3.00) | 3 (3.00) | 8 (8.00) | 1 (1.00) | 4 (4.00) | - | - | - |
| | E | 7 (7.00) | - | 5 (5.00) | - | - | - | - | - | - |
| Colitis | G | 3 (3.00) | 2 (2.00) | 14 (14.00) | 4 (4.00) | 1 (1.00) | 2 (2.00) | 1 (1.00) | - | - |
| | F | 11 (11.00) | 3 (3.00) | 4 (4.00) | 8 (8.00) | 2 (2.00) | 4 (4.00) | - | - | - |
| | E | 6 (6.00) | - | 4 (4.00) | 1 (1.00) | - | 2 (2.00) | - | - | - |
| Ulcers | G | 5 (5.00) | 2 (2.00) | 16 (16.00) | 8 (8.00) | 6 (6.00) | 5 (5.00) | 1 (1.00) | - | - |
| | F | 8 (8.00) | 2 (2.00) | 4 (4.00) | 5 (5.00) | 4 (4.00) | 1 (1.00) | - | - | - |
| | E | 8 (8.00) | - | 10 (10.00) | 2 (2.00) | 1 (1.00) | 2 (2.00) | - | - | - |
| Skin Disease | G | 3 (3.00) | 2 (2.00) | 10 (10.00) | 4 (4.00) | 2 (2.00) | 4 (4.00) | - | 1 (1.00) | 1 (1.00) |
| | F | 10 (10.00) | 2 (2.00) | 4 (4.00) | 8 (8.00) | - | - | - | - | - |
| | E | 6 (6.00) | 2 (2.00) | 6 (6.00) | 2 (2.00) | - | 1 (1.00) | - | 1 (1.00) | - |
| Arthritis/ Gout | G | 3 (3.00) | 3 (3.00) | 14 (14.00) | 5 (5.00) | 3 (3.00) | 5 (5.00) | - | 2 (2.00) | 2 (2.00) |

| | | | | | | | | | | |
|---|---|---|---|---|---|---|---|---|---|---|
| | F | 12 (12.00) | - | 5 (5.00) | 6 (6.00) | 2 (2.00) | 2 (2.00) | - | - | 2 (2.00) |
| | E | 5 (5.00) | | - | - | - | - | - | - | - |
| Heart Murmur | G (4.00) | 4 (2.00) | - | - | 2 (2.00) | - | 2 | • | | |
| | F (8.00) | 8 (8.00) | - | 8 | 4 (4.00) | - | 2 (2.00) | 2 (2.00) | - | - |
| N | | | | 100 | | | | | | |

In general, from the above table we find that Ayurveda and Homoeopathy are the systems of medicines which have been found to be effective in almost all types of health problems which result stress and strain. Nature cure, dietary habits and Yogic exercises are also useful in combating some of the diseases. In particular, Ayurveda has shown excellent results in 8.00 per cent cases, good in 5.00 per cent and fair in 8.00 per cent of cases for treating allergies. For diabetes these figures are 10.00 per cent (excellent), 4.00 per cent (good) and 4.00 per cent (fair). Again in treating kidney stones/disease 8.00 per cent have shown excellent results, 4.00 per cent good and 9.00 per cent fair results. Similar trend can be seen in cases of urinary infection, colitis, skin diseases etc. Homoeopathy has been particularly useful in treating diabetes with 4.00 per cent (excellent), 9.00 per cent good), and 11.00 per cent fair, high blood pressure with 3.00 per cent (excellent), 13.00 per cent (good) and 7.00 per cent (fair), skin diseases with 10.00 per cent (excellent), 10.00 per cent (good) and 4.00 per cent (fair) and so on. It is interesting to note that for certain diseases, few cases of poor performance of homoeopathy have been reported although these have not been shown in the table. Similarly for alcoholism, allergies, high blood pressure and smoking the failure is 1.00 per cent each whereas for migraine it is 2.00 per cent. Nature cure, dietary habits and yogic exercises have also contributed in controlling a number of diseases. Nature cure has been found to be helpful in treating migraine with 4.00 per cent excellent results, 7.00 per cent good and 2.00 per cent fair results. For skin diseases these figures are 2.00 per cent, 4.00 per cent and 8.00 per cent respectively. In 10.00 per cent of cases good success has been achieved in controlling obesity through diatary habits. Similarly with the help of yogic and breathing exercises ulcers have been found to be controlling with 2 per cent excellent results and 5 per cent good results. The other therapies like relaxation techniques, physical exercises and physiotherapy have very little inpact in treating these diseases except that physical exercises has helped in controlling obesity with 2.00 per cent excellent results, 5.00 per cent good and 4.00 per cent fair results. In 3.00 per cent of cases good results have been obtained in treating stroke through physiotherapy. Physiotherapy has also helped for treating arthritis/gout with good (2.00%) and fair (2.00%) amount of successes.

## C. Leisure Activities And Physical Exercises

Opinions on the need for leisure activities and physical exercises to relieve stress and strain and strain of the working executives were sought from the doctors. Their response are given in Table 104.

**Table 104: Need For Leisure Activities And Physical Exercises**

| Response | Leisure activities | Physical exercises |
|---|---|---|
| YES | 83 (83.00) | 82 (82.00) |
| NO | 17 (17.00) | 18 (18.00) |
| N | 100 | 100 |

The necessity of leisure activities in controlling stress and strain have been felt by 83.00 per cent of doctors and that of physical exercises by 82.00 per cent.

Next, the doctors who have felt the need of leisure activities (83.00%) were then asked to give their opinions on various leisure activities essential to the executives. Their responses have been shown in Table 105. Similarly the reactions of those who felt the necessity of physical exercises (82.00%) on various types of physical exercises like swimming, jogging, welkins, cycling, gardening etc. have been summarized in Table 106.

**Table 105: Opinion On Various Leisure Activities**

| Activity | Respondent |
|---|---|
| Giving more time to children | 38 (45.78) |
| Social activity | 38 (45.78) |
| Cultural activity | 38 (45.78) |
| Spending more time with the family | 42 (50.60) |
| Going for holidays/vacations | 39 (46.99) |
| N | 83 |

A large majority of 50.60 per cent feel that the executives should utilize more of their leisure time with the families. About 47 percent prefer that executives should go for outing in holidays and vacations. Giving more time to children; to keep oneself associated with social or cultural activities are some of the other pass times suggested by 45.78 per cent of doctors.

**Table 106: Opinions On Various Physical Exercises**

| Exercise | Respondent |
|---|---|
| Swimming | 60 (73.17) |
| Cycling | 27 (32.92) |
| Running | 26 (31.71) |
| Squash | 9 (10.98) |
| Karate | 9 (10.98) |
| Steam Bath | 37 (45.12) |
| Archery | 8 (9.76) |
| Cricket | 11 (13.41) |
| Slimming exercises | 39 (47.56) |
| Badminton | 33 (40.24) |
| Rowing | 20 (24.39) |
| Turkish/Sauna Baths | 25 (30.49) |
| Gardening | 50 (60.98) |
| Walking | 63 (76.83) |
| Dancing (Aerobics) | 38 (46.34) |
| Mountain Climbing | 5 (6.10) |
| Fishing | 25 (30.49) |
| Skiing | 5 (6.10) |
| Tennis | 26 (31.71) |
| Skating | 7 (8.54) |
| Jogging | 41 (50.00) |
| N | 82 |

Walking appears to be one of the very good form of physical exercise for controlling stress and strain and this view has been confirmed by 76.83 per cent of doctors. Swimming, gardening and jogging are few other exercises preferred by 73.17 per cent, 60.98 per cent and 50.00 per cent of them. Again 47.56 per cent are for slimming exercises, 46.34 per cent for dancing and 45.12 per cent for steam bath. Skiing, mountain climbing and skating seem to be the least favourite ones, these are recommended by 6.10 per cent, 6.10 per cent and 8.54 per cent of the doctors respectively.

## D. Behavioural Changes/Changes In Attitudes

We now consider yet another method which may reduce stress and strain viz. behavioural changes/changes in attributes. It was felt that changes in behaviour like behaving decently, working sincerely, learning from mistakes, avoiding bossism etc. may be helpful in controlling stress and strain. Keeping this in view doctors were asked to give their opinions as to whether they agree with the statement that such behavioural changes/changes in attitudes can bring reduction in stress and stress. It was found that all of them agreed with the statement. However, their reaction on various types of behavioural changes which they feel are helpful in combating stress and strain vary and are given in Table 107.

**Table 107: Behavioural Changes/Changes In Attitudes**

| Type of Change | Respondent |
|---|---|
| Behaving decently | 32 (32.00) |
| Working sincerely | 40 (40.00) |
| Sleeping sufficiently | 88 (88.00) |
| Planning orderly | 52 (52.00) |
| Earning honestly | 72 (72.00) |
| Learning from mistake | 44 (44.00) |
| Believing in hard work | 40 (40.00) |
| Doing good to others | 44 (44.00) |
| Avoiding animosity | 44 (44.00) |
| Avoiding bossism | 28 (28.00) |
| Avoiding ego | 16 (16.00) |
| Avoiding false prestige | 60 (60.00) |
| Avoiding selfishness | 56 (56.00) |
| Avoiding irregular habits | 60 (60.00) |
| N | 100 |

Examining the Table we find that 88.00 per cent of doctors feel that sleeping sufficiently relieves stress and strain. Another 72.00 per cent suggest that earning honestly which gives lot of peace of mind can contribute in reducing stress. Similarly 60.00 per cent of them recommend that for reducing stress and strain, false prestige and selfishness should be avoided. Again 44.00 per cent feel that learning from mistakes, doing good to others and avoiding animosity are some of the traits which and strain. Working sincerely and believing in hand work are also favoured by 40.00 per cent of them. Of course, very few are in favour of avoiding bossism (28.00%) and avoiding ego (16.00%).

## E. Importance Of Complementary Medicines

We know that various therapies exist under complementary systems of medicine and it would be interesting to ascertain from the doctors as to how much importance they attach to each of these therapies. According they were asked to give their responses as per the degree of importance viz., 'Most Important', 'Important', 'Neither Important nor Unimportant', 'Unimportant' and 'Most Unimportant'. Their responses under ten broad categories of therapies (same as given Chapter 4), each category in turn having several therapies are shown in Table 108. The last but one column in the table shows the weighted average score of each therapy. For the calculation of weighted average score reference is made to Chapter 3. The ratings given on the basis of weighted average scores are shown in the last column. However, several of the therapies are having identical ratings since their weighted average scores are same.

## Table 108: Opinion on Various Therapies By Degree of Importance

| Therapy | Degree of Importance: Most Important | Important | Neither Important nor Unimportant | Unimportant | Most Unimportant score | Weighted average | Rating |
|---|---|---|---|---|---|---|---|
| **A. Traditional** | | | | | | | |
| Ayurveda | 24 (24.00) | 30 (30.00) | 42 (42.00) | 3 (3.00) | 1 (1.00) | 0.73 | 13 |
| Unani | 15 (15.00) | 23 (23.00) | 57 (57.00) | 4 (4.00) | 1 (1.00) | 0.47 | 23 |
| Siddha | 10 (10.00) | 23 (23.00) | 64 (64.00) | 1 (1.00) | 2 (2.00) | 0.38 | 26 |
| Trinal | 6 (6.00) | 13 (13.00) | 72 (72.00) | 8 (8.00) | 1 (1.00) | 0.15 | 40 |
| Herbal | 9 (9.00) | 39 (39.00) | 48 (48.00) | 3 (3.00) | 1 (1.00) | 0.52 | 18 |
| Home made (Indigenous) | 12 (12.00) | 19 (19.00) | 61 (61.00) | 7 (7.00) | 1 (1.00) | 0.34 | 29 |
| **B. Oriental/Chinese** | | | | | | | |
| Acupuncture | 14 (14.00) | 37 (37.00) | 43 (43.00) | 5 (5.00) | 1 (1.00) | 0.48 | 22 |
| Acupressure (Shiatzu) | 14 (14.00) | 46 (46.00) | 34 (34.00) | 5 (5.00) | 1 (1.00) | 0.67 | 14 |
| Electro-Acupuncture | 8 (8.00) | 32 (32.00) | 52 (52.00) | 6 (6.00) | 2 (2.00) | 0.38 | 26 |
| Ear Acupuncture | 10 (10.00) | 32 (32.00) | 51 (51.00) | 3 (3.00) | 4 (4.00) | 0.41 | 25 |
| Moxibustion | 6 (6.00) | 20 (20.00) | 61 (61.00) | 7 (7.00) | 6 (6.00) | 0.13 | 41 |
| **C. Homoeopathy** | | | | | | | |
| Homoeopathic Remedies | 29 (29.00) | 32 (32.00) | 33 (33.00) | 5 (5.00) | 1 (1.00) | 0.83 | 10 |
| Biochemic Remedies | 20 (20.00) | 39 (39.00) | 38 (38.00) | 2 (2.00) | 1 (1.00) | 0.75 | 11 |
| **D. Natural Remedies** | | | | | | | |
| Hydrotherapy | 12 (12.00) | 38 (38.00) | 40 (40.00) | 8 (8.00) | 2 (2.00) | 0.50 | 20 |
| Message | 11 (11.00) | 55 (55.00) | 31 (31.00) | 2 (2.00) | 1 (1.00) | 0.73 | 13 |
| Reflexo-Logy | 9 (9.00) | 42 (42.00) | 44 (44.00) | 3 (3.00) | 2 (2.00) | 0.53 | 17 |
| Nature Cure | 26 (26.00) | 49 (49.00) | 24 (24.00) | - | 1 (1.00) | 0.99 | 5 |
| Psychoso matic Therapy | 17 (17.00) | 42 (42.00) | 40 (40.00) | 1 (1.00) | - | 0.75 | 11 |
| Mud Therapy | 6 (6.00) | 35 (35.00) | 51 (51.00) | 6 (6.00) | 2 (2.00) | 0.31 | 32 |
| Colour Therapy | 6 (6.00) | 26 (26.00) | 61 (61.00) | 5 (5.00) | 2 (2.00) | 0.29 | 33 |
| **E. Nutrition** | | | | | | | |
| Nutritional Therapy | 20 (20.00) | 50 (50.00) | 26 6.00) | 3 (3.00) | 1 (1.00) | 0.85 | 8 |

| | | | | | | | |
|---|---|---|---|---|---|---|---|
| Dieteties | 20 (20.00) | 49 (49.00) | 30 (30.00) | 1 (1.00) | - | 0.88 | 7 |
| Fasting | 13 (13.00) | 42 (42.00) | 42 (42.00) | 2 (2.00) | 1 (1.00) | 0.64 | 15 |
| Vegetari-Anism | 19 (19.00) | 40 (40.00) | 39 (39.00) | 1 (1.00) | 1 (1.00) | 0.75 | 11 |
| Veganism | 8 (8.00) | 28 (28.00) | 55 (55.00) | 6 (6.00) | 3 (3.00) | 0.32 | 31 |
| **F. Yoga** | | | | | | | |
| Yogic Exercises | 43 (43.00) | 40 (40.00) | 15 (15.00) | 2 (2.00) | - | 1.24 | 1 |
| Breathing Exercises | 40 (40.00) | 44 (44.00) | 15 (15.00) | - | 1 (1.00) | 1.22 | 2 |
| Pranayama | 34 (34.00) | 39 (39.00) | 25 (25.00) | 2 (2.00) | - | 1.05 | 4 |
| **G. Spiritual** | | | | | | | |
| Faith Healing | 11 (11.00) | 36 (36.00) | 47 (47.00) | 5 (5.00) | 1 (1.00) | 0.51 | 19 |
| Spiritual Healing | 16 (16.00) | 34 (34.00) | 40 (40.00) | 9 (9.00) | 1 (1.00) | 0.55 | 16 |
| Mantras | 12 (12.00) | 32 (32.00) | 44 (44.00) | 5 (5.00) | 7 (7.00) | 0.37 | 27 |
| Meditation | 27 (27.00) | 41 (41.00) | 29 (29.00) | 2 (2.00) | 1 (1.00) | 0.91 | 6 |
| Tantras | 9 (9.00) | 26 (26.00) | 51 (51.00) | 7 (7.00) | 7 (7.00) | 0.23 | 37 |
| **H. Manipulative** | | | | | | | |
| Manipulative Therapies | 9 (9.00) | 26 (26.00) | 58 (58.00) | 6 (6.00) | 1 (1.00) | 0.36 | 28 |
| Chiropractic | 6 (6.00) | 22 (22.00) | 63 (63.00) | 8 (8.00) | 1 (1.00) | 0.24 | 36 |
| Osteopathy | 5 (5.00) | 23 (23.00) | 62 (62.00) | 7 (7.00) | 3 (3.00) | 0.20 | 38 |
| Bone Setting | 2 (2.00) | 18 (18.00) | 64 (64.00) | 11 (11.00) | 5 (5.00) | 0.01 | 43 |
| Postural Integration | 8 (8.00) | 37 (37.00) | 47 (47.00) | 6 (6.00) | 2 (2.00) | 0.43 | 24 |
| Postural Remedies | 11 (11.00) | 37 (37.00) | 44 (44.00) | 6 (6.00) | 2 (2.00) | 0.49 | 21 |
| **I. Behavioural** | | | | | | | |
| Biofeedback | 8 (8.00) | 23 (23.00) | 63 (63.00) | 4 (4.00) | 2 (2.00) | 0.31 | 32 |
| Relaxation Techniques | 22 (22.00) | 42 (42.00) | 34 (34.00) | 2 (2.00) | - | 0.84 | 9 |
| **J. Others** | | | | | | | |
| Physical Exercises | 39 (39.00) | 46 (46.00) | 13 (13.00) | 1 (1.00) | 1 (1.00) | 1.21 | 3 |
| Electrical Therapy | 9 (9.00) | 25 (25.00) | 51 (51.00) | 13 (13.00) | 2 (2.00) | 0.26 | 35 |
| Magnetic Therapy | 6 (6.00) | 35 (35.00) | 47 (47.00) | 10 (10.00) | 2 (2.00) | 0.33 | 30 |
| Bach flower Remedies | 3 (3.00) | 22 (22.00) | 65 (65.00) | 9 (9.00) | 1 (1.00) | 0.17 | 39 |

| | | | | | | | |
|---|---|---|---|---|---|---|---|
| Hypnotherapy (Hypnosis) | 5 (5.00) | 31 (31.00) | 61 (61.00) | 3 (3.00) | - | 0.38 | 26 |
| Physio-Therapy | 17 (17.00) | 43 (43.00) | 38 (38.00) | 1 (1.00) | 1 (1.00) | 0.74 | 12 |
| Art Therapy | 4 (4.00) | 28 (28.00) | 60 (60.00) | 7 (7.00) | 1 (1.00) | 0.27 | 34 |
| Organic Remedies | 1 (1.00) | 21 (21.00) | 65 (65.00) | 10 (10.00) | 3 (3.00) | 0.07 | 42 |
| Music Therapy | 12 (12.00) | 37 (37.00) | 44 (44.00) | 5 (5.00) | 2 (2.00) | 0.52 | 18 |
| Speech Therapy | 4 (4.00) | 33 (39.00) | 55 (55.00) | 8 (8.00) | - | 0.33 | 30 |
| N | | | 100 | | | | |

Examining the table we first observe that a considerable majority of doctors are undecided about the importance of several of these therapies. The percentages of such doctors mostly vary between 40.00 per cent to 60.00. For example it is 43.00 per cent for Acupuncture, 51.00 for Mud Therapy, 55.00 per cent for Veganism and so on. Of course, there are exceptions like Tribal medicine for which the percentage is as high as 72.00. Similarly for Yogic exercises and Physical exercises these are as low as 15.00 per cent and 13.00 per cent respectively.

Secondly there are very few who think that these therapies are unimportant or most unimportant, their percentages for most cases are between 6.00 to 12.00. Lastly, those who consider these therapies to be important or most important comprise the rest of the population of doctors. It is interesting to note that Physical exercises, Yogic exercises and Breathing exercises are the therapies considered to be important by a very large majority viz. 85.00 per cent, 84.00 per cent and 83.00 per cent of doctors respectively. The least favoured ones are Bone setting (20.00%), Organic remedies (22.00%) and Bach flower remedies (25.00%). For other therapies the percentages vary between 45.00 to 65.00 barring few exceptions. Regarding weighted average scores, we find all the scores to be positive thereby slowing that on the whole all the therapies have been considered to be important. The highest score 1.24 is given to Yogic exercises followed by 1.22 to Breathing exercises and 1.21 to Physical exercises. On the basis of these scores the first three ratings have been given to these therapies. This more on less confirms the conclusions arrived at by considering the percentages, except that the order is slightly different. Similarly Pranayama, Nature cure and meditation are rated as fourth, fifth and sixth respectively. Finally, the last two ratings are given to organic remedies (42nd) and Bone setting (43rd) which again confirms the conclusions based on percentages. Some of the therapies having identical ratings are e.g., Biochemic remedies, Vegetarianism and Psychotherapy all rated as 11 and Siddha and Electro acupuncture both rated as 26.

In conclusion we may make the following observations.

1. Most of the doctors are practicing allopathy, homoeopathy, ayurveda, naturopathy and are having sufficient professional experience.
2. According to them, complementary medicines are cheaper, safer, have no side effects, involve less technicalities, are less time consuming and curative in nature.
3. The majority of them feel that financial problems, socio-economic changes conflict, in family are some of the most important factors which cause stress and strain to the executives.
4. Ayurdeva and homoeopathy are the systems of medicines which have been found to be most effective in almost all types of stress related problems. These are followed by nature cure and yogic exercises.
5. Most of the doctors are of the opinion that leisure activities and physical exercises play an important role in reducing tension of the executives.
6. Lastly, physical exercises, yogic exercises and breathing exercises are the therapies considered to be most important by majority of doctors. Nature cure, meditation, massage and acupressure have also been found to be quite helpful in reducing stress and strain.

# CHAPTER 9 Research Findings

The working executives invariably face stress and strain problems in their career. The present study has been undertaken to examine the causes of stress and strain to the executives and their management through complementary system of medicines. The specific objectives of the study are:

(1) To trace and document the historical development concerning health problems of executives with emphasis on stress management.

(2) To study and review the various research findings in India and abroad on complementary medicines available for coping up with health problems of professionals and counteracting occupational stress.

(3) To analyse the executives/patients opinion regarding their health problems, specially stress management.

(4) The analyse the various methods applied by different health professionals in coping up with health problems of executives/managers concerning stress management.

(5) To draw an action plan for coping with stress for working executives.

For the purposes of the study, two opinion surveys on executives and health professionals have been conducted separately. The opinion survey on executives was conducted on 150 individuals selected at random from metropolitan city of Delhi. Similarly, the survey on health professionals was based on the opinion of 100 doctors practicing different systems of medicine in Delhi. The findings of these surveys are discussed briefly in the subsequent sections. Finally, suggestions have been made on future action plans for tackling stress and strain problems through complementary medicines.

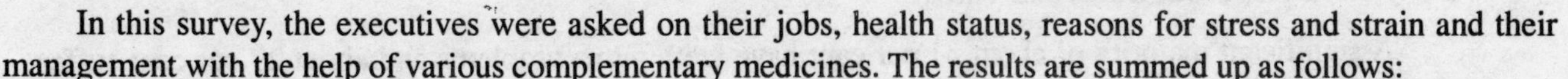

## OPINION SURVEY OF EXECUTIVES/PROFESSIONALS

In this survey, the executives were asked on their jobs, health status, reasons for stress and strain and their management with the help of various complementary medicines. The results are summed up as follows:

(1) The sample consists of 126 males and 24 females executives out of which 132 are married and mostly belong to the age group '31-50 years'.

(2) Among them there are graduates, postgraduates and professionally qualified individuals.

(3) Interestingly, 120 out of 150 are employed as administrators/managers/managing directors irrespective of the type of qualifications they possess.

(4) Most of them are working executives either in private companies, in public/limited organisations, in government organisations or in government undertakings. Very few are having their own business.

(5) About two-thirds of the executives belong to the income group Rs. 3,000–7,000 and a little less than half of them are having their own houses.

(6) They have small families consisting mostly of 1 to 2 children.

(7) Most of them are satisfied with their jobs and very few seek change.

(8) The jobs which require frequent touring/travelling may cause stress and strain and the majority of the executives whose jobs involve such touring/travelling are in agreement with this view.

(9) It has been found that the complementary system of medicines which the executives have generally consulted are homoeopathy, naturopathy and yogic therapy.

(10) In about 65 per cent of cases, expenditure or medical services are fully or partly borne by the companies/ organisations in which the executives are working. The rest make their own arrangement.

(11) For majority of them the daily intake of food is milk, bread, cereals, green vegetables, salad, potatoes, pulses, ghee and fruits. This appears to be quite balanced and nutritive diet. Some of them take seasonally ice-cream, fruit juices, peas, peanuts and eggs. There are a number of executives who have never tasted red meat, fish, poultry and eggs.

(12) Very few among them smoke, chew tobacco or drink. These who drink do it either once a week or only occasionally.

(13) There are various reasons which may cause stress and strain to a varying degree. Thus some may cause 'always stress', some 'frequent stress', some 'occasional stress', some 'rarely any stress' and some 'no stress at all'. A comprehensive list of 37 possible causes of stress was made and opinions sought on them from the executives. Weights were then allotted to above 5 types of stress in order to have a common index viz. weighted average scores and thereby, ratings for a comparative study of the various reasons with respect to degree of stress they cause. The analysis has shown that 'controlling staff' and 'disciplining the staff' causes maximum stress to the executives. These are followed by 'planning', 'managing with objectives' and 'managing conflict'. Similarly, 'telephoning', 'reading – research findings, etc.' and 'your monthly check up (medical)' are some of the reasons which cause minimum stress.

(14) The executives in general appear to possess good health and most of them have not encountered any serious medical problems during past one year. However, their responses towards various diseases are given here in brief.

(a) Appetite, Body Weight, Fever and Sweats

About 19 per cent have appetite problem and 22 have sweats and another 2 per cent have suffered from fever.

(b) Skin Rashes and Allergies

The individuals suffering for skin rashes/allergies are negligible.

(c) Ears, Eyes, Teeth/Gums and Throat

A significant majority of about 31 per cent have teeth/gums problems and about 29 per cent suffer from eye diseases.

(d) Respiratory System

Most of the executives have no respiratory troubles.

(e) Cardiac

Only 13 per cent have some pain or tightness in chest.

(f) Gastro-intestinal

The main problems in the gastro-intestinal diseases faced by them are constipation (28.00 per cent) and stomach pains (23 per cent).

(g) Genito-urinary

About 33 per cent urinate at night and 26 per cent get up more than once at night. Feeling burning sensation during urination, trouble in starting and stopping urine and loosing urine while coughing or sneezing are quite rare.

(h) Musculoskeletal

About quarter of the population suffer either from pain in back on pain in legs and joints.

(i) Neurologic Hematologic

Only 22.00 per cent are bothered by frequent headaches.

(j) Emotional

There are about 35 per cent executives who often feel depressed or sad due to tension, back pain, etc. Again 26 per cent are upset or nervous, one of the reason for this may be excessive strain.

(k) Male Sexual

Majority of them do not have any major problems of their male sexual organs.

Besides the above problems, there are certain problems exclusive to female like menstrual period, bleeding, vaginal discharge or itching and lump on breasts. Most of the female executives are free from such complications.

(15) Interestingly only 1 per cent of the executives are dissatisfied in sexual activities.

(16) The executives spend their leisure time in reading, watching TV/Movies, shopping and doing miscellaneous jobs like cooking, teaching/playing with children, meeting friends, etc.

(17) Most of the executives take a vacation in a year for recreation.

(18) Nearly half of the population is engaged in some form of physical exercises like jogging walking, swimming, playing tennis/badminton, playing golf/hockey, cycling and yogic asanas.

(19) Some of the health problems faced by the executives are bronchial asthma, blood urea, backache, headache, heart trouble, cold, obesity and these have been successfully tried mostly through ayurveda, homeopathy, massage, fasting, nature cure, yogic asanas and breathing exercises.

(20) According to the executives, the therapies which have given best results in controlling their stress and strain problems are yogic exercises, nature cure homoeopathy, meditation, ayurveda and massage. Small percentages of them have also tried successfully fasting, hydrotherapy, music therapy, physical exercises, mud therapy and primitive medicine.

(21) Regarding health care management, about 31 per cent feel that it should be the responsibility of the individuals. Few others feel that it should be the government's responsibility.

(22) Pregnancy and child birth cause lot of stress to women and about 50 per cent of the female executives agree with this. For combating this stress, they have successfully tried homoeopathy and naturopathy.

(23) An ideal family, according to 75 per cent of the female executives should consist of two children, one female and one male child. Further, a large majority of them have recommended spacing between children to be 3 to 4 years.

From above the following conclusions can be drawn.

(1) The executives are of the opinion that handling of staff causes maximum stress to them.

(2) The majority of them feel that complementary medicines can play an important role in controlling stress and strain.

(3) The therapies which the executives have successfully tried in treating some of the stress-related health problems are homoeopathy, ayurveda, naturopathy, yogic asanas, meditation and massage.

(4) Most of them are engaged in various kind of leisure activities and also doing some sort of physical exercises. These help them in reducing tension.

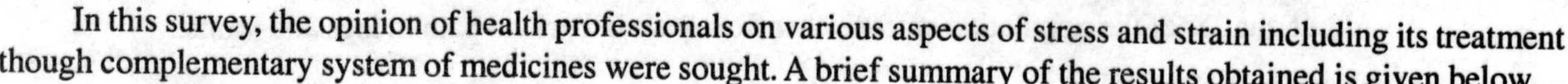

## OPINION SURVEY OF HEALTH PROFESSIONALS

In this survey, the opinion of health professionals on various aspects of stress and strain including its treatment though complementary system of medicines were sought. A brief summary of the results obtained is given below.

(1) There are 69 male and 31 female doctors out of 100. Among them 60 male doctors and 21 female doctors are married.

(2) More than half of them belong to the age group '31-45 years'. For males and females separately also the same trend can be observed.

(3) Among the doctors, mostly are homoeopaths, allopaths, naturopaths and ayurvedic practitioners with very few yogic therapists and physiotherapists. In case of ayurvedic practitioners, almost all of them are either doctorates or graduates. Most of the homoeopaths are holding diplomas. The allopaths have an even distribution of doctorates, post-graduates, graduates and diploma holders. There are naturopaths who are having either doctorate degrees or diplomas.

(4) About 10 per cent of them have undergone specialised training in acupuncture and about 5 per cent in yoga.

(5) The majority of the doctors are having professional experience ranging between '5 to 20 years'. However 22 per cent and 17 per cent have experience 'less than 5 years' and 'above 20 years' respectively.

(6) Almost all of them are in accordance with some general comments about complementary medicines. For example, majority agree that these medicines are non-expensive, having no side-effects, can be easily administered and curative in nature. The only draw-back they feel that these take more time for recovery.

(7) Forty- nine statements on possible causes for stress and strain to executives were listed and the doctors asked to give their responses towards them under 5 levels of agreements viz. (i) strongly agree, (ii) agree, (iii) neither agree non disagree, (iv) disagree and (v) strongly disagree. As before, weighted average scores and thereby ratings of these statements were calculated. The doctors have given first three ratings to financial problems, socio-economic changes and conflict in family, respectively. The rating 4 has been simultaneously given to children's education, housing and decision-making. Plant closing, relocation, biochemical imbalance are some of the statements which have been rated very low, the lowest rating being given to military crisis.

(8) Doctors have found ayurveda and homoeopathy to be the most effective systems of medicines in controlling almost all types of health problems which result in stress and strain. Nature care, dietary habits and yogic exercises are few more which are also useful for reducing stress and strain. In particular, ayurveda has shown excellent results in curing allergies, diabetes in few cases and good results in other cases. Homoeopathy accounts for treating diabetes and high blood pressure. Nature cure has been particularly helpful in treating migraine with results varying from excellent to fair.

(9) The need for leisure activities and physical exercises have been emphasised by more than 80.00 per cent of the doctors. Some of the leisure activities which most of them feel may be beneficial for relieving stress are spending more time with the families, going for holidays/vacation, cultural activities, etc. Similarly, about 60.00 to 75.00 per cent of them recommend walking, swimming and gardening as the best forms of physical exercises for reducing stress. A lesser number of them also suggest jogging, slimming exercises, steam bath, dancing etc.

(10) Another factor which has been considered in this survey is the behavioural changes/changes in attitudes of the executives and whether this can bring some relief in stress and strain problems. A majority of doctors are earning honestly, avoiding false prestige, and believing in hard work are some of the behavioural changes/ changes in attitudes that the executives should practice for relieving their stress.

Finally, opinions of the doctors about how much importance they attach to therapies existing under complementary system of medicines were sought. They were asked to give their responses as per the degree of importance viz. (i) Most important, (ii) Important, (iii) Neither important nor unimportant, (iv) Unimportant and (v) Most unimportant. Weighted average score and rating for each have rated yogic exercises as highest followed by breathing exercises and physical exercises. Forth, fifth and sixth ratings are given to pranayama, nature cure and meditation respectively. Massage and acupuncture get 13th rating and 14th rating. Tribal medicine, moxibustion and organic remedies are rated very low. However, the lowest rating goes to bone setting.

In conclusion, we may observe the following:

(1) The doctors are mostly homoeopaths, allopaths, naturopaths and ayurvedic practitioners having considerable professional experience. There are also few yogic therapists and physiotherapists.

(2) Most of the doctors feel that complementary medicines are cheaper, safer, having no side-effects and can be easily administered.

(3) They have attributed the possible reasons of stress and strain for executives to financial problems, socio-economic changes, conflict in family and children's education.

(4) In treating the stress and strain problems of executives, the doctors found homoeopathy, ayurveda to be the most effective systems followed by nature cure, dietary habits and yogic exercises though to a lesser degree.

(5) The doctors have emphasised the need of leisure activities and physical exercises in controlling stress. The leisure activities may include spending more time with the family, watching movie/T.V., going out, etc. Walking, swimming and jogging are few physical exercises suggested by them.

(6) Doctors also feel that behavioural changes/changes in attitudes like sleeping sufficiently, earning honestly, etc. can bring down the tension considerably.

(7) Commenting on the importance of various complementary medicines in treating stress and doctors have rated yogic exercises, breathing exercises, physical exercises, nature cure and meditation in that order.

On the basis of the main findings arrived at on the two opinion surveys we may conclude the following:

(1) The executives and the doctors both have given their opinions on the causes of stress and strain. Whereas the executives feel that factors responsible for stress are controlling and disciplining the staff, planning, etc., the doctors attribute them to financial problems, conflict in family, children's education and so on.

(2) Both executives and doctors agree that complementary therapies can play an important and positive role in stress management. These therapies can be used successfully either singly or by combination of several of them.

(3) Both found that stress can be managed successfully through homoeopathy, ayurveda, nature care and yogic exercises.

(4) Doctors are of the opinion that leisure activities and physical exercises are essential for relieving stress. On this account, the responses of the executives are noteworthy. Infact, their responses have shown that mostly the executives are engaged in some sort of leisure activities like spending time with family, teaching children, watching movie/T.V. and going out with family during for vacation. Again, majority of them do various types of physical exercises like walking, swimming, playing tennis and badminton and jogging.

(5) The doctors have also felt that behavioural changes/changes in attitudes of working executives will lesson tension. They thus recommended that executives should have sufficient sleep, they should plan orderly, earn honestly, avoid bossism, avoid irregular habits, and learn from mistakes.

Most of the executives have stressed that health care management should be the individual's own responsibility. In view of this, an individual executive may benefit by making behavioural changes/changes in his attitudes as recommended in para 5.

## Suggestions

### Future Research Work

Following recommendations are made for carrying out future research investigations.

- Separate stress management studies needed for individuals working under different work atmosphere since stress may vary from job to job, industry to industry, etc. Similar studies are necessary for women engaged in various fields viz. those doing social work, those working in the office since they are subjected to varying degrees of stress.
- Various complementary medicines are available and it is needed that from each of these medicines e.g. homoeopathy, naturopathy, yogic exercises, meditation, etc., case studies should be carried out separately to ascertain their efficacies in managing stress and strain related health problems.

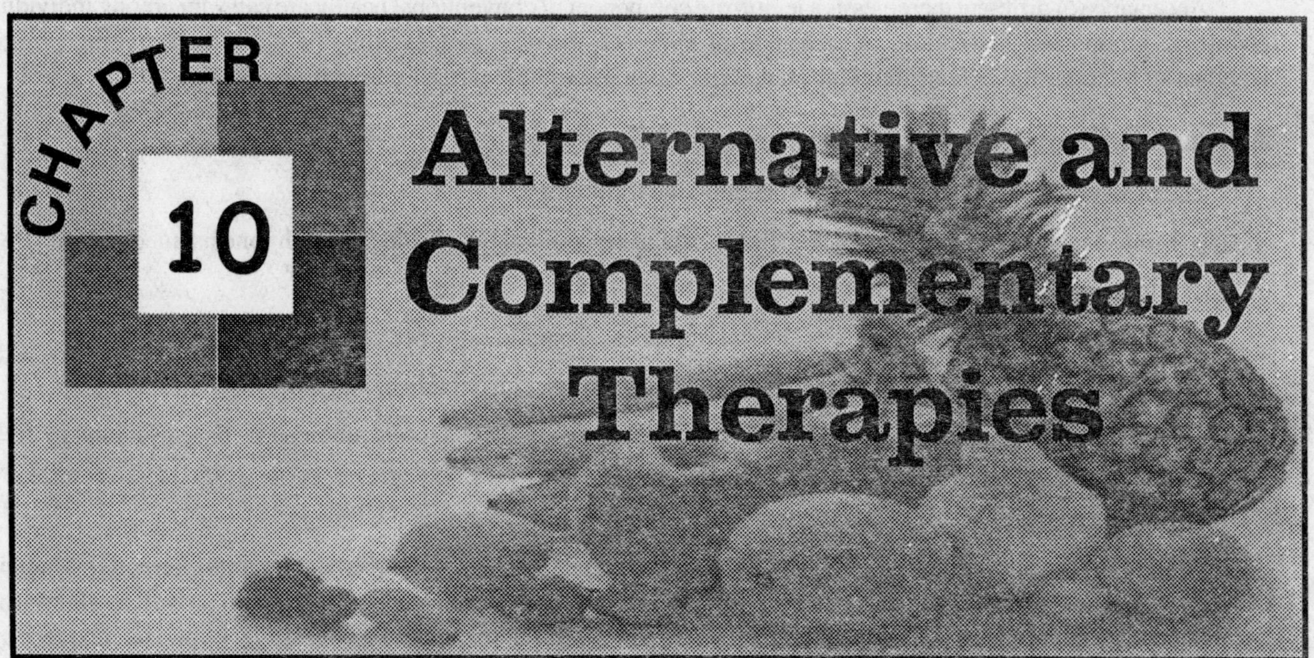


## WHAT ARE ALTERNATIVE/ COMPLEMENTARY THERAPIES (ACTs)

Alternative/complementary therapies refer to a broad range of philosophies, approaches and therapies that are usually developed and offered outside of traditional or conventional healthcare (National Centre for Complementary & Alternative Medicine 1999). They are heterodox therapies, that is, they may be considered to present unorthodox positions when contrasted with conventional medicine.

ACTs are also sometimes referred to as 'holistic' therapies, because the approach addresses the physical, mental, emotional and spiritual needs of the person and places a greater emphasis on prevention than on treatment (National Centre for Complementary and Alternative Medicine 1999a).

In the past, these therapies were not usually taught in medical or health-profession schools. However, the past decade has seen the inclusion of interventions such as acupuncture into physiotherapy and medical curricula, as well as in continuing education on programmes.

There is some overlap between conventional health interventions and alternative/complementary therapy. For example, hypnosis and visualisation can be viewed as both conventional health-care and alternative/complementary care. There are several issues that determine whether an intervention might be considered as conventional or alternative. Whether the intervention is used in conventional healthcare therapy or for an unusual purpose not generally accepted by conventional healthcare or delivered by someone not recognised for that specialty.

For example, hypnosis and visualisation would be considered as conventional interventions for treatment of pain but alternative for treatment of enuresis. These therapies might be considered as alternative even when they are used for pain, if the practitioner is not a person recognized in as conventional health professions. In this case, may be using a therapy somewhat differently from the way in which it would be used by a conventional health professional.

Other therapies may be largely considered as ACTs even when they are provided by conventional health professionals such as physiotherapists, occupational therapists or nurses (e.g., Alexander technique, Feldenkrais, therapeutic touch and others), because the underlying theoretical rationale is not widely accepted in conventional healthcare.

Acceptance of different therapies as a legitimate component of conventional healthcare can vary among individuals countries, groups and institutions. The degree of evidence for effectiveness may be a key determining point of whether an intervention is considered as an ACT or as an acceptable part of conventional healthcare.

## Alternative/Complementary Approaches for Pain

The most common ACTs used for pain include the following:

(1) Mind-body behavioural therapies such as visualisation, relaxation, biofeedback, hypnosis, meditation

(2) Alternative medical systems (e.g., acupuncture)

(3) Biologically-based therapies (e.g., herbal remedies, aromatherapy, bee stings)

(4) Manipulative and body-based systems (e.g., body works, chiropractice, TENS)

(5) Biofield therapies using metals (e.g., chelation, copper bracelets, coin rubbing) or based on energy fields (e.g., Reiki, therapeutic touch, vibrational medicine)

(6) Bioelectromagnetics (e.g., magnetic therapy)

This list was developed in the United States by the National Centre for Complementary and Alternative Medicine (1999b). Some of the therapies listed are an important part of conventional healthcare for pain as well as alternative/complementary interventions. Therapies such as acupuncture, spinal manipulation, massage, hypnosis, imagery and relaxation are more widely accepted in conventional healthcare (Ernst et al. 1995). The mind-body approaches are used by occupational therapists, psychologists, and by many physiotherapists. TENS and several other interventions are commonly used by many physiotherapists.

In some cases, specialised training and certification is required (e.g., chiropractice, acupuncture and hypnosis). Other therapies are easily available to a client without (e.g., herbs, diet supplements). These differences affect how widely they are used and the potential benefit or harm.

## USAGE OF ACTs

Alternative/complementary therapies are widely used. In conventional healthcare, at times, cure in accompanied by certain side-effects, resulting in a person's frustration and disillusionment (Berman et al., 1998). In chronic or progressive health problems, especially if they involve pain of mood disturbances*, (Eisenberg et al. 1993). For example, Krauss et al. (1998), found that 57 per cent of adults with physical disabilities used ACTs compared to 34 per cent of the national general population. primarily to obtain pain relief and secondarily to relieve depression or anxiety.

Approximately, 31-94% of adults with arthritis also use some form of ACT (Southwood et al. 1990). Rao et al (1999), found that two-thirds of patients at six rheumatology clinics used these therapies. Use of ACTs is also associated with higher education (Eisenberg et al. 1993, Warrick et al. 1999). Clients with more education may have more access to sources of healthcare information, particularly the Internet, where considerable information about ACTs is readily available.

People with cancer are also frequent consumers of ACTs with 7-64 per cent reporting use of one or more ACTs (Cassileth 1999). Thirty-seven per cent of cancer outpatients attending a pain and symptom clinic (Oneschuk et al., 1998), and 22 per cent of patients with head and neck cancer use ACTs (Warrick et al., 1999). Nam et al. (1999), reported that 25-80 per cent of patients with prostate cancer used ACTs. People with cancer who are in pain and faced with a threat to their life seem to trust ACTs for relief possible cure.

While the major groups of ACT consumers are adults; ACTs are frequently used by adults for children. Sixty-nine per cent of parents who use ACTs for their own healthcare also use them for their children's health problems (Spigelblatt et al. 1994). The number of different ACTs used for children by their parents' increases with the child's age, particularly when the child is assailed by some chronic ailment (Southwood et al.1990). A 1994, 39-86 per cent of children with arthritis from Sweden, Australia, New Zealand or Canada have used an ACT for the management of this condition (Hoveraal et al. 1984; Southwood t al 1990).

## WHY ARE ACTs POPULAR?

Many clients that we meet in our professional practice will be faced with situations similar to the one that is described in the Reflective exercise.

Often clients will find that conventional healthcare is unable to effectively treat all the problems associated with a persistent pain or a progressive health problem. As in case of, rheumatoid arthritis, sometimes, the disease is responsive to medication and at others may even cause serious health side-affects. This unpredictable course might make the client seek out an ACT. Frustration with conventional care, progressive illness and easy access to ACTs are making A.C.T's more and more popular.

ACTs also seem to be more natural safer and without any side effects. A person with cancer may have concerns about the side-effects of chemotherapy or radiation. Such experiences increase the appeal of ACTs.

Most ACTs, promote a holistic view of health, and an enhancement of the mind body connection,thereby enabling a person to regain more control and relief over his health problems.

Many ACTs emphasise the interpersonal relationship between the client and the practitioner. Thus may make, the client feel better understood . This is particularly for people with persistent pain. Often, in conventional healthcare, a person with pain will have encountered considerable doubt about the legitimacy of the pain. Consequently, more energy may be expended on trying to prove the existence of the pain than on recovering from the pain. A practitioner of ACT allows the client to believe and finds ways to make him get on with it (Kenny & Guy 2001).

People who use ACTs and feel that they have been helped often advocate the use of ACTs to others with similar problems. This is borne out in a survey about the use of alternative treatments by parents (Spigelblatt 1995). Hearing about ACTs by word of mouth was the most common reason given by these parents for using an ACT for their children.

Lastly, some people use ACTs as an adjunct to other health behaviours. Vitamins and other herbal remedies are sometimes used in this way to.

Clearly, there are many reasons for the appeal of ACTs. ACTs provide relief from prsistent pain at a low cost and with seemingly fewer risks of harm (Boisset & Ftzcharles 1994, Eisenberg et al 1993).

### Acceptance of ACTs by conventional health professionals

Physiotherapy approaches to care. Many accepted techniques employed in rehabilitation for complex health problems were at one point considered 'alternative'.

An example from physiotherapy comes from Elizabeth Dicke, a German physiotherapist, who developed circulatory complications after a leg infection. Ms. Dicke discovered that deep massage to her back resulted in improved circulation to her leg. Amputation was avoided and connective-tissue massage was born (Gifford & Gifford 1994).

Sensory integration was developed by Mr. Ayres, an American occupational therapist, as an approach for treating children with learning disabilities (Spitzer et al 1996).

Often, health professionals have had to come up with innovative approaches to cope with the health problems of their clients. Their perspective is quite different from medicine where the primary goal is to cure disease and provide relief of symptoms. Possibly for these reasons, the number of professionals such as physiotherapists, occupational therapists and nurses, accepting ACTs, in some cases even including some of them as a legitimate aspect of conventional practice, is on the increase.

Some ACTs are gaining acceptance by conventional health professionals. For example, when health professionals with expertise in low back pain were surveyed abut ACTs, they rated osteopathy and chiropractic as effective for acute uncomplicated low back pain, and acupuncture as effective for chronic, uncomplicated, low back pain, but neither homeopathy or herbalism was considered effective (Ernst & Pittler 1999).

In a Canadian survey, general practitioners perceived that alternative therapies were useful for musculoskeletal problems, chronic pain and chronic illness (Verhoef & Sutherland, 1995).

As noted previously, the ACTs that are most readily accepted in conventional healthcare are those therapies that 'fit' most easily into conventional frameworks. For example, cognitive-behavioural therapies, relaxation and hypnosis fit comfortably into conventional pain management programmes and generally would not be considered as ACTs.

Other therapies, such as massage, may be accepted intuitively because many health professionals have experienced personal benefit from them. When the ACT is relatively new, its underlying theory is foreign to conventional healthcare, then the ACT is treated with more skepticism. For example, interventions based on shifts in the circulation of an undetectable energy in invisible conducts (i.e., vibrational medicine) will not readily gain acceptance.

## Accessing information about ACTs

Obtaining accurate information about any ACT is challenging. Until recently, they have not been well researched or published in healthcare journals (as the principles governing them sometimes go against the conventional medicine) Discussions are mostly found in books concerned with health and wellness, in health-related magazines, and through organizations or businesses concerned with alternative/complementary healthcare.

In the last decade, two very powerful and efficient ways of information-gathering have emerged. One approach is to gather information via a computerised search of electronic databases (e.g., Cochrane Library, Medline & CINAHL). Such searches can be done at university or hospital libraries. The second approach is to use a search engine on the Internet to find information about a particular strategy. It is important to recognise that the way in which one searches for information, and the reason for conducting the search, will determine the kind of information that is retrieved.

Accurate information about ACTs may exist both in electronic databases of traditional medical and health-related journals, and on the Internet. However, potential bias exists. Conventional literature sources may give greater attention to identified risks than to the benefits associated with ACTs. Conversely, literature emanating from ACT practitioners or producers may be biased towards publication of benefits with minimization of risks. The reason for the search also influences the type of information that the searcher may be looking for. A client's search is for more reasons. A therapist may search for information to be helpful or to broaden his or her understanding of an ACT.

The Reflective exercise present two scenarios about an ACT that illustrates how questions about an ACT might emerge for a client or a therapist. Exercise describes a therapist scenario from the client's perspective.

One of the authors (A.U.) first became aware of bee-sting therapy for pain in the process of conducting a large community survey of the way people appraise and cope with a recent pain event. Several respondents spontaneously commented that they were using bee-stings to relieve chronic pain. There is no known prevalence data about how widespread the use of bee-sting therapy for pain might be. Bee-sting therapy is a good illustration of an ACT that is not well-known among conventional health professionals, but may be known to people who experience chronic pain.

Let's consider the information that might be retrieved on bee-sting therapy for pain. We conducted a search via CINAHL, Medline and the Internet. A search of CINAHL and Medline identified two papers related to bee-sting therapy. A search of the references of these two papers identified one additional publication. The first paper was a letter to the editor expressing concern about the increasing usage of this ACT in the writers' own country (Italy) because of the risks of granulomata due to retention of stinger fragments, and the possibility of anaphylactic shock (Altomare & Capella 1994). The second paper presented a case of painful nodular lesions in a 65-year-old man (Veraldi et al. 1995). He had used bee-sting therapy for 1 month for pain due to arthrosis of the spinal column. Conventional treatment was used to treat the lesions, but after 1-year follow-up, there was only partial regression of the lesions. The third paper described the following types of reactions associated with bee stings: urticaria and generalised oedema, local swelling, shock and collapse, laryngeal oedema, bronchospasm, angioneurotic oedema, partial or complete coma, tachycardia, itching, rash, faintness, face swelling, vomiting and cyanosis (Ordman 1968).

These reactions may occur with a bee-sting or with injection of the bee venom. In addition, Ordman (1968) discussed the way in which increased exposure to bee venom can increase sensitivity and increase the probability of adverse reactions and their severity. These papers gave the impression that bee-sting therapy or apitherapy as it is also termed is dangerous, and that it was once a common therapy for arthrosis, rheumatic diseases and sciatica, but has now fallen into disuse (except perhaps in Italy).

In contrast, a 10-minute search of the Internet located two apitherapists, five books directly concerned with bee-venom therapy, two electronic discussion lists, an American Apitherapy Society, and four testimonials about the effectiveness of apitherapy. These sources did emphasise the need for allergy-testing in advance of using apitherapy, but there was no discussion about other possible side-effects or the risk of sensitivity with increased use. Evidence of effectiveness was presented in an anecdotal format. There were no testimonials from anyone for whom the therapy was ineffective or harmful. The apitherapists presented themselves as nurturing individuals concerned about the welfare of others and convinced that bee-venom therapy was an effective remedy for many problems.

An occupational therapist or physiotherapist who conducted these two searches might conclude that bee-sting therapy is uncommon, has a number of serious risks, and is without any scientific evidence of effectiveness. In contrast, a client who is suffering from pain due to arthritis, multiple sclerosis or sciatica might conclude that conventional medicine knows little about this therapy, the risks were possibly over-stated and rare, and that the therapy was helpful for people with similar problems.

The therapist and the client, will do well to search both the conventional and the alternative health literature to obtain the most balanced and comprehensive understanding of the benefits, limitations and possible risks of any health intervention (Newall et al. 1996).

Very often an ACT is based on a theoretical foundation by the originator or a master teacher, and it should state clearly that the approach is not intended to replace conventional medicine or healthcare. It should provide discussion about possible harm and how to monitor for side-effects. Claims about research-evidence of effectiveness should be treated cautiously.

## Benefits and limitations of ACTs

Alternative/complementary interventions may be beneficial, ineffective or harmful, in the same way as interventions that are used in conventional healthcare. In this section, we will examine the potential benefits and harm of alternative/ complementary approaches, and then, in the following section, we will receive the data on some of the more common ACTs used for pain.

### Benefits

There are a number of potential benefits of ACTs. Some of these benefits are psychological and others are physiological. In large part, the psychological benefit can be attributed to the emphasis on the interaction between the mind and the body. The mind-body medicine approaches are more likely to decease feelings of helplessness and to promote feelings of hopefulness and optimism about recovering from pain. By emphasising the client-therapist relationship, the client feels that she or he is treated with more perception. The perception that many of these therapies are more natural than those associated with conventional healthcare leads to the conclusion that they can not cause no harm. Both directly and indirectly, these three factors promote, a sense of well-being.

Some ACTs have a physiological benefit in reducing pain. Some of this benefit may be due to reduced stress, improved muscle relaxation and attention to environmental or lifestyle factors that aggravate pain. Other therapies have a more direct physiological benefit on reduction of pain. For example, there is sufficient research to demonstrate that acupuncture is effective in reducing some types of pain (Alltree 1994, Baldry 1989, Gadsby & Flowerdew 1997, 1999, Patel et al. 1989, Pomeranz 1995, Ter Reit et al. 1990, Winlentz 1998).

Unfortunately, for other ACTs, there is insufficient research to demonstrate whether or not the therapy is beneficial. Much of the evidence is only at the level of case stories. which are biased because they are used to sell the product or the approach. Some therapies will have evidence of correlational relationships between the product or therapy and beneficial outcomes, such as reduction of pain. However, correlational studies do not provide evidence that the reduction in pain is caused by the use of the ACT. The beneficial effect may be due to something else that the person was doing in addition to using the ACT, or some other factor. With the growing emphasis on evidence-based practice, in the next few years there will likely be a significant increase in the number of studies assessing the efficacy of ACTs.

Aside from any direct therapeutic (psychologic or physiologic) effect on pain, the holistic approach of ACT encourages the reduction of unhealthy habits such as a sedentary lifestyle, smoking and consumption of high-fat foods, and suggest ways to improve of health through a nutritionally balanced diet and an active lifestyle. This positive change in health may enable the consumer to cope more effectively with pain. Improved coping is an important positive benefit.

## Harm

There are a number of ways in which ACTs can be harmful. Harm may come if it is used as an alternative rather than as a complementary therapy. Harm may also result from problems in the regulation of products.

ACTs that are used as alternative strategies may exacerbate the underlying cause of the pain, even if the ACT is effective in providing some pain relief or relief from other symptoms. This can be a significant problem for diseases such as arthritis, cystic fibrosis, diabetes, cancer and others. ACT practitioners may not be trained to identify malignancy or other underlying problems. With some chronic or life-threatening conditions (e.g., rheumatoid arthritis, morbid obesity, cancer), the timing of effective intervention may be critical to prevent the development of side-effects or further complications of the disease.

The potential for physiological harm is more for children, whose developing nervous system may be at greater risk. The most common pain problem in children that parents treat with ACT is juvenile arthritis (Hoyeraal et al 1984, Southwood et al. 1990). Deterioration in management and control of arthritic diseases, growth retardation, very early onset of puberty and life-threatening starvation have been reported as consequences of alternative/complementary diet manipulations and medicines (Southwood et al 1990, Spigelblatt 1995).

Mercury poisoning, hyponatremia, oedema, and urticaria have been reported in children treated with homeopathy (Spigelblatt 1995). Careful monitoring of benefits and possible side-effects will assure the parent that the benefits of therapy are maximised, particularly if conventional health professionals remain involved with the child's care.

Some ACTs are not well-regulated. Most therapies are not systematically tested so there is no formal mechanism to monitor benefits or harmful effects. Also, there are no controls to ensure that the product actually contains sufficient active ingredient to achieve a positive effect and no mechanism to alert the consumer on the product labels about possible side-effects.

Many alternative therapies (e.g., herbal remedies, diet supplements, ointments and homeopathic remedies) can be administered independently by a client without the guidance of an alternative or a conventional health practitioner. An individual who uses these strategies in this way is typically more attentive to noting positive effects, in part because the strategy is considered natural and therefore safe. Negative consequences may take some days to emerge. An individual may not make the connection between the intervention and any negative health effects.

However, the current interest in ACTs may result in significant changes to the control of these therapies and may provide better consumer protection.

Some therapies have the potential to become more personal and intimate. Relaxation, hypnosis, or therapies which involve physical contact (e.g., massage) are the case in point. Clients who have a history of abuse require sensitivity and considerable professional skills before such therapies are attempted.

Most ACTs have exorbitant price tags and they are not governed by governmental programmes. If the therapy has a known benefit, then the cost may be reasonable. For ACTs with unknown or questionable benefits, the high cost of treatment can be an unnecessary burden.

Unfortunately, the lack of regulation of many ACTs enables unscrupuleus people to enter this area of practice. The potential for exploitation is also increased by the easy access to the Internet for clients and charlatans. It is often difficult to dissociate useful information from fraudulent material.

To sum up, ACTs can be beneficial and harmful to the client. This dissociate is also true for many interventions offered in conventional healthcare for pain. For example, surgery for back pain often causes more pain; indeed one study found that 15 per cent of patients were worse after spinal surgery (Waddell et al.1979). Accessing multiple sources of information, attending to positive and potentially harmful effects, consultation with conventional health professionals and ACT practioners, and exercising caution against exploitation, will enable a client to make informed choices.

## Evidence for effectiveness or harm for common ACTs for pain

In this section, we refer to Cochrane reviews, meta-analyses or systematic where they exist, and other sources of evidence, to examine the benefits or harm for some of the more well-known ACTs used for pain.

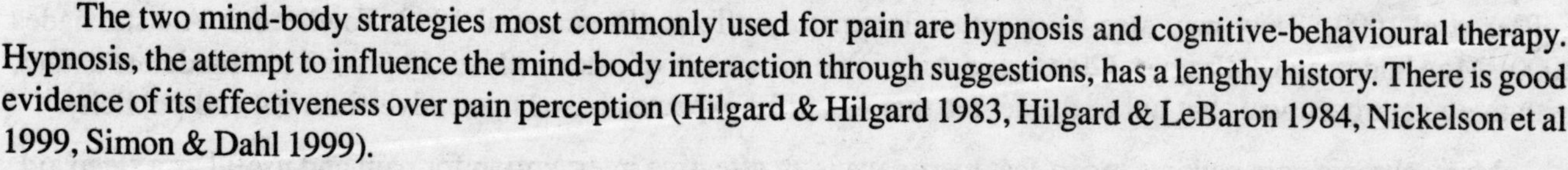

## MIND-BODY APPROACHES

The two mind-body strategies most commonly used for pain are hypnosis and cognitive-behavioural therapy. Hypnosis, the attempt to influence the mind-body interaction through suggestions, has a lengthy history. There is good evidence of its effectiveness over pain perception (Hilgard & Hilgard 1983, Hilgard & LeBaron 1984, Nickelson et al 1999, Simon & Dahl 1999).

Recently, Rainville et al. (1999), demonstrated that hypnosis was successful in modulating pain perception. Hypnotherapy out-performs physical therapy in clients with fibromyalgia who do not respond well to most other forms of treatment (Haanen et al. 1991).

The principle governing cognitive-behavioural therapy is based on the premise that behavioural responses to illness are influenced by both positive and negative reinforcement and treatment is aimed at improving management and coping strategies. Cognitive-behavioural therapy and hypnosis are effective in decreasing pain and pain-related anxiety in children undergoing bone-marrow transplantation (Liossi & Hatira 1999). Studies revealed that cognitive coping strategies were effective at reducing the perception of chronic pain (Fernandez & Turk 1989).

Another ACT, imagery, uses of the senses to evoke images that will have a positive effect on clients' interpretation of symptoms. Imagery is thought to affect the autonomic nervous system (Hawk 2000). Imagery is used to modify or relieve pain (Roberto 1994) and is not usually used alone but in combination with relaxation strategies. Relaxation therapies are broadly employed by healthcare practitioners. In a critical review of relaxation techniques, Kerr (2000) concluded that relaxation strategies (including physical and non-physical approaches) had a positive effect on physiologic indicators of stress (as shown by heart-rate electromyography and blood pressure) and psychological markets.

Mind-body therapies influence the way people think, feel and behave. When a person is willingly placed under the influence of suggestion, he or she is in a vulnerable state; therefore appropriate training and ethical practice are imperative as necesssary.

## Biologically-based therapies

Increasing awareness about herbal remedies, also known as nutraceutical, has lead to the proliferation of anecdotal reports regarding the benefits of such products for pain. Unfortunately, as Towheed and Anastassiades (2000), have written, these remedies are often less beneficial than what the labels proclaim:

Pharmacists may also not be sufficiently knowledgeable about ACT products.

Chrubasik and Roufogalis (1999) listed the following biologically-based products for pain: devil's claw, stinging nettle, willow bark, blackcurrant leaf, black-currant seed, evening primrose seed, borage seed, goldenrod herb, aspen bark with ash bark, capsicum, arnica flower, comfrey herb and root, white mustard seed, sweet clover herb, tea tree oil, feverfew, butterbur, peppermint oil, (St. John's Wort, and Kava-Kava). Chrubasik and Roufogalis (1999), argued that in a number of clinical studies, herbal products have demonstrated greater effectiveness than a placebo with a lower incidence of side-effects than conventional medications used for pain.

Currently, of these herbal products, only St John's Wort has been examined in a Cochrane review. This herb does have a positive impact on depression. It may also have a direct benefit on pain-relief but this outcome has not been well-researched. There are also some side-effects.

There are a few compounds that merit special mention. Selenium deficiency may contribute to the muscle pain of fibromyalgia (van Rij). A study using selenium supplements resulted in improvement after 12 weeks in nearly 60 per cent of the subjects in a double-blind study (Robinson et al. 1981).

Caffeine is an additive in many over-the-counter analgesic preparations and is present in many popular drinks and foods. Many clinical trials have investigated the effectiveness of caffeine for pain. It is recommended that caffeine does should not exceed 200 mg and should not be taken more frequently than every 3-4 hours (Food and Drug Administration 1975).

Glucosamine sulfate and chondroitin sulfate have received public and research attention. The studies of these compounds have led to the conclusion that they may aid in cartilage production and repair (Burkhardt & Ghosh 1987, Leffler et al 1999). They may also have anti-inflammatory effects (Ronca et al 1998, Towheed & Anastassiades 2000). McAlindon and colleagues (2000), concluded that symptoms of osteoarithritis improved to a moderate extent, with these neutroceuticals but not to the degree that would be expected based upon advertisement and publicity.

Many chronic pain patients report that marijuana is an effective intervention for pain and useful as a sleep aid. Clinical trials have demonstrated the value of cannabinoids for their analgesic effect, however there is a high incidence of side-effects (drowsiness, hypotension and bradycardia) (Herzberg at al 1997). These substances are not available in most countries by prescription, but patients gain access through illegal 'street' markets (determination of dose is even more uncertain in the illegal market than with unregulated herbal remedies).

Aromatherapy uses essential oils from herbs, plants and flowers to relieve pain (Urba 1996). It is often used to treat pain due to arthritis (Brownfield 1998), cancer pain (Urba 1996) and chronic pain (Buckle 1999). It has also been used to treat nausea, vomiting and pain due to labour in children, and improve mood during labour (Burns & Blamey 1994). There is little evidence that aromatherapy has a positive benefit on pain or sleep, but aromatherapy in combination with massage may improve subjective perceptions of well-being (Brownfield 1998).

## Manipulative and body-based systems

Touch plays a powerful role in human health and well-being (Montague 1971). The body-works approach uses external manual techniques, along with increased self-awareness, to achieve a posturally balanced, flexible and strong body alignment (McPartland & Miller 1999).

The number of forms of body works is rapidly increasing, with 197 named techniques thus far in the USA (McPartland 1992). There is no common nomenclature for these therapies. For example, Reiki may be considered as a 'body-work', but it is also a 'biofield' approach. The goals of the therapy and the amount of physical force that is used in treatment are important considerations to determine if there are any contra-indications (e.g., someone with osteoporosis should not undergo therapies that involve significant forces, particularly through bones or joints).

Balanced energy flow is a common objective to these therapies and is generally achieved through gentle techniques. Some techniques target the circulation of fluids. Other techniques focus on muscles, tendons and fascia. These techniques closely overlap with physiotherapy. Many types of massage fall into this category, along with techniques such as shiatsu, myofascial release and rolfing. These latter techniques involve direct movement and manipulation of bones and joints. Nevertheless, none of these therapies, with the exception of massage, have been sufficiency examined in empirical research to provide convincing evidence of effectiveness.

The amount of force applied by the practitioner varies with the technique. Generally, lighter forces are used when influencing energy or cerebrospinal fluids (CSF) flow, and increased forces when the target is connective tissues. Joint manipulation requires significant force, but delivered under controlled conditions limiting the force transmission to specific joint structures.

Craniosacral therapy is based upon the undemonstrated belief that a practitioner can feel the pulsations of CSF and through subtle cranial bone movement can influence its circulation. Measurement can be difficult as the targets of the craniosacral therapy become less and less tangible, therefore reports of effectiveness must be examined carefully.

Myofascial release uses sustained postures, stretching and deep massage, targeting fascia that has shortened due to injury and faulty posture. Myofascial release techniques target the entire body facia; typically one area is not treated in isolation. A physiotherapy technique might single out a shortened hip extensor muscle and target it specifically. ROM is more likely to improve when the affected muscle group is targeted specifically.

Massage is frequently used to relieve stress and ease musculoskeletal pain, back pain, and headaches. A systematic review was conducted on massage for low back pain and found that although massage seemed to have some potential as a therapy for low back pain, the existing research had too many major methodologic flaws to provide evidence for or against its efficacy (Ernst 1999).

In a different review, Ernst (1998) found that massage had some potential to relieve pain associated with muscle soreness following exercise. Massage was also included in a review of non-pharmacological therapies for cancer pain, but in this review massage did not appear to have a beneficial effect on pain relief (Sellick & Zara 1998).

Back massage was included with bath and mobilisation for low back pain associated with labour, but this intervention was not as effective as intracutaneous sterile water injections (Labrecque et al.1999) in relieving pain intensity or unpleasantness of the pain. Interestingly, although water injections provided significantly more pain relief, fewer women in this group indicated that they would choose this treatment again if they experienced back pain in another delivery.

A trial was conducted, massage, for staff in a hospital setting (Katz et al. 1999). The Swedish massage technique was used and carried out by registered massage therapists. This study demonstrated that massage may have an impact on pain relief for common pains that are experienced in the workplace and that massage can decrease tension and improve mood.

Research about massage thus far has only provided limited evidence regarding the benefits of massage for pain. However, other studies have shown a positive effect of massage on depression, anxiety, fatigue and confusion (Field 1998, Field et al. 1996, 1997). Improvement of mood may be very important to enable clients with chronic pain to readjust to daily life and maintain a better quality of life while managing persistent pain. These studies do not report negative effects associated with massage, but massage may be contraindicated for clients with a history of physical or sexual abuse, or who are otherwise uncomfortable with this degree of physical contact.

## Biofield therapies

This category includes the field of vibrational medicine, It includes encompasses many types of therapy. The notions of energy balance clearly echo traditional Chinese medicine. The foundation of the field of study is the Einsteinian paradigm, which sees 'human beings as networks of complex energy fields that interface with physical/ cellular systems' (Gerber 1988). The flow of this energy is considered central to wellness. Its interruption or change heralds illness, and its correction, a return to balance and health.

Therapeutic touch is a well-known biofield approach. The technique attempts to achieve a balance by manipulating a person's energy field using specific hand placements and strokes, without actually making any physical contact with the client. Preliminary research suggests that therapeutic touch may decrease anxiety. (Quinn & Srelkauskas 1993) and may have some effect on improving pain and function in clients with osteoarthritis of the knee (Gordon et al 1998); however, there is no clearly convincing evidence of positive benefit.

There are also several other therapies based on energy flow. Reiki is believed to be a 2500-year-old therapy originally developed in Tibet. With this technique, the practitioner lightly places his or her hands on a client's body, directing healing energy in 12 places.

Polarity therapy uses massage to seek balance in the circulation of *prana* or energy through channels similar to the meridians of traditional. Chinese medicine (McPartland & Miler 1999).

None of the interventions mentioned in this section have been examined in randomised controlled trials. Their effectiveness or risk for harm similarly remains unknown.

## Bioelectromagnetics

The use of magnetic therapy dates to Paracelsus in the fifteenth century (Livingston 1998). Paracelsus argued that magnets could attract disease out of the body, in much the same way that they attracted iron. Franz Anton Mesmer (1734 – 1815), is famous for his work which laid the foundation for modern-day hypnosis. In his sessions, patients sat around a tub filled with water and iron filings, and held iron rods through which his magnetic influence might reach their bodies. Magnets have been used in various fashions to draw disease and illness out of the body, although their popularity has also come and gone through the centuries.

At present, magnets for therapeutic purpose are sold in band-aid-like patches, as belts, wraps, insoles, headbands, earrings, necklaces, bracelets, cushions, pillows and mattresses (Living 1998). There is no research demonstrating the effectiveness of magnetic therapy for pain. However, a recent study comparing magnetic therapy with sham magnets to relieve post-polio pain found a significant relief in pain through magnetic therapy as compared to controls (Vallbona et al 1997). More research is needed to determine whether magnetic therapy is indeed beneficial for post-polio pain or for any other type of pain.

## Implications for physiotherapists and occupational therapists

There are two important considerations concerning ACTs for physiotherapists and occupational therapists.

Whether the intervention is considered conventional practice or ACT, a therapist should be cognizant of the degree of evidence of benefit that exists for any intervention that is offered to a client, and any associated harm. As noted, some ACTs, such as cognitive-behavioural therapies, chiropractic and acupuncture, have some degree of evidence for positive benefit and fewl side-effects when provided by qualified practioners: and they are generally well-accepted in conventional healthcare. However, the evidence for other therapies such as biofield strategies or bioelectromagnetic interventions is weak.

Secondly, occupational therapists and physiotherapists will likely have clients with pain who are using ACTs. In most of these therapies will be used as complementary to the interventions used by the therapist and other conventional treatments. However, occasionally the client may indicate his or her intention to terminate conventional care for alternative therapies. Nevertheless, it is important that the therapist avoid endorsing a therapy about which he or she may have insufficient knowledge or expertise. The therapist should ensure that the client has access to accurate information.

# ACUPRESSURE: AN INTRODUCTION

Aupressure is a blanket term, populary used to cover all types of pressure therapies that use finger or thumb pressure at specific pointes on the body. It has its own technique and is a specific science on its own merits. "Acu" means pointed or concentrated, and so acupressure. Means pointed or concentrated pressure. Acupuncture treatment is given by needles, having points to be punctured all over the body. We can roughly say that acupuncture without needle is Acupressure, the points being almost similar in both. The points Acupuncture are used on Meridianology. According to this there are 14 Energy flows or 14 rivers are flowing in the body, points being on the particular flow. And these points are present, all over the body. In Japan body pointed are being used in SHIATSU" Therapy. This therapy is recognized by Japan Government. Trained person in this therapy are working as professional practitioners in Japan. There "SHI" means pressure and "ATSU" means finger i.e. "SHIATSU" means finger pressure.

In zonology, this was studies by Dr. Fitzerland of USA, after studying many different oriental therapies and experimenting for long by himself and his associate for fifty for long years. According to zonology (zone may be feet zone, sole zone etc.) the human body is divided into 10 zones, one zone relating to toe or finger. A specific point pressed in that zone will have a reflex action for correcting the defect in the organ covered by that zone. There are different banches like Foot Reflexology, Hand Reflexology, Eye Reflexology, Ear Reflexology etc., the named suggesting the zones covered. Foot Relexology, which has all the points located on the soles of the feet, is a main branch of study. With this one can become one's own doctor for day to day health problems, by pressing the different points. One of the principle of Accupressure is that there is a continuous flow of Energy in human body, known as 'chi' in 'Ki' in Japan, and 'Adya' or 'Ojas' or 'Pran' or 'Shakit' in India etc. Some cointries name it as Bio-Electro-Magnetic current or 'Mana' or 'Vital' energy also. This energy has positive and negative properties. Its imbalance is the DISEASE and its balancing, knows as 'Homeostasis', is health. The blocking of flow of this energy causes sickness of cells in the respective organ as it affects neural flow and blood flow adversely. Acupressure treatment improves Nerve flow and Blood flow and ultimately organs are repaired. Thus it works from the subtle level of cells for the ultimate correction of organs, and hence more effective.

Foot reflexology covers points on the soles of the feet only. As explained before, the body is devided into 10 zones, 5 on left side of the body and 5 on right side, each zone passing to a Big toe or others.

All the theories now lead to following conclusions:

1. All the organs on the left side of the vertical central line of the body are having reflex points. On the left feet.
2. Similarly right sided organs have its reflex pts. On right feet.
3. The organs covering the area of right as well as left have their treatment points on both the feet.
4. Nature's symmetrical arrangement has also provided that the Acupressure reflex points for the organs on upper areas of the body are located around the top area of the feet.

The pressure is applied for 10 sec. for 3 times is one sitting. If you press at a wrong place it does not harm, but there won't be benefit. To know that you have pressed at right location, there will be a tenderness or pain on pressing it. Just 30 secs. Per point per day can make the difference. One can use this, even though one is not sick, for prevention of disease. And this is how you can become your own Doctor for day today ailments.

The roots of the pressure therapy are in hoary past of the oriental culture, where almost all such healing, depth searching, self development arts and sciences were cradled. It was used in Himalayan areas but in different forms and names. A 2330 B.C. painting of Egypt shows Acupressure Treatment. It is actively practiced in China and Japan. American Doctors systematize. It making it suitable to use by a layman after small training. About Results? Yes, they are wonderful and out of 100 patients 5 get miracles. Like a woman, diagnosed by Doctors as uncurable and totally bed ridden for life could travel in different parts of India, and specifically it is wonderful in all types of pains and also problems of Glands and Brain. The reason is that very subtle nerve flow are taken care of in the respective regions like brain and nervous system and glands where relatively less subtle drugs can not reach. Due to this, the result in

Lumbago, spondylosis, sciatica are very good by Acupressure Treatment. A crippled and sickly becomes energetic, a hypertensive is controlled, what more you want ? it is not without reason that the people of India had different rituals like Tilak, Strings on the wrist, Janeyu, Cord around big toe of both the feet, the Bangles, Bajuband, Neckless, Kardhani, Ornaments, pajed on the feet etc. It is very interesting that the ears and nose were pierced at particular points. Similarly the tattoos on particular points help in the function and control of the organs of the Body.

More and more people go for Acupressure due to its simplicity and results. It is simple, straight forward, pure and is without drugs, it is inexpensive and hence very good specially for rural masses of India. It needs less time and space. It is non-violent and without any side effects. Disgusted with durgs and Hopitals more and more people, these days, are (unless in Emergency) turning to one or other form of therapy. Modern world has started realizing the worth of 'Alternate Medicine', like Acupressure therapy. World Health Organisation also has appreciated Acupressure in its tradition Health Programme. The Acupressure in general improves Nerve flow, Blood flow and removes nerve flow, Blood flow. It releases Tension also. The Doctors agree that 75% of the diseases are hence tension releasing helps much for cure and prevention of many diseases.

In the end, I shall like to emphasise that there is a great similarity between Naturopathy and Acupressure. As a matter of fact Naturopathy helps a person to be healthy by being very close to the nature and by proper utilization of the nature and by proper utilization of the five elements, namely Akash, Vayu, Agni, Jal and Prithvi. There is a popular saying :"Sab Rogon ki ek Dava, Mitti, Pani, Dhoop Hava,"

Along with Naturopathy acupressure strengthens the vital forces to keep you not only healthy but also prevents you from falling sick.

## NATUROPATHY – KEY TO HAPPY, HEALTHY & PROSPEROUS LIFE

1. Everyone ASPIRES to have these virtues

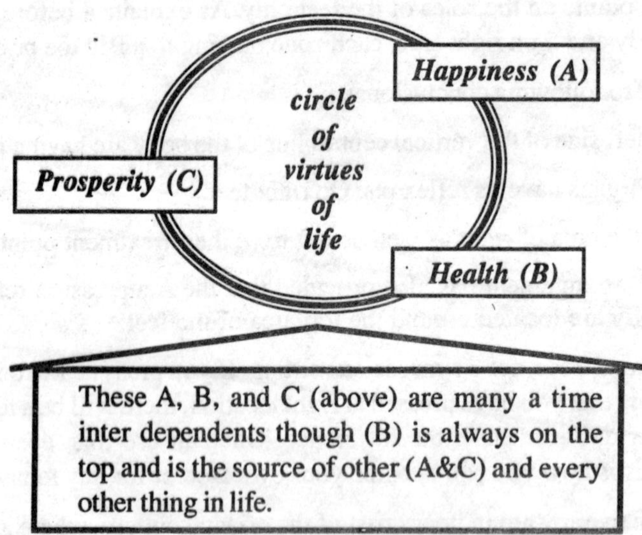


2. But, they keep eluding us.
3. Why ?
4. Because……

A. (i) We are not alive (living mean following some rules, principles etc.) since we obey no principles and/or ethics in life;

(ii) We don't have time for such living for such living, neither for self nor for welfare i.e. for others.

(iii) We don't understand happiness and don't even think of living for it but live to earn and hoard money and materialism and live for what others would think and say.

(iv) We don't know who we are and what for have we been thrown on earth by God the Almighty. And instead of endeavouring to know this we keep chasing certain unknown and meaningless objectives/GOALS;

B. (i) We do not know about our body and its needs;

(ii) We do not care that it is a living organic machine and as against other machines it needs care and adequate maintenance, REST, DIET, 5 elements (TATWAS) and YOGA.

C. (i) Since, neither do we have (A) nor (B) HOW can we have (c) above;

(ii) We not being healthy spend a lot on MEDICATION-denting our prosperity;

(iii) In our bid to purchase happiness through LUXURY goods we invite an unending chain of problems, expenses a tension-denting our (A) and (C);

(iv) We do not understand that nothing in this world can give happiness if we are healthy;

(धर्म) -- पहला सुख निरोगी काया, दूसरा सुख गन्ठी में माया (अर्थ)

(काम) -- तीसरा सुख इन्दर घर नारी, चौथा सुख पुत्र की छाया (मोक्ष)

(v) We are in a false belief that money is GOD and is everything. Thus, we are also its race. Whereas, it is NUMBER 2 in value;

(vi) Health, therefore, should get top priority in life;

(vii) For the sake of money we leave behing all the dignities of life and don't respect and observe any ethical, moral or spiritual values –viz. YAM, NIYAM etc.;

WE, THEREFORE, should introspect independently with cool, quiet and under prejudiced mind and attempt for improvement on the following lines seriously and since for our own HEALTH; and happiness and prosperity.

All these may not be adoptable at once definitely slowly and in stages. If followed we patience and faith and like a KARM-YOGI of HOLY GITA i.e., without expecting result (overnight) one will definitely be able in unlocking the treasure of life.

## SCHEDULE

A. Plan to sleep early to get up early in the morning.

EARLY to bed and early to rise

Makes a man Healthy, Wealthy and Wise.

B. Wake up at 4.30 A.M.....

(1) Activate your body tissues—vigorously stretching and pulling your arms and legs to the maximum on each side and twisting the body in a similar manner before coming to the sitting position the bed.

(2) Give light massage gently to the scalp and pull the blood upwards near the ears temple region with your fingers. Pull the hair upward gently with your fingers.

(3) Offer your prayer to GOD, also thanking HIM for blessing you with this NEW MORNING.

(4) Before putting your feet down on the earth, the mother earth, touch HER with your hands and pay due respect to her.

(5) Now is the time to take some oath etc. to remember and observe some ethical principles, yam and niyam etc. during the day to follow.

C. Leave the bed at 4.40 A.M.

(1) Drink 2-3 glasses of water (for kidney flushing and cleansing)

(2) Water from copper vessel kept overnight is preferable.

(3) Go to toilet and take bath in live cold water. Live water is one which is either flowing/stream/running through pipes or stored in metallic container/tank. Since, cooling comes from top start pouring water on your head during bath. During toilets/urination keep teeth pressed against each other.

….. at 5.01 A.M…

(1) Sit down on a clean 'ASAN' in a cool, quiet, pleasant place with open fresh air and do….

(a) Nadi Shodhan, b) other Pranayams and c) Meditation for 30 minutes.

(2) Eat one spoonful of BUTTER/Desi Ghee

(3) 6 A.M. Go out for the morning walk and for acquiring 5 TATWAS. The park should be such which is well maintained and clean having thick greenery (Good grass, plants, bushes and tree). Your body should have minimum clothes so that body is exposed the maximum. Coarse, Khadi types, Airy clothes should be preferred.

- Do some yogasanas on a bed sheet/blanket laid out on grass.
- Surya Namaskar – 2 or 3 rounds.
- Bare feet walking on the dew-clad/otherwise moist grass and running for at least 15-20 minutes.
- Deep breathing (Abdominal) in fresh air 15-20 minutes.
- Sun Bath in the rising sun –15-30 minutes.
- If cool breeze blowing, run against this breeze to acquire air element through skin.
- Do invariably the Shavasana after the above exercise session.

(4) Sit down for readings – newspaper and others on returning from the park.

(5) Take 4-5 Tulsi leaves, wash its surface dust and gulp down the food price with water or milk before starting your breakfast.

(6) It is 7 A.M. — Time for breakfast

- Sprouts of soyabean, alfalfa seeds, black-TIL, Gram, Kidney Bean etc.
- Just the soaked seeds if sprouts not available.
- Chew them properly (it is drinking the meals).
- Eat the milk i.e. do not gulp down in a gasp/flow.
- Vajrasana for 5-15 minutes.

(7) At 7.30 A.M. you are ready for the day.

(8) During your working hours keep your body in straight upright posture

(9) Meals : take early, say 12.30 P.M. to 1 P.M.

- Eat only when hungry.
- Eat when Surya Nadi is running.
- Light strolling before meals to stimulate the system.

- Wash not only the hand but also mouth, face and eyes before meals.
- Pass urine before and after the meals.
- Drink water ½ and hour before and one hour after the meals.
- Avoid spicy, fried and un-natural food.
- Avoid chillies (especially red) and 'KHATAI' (powder of dried undraped mangoes), sugar and salt to the extent possible.
- Take a few sips of water (AACHMAN) before meals.
- Do Vajrasana for 10-15 min. after meals.
- Eat in squatting position.
- Keep an Alkaline; Acidic balance of 80.20 in the diet.
- Eat at cool, quiet place with peaceful/restful mind.
- Eat upto 75% of your stomach capacity so that the space necessary for digestive activities and air TATWA is available.
- Eat one type of food at a time and avoid mixing up of proteins, fats carbohydrates with one another.
- Avoid mixing up of fresh vegetables with fruits.
- Do not talk during meals.
- Take light; Satwik; Nutritive, easily digestible, balanced diet.
- Include sprouts in your meals.
- Take yogurt/curd.
- Roughage should invariably be included in meals.
- Eat raw, unpolished and natural.

D. DIET

Sprouts of wheat, gram, soyabean, beans, til, etc.

Raw Vegetables – Carrot, cabbage, beet, radish, onion, cucumber, tomatoes, amla, spinach, bathua and methi leaves etc.

Take all seasonal fruits

Cooked pulses and begetables.

Curd.

E. Evening should be kept for social interactions and family needs.

F. Dinner at around 7.30 P.M. – 8 P.M.

G Sleep at 9 P.M.

- Prayer, Pranayamas and Meditation before sleep.

H. Take weekly fast

- During fasting take rest
- Consume a lot of water (preferable juices of alkaline vegetables/fruits)

- Lemon juice and pine-apple juice are useful.

I. Fortnightly/monthly massage with mustard, til, olive oil. Oil used may be one already prepared in sun-light.

J. Mental & Spiritual :

- Inculcate the habits and imbibe the characteristics of a SADHAK.
- Observe and follow YAM and Niyam.
- Yoga, Pranayama and Dhyana.
- Develop patience —the root of FAITH.
- Faith is the biggest asset ...Faith in self and in GOD.
- Surrender totally in the lotus feet of THE ALMIGHTY.
- DON'T get excited in any situation—happiness, gloom, tragedy, horror etc.
- EGO should be killed; this being the strongest wall between self and the GOD. But maintain positive self respect.
- Be human and kind-hearted to all.
- Believe in forgiveness and charity.
- Exercise control on sense organs especially those for speech, taste and sex.

Complementary Treatments

**Acupuncture**

A practitioner will address the underlying weakness or blockage in the patient's energy system.

- Lifestyle and eating habits will also be examined. Hereditary aspects will be taken into consideration.
- Pressure points on the bladder, conception and governor meridians may be used, and moxibustion may be suitable.

**Naturopathy**

Prostatic massage, a special technique carried out by a qualified naturopath, can alleviate BPH.

- Nutritional and dietary management will be undertaken with herbal medication.
- Hot and cold compresses and sitz baths may be helpful, as may zinc supplements to reduce prostage enlargement, and drinking plenty of fluids (except diuretic drinks).

**Homoeopathy**

Treatment will be according to the cause of the problem, but some very helpful remedies include:

- Sabal for an enlarged prostate and difficult, painful urination.
- Baryta for a frequent urge to urinate although the stream is weak, and the person is thin and perhaps prematurely impotent. For prostatitis, homoeopathic treatment is constitutional but in an acute attack the following remedies may help:
- Sabal, if the prostate is enlarged but the area around it feels cold and intercourse is either impossible or painful.
- Thuja if there is a burning sensation at the neck of the bladder and a frequent urge to pass water.

## Western herbalism

Treatment can be very helpful in reducing BPH and also any information or infection that affects the prostate gland. Herbs that have diuretic can be given to help encourage a person to urinate.

## Other therapies

**Cymatic** is extremely useful for the treatment of prostate of problems, as it is for most endocrine system function problems. Kinesiology and shiatsu may be useful for BPH. Crystal and gemstone therapy may help to strengthen the immune system and in turn activate the body's natural healing process. Macrobiotic treatment may advise a standard macrobiotic diet, in which there is no chicken, egg, meat, salmon or backed foods, and which features a reduced intake of salt. Herbs with hormonal effects and kidney tonics may be suggested by a Chinese herbalist. A yoga practitioner may recommend gentle asanas, relaxation, pranayama, meditation and shat kriyas. In Ayurvedic medicine treatment may consist of Ayurvedic oral preparations and panchakarma therapy. Reflexology will be aimed at treating points for the endocrine gland and bladder. An aromatherapist will incorporate oestrogen-like oils such as clary sage and geranium in an all-over body massage.

## YOGA CAN HELP YOU

1. To reduce nervousness, and psychomatic diseases.
2. To reduce depression and gain more self assurance and contentment.
3. To reduce irritability and gain more tolerance in frustrating situations.
4. To reduce tendency to unnecessarily dominate, to gain and deserve more respect, cordiality and tolerance.
5. To decrease the breath rate, resulting in a more co-ordinated and rested state of nervous system.
6. To reduce cardiac output, resulting in reduction in the work-load of the heart.
7. To increase the natural tendency of the mind to progress and go beyond all limitations and gainunbounded awareness.
8. To solve all problem whwich hinder to achiev profound physical fitness.
9. To alter the daily routing of life and realize one's ability to reconcile opposites and the ability to harmonise and make maximum use of divergent values.
10. To increase the levels of rest by decreasing the consumption of oxygen and metabolic rate. (there comes a natural physiological changes due to lowered requirement of oxygen by the cells in the human body during YOGA NIDRA).
11. To improve learning ability, academic performance, integration of emotions/thinking.
12. To improve performance, and more job satisfaction, more stability in job and better inter-personal relationship with the superiors, co-workers.
13. To increase mental healt, improve ability to concentrate, and gain emotional stability.
14. To improve the condition of the hypertensive patents.
15. To help the drug addicts in reducing their desire for drugs initially and finally in getting rid of it.

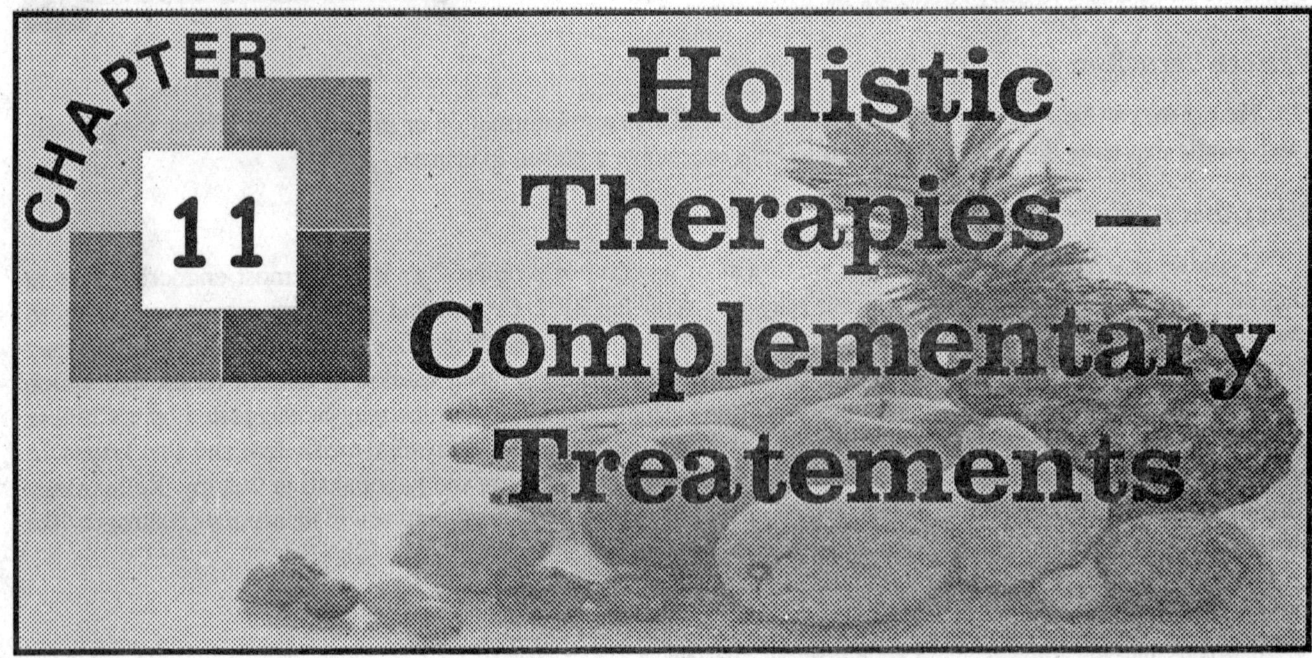


## UNDERSTANDING IMBALANCE

It is important to understand that the terms used to describe yin and yang are ***relative*** rather than absolute states. There is nothing that is purely yin or purely yang; each contains a part of the other in order to represent wholeness.

Everybody, despite their gender, possesses varying degrees of yin and yang characteristics. The subtle balance is constantly changing and, in the same way, every aspect of the universe changes. There are cycles of light and seasons, which reflect the constant shift between the polar opposites.

Understanding the energetic roles of yin and yang is the key to any therapeutic application

***KEY NOTE:*** The primary function of yin is to cool, moisten, relax and promote sleep. The primary function of yang is to warm, energise and stimulate.

When yin and yang are balanced within your life, you experience health. When they are imbalanced, ill-health can arise. If a person's yin energy is deficient, the symptoms are likely to be a feeling of heat, thirst and restlessness. If a person's yang energy is deficient they are likely to feel chilly, tired and unmotivated.

A person's condition, whether excessively yin or yang, will have a direct impact on how the energy flows in the meridians. An excessively cold condition may restrict the flow of energy along a meridian, while too much heat may cause an excess of energy to flow along a meridian.

The concept of yin and yang may be used as a guide when helping clients to restore balance and overall health. The application of this ancient theory is discussed below.

### The Application of Yin and Yang

Yin and yang can be defined with reference to the eight principles of change:

| Yin | Yang |
|---|---|
| • cold | • hot |
| • empty | • full |
| • deep | • surface |
| • imbalanced towards the yin | • imbalanced towards the yang |

To illustrate this in simple terms, if a person is feeling chilly and lacking in energy, they will be imbalanced towards the yin. The condition is likely to be longer-term and chronic. If a person has a fever and a full feeling in the chest, the condition is imbalanced towards the yang. The symptoms arc likely to be short-term and acute.

These are extreme examples of excessive yin and yang states. However, in practice most people are likely to suffer from combinations of yin and yang conditions.

For example, when touching a client's back, you find the upper back to be **hot** (yang) and the lower back to be cool (yin). Relating this to the eight principles of change, the upper back would be considered full (yang) with the tension being very much on the surface. The lower back **would be** considered empty (yin) with the tension being so deep that it has a hollow or empty feeling.

In order to restore health, we need to balance the opposing extremes. In other words the extreme yang part must relax and become more supple (or more yin) and the extreme yin must become more active, vital and full (or more yang).

***KEY NOTE:*** With any form of bodywork, it is important to understand that we are not only dealing with surface tension, but also with the underlying organs and the meridians that supply these organs with energy. Problems arising with organs, nerves, muscles and meridians are all connected. We should never forget the whole, as one problem may affect the body in the form of a compensatory imbalance elsewhere.

Having a deeper understanding of meridians can **help us to recognise that problems in a *certain* part of the body correspond to problems in specific organs. We can work on these areas in order to address the imbalance.**

## MERIDIANS

The human body is a natural energy source which generates electrical energy within the ionic environment of the cells and tissues. Body fluids contain electrically-charged ions which can cause a current to flow. Body meridians are thought to contain a colourless, free-flowing, non-cellular fluid, which conveys this electrical energy throughout the body.

Although the meridians are categorised in terms of the organs and tissues that they supply they are thought to form a single continuous circuit which conveys electromagnetic energy throughout the body.

The body's circuit of electrical energy is divided into 14 major meridians; there are it organic meridians and two storage meridians. Body meridians are named according to the internal structures they supply. Each of the organic meridians supply a group of muscles in the body, as well as a group of internal tissues.

## Organic Meridians

### Yin Meridians

Six of the organic meridians are called yin meridians. The yin circuit conveys negative electro magnetic energy throughout the body and supplies the yin organs:

- heart
- lungs
- liver
- spleen
- kidney
- pericardium.

The yin meridians have a common purpose which is to alter, circulate and store blood and energy (chi). They are located deep in the body.

### Yang Meridians

The remaining six organic circuits are called yang meridians. The yang meridians convey positive electromagnetic energy throughout the body and supply the yang organs:

- stomach

- small intestine
- large intestine
- gall bladder
- urinary bladder
- triple warmer (the three zones of energy in the torso).

The yang meridians are closer to the surface and are all part of the digestive system.

It is important to understand that no organ operates independently within the meridian network. Each yin organ and its meridian, works in line with a corresponding organ and meridian. So, the meridians function in pairs, each one being made up of one yin meridian and one yang meridian. Energy or chi, moves from the head towards the feet through the yang meridians on the back of the body and from the feet to the head through the yin meridians on the front.

## The Storage Meridians

The storage meridians (the conception vessel and the governing vessel) both help to create balance among the 12 organic meridians by dispersing excess chi to deficient meridians. They also help to unite the organic meridians by allowing chi flow to adjust when there is a blockage.

*KEY NOTE:* When working along a specific meridian, remember that you are also working on a related organ. When pressing on a point along a meridian, energy is boosted along the pathway to the corresponding organ.

## Yin, Yang and Emotional State

It is important to realise that emotions can upset the natural balance and flow of electromagnetic energy in the body, by subtly altering the chemical state of the body's tissues and their ionic conductivity. Yin emotions such as depression, fear, disappointment, grief, withdrawal and shame can cause the body's tissues to be flooded with negative electromagnetic energy. The negative energy that permeates the body's system then causes negative congestion. This deprives the yang circuit and the corresponding muscles and tissues of positive energy.

Conversely, an excess of yang emotions such as anger, agitation, impatience, frustration, jealousy, hostility, envy and defensiveness can flood the tissues with positive electromagnetic energy. This depletes the yin circuits along with the muscles and tissues supplied by them.

## The Heart Meridian

The heart meridian begins at the heart and surfaces in the centre of the axilla. The meridian passes down the inside of the arm, crosses the inner point of the elbow fold, and runs through to, the tip of the little finger.

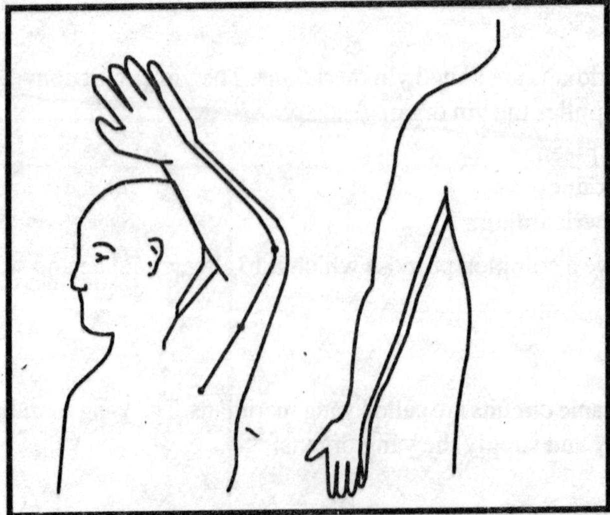

**Fig. 33 : The Heart Meridian**

## Common Symptoms of Imbalance

| PHYSICAL | EMOTIONAL |
|---|---|
| hot or cold hands and feet | excessive laughter |
| red complexion | hysteria |
| nervousness | lack of joy |
| irritability | expressionless appearance |
| mental or emotional disturbance | |
| insomnia, disturbed sleep or excessive dreaming | |
| cardiovascular disorders | |
| brain or nervous system disorders | |
| speech problems | |
| spontaneous sweating | |
| poor memory of important life-events | |

**KEY *NOTE:* The heart meridian is the centre of emotional and mental consciousness. It is associated with passion, mental clarity and joy.**

### The Lung Meridian

**The lung meridian runs from deep in the body within the lung to surface in the hollow area by the front shoulder. It then passes over the shoulder and down the front of the arm, running along the biceps muscle. It goes down the arm to the wrist just below the base of the thumb and ends at the thumbnail.**

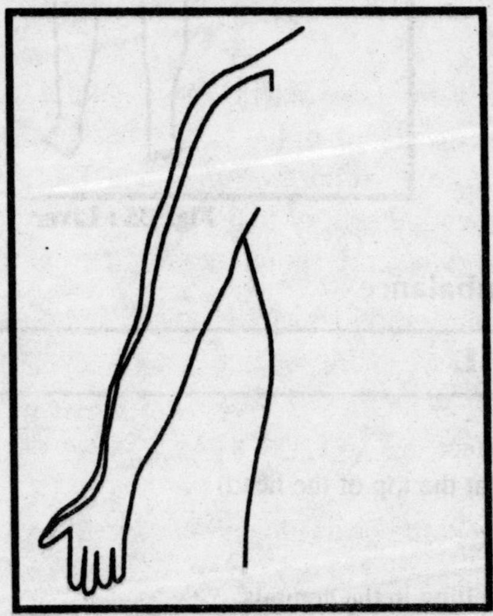

**Fig. 34 : Lung Meridian**

## Common Symptoms of Imbalance

| PHYSICAL | EMOTIONAL |
|---|---|
| asthma | chronic or long-term grief, sorrow |
| bronchitis | claustrophobia |
| congestion in the chest | compulsive behaviour |
| coughing | restlessness |
| breathing difficulties | |
| pneumonia | |
| excessive mucous | |
| sore throat | |
| loss of voice | |
| deficient or excessive perspiration | |
| collapsed or hollow chest | |

***KEY NOTE:*** In Chinese medicine, the lungs are the rulers of energy. How deeply we breathe shapes the energy and gives it its definition to provide the quality and quantity of energy required for respiration.

## The Liver Meridian

The liver meridian begins at a point inside the big toenail, passes over the top of the foot, continues above the inside of the ankle, runs past the inside of the knee and along the inner thigh. It proceeds through the genital region, upwards to the sides of the body and then ends at the ribs just over the liver (for the meridian on the right side of the body) and just over the spleen (on the left side).

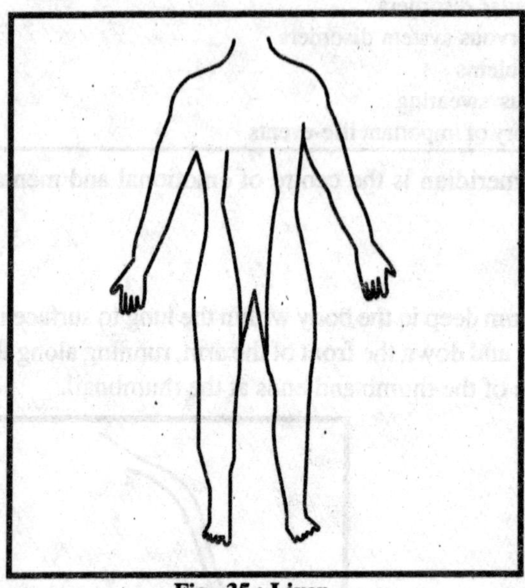

**Fig. 35 : Liver**

### Common Symptoms of Imbalance

| PHYSICAL | EMOTIONAL |
|---|---|
| red face | anger |
| pale, drawn face | frustration |
| headaches (at the top of the head) | depression |
| migraines | lack or will |
| dizziness | |
| pain and swelling in the genitals | |
| menstrual pain, irregular periods, premenstrual syndrome | |
| disorders of the eye and vision | |
| muscle spasms, seizures, convulsions | |
| pale fingernails, ridges in nails, cracked nails | |
| pain relating to tendons | |
| allergies | |
| easily bruised | |
| dandruff and hair loss | |

***KEY NOTE:*** In Chinese medicine, the liver and liver meridian are considered to control the life force. The liver meridian is associated with expression of the will and with creativity - when life energy is weak it is usually indicative of a troubled liver.

## The Spleen Meridian

The spleen meridian begins at the inside of the big toe at the nail and then runs along the inside of the foot, it turns upward in front of the ankle bone, then ascends along the inside of the calf to the knee. From there, the meridian runs up through the genital region, through the abdomen, proceeds to the spleen itself, and then to the stomach. The meridian continues upwards, along the side of the body and chest area to the outside of the breast.

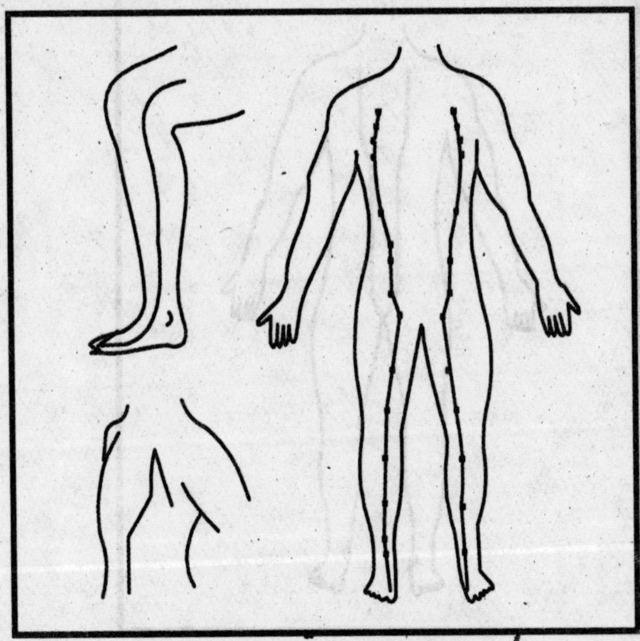

Fig. 36 : Spleen Meridian

### Common Symptoms of Imbalance

| PHYSICAL | EMOTIONAL |
|---|---|
| digestive problems - dyspepsia, constipation and diarrhoea | excessive worry |
| heartburn, acid indigestion | sensitivity |
| nausea | obsession |
| belching and gas | lack of awareness |
| immune deficiency or disorders | |
| lymphatic problems (swollen lymph nodes) | |
| abdominal distension | |
| appetite imbalance | |
| hypoglycaemia or diabetes | |
| heavy, aching body | |
| knee or thigh problems | |
| memory problems | |
| vomiting after eating | |

***KEY NOTE:*** In Chinese medicine, the spleen is regarded as the primary organ of digestion, passing chi to the small and large intestines. When the spleen is weakened by excessive consumption of sugar and acidic foods, it is unable to pass sufficient energy to the intestine. This often results in chronic indigestion and constipation.

## The Kidney Meridian

**The kidney meridian starts at the little toe and crosses under the foot to the inner edge of the instep. It circles the anklebone towards the heel, then rises along the inside of the calf to the inner thigh. At the pubic region it goes external for a short distance and re-emerges over the abdomen and chest extending to the clavicle.**

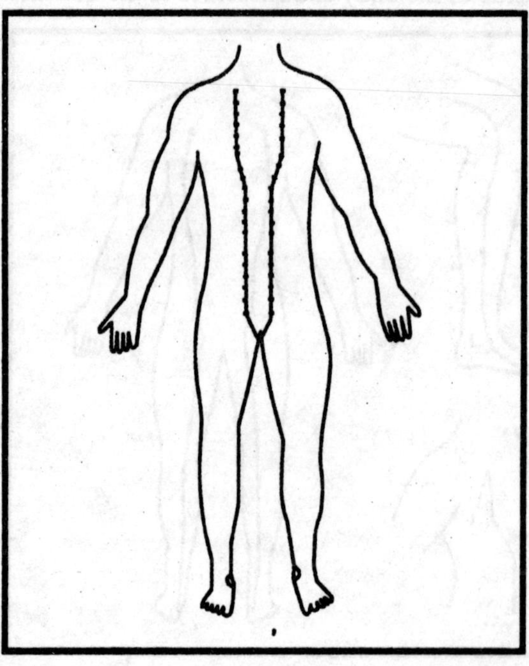

**Fig. 37 : Kidney**

### Common Symptoms of Imbalance

| PHYSICAL | EMOTIONAL |
|---|---|
| cold extremities (especially the feet)<br>achy or weak bones<br>darkness under the eyes<br>drowsiness, lack of energy<br>diarrhoea<br>dizziness on standing<br>tinnitus<br>oedema<br>hearing loss<br>low back pain<br>irregular menstruation<br>premenstrual syndrome<br>reproductive problems<br>painful or hot soles of feet<br>urinary incontinence<br>sexual problems<br>hypertension<br>hair loss | fearful, easily frightened<br>chronic anxiety<br>foolhardiness |

***KEY NOTE:*** **In Chinese medicine, the kidneys are responsible for strength and constitutional vitality of the body. They control the essential energy within each cell of the body and thereby, maintain the health, vitality and function of every organ, system and sense.**

## The Circulation or Pericardium Meridian

The circulation or pericardium meridian starts internally at the surface of the heart and emerges just outside each nipple. It follows around the axilla and travels down the inside of the arm to the wrist ending at the thumb-side corner of the middle fingernail.

### Common Symptoms of Imbalance

| PHYSICAL | EMOTIONAL |
|---|---|
| stiffness of spasm in the arm and elbow | timidity |
| distended chest and ribs | anxiety |
| discomfort in chest | nervousness |
| hot plams | insensitivity |
| red face | rude behaviour |
| sexual dysfunction | excessive laughter |
| painful or swollen underarm area | |
| tension in upper chest | |
| painful, stiff head and neck | |

***KEY NOTE:*** **The circulation or pericardium meridian does not correspond directly to an organ.**

## The Stomach Meridian

The stomach meridian starts below the eyes, descends to the sides of the mouth and the jaw, from where a branch rises to the forehead. It also continues along the side of the throat to the collar bone and over the chest and abdomen to the pubic area. From there, it passes along the front of the thigh to the outside of the kneecap. Below the kneecap, the meridian divides into two branches, one that ends at the second toe and one that ends at the third toe.

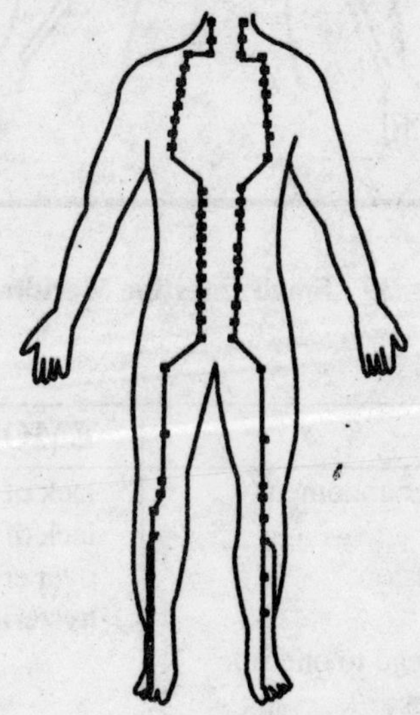

**Fig. 38 : Stomach Meridian**

### Common Symptoms of Imbalance

| PHYSICAL | EMOTIONAL |
|---|---|
| distension of the upper abdomen | critical |
| abdominal pain | lack of understanding |
| jaw tension | lack of compassion |
| knee pain | anxiety and nervous tension |

| | |
|---|---|
| lip or mouth sores<br>vomiting<br>frequent hunger or thirst<br>neck or throat swelling<br>yawning<br>groaning | emotionally unstable |

***KEY NOTE:*** In Chinese medicine, the stomach and spleen are considered to be connected, one providing energy to the other. As the stomach meridian begins at the mouth, it is said to govern the mouth, tongue and oesophagus, thereby controlling the preparation of food for digestion.

## The Small Intestine Meridian

The small intestine meridian begins at the outside of the nail on the little finger, trails the back of the hand to the wrist and flows from the outside of the ulna to the elbow. It follows the back of the arm up to the shoulder joint, where it crosses the scapula to the clavicle. From here, the meridian continues up the side of the neck and over the cheek to the ear.

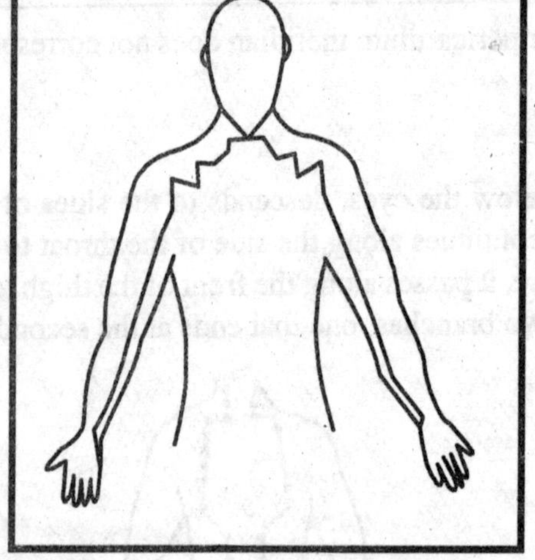

**Fig. 39 : Small Intestine Meridian**

**Common Symptoms of Imbalance**

| PHYSICAL | EMOTIONAL |
|---|---|
| distension of the lower abdomen<br>arm pain<br>shoulder pain and tension<br>swollen cheeks<br>difficulty in turning head to one side<br>eye soreness or redness<br>disorders relating to the small intestine | lack of mental clarity (deficient chi)<br>lack of joy (deficient chi)<br>over emotional (excess chi)<br>hysteria (excess chi) |

***KEY NOTE:*** In Chinese medicine, imbalances in the small intestine prevent the smooth transfer of energy from the food to the stomach, resulting in digestive disorders. The small intestine is considered to be linked with the heart, helping to bring clarity of mind.

## The Large Intestine Meridian

The large intestine meridian starts at the index linger on the outside of the nail (towards the thumb), runs through the crease between the thumb and the index finger, then passes up the thumb-side edge of the arm to the edge of the shoulder. It then crosses the shoulder and neck to the cheek, touches the upper lip and ends at the nostril.

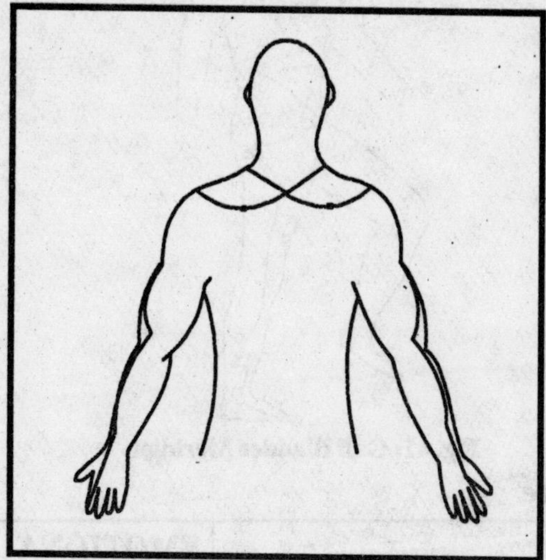

Fig. 40 : Large Intestine

### Common Symptoms of Imbalance

| PHYSICAL | EMOTIONAL |
|---|---|
| constipation<br>diarrhoea<br>headache<br>shoulder pain<br>nasal congestion<br>toothache | excessive worry<br>grief and sadness<br>compulsive attention to detail<br>stubbornness |

***KEY NOTE:*** In Chinese medicine the large intestine is considered to perform the function of elimination, both in a physical and metaphysical sense. That is, the condition of the large intestine reflects the mind and body's capacity to eliminate those experiences, beliefs and emotions we no longer need. This enables us to grow as individuals. The **large intestine is also responsible for sending energy downwards** into the body and, thus, grounds us to the earth.

## The Gall Bladder Meridian

The first thing to notice about the gall bladder meridian is that it zigzags back and forth over the head and that it zigzags down both sides of the body. Secondly, it is one of the longest meridians. The meridian begins at the outside corner of each eye, loops around the ear to the neck, goes back over the head to the forehead above the eyes, then over the head again to the back of the neck. From there it drops down the neck and over the front of each shoulder. It then zigzags down the sides of the body, along the outside of each leg, over the front of the ankles, and ends at the fourth toe.

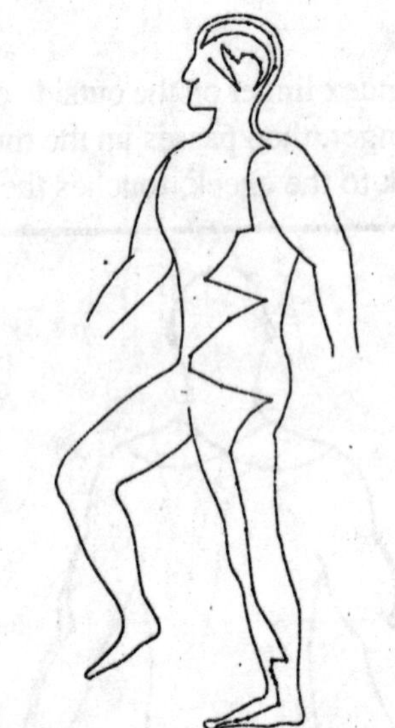

Fig. 41: Gall Bladder Meridian

**Common Symptoms of Imbalance**

| PHYSICAL | EMOTIONAL |
|---|---|
| headache (temple) and migraine<br>eye and ear pain<br>joint stiffness and pain<br>tightness and pain in the sides of the chest<br>nausea and vomiting<br>yellow colour in eyes<br>stiffness in fourth toe<br>gall stones | anger and frustration (excess chi)<br>depression and lack of will (deficient chi) |

***KEY NOTE:*** **In Chinese medicine, the gall bladder is seen as an external motion of the liver energy. Therefore, liver symptoms become more pronounced when the gall bladder is imbalanced. The Chinese say that when the gall bladder is balanced, good judgement and clear thinking is made possible;when the organ is unbalanced frustration and clouded judgement will result.**

## The Bladder Meridian

**The bladder meridian begins at the inside corner of the eye. passes over the forehead and the top of the head, then continues down the back in four lines, two on either side of the spine. The four lines continue over the buttocks and down the legs, where two meet behind each knee. A single line then passes down each leg along the centre line of the calf behind the outer ankle, and ends at the outer tip of the little toe.**

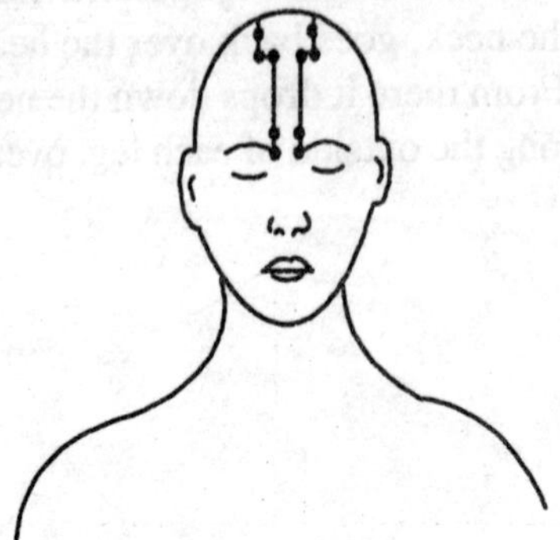

Fig. 42: Gall Bladder M

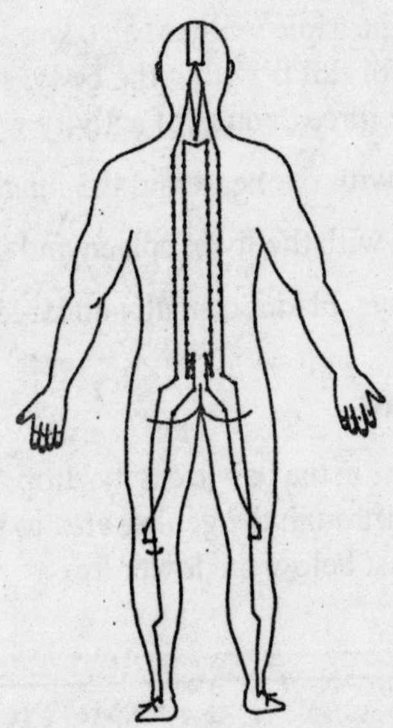

Fig. 43 : Bladder Meridian

**Common Symptoms of Imbalance**

| PHYSICAL | EMOTIONAL |
|---|---|
| back problems<br>bladder infections<br>incontinence<br>hip or sacrum problems<br>pain on inside corner of eye<br>rounded shoulders<br>spasm or pain at back of calf<br>stiffness in little toe<br>aching feet after standing | paranoia<br>jealousy<br>excessive suspicion<br>fear<br>chronic anxiety |

***KEY NOTE:*** **In Chinese medicine, the bladder is part of the system that includes the kidneys and the reproductive organs. By boosting energy along the Meridian, you strengthen not only the bladder itself but every organ in the body.**

## The Triple Warmer Meridian

**The triple warmer meridian begins on the outside corner of the nail on the fourth finger and runs up the middle of the outside of the arm to the top of the shoulder. It continues over the shoulder to the clavicle, up the back of the neck and circles around the back of the ear. It then continues to the outer corner of the eyebrow.**

**Common Symptoms of Imbalance**

| PHYSICAL | EMOTIONAL |
|---|---|
| distended abdomen<br>colds and fevers<br>deafness<br>pain behind<br>elbow problems<br>swollen jaw<br>slow metabolism, overweight<br>fast metabolism, hyperactive | none |

*KEY NOTE* In Chinese medicine, the triple warmer, also known as the triple heater meridian, does not relate .to a specific organ, but is believed to control fluids within the body, specifically water and the endocrine system. The triple warmer receives its name from the three centres of activity within the body that, as they function, create heat:

- the upper warmer is associated with the heart and the lungs
- the middle warmer is associated with the liver, spleen and stomach
- the lower warmer with the kidneys, bladder, small and large intestines.

## The Conception Vessel Meridian

The conception vessel meridian starts in the pelvic cavity, drops down and emerges in the perineum, just between the anus and the genitals. It then crosses through the genital area to the top of the pubic bone, runs up the midline of the abdomen, chest and neck and ends just below the lower lip.

**Common Symptoms of Imbalance**

| PHYSICAL | EMOTIONAL |
|---|---|
| asthma<br>coughing<br>epilepsy<br>eczema<br>hay fever<br>head and neck pain<br>laryngitis<br>lung problems<br>mouth sores<br>pneumonia<br>genital disorders<br>itching<br>painful abdominal skin | none |

*KEY NOTE:* In Chinese medicine, the conception vessel is seen as the regulator of the peripheral nervous system and along with the governing vessel (see below), it controls the other 12 meridians. It creates balance by uniting the organ meridians, allowing energy flow to adjust when there is a blockage. In addition to providing energy to all of the peripheral nerves, the conception vessel also governs menstruation and the development of the foetus in women.

## The Governing Vessel Meridiam

The governing Vessel Meridiam begins in the pelvic cavity and then drops down and emerges below the genital area. It then passes to the tip of the coccyx. From here, it moves upward across the sacrum and along the spine, up over the head towards the upper lip. It then goes under the lip to the upper gum.

**Common Symptoms of Imbalance**

| PHYSICAL | EMOTIONAL |
|---|---|
| headaches and pain in the eyes<br>stiffness in the spine<br>back pain or tension<br>dizziness<br>eye problems<br>cold extremities<br>fevers | none |

| haemorrhoids<br>insomnia<br>neck pain<br>spinal problems<br>rounded shoulders, heavy head | |
|---|---|

***KEY NOTE:*** **In Chinese medicine, the governing vessel is the regulator of the nervous system and, along with the conception vessel, it controls the other 12 meridians. Like the conception vessel, it allows excess energy to pass through it to other meridians that may be deficient in energy. The Chinese think of this as an 'extra meridian'.**

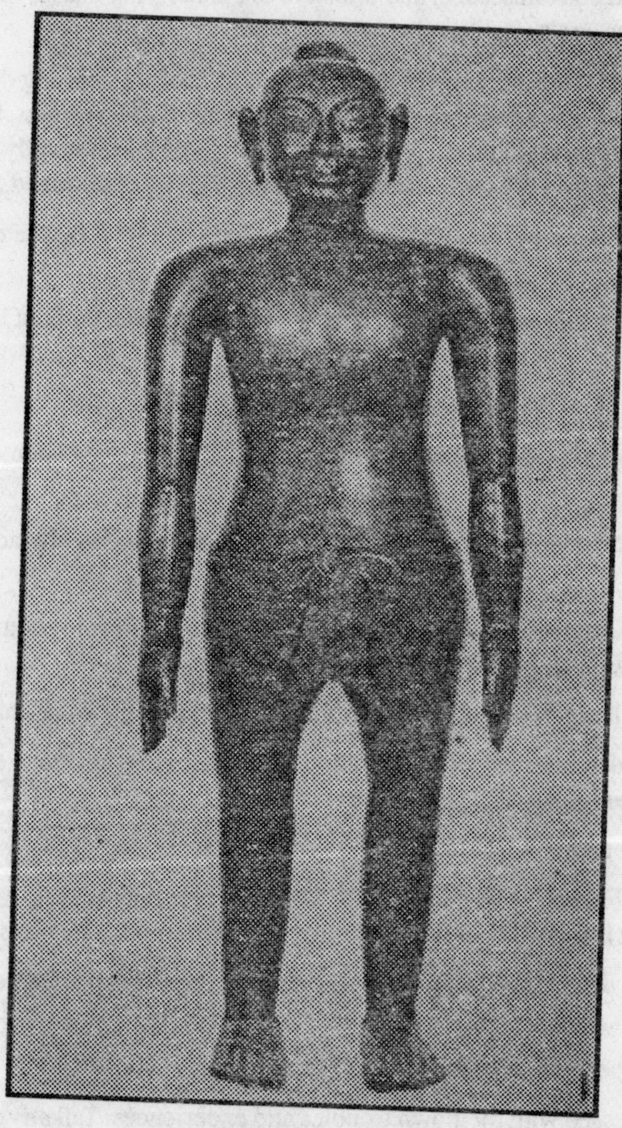

## BACH FLOWER REMEDIES

This unique healing system consists of essence made from thirty-eight different flowers, each having a specific action upon a certain mental attitude. Just as the body has its own self-healing properties regarding diseases and wounds, the mind and spirit have their own self- healing capacities, which the Bach Flower Remedies stimulate. The remedies used are all prepared from the flower of wild plants, bushes, and trees, and none of them is harmful or habit forming.

They are used for worry, apprehension, hopelessness, irritability, and so on, because these states of mind or moods hinder recovery of health, retard convalescence, and often are the underlying causes of sickness and disease. A long continued worry or fear depletes one's vitality.

It is important to identify the nature of the individual's unique "patterns" before selecting the appropriate remedy. Consider the persons' attitudes, feelings, worries, indecision, timidity, vexations, possessiveness, hopelessness, lethargy, hatred, overpowering or demanding nature, intolerance, tenseness, etc., and, most importantly, the reason behind the apprehension, worry, and fear. Only then can the correct remedy or remedies be determined.

**AGRIMONY**. Those who suffer inner torture, which they try to hide behind a façade of cheerfulness. Often used for no known reason.

**ASPEN.** Apprehension, the feeling that something dread ful is going to happen without knowing why. Anxiety for known reason.

**BEECH.** Critical and intolerant of others. Arrogant.

**CENTAURY**. Weakness of will, those who let themselves be exploited or imposed upon, they have difficulty in saying "no." A human doormat.

**CERATO**. Those who doubt their own judgment and intuition, always seeking the advice of others. Often influenced and misguided.

**CHERRY PLUM**. Uncontrolled, irrational thoughts, fear of losing control and doing something terrible, fear of "going crazy". Uncontrolled bursts of temper. Impulsively suicidal.

**CHESTNUT BUD**. Refused to learn by experience, continually repeating the same mistakes.

**CHICORY**. Overly possessive, demands respect or attention likes others to conform to their standards, makes martyr of oneself. Interference and manipulates.

**CLEMATIS.** Indifferent mental escapist from reality.

**CRAB APPLE**. "The Cleanser Flower." Feels unclean or ashamed of ailments. Self- disgust/ hatred. House proud ELM. Temporarily overcome by inadequacy or responsibility, though normally very capable.

**GENTIAN.** Despondent. Easily discouraged and rejected. Skeptical, pessimistic. Depression, when its cause is known.

**GORSE.** Desperate, without hope: "Oh, what's the use?" Defeatism.

**HEATHER** People who are obsessed with their own troubles and experiences. Talkative bores, poor listeners.

**HOLLY**. For those who are jealous, envious, revengeful, and suspicious.

**HONEYSUCKLE.** For those with nostalgia who constantly dwell in the past. Homesickness.

**HORNBEAM**. "Monday morning" feeling, but once started, task is usually fulfilled. Mentally tired. Procrastination.

**IMPATIENTS.** Impatience, irritability, Reacts in an exaggerated manner.

**LARCH**. Despondency due to lack of self- confidence; expectation of failure, so fails to make the attempt. Feels inferior, yet has the ability.

**MIMULUS.** Fear of known things, fear of the world. Shyness, timidity, bashfulness.

**MUSTARD**. Dark cloud of depression that descends for no known reason, which can lift just as suddenly, making one downcast, saddened, and low.

**OAK.** Brave determined type. Struggles on in illness and against adversity despite setbacks. Plodders, never resting.

**OLIVE**. Drained of energy, everything an effort. Physically fatigued.

**PINE.** Feelings of guilt. Blames oneself for the mistakes of others. Feels unworthy.

**RED CHESTNUT**. Excessive care of and concern for others, especially those held dear.

**ROCK ROSE.** Alarmed, panicky, full of trepidation.

**ROCK WATER**. For those who are hard on themselves and often overwork. Rigid, self-denying, ascetic.

**SCLERANTHUS.** Uncertainty, indecision, vacillation. Fluctuating moods.

**STAR OF BETHLEHEM**. For all the effects of upsetting news of fright following an accident. For release from trauma, no matter how old it is.

**SWEET CHESTNUT**. Absolute dejection. Feels as if one has reached the limits of what one can stand.

**VERVAIN**. Over enthusiasm, over effort, straining. Fanatical and highly strung. Incensed and frustrated by injustices.

**VINE**. Dominating/ inflexible/ambitious/tyrannical/autocratic. Arrogant pride. Considered to be good leaders.

**WALNUT**. Protection remedy against powerful influences; helps adjustment to any transition or change, e.g., puberty, menopause, divorce, new surroundings. Unlike Centaury, the person knows what he wants but is easily influenced by other people to do something else.

**WATER VIOLET.** Proud, reserved, sedate types, sometime feel "superior." Little emotional involvement but reliable, dependent.

**WHITE CHESTNUT.** Persistent unwanted thoughts. Preoccupation with some worry or episode. Mental arguments. Constant inner dialogue

**WILD OAT.** Helps determine one's intended path of life.

**WILD ROSE.** Resignation, apathy. Drifters who accepts their lot, making little or no effort for improvement; lacks ambition.

**WILLOW.** Resentment and bitterness with "no fair" and "poor me" attitude.

**RESCUE REMEDY**. Dr. Bach combined five specific remedies (cherry plum, clematis, impatiens, rock rose, star of Bethlehem) to formulate an emergency composite that he called Rescue Remedy. Its purpose is to comfort, reassure, and calm those who have received upsetting news or have experienced a trauma. Rescue remedy is unvaluable to keep on hand for immediate emergency use; however, it does not take the place of medical attention. It is taken orally (4 drops) in a glass of water but can also be applied externally either in liquid or cream form.

The Back Remedies are useful in their action without unpleasant side effects; thus, they can be taken by anyone. Stock concentrate remedies will keep indefinitely; a 10 ml concentrate bottle will make approximately sixth treatment bottles. More than one remedy can be taken at the same time. Place 2 drops of each chosen remedy in a glass of water and sip at intervals during the day or prepare a treatment bottle: fill a 1-fluid- ounce dropper bottle with spring water, add 2 drops of each chosen remedy, and place 4 drops of this mixture directly on the tongue at least four times a day.

## BIOFEEDBACK

The term biofeedback has come into popular usage in recent years in both scientific and popular circles. While still its infancy, a considerable body of scientific research is fast developing which serves to clarify the role of biofeedback in the treatment of chronic pain (including migraine and muscle – contraction headache.) First, biofeedback is not a product of our contemporary scientific age but is as old as mankind. Second, biofeedback is not a miracle cure, and it will not revolutionize health care. It will not cure cancer, leukemia, heart disease or the common cold! Biofeedback is simply a treatment technique – a proven, effective treatment technique in carefully selected patient suffering a limited number of medical disorders medical practices. It is not a "cure- all," but it is just technique in a practitioner's armamentarium.

To understand biofeedback, a careful distinction must first be made between the terms "biofeedback" and "biofeedback training". Biofeedback is a natural, usually unconscious learning process. For example, how did you learn the complex mind- body coordination required to pick up a pencil, to write your name, to walk, to read, to feed yourself without making a mess, to throw a baseball, to play golf or drive a car? The answer is biofeedback. Through trail – and – error effort we receive feedback from the environment and our body which we then use to modify and perfect future efforts. For instance, the proper swing of a golf club requires the complex coordination of our muscle, nervous system and sensory system of sight and touch. Through repeated trial- and error feedback we refine and improve our coordination and are eventually rewarded with a lower golf score. Slightly more sophisticated types of biofeedback include listening to your heart rate with a stethoscope, weighing yourself on a bathroom scale, taking your blood pressure and taking your temperature with thermometer. Biofeedback, then, is the measuring or recording of a biological process which is fed back (or made available) to the individual.

If an individual takes a biological process which is measured in some way and continuously "feed back" to him, and he attempts to use the information to guide his trial- and- error efforts to modify a targeted biological process, he is using biofeedback training. For instance, suppose you wanted to learn to decrees your heart rate. You might sit in a chair with a stethoscope to your chest and, through trail and error, attempt different mental strategies until you audibly detected a noticeable decrease. While this is a crude and simplistic example of biofeedback training, it does qualify under our definition. However, if your doctor refers you to a biofeedback specialist for training, don't expect your treatment to be this elementary.

Today biofeedback training for selected medical disorders refers to a variety of techniques utilizing sensitive and highly sophisticated biological recording instruments. To look at a fully equipped biofeedback facility is to be reminded of endless stereo components stacked one on the other with meters, dials and flashing lights. These instruments assist individuals in gaining control over biological processes generally thought not to be under voluntary control. Through electronic measurement, integration, amplification, and transformation into easily perceived visual and audio signals, one can sit passively and watch one's blood pressure vary from moment or observe the electrical activity of painful muscle in the neck and back. Combined with other proven effective treatment techniques, biofeedback training is a useful component in the treatment of chronic pain.

## HISTORICAL PERSPECTIVE

Scientist and laymen alike have long been fascinated with far east yogis who reportedly can walk on broken glass and survive extended periods of time submerged under water without oxygen. The ability to achieve such voluntary control of physiological mechanisms has reminded a mystery until about twenty years ago when science began its first serious look at medication and associated forms of mind- body interactions. Experimentation first began with laboratory animals, but as research and understanding grew, the use human subject became common place. Let's look at some of the historical highlights in the development of biofeedback from an early mystic phenomenon to an accepted and effective treatment techniques.

The roots of the scientific study of biofeedback training can be traced back to the 1960's when Dr. Neil Miller, a psychologist, and his colleagues reported they had successfully trained a number of laboratory rats to voluntarily control their heart rates, blood pressures and formation of urine. Dr. Miler, in fact, claimed that the rates could even be trained to increase the blood flow to one ear while maintaining the natural flow of blood to the other! Needless to say, this report sparked the interest of the scientific community, and the scientifically controlled experimentation of biofeedback began.

Early report of laboratory animals taught to raise and lower blood pressure, alter blood flow, and increase and decrease their heart rates also met with much skepticism. Biofeedback was in direct contradiction to what had long been accepted as scientific fact: that our bodily processes are controlled by either the voluntary nervous system (e.g., arm and leg movement) or the involuntary nervous system (e.g., heart rate, digestion, blood pressure, etc.), it is true that our hearts will beat without our conscious effort and that our blood pressure will vary from moment to moment "automatically". However, early biofeedback research demonstrated that we can learn to exert some conscious control over biological processes previously assumed to be totally beyond our control. This was considered a major scientific breakthrough, and the number of researchers investigating biofeedback grew rapidly.

Some twenty years after the beginning of serious scientific investigation of biofeedback, we find that the treatment modality is no longer only speculative laboratory research, but a proven clinical treatment technique. Once a counterculture fad with interest targeted toward achieving nirvana and inner pace through alpha wave feedback, biofeedback training is today performed by thousands of doctors and therapist in training a variety of chronic- pain, Raynaud's discase and temporomandibular joint pain. Biofeedback training has come of age and has gained wide acceptance…

## BIOFEEDBACK TRAINING: TECHNIQUE

The most effective use of biofeedback training in the treatment of chronic- pain conditions has focused on learning voluntary control of one of the following physiological processes: electromyography biofeedback and thermal biofeedback. Electromyography (more commonly referred to as EMG) biofeedback is most frequently employed in the treatment of musculoskeletal disorders. Electrical activity of targeted muscle groups is recorded and made continuously available to patients who use this information, along with instructions from the therapist to gradually learn better control of "tight" or "tense" muscles.

A second frequently employed type of biofeedback in the treatment of chronic pain is know as thermal or temperature biofeedback. Thermal biofeedback is most often the treatment of choice with vascular disorders involving impaired blood circulation in the body, usually the head, hands or feet. Blood flow from an affected body part is recorded and made continuously available to patients who combine the knowledge with instructions from the therapist to increase or decrease circulation to the (head).

Most patients who undergo biofeedback training are referred by their physician to a biofeedback therapist or doctor who use biofeedback as one of several techniques in the treatment is much different than other forms of health care to which you may be accustomed. In biofeedback training, the patients must assume responsibility for his health care and expend the effort required to learn and effectively utilize biofeedback skills. Of course, the doctor or therapist will assist you in your training, but the final responsibility falls on the patient. The doctor or therapist acts much like coach, teaching and directing you as you learn a new skill to combat chronic pain. This approach is in sharp contrast to traditional health care. Rather than handing your pills to take for your pain, the biofeedback therapist will help you learn ways to manage your pains.

Should you decide that biofeedback is worth a trial, you will learn that biofeedback training involves several phases. The order of the phases and the specifics of treatment will vary with the doctor or therapist and the type of (Headaches) you have. However, the following protocol should give you some idea of what to expect from biofeedback training.

The first phase of biofeedback training is termed the baseline phase. After you doctor or biofeedback therapist conducts a careful evaluation of your pain and before feedback training begins, you may be asked to keep a "pain diary" for a week or two. Careful daily charting of your intensity and the name and amount of any medication taken will give your doctor or therapist valuable information. For example, in addition to obtaining a baseline measure of your pain intensity and medication in take (which can be used comparison as you progress in biofeedback training), important pain patterns or trends can often be identified. Baseline measurement prior to beginning biofeedback training is an attempt to provide a degree of control and objectivity to your self- reported pain complaints. It is to the patient's benefit to cooperate and carefully complete the daily pain diary as requested.

Once a baseline has been established, your doctor or therapist will orient you to the biofeedback equipment. You will likely be requested to sit in comfortable chair, usually located in a dimly lit, sound- resistant room. Your doctor or therapist will explain the operation of the biofeedback equipment, which looks like a collection of stereo components complete with meters, lights and calibration gauges. Depending on where you are experiencing your pain, the skin around the affected body part will be cleaned with alcohol or acetone. This will cleanse the skin of oil and promote the best contact between you skin and the electrodes.

The electrodes (which measure muscle activity or blood flow, depending on the type of biofeedback employed) are next secured to the skin with an adhesive collar. The placement of the electrodes is often directly on the painful body part. Two or there electrodes may be used, with a electrodes surviving as a ground. You will then be asked to relax while the biofeedback equipment is calibrated and checked.

The next step involves measuring the normal or resting level of the biological process targeted for training. For instance, if you pain problem is chronic muscle- tension headaches, you would be asked to simply relax while the measurement taken of the muscle in the forehead. This measurement is the resting level is considered a starting point of training. You will gradually learn to control the forehead muscle so that the resting level after successful completion of eight to ten training session is greatly decreased when compared to initial pre-training resting levels.

Once a baseline has been established, it is time to began biofeedback training. The basis of biofeedback is a process known as shaping. Shaping is a basic learning technique where by progress towards and identified goal is accomplished through small, incremental step. Once step must be successfully mastered before proceeding to the next. Again using muscle tension headache as an example, reduce muscle activity or "tightness" is the ultimate goal of EMG biofeedback training. Therefore, your doctor or therapist sets a threshold for you so that a soft tone continuously sounds. Successful muscular relaxation will terminate the tone, thereby signaling that you have successfully decreased your muscle tension. A few threshold for you to work towards is set, and your job is to again terminate the tone by further relaxing your frontalis muscles. Step-by-step levels of muscles tension are decreased through shaping until the patient achieves a resting level muscle tension which does not result in head pain.

After you begin to demonstrate moderate control of the target biological process, your doctor or therapist may introduce a voluntary control phase to the training protocol. During the voluntary control phase, you will not be given feedback. Rather, your doctor or therapist monitors your progress while you exert passive voluntary control of the target physiological process. Voluntary control phase instituted in the overall training protocol prohibit excessive depending on continuously feedback to control biological process and help generalise the patients ability to control the targeted process out side of the doctor's office where cmntinious feedback is not available. When you are able to control successfully the targeted biological process during voluntary control phase, your doctor may ask you to begin practicing your control technique at home between training sessions.

After a number of biofeedback training sessions, which will very depending on what type of (headache) you have and how quickly you learn, you should find that your ability to control the targeted response has increased while the time effort required for voluntary control has decreased. The greater control you develop, the greater effect it should have on your (headaches). While voluntary control of muscle activity may be relatively easy to learn, control of blood flow may take longer to accomplish and is somewhat more difficult for most people.

Exactly how does one go about learning voluntary control of muscle or blood flow? If you asked most successfully biofeedback patients how they voluntarily exercise control over biological process long thought to be involuntary, they would respond with, "I'm not sure!" Some report relaxing deeply while thinking of their body being warmed by a penetrating heat. Other report conjuring up images of peaceful landscapes. They described it as a "Knack" or "Sense" that is most unconsciously produced. They describe as "will" that, during early training, requires deliberate and careful thought and effort but over time becomes a technique requiring very little consciousness.

## Biofeedback with Chronic (Headaches)

Biofeedback is currently most widely recognized as effective in the treatment of chronic-pain states. A review of the scientific literature evidences the use of biofeedback in the treatment of a variety of painful medical disorders with varying degrees of success. At this time, it appears that biofeedback training has proven most beneficial in the treatment of migraine and muscle-contraction headaches...... let's take a closer look at how biofeedback is effectively utilized in the treatment of these troublesome chronic-pain disorders.

## Migraine Headache

Simply defined, migraine or vascular headache is disorders characterized by excruciating pain usually located on one side of the head and often accompanied by nausea, vomiting cognitive impairment, depression, and, occasionally, even suicidal thoughts. Migraine attack are usually preceded by an aura of prodromal stage during which the victim experiences blurred or double vision, or even temporary blindness. At time there are vision of bright flashing lights, strange shapes or dazzling colours.

A migraine attack usually comes in three states: prodormal, the actual attack and the aftermath. An attack may last anywhere from a few hour to several days, and the pain is nothing less than horrible. Twice as many women suffer migraine headaches as men and, although rare, migraine can affect children as well as adults. Many victims of migraine find that the attack cease to occur when they reach middle age, although other victims endure migraines all their lives.

A fortunate discovery at the Menninger Foundation in Topeka, Kansas, in the last sixties led to the development of the thermal biofeedback technique of treating migraine. During test of the ability to lean control of blood flow to the extremities, a subject who happened to be experiencing a migraine at the time of the investigation reported an unexpected side effect. The subject claim the she experienced a sudden decrease in the intensity and severity of her headache, which the researchers noted coincided with a dramatic increase in the blood flow to the subject's hands. This discovery was the catalyst for an intensive five- year study of thermal biofeedback as a treatment technique for migraine headaches.

Thermal biofeedback involves attaching a small, sensitive thermometer to the tip of the index finger. Thermometer measures the warmth of the skin, the shin temperature being associated with blood flow. In either words, the greater the warmth of the hands, as measured by a special thermometer, the greater the blood flow to the extremities. The patient is instructed to watch a meter that gives continuously visual feedback of hand temperature. Through trial-and-error practice and with instructions from the doctor or therapist, the patient soon learn to increase the warmth of the hands, thereby increasing the blood flow to the hands. After several training Sessions, many patients learn to increase the warmth of their hands by as much as 80-10 °F (about 4 °C). Of course, voluntary control of extremity blood flow is associated with a decrease in frequency, intensity, and duration of migraine attack.

Research and clinical or thermal biofeedback effectiveness in the treatment of migraine headache have been mixed. While some studies report that as many as 60 to 80 percent to patients benefit for thermal biofeedback, perhaps a more accurate estimate may be closer 40 to 50 percent. However, when thermal biofeedback is combined with relaxation exercise and modifications in life- style, the technique offers hope to many migraine victims who otherwise continue to suffer despite the best effort of medical science.

## Muscle- Contraction Headaches

The advertising world does not hesitate to suggest possible reason and remedies for muscle –contraction (tension) headaches. We usually are shown a stress situation, such as a housewife reusing to prepare dinner while two or three children scream and cry, the telephone rings, the doorbell rings and the roast meat burns. The frantic housewife clutches her head in obvious distress as the television announcer recommends taking brand X pills "for last headache relief". In reality, this often does prove to be the case. Many of us are subject to occasional headaches when there is unusual pressure at home or work, when we are enduring a particularly frustrating period, or suffering from glare combined with heat. For this type of occasional head pain, "Brand X" analgesic pills probably work well. But what if the headaches occur more and more frequently, even daily, and the consumption of analgesics creep up steadily? Medical attention is then usually required.

Tension headaches affect both of the head symmetrically in approximately 90 percent of tension- headache patients, unlike migraine which is usually located only on one side of the head. The quality of the headache is remarkably consistent and characteristic. It is often described as a tightness, more of an uncomfortable feeling of pressure than pain. It is also described as a dull ache in the forehead, or the temples, or the back of the heads, or the neck, or even "all over the head". Approximately one in the muscle- contraction- headache suffers also plagued with vascular involvement. Known as "combined muscle contraction-migraine" headaches, the disorders appears to be a link between the two maladies and frequently complicates an accurate diagnosis.

The victim of a chronic tension headaches experiences pain not only during tense or stressful situations, but also may endure head pain in anticipation of any unpleasantness. The symptoms may later being in advance of a day's work, a routine shopping trip, a visits to friends or any of other aspects of daily life. In time, the patient's activity level and optimism decrease as the consumption of analgesic medication increases. The product is a distressing cycle of chronic pain and, as a result, further muscle tension and pain. Tense muscle cause pain because prolonged muscle constriction depletes the muscle of oxygen and decreases blood flow. As a result, toxins build up in muscle tissue, resulting in a pain.

Biofeedback treatment of muscle- contraction headaches is based on the following premises: if muscular tension in the shoulders, neck and head can be decreased or prevented before it begins, and maintained at reduced levels, headache frequently can be reduced or even eliminated. Muscles give up electrical discharges which can be measured and recorded with biofeedback instruments. Electrodes are attached to the frontalis muscles in the forehead or to the neck and shoulders. The patients then uses continuous audio or visual feedback of muscle to learn techniques to reduce muscular tension. Specific relaxation exercise are frequently included as part of the treatment regimen, and successful elimination of tension headaches can usually be accomplished within five to ten training sessions. Once treatment ends, the patients must continue home practice of the relaxation technique to guard against relapse.

## IRIDOLOGY

Iridology is the study of health and illness by diagnosing changes to the iris, or coloured part of the eye. The eyes have always been considered of some importance as indicators of internal health, or ill- health, but iridology as a distinct system dates back to the nineteenth century, to a Hungarian doctor called Igantaz von Peczely. He noticed that a thin blank line which he had observed in the bird's iris gradually faded to little marks around a small dot.

He published his finding in 1881, and they caused much interest through out European and later American medical circles. In the 1950's in the US, Dr. Bernard Jensen produced a detailed chart of iris, locating each organ in the body to a specific part of the iris. His mapping system is quite complex, with various rings or zones relating to different systems, such as digestive, circulatory, lymphatic, muscular, skeletal and so on. Overall the left eye the up problems on the left side of the body, and the right eye the right side, although many disturbances seem to produce changes in both irises.

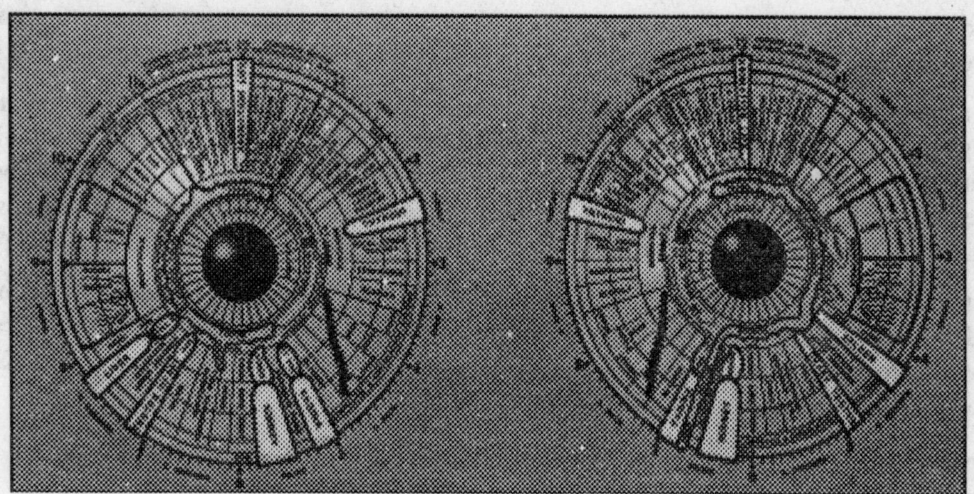

The map that Jensen and others developed divides the iris into various sections, rather like a wheel divide by spokes. In each segment any marking within the iris are thought to be linked to different parts of the body, or else varying functions. Overlapping these divisions are the concentric rings mentioned above, which radiate from the centre of the eye outwards and are believed to show disturbances in the stomach, the glands and inner organs. The muscles and skeleton and finally the skin and eliminative process.

In the last 30 years or so, the knowledge of what an iris is able to show has increased and some different schools of thought amongs iridologists and, in the eye-yellowing, dullness or unnatural brilliance, for example-an yellowing, unnatural brilliance, for example-an indication of ill health, conventional medicine dismissers completely the concept of specific, detailed linkers between parts of the body and making in parts of the irises. Nevertheless, iridology has steadily grown in popularity among a number of therapists, who will use the technique as on of their diagnostic methods and as a non-invasive way of checking out internal functioning. An iridologist will diagnose rather than treat, and if any signs of degeneration, malignancy or disease are detected, patients are advised to see their GP.

Although many naturally therapists are themselves skeptical of some of the claims of iridology, it is an area for fruitful research-our eyes are, after all, windows to the soul.

## CHIROPRACTIC

Chiropractic is a well- established system of treatment major forms of manipulative therapy. It is based upon the premise that structure affects functions, and in particular that displacement of the structure of the spin can cause pressure on nerves which in turn affect other parts of the body. In the US there are currently more osteopath than chiropractors, but both are accepted by the medical profession.

In 1895, in Iowa, a self- taught "magnetic healer" named Daniel David Palmer treated his office janitor, who had become deaf after bending over and feeling a click in his back. Palmer discovered a slight misalignment of the alignment; this led to the hearing being restored. Subsequently, Palmer went on to found a school of chiropractic – the word derives from two Greek words meaning practical use of the hand.

Chiropractors use a variety of manual adjustment techniques to help correct faulty alignment, and following a thorough physical examination, plus questioning about your general health, are likely to take X-rays to establish precisely what is happening to your skeleton. Manipulation is then carried out to give normal movement back to any affected joints, and you will probably be re-examined to make sure that the joints are now moving more freely. In chronic or series cases, a series of treatments may be necessary.

The vast majority of people seeking chiropractic treatment suffer from some kind of musculoskeletal pain, especially in the neck or lower back. A common injury caused by car accidents is whiplash, where the head and neck are abruptly jerked, and chiropractors can often correct the trauma caused to the structures. Frequent headaches may also be a reason for a visit to a chiropractor, and relief is often reported from the manipulative adjustments.

Although some chiropractors restrict themselves completely to spinal adjustments, many practitioners, especially in the US, may give advice on exercise and nutrition, and even prescribe dietary supplements. This is similar to some schools of training in osteopathy which combine advice with naturopathy for all- round health benefits. The manipulative treatments have been the subject of some research and in American, English and New Zealand studies, for instance, chiropractic has been shown to be one of the most effective forms of treatment for musculoskeletal problems.

The differences between chiropractic and osteopathy are largely historical and both systems accept modern physiological ideas, mainly differing in the specific techniques used to achieve similar aims. That chiropractic treatment is covered by Medicare, Medicaid and most health insurance schemes in the US, and some in the UK, is a sure sign that the manipulative therapies have established their credentials.

## OSTEOPATHY

Osteopathy is one of the two major systems of manipulative therapy, together with chiropractic. Its origins date back to the nineteenth century, but it has philosophical connections right back to the Hippocratic school of medical thought in the fourth century BC. It was founded by an American doctor, Andrew Taylor Still, in 1874, after several years of trying to find a better way of treating his patients than bleeding and purging. He based his ideas on the ancient notion that the body can cure itself, and on the concept of the need for the structure of the body to be correctly aligned in order to release our innate self- heading power.

Although we stand upright our anatomy is still basically that of a creature which moves on all fours, and there is a constant strain on the whole frame- work. Still recognized that the affect of gravity is particularly severe on the spine, the vertebrae and the cushioning discs between them. Still's earlier training as an engineer helped him in his assessment of the problems that could result from misalignment of the patient's skeletal structure and his philosophical outlook emphasized the interconnectedness of the body and its self- hearing potential.

Still therefore developed the use of manipulative techniques to treat not just the spine but the whole body. Structure and function were seen as interdependent and attention to the former would improve the latter. In 1892, he founded the first school of osteopathy, in Missouri. One of his students, John Littlejohn, subsequently founded the British School of Osteopathy in 1917. In the US, osteopaths are also medically trained and represent some five per cent of American doctors, in the UK they considerably outnumber chiropractors, and have recently been granted State Registration as a recognized and statutorily regulated profession.

Osteopathic treatments will involve a detailed case history of our general health, as well as particulars of any accidents/ injuries and the current problem and then a complete physical examination to asses the range and freedom of movement of the body. Manipulative techniques, perhaps accompanied by some deep neuromuscular massage, may be used to help to restore normal structure balance and functioning.

A number of specific techniques have been developed over the last hundred years or so, ranging from gentle, repeated movements of joints to increase their mobility, to quick thrust movements which rapidly guide the joint through its normal range. These latter manipulations can often cause the characteristic cliking noise that many people experience during a session. They may also temporarily irritate surrounding tissues and give some extra discomfort until the areas settles down again.

A fairly recent development within some schools of osteopathy has been the use of cranial- osteopathic treatment. This involves very gentle movements to help the flow of cerebra- spinal fluid, a lymph-like fluid which moves rhythmically around the brain and spinal cord, bathing and nourishing the nerve tissues. Any impediment in this rhythm is seen as creating imbalance within the body, with subsequent ill- health Cranial- osteopathic treatments are especially helpful for infants- say, after a difficult birth- and in London, for example, there is an osteopathic hospital centre for children that uses these gentle methods in such circumstances.

Since osteopaths in America may also be family doctors and in the UK they are not only State Registered but are starting to work in doctors' surgeries or even hospitals osteopathy has become well integrated into conventional medicine; however, not all doctors accept that it is anything more than just a "back treatment".

## ALEXANDER TECHNIQUE

The Alexander Technique is a method of training in posture, body movement and positioning. It was originally devised by Frederick Alexander, an Australian actor, around the turn of the twentieth century. He found that when he was giving an important Shakespearean speech on stage, his voice, continually faltered. The only advice given to him was to rest his voice, which only helped until the next large role. Eventually, he set about studying exactly how he was using his body by watching himself in a mirror and discovered that he tensed his body when performing. The effort of projecting his voice made him bring his head down, restricting his vocal cords and impairing deep breathing or voice control.

Over a period of time Alexander slowly adapted the way he held his body when acting on stage and overcome his "startle reflex pattern" as he called it. Gradually he developed the idea that body use – how we hold ourselves, move and so forth- can affect the functioning of our internal organs and overall health. He started to reach his methods of body realignment, moving to London in 1904 and subsequently going to the US gaining widespread recognition. The techniques he devised are based upon the principle of extending the spine, allowing it to reach its optimal length and generally to redeploy the body's entire muscular system. Exercises are thus geared to restoring natural posture and ease of movement, with minimal muscular effort. A common phrase used to describe the ideal movement is, "the head leads, the spine follows".

Animals and young children usually move naturally with a lengthened spine and a sense of poise. Unfortunately, we often acquire bad habits as we get older and additional stresses can lead to imbalance and excessive muscular effort in movement. If chronic tensions build up, the neck and back muscles contract, leading to rounded shoulders, a lowered head and an arched back, which causes further tension build up, the neck and back muscles contract, leading to rounded shoulders, a lowered head and an arched back, which causes further tension and so the problem gets worse and worse. Alexander teachers seek to help re-educate us to change these patterns and regain positive, easy body use.

Alexander schools have often been associated with drama or music establishments, echoing the man's back ground, but the techniques are suitable for all kinds of occupations. Improvements in posture can be accompanied by health benefits such as greater mental alertness, better sleep, increased resistance to stress and enhanced performance of physical tasks. The techniques are learned from a teacher, in the form of lessons rather than treatment sessions and may initially involve sample actions such as sitting down and getting up from a chair or waling to and fro, with corrective advice on how to use the body more efficiently.

Self-help measures may be of benefit in the first instance; copying Alexander's example and looking closely at your posture in the mirror might be valuable in identifying obvious imbalances. However, since bad habits can be difficult to change, or even spot sometimes, a series of lessons from a teacher is likely to be the most helpful way to correct these.

The Alexander technique is not a cure-all, but improvements in the way we hold and use our bodies can improve many people's overall health and movement.

## AN ENERGETIC SYSTEM

Ayurveda is an energetic system and that such systems utilise the qualities of things to categorise them. Also, bringing to mind the 'as above, so below' principle, we must look at how the qualities of Air, Fire and Water as they exist' out there relate to 'in here', that is in our body, mind and spirit.

If it seems that I have made a subtle but profound leap from talking about elemental Air/Ether, Fire/Water and Water/ Earth to air, fire and water 'out there', it is because all of these things are related (as you will, of course, have grasped). Now that we are talking about the gross physical plane it helps to relate the Doshas somewhat to this level of creation, though they are not themselves air, fire or water any more than they are Air, Fire or Water. They are functional energies with certain properties.

If I am belabouring this point it is because understanding the quality of Vata, Pitta and Kapha will assuredly enhance your understanding of yourself, others and the whole of life. The ability to apply this understanding gives you the choice of creating balance in yourself.

**The Qualities of Tridoshas**

| Vata | Pitta | Kapha |
|---|---|---|
| Air/Ether<br>Erratic, for example wind that is changeable. The digestion may be erratic | Fire/Water<br>Intense, as in the heat of a flame. Anger | Water/Earth<br>Stable/Static, that is not easily changed. Not easily perturbed. |
| Light (opposite of heavy), for example a birch tree or a small-boned person | Light (not dark), for example sunlight. Blonde to red hair | Heavy, as in the mass of mountains or big-boned or heavy-headed/ sluggish |
| Cold, as in chilly weather and poor circulation | Hot, as in summer and body temperature | Cool, as in weather and skin temperature |
| Mobile, as in always in motion, activity-oriented | Spreading as in fire or a rash | Smooth, as in the texture of fats/ oils Complexion |
| Rough(ening), as in the effect of wind erosion Hair or Skin | Oily, as oil feeds fire and skin type | Soft as in the sponginess of a peat bog or a mellifluous voice |

| | | |
|---|---|---|
| Dry, as in climate, hair, mouth<br>Clear as in unclouded or clairvoyant | Liquid as in acids, melted solids<br>Sharp as in memory, a pointed nose or a spear-shaped tree | Moist as in marsh lands, saliva<br>Cloudy as in skies, urine, thinking |
| Subtle, that is non-material, a thinker/ ponderer | Sour taste and fleshy smell | Dense as in concentrated substance or physical build |
| Astringent taste | | Sweet and salty tastes |

## HOW THE BODY WORKS: THE TRIDOSHAS AS PHYSIOLOGY

We have seen earlier how the elements relate to the structure of the body. We can now go on to how the biological energies that they combine to create relate to the body's functioning. There are three types of activity going on in the body continuously:

1. Natural functioning is maintained in cells and entire organ systems.
2. Growth, maintenance and repair of tissues (*Dhatus*, of which there are seven).
3. Excretion of wastes (*Malas*) from cells and organs.

The functioning of the body is maintained by the interaction of the three Doshas. The word 'Dosha' in Sanskrit means a fault, not as in blame but as in some flawed thing liable to malfunction at any moment.

The Doshas are (paradoxically) both essential to the body's functioning and liable to throw it out of the kilter. When performing their ascribed tasks and moving on and out of the body and staying in relative balance one with the other, they are the foundation of health. If any one of them accumulates it will eventually and inevitably give rise to problems of a physical and/or mental-emotional nature. How they do this and what problems they can cause will be considered later on.

The Doshas respond to external causes such as beans in your diet or a rushed lifestyle. What our minds and bodies experience as a result is the increase of a Dosha (Vata in the examples give above), not the direct effect of an outside force. If the functional integrity of the body is good it will cope well with this temporary increase and eliminate it.

*Vata* in the body is responsible for all movement. Indeed, Vata embodies the principle of movement. Th , sensory and motor nerve conduction is due to the presence of Vata.

Pitta in the body is responsible for metabolism, being as it is the principle of transformation from one state to another. This includes the transformation of food, air, water, from external substances to the biological substances our bodies can utilise. Thought is also metabolised (if Pitta is in a good balanced state) and integrated.

Kapha builds substance, being the principle of stability, solidity and cohesion.

**Psycho-physiological Functions of Tridoshas**

| Vata | Pitta | Kapha |
|---|---|---|
| Respiration | Digestion (the action of enzymes, acid, etc. on food) | Creation, repair and maintenance of body tissues |
| Swallowing(liquids and food) | Absorption (the biochemical aspects of the process) | Nutrition of the tissues |
| Elimination (urine, faeces, flatus and foetus) | Assimilation (the act of making what you have taken in – food or information – part of yourself) | Strength |

| | | |
|---|---|---|
| Movement (all voluntary and involuntary movement) | Vision | Stamina<br>CalmnessImmunity |
| Absorption (the movement of food in the digestive tract and of molecules from it into the bloodstream) | Comprehension, Appreciation, Recognition, Evaluation, Discrimination and Discernment | |

We can see from the lists relating the Doshas to qualities and functions that these energies have attributes that can be both the things they *are* and the things they *do*. So, Vata is light and makes things lighter, it is cold and chills things down, it may not be rough, per se, but as wind it roughens as it erodes.

The Psycho-physiological functions of the Doshas seem to separate them into activity-oriented Vata, transformational Pitta, and substance-building Kapha. But this is over-simplistic. Yes, Vata has movement, but it also intitiates transformation including metabolism, which is governed by Pitta. It is so easy to see Kapha as only structure and matter because of its relative density, but it is also the energy that maintains the body. It creates the physiological energy to kep the organism going, maintain it and repair it. The three Doshas are inextricably linked and must maintain a balance for health to prevail.

## WHERE ARE VATA, PITTA AND KAPHA?

As biological energies that can be balanced or imbalanced, the Doshas have homes in the body parts where they will first start to increase if they are going to go out of kilter, and to where they must be brought back before excess can be eliminated. They can only be directly eliminated from their main sites, their true homes, and not from parts of the body to which they may go walk-about when they overrun.

**Sites of the Doshas in the Body**

| Vata | Pitta | Kapha |
|---|---|---|
| Colon (main site) | Small intestines(main site) | Stomach(main site) |
| Pelvic cavity | Stomach | White mater of brain |
| Thighs | Sweat glands | Meninges |
| Ears | Blood (red blood cells) | Cerebro-spinal fluid |
| Bones | Fascia | Saliva |
| Skin (organ of touch) | Eyes (organ of sight)Subcutaneous fat | Sinus secretionsPeri-pleural, cardial fluid |
| | Skin | Gastric mucous membrance |
| | Liver (main organ of metabolism) | Synovial fluid Serum |

### Vata, Pitta, Kapha

If Vata, Pitta and Kapha are biological energies within the body and mind which are responsible for their structure and function, then similar forces must exist 'out there' in places, foods, plant medicines, etc. So, at this level of creation, Vata, Pitta and Kapha are organising principles in external world of matter and in the psychic world of spirit and mind as well as in the body.

Time is movement. Choronological time is based on the movement of the earth round the sun, the diurnal rhythm of day and night. Biological time is related to the biological Doshas, when the various organs are most active – activity is movement. The various stages of human life are also related to the Doshas. They are the seasons of our lives and are often referred to as such. The Tridoshas relate to all these different sort of time.

Likewise, psychological time is the movement of emotions and feelings and, of course, these too are governed by the functional energies of Vata, Pitta and Kapha.

The following diagram links the times of day presided over by each of the Doshas with the organs they are sited in and therefore when the said organs are most active. This is because *prana* (the life-force) is highest in the various organs at the times of the day indicated.

Looking at the diagram, we can relate health problems involving certain organs to the time of day or night. For example, gastric ulcers are more likely to perforate in the early hours, because that is when prana is most active in the stomach. Early morning and evening are when mucus collects in the bronchial system under the influence of Kapha and certain types of asthma are likely to be worse. During Pitta times hepatitis sufferers will suffer itching, while gastritis and colitis will be provoked. Similarly, degenerative arthritis and irritable bowel may make their presence felt most during Vata times.

## Doshas and Manas (THE MIND)

When well-balanced, the Doshas exert positive mental-emotional effects, otherwise they manifest as negative qualities, traits or attitudes.

**The Doshas and Positive and Negative Mental States**

| Vata | | Pitta | | Kapha | |
|---|---|---|---|---|---|
| ***Positive*** | ***Negative*** | ***Positive*** | ***Negative*** | ***Positive*** | ***Negative*** |
| Active<br>Creative<br>Friendly<br>Clear<br>Inspired<br>flexible | Anxious<br>Depressed<br>Insecure<br>Ungrounded<br>Restless<br>Unstable<br>fearful | Knowledgeable<br>Decisive<br>Ambitious<br>Discriminating<br>logical | Critical<br>Angry<br>Envious<br>Jealous<br>Irritable<br>Judgemental | Peaceable<br>Loving<br>Compass-<br>ionate<br>Caring<br>Inclusive | Possessive<br>Greedy<br>Acquisitive<br>Overly<br>attached |

As the diagram indicates, the various times of the day relate to how the Doshas affect the mind as well as the body. So if we are unbalanced in the direction of Vata, for example, then the negative emotions that relate to Vata will manifest more determinedly at Vata times – dawn and dusk. Likewsie, Pitta and Kapha negative emotions will be most likely felt at midday/midnight and early morning/evening respectively. Between 4 and 8 both morning and evening are times governed by both Vata and Kapha as far as bodily functions are concerned, and also when *Sattva*, the principle of clarity and balance, is predominant in the mind. This is obviously a good time to meditate and do yoga, since these qualities enhance our inner awareness. For the remainder of daylight hours (from 8 a.m. till 4 p.m.) our minds are too rajastic (*Rajas* is the principle of dynamic energy and movement) for them to be conducive to meditation. Night hours from 8 p.m. to 4 a.m. are tamasic (*Tamas* is the principle of darkness, inertia and dullness) and again meditation will not come easily and we would be inclined to 'drop off'. Winding down after the day's activities and sleep are what those hours are for.

Stages of life have already been mentioned as a form of time governed by each of the three Doshas. Kapha governs the early years up to adolescence, gradually easing into Pitta time from early adulthood to the onset of old age, when Vata governs. It is quite easy to see the qualities of the Doshas in these life stages. The early years are years of growth (anabolism), plumpness (known as 'puppy fat'), moistness as in the dewy complexion of children and the predisposition to snuffly noses. Gradually, Pitta takes over and striving ambition, drive, activity, energy and achievement are characteristic of our adult years. This is the time of 'doing'. As we move towards retirement or at least the change of pace in life that most people desire (circumstances permitting), Vata takes over as the force governing our body/mind and experience. Vata time is characterised by breakdown (catabolism) as the ageing body replaces cells less rapidly and less efficiently, dryness as the tissues dehydrates, and lightness as body mass and bone density decrease.

Seasons too have their Dosha. The relative heat of the summer sun, the bright light of sunlit days, the intense colours of summer flowers all reflect the qualities of Pitta. Pitta time includes the late spring. Winter and early spring reflect the qualities of Kapha, the time of wet and cold, of dull, heavy skies. It is a time when we find it more difficult to rise and hibernation beckons – Kapha-related qualities. Autumn is the Vata season when the temperature and climate are erratic; leaves are turning and drying out and are on the move – off the trees.

These Doshas expressed in Nature have an effect on the creatures living through the seasons. During each season the qualities it possesses build up within us and often result in imbalances that manifest at the end of the season. One good example is spring colds. Just as the weather seems to herald the arrival of spring many people succumb to colds. These are the result of the build-up of Kapha during the winter months. To get rid of such accumulated Doshas, seasonal purification is advised.

## SUB-DIVISIONS OF THE TRIDOSHAS

The three Doshas are subdivided according to function, area of action and (in the case of Vata, as principle of movement) direction of movement. Each dosha has five subdivisions.

### The Five Subdivisions of Vata

1. Prana
2. Udana
3. Vyana
4. Samana
5. Apana

The term Vayu is often used to denote Vata in combination with the names of its subdivisions.

### Prana Vayu

Prana Vayu moves in and down and is responsible for all higher sensory functions of the body including recent memory, breathing in, swallowing, central and peripheral nerve conduction, the movement of ideas and thoughts. Its area of functioning is mostly above the diaphragm, though the ascending and descending nerve tracts of the spinal cord are governed by Prana. The name 'Prana', the breath of life, is also given to the life energy, life-force or vital force known in Chinese medical philosophy as 'Chi', and is different from Prana Vayu.

### Udana Vayu

Udana Vayu functions in the same area of the body as Prana Vayu, but up and out. So, exhalation, spitting, crying, sweating, vomiting and remote memory are functions of udana. And, as it rules the throat area, modes of self-expression like speaking out, communicating, singing, whistling, sobbing and laughing are similarly in its domain. Expression of will is also the province of Udana, as exemplified by the ability to express one's belief, needs and desires. The balance necessary between Prana and Udana is clear. For example, breathing must be co-ordinated.

### Vyana Vayu

Vyana Vayu is centered in the heart and is responsible for the movement of all circulation (blood and lymph) round the entire body and the maintenance of blood pressure. It also governs the actions of the joints. Altered forms of it circulate in the body. These toxins seek homes in weakened body parts to create disease.

The traditional view of Pitta as the container of Agni reflects their intimate connection. Agni is the heat energy within Pitta which performs the digestive function; they therefore share some characteristics. They are both hot and sharp and light, but whereas Pitta is oily and liquid, Agni is dry and subtle. It is responsible for changing the state of ingested substances into what our body/mind can use.

There are 13 Agnis that transform raw substances (food or thoughts) that are presented to them. They are:

1. Jathar Agni, the gastric fire.

2-6 Bhutagni – one to convert each of the elements (Ether, Air, Fire, Water and Earth) existing in material substances into their biologically-acceptable counterparts.

7-13 Dhatu Agnis – each associated with one of the body tissues and partly responsible for its proper formation

It is also necessary to mention that some authorities add to this list:

- The five Pitta Agnis (one for each of the subdoshas).
- Two Pilu and Pithar cellular Agnis, which work at the atomic and chromosomal level and beyond, converting the subtlest forms of nutritive substances into consciousness. That is why what we eat determines who we are.
- One Brahmagni, the fire of awareness which transforms.

The subtler forms of Agni are more easily understood if you keep in mind the transforming power of fire. It also pays to remember to give total attention to the food you are eating, because it affects your consciousness. Do not eat when you are upset or angry, do not eat while watching television or reading a newspaper; these things are absorbed and digested along with the food and affect the functioning of Agni.

As you will see in later sections, the strength of Agni is a major factor in disease-formation. To maintain health requires well functioning. Agni which affects life span, immunity, strength and energy level, colour and lustre of skin, correct condition in the gut for friendly flora to thrive and therefore, optimum digestion, absorption and assimilation.

## Subtle digestion and taste

There are six tastes in Ayurveda, sweet, sour, salty, pungent, bitter and astringent. Each one is associated with a pair of the great elements and its effects therefore are due to the qualities of its constituents elements.

1. The Sweet taste gives energy and increases body bulk. It increases blood sugar levels, slows metabolism and makes one heavy and sleepy after meals. It is associated with Kapha Dosha and the elements of Water and Earth is easily recognised.

2. **Sour** has the elements of Earth and Fire. It increases digestive enzymes, which , of course, are Pitta substances. It increases salivation (think of biting into a lemon and see what happens). The Earth increases the thickness of mucus secretions in the respiratory tract.

3. The **Slaty** taste consists of the elements Fire and Water. The salty taste increases salivation and the flow of gastric juices, thereby, improving digestion, absorption and assimilation. It eases gases and spasm in the colon.

4. **Pungent** holds the elements of Air and Fire; Air feeds Fire and produces the heat that is characteristic of this taste. There is no problem understanding that it improves circulation. Agni is stimulated in the digestive tract, and there digestion is assisted.

5. **Bitter** contains the Earth and Air elements and is therefore cooling in its action. Its reduces sugar level in the blood and lowers fever. It enhances all the other tastes.

6. The last taste, **astringent**, comprises Earth and Air. It reduces bleeding time, tones tissues and dries out the food mass to be eliminated as faeces.

You will encounter the word *Rosa* in subsequent sections. It has numerous meanings, many of which are linked at deeper levels of understanding. Many 'Eureka!' – type experiences are likely to be part of your travels with Ayurveda as you integrate it into your life as lifestyle, diet, meditative practices or self-healing techniques.

Rasa is used here to refer to the initial taste something has when your taste buds relay information to the brain via sensory nerves and you perceive the flavour of something, which is a combination of all the tastes it stimulates. This taste correlates with the effect given above.

The delay effect of taste is called *Virya* and means strength or potency (as in virility). At this stage in our exploration of Ayurveda it is sufficient to restrict the potencies looked at to 'hot', which increases digestive capacity, and 'cold', which reduces it. The other qualities of substances will be subsumed under these two. Three of the initial taste have hot Viryas and three have cold ones. Can you work out which has which?

The long-term effects of substances on the body are Vipaka, or post-digestive taste. There are three : sweet, sour and pungent.

**Rasa, Virya and Vipaka**

| *Initial taste (Rasa)* | *Elements* | *Delayed effect (Virya)* | *Long-term effect (Vipaka)* | *Increase/Decrease in Dosha* |
|---|---|---|---|---|
| Sweet | Earth + Water | Cold | Sweet | Decrease in Vata and Pita, Increase in Kapha |
| Sour | Fire + Earth | Hot | Sour | Decrease in Vata, increase in Pitta and Kapha |
| Salty | Fire + Earth | Hot | Sweet | Decrease in Vata, Increase in Pitta and Kapha |
| Pungent | Air + Fire | Hot | Pungent | Increase in Vata and Pitta, Decrease in Kapha |
| Bitter | Air + Ether | Cold | Pungent | Increase in Vata Decrease in Pitta and Kapha |
| Astringent | Air + Earth | Cold | pungent | Increase in Vata Decrease in Pitta and Kapha |

Finally, with regard to 'taste' there is the Ayurvedic concept of *prabhava*, which is idiosyncratic effect of some substances. Some things just don't follow the rules indicated by the initial taste, delayed effect and the post-digestive (long-term) taste or effect. their ultimate effect on the mind/body is varied depending on the person's constitution and imbalance, and can only be learned by experience.

## STAGES OF SUBTLE DIGESTION

In Ayurveda, the movement of food through the digestive system is described as the phase governed by each of the six tastes. So, the sweet taste is stage one of digestion., starting in the mouth and stomach (first hour and a half). It is governed by Kapha and it releases sweetness (Earth and Water) into the bloodstream.

Stage two is sour and lasts through the remaining 90 minutes or so in the stomach. Acidity is released into the bloodstream. This and stages three and four (salty and pungent) are governed by Pitta.

The final two stages (five and six) of the subtle digestion, bitter and astringent, are governed by Vata. Bitter enzymes characterise the fifty stage; in the colon the astringent taste binds the content to form stools (Air, being drying, enables the reabsorption of much water and the Earth brings solidity to the content).

### The Tissues

Unlike the Doshas and subdoshas, the tissues (Dhatus) have a specific and sequential order of appearance. Each of the seven Dhatus received sustenance from and is stimulated to grow by the Dhatu prior to it in this chain. that is, each is a prerequisite of the subsequent tissues.

Also produced at each stage are secondary tisse (*Upadhatus*), which differ from the primary tisse in that they are physiology a dead end. They do not contribute to the formation of the next tissue in line, though they are useful to the organism while they are around.

The third category of substances produced in tissue manufacture is waste (*Malas*). No manufacturing plants produces only high-quality finished end-products. All have by-products, including wastes. However, the more efficient the plant, the less waste and the more top quality products are produced. Likewise here in the Dhatu factory : when each of the seven Dhatu, Agnis is working efficiently, healthy tissue and secondary tissue production is optimal and waste is minimal. There is a relationship between Doshas and Dhatus.

The Doshas are responsible for the formation of the Dhatus. Kapha Dosha is responsible for all but two of the seven Dhatus. As Kapha is physiologically the one associated with growth, maintenance and repair. However, Pitta is responsible for blood (*Rakta*), and Vata for bone (*Asthis*). The seven Dhatus and associated by-products are listed below.

**The Dhatus System**

| *DHATU* | *SITE* | *FUNCTION* | *UPADHATU* | *MALA* |
|---|---|---|---|---|
| Rasa Lymph/ Plasma | Entire body | Nourishment body and mind; life's juice | Breast milk and menstrual flow | Physical Kapha – phlegm, mucus |
| Rakta Red blood cell | Blood | Invigoration, body and mind | Blood vessels, tendons | Physical Pitta – bile |
| Mamsa Muscle | Skeletal and visceral muscle | Plastering skeleton, protect, contains | Ligament and skin snot and smegma | Ear wax, navel line, |
| Meḍa Fat | Adipose tissue in limbs and torso | Lubrication body, voice Feeling loved | Omentum | Sweet (the greasy part of it) |
| Asthi Bone | Bones, especially growing ends | Support, strong foundations to body, and security | Teeth | Nails, body and head hair |
| Maja Marrow and nerve tissue | Marrow, nerve tissue including brain and spinal cord | Filling, of bond and nerve channels. Also sense of fullness | Sclerotic fluid in eyes (some say head hair) | Tears and secretions form ducts |
| Shukra Reproductive fluids | Reproductive tissues | Procreation and creativity | None | None |

The Dhatus are formed sequentially over a period of approximately 35 days. The first, Rasa, is formed within five days;' each subsequent tissue takes a further five days. this must be taken into consideration in the treatment of health imbalances as medicines such as herbs or dietary charges will inevitably take time to have an effect on the various tissues.

The process of tissue formation is as follows. Until the food you eat is absorbed from the stomach or duodenum into the blood and lymph, it is not part of you. Think of a child swallowing a bead. Assuming it does not lodge anywhere, it passes through and out.

What is absorbed is called nutrient cycle or *Ahara Rasa*. This is the raw materials, which is 'cooked' by *Rasa Dhatu Agni* and turned into mature Rasa tissue, the secondary tissue (breast milk and menstrual fluid is female), and waste. It also produces a refined form of the war material which goes on to be the stuff that is transformed into red blood cell (Rakta), secondary tissues ( blood vessels and tendons), and waste. This goes on down the line.

If a prior tissue is substandard or if a tissue's Agni is deranged, then obviously that tissue will not be well formed. There are several ways that Dahtu formation can be negatively affected. Inherited tissue weakness as well as that incurred by faulty living (including a poor diet) are among them.

The translations of the Sanskrit names of the Dhatus incline us to think of them as less than they are. Rasa is more than just the substance of lymph, and Rakta is more than red blood cell. These Sanskrit terms are meant to include all the enzymes, hormones and metabolic pathways in the formation of particular tissues.

Traditionally, the Vedic texts talks about three ways a tissue may be involved in the creation of the next in line. These are:

1. 'Seeding', when one tissue sows the seeds for the next (used to describe the less apparent links between muscle and fat, for example).
2. 'Irrigation', which is a connection like water feeding a field of crops through channels. Rakta demonstrates this as it flows through the blood vessels and carries the required nutrients for formation of Mamsa (muscle).
3. 'Direct conversion' covers such obvious examples as the nutrients plasma containing all the necessary substances for the formation of red blood cells.

The emotions that most typify Pitta are the hot fiery one like anger, jealousy and (at an extreme of imbalances) hatred. I had a client who decided to become vegetarian and from that day on continously told me that he hated meat eaters. He would laugh and say that he knew it sounded odd, but is did ! This response reflects the emotional intensity of the Pitta nature.

## The Kapha Person

The stereotypical Kapha person is large, bulky, slow moving and easy going. She is slow to anger but once aroused to it is an implacable enemy. Kapha holds on to things like this because it is created from the elements Earth and Water, the most stable and solid of the elements, and is thus not going to move location or change opiñion easily.

Kapha loves to sit and, preferably, eat. She has soft, pale, cool skin, large, dewy eyes and a good head of thick hair. Generally, Kapha is colour than Pitta but no so cold as Vata, and her sitivity is less related to her nervous and digestive system and more to her emotional nature. The emotions that predominate when Kalpa is out of Kilter are holding-on and gathering-to-us kind, like possessiveness, greed and acquisitiveness. However on the positive side she calm, compassionate and loving. Kapha is good at calming down heated situations and makes for an office manger who 'oil the wheels'.

As stated earlier, someone whose constitution is of the duo-Doshic variety (whichever two are involved) will have some of the attributes of each of their constituent elements (two for each Dosha). Considering how many ways each attribute can be expressed, the possible permutation of physical, mental and emotional characteristic are legion. Nature has no difficulty producing unique individuals.

There are various methods of assessing Prakruti. A highly skilled Ayurvedic physician can read it in the pulses (we will take a brief look at pulse diagnosis. At this stage, by far the most reliable method of self-assessment is to look at your fixed physical attributes like your skeletal frame, your weight, the colour of your hair and eyes and so on. These, together with longstanding emotional and behavioural patterns and disease tendencies, will produce a reliable measure of your constitution.

At the end of this chapter there is a questionnaires to use in making your self-assessment. Many of us are prone to self-deception and you may be tempted to answer according to how your would like to be or feel. Knowing how you are, fundamentally, will enable you to implement changes that can have a profound effect on your physical and emotional health and on your relationships.

## On Using The Questionaire

The best way to do the following questionnaire is to enlist the help of someone who has known you of a long time. Someone like a family member who has watched your physical transformation as you grew up and has known you though the various stages of development as your mind and emotions took shape. Someone who can help you distinguish 'you' from your imbalances.

For this reason it is very important that your' score these items according to how you have been for most of your life and/or when more balanced, more 'yourself'. It is a work picture of your 'self' we are aiming to elicit, not a picture of your imbalances or disease. Not all of us have recourse to old friends and family, we must do what we can, this is a counsel of perfection.

## Ayurvedic Body/Mind Constitution (Prakruit) Questionnaire

When filling in this questionnaire:

- If possible, enlist a helper who has known you for some time (like a family member).
- For each characteristic listed in the left-hand column, mark with an 'A' the Vata, Pitta or Kapha description that best matches you (not all the words in any one description will apply), as you have been for most your life.
- If you and your helper do not agree on which applies most to you, leave that whole constitutional characteristic out (do not score that one at all) and go on to the next.
- If more than one description of a specific characteristic seems equally applicable to you, put an 'A' at each.
- Mark with a 'B' any description that seems to apply only slightly less than your 'A' choice.

| | *VATA* | *PITTA* | *KAPHA* |
|---|---|---|---|
| ***PHYSICAL CHARACTERISTICS*** | | | |
| Skeletal Structure | Light frame | Medium frame and bones | Large frame and bones |
| Musculature | Underdeveloped tendons quite visible | Rather athletic well develop | Bulk, fleshy |
| Weight | Light-weight | Medium for height | Tends to overweight |
| Height | Extremely tall and lanky or short and petite | Medium, average | Tall or short but proporotionately sturdy |
| Colouring/Complexion | Darkish skin or tans easily | Fair skin tones, freckles, burns easily | Pale, like alabaster, tans slowly |
| Skin Texture | Dry and rough, crackles in cold/dry conditions | Soft, fine and moist, may be oily | Thick, soft and smooth, moist or oily |
| Iris Colour | Grey, violet, dark brown | Light, blue, green, hazel, electric blue | Milk chocolate brown or dark blue |
| Eyes | Small, dull, eye whites – darkish | Medium, bright, prone to redness | Large, lustrous, clear whites |
| Teeth | Uneven or gap between front teeth, receding gums | Medium-sized, soft teeth prone to decay, gums bleed easily | strong white, even - sized, large teeth good gums |
| Hair | Coarse, dark brown to black, dry, curly/wavy | Fine, thin, fair to red, can go grey early | Thick, heavy, wavy, oily, shiny mid to dark brown |
| Speaking Voice | Rather weak or hoarse | Penetrating can't whisper | Low-pitched, pleasant tone |

## Body Functions

| | | | |
|---|---|---|---|
| Appetite | Variable | Keen, can't miss a meal without feeling irritable or dizzy | Consistently good |
| Digestion | Erratic, no discernible pattern | Very good balances desires to eat and ability to digest | Can feel that it moves though very slowly |
| Elimination | Erratic, but more often constipated than loose, dark, gassy | Regular, loose, yellowish, at times gives a burning feeling on passing | Regular, slow, solid bulky mucus in faecas at times |
| Sex Drive | 'If the head' variable, has desire but low in energy | Strong appetite, passionate, sufficient energy | Moderate to low desire, steady and strong energy |
| Stamina | Poor, yet dissipates energy | Medium over-experts competitively | Good, conserves energy unnecessarlity |

| Pace | Everything done at high speed | Everything done at a controlled rate | Everything done slowly and deliberately |
|---|---|---|---|
| Temperature | Likes hot weather and rooms | Likes cool weather and rooms | Likes warmth but not humidity |
| Sleep | Difficulty getting to sleep, sporadic wakes tired | Light but sufficient wakens alert | Heavy, difficulty waking |
| Exercise | Aerobic, frequent and high energy expenditure | Completive balances amount with energy available | Gentle walking in countryside infrequently |

## Mind and Emotions

| Learning | Fast learner even if only superficial interest | Has to be really interested, then can learn easily | Slow to learn but at a steady pace |
|---|---|---|---|
| Memory | Short-term recall good, long-term variable, tends to forget quickly | If interested integrates materials and retains what is learned, sharp recall | Excellent long-term memory, tends to hold on to thoughts and emotions |

## Principles of Ayurveda

| Beliefs | Changeable | Strongly held, acts accordingly to belief | Consistent, unweaving, difficult to change |
|---|---|---|---|
| Lifestyle | Spontaneous, erratic | Busy and organised | Static and repetitive |
| Predominant | Anxiety, fear, | Anger, irritability | Progressiveness |
| Emotion | Insecurity | Judgemenialism, (self-)criticism | acquisitiveness and greed |
| Dreams | Nightmares, being chased, running, flying, fear-filled, much movement, variable recall | Violence, fire, passion, also transformation from one thing or state into another exchange of information, money or anything and sharp recall | Romantic events, water-river, sea, swimming also mundane about everyday events, often unmemorable |
| Work/projectPreference | Creative thinker likes 'ideas' stage, a planner | Putting plans into action, making thing happen, an executive | Peace-making, keeping things running |
| TOTAL 'A's | Vata | Pitta | Kapha |
| TOTAL 'B's | Vata | Pitta | Kapha |

When assessing your constitution from this questionnaire :

- Add up all the 'A's in each column. The Dosha which has the highest score is your constitutional type and the next highest is your secondary type.
- If there is nay doubt about which is highest, add on the 'B' scores to decide which is over all most descriptive of you.
- Remember, you can have two Dohas equally prominent in your constitution. A few people are tri-doshic.

## VIKRUTI : THE STATE OF IMBALANCE

Now that you have made an assessment of your basic constitution, the next step is to look at how you have gone out of kilter. This does't necessarily mean your have any symptoms of what we would generally call 'illness', but includes all physical, psychological/emotional and spiritual distress you experience as a result of imbalance.

Usually imbalance is brought about in a general sense by an increase in one of the Doshas. the pithy Ayurvedic sutra that explains how this happens says, 'like increases like'. Whatever you eat, imbibe, look at, think about, smell or tough is taken into your 'self' either physically or as sensory perceptions, and the Doshas of these things will increase the same Doshas in you. They will do this by increasing certain of the qualities or actions that are characteristic of the Doshas in question.

If you live in high, dry, cold area, eat raw, cold, dry, light food like salads and frequently travel by air with your very tall, dark, nervous partner – guess which Dosha is going to be provoked ? Right, Vata ! All the things we take into ourselves are going to build up and affect the balance of the Doshas.

Major traumas like the loss of a partner or your home, bankruptcy or accidental injury have the effect of suddenly and severely altering the balance of the Doshas.

Often minor imbalances are caused by one-of events like getting caught in a heavy rainstorm with inadequate clothing and having to continue walking for hours in the cold. Such cases may be sufficiently redressed by spontaneous acts of caring and common sense on the part of parent or partner who may provide warm towels, an open fire and warm, spicy goods upon our return; they may then be no repercussions.

However, our habitual diet and patterns of thought and emotions, where we live and with whom; our lifestyle (including exercises or the lack of it) and work stress levels have a cumulative effect on our doshic balance.

We are frequently obvious to the fact that how we are living is unsuited to our type. Since our culture subscribes to the cult of the individual on the one hand but tells us we all need the same food and lifestyle to remain healthy and the same medicines when we have the same named illness, our lack of awareness is perhaps understandable.

Knowing your Prakruti gives your this awareness', and knowing that 'like increases like' enables you to balance the Doshas in your environment (everything that is outside of the self).Everything you take in and every action you take (in other words, every interaction between you and your environment) is going to alter your doshic balance.

Provided the Doshas are well-enough balanced and the deviation actions that occurs as a part of just being above and interacting with the environment are small for the normal elimination process to deal with, all will be well! If you remember that your Prakruti is the individual, inborn constitution that is your unique balance of the Tridoshas, then you will realise that you are most likely to go out of balance on the direction of your predominant Dosha.

A variation on the theme of 'like increases like' is 'like attracts like'. Vata people are people in whom two characteristics, qualities and actions' of Vata predominate. They are also down to vata-increasing activities and substances-particularly when out of balance. A balanced Vata individual may see the point of early nights to compensate for the busty days. Memory, discrimination and determination are functioning well. However, since Vata is almost 'out-of-balance' personified, it is more often the case that the excessive physical execise, the frenetic lifestyle and the late nights that disturb Vata are going to be part of that individual's (non) routine !

Likewise, Pitta-predominant folk may be tempted by the red meat, Mexican food, competive sports, fiery relationship and workholism that provokes Pitta to rise and spills over into a state of imbalance – their present Vikruti.

Kalpa, being thte Dosha least inclined to change, has potentially the best chance of remaining balanced (all another things being equal). However, the only thing that remains equal is the certainty that Kapha individuals are going to be attracted to the very things that will throw Kapha Dosha out of Kilter – baked bananas and cream, lounging on the sofa, eating ice-cream nad watching soaps operas.

In later chapters there is information on how you can achieve balance. At present we will look how to recognise your impending imbalances before they become recognisable diseases.

## THE FIRST SIGN OF IMBALANCE : INDIGESTION

The first sign that all is not well in your internal state is indigestion, which in Ayurveda is, of course, divided into Vata, Pitta and Kapha types. Depending upon which Dosha is beginning to affect your internal balance by the 'like increases like' principle, you will start to experience one or other types of indigestion.

We are likely to think that indigestion is not much of a problem and thus it is unrelated to real health issues. However, this represents only the first stages in the development of disease (which we will look at later in more detail), and unless resolved will progress through later stages, manifesting in very different guises and becoming more and more entrenched. Of course, often we deal with these imbalances in a similarly commonsensical way to the treatment of the cold, wet returnee suggested above. Then all will be well and our Doshas are kept in check. But when we know what we are looking for ('awareness' again, we are much more likely to do the correct things to keep us balanced or to reduce minor imbalances.

### Vata Indigestion

When Vata starts to accumulate, its changeable, erratic nature express itself in variability. the digestion is fine some days and distinctly off on others, with the same foodstuffs and no recognisable differences in events. Likewise, the bowels are alternately constipated and loose, the toxic presence of Ama appears and disappears erratically and the appetite comes and goes. This is Vata indigestion. Flatulence is troublesome.

### Pitta Indigestion

As Pitta starts to go awry, cold food, drinks and environment are appealing. Stomach acid, heartburn and sour taste in the mouth are present. the hear of increased Pitta liquefies the intestinal contents and produces diarrhoea. Agni (the digestive fire) is negatively affected, as any excessively liquid, hot or cold, will douse Agni. Digestion is impaired by the increase in Pitta Dosha (a point worth taking special note of, as often there is an initial confusion between the fire of Pitta and that of Agni). As you have correctly deduced, the hot emotion of anger will increasingly spew forth as Pitta wrests control. It is therefore worth nothing how you are relating to others. If your loved ones are increasingly running for cover or taking a 'there, there' approach in conversation, which seems amore and more a contest of wills….. think Pitta!

### Kapha Indigestion

The wet, heavy and dull qualities of Kapha ensure that the dry lightness of Agni is somewhat doused, and Kapha indigestion follows. What appetite remains desires light food with the astringent and bitter tastes, and the mouth waters in the way it often does before vomiting occurs – not in anticipation of some culinary delight ! The heaviness is felt both in the stomach (primary home of Kapha) and in the limbs. The mind feels dull and a lack of enthusiasm of life is obvious. The desire for any exercise of body or mind is definitely not on the increase and a 'hey, who needs to work ( or play) anyway!' attitude reigns.

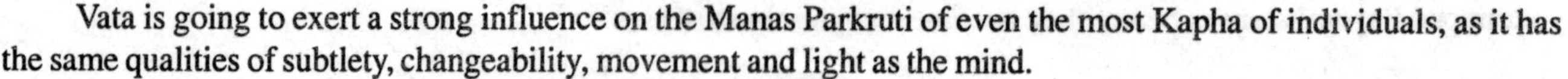

## IMBALANCES – THE ROLE OF THE MIND

Vata is going to exert a strong influence on the Manas Parkruti of even the most Kapha of individuals, as it has the same qualities of subtlety, changeability, movement and light as the mind.

The dominant culture in the West is fast, changeable and stress-including as everyone, including the most phlegmatic of individuals. Some people recognise the mismatch between their natures and that of the dominant culture and 'opt out'. Most of us struggle to adapt to the demands of our tribe, and in doing so bring about doshic imbalances that are mostly Vata. The pressures of modern living have profound effects on the mind.

Mind is more subtle and therefore, more pervasive that the physical aspects of our being. This being so, mind plays a fundamental role in the causation of disease.

In Ayurveda, the body is directed by the mind and, although there are physical causes like accidents that are outside our conscious control, many of the physical repercussions we experience are the result of a perverse and willful determination to ignore what we know we should do. We seem to imagine that we can contravene the laws of Mother Nature and get away with it ! this too has its roots in the idea, characteristic of our times, that humans are somehow above Nature and can either ignore her or command her at will.

Other information that may help in your assessment is awareness of the external factors relevant to your imbalance. For example:

- In which season did your symptoms start and at what time of year do they now occur?
- What age were you and what stage were you at in life when they started?
- At what hour of day or night do you have most awareness of the problem? For example, noon and midnight gastric burning might indicate Pitta.
- What climatic conditions make your health problem worse or better? For example, some people's psoriasis disappears when they are on holiday in a sunny location by the sea.
- How do the geography of your environment, the people you live with or your occupation affect you? It is not a matter of 'do they'? but only 'how do they?' affect you.

What qualities does each of these areas of your life exhibit? Looking at your life now and leading up to the time when the health problem started should give you a working hypothesis about the Dosha that needs treating.

As mentioned earlier, the presence of the Doshas can go through the stages of accumulation, provocation and spread and result in imbalances even though they may not find entrance into the tissues because the Dhatus and their Agnis are strong. This means that they will not go on to the stages of what we in the West think of as 'disease'. But life with excess Doshas is not living in health, and eventually these excesses will very likely find a chink in the Dhatu armour.

The tables that follow may help you recognize the excesses of Vata, Pitta and/or Kapha that you might be living with. The first lists signs and symptoms associated with increases of each of three Doshas. The second table gives signs and symptoms of the Doshas in each of the seven Dhatus (tissues).

**Signs and Symptoms of Increased Doshas**

| | |
|---|---|
| **Increased Vata** | Dry, rough skin with dark discolouration, emaciation; constipation, motions like sheep's droppings, flatulence; tremors, muscle twitching; tingling, numbness, dizziness and tinnitus; cracked nails, lips, nipples and anus; scanty urine and menstrual flow; desire for hot food, drinks, atmosphere and clothing; inability to slow down; pain that is radiating, fluctuating, shooting, traveling, throbbing, gripping and griping; fear of the unknown, jumping to conclusion, mood swings. |
| **Increased Pitta** | Yellow tinge to the skin, whites of eyes, stool and urine; insomnia – sleep till early hours only; tired, bloodshot eyes, fainting, acidity, diarrhea, vomiting, nausea, acne, hives and urticaria, boils and abscesses; metallic smell on breath and taste in mouth; bleeding gums; profuse menses; hypoglycaemia (low blood sugar), sugar craving, candidiasis (proliferation of the fungal organism Candida); emotionally judgemental, aggressive, perfectionist, competitive, ambitious, depressed as a result of even slight failure, perhaps suicidal, jealous, angry, impatient, irritable |
| **Increased Kapha** | Pale skin, nails, stools and urine; mucus in stools and urine; skin moist, swollen, cold; heaviness, sluggishness; water retention, oedema and swelling; loss of appetite; excessive and thick saliva; lethargy, excessive sleep and drowsiness; cold, cough, congestion and breathlessness. |

**Tridoshas in The Seven Dhatus**

| DHATU | DOSHA | TYPICAL SYMPTOMS AND CONDITIONS |
|---|---|---|
| Rasa | Vata | Skin is dry, rough, cracked, cold, hard, dark and discoloured. Dehydration. |
| | Pitta | Skin rashes, hives, acne, dermatitis and eczema, fever. |
| | Kapha | Skin is pale, cold and clammy. Lymphatic congestion and oedema, sinus and bronchial congestion, mild fever, cellulite. |
| Rakta | Vata | Circulation poor, cold hands and feet, blood clots, varicose veins and gout, anaemia. |
| | Pitta | Jaundice, cholecystitis, enlarged liver and spleen, psoriasis, eczema. |
| | Kapha | Thickening of blood, cholesterol, embolism, megaloblastic anaemia, high blood pressure. |
| Mamsa | Vata | Muscle spasm, tremors, pain, stiffness, wasting, paralysis, multiple sclerosis. |
| | Pitta | Inflammation of the muscles and bursitis. Ulcers, colitis. |
| | Kapha | Tumours composed on muscle tissue, cystic swellings in tendons, abnormal enlargement of muscle tissue. |
| Meda | Vata | Lack of lubrication, loose joints, dislocation of joints, low backache, lack of fat. Enlargement of spleen. |
| | Pitta | Boils, abscesses, urinary tract infections. |
| | Kapha | Enlargement and degeneration of the liver, diabetes, obesity. |
| Asthi | Vata | Joint pain, osteoporosis, osteoarthritis, dental cavities, brittle hair and nails. |
| | Pitta | Arthritis with much inflammation, rheumatism, inflammation of the bone or marrow. |
| | Kapha | Oedematous joint swellings and Kapha-related arthritis, bone-like tumours. |
| Majja | Vata | Leukaemia, anaemia, osteoporosis, paralysis and other neuromuscular problems, coma. |
| | Pitta | Sickle cell anaemia, multiple sclerioses, leukaemia, microcytic anaemia. |
| | Kapha | Tumours of the brain including the pineal gland, tumours in nerve tissue. |
| Shukra | Vata | Pulmonary tuberculosis, premature ejaculation, absence of sperm, depression, anxiety and other mental/ emotional problems. |
| | Pitta | Inflammation of the prostrate or ovaries, lack of sperm, sterility, menstrual haemorrhaging. |
| | Kapha | Enlarged prostrate, stones in prostate, tumours of the testicles. |

Because you are dependable and so good at smoothing ruffled feathers, team sports and activities like climbing allow you to exhibit wonderfully positive Kapha qualities and give you the motivation to continue. If you do not exercise at all at present, join the local ramblers group (one that does graded walks) and enjoy being out in the elements and letting the elements feed you. Your warm, compassionate, earthy disposition will soon ensure that other group members look forward to your company and remind you about prospective walks. You too can enjoy gardening, being at one with the earth. The more strenuous aspects of this activity will use up much of the stored energy that Vata people lack and would so love to have.

If Vata finds it impossible to create a routine (life is so full of surprises and one has to be ready to embrace them all) and Pitta organises everything and everyone (only by controlling the world can things get done), Kapha has a routine that is the route to a rut! Try a tiny change in your usual timetable. Vary something small, just try it and see that the world will still turn on its axis and that you feel a little more alive. Phone your most Vata friend and arrange to spend a few hours together (could either of your cope with more?).

Meditation has a place in Kapha's life too, but make sure that you sit your spine erect and that you choose a time when you are fully awake, to minimise the possibility of dropping off. Though early morning is generally the best time to meditate, before the activity of daily life builds up, it is probably best for you to use the early evening Vata time of 2 to 6 p.m. if you are just introducing meditation into your daily regime. Later you could try another session early in the day. Also, the small of incense will appeal to the Kapha person, as the sense of smell has such a strong affinity with Earth. The smell of incense will become a stimulus to which your mind and body become conditioned, and the peace and calm of meditation will be enhanced – more on this in the section on mantra and meditation.

In the realm of work Kapha brings consistency, diplomacy, perseverance, empathy and caring. The arenas best suited to making the most of Kapha's strengths are the caring professions like counselling and nursing, office management, construction work, conservation and archaeology, and the hotel and catering services.

When you take a holiday including some activities that stimulate your, body and mind. A walking holiday, sailing in a small craft convoy round the Greek islands or touring with some sightseeing done on foot are all good options; and you can always opt for an additional few days of self-indulgence on a beach or by a lake.

## DIET: YOU ARE WHAT YOU EAT

Let me recap the information about the six tastes introduced before examining the foods that are best suited to each Dosha.

Sweet sour and salty pacify Vata,

Sweet, bitter and astringent soothe Pitta.

Pungent, bitter and astringent soothe Kapha.

The therapeutic effects of tastes are as follows:

- Sweet is mildly cooling, the most moistening, and adds the most heaviness. It is nutritive, strengthening and balancing to the mind and soothing to the body's mucous membranes (the protective membrances that line organs such as the stomach intestines, mouth and gullet). It calms down burning sensations.
- Sour is moderately heating, mildly moistening, and increases lightness to the greatest extent. It is stimulating to the palate and to saliva. It dispels flatulence, improves circulation (is heating) and is nutritive to tissues (with the exception of the reproductive tissues).
- Salty is mildly heating, moderately moistening, andis moderately heavy. It is stimulating to the digestive tract – in small amounts promoting digestion, in medium amounts acting as cathartic and in large amounts causing vomiting. It is sedative to the nervous system.
- Pungent is the most heating and drying of tastes and has a moderately lightening effect. It has a generally stimulating effect on digestion, metabolism and circulation. Therefore, it is useful in flatulence, colic, indigestion and poor circulation, and to induce sweating in fevers.
- Bitter is the most cooling and lightness-inducing, and is moderately drying. It reduces fevers, kills bacteria and parasites and, in small amounts, stimulates the secretion of digestive juices. To this end it is commonly an ingredient of pre-dinner drinks (as in Angastura bitters).
- Astringent is moderately cooling and moderately heaviness and dryness-inducing. It has a contracting effect on tissues and thus stops bleeding, diarrhoea, catarrhal discharges, sweating and inflammation.

The six tastes are found mixed in substances but in differing amounts. The predominant taste in some common foods are listed below.

| *Predominant-taste* | *Foods/Food Categories* |
|---|---|
| Sweet | Sugars (cane and beet), fruits sugars (e.g. date sugar), milk sugar, maple, syrup, molasses, honey. Also in fats and complex carbohydrates such as grains and root vegetables. |
| Sour | Acidic fruits such as the citrus fruits and tomatoes, and sour varieties of other fruits such as apples, berries, plums and grapes. All fermented foods such as pickles, vinegar and alcohol. |
| Salty | All sea food (including seaweeds) and sea and rock salt. |
| Pungent | Tea, coffee and spices such as ginger, cinnamon, black pepper, cayenne pepper and paprika. |

| | |
|---|---|
| Bitter | Though not a predominant taste in foods (indeed it is often a sign that a food is 'off'), it can be found in many medicinal herbs to good effect. |
| Astringent | Commonly predominant when fruits (such as bananas) are unripe. Predominant in pomegranates and lettuce. |

## General Advice on Diet and Dosha

If your scores for the Prakruti questionnaire indicate that you are a close mix of two Doshas or even a Tridoshic person, then you must take other information into account when masking dietary choices. For example, a Vata/Pitta person should stick to the Vata diet during the seasons that are cold (remember, autumn is particularly Vatagenic) and should use Pitta-soothing foods in the summer and late spring. It is also important to take Vikruti (the state of imbalance) into account. Using diet to decrease the aggravated Dosha is a safe and effective if somewhat slower treatment than others that require more specialist knowledge.

It is because it is slow relative to herbal treatment, for example, that diet is so safe and radical (in the sense of getting to the root of a problem). Such effects are sure to be long lasting and give the mind as well as the body time to adjust. Generally, the body does not take well to drastic and speedily implemented changes. The body takes time to change its habits – foods and activities that it has become used to. A couple of inconsistent changes in how and what you eat are worth innumerable abortive attempts at changing your entire daily dietary regime.

Take care to remember that the food lists for each Dosha are given as general advice. You may be sensitive to certain foods and, of course, must not eat them just because you discover that your Doshic type can eat these foods. Also, foods that you are addicted to and that you would be miserable about dropping entirely can and should be reduced in quantity and frequency rather than eliminated entirely, at least initially. Removing items suddenly may provoke reactions, particularly if you start to reintroduce them after a period of withdrawal.

As an example, think of the case of a person who is sensitive to dairy but who may not actually be aware of this because he has always loved it and eaten it everyday. The catarrhal congestion he has experienced for years has been an inconvenience he has grown to accept. Because he is predominantly Kapha he decides to eliminate dairy from his diet and does so consistently from the day he makes his decision. After a few days he may find that he craves the eradicated foods and that he is getting headaches as his body, released from the daily dose of dairy, turns the energy previously used to cope with a state of allergy to eliminate accumulated wastes. It he stays with it these symptoms may diminish and, after a few months, he may forget how bad he used to feel and decide to reintroduce his beloved dairy ('After all, where's the harm in it?'). Rather rapidly, he may feel worse than he did before he tried cutting dairy out of his diet as his body rebounds in its reaction to a substance it is sensitive to. Be kind to yourself, this is not a punishment and feeling miserable is not conducive to health.

Be aware that it is your daily diet that counts – the occasional indiscretion is dealt with by a healthy person. Make up the bulk of your diet from fresh, seasonal, organically grown, non-genetically modified foods. Home-grown and home-cooked are best – think of the love that is being ingested along with the food. In Eastern traditions, the position of cook is revered and honoured, as someone who is well-progressed on the spiritual path has the most to add to the diets of those he cooks for.

Too much food is merely converted into Ama. What constitutes 'too much' is determined by the state of your digestion – therefore, if you are Vata or have a Vata imbalance, eat small meals and watch for signs of not digesting properly. Foods cooked together such as soups and stews are generally most easily digested.

Food combining is an important subject in Ayurveda. Here are some general combinations to avoid :

- Fruit is a food that is best eaten on its own. That is, you can mix fruits that are suitable for you, but do not have them at the same sitting as other types of food. It makes a good breakfast or you can have it as a mid-morning or mid-afternoon snack.
- Sour dairy such as yoghurt should not be eaten at the same meal as sweet dairy such as milk or cream.

- Raw foods such as salads or muesli should not be taken at the same meal as cooked foods.
- Dairy should not be eaten with starches.

Apart from drinking a little water or a small amount of wine with a meal, drinks are best taken between meals. The rule is one-third fluid, one-third food and one-third empty to allow good mixing.

Do not exercise until a couple of hours have elapsed after a meal, apart from a short stroll enabling the contracting and relaxing abdominal muscles to massage the intestinal contents as you walk. The process of digestion takes energy, the activity of a specific part of the nervous system and blood flow to the digestive organs, all of which necessitate a certain degree of passivity in other parts of the body and mind.

Finally, remember that food is intended to supply Prana in a gross form, to nourish the body and maintain its physical existence, while the subtle components of food feed the mind. As the subtle energies that enter the organism are so important, always eat mindfully. Eating while watching television, reading the paper or having a heated discussion will compromise digestion and permit these materials to be absorbed along with the food – bitter fruits indeed!

**Dietary Guidelines for the Doshas-Animal Products**

| | |
|---|---|
| **VATA** | |
| YES | AVOID |
| All are good in moderation for grounding Vata. | |
| The dark meat of chicken and turkey in preference to the white meat. | |
| **PITTA** | |
| YES | AVOID |
| Chicken (white meat) | All other animal products, including egg yolks |
| Egg whites | |
| Fresh water fish | |
| Rabbit | |
| Turkey (white meat)Venison | |
| **KAPHA** | |
| YES | AVOID |
| Chicken (White meat) | Beef |
| Eggs | Duck |
| Freshwater fish | Lamb |
| Rabbit | Pork |
| Turkey (white meat) | Sea fish/food |
| Venison | |

**Condiments**

| | |
|---|---|
| **VATA** | |
| YES | AVOID |
| Most | Horse radish |
| Chocolate (occasionally) | |
| Chilli peppers (in moderation) | |
| **PITTA** | |
| YES | AVOID |
| Black pepper (occasionally) | All others including : |
| Coriander leaves | Chillies |

| | |
|---|---|
| Mango chutney (sweet)<br>Lime, fresh (occasionally)<br>Salt (in moderation) | Chutneys<br>Horse radish<br>Mustard<br>Lemon<br>Mayonnaise<br>Pickles<br>Tomato<br>Ketchup<br>Vinegar |
| **KAPHA**<br>**YES**<br>Black pepper<br>Chilli pepper<br>Coriander leaves<br>Horseradish<br>Ketchup (occasionally)<br>Lemon (in moderation)<br>Mango chutney (spicy)<br>Mustard<br>Seaweeds (in moderation) | **AVOID**<br>Chutneys (sweet)<br>Pickles<br>Mayonnaise<br>Salt<br>Soya sauce<br>Tamarind<br>Vinegar |

**Culinary Herbs and Spices**

| | |
|---|---|
| **VATA**<br>**YES**<br>All spices | **AVOID**<br>Horseradish |
| **PITTA**<br>**YES**<br>Black pepper (occasionally)<br>Caraway (occasionally)<br>Coriander leaves<br>Cumin<br>Dill<br>Fennel<br>Ginger, fresh<br>Mint<br>Orange peel (occasionally)<br>Peppermint<br>Saffron<br>Spearmint<br>Turmeric<br>Vanilla (occasionally) | **AVOID**<br>All others |
| **VATA**<br>**YES**<br>All spices<br>Fennel (in moderation)<br>Vanilla (in moderation) | **AVOID** |

## Dairy Food

| | |
|---|---|
| **VATA** | |
| **YES** | **AVOID** |
| All fresh dairy. Dilute and add spices to yoghurt Ice-cream (in moderation) | All dried products and yoghurt with fruit |
| **PITTA** | |
| **YES** | **AVOID** |
| Light and sweet | Salty and sour |
| Milk | Buttermilk |
| Cottage cheese | Hard cheese |
| Cream | Salted butter |
| Ghee | Sour cream |
| | Yoghurt |
| **KAPHA** | |
| **YES** | **AVOID** |
| Ghee (in moderation) | Most |
| Unsalted goats' cheese | |
| Goat's milk (in moderation) | |

## Drinks

| | |
|---|---|
| **VATA** | |
| **YES** | **AVOID** |
| Juices : | Apple |
| Apricot | Mixed veg |
| Berry (except cranberry) | Pear |
| Carrot | Pomegranate |
| Cherry | |
| Grape | |
| Grapefruit | |
| Mango | |
| Orange | |
| Peach | |
| Pineapple | |
| Hot Drinks: | |
| Chai (hot, spiced milk) | Caffeinated tea/coffee |
| Grain coffee | Chocolate |
| Soya milk (hot, spiced) | Cocoa |
| Cold Drinks: | |
| Almond milk | Carbonated iced drinks |
| Fresh lemonade | Soya milk (cold) |
| Alcoholic Drinks: | |
| Beer (in moderation) | Spirits |
| Cider (in moderation) | |
| Wine (in moderation) | |
| Herb Teas: | |
| Most, the following | |

| | |
|---|---|
| occasionally: | |
| Jasmine | Blackberry |
| Lemon balm | Ginseng |
| Nettle | |
| Passion flower | |
| Strawberry | |
| Mate | |
| Raspberry (in moderation) | |
| PITTA | |
| YES | AVOID |
| Juices: | |
| Apple | Carrot |
| Apricot | Cranberry |
| Grape | Grapefruit |
| Mango | Orange |
| Mixed veg | Pineapple |
| Peach | Sour berry |
| Pear | Sour cherry |
| Sweet berry | Tomato |
| Sweet cherry | |
| Hot Drinks: | |
| Bouillon | Caffeinated tea/ coffee |
| Chai (occasionally, hot, | Chocolate |
| spiced) | Cocoa |
| Grain coffee | Iced drinks |
| Cold Drinks: | Lemonade |
| Almond milk | |
| Carob milk | |
| Cows' milk | |
| Lassi (diluted yoghurt) | |
| Rice milk | |
| Soya milk | |
| Alcoholic Drinks: | |
| Beer (occasionally) | Cider |
| Herb Teas: | Spirits |
| Most | |
| | Cinnamon |
| | Ginger (dried) |
| | Ginseng |
| | Hawthorn |
| | Rosehip |
| | Mate |

| KAPHA<br>YES | AVOID |
|---|---|
| Juices:<br>Apple<br>Apricot<br>Berry<br>Carrot<br>Cherry, sweet<br>Cranberry<br>Mango<br>Mixed veg<br>Peach<br>Pear<br>Pomegranate | All sour |
| Hot Drinks:<br>Caffeinated tea/coffee<br>(in moderation)<br>grain coffee<br>Soya milk (hot, spiced)<br>Veg bouillon | |
| Cold Drinks:<br>Carob drinks | Rice milk<br>Soya milk (cold)<br>Iced drinks |
| Alcoholic Drinks:<br>Cider<br>Wines (dry) | Beer<br>Spirits<br>Wines (sweet) |
| Herb Teas:<br>Most, the following<br>Moderately:<br>Comfrey<br>Fennel<br>Ginseng<br>Liquorice<br>Rosehip (occasionally) | |

**Fruit**

| VATA<br>YES | AVOID |
|---|---|
| Most sweet fruit. If in doubt, cook. If dried, soak overnight and preferably cook. | All dried<br>Apples (raw)<br>Cranberries<br>Pears<br>Watermelon |

| | |
|---|---|
| **PITTA**<br>YES<br>Most sweet and astringent fruit, including dried.<br>Also:<br>Grapes (except green)<br>Limes (in moderation) | AVOID<br>Sour fruit and sour varieties:<br>Apricots<br>Berries<br>Cherries<br>Oranges<br>Pineapples<br>Plums |
| **KAPHA**<br>YES<br>Most astringent and dried fruit<br>Figs (dried, in moderation)<br>Grapes (in moderation)<br>Lemons (in moderation)<br>Limes (in moderation)<br>Mangoes (occasionally) | AVOID<br>Most sour and sweet fruit, including:<br>Coconut<br>Figs, fresh |

**Grains**

| | |
|---|---|
| **VATA**<br>YES<br>Cooked:<br>Durham wheat<br>Oats (cooked)<br>Quinoa (in moderation)<br>Rice (vary all types)<br>Rice cakes (occasionally)<br>Wheat pasta (occasionally) | AVOID<br>Dry as in muesli/ breakfast cereals:<br>Barley<br>Buckwheat<br>Maize<br>Millet<br>Oats (dry)<br>Oat bran<br>Rye<br>Sago<br>Spelt<br>Tapioca<br>Wheatbran |
| **PITTA**<br>YES<br>Barley<br>Oats (cooked)<br>Oat bran<br>Rice (brown, only occasionally)<br>Sago<br>Spelt | AVOID<br>Buckwheat<br>Maize<br>Millet<br>Oats (raw)<br>Quinoa<br>Rye |

| | |
|---|---|
| Tapioca<br>Wheat<br>Wheat bran (in moderation) | |
| **KAPHA** | |
| YES | AVOID |
| Barley<br>Buckwheat<br>Durham wheat<br>Maize<br>Millet<br>Quinoa (in moderation)<br>Rye | Oats (cooked)<br>Rice (brown/white)<br>Wheat grains<br>Wheat flour |

## Nuts and Seeds

| | |
|---|---|
| **VATA** | |
| YES | AVOID |
| All nuts and seeds (in moderation)<br>sesame seeds (roasted) | |
| **VATA** | |
| YES | AVOID |
| All nuts and seeds (in moderation)<br>sesame seeds (roasted) | |
| **PITTA** | |
| YES | AVOID |
| Almonds (skinned, occasionally)<br>Pumpkin seeds (roasted, in moderation)<br>Sunflower seeds (roasted, in moderation) | All nuts<br>Sesame seeds |
| **KAPHA** | |
| YES | AVOID |
| Coconut<br>Pumpkin seeds (roasted, in moderation)<br>Poppy seeds<br>Sesame seeds<br>Sunflower seeds (roasted, in moderation) | All nuts |

## Oils/Fats

| | |
|---|---|
| **VATA** | |
| YES | AVOID |
| All oils except blended vegetable oil | |
| **PITTA** | |
| YES | AVOID |
| Canola | Almond |
| Coconut | Animal fats |
| Olive | Corn |
| Sunflower | Sesame (dark) |
| Safflower (in moderation) | |
| Soya (in moderation) | |
| walnut | |
| **KAPHA** | |
| YES | AVOID |
| Small amounts only of: | Most, especially: |
| Canola | Apricot |
| Corn | Avocado |
| Ghee | Coconut |
| Safflower | Olive |
| Sunflower | Sesame |
| | Soya |
| | Walnut |

## Pulses

| | |
|---|---|
| **VATA** | |
| YES | AVOID |
| Mung dal | Most, including soya flour |
| Red lentils | and cold tofu |
| Soya derived products: | |
| Milk | |
| Cheese | |
| Sauce | |
| Sausages | |
| Tofu (cooked) | |
| **PITTA** | |
| YES | AVOID |
| Most, especially: | Fermented products such |
| Aduki | as Miso and soy sauce |
| Mung dal | |
| Tofu (cooked) | |
| due to their sattvic influence | |
| **KAPHA** | |
| YES | AVOID |

| | |
|---|---|
| Most pulses<br>Soya milk (best spiced)<br>Tofu (cooked only) | Soya beans and their products including cold tofu |

## Sweeteners

Honey must be used uncooked as heated it produces Ama.

| | |
|---|---|
| **VATA**<br>**YES**<br>Most | **AVOID**<br>Saccharine<br>White sugar |
| **PITTA**<br>**YES**<br>Most | **AVOID**<br>In excess:<br>Jaggery<br>Honey<br>Molasses<br>Saccharine<br>White sugar |
| **VATA**<br>**YES**<br>Honey (in small amounts) is best. Also, but sparingly:<br>Barley malt<br>Brown rice syrup<br>Fruit juice concentrates<br>Maple syrup | **AVOID**<br>All others |
| **VATA**<br>**YES**<br>Well cooked. Use spices and add ghee as a condiment.<br>Artichoke<br>Asparagus<br>Black olives<br>Broccoli (occasionally)<br>Cabbage (occasionally)<br>Carrots<br>Cauliflower (occasionally)<br>Courgettes<br>Daikon radish<br>Fennel<br>Green beans<br>Kale (occasionally, well-cooked)<br>Leeks (cooked)<br>Onions (cooked)<br>Pumpkin<br>Parsnips (in moderation)<br>Radishes | **AVOID**<br>Raw and cold as in salads.<br>Aubergine<br>Bell peppers<br>Brussels sprouts<br>Celery<br>Green olives<br>Kohlrabi<br>Leeks (uncooked)<br>Lettuce<br>Mushrooms<br>Onion (raw)<br>Potatoes (white)<br>Turnips |

| | |
|---|---|
| Spinach (in moderation)<br>Sprouts (in moderation)<br>Squashes (in moderation)<br>Sweet corn (in moderation)<br>Sweet potato<br>Tomatoes (occasionally) | |
| **PITTA**<br>YES<br>Most sweet and bitter veg<br>Only cooked:<br>Beets<br>Carrots<br>Leeks<br>Onions<br>Radishes<br>Spinach (occasionally)<br>Sweet corn (occasionally)<br>Also, cooked or uncooked, as suitable:<br>Artichoke<br>Asparagus<br>Broccoli<br>Brussels sprouts<br>Cabbage<br>Cauliflower<br>Cucumber<br>Endive<br>Green beans<br>Kale<br>Ladies fingers<br>Lettuce<br>Parsnips<br>Peas<br>Potatoes<br>Sprouts<br>Sweet peppers<br>Squashes<br>Watercress | AVOID<br>Pungent veg<br><br>Chillies<br>Garlic<br>Mustard greens<br>Tomatoes<br>Turnips |
| **KAPHA**<br>YES<br>Most pungent and bitter veg<br>Artichoke<br>Aubergine<br>Asparagus<br>Bean sprouts<br>Cabbage<br>Carrots<br>Cauliflower<br>Celery | AVOID<br>Sweet and watery veg<br>Courgettes<br>Cucumber<br>Mushrooms<br>Pumpkin<br>Squashes<br>Sweet potatoes<br>Tomatoes (raw)<br>Also, sour, pungent and |

| Daikon radish<br>Fennel (in moderation)<br>Garlic<br>Green beans<br>Kale<br>Ladies fingers<br>Leeks<br>Mustard greens<br>Onions<br>Peas<br>Spinach<br>Turnips<br>Watercress | salty veg such as olives and pickles |
|---|---|

There are some very useful textbooks that can give you more detailed information and advice on diet, including suitable menus for the Doshic types. Several of these are listed in the Bibliography. Please investigate these and implement the cumulative suggestions, because consistent dietary changes alone will have a profound effect on your well-being - given that all-important element of time.

If what you eat is important in Ayurveda, then so is what and when you avoid eating. Fasting has an honourable and venerated place in lifestyle and treatment as recommended by traditional Ayurveda. And, as with almost everything else, how you go about it depends upon your constitution.

If Vata is your Prakruti or is the Dosha that is vitiated, then the hot-house plant technique should be applied – easy does it! About once a fortnight choose a day when you can take it easy and avoid solid food. Drink diluted fruit juices (check the food lists), spiced milk or lassi, or hot water with lemon and honey. Avoid trying to drink water alone and do not extend the fast.

If Pitta is your type or is deranged, then take a day a week to eat a mono diet. This is when you rest the digestive tract by eating only one sort of foodstuff such as grapes, but you eat them in the quantity you desire. Pitta also benefits from eating raw fruit or raw vegetable salads only, or their diluted juices. A third type of fast that suits Pitta is eating kichadi only. This can be extended for several days but not beyond feeling that you never want to look a mung bean in the face again! As with Vata, do not indulge in water-only fasts.

Kapha digestion benefits greatly from regular weekly fasts taking only suitable juices or warm water and (the unfairness of it!) Kapha can undertake longer fasts, particularly at the turn of the seasons.

## Household Herbs

There are several culinary herbs and spices that you will probably have in a cupboard which can be used in self-help Ayurveda. Perhaps you already keep a few other substances, such as ghee, that will be useful in Ayurvedic cooking and can be used as household cures. Very likely the difference between how you have hitherto used them and how you can use them for self-healing is to do with quantity and frequency.

## Black Pepper

Black pepper can be used to good effect as follows:

Black pepper will decrease Vata and Kapha but increase Pitta, so watch out for signs of high Pitta like redness, heat, irritability or anger.

- A pinch of black pepper with teaspoonful of honey acts as a natural antihistamine and is very good for sinus congestion.

- In a mixture with ginger and long pepper (Trikatu or three peppers) it increases Agni (digestive fire), improving appetite and digestion.
- A pinch with a teaspoonful of ghee is anti-allergic and therefore useful for symptoms of the hay fever variety.

## Turmeric

Turmeric, the yellow root powder used in the preparation of curries, is a powerful antibiotic. It helps kill off viruses, bacteria, fungal organisms and even worms. It has many uses:

- For chronic bronchitis: 1 teaspoonful in a cup of milk, boiled and taken daily.
- For a sore throat: 1 teaspoonful in a cup of milk, boiled and taken daily.
- For iron-deficiency anaemia: ¼ teaspoonful in a cup of yoghurt,
- For eczema, dermatitis or psoriasis: Make a paste with ghee and apply. Cover with care to avoid yellowing your clothes and bedding!
- For fungal infections of nails or athlete's foot: 1 teaspoonful of Aloe vera gel and ¼ teaspoonful of turmeric. Apply and cover.

## Asafoetida

Asafoetida is also used to flavour curries. The smell and taste of it is sulphurous, so you may regard the cure as worse than the problem! – but it can be used in self-help.

- For chronic dyspepsia (indigestion) : 1 teaspoonful of ghee with a pinch of asafetida.
- For sexual debility: 1 teaspoonful of ghee with a pinch of asafetida.
- Cavaties: Until you can get dental treatment for a cavity, use a toothpick to fill the offending hole with asafoetida powder.

## Ginger

Ginger is the digestive aid par excellence:

- To sharpen appetite and aid digestion: Chew a sliver of fresh ginger before meals.
- To relieve trapped gas or colicky pains: Make a tea with 1/8 -1/4 teaspoonful of ginger powder; sip. You can use 1 teaspoonful of grated fresh ginger and boil it for 5 minutes. Honey can be added before drinking ginger tea, but wait until it has cooled to drinking temperature.
- For a fever that starts in the morning or evening with goosebumps and shaking, a generalised body ache, constipation, stiff, joints and a rapid pulse: 1/3 teaspoonful ginger powder plus equal amounts of cumin powder and myrrh powder (which you probably will not have in your cupboard – yet!). Keep the herbs in a cup of hot water for 10 minutes before drinking. It will help induce a healing sweat to reduce the temperature.
- *For headache*: Make a paste with 1 teaspoonful of ginger powder and water, apply to the forehead and lie with it in place for half an hour. This can help some types of migraine too – try it.
- *For colds, cough, congestion, runny nose, post-nasal drip, fever with chills and dull heaviness in the head* : Take a tea of ginger, cinnamon and fennel. Make up a mixture of equal parts of these and store it in a tightly sealed jar in a cool, dark cupboard. When needed make a tea with 1 teaspoonful of the mixture in hot water, two to three times daily.

## Pippali

If you can obtain pippali (long pepper) to use in trikatu (three peppers), then it can be used as follows :-

- *For hayfever* : Make a tea with pippali, liquorice and lemongrass (powdered): 1/3 teaspoonful of each in hot water.

- *To help burn fat molecules* : Used alone or as trikatu, a pinch of the spice with 1 teaspoonful of honey, followed after 10 minutes by a cup of hot water and no other food or dink for atleast one hour.
- *For Kapha conditions and problems where Ama is a major component, when you cannot obtain long pepper*: Make a mixture with 1 part bay leaves, ¼ part black pepper, 1/8 part cloves and 1/16 part cardamom. Use 1 teaspoonful to make 1 cup of the tea.

Using the list of herbs and spices, concoct mixtures that will benefit your Dosha or calm the Dosha you know is increased. You can make your own tea bags of herbs and spices – ground like ginger, whole like cloves and cinnamon sticks, or as sticks like fennel or cumin – by making a small bundle of the amount required in a square of unbleached muslin. They are health- and environmentally-friendly and recyclable.

## Aromatherapy

Another beneficial addition to your balancing act is the use of essential or volatile oils. A little was said about these wonderful herbal extracts when we were looking at lifestyles, and suggestions were given as to how to use them (in oil burners, in baths, on pads in your pillowcase at night, as steam inhalations or in massage oil).

There are libraries full of books with good suggestions as to how most effectively to combine these oils for various conditions of body and mind. Here I will restrict the advice given to which oils are suited to each Dosha. In general, two to three drops of two to three essential oils can be used in two treatments (say in a massage and in a bath) on the same day. Never take volatile oils by mouth. Some practitioners are trained in the internal use of essential oils and their advice can be followed, but for self-help purposes leave well alone. The reason for this is the extremely concentrated nature of these oils. Chemically they are oils but they do not appear oily. Their intensity and oily nature are signatures of Pitta and they can burn (only very few essential oils can be used undiluted on the skin, so do not use them except in a carrier oil, cream or mixed well with bath water). Also, being so concentrated, very little can be too much and taken internally can be very toxic.

**Essential Oils for the Doshas**

| Oil | Dosha(s) |
|---|---|
| Camphor | Vata and Kapha |
| Cinnamon | Vata and Kapha |
| Eucalyptus | Vata and Kapha |
| Frankincense | Vata and Kapha |
| Lavender | Vata and Kapha |
| Lemon | Vata and Kapha |
| Lime | Pitta |
| Peppermint | Vata and Kapha |
| Rose, red | Vata |
| Rose, white | Pitta |
| Rose, yellow | Kapha |
| Rosemary | decreases Vata, Pitta (only if weak Agni), Kapha (for headaches) |
| Saffron | Vata, Pitta and Kapha |
| Sage | Vata and Kapha |
| Some other essential oils of particular benefit to each of the three Doshas include: | |
| Vata | Cederwood |
| | Geranium |

| | |
|---|---|
| | Juniper |
| | Myrrh |
| | Patchouli |
| | Ylang-ylang |
| Pitta | Gardenia |
| | Jasmine |
| | Lotus |
| | Sandalwood |
| | Vetivert |
| Kapha | Basil |

Carrier oils for the Tridoshas differ, as they too have qualities that are needed by some types and best avoided by others.

Vata types can use oil of all varieties as the heaviness that is characteristic of all oils is grounding to Vata. However, good-quality cold-pressed sesame oil is warming to the Vata individual, and for this is particularly recommended by traditional Ayurveda. Castor oil is also very useful for Vata and is penetrating and healing. Light, gentle massage with long, flowing, stroking movements (effleurage) is beneficial to Vata.

Pitta needs far less oiling, but sunflower oil or coconut oil are recommended for their more cooling qualities when massage is required. More kneading and wringing movements can be incorporated into the massage for a Pitta individual, while keeping the stroking movements.

Kapha needs little oil, and indeed dry massage can be used to effect. If oil is used to facilitate the gliding of hands over skin, then use corn oil or mustard oil. Deep massage is good for Kapha using the friction of knuckles and thumb rotation as well as wringing and kneading movements.

The treatments dealt with so far have had their primary focus on the body – they are physical treatments. Those that follow are more subtle contributions to the restoration and maintenance of health. Treatments that are directed at the subtle bodies affect the physical body, as the subtle does not merely surround the body but suffuses it – anything that exists in the physical world must first exist in the subtle realms. Therefore, treatments that are directly connected to the subtle may work indirectly on the physical. Also, it may take time for the effects of these treatments to appear on the physical plane, and the cause-and-effect relationship may be more difficult to explain in what is termed 'scientific language'.

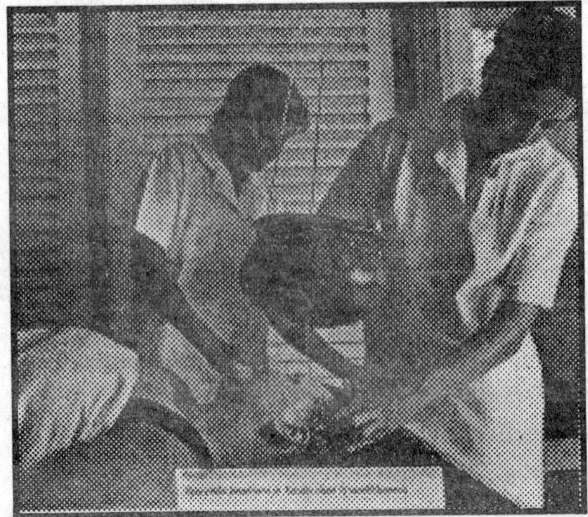

*A steady stream of warm oil may be poured onto the forehead to induce deep relaxation. The oil is stroked into the hair and massaged into the scalp.*

**Fig. 44 : Indian Massage**

## THE POWER OF HEALING PLANTS

### Plants in Poetry

**The Acorn and the Gourd**

Jean de La Fontaine, 1671

The extraordinary complexity of plants is not limited to their powers of healing. French poet, Jean de la Fontaine illustrated the cleverness of nature through a fable.

*All that love does is wise and good*
*I need not travel for abroad*
*'To make this maxim understood.*
*But take example from a Gourd.*
*Observing once a pumpin,*
*Of bulk so huge on stem so small,*
*What meant he ? Cried a bumpkin,*
*"Great love, I mean, who made us all,*
*By such an act capricious ?*
*If my advice were asked by heaven,*
*To yonder oaks the gourds were given,*
*And it would have been judicious;*
*For sure it is good taste to suit*
*To monstrous trees a monstrous fruit....*

*The more I view this sad abortion*
*If all the laws of true proportion,*
*The more I am sure the Lord of Thunder*
*Has made a very serious bluder'.*
*Teased by this matter, tony cries,*
*'One soon grows weary when one is wise',*
*The dozing ' neath an oak he lies.*
*Now, as he slept, an Acorn fell*
*Straight on his nose, and made it swell,*
*At once awake, he seeks to trace*
*With eager hand what hurt his face,*
*And in his beard the Acorn caught,*
*Discovers what the pain had wrought.*
*And now, by injured nose induced.*
*Our friend takes u; a different tone.*
*'I bleed, I bleed ! if from the tree, instead.*
*A full grown Gourd had struck my head!*
*Ah! Jove, most wise, has made decree*
*That acorns only deck the tree,*
*And now I quite the reason see!*
*And now I quite the reason see!*
*Thus in a better frame of mind*
*Homeward went our honest hind.*

## PROTECTING OUR PLANTS

The secret language of nature

David Bellamy and Andrea Pfister

David Bellamy, botanist, writer and broadcaster, has become one of the best-known personalities in Britain. Andrea Pfister, a graduate in botany and ecology, works on the human and social aspects of conservation. They took this quotation from an adverstisement that appeared in the *International* Herald Tribune and other leading American newspapers in 1990.

Imagine your fate is entwined with that of a South Ameican, vine, or a fragile pink flower in far off Madagascar. If these plants were threatened with extinction, you would spring to their defence.

What if we told that many patients facing major surgery rely on a muscle relaxant extracted from an Amazonian vine, *Chrondroendron tomentosum ?*

Or that four out of five children with leukaemia survive, thanks to the chemicals vincristine and vinblastine, donated by the rosy perjwinkle?

Would the fate of these plants raise your concern? If so, read on.

It is essential that you be aroused beyond mere concern, to action…

Extracts from an Amazonian oak tree coagulate proteins, immensely helping scientistsin the search for an AIDS vaccine . People sleep deeply and breathe easily during operations thanks to scopolamine derived from mandrake, henane, and thorn applies. Cancer of the lung, kidney and testies responds to Etoposide, a drug synthesizes from May apples….

Women who take the contraceptive pill for granted would not be taking it at all were it not for the yam. This large tuber is the source of the Pill's active ingredient, diosgenin.

Peptic ulcer heal faster thanks to the pale blue petals and flat brown pods of liquorice flower origin of carbenoxaline.

Now this vast store of known and potential medicines is under threat and we are fll of us obliged to protect it.

Ladies and gentlemen, this is our last chance. The world, our world, is dying from an latrogenic disease caused by a pathogen called Home sapiens, which is destroying the life support system of the Earth and the best stocked pharmacy there has ever been: If the medical profession in all its guises can't see that its way ahead is through a new eclectic,. The best of the old with the best of the new working in symbiosis to solve the real problems of this, the saddest of centuries, the future hasn't a chance. We must use the green print of medicare handed down to the West over more than 30,000 years to reach a very attainable and respectable goal : every child a wanted child, growing up into an individual who can aspire to the dignity of a truly civilised world and an average active life of perhaps a little more than three score years and ten, leading on to an active old age, not sans eyes, sans teeth, sans everything, but sans pain and the anguish of geriatric syndromes.

## PLANTS TO CURE EMOTIONAL ILLS

Some doctors have developed original views on plants. French doctor, Bernard Vial believes that plants are capable of curing the emotional problems that could be the cause of numerous diseases. An article published in the magazine *Medicine Douce* (alternative medicine), July-August 1993 written by Francoise Nahmias, sums up this surprising take on herbalism. Here are a few extracts.

### What is emotional medicine?

'Every disease is a state of uneasiness, an inability to express an emotional disorder or the failure of it being understood' this idea, proposed by Doctor Vial, underpins the logic of ' emotional medicine'. Thus, behind bronchitis is often hidden ' an unhappy family environment ' and asthma masks 'a stifled love song' Doctor Vial's theory led him to explore the relationships between emotions and disease and the possibility of removing the blockages causing disease with the use of appropriate medicinal plants.

This treatment rests on two hypotheses. On the one hand, a well – targeted remedy can change the emotional mood of a patient and can thus, help him with his problems. On the other hand, proteins in blood serum provide the biological support for this change. These serum proteins are sensitive to failures and disappointments. They carry the emotional's scars of each person. Once the events have been imprinted, these blood molecules transmit the negative information to the ogans, the souce of psychosomatic symptoms.

By using specific plant remedies that carry new information to the serum proteins, it is possible to target the disturbed emotions and to help them emerge. This information stops the emotional disturbance and diminishes the risks of psychosomatic symptoms. Cured from its 'emotional wound; the protein structure is once again open to other emotions. To benefit from this particular treatment, the patient can take the plant in tablet or tincture form, or inhale it .

This medical practice stems from a series of observations and experiments carried out in the field by more than 200 general practioners in France over a period of 20 years. To date the ' emotional impact ' of 1,200 plants has been identified.

## Discover your plant

Bering in mind the theory of plants helping to cure our emotional ills, select the plants you like best from the following tables. Your choice will speak volumes about your emotional state. You can then read about the strength of your chosen plant to modify your emotions, guiding them in a more positive direction.

| | FLOWERS | |
|---|---|---|
| PLANTS | YOU ARE | YOU WILL BECOME |
| ROSE | Rigid, intolerant, cut off from happiness, closed to others. | Generous but very attached to your principles. |
| LILY | Subject to continuous anguish which paralyses your spontaneity. | Endowed with a subtle sense of humour which will temper your seriousness. |
| POPPY | ..very shy, the eternal adolescent, you feel unable to cope with adult life. | Open to new experiences, open emotionally. |
| NARCISSUS | …lacking in self regard | Indulgent towards other and self aware. |
| PERWINKLE | Emotionally insecure, verging on arrogance : cynical, you like challenges in order to prove your superiority. | … sure of yourself, without feeling the need of competition with others and yourself. |

| | TREES | |
|---|---|---|
| OAK | | |
| Olive tree | .. difficulties in affirming your autonomy within the family , tapped between insecurity and authority | Independent, responsible, sold, you will learn how to help others to overcome their problems. |
| Maritime pine | .. In the grips of savage resentment, you are merciless in battle. | Clear headed, thoughtful, kindly and courteous, without excessive familaity. |
| Palm tree | Sensitive to praise and like to be protective | Courageous , altruistic, with a need to be recognised but still wanting to defend the helpless. |
| Birch | .. found it difficult to recover from the failure of a first love- affair and have renounced sexually for the intellect. | Endowed with a great understanding of feeling and the heart, without being pedantic |

| | HOUSEPLANTS | |
|---|---|---|
| PLANTS | YOU ARE/HAVE | YOU WILL BECOME |
| Rubber plant | A tendency to be hard- hearted through lack of contact with reality | Attentive towards your friends and see material issues in the right perspective. |
| Mother in law plant | .. a feeling of constantly being betrayed or slandered, you oscilliate between anger and confusion. | Capable of refusing easy solutions, you will break away from situations which do not suit you. |
| Begonia | A perfectionist with confused desires. | .. capable of learning from your mistakes and will make commitments in spite of doubts. |
| Hydrangea | ..a prisoner of family quarrels. | .. an idealist who refuses the trappings of power. |

| | | |
|---|---|---|
| **Gemanium** | An agitated mind and unachievable goals. | .. independent and courageous, capable of affirming yourself no matter the situation or company. |

**SPICES**

| PLANTS | YOUARE/HAVE | YOUWILLBECOME |
|---|---|---|
| **Cinnamon** | .. the feeling that you are diminished if other are not fullsome in their praise of you. | .. modest , love honesty, detest a lack of sincerity. |
| **Nutmeg** | Susceptible, infantile in amorous relationships, tyrannical because of your hidden fragility. | Playful and charming, drawing on the world of children to live up the daily round. |
| **Cloves** | Changeable, varying from being inordinately over-confident to totally self deprecating. | Capable of doing without others' approval and of adapting to any situation. |
| **Pepper** | Incapable of expressing your desires for fear of breaking the rules. | Inspired by a deep sense of values and able to make long-term commitments when you are sure of your feelings |
| **Ginger, curry** | Unhealthy shy, you feel the need to feel protected by those around you. | Capable of living your own life whilst managing your nearest and dearest yet you will still be able to dispense with convention if need be. |

**HERBS**

| PLANTS | YOU ARE/HAVE | YOU WILL BECOME |
|---|---|---|
| **Borage** | .. convinced that you must atone for mistakes committed by the people around you. | .. capable of looking at other tolerantly and without prejudice. |
| **Clover** | A tendency to lose yourself in daily preoccupations to escape from reality. | .. organised, efficient, open, broad – minded. |
| **Lavender** | Worn out by an incessant steam of petty family disputes. | A peacemaker who knows the just measures of things. |
| **Horsetail** | Eternally misunderstood, too vulnerable to defend yourself. You have a constant sense of injustice. | .. acceptable and capable of taking an objective look at life |
| | under the impression that you are a victim and remain traumatised by painful emotional experience | … warm and ironic, will not let yourself be easily tamed. |

## A few preconceptions clarified

Much has been said about herbal medicine, some of it contradictory and some false ideas die hard while certain truth are not easily accepted. Here is the low – down on a few common preconceptions.

| | | | |
|---|---|---|---|
| 1. Herbalists no longer exist. | | 5. New method of administering plants have made them flavour of the month again | |
| **TRUE** | **FALSE** | **TRUE** | **FALSE** |
| 2. Herbal medicine is not a ' soft ' option | | 6. Plants are less effective than chemical medicine. | |
| **TRUE** | **FALSE** | **TRUE** | **FALSE** |
| 3. Herbal medicine is an old – fashioned medicine. | | 7. All diseases can be cured by plants. | |
| **TRUE** | **FALSE** | **TRUE** | **FALSE** |
| 4. Plants should not be used to treat children and old people. | | | |
| **TRUE** | **FALSE** | | |

**1. FALSE**

**2. TRUE:** Although it is a natural medicine it can be toxic and dangerous. This is why it is not advisable to follow treatment, without the advice of a specialist ( herbalist, pharmacist, doctor or therapist ) and why it is important to follow the directions scrupulously. Even non-toxic plants can cause problems if they are wrongly used, e.g., Too much liquorices can increase blood pressure and excessive dandelion can drain potassium reserves.

**3.FALSE:** Herbal medicine is certainly very old- its origins are lost in the proverbial mists of time. However , modern science has confirmed the therapeutic efficacy of plants, in the majority of cases, discovering substances within plants that confirm and explain their traditional uses.

**4. FALSE:** Plants are suitable for people of all ages. However, it is especially important that children and old people follow carefully the advice of a specialist and do not improvise the dose or treatment. The reason for this is that the negative side-effects of certain plants are stronger in the very young and the very old.

**5. TRUE:** Plants today are packaged in capsules, ampoules and drop that are simpler and easier to use and better adopted to the modern lifestyle.

**6. TRUE AND FALSE:** Plants provide ingredients for nearly 70 per cent of conventional medicines. Medicinal plants contain active substances that have a direct biological effect on the body, as to conventional medicines. Conventional medicines often contain a single active substance, whereas plants have a more complex structure. Conventional medicines have a more precise and rapid action but are often linked with troubling secondary effects, wheras plants act more slowly but are tolerated better by the body.

**7. FALSE:** We shouldn't ask too much from plants. They are powerless in curing some serious illness ( e.g., Cancer, AIDS, auto-immune diseases). However, they do offer useful complementary treatments. Moreover, we mustn't forget that scientists throughout the world are searching the plant world for medicines capable of curing today's incurable diseases.

The philosophy (logical positivism) that lies behind Western science in the way that Sankhya philosophy underpins Ayurveda, ensures that only phenomena that can be subjected to experimental observation are deemed worthy of consideration. This had led to the acceptance of the ideal of the double-blind trial as the arbiter of scientific truth. Each of us has to decide for ourselves whether or not to accept the premises of this science as the only truth. Ayurveda (among several indigenous philosophies and sciences) offer other truths that do not force us to reject the Western scientific approach but invite us to see it as one among various important bodies of theory, each of which is useful in explaining some of the world around us.

## HERBAL TREATMENTS FOR STRESS

It a period of strees is predictably about to occur, it can be prepared for ahead of time, as herbs, diet, and any appropriate lifestyle changes will minimize the impact. Nervine relaxants can be used regularly as gentle soothing remindes. The following herds can be taken as teas, cold drinks, infused in massage oil, or used in relaxing footbaths or full baths.

| | | |
|---|---|---|
| Balm | Linden | Red Clover |
| Chamomile | Mugwort | Skullcap |
| Lavender | Oats | St. John's Wort |

A daily supplement of vitamin B complex and vitamin C is also suggested. By using herbs and improving the diet, you are responding to stress in a healthy way, and the impact of the various stressors can be ameliorated. Relaxation exercises and an honest reevaluation of both lifestyle and life goals are invaluable. This is not always easy, but remember that people can change, change their lives, and reevaluate their choices.

The line between chronic stress and the daily levels we all seem to put up with is fuzzy. A gentle soul with a delicate constitution will cross the line sooner than a stronger person who copes well. Neither of these extremes is better that the other; they merely reflect the fact that we live in a world of human diversity. That's sometimes a joy and sometimes an actual cause of stress! The advice given above holds for chronic stress, but in addition, adaptogens become pivotal in this situation. Important examples are ginseng, Siberian ginseng, and ashwaganda.

Perhaps Siberian ginseng is the most highly recommended because it has no toxicity and lacks the stimulating effects some people experience with korean or American ginseng. The usual dosage of the tincture is ½ to ¾ teaspoon three times a day. Commercial products are increasingly made from a highly concentrated dry extract. First they are extracted using a liquid, which is dried to a powder and then made into tablets. An equivalent dosage using a solid extract concentrated at a ratio of 20:1 would by 100 to 200 mg. The recommended regime is usually for a six-week course followed by a two-week break. This regime can be repeated for as long as is necessary.

In addition to adaptogens, every attention must be given to general health as the body will often show its stress through some physical symptom. This may be a long-standing complaint that gets worse, an old problem that reappears, or just a speeding of the aging process.

There are times in most people's lives when things get to be too much and the pain of existence buildsto a crescendo. Immediate herbal relief may be needed in a whole range of traumatic situations-from being involved in a car accident to some personal emotional crisis. In all cases, herbs will take the edge off the trauma but will rarely remove it. At such times, herbs can be only an aid, just one element of the approach taken to deal with the difficulties being faced. This approach may also include seeking help from a health professional, going on vacation or a retreat, or even checking into a hospital.

The plants that are capable of easing intense stress are considered dangerious in our society, and because they are restricted drugs, they will not be discussed here. However, in addition to the herbs previously mentioned, the following remedies might be considered: passionflower, valerian, will lettuce.

**Basic Stress Formula**

1. 2 parts skullcap
2. 2 parts valerian
3. 1 part oats

*Take 1 teaspoon of tincture as needed.*

Noticethe doswatge here (1 teaspoon of tincture as needed). This is a recognition that the stress response has a cyclical nature and each person will find certain times of the day more challenging that others. As this is largely symptomatic medication, it may be increased until the desired relief is experienced. The dosage regime may be altered as necessary, varying time of day and quantity of dose to suit individual needs. For example this may be a large dose first thing in the morning, or smaller amounts at frequent intervals throughout the day. The patient's experience is the guiding principle here. Always treat the human being and not the theory about the disease.

*A possible prescription for acute stress associated with indigestion and palpitations:*

- 2 parts skullcap
- 2 parts valerian
- 1 part motherwort
- 1 part chamomile
- 1 part mugwort

*Take 1 teaspoon of tincture as needed. The motherwort supports relaxation but also has a specific calming impact an nalnitations*

## Anxiety

When the level of stress goes beyond the point of being a healthy stimulantand starts to adversely affect our health, it often takes the form of anxiety. It might surface as fear, apprehension, or a wide range of bodily symptoms. These are most prominent in the early stages of the illness and represent a reasonable reaction to the onset of illness and the related uncertainties.

Generalized anxiety disorder (GAD) is much more than the normal anxiety people experience day to day. It is chronic and exaggerated worry and tension, even though nothing seems to provoke it. Having this disorder means always anticipating disaster, often worrying excessively about health. Money, family, or work. Sometimes, though, the source of the worry is hard to pinpoint. Simply the through of getting through the day might provoke anxiety. People with GAD realize that their anxiety is more intense than the situation warrants. They also seem unable to relax and have trouble falling or staying asleep. Their worries are accompanied by any of the physical symptoms listed on the following page.

There may be no recognizable basis for the fear or feeling of threat, or that actual stimulus may be completely, the symportion to the emotion it provokes. Nevertheless, the symptoms it provokes are very real. For some people, anxiety takes the form of attacks that, through they occur unpredictably, may become associated with specific situations. They start with a sudden, intense apprehension, often combined with a feeling of impending doom and sometimes with feeling of unreality. Any of the symptoms described below may occur. An "anticipatory fear" or loss of control often develops, so that the person experiencing the attack becomes afraid of, being left alone in a public place. The anticipatory fear may itself precipitate other symptoms that escalate the attack.

People with panic disorder have feeling of terror that strike suddenly and repeatedly with no warning. They can't predict when an attack will occur, and many develop intense anxiety between episodes, worrying when and where the next one will strike. In between times there is a persistent, linger most attacks averages a couple of minutes, occasionally they can go on for up ten minutes. In rare cases, they may lat an hour or more.

## Symptoms of Anxiety

There are a whole range of reactions associated with anxiety.

Anxious mood. Worrying, apprehension, anticipation of the worst, irritability. The remedies. The herbal approaches described in the following section will be generally helpful, but the beach flower remedies are especially relevant. For example, aspen and rock rose are indicated in states of apprehension.

Fear. Of the dark being left alone, traffic, strangers, large animals, crowds.

The remedies. Again, it is the back flower remedies that shine here, especially cherry plum and minibus.

Cognitive symptoms. Difficulty in concentration, poor memory. Adapted from. Hamilton, M "The Assessment of Anxiety States by Rating" British journal of Medical Psychology, 32,1959,pp.-50-55.

The remedies. The specifies suggested for stress management' given in the following pages are indicated with the possible addition of gink go and rosemary to help with difficulty in concentration and poor memory Basil essential oil can be used to aid concentration as an inhalation. A "brain tonic" tea can easily be made to increase memory and improve the ability to concentrate. Mix in a cup of boiling water for ten to fifteen minutes. Drink three times a day.

- Rosemary, 1 part.
- Yerba mate, 1 part.
- Ginkgo leaves, 4 parts.
- Gout kola, 2 parts.

Depressed Mood. Loss of interest, depression, depression, diurnal mood swings, lack of pleasure in hobbies, early waking.

The remedies. In addition to the humbly suggestions that follow, the Back flower remedies can be especially relevant. Consider gentian, gorse, mustard, olive, sweet chestnut, and wild rose.

Generally body Sensations. Tinnitus, hot and cold flushes, prickling sensations, blurred vision, feeling of weakness.

The remedies. All of the relaxing nerviness and relaxing exercises will ease this group of symptoms.

Respiratory Symptoms. Pressure of construction in chest, tightness of breath, feelings of chocking, sighing.

The remedies. All of the relaxing nervines and relaxing exercise will ease this group of symptoms.

Genitourinary symptoms. Frequency in urination, suppressed menstrual periods, frigidity, premature eaculations, impotence, urgency of urination, excessive bleeding furing period, loss of erection.

The remedies. These symptoms can be treted with herbal medicines that are not directly relevant to the topic of steer management. This highlights the need for competent diagnosis to ensure appropriate treatment. See herbs for women's Health by Me's Brove, N.D. And Linda Condtrella, n.D. and Herbs for men's Health by CJ Puptiopns (keats publishing).

Physiological Symptoms. Tremor of hands, strained face, swallowing swwating, furrowed brow, facial pallor, belching, eyelid twiching.

The remedies. All of the antispasmodics, relaxing nervines. And relaxing exercise will ease this group symptoms.

Tension. Feeling of tension, inability to relax, easily moved to tears, feeling of restlessnes, fatiguc, startled response, trembling.

The remidies. Again, the relaxing nervines and relaxing exercise, will help, but in addition, the essential oils of lavender and rose geranuum are especially helpful. The back flower Remedies hornbeam, olive, and rock should alod be considered.

General Sonatic symptoms. Muscular aches and paints, muscular twitching, musccular stiffness, grinding teeth.

The remedies. Muscle-relaxing antispasmodies such as crampbark and the stronger relaxing nervines such as valerian are effective here.

Cardivascular Symptoms. Tachcardia, chest pain, feelings of faintness, palpitations, throbbing of blood vessels, skipped heartbeats. The remedies. Herbal medicine has much to offer for the gentle treatment of heart probles in this body system and are discussed in Herbs for the Heart by CJ uotion (keats publising).

Gastrointestinal symptoms. Difficulty in swallowing idigestion. Hertburn, loosenes of bowels, constipation, gas, burps, bloating, weight loss.

The remedies. One of the strengths of herbal medicine is its efficary in the treatment of digestive system problems, and especially those that are stress-releated. This is discussed below and in much more depth in Herbs to improve Digestion by CJ Puotien (Kets publishing).

Autonomic nervous system symptoms. Dry mouth, pallor, giddiness, flushing, tendency to sweat.

The remedies. All of the relaxing nervines and relaxing exercise will ease this group symptoms.

## Depression

Depression is a state of mind familiar to almost everyone, but this very familiarity becomes problematic when approaching clinical depressive states. In ordinary usage, the word refers to a mood state that in medicine is called dysthymia, as constrasted with the normal state of elation. In psychiatric usage, disorders of mood are called effecive disorder, depression can be such a disease in itself or a symptom of another mental disorder. Normal human response to some situations may also include transient depression.

Major depression occurs in 10 to 20 per cent of the world's population in the course of a lifetime. Woman are more often affected than men by a two-to-one ratio, and they seem to be at particular risk in the period prior to menstruction or following childbirth. Relatives of patients with major depression also seem to be at home higher risk of becoming depressed, and about 2 per cent of the population may have a chronic disorder known as a depressive personality.

Depression is defined by a standard set of symptoms described in the American Psychiatric Association's Diagnostic and Statistical manual of mental Disorders. They are:

- Poor appetite and significant weight loss, or increaed and significant weight loss, or increased appetite and significant weight gain.
- Insomnia or increased sleep.
- Agitation or retardation of movement and throught.
- Loss of interest or pleasure in usual activities or decrease in sexual drive.
- Fatigue and loss of energy.
- Feelings of worthlessness, self-reproach, or excessive or inappropriate guilt.
- Diminished ability to think or concentrate, indecisiveness.
- Recurrent throughts of death or suicide, or sucide attampts.

Not all of these characteristics occur in each individual who becomes depressed. For purposes of psychiatric treatment, a person is considered to have experienced a major depressive episode if he or she exhibits a loss of intrest or pleasure in all or almost all usual activities day for a period of at least two weeks. The term "depression" is often modified by words that imply either some specific factor, or some chemical mechanish is cause of the state.

- Depressions that are reactions to some loss of or separation from a valued person or object are called reactive (or exogenous) depressions.
- This contrasts with the usually more serve depressions, without apparent cause, called endogenous depressions, or those accompanied by delusions.

## Specific Ramedies for Depression

St. John's wort (Hypercricum) has a long tradation of use in Europe, and while it sometimes gets remarkable results. It is also sometimes ineffective. It takes time to work, so it must be taken for at least a month.

A double-blind clinicl trial was conducted in 1993 testing the antidepepressent effects with depressions of short duration were treated in a double-blind study either with 300 mg of St. John's wort extrat thre time a day or with a placebo. After four weeks of treatment, 67 per cent of the participants experienced a positive improvement.

Other lifestyle issues must also be addressed in the treatment of depression. From green salads to relaxation,from spinal adjustments, from spinal adjustment to listening to music, the list is endless. Exercise is especially important.

*Basic Formula for Depressions*

- 2 part S. John's wort
- 1 part oats
- 1 part lavender
- 1 part mugwort

*Take 1 teaspoon of tincture three times a day at least one month.*

The Textbook of natural Medicine by joseph Pizzorno and michael Murray, N.D. Suggests the following nuttitional supplements.

- Vitamin B complex, 50 to 150 daily
- Vitamin C, 1 gram three times daily
- Folic acid, 400 mcg daily
- Vitamin $B_{12}$, 250 mcg dily
- Magnesium, 500 mg daily

## Indigestion

Digestive system symptoms can be unpleasant way for the stress response to manifest.

Every herbalist and every culture have their favorite remedies for indigestion. European specifis include gentian, peppermint, chamomile, balm, hops, and valerian. Often a tea made from a single fresh remedy is best. This should be an herb with a taste and atoma. Ideally, it should be plant you could easily cultivate, thus providing a steady supply of fresh leaves. These simple teas can be augmented By using a combination of tinctures to aid the digestive system in general.

**Indigesion Tincture**

Mix equal parts.

- Gentian
- Chamomile
- Valerian
- Peppermint

*Take ½ teaspoon tea minutes before eating.*

## Hypertension

There are over 35 million hypertensives in the united States, with twic as many african American for this are not know-Although hypertension is a common problem in our culture, it is rare in cultures that are relatively untouched by the Western lifestyle. Stress plays a major role in causing and maintaining hypertension. Dietary, psychological, and social factors must all be addressed any real change to occur.

Hypertension Formula

- 2 parts hawthorn
- 1 part linden
- 1 part yarrow
- 1 part crampbark
- 1 part valerian

*Take plants of tincture three times a day. Other plants might also be included depending upon the specific symptoms. Here is a possible mixture for hypertension where strees is a major factor.*

- 2 parts hawthorn
- 1 part lin den
- 1 part yarrow
- 1part Siberian ginseng
- 1 part skullcap
- 1part crampbark
- 1 part valerian

*Take 1 teaspoon of tincture three times a day.*

A number of herbs are specific hypertension, unsually working because of their impact on one or another of the processes involved in conditions development. The most important plant remedy within western medicine is hawthorn, probably followed by linden. Garlic is also effective for lowering hingh blood pressure and should be used in cooking and as a dietary supplement.

## Premenstrual Syndrome (PMS)

This describes a broad range pf symptoms that occur cylically and which are severe to disturb a women's life patterns or cause her to seek help from a health practitioner. Most women experience some body change cyclically during the menstruating years corresponding to the pattern of cycling hormones.

From my clinic experience, I would suggest skullcap as ideally suited for relief of the psychological symptoms, though various other remedies may pct as well for specific women, so generalizations are problematic. Longer-term, hormonally focused herbal treatments are very effective but beyond the scope of this book.

# HERBAL TREATMENT TO RELIVES STRESS

Herbs can help the body and mind cope with the stress response in a number of ways, in addition to the rather simplistic ones of stimulation and relaxation. In Western herbalism today, it is common to differentiate between groups of herbs that have similar physiological effects on people. Herbs that act on the nervous system are collectively called nerviness, and are grouped into nervine tonics, nervine relaxants, and nervine stimulants. There are also muscle-relaxing antispasmodics and sleep-inducers known as hypnotics. Of most direct relevance for stress management are the adaptogenic herbs.

## Types of Herbs

### Adaptogens

As we approach the twenty-first century, we live in a world of stress, pollution, lack of meaning, and lack of purpose. In the face of such a cultural alienation from nature, the plethora of diseases assailing the "civilized" world should come as no surprise. To heal these ills, the underlying causes must first be addressed and these causes are not only within the individual but within our culture as a whole. When a health problem is related to lowered resistance due to the impact of a hostile environment, we must first heal the hostile environment. In other words, even if there were a remedy that offered individuals protection against toxic chemicals, it would be preferable to remove the toxic chemical from the environment. This makes economic sense, is the right stance in Hippocratic terms, and is right action in spiritual terms.

When attention is given to appropriate support for the body under stressful conditions, nature comes to our rescue. Technically, what is needed is an increase in nonspecific resistance to damaging man-made factors and illnesses. A range of herbal remedies are coming to light that do this. Soviet scientists coined the term "adaptogens" to describe herbs that produce this wonder increase in resistance and vitality, defining them like this:

- An adaptogen must show a nonspecific activity, i.e., increase in power of resistance against physical, chemical, or biological noxious agents.
- An adaptogen must have a normalizing influence independent of the nature of the pathological state.
- An adaptogen must be innocuous and must not influence normal body functions more that required.

In this sense, adaptogens reinforce the nonspecific power of resistance against stressors, increase general capacities to withstand situations of stress, and hence guard against disease caused by overstress of the organism. The general aim of adaptogen treatment is a reduction of stress reactions during the alarm phase of the stress response, prevention or at least delaying of the state of exhaustion, and hence a certain level of protection against long-term stress.

A number of herbs that can be described as adaptogens include ginseng, Siberian ginseng, ashwaganda, shiitake, and schizandra. It is worth looking at the evidence for adaptogenicity in a little depth. Rather than exploring the back ground for all these adaptogenic herbs, we will focus on Siberian ginseng.

## Siberian ginseng

*(Eleutherococcus senticosus)*

Siberian ginseng, one of the most remarkable of the adaptogenic plants, has a wide range of uses and very low toxicity. There has been a great deal of excellent clinical and laboratory research conducted in the Soviet Union, where Professor Brehkman and his team have been studying the herb for over thirty years. Large-scale clinical trials have been undertaken on both healthy and sick people with more than 1,000 published research papers devoted to its application, the mechanism of action, and investigation of its active principles.

Pharmacological research suggested that the active principle of the adaptogenic plants – the eleutherosides from Siberian ginseng and the panaxosides from ginseng – are saponin glyhcosides, which increase the general nonspecific resistance of the body to a whole range of diverse chemical, physical, psychological, and biological factors. Its safety and ability to increase the resistance of the normal human body to extreme conditions make Siberian ginseng a remedy of great importance.

Studies on Siberian ginseng provide some of the best clinical trials done on herbal medicines so far. Large numbers of people including control groups were involved in these studies. Between 1973 and 1975, 1,200 drivers from the volgaies automobile plant were given 8 to 12 mg of Siberian ginseng extract daily with tea for two months each year in the spring and autumn. By the end of the experiment, illness among the drivers had decreased by 20 to 30 per cent, while the total disease incidence among other workers at the plant increased by 20 per cent. Based on these results, the authorities at the factory undertook a mass program of preventive medicine with the herb in the winter of 1975. In was included in the diet as Siberian ginseng sugar at a per day dose of 2 ml. Altogether, 13,096 persons were engaged in the experiment. The overall disease incidence dropped by 30 to 35 per cent as compared to a control group that did not use the remedy.

In another clinical trial, a group of fifty-four miners received the extract before the beginning of their shift daily in June and July of 1976. The number of people reporting sick dropped by 33.3 per cent and the number of days lost through illness dropped by 45.6 per cent. Reduction of the incident of influenza and acute respiratory diseases was particularly impressive. In a strict medical sense, Siberian ginseng is an adrenal stimulant and not an antiviral remedy. However, the Russians have accumulated much data on the anti-influenzal effect of the herb as well. Such findings imply that either it possesses an invingorating and tonic action on natural immunity or it has direct antivirus activity.

**Conditions shown to improve with Siberian ginseng**

There is an ever-lengthening list of pathologies that have been demonstrated to improve with the use of this adaptogen. Here is a short list based on published results:

- Neurasthenia
- Hypertension
- Chronic gastritis
- Diabetes
- Atheroscherosis
- Tuberculosis
- Brain Injuries
- Infectious diseases

## Cancer

Siberian ginseng is also being used in Russia for the postoperative treatment of cancer patients. Not only does it speed it speed postoperative recovery, but it ameliorates the stress response that can aggravate metastasis, the spreading of cancer cells around the body. The ability of Siberian ginseng to potentiate antitumor immunity has also been discovered recently. It increases antineoplastic white blood cells (natural "killer cells") and induces the synthesis of γ-interferon by leukocytes. It is well known that stress decreases the activity of the immune system and particularly that of the natural killer cells. An obvious association exists here on a biochemical level between stress, immune function, and the herb Siberian ginseng.

In these times of pollution and exposure to strange and dangerous chemicals, this fascinating plan may prove of vital help as it also reduces the toxic impact of a number of chemical compounds. In laboratory tests, Siberian ginseng was shown to decrease the sensitivity of mice and rats to the toxicity of a range of chemicals. When the animals were treated with cytotoxic drugs combined with Siberian ginseng, they lost weight and their white blood count was higher the drugs alone. The implications for using this herb as support in anticancer chemotherapy are clear and exciting.

A fundamental problem with the use of cytotoxic drugs in cancer therapy is that they destroy not only cancer cells but healthy ones as well. In the test, lethal doses of the drugs resulted in the animals, death, but when Siberian ginseng and drugs were used in combination, the death rate dropped. In a group of mice given thiophosphamide in a dose of mg./kg, 53 per cent of the animal died. Similar results were obtained in group of animals given ethymidin in a does of 1.5 mg/kg. Thirty per cent so treated died, while all those receiving both the herb and drug remained alive.

Siberian ginseng also appears able to reduce the narcotic effects of a number of drugs. For example, it shortens the duraprophylactic of sleep induced by sedatives. It may also prove useful for prophylactic and therapeutic application in acute and chornicpoisoning with some insecticides and industrial poisons. This ability of Siberian ginseng is linked with its ability to activate. This body's own metabolic system for inactivating toxins. Therefore, Russian pharmacologists advise the use of the extract in different drug formulae to reduce their inherent toxicity.

It is clear that Siberian ginseng is a very special remedy indeed. It can increase individual resistance to the whole spectrum of factors that contribute to stress reactions and exhaustion. Apparently, the herb will help whether the stress is from extremes of weather or from psychological exhaustion. Its universal properties make this herb one of the most efficacious and promising medicines for increasing hardiness against the many stresses of contemporary life.

### Nerviness

A nervine is plant that has an effect upon the nervous system in some way: there are nervine tonics, nervine relaxants, and nervine stimulants. Remember that any successful treatment of nervous system problems with herbs must involve treating the whole body, heart, and mind, not simply the sings of agitation and worry. Of course, the agitation can be reduced greatly by the appropriate herbs, but the whole system must be strengthened in the face of the storm as well.

## Nervine tonics

Perhaps the most helpful contribution herbal medicine can make is to strengthen and *"feed"* the nervous system. In cases of shock, stress, or nervous debility, the nervine tonics strengthen and restore the tissues directly. On the other hand, they can contribute to the healing of damaged nervous tissue, whether this is due to a pathological process or physical trauma. This invaluable group of remedies is best nervous system but appears to work via its vasodilating action on the blood.

| MILD RELAXING NERVINESS | | |
|---|---|---|
| *Balm* | *Chamomile* | *Lavender* |
| *Black cohosh* | *Hyssop* | *Red clover* |
| **MEDIUM RELAXING NERVINESS** | | |
| *Damiana* | *Motherwort* | *Skullcap* |
| *Linder* | *Mugwort* | *St. John's wort* |
| *Lobelia* | *Pulsatilla* | *Vervain* |
| **STRONG RELAXING NERVINES** | | |
| *California poppy* | *Passionflower* | *Wild lettuce* |
| *Hops* | *Valerian* | |

Vessels of the brain, thereby increasing oxygen availability to brain cells, other nervine tonics can have, in addition, a relaxing effect. Skullcap is often the most effective, particular for problems related to stress.

## Nervine relaxants

This group of nerviness are extremely useful in our times of stress and confusion, alleviating many of the accompanying symptoms. They should always be used in a broad holistic way, not simply to tranquilize. Too much tranquilizing, even that achieved through herbal medication, can in time deplete and weigh heavily on the whole nervous system.

Many of the nervine relaxants also have other properties and can be selected to aid in related problem. This is one of the great benefits problem. The physical symptoms to help in stress and anxiety may be treated with herbs that work on the anxiety itself. They can also be grouped in terms of their relative stregth, bearing in mind that not all people respond to herbs in the same way.

Since each system of the body has plants that ate particularly suited to it, relaxing nervous can be selected based on their affinity for the various system.

- **Circulatory system.** Balm, linden, and motherwort are generally helpful to the cardiovascular system. However, most remedies that reduce over activity in the nervous system will and the heart and ameliorate problem such as high blood pressure.
- **Respiratory System.** Most sedatives will help in asthma, but black cohosh, lobelia, motherwort, and wild lettuce are especially helpful.
- **Digestive System.** All the relaxing and antispasmodic remedies may be of a value here to ease colic, but sedatives that actively digestion include balm, chamomile, and lavender.
- **Reproductive System.** Black cohosh, blue cohosh, crampbark motherwort, and wild lettuce all have an affinity for this system.
- **Muscles and Skeleton.** All sedative remedies will ease muscular tension and thus pain in this complex system. Black cohosh is especially helpful.
- **Nervous System.** All the remedies mentioned above relate here.
- **Skin.** All these nerviness may help the skin in an indirect way, but the following herbs are especially beneficial for the skin red clover, St. john's wort, pulsatilla and black cohosh.

While any of the above nerviness will be generally relaxing another way to select the herb (or herb) that will prove most appropriate is to take into account their other properties. The range of options and the various subtleties can be daunting and complex, but as example consider the list below. It combines the need for relaxation with other common symptoms as an indication for relevant herbs.

- **Delayed menstruation.** Black cohosh, motherwort, mugwort.
- **Diarrhea.** Black haw, cramp bark hops, linden.
- **Muscle tightness.** Black cohosh, black how, cramp bark hops, lavender, lobelia, valerian.
- **Colic.** Balm, black haw. Chamomile, hops, hyssop, lavender, linden, mugwort, valerian.
- **Sinus congestion.** Chamomile, hyssop, linden.
- **Heartburn.** Balm, cohosh, Jamaician dogwood.
- **Skin problem.** Red clover
- **Flatulence.** Balm, chamomile, hopes, hyssop, lavender.
- **Hypertension.** Linden, motherwort, passionflower, skullcap, valerian,
- **Asthma.** Lobelia, motherwort, wild cherry bark wild lettuce.
- **Menstrual cramps.** Black cohosh, blue cohosh, crampbark motherwort, skullcap, valerian, wild lettuce.

## Nervine stimulants

Direct stimulation of the nervous tissue is not often needed in out times of hyperactivity. It is usually more appropriate to stimulate the body's innate vitality with the help of nervine or bitter tonics, which work by augmenting bodily harmony and thus have a much deeper and longer-lasting effect than nervine stimulants. In the last century, much more emphasis was placed by herbalists upon stimulant herbs. It is perhaps, a sign of the times that our world is supplying us with more than enough stimulus.

When direct nervine stimulation is indicated, an herb to use is kola nut, although guarana, coffee, mate, and tea should also stimulants is that they have a number of side effects and can themselves be involved in aggravating psychotically problems such as anxiety and tension.

Some of the herbs rich in volatile oils are also valuable stimulants; among them the commonest and best rosemary and peppermint.

## Antispasmodics

In addition to the herbs that work directly on the nervous system, the antispasmodic herbs – which affect the peripheral nerves and the muscle tissue – can have an indirect relaxing effect on the body. When the physical body is at ease, a relaxed psych follows. Many of the nervine relaxants have this antispasmodic action. The autonomic nervous system and not necessarily the central nervous system. This allows a physical relaxation of muscles without a sedative effect upon consciousness.

### ANTISPASMODIC

| | | |
|---|---|---|
| Balam | Jamaicn | Roman |
| Black cohosh | Dogwood | Chamomile |
| Black haw | Lavender | Rosemary |
| Bugleweed | Licorice | Skullcap |
| California | Linden | Skumk cabbage |
| Poppy | Lobelia | St.john's wort |
| Catmint | Motherwort | Sundew |
| Celery seed | Mugwort | Thyme |
| Chamomile | Mullein | Valerian |
| Crampbark | Parsley | Wild cherry |
| Damiana | Pasque flower | Wild lettuce |
| Ginger | Passion flower | Wild yam |
| Hyssop | Peppermint | |
| Hops | Red clover | |

Listed below are some common conditions and the appropriate antispasmodic herbs for relieving them:

- **Delayed menstruation.** Black cohosh, caraway, motherwort, mugwort, pennyroyal.
- **Diarrhea.** Black haw, bugleweed, crampbark, ground ivy, hops, linden, red sage, rosemary, St. John's wort, wild cherry.
- **Muscle tightness.** Black cohosh, black haw, crampbark hops, lavender, lobelia, Valerian.
- **Colic.** Angelica, aniseed, balm, caraway, cardamom, catnip, chamomile, dill, fennel, fenugreek, ginger, hops, hyssop, lavender, motherwort, mugwort, parsley, pennyroyal, peppermint, red sage, Roman chamomile, rosemary, thyme, valerian, Vervain, wild carrot.
- **Sinus congestion.** Betony, catmint, chamomile, coltsfoot, elder, fenugreek, ginger, hyssop, lavender, linden, mullein, peppermint, red sage, thyme.
- **Heartburn.** Coltsfoot, fenugreek, licorice, mullein.
- **Arthritis.** Angelica, black cohosh, celery seed, elder, lavender, licorice, linden, wild yam.
- **Skin problems.** Black cohosh, red clover.
- **Flatulence.** Balm, chamomile, hops, hyussop, lavender, motherwort, mugwort, valerian.
- **Hypertension.** Linden, motherwort, passionflower, skullcap, valerian.
- **Asthma.** Labelia, motherwort, wild cherry bark wild lettuce.
- **Menstrual Cramps.** Black cohosh, black haw, crampbark motherwort, skullcap, valerian, wild lettuce.

## Hypnotics

Hypnotics are herbal remedies that will help to induce a deep and healing state of sleep. They have nothing at all to do with hypnotic trances. Herbs that promote sleep have modes of action that vary from mild, muscle relaxing properties, through volatile oils that ease psychological tensions, to remedies that contain strong alkaloids that work directly on the central nervous system and put you to sleep. Some of the most effective plant hypnotics are illegal for the very reason of their effectiveness. This includes the whole range of opium poppy derivatives. The remedies mentioned here are entirely safe and have no addictive properties. When treating sleep problems, hypnotic herbs should always be used in conjunction with attention to relaxation, diet, and lifestyle.

Each system of the body has plants that are particularly suited to it, some of which are hypnotics of varying strength. It is safe to say, however, that all the hypnotic remedies can help the whole body in that sleep is such a vital health process.

- **Circulatory system.** Motherwort, linden, balm. They are all in the milder group.
- **Respiratory system.** All the hypnotics can help as antispasmodics in conditions such as asthma, if used at the right does. Wild lettuce eased irritable coughs.
- **Digestive system.** The relaxing nerviness and carminatives are important, especially balm, chamomile, hops, and valerian. The antispasmodic herbs will help with intestinal colic, for example, hops, Jamaican dogwood, passionflower, and valerian.
- **Muscles and skeleton.** All hypnotics will aid and in reducing muscle tension and even the pain associated with problems in this system. They may be used internally or as lotion. Especially important are Jamaican dogwood and valerian.
- **Skin.** Chamomile and cowship are healing, but otherwise the value of hypnotics here is to ensure that the body has a good recuperative rest each night.

| MILD HYPNOTICS | MEDIUM HYPNOTICS | STRONG HYPNOTICS |
|---|---|---|
| Chamomile | California poppy | Hops |
| Linden | Motherwort | Jamaican dogwood |
| Mugwort | Pulsatilla | Passionflower |
| | Skullcap | Pulsatilla |
| | | Valerian |
| | | Wild lettu |

## Herbal Medicine for Natural Healing

### Thankuni or Mandukparni

Centella assiatica is a small herbaceous annual plant of the family Apiacease, native to Asia. It has been used as a medicinal herb for thousands of years in in india, China and Indonesia.

- Its ability to heal wounds, improves mental clarity, and treat skin conditions such as leprosy and psoriasis are important reasons for its extensive use.
- As per Ayurveda, the herb is one of the chief herbs for revitalising the nerves and brain cells; hence primarity known as a brain food in India.
- Its has been used for the purposes like boosting memory, wound healing, a mild diuretic, increasing concentration, alertness, as well as anti-anxiety and anti-stress.

## Brahmi

Brahmi represents the creative energy of this Universe. The plant Brahmi stands for the personified energy of Brahma which induces all creativity specifally those of sensory organs in the body.

- It is the main revitalising herb for the nerves and the brain cells.
- It increases intelligence, longevity, circulation in the brain and improves both short term and long term memory;
- It decreases senility and aging. It fortifies the immune system, both cleansing and feeding it and strengthens the adrenals
- At the same time, it is a powerful blood purifier and is specific for chronic skin diseases, including leprosy and syphilis, as well as eczema and psoriasis.
- It is cerbrovascular stimulating, a circulatory stimulant, and it accelerates wound healing.

**Basil**

Basil of the Family Lanmiaceae, is perhaps the most sacred plant sacred plant of India.

- It contains natural mercury, which, as the semen of Shiva gives the Shiva, gives the seed power of pure awareness.
- Basil is an effective diaphoretic and febrifuge in most colds, flus and lung problems.
- It removes excess Kapha from the lunge and nasal passages, increasing Prana and promoting sensory acuity.
- It also removes high Vata from the colon, improves absorption and strengthens the nerve tissue, increasing memory, It has the property of destroying bacteria and insects.

**Amlaki / Anola**

A deciduous tree with small leaves which are very closely set in pinnate fashion. Flowers are pale green, so are the fruits. They are the remedies for-

- Indigestion
- Jaundice
- Rich source of vitamin C, hence prevents asthma.
- Root bark is astringent and useful in ulcerative stomatitis
- Leaves are useful for conjunctivits, dyspepsia, dysentery.
- Fruits are useful for stomachic, laxative, aphrodisiac, bronchits, skin diseases and graying hair.

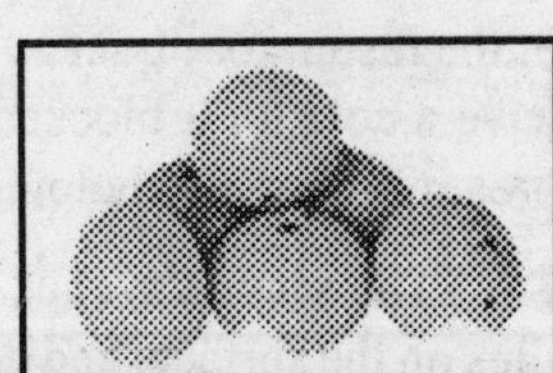

Ayurveda ascribes amazing curative powers to the Neem. This is reflected in the term- "Neem-Hakim". Then there is the Neem-panehang- (1) Roots (2) Bark (3) Gum (4) Leaves (5) Fruits Kernel and Oil-which furnishes a variety of antivirals-antibacterials, fungivides and other bioactive substances. These have been found effective against a host of ailments ranging from chages diseases to Malaria.

Countless Indians today use Neem-twigs called "datun" - as disposable tooth-brushes-for white healthy teeth. Dried neem leaves are put in stroed-grain-clothes and books to protect them from pests. Neem leaves are used for skin-ailments and rituals. Neem oil-cakes curb pests, improve the soil and serve as a nourshing animal feed.

All this explains why the Africans call Neem- "Muarubaini" means Forty-uses of cures". The sanskrit name for the Neem "Arishta" means wonder-off of evil and pestilence. Parsians-they called it- "Azad-dirakht-Hind"- which literally means- "Free-tree of India".

So salute the Neem next time you see the tree.

# CHAPTER 14 Aromatherapy, Rekhi

## THERAPEUTIC APPLICATION

The second part of the word aromatherapy implies a kind of action. How do we apply these special natural fragrances? Well, there are two pathways for essential oils to enter the human body.

First, there is the avenue provided by breathing and the lungs. We have just explored the sense of smell via the nose, but of course we also breathe through the mouth. Essential oils can travel through the mouth into the passageways of the respiratory tract as far as the lungs. Pungent oils such as Eucalyptus are a good example of this at work; if you have a cold, or a blocked nose, inhaling such a powerful aroma will open up the respiratory passages, improving breathing and also helping to loosen mucus, making it easier to cough.

The second avenue of entry is via the skin. The skin has many layers; overlapping cells like microscopic roof tiles on the surface, and deeper layers richly supplied with blood vessels, nerves, sweat glands and oil glands. Taking baths with essential oils as well as using massage brings these oils into direct contact with your skin. The warmth of bath water or the friction heat generated by massage helps the tiny essential oils molecules to pass through the top layer of the skin and enter the bloodstream. From there they can be used by the body where needed, passing out of the system via the kidneys. Massaging an aching back with Rosemary, for example, will give a feeling of warmth to the muscles, improving local blood supply and easing away stiffness.

Essential oils fall into different groups according to what they do. Calming oils such as Lavender or Orange Blossom help to ease physical pain, soothing aching muscles or headaches, and have a sedative effect on body and mind. Pungent oils such as Black Pepper or Cardamon have an energising effect, warming poor circulation, producing a feeing of physical vituality. Fresh oils such as Peppermint or Rosemary are stimulating, cleansing the body and removing toxins as well as improving concentration. Citrus aromas such as Lemon or Mandarin aid the flow of digestive juices, tonifying the system; they also help combat depression.

# THE POWER OF SMELL

We are often unaware of our sense of smell: many people only notice it when it is temporarily absent. For example, during a heavy cold we notice that everything feels *remote,* and that food has no taste. This is because 80 percent of what we taste comes from our sense of smell; only 20 per cent comes from the tongue. If someone loses their sense of smell permanently, this can actually cause severe depression. Why? Because we rely very deeply on the sense of smell to add richness and vitality to our experience of the world around us.

Smells register via the nose as we breathe, travelling up the nostrils and triggering nerve impulses which fire instantly into the brain. Thousands of these reactions occur daily, even when we are asleep. Smells have a strong influence on our well-being because they affect areas inside the brain linked to moods, emotions or feelings, as well as chemical balances in the body. So, aromas which make you feel mentally calm also trigger internal chemical changes, relaxing your body. Fragrances which are more revitalising stimulate the brain, wake you up and give you a feeling of energy.

Some impulses received by the sense of smell affect areas deep inside the brain which are beyond conscious awareness; very often reactions to smells are expressed as non-verbal sounds such as 'mmmm" or 'urgh!" These show that our responses to smells are instinctive, a simple "like" or "dislike". This is evident in small children who automatically reach toward what smells good and move abruptly away from what smells bad.

In adults, strong instinctive responses to aromas usually stem from associated memories. The French writer, 'Marcel Proust's epic novel, *Ala recherche du temps perud* (In Search of Lost Time) centres on one smell - a Madeleine cake dipped in lime-flower tea - which triggers powerful, detailed memories of his early life.

If you have never before paid much attention to your sense of smell, it is fun to start observing it more closely. For example, simply go outside and walk about for 20 minutes, to see how many scents you detect. You may be surprised by the number of aromas there are!

## Essential oils

Learn how to use essential oils and extracts of aromatic plants to heal the body and calm the soul, by using floral remedies and flower extracts.

| | **PLANT EXTRACTS** | | |
|---|---|---|---|
| ***OIL*** | ***PROPERTIES*** | ***INDICATIONS*** | ***HOW TO USE*** |
| Basil (Ocimum basilicum) | Analgesic, expectorant, tonic | Fatigue, migraine, colds, coughs, nausea | Inhalations, oral consumption, massage, baths. |
| Bergamot (Citrus bergamia) | Antiseptic, stimulant | Depression, fatigue, skin problems. | Inhalations, compresses, baths, massage. |
| Bois de rose (Rosa centifolia) | Antiseptic, sedative. | Skin problems, wrinkles, stress | Massage, baths. |
| Camomille (Matricaria) | Anti-inflammatory, sedative, antispasmodic. | Stress, anxiety, insomnia, inflammation, stomach problems. | Compresses, oral consumption, baths. |
| Cinnamon (Cinamomum) | Antiseptic, analgesic, anti-inflammatroy, tonic | Infectious diseases, respiratory diseases, fatigue | Oral consumption, inhalations, massage. |
| Cumin (Cuminium cyminum) | Digestive | Indigestion, liver problems | Oral consumption, massage |
| Eucalyptus (eucalyptus globules) | Antiseptic, anti-inflammatory, analgesic, expectorant, balsamic. | Bronchial diseases, herpes, cystitis, rheumatism. | Massage, inhalations, baths. |

| | | | |
|---|---|---|---|
| Garlic (Allium sarivum) | Antiseptic, lowers blood pressure, antiviral | Wounds, high blood-pressure, coughs, colds. | Massage, oral consumption |
| Jasmine (Jasminum officnale) | Sedative, tonic, moisturising. | Stress, nervousness, depression, dry skin. | Oral consumption, message, baths. |
| Juniper (Juniperus communis) | Antispasmodic, antiseptic, stimulant, carminative, diuretic. | Liver problems, urinary infections, rheumatism, cellulite. | Baths, oral consumption, massage. |
| Lavender (Lavandula officinalis) | Antiseptic, tonic, diuretic, astringent. | Fatigue, skin problems, infections, warts. | Compress, baths, gargles, oral consumption, massage. |
| Lemon (Citrus limonum) | Antiseptic, antiviral, analgesic, sedative. | Burns, skin infections, stress, insomnia, anxiety, headaches. | Massage, baths, oral consumption. |
| Oregano (Origanum vulgare) | Antiseptic, antiviral, inhalations, anti-inflammatory, appetite-stimulant | Respiratory problems, viral infections, loss of appetite. | Oral consumption, compresses, massage. |
| Peppermint (Mentha piperita) | Stimulatnt, analgesic, antiseptic, helps the liver. | Nausea, headaches, colds, tiredness, emotional shocks. | Oral consumption, inhalations, compresses, massage. |
| Rosemary (Rosmarinus officinalis) | Antiseptic, fungicide, diuretic, stimulant, antidepressant. | Fatigue, sprains, water retention, rheumatism. | Oral consumption, massage, baths |
| Seville orange (Citrus aurantium) | Sedative, hypnotic, antiseptic, lowers blood-pressure | Skin problems, stress, insomnia, high blood pressure | Baths, massage, compresses. |
| Tea tree (Melaleuca altemifolia) | Antiseptic, fungicide, antibiotic, antiviral | Fungal diseases, thrush, infectious diseases | Inhalations, compresses, baths, massage |
| Thyme (Thymus vulgaris) | Antiseptic, antiviral, anti-inflammatory, tonic | Infectious diseases, viral illnesses, fatigue rheumatism | Oral consumption, inhalations. |
| Vervain (Verbena officinalis) | Tonic, digestive,antiseptic | Fatigue, indigestion | Oral consumption, massage |
| Ylang-Ylang (Cananga bdorata) | Sedative, antidepressant, lowers blood-pressure | Stress, nervousness, depression, high blood pressure | Baths, massage, diffusion in atmosphere. |

## Dr. Bach's 38 floral remedies

### THE SUBTLETY OF FLOWERS

| REMEDY | FLOWER OF ORIGIN | INDICATIONS |
|---|---|---|
| Agrimony | *Agrimonia eupatoria* | Helps those who hide their malaise under an exterior of cheerfulness to regain inner peace and harmony. |
| Beech | *Fagus sylvatica* | Quietens intolerant, critical people who believe themselves always in the right. |
| Centauria | *Centaurea* | Strengthens the will, reinforces the capacity to assert oneself and to find one's rightful place. |
| Cerato | *Ceratostigma willmottianum* | Helps those who find it difficult to take the initiative and rely on others. Helps one to make choices and to carry them through. |

| | | |
|---|---|---|
| Cherry plum | *Prunus cerasifera* | Helps those who are frightened of losing control of themselves and who feel at the end of their tether. |
| Chicory | *Cichorium intybus* | Helps those who are possessive, stubborn or egocentric; helps them to forgive |
| Clematis | *Clematis vitalba* | For those who have their head in the clouds, helps them to focus and live in the present and to carry out their daily tasks. |
| Common rock rose | *Helianthemum nummularium* | Remedy for emergencies. To help overcome fear and trauma, to find the courage to act. |
| Crab apple | *Malus pumila* | For those who are preoccupied by cleanliness and purity and who make mountains out of molehills. |
| Dog rose | *Rosa canina* | Combats lethargy and apathy and brings back a lust for life. |
| Elm | *Ulmus procera* | For those who take on important responsibilities but feel that they have bitten off more than they can chew. |
| Gentian | *Gentiana* | Combuts pessimism and discontent and brings back confidence and will. |
| Gorse | *Ulex europaeus* | Helps those who have lost all hope to accept life's difficulties. |
| Heather | *Calluna vulgaris* | Curbs the excesses of the ego, brings relaxation and inner calm. Encourages consideration of those around you. |
| Holly | *Ilex aquifolium* | A remedy for jealousy, mistrust and suspicion. Awakens sincere love. |
| Honeysuckle | *Lonicera caprifolum* | Helps those nostalgic for the past to rediscover the joys of the present and to contemplate the future with serenity. |
| Hornbeam | *Carpinus betulus* | Reinforces motivation, revives enthusiasm in cases of mental fatigue. Reinforces capacity for adaptation, gives back a taste for life. |
| Horse Chestnut bud | *Aesculus hippocastanum* | Calms irritability, impatient, anger and edginess born of inner tension. Allows one to take one's time to do things properly. |
| Impatiens | *Impatiens* | Adjusts self-confidence. Helps one to accept failure more easily, but also to expect disappointment less often. Helps shy and sensitive people who suffer from constant feelings of insecurity and suppressed fear. |
| Larch | *Larix deciduas* | Helps shy and sensitive people who suffer from constant feelings of insecurity and fear. |
| Monkey flower | *Mimulus guttatus* | Relieves recurrent but short-lived bouts of melancholy, sadness and even deep depression. |
| Mustard | *Brassica hirta* | Helps hard workers and those who shoulder other people's burdens to recharge their batteries and gain a sense of proportion. |
| Oak | *Que3rcus robus* | Helps those who suffer from non-constructive self-criticism and constant feelings of guilt. |
| Pine | *Pinus sylvestris* | Helps those who are always worried about others, even without reason, and who tend to fear the worst. |
| Red chestnut | *Aesculus carnea* | Helps to overcome physical and mental shocks and to cope with emergency situations. |
| Rescue Remedy | *Rock rose, Star of Bethlehem, impatiens, plumand clematis* | Relieves daily feelings of inexpressed insecurity and anxiety, especially in shy and sensitive people |
| Scarlet monkey musk | *Mimulus cardinalis* | Calms repressed anger and aggression and aids self-assertion. For those who suffer from mood swings and are constantly in a melancholy and doubting frame of mind. |
| Scleranthus | *Scleranthus anuus* | Stabilises them and helps them to make decisions. |
| Spring water | *Pure water from protected sources* | Helps those who are too strict them themselves to rediscover the pleasures of the senses and feelings; helps with find in inner peace. |
| Star of Bethlehem | *Ornithogalum umbel/atum* | 'Great comforter'. To help recover from physical and mental shocks, recent or old. |
| Sweet chestnut | *Castanea sativa* | Revives 'hope in moments of extreme anquish and despair. |

| Sweet violet | *Viola odorata* | Remedy for very shy, self-effacing, sensitive people who find it hard to impose themselves and who retreat in order to protect themselves. |
|---|---|---|
| Vervain | *Verbena officinalis* | Curbs the optimism of those who always think they are right and want to impose their views on others. Makes people more tolerant and reflective. |
| Vine | *Vilis vinifera* | Mellows inflexible, proud, over-assertive people and helps them learn to listen and develop respect for others. |
| Walnut | *Juglans regia* | 'Chain breaker', which helps people break out of old situations and deal with new ones better. Facilitates change. |
| White chestnut | *Aesculus hippocastanum* | Calms over-active minds helping to develop moments of mental relaxation and peace. |
| Wild oat | *Bromus ramosus* | Helps those who, in spite of their great capabilities, have difficulty in finding their way; helps them to make the right choices and to give free rein to their real qualities. |
| Willow | *Salix* | Helps those who bear grudges and who always silentlv blame others. |

## The Beneficial Effects of Tea

Tea is the most popular beverage derived from a plant in the world and is the number-one breakfast drink. It is so popular that it is easy to forget its therapeutic qualities. However, tea is a truly medicinal plant and science has recently discovered some more of its therapeutic properties.

## Black or Green ?

Whatever the colour of the tea, the plant from which it comes is the same, Camellia sinensi : the different between black and green teas lies in the method of harvesting. The best tea (Pekoe) is harvested when the bud is just beginning to lengthen into the shape of a small cigar. If it is harvested later or when the bud has a large bouquet of leaves the quality is inferior.

## Green Tea

This is very rich in tannins, especially catechin which slows down the build-up of cholesterol and also acts as an antidiuretic. Studies on mice have shown that daily consumption of green tea halts the growth of 87 per cent of skin cancers, 58 per cent of stomach cancers and 56 per cent of lung cancers. This antitumour action is due to a high concentration of polyphenols (antioxidants which prevent cell degeneration) and of epigallocatechin gallate (ten times higher than in black tea), a substance that slows down one of the enzymes responsible for the growth of tumours. (Professor Conney, University of New Jersey; Professor-Fujiki, Japan National Cancer Research Institute).

## Exotic Origins

According to legend, in 2737 BC, the Chinese Emperor Chin Nong, the father of Chinese medicine, was getting ready to drink his daily bowl of hot water when a few leaves from the tea bush under which he was resting fell into his cup. The rest is history and a cup of tea has become a symbol of conviviality and hospitality everywhere; witness our own British tea time, Indian 'chair' Arabian 'mint tea' and the Japanese 'tea ceremony', to name but a few.

## Healing with Reiki

There is not a single situation in life in which you cannot bring in the connection of Reiki. Its healing energy works on all levels - spiritual, mental, emotional and physical.

## The effect of Reiki

An individual's experience during a treatment depends on what he needs at that moment and how sensitive he is to subtle energy. Some people may just feel a general relaxed state of well-being, while others have strong physical and emotional reactions, indicating that the body's healing processes are working. Reiki is very good at detecting weaknesses in the body. It works like a flood of energy, moving blocks, increasing the circulation on both a subtle and physical level, and balancing the system. On a physical level, Reiki clears toxic waste accumulated in the body, while emotionally it allows hidden feelings of vulnerability, irritability and sadness to surface. This is what is usually called a 'healing crisis' and is part of the purification process that will leave the person lighter and more balanced.

## Reiki as meditation

Many people like to have Reiki treatment even if they do not have any particular health problem. Their experiences might be akin to meditation because Reiki is a spiritual force. I had one patient who came to me because he wanted Reiki to help him connect to his inner being. On this level, the experience might be an altered state of consciousness, seeing bright colours, or light, feeling an openness of heart, having visions and even hearing mantras.

## Treating ailments

All emotional problems generally respond very quickly to Reiki. Physical conditions linked to stress and tension including headaches, cramps, sleeping problems, and high blood pressure, also respond well because of Reiki's profound centring and balancing effect. As a matter of fact, most of my early clients had emotional problems or bad backs. I found that a back that had 'gone out' or into spasm would usually be relieved within three treatments. Reiki can also have good results with acute problems. It can speed up the healing of broken bones and relieve acute pain. The mother of one of my students was in hospital waiting for surgery because her intestines were cramped into a knot. Her daughter had just learned Reiki and went to visit. She discreetly put her hands on her mother's stomach for some time. The doctors were amazed to see that the problem the mother came in with had disappeared. She went home without having the operation.

## Overcoming addiction

Changes on a mental level are more subtle and generally seem to happen over a longer period after the initiations. Eva, a friend of mine, wanted to learn Reiki in order to quite smoking. I told her that I could not guarantee anything, but if she really wanted to stop smoking, Reiki would certainly help her. So much was happening for Eva during the Reiki workshop that we both forgot about the smoking. Later, when I remembered, I asked her about her smoking habit. Eva said that she had cut down her daily consumption to half without thinking about it. Reiki helps to balance the whole system. As we open up to Reiki we get more sensitive and more in touch with what we do to ourselves. We can sense how unnatural it is to overload our systems with alcohol, drugs and too much or the wrong kind of food. Reiki also fills the spiritual emptiness or disconnection that often is at the core of the addiction.

## Reiki for children

Children usually love Reiki and respond quite quickly. If their parents have been initiated into Reiki it becomes very natural for children to ask for treatment when they feel unwell, for example if they have a headache or a stomach upset. Treatments are usually informal and shorter than adult treatments because children get restless if they lie still for a long time. They also tend to become quite hot during Reiki. A good way to give Reiki to a child is to do a spot treatment on the aching part. Another good idea is to have the child on your lap reading a story and put one hand on their stomach.

## Reiki in pregnancy

It is great to give pregnant women Reiki to relieve the tension they get carrying around so much extra weight. The baby in the womb also benefits enormously. One of my editors, *Diana,* treated her sister who was having some pain and tiredness late in her pregnancy.

As soon as she put her hands on her sister's leg, they both felt the baby moving around inside the womb. I have initiated many pregnant women into Reiki so that they are able to communicate with their unborn child in a unique way.

## Dying with the support of Reiki

Since Reiki is a spiritual energy, it can help people reconnect to their spiritual selves, and help them to accept their transition. It can also help to ease the pain and fear of dying. In Lyon, France, where I used to go regularly, I taught Reiki to a nurse, Isabelle. Through word of mouth, other nurses heard about it and many of them came for initiations. Now in the hospital where they work, the nurses have permission to use Reiki for dying patients, who frequently ask for a nurse who knows Reiki to sit with them.

## Is Reiki safe?

There is really no contraindication for treating with Reiki as long as the patient is willing to take responsibility for his or her reactions. Nobody can promise that a healing will occur. Only by trying can you see how a person responds.

## Benefits of Reiki

As the life energy flows into the patient, it brings about a wide range of healing effects including:

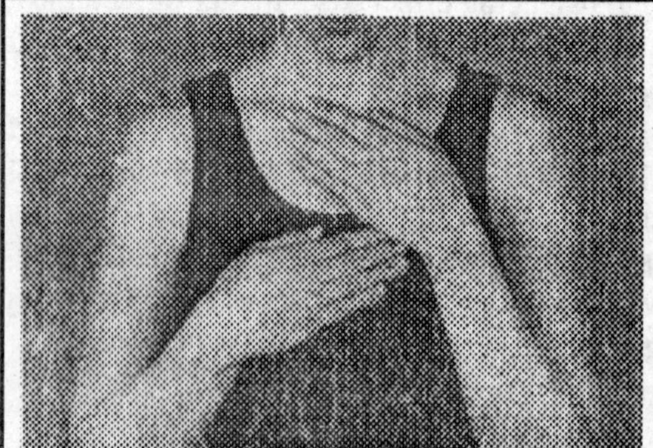

is an ancient hands-on healing system based

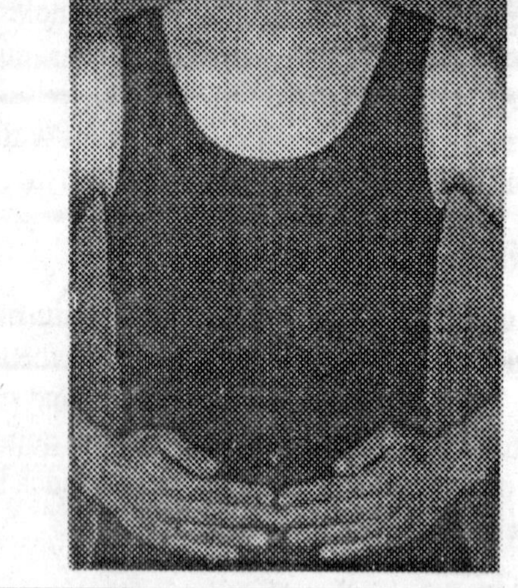

Physical effects

Reduces muscular tension

Lifts headaches

Soothes stomach aches

Eases pain

Balances energies

Clears toxins

Relieves fatigue

Increases Energy

Promotes refreshing sleep

Strengthens natural self-healing mechanisms

Emotional and mental effects

Promotes calm and well-being

Relaxes body and mind

Aids meditation

Relieves stress

Enhances creativity

Encourages emotional release

Soothes emotional distress

Helps unlock suppressed feelings

Promotes a peaceful, positive outlook.

Reiki and other complementary therapies

## Bach

Flower Remedies are infusions of flowers of plants in homeopathic dilutions that are given to help negative emotional states.

I know a Reiki practitioner who sends many of her patients to get homeopathic remedies from another practitioner and finds that Reiki and homeopathy make an excellent combination. The only problem when doing combined treatment is being able to tell which treatment did what, if that is important to you.

A way to increase the efficacy of a homeopathic, herbal, or other remedy is for a Reiki practitioner to hold the bottle or herbs in their hands so that Reiki energy is absorbed into the remedy. Some people use this technique even for orthodox drugs to minimise any bad side-effects. Crystals can also be empowered by Reiki, by holding them in your hands or by using mental programming on them.

## Reiki with orthodox medicine

It is important when practicing complementary medicine not to prevent people from taking orthodox medicine. On no account should you tell them to stop conventional drug treatment. This is a matter between them and their doctors. Reiki sometimes has miraculous results, but healing is not something that you as a practitioner can promise your patient - it is not in your hands.

If a person wants to use only complementary methods to help the healing process, it is his or her personal choice. Apart from Reiki, there are many other ways to improve health, for example making changes to diet and lifestyle, looking at the spiritual dimension of life and starting to practice systems such as yoga or Qigong. Also, a combination of complementary therapies might be helpful.

There is no contra-indication to using Reiki alongside conventional medicine - in fact it can greatly help those undergoing conventional treatment. Jane, of example, a woman in her early fifties, had cervical cancer. As surgery was not an option, a series of 30 sessions of radiotherapy was planned. Halfway through her treatment she started having Reiki, but by this time she was feeling very unwell. Because of Jane's poor condition, Migi, her practitioner, suggested to Jane that she should take the Reiki initiations so that she could treat herself every day. A few weeks later, Jane was initiated by me into first degree Reiki. Even though Jane gave herself Reiki everyday, she continued her Reiki sessions with Migi once a month. Slowly during the summer, Jane started to regain her strength and the burns she had suffered as a side-effect of the cancer treatment began to heal.

Jane believes her recovery from the damaging effects of radiotherapy was accelerated through Reiki treatments. She thinks that Reiki minimised some of the possible damage to her bowel and her bladder, and that it helped to shrink the tumour and heal the effects of the radiotherapy. The latest scan shows no sign of the tumour. Another benefit of the Reiki is that Jane is no longer experiencing headaches, which had been a long-term problem. Now Jane looks great!

## The Five Reiki Spiritual Principles

Here are Dr Usui's five spiritual principles of Reiki, which are guidelines on how to live. They might seem simple, but they are not always so easy to follow. Use them as a focus for meditation.

**Just for today do not anger:** This does not mean that we should repress anger. It means that we should be conscious of our feelings and try to communicate them in a constructive way - not dump our anger on people who have nothing to do with it. Whenever there is a mismatch between the intensity of the feelings and the event that has taken place, we know there are a lot of unconscious feelings bubbling to the surface. The more we connect to the real love inside, the faster we can let go of anger and other negative emotions. There is nothing wrong with feelings. Emotion is just energy that keeps moving. It is when it gets stuck that we become ill.

**Just for today do not worry:** Worrying does not help any issue or situation. It only creates tension and stress. If we truly realise this, we can drop the worrying like a bad habit. Just for today, we can try to experience the support that is all around us. If we worry a lot, it shows our discnnectedness from the divine; there is a lack of trust. Use whatever means you know to connect again: prayer, meditation, and Reiki.

**Honour your teachers, parents and elders:** We learn from our parents and teachers. When we take their knowledge inside us, it becomes part of us. So to honour parents and teachers is to honour ourselves.

My parents always supported me, even if sometimes they did not understand what I was doing. I will always be grateful for that. Even if you do not agree with everything your parents did, they in their turn were victims of their parents. So you have to look upon them with understanding and compassion. To keep blaming is to be locked into a reactive pattern.

Thinking of my teachers, I feel enormous gratitude. There is no way that I can pay them back for their precious gifts. I can only try to follow their teachings.

**Earn your living honestly:** We must live our lives in a way that keeps us true to ourselves. The moral way in which we conduct our lives will, in the widest sense, reflect on our health. Honesty is no just about keeping to the facts. It is about honouring our deepest feelings and beliefs and being aligned to the divine power inside.

**Show gratitude to all living things:** In Reiki we always end a treatment by saying, 'Thank you, thank you, thank you!' This acknowledges the work of the spiritual energy. We are only its channels. People, animals, plants - we are all interconnected by Reiki energy. When we truly realise this, we start living with compassion and love, entering our true state of being.

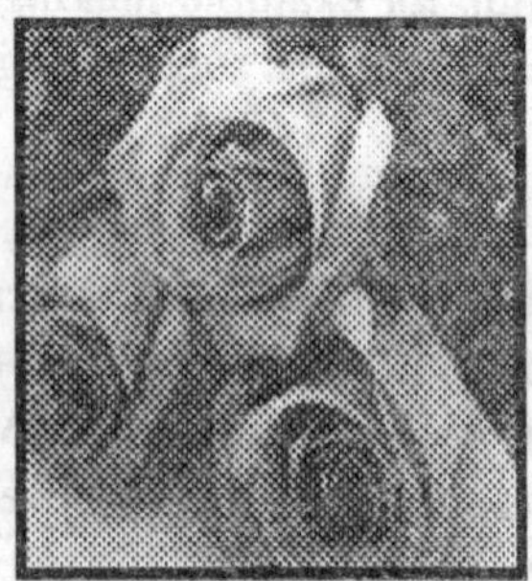

***ROSE***

*Essential oils are highly concentrated; it can take 5,000 roses to produce just one teaspoonful of oil.*

***MOGRA***

*Aromatherapy are now widely available and can be mixed with pure vegetable oils for use in massage.*

**Fig. 45 : Rose-Oils-use in Massage**

**One of the most primitive forms of medicine involved burning aromatic plants in order to "smoke" illness out of a patient, This process was frequently interlinked with various rituals and religious practices, and sometimes plants with; mind altering properties were burnt too, to create a mystical, other-worldly experience as part of the healing ritual. The use of incense in the ceremonies of diverse religions through the centuries has perpetuated this aspect; many of the gums and resins that are used in incense have powerful therapeutic properties - for example, as respiratory anti-septics as well as inducing a meditative, reflective state of mind in the worshippers.**

**Aromatic plants and extracts have been highly regarded by all the greater ancient civilizations, stretching through the Middle East from Babylonia and Persia to India and China. The oldest medical texts from these countries, dating back at least 3,000 years, list many aromatic plants and their uses. Some of the most detailed descriptions are to be found in ancient Egyptian writings; fragrant plants were employed in all aspects of life, from perfume and cosmetics to medicine and in the rituals for embalming the dead. Some of the oint-ment jars excavated from Tutankhamen's tomb contained Ppreservative resins such as frankincense which still had an odour after some 3,200 years.**

**The Egyptians were very aware of the value of fragrance in enhancing mood, and developed a reputation as masters of perfumery; Cleopatra may have owed something of her fabled attractiveness to Julius Caesar and Mark Antony from her use of vast amounts of rose petals to scent her living quarters: Interestingly, however, the Egyptians do not appear to have discovered the process of distilling the essential oils from plants, relying instead on infused oils and ointments. These were later widely used by the Greeks and Romans, both as medicine and as part of the daily ritual of public bathing, which the Romans in particular so enjoyed.**

Many Greek physicians were employed by the Roman armies, and they carried the knowledge of aromatic, and other, plants across many countries. Galen, who rose to be the personal physician to the Emperor Marcus Aurelius, invented the original cold cream and was a great writer on all matters concerning health and medicines. His and other works formed the basis of medicine for many centuries, and with the decline of the Roman Empire much of this knowledge went eastwards into Byzantium. It was the Arabic countries that made the next great leap forwards in aromatherapy. By the ninth century, Baghdad was thriving partly due to being the centre of the rose industry, exporting rose water as far as India. The principle of distillation was first applied to roses and is generally credited to Abu Ali Ibn Sina, better known as Avicenna (980-1037), a philosopher and physician from Uzbekistan. Steam distillation enabled the pure essential oil to be extracted from many plants.

In the West, aromatic infused oils had continued to be used, and during the period of the Crusades, essential oils, or "perfumes of Arabia" as they were known, spread extensively throughout Europe. As the gums and resins of Asia were not easily available, native Mediterranean plants such as rosemary and lavender were used for making essential oils too. The French were particularly enthusiastic in adopting these oils, laying the foundations for today's perfumery industry as well as therapeutic uses.

Burning antiseptic herbs such as thyme and rosemary, to fumigate the air and ward off disease, was carried out in several French hospitals until well into the twentieth century. Indeed, it was a Frenchman, Rene Gattefosse, a chemist working in the perfumery industry, who coined the term aromatherapy some 50 years ago. He burned his hand badly in an accident in his laboratory. He used essential oil of lavender to cool the tissue and found it healed the burned flesh remarkably quickly, with no infection or scar. During both World Wars, essential oils were used to treat wounds and infections, and one of the pioneers of this work was Dr. Jean Valnet, who published his findings in the late 1960s.

Respected medical establishments in France' are now looking at the medicinal aspects of essential oils.

It should not be forgotten, however, that the power of aromatic plants extends beyond antiseptic or anti inflammatory properties. It is well established that scent can evoke memories, change people's moods and make them feel good. Aromatherapy has developed in the UK, the US and many other countries in the last 20 years into a holistic system that tries to heal and balance the whole person. The oils are often incorporated into massage, or used in baths, or simply evaporated into the air in a burner to improve physical and emotional well-being. These methods would be familiar to the ancients, and show a continuing tradition of usage of aroma in therapy. There are also more aromatherapy practitioners than ever before offering complete treatments.

Sandalwood

# Yoga Mantra Meditation

'Man shall not live by bread alone…' Food feeds the physical body, what we take in via the senses feeds the mind, and meditation feeds the spirit. Meditation should be an important part of your daily routine – a part that feeds the spirit and which has a knock-on beneficial effect on the mind and body. Listening to the sound of silence is essential to holistic living and is vital to a lifestyle that supports the trinity of humanness – body, mind and spirit.

Food and the senses bring sustenance from the external environment, whereas in meditation your focus is internal. Since you are in truth spirit in physical clothing and part of the One, it is vital to your complete health to contact that One within by regularly turning your focus inwards.

To meditate is to detach your awareness from external concerns and allow it to seek the God within. To facilitate this you can use many tools, from focusing your attention on a candle flame to the use of *mantra* (a Sanskrit word referring to syllables/sounds that have subtle energies). The point is to use these tools in meditation to assist in easing the mind from its usual treadmill of thoughts; therefore, a main characteristic of such tools is simplicity. Something that has many associations will lead the mind off on another excursion. Therefore, visualisation techniques and shamanic journeying, useful though they are for contacting subtle parts of the Self, is not meditation. Talk to God by all means, regularly. Ask for blessings and grace – this is supplicatory prayer. Ask also for blessings for others – this is intercessionary prayer (and there are plenty of examples of its beneficial effects). Use prayers of praise to express your gratitude for personal and global blessings. However, another aspect of communion with Spirit is allowing space and stillness of mind to receive the Divine response – this is meditation.

The usefulness of mantra in meditation is that the Sanksrit sounds produce subtle energies that reverberate with certain parts of our subtle bodies.

A simple mantra meditation is 'So-Hum'. In this meditation the 'So' syllable repeated internally on the in-breath represents universal consciousness, and the 'Hum' on the out-breath stands for 'self' consciousness. So-Hum is breathing in the universal and breathing out the ego. This is a meditation that can be used by anyone.

Sit comfortably, spine erect, on a cushion in the lotus or half lotus posture or on a straight-backed chair, feet flat on the floor with the hands resting lightly on the thighs. Please be comfortable. If you cannot sit cross-legged without being painfully aware of it – don't!

Feel, imagine, visualise, 'intend' the breath rising from the base of the spine and moving up the front of the body through each *charka* (Sanskrit for 'wheel'). On reaching the crown charka, pause and then breathe out while imagining the breath moving down through the third eye and crossing to descend the spinal column back to the base.

Our problems as humans being, as described in the Sankhya philosophy, with the belief in the myth of separateness. Our quest is to seek our own godliness within and thereby, to unite and end the pain (physical, mental-emotional and spiritual).

## CHAKRAS AND MANTRAS

The Bija mantras (literally, seed mantras) are the sounds of the letters of the Sanskrit alphabet that are associated with the seven main charkas (energy centres of our subtle bodies that, of course, permeate and affect our physical existence). Because they permeate from the subtle to the gross of our existence, the charkas affect our physiology and our emotions. Below is a list of the seven main charkas in the order in which they exist, from the bottom of the spinal column to the crown of the head. They are envisaged as lotus flowers with varying numbers of petals. The main physiological and emotional associations of the various charkas and the primary Bija mantra relating to each is given. Benefit to the body and mind can be achieved by use of these simple mantras.

1. Root charka (*Muladhara*), Earth element. It is centred at the base of the spine. Associated with the rectum, prostate, cervix and gonads. The main function of this energy centre is physical survival and groundedness. Ungroundedness is the dysfunction. Can lead to problems like food addiction (dissatisfaction associated with physical matter/Earth) and dysmenorrhoea. The Bija mantra is *Lam* and the associated colour and gem are red and the ruby respectively.
2. Self-Place (*Svadhisthana*), Water element. It is centred round the lower belly. Associated with the kidneys and adrenal glands. The main function of this centre is self-esteem, creativity (including reproduction) and personal sexuality. Its dysfunction manifests as over-attachment and low self – esteem. Can involve problems to do with fertility and premature ejaculation. The Bija mantra is Vam and the associated colour and gem are orange and red coral.
3. City of Gems (*Manipura*), Fire element. It is centred in the solar plexus and is associated with the digestive system including the pancreas. It has to do with the marriage of the male and female energies. Its functions are to do with personal power, dominating energy and competitiveness, and include the qualities of pride, confidence and achievement. The stress related to unfulfilled ambitions/lack of achievement can produce anger and hate as extremes of dysfunction. The Bija mantra is *LAM* and the colour and gem are yellow and the topaz.
4. The Heart Chakra (*Anahata*), Air element. Associated with the cardio-vascular system and the thymus gland (related to immunity). It is the bridge between the lower three bodily and 'tribal'-related charkas and the upper three transpersonal ones. The main function is personal love of a higher nature than sex and it is the seat of love as emotion and compassion. Its dysfunction is lack of love. Stress based here may be to do with rejected love. The Bija mantra is *YAM*, which is also the name of the god of death, in this instance the death of the Ego as the energy of Anahata bridges the lower Self and the higher Self. The colour is green and the gem is emerald.
5. Throat Chakra (*Vishuddha*), Ether element. This charka is associated with the respiratory system and metabolism, and thus involves the thyroid and parathyroid glands. Its main functions are the expressions of emotion and will-power, but all forms of communication are connected to this charka, with the associated qualities of clarity and sharing. Unprocessed emotion can cause problems in this area, and lack of communication is its dysfunction. The Bija mantra is *HAM*, the colour is blue and the gemstone is the blue sapphire.
6. The Third Eye (*Agya or Ajna*), Consciousness is the element. It is centred behind the eyebrows and is associated with the ANS (Automatic Nervous System, dealing with processes such as digestion which are usually beyond voluntary control) and the pituitary gland (the conductor of our hormonal system, which is the carrier of longer-lasting instructions to our body and emotions than the fast-acting nervous system). This is

where gross and subtle, matter and mind meet and merge. The function is intuition and the dysfunction is refusal to see things as they really are. Its works closely with the seventh charka to keep logic and intuition balanced. The mantra is *SAM* (on the in-breath) and *KSHAM* (on the out-breath), the colour is indigo and the stone amethyst.

7. Crown Chakra (Sahasrara), Bliss is the element. It is centred on the pineal gland and holds sway over the CNS (Central Nervous System- the activity of the brain and spinal cord). The seventh chakra's function is to initiate and stimulate the spiritual journey, to instill divine discontent so that we seek to transcend our physical human existence. Its dysfunction is mental imbalance, psychosis and depression. As stated in the previous paragraph, these two uppermost charkas of the body are where the logic of the left brain and the creativity and intuition of the right brain must balance and work together. Cold logic needs the warmth of love and compassion. We need the left brain's capacity for clear, abstract and logical thought but only in the service of spirit. The Bija mantra is *OM*, the colour violet and the stone the alexandrine.

You can work with the Bija mantras to help with the dysfunctions mentioned under each chakra. Envisage and feel the electro-magnetic current vibrating between the front and back of your body at each of the levels indicated by the descriptions of where the charkas are centred.

## Yoga: Breathing, Exercises and the Doshas

Yoga (meaning 'union') is another of the main Vedic sciences and as such has an age-old connection with Ayurveda. It is so much more than the exercise form that many of us in the West enjoy. Yoga is the ultimate in experiencing reality, as one of its main precepts states that only in uniting with whatever it is that you are trying to comprehend can you know it. As stated earlier, all human problems stem from not knowing our true nature, which is as part of the great One. Thus, Yoga and Ayurveda place knowledge of the true nature of Self and Reality at the centre of what it means to be healthy. Knowing oneself is essential to health. I encourage you to explore the science of Yoga, for here I only make certain health-giving and helpful suggestions.

In Ayurveda, Yoga Asanas (physical postures) and the Pranayama (breath control) are often used therapeutically. These are only two of the eight branches of classical Yoga, but are the ones most directly affecting the physical body.

Asanas can be used to balance the Doshas generally or chosen for specific problems. Both Asanas and Pranayama (which works with the breath of life, Prana) boost vitality.

Vata individuals could benefit from alternate nostril breathing. Using the thumb and middle finger to open and close the two nostrils, first block one and breathe in through the other, then change over and breathe out. The next in-breath is via the same nostril you just breathed out through, and so it goes on.

Pitta people can reduce the heat and intensity of Pitta by breathing in via the left nostril and out via the right and repeating that sequence. Since the left nostril is related to the cool, compassionate, female, lunar energy it will induce related qualities in the individual.

Conversely, Kapha individuals who need the addition of some solar, masculine, heating, assertive energy should close the left nostril and breathe in through the right, release and breathe out via the left and continue that cycle.

Likewise, solar or lunar energy can be encouraged in the individual during sleep by lying on the left side (which blocks lunar energy) if Vata or Kapha are predominant, or choosing the right side (blocking solar energy) if Pitta is predominant. Similarly, lying on the right side will help reduce fever (should that be excessive) until more curative treatments can be given or taken.

Below are Yoga Asanas which are particularly suitable for problems related to each of the three Doshas. These are enlisted according to degree to difficulty. Postures that are useful for balancing each Dosha are in boldface. If you have never practiced Yoga, find a good class locally (the Useful Addresses and Resources chapter will be of help_ and learn the basics. You will probably find that the majority of postures mentioned will be incorporated in most Yoga classes. If you are in any doubt about a posture, ask for help and a demonstration.

| VATA | PITTA | KAPHA |
|---|---|---|
| **BASIC:**<br>**Cobra** – helps with insomnia, constipation, spinal circulation and menstrual problems.<br>**Corpse** – conserves energy and balances blood pressure. Helps Vata type asthma, insomnia, depression and varicose veins. Forward Bend – improves circulation, particularly pelvic.<br>**Knee to Chest** – helps constipation and flatulence. Helps backache, sciatica.Palm Tree – improves circulation, depression,Pose of the Child – relieves constipation and improves circulation.Yoga Mudra – tones nerve centres in the pelvis helping with menstrual problems. Alleviates headache and sciatica. Helps in depression.<br>**INTERMEDIATE:**<br>**Locust** – helps constipation and stimulates kidney function.<br>**Plough** – stimulates the thyroid and circulation and relieves constipation. Good for backache, headache, sciatica, menstrual disorders and depression. Shoulder Stand – improves circulation, particularly in the upper body, and relieves constipation.<br>**ADVANCED:**<br>**Head Stand** – balances the nervous system. Helps varicose veins.<br>**Lotus** – tones pelvic nerve centres and helps in depression. | **BASIC:**<br>**Boat** – helps relieve gastritis, peptic ulcer and irritable bowel.<br>**Bow** – stimulates the kidneys and neighbouring organs and the adrenals.<br>**Bridge** – relieves flatulence and constipation and stimulates spinal circulation.<br>**Cobra** – stimulates the kidneys and surrounding organs and the adrenal glands. Benefits high blood pressure.<br>**Fish** – improves asthma, migraine, malabsorption and liver and respiratory problems.<br>**Knee to Chest** – relieves flatulence and constipation.<br>**Locust** – stimulates the kidneys and surrounding organs and the adrenals. The effects are increased if practiced consecutively with the Bow and the Cobra. Also good for malabsorption.<br>**Sheetali** – encourages the flow of Prana and is cooling. Useful for peptic ulcer and migraine headaches.<br>**INTERMEDIATE:**<br>**Shoulder Stand** – improves thyroid function in hyper thyroidism. Benefits high blood pressure and migraines. Benefits the liver. Cools the emotions of anger.<br>**ADVANCED:**<br>**Hidden Lotus** – tones pelvic nerve centres. Helps with peptic ulcer and liver malfunction. | **BASIC:**<br>**Boat** – helps relieve sinus congestion and asthma. Useful in diabetes.<br>**Bow** – stimulates the kidneys and surrounding organs including adrenals. Helps in sinus congestion and asthma.<br>**Cobra** – stimulates the kidneys and surrounding organs including the adrenal glands. It helps with constipation and asthma.<br>**Fish** – improves asthma and other respiratory problems like bronchitis, sinus congestion with related headache and asthma.<br>**Forward Bend** – tones the nervous system and facial muscles. Useful in bronchitis and diabetes.<br>**Lion** – rejuvenating, energizing and encourages the flow of Prana. Stimulating to the throat and larynx.<br>**Palm Tree** – improves circulation generally, warming. Good for asthma.<br>**INTERMEDIATE:**<br>Backward<br>**Bend** – improves mobility, circulation and works on the nervous system. Helps with bronchitis and diabetes.<br>**Plough** – stimulates the thyroid. Relieves constipation and helps with sinus congestion and bronchitis.<br>**Shoulder Stand** – helps with asthma, emphysema and relieves constipation. |

**The Pranic Benefits of Yogic Breathing:** Breath is seen as the outward manifestation of prana, the vital force or energy that flows through the physical body but is actually in the Austral Body. By exercising control over breathing, you can learn to control the subtle energies within the body, and ultimately gain full control over the mind.

**Outward Signs of the Invisible:** We can not see the wind, but we can infer its movements from the swaying of the trees. Prana, too, is invisible, but we can observe its state by looking at the state of the breath, since the breath is the outward manifestation of prana.

**Pranic Benefits:** The prana, when consciously controlled, is a powerful vitalising and regenerating force. Once you are able to control the prana, it can be manipulated for self development. For healing yourself of seemingly incurable diseases, and to help you to heal others.

## Why Meditate?

Meditation is a state of consciousness that can be understood only on a direct, intuitive level. Ordinary experiences are limited by time, space, and the laws of causality, but the meditative state transcends all boundaries. While you meditate, past and future cease to exist. There is only the consciousness of I am in the infinite, eternal, Now.

## What is Happiness?

Everyone wants to be happy; this is a universal fact. Most people believe that some material object will bring this happiness-money, the perfect spouse, the dream job, a new car, a big house with swimming pool- but in truth the list of what would make you completely happy is never-ending. Each "thing" will please only for a short time, until the novelty wears off. As long as you think that happiness will come from something outside yourself, you will never be happy. Happiness, the blissful state, comes from within your own self. Anyone who believes otherwise is like a person wandering in the desert, constantly disappointed by mirages of water and shade. Worldly happiness is equally elusive, always just beyond our grasp. Two famous stories, told below, illustrate the reason why.

**Physical Benefits:** Meditation provides a lasting spiritual rest, which must be experienced to be understood. Once you can meditate, the time you normally devote to sleep can gradually be reduced to as little as three hours per night, and you will still feel more rested and peaceful than before. By reducing heart rate and consumption of oxygen, meditation greatly reduces stress levels. It seems that each part of the body, even down to the individual cells, is taught to relax and rejuvenate. Meditation helps to prolong the body's period of growth and cell production, and reduces the decaying process. After the age of 35, our brain cells die off at a rate of 100,000 per day, and they are not replaced, but meditation can reduce this decline, as it changes the vibratory make-up of both the body and the mind. In this way, meditation can prevent or minimise senility.

**Mental Benefits:** We each posses vast inner resource of power and knowledge, much of it brought with us from past lives. In meditation, new patterns of thinking come to the surface and develop as we experience a new view of the universe, a vision of unity, happiness, harmony, and inner peace. Negative tendencies vanish, and the mind becomes steady. Meditation brings freedom from fear of death, which is seen as a doorway to a new name and form. People who mediate regularly tend to develop magnetic and dynamic personalities, cheerfulness, powerful speech, lustrous eyes, physical health, and boundless energy. Others draw strength from such people and feel elevated in their presence.

Meditation is only possible when all mental modifications (thought waves) have been stilled, and with this comes mental peace.

## Charting Your Progress in Meditation

*"An ounce of practice is worth tones of theory."* – *Swami Sivananda*

Do not abruptly change your way of life. Begin to evolve bit by bit, thus developing your willpower.

Keep a spiritual diary; it may prove to be an eye-opener. It is a simple practical aid to help you to be regular in your practice and to make the most of limited time available.

Make a daily routine and stick to it.

Nightly, just before going to bed, review what you have done that day. Keep the spiritual diary for six months and compare your progress.

Remember that regularity and sincerity are the most important secrets to success.

Only you can evaluate whether you are making progress. There are no objective tests or guidelines. No-one else can tell you this; it is completely subjective.

Do your body and mind seem to be shedding a kind of dullness or heaviness?

Do you feel more peaceful, happier with yourself, and less prone to emotional outbursts? Are serenity of mind and a sense of deep-seated contentment starting to manifest themselves?

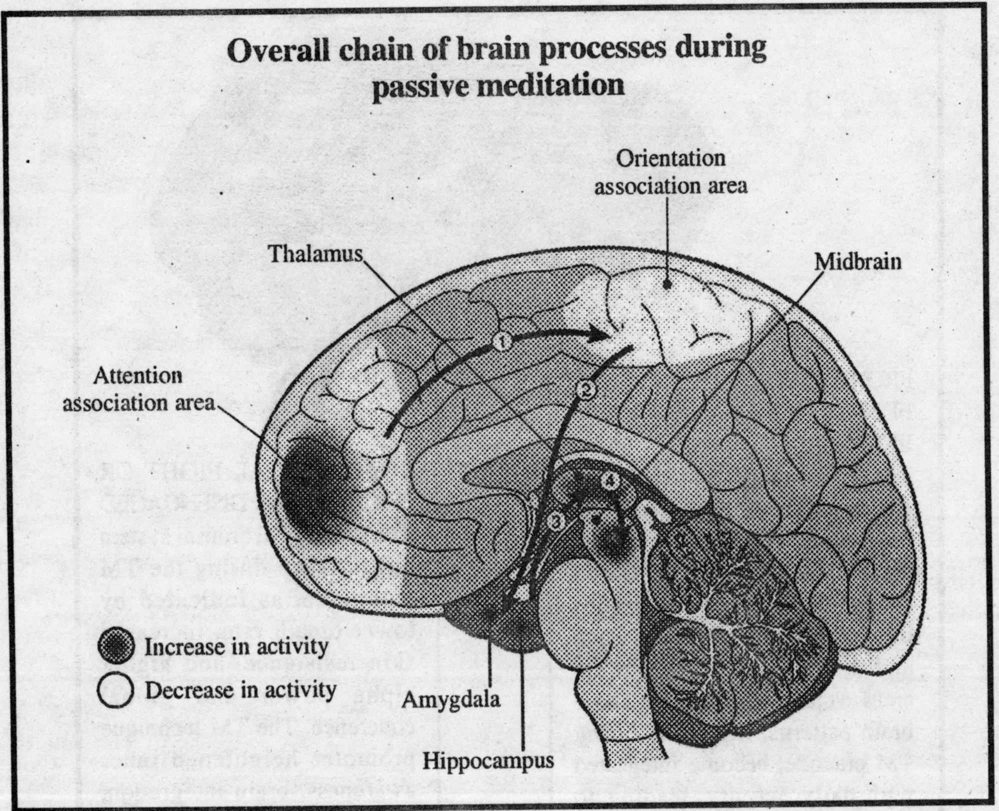


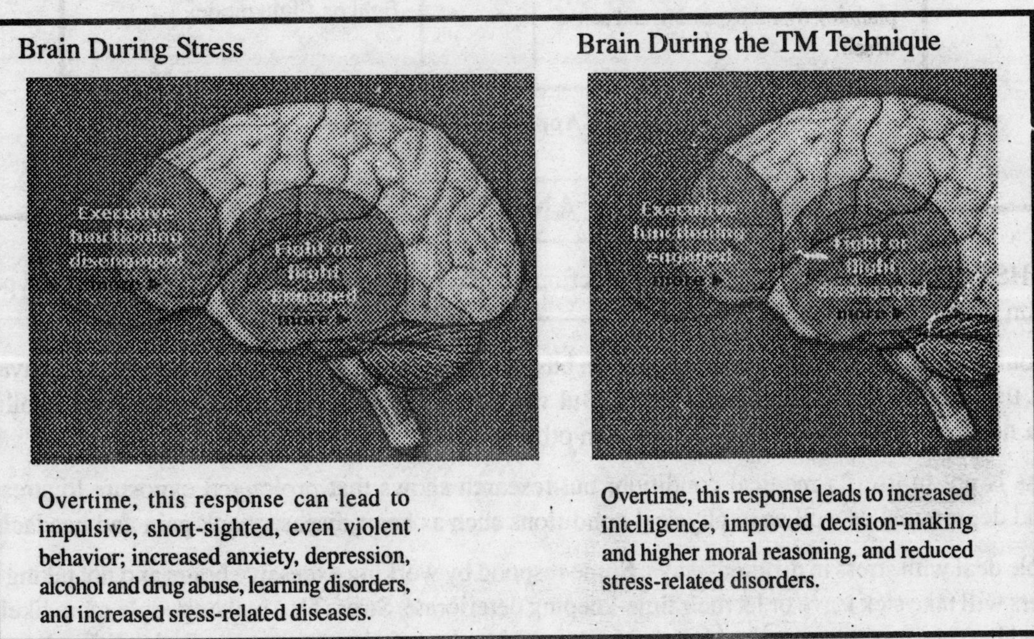


Overtime, this response can lead to impulsive, short-sighted, even violent behavior; increased anxiety, depression, alcohol and drug abuse, learning disorders, and increased sress-related diseases.

Overtime, this response leads to increased intelligence, improved decision-making and higher moral reasoning, and reduced stress-related disorders.

**Fig. 47**

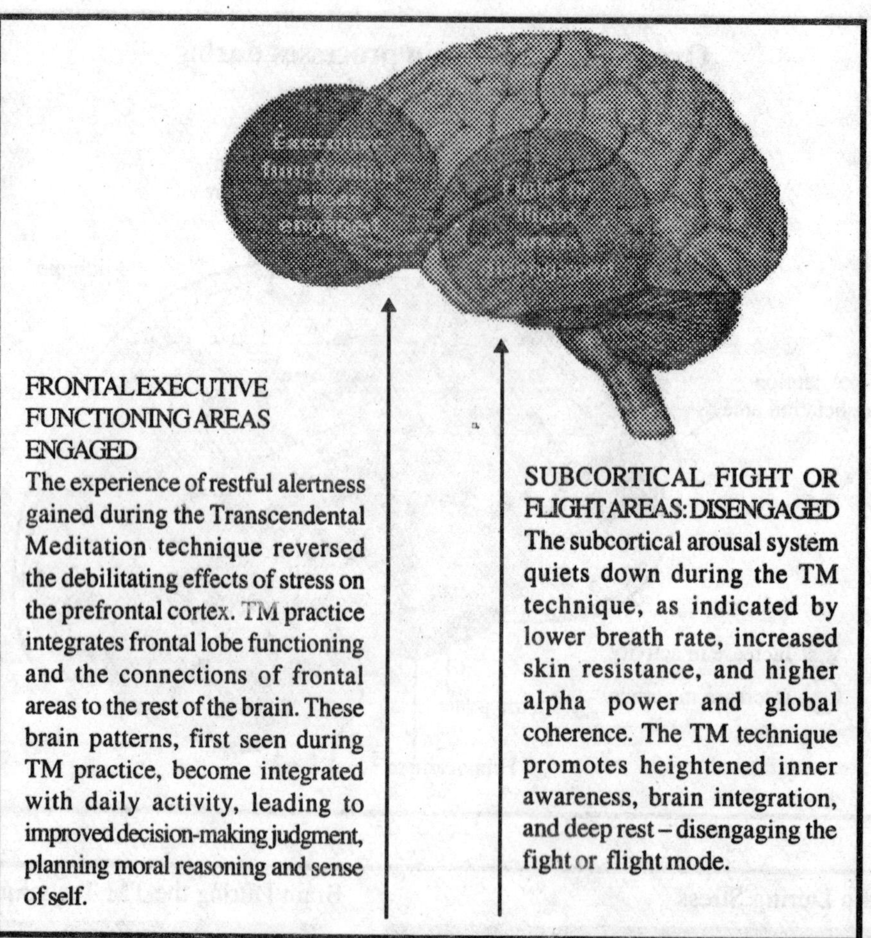


**Fig. 48 : Applied 'TM' Techniques**

## STRESS, YOGA AND HOLISTIC HEALTH

The HSE defines stress as, "the adverse reaction people have to excessive pressure or other types of demand placed upon them".

Of course, a certain level of pressure in life on business environment is desirable. It helps to motivate people and will boost their energy and productivity levels. But when pressure starts to exceed individuals' ability to cope, it becomes a negative rather than a positive force-in other words, stress.

Stress is not in itself a medical condition, but research shows that prolonged exposure to stress is linked to anxiety and depression, as well as to physical conditions such as heart disease, back pain and headaches.

People deal with stress in different ways. Some respond by working excessive hours and not taking any holidays, while others will take sick leave or let their time-keeping deteriorate. Stress also makes people more likely to lose their tempers and become less tolerant of criticism. Many individuals suffering from stress find it difficult to sleep because adrenaline and cortisol-two of the 40 hormones produced by the body when it is stressed-will interfere with their ability to switch off and relax. Yoga, the ancient treasure of our nation has stood the test of time. The various definitions of Yoga, ***"Yoga Karmasu Kausalam" "Yoga Samatvam uchyate," "Yoga citta vritti Nirodlia"*** etc. teach us-

What we should derive from life; and

What should we give to others.

In modern times, the education is much inclined towards Western bent of ***"Learn only to earn."*** But education can not become only the source to livelihood, because human life has more precious and gracious purpose. The value-based education leads us steadily towards that purpose. The basic ***Sanskaras*** of *Ahimsa, Satya, Asteya, Aparigraha, and Bramhamacharya* form the foundation of values which are the part of Ashtanga Yoga. The ***Yama- Niyama*** concept, if deeply rooted in ***early primary education*** would mould the soil to the desired shape at the right time. The *Asanas, Pranayamas, Kriyas, Bandhas, Mudras* are not only beneficial for body but also for the mind. The healthy mind resides in healthy body. When integration of body, mind and spirit is achieved, one's personality blossoms. Number of such personalities can be created with the help of Yoga education.

The Ancient Science and Art of Yoga is the real, time-tested, comprehensive, long-term solution to all human problems. The greatest advantage of Yoga lies in the fact that it addresses human problems at individual and collective levels. It helps create harmony within the person and the society in which he lives. It integrates body, mind, intellect, emotions and spirit, which bring harmony, happiness and peace.

***Yoga*** works as a ***tool for Modification of Behaviour, Emotion & Personality.*** Patanjala Yoga explains the real significance of emotional intelligence by way of complete cessation of modification of mind (P.Y.S.-I:2). In fact, yoga practices work at the visceral and the emotional level in following psycho-physiological principles and tackles functional disturbances of the neuro-vegitative system, attitudinal and emotional domains of human personality.

Relaxative asanas work for *chitta vishranti* i.e. tranquility and peace. Corrective asanas develop stability, steadiness and lightness of the body. Emphasis on relaxation, taking help of gravity to ensure eternal effects of tackling mento-emotional states. Asanas, Bandhas, Mudras, Kriyas and Pranayamas may have beneficial effects on autonomic nervous system, brain and the mind. Along with yoga practices, yogic diet comprising simple vegetable proteins, low in salt content and moderately rich in cereals, vegetables and fruits and adequate minerals and vitamins seem to have been prescribed for better health. Such type of food influences the awareness and overall feeling, thinking, being and behavior. Yoga aims at improving the emotional control in overcoming imbalance. Yoga ultimately enriches our emotions, value systems and attitude to life as a whole and influences our personality.

## Introduction

This diagram shows how the effect of stress or pressure can be positive or negative. Stress is beneficial when we feel challenged and stimulated, but negative if we feel overloaded or under stimulated. At opposite ends of the spectrum we can suffer from 'burn out or 'rust out'. It is part of good management to keep the amount and nature of people's workload at or near the optimum point.

Stress can be positive or negative. Some pressure can be a very good thing. The tasks and challenges we face every day can keep us motivated, give us a sense of achievement, and provide job satisfaction, but inappropriate levels of pressure - too much or too little - can lead to negative stress. The following definitions may help you to get a clearer understanding of negative stress.

Negative stress is a result of: A mismatch between the demands made on us and our real or perceived ability to cope.

Getting married, suffering a bereavement, even buying a house: all sorts of events add to the worry. Hundreds of thousands of teenagers have had their first taste of extreme stress first with exams then the long wait for results. If grades do not meet expectations, they can become a source of depression, of humiliation. In a few cases, the disappointment can lead to suicide.

## Symptoms of Stress

Stress is a pressure people feel in life. When stress persists and becomes excessive, it culminates to strain and, in turn, adversely affects a person's physique, psychology and behaviour. The body prepares itself for "fight or 'flight'. The excessive stress develops various symptoms that harm the employee's job performance and health, and threaten their ability to cope with the environment. The various symptoms of stress are as below:

- Emotional instability
- Excessive use of alcohol or drugs
- Feelings of inability to cope
- Unco-operative attitude
- Sleeping problems absentiasm
- Chronic worry
- Inability to relax
- High blood pressure
- Digestive problems
- Nervousness and tensions

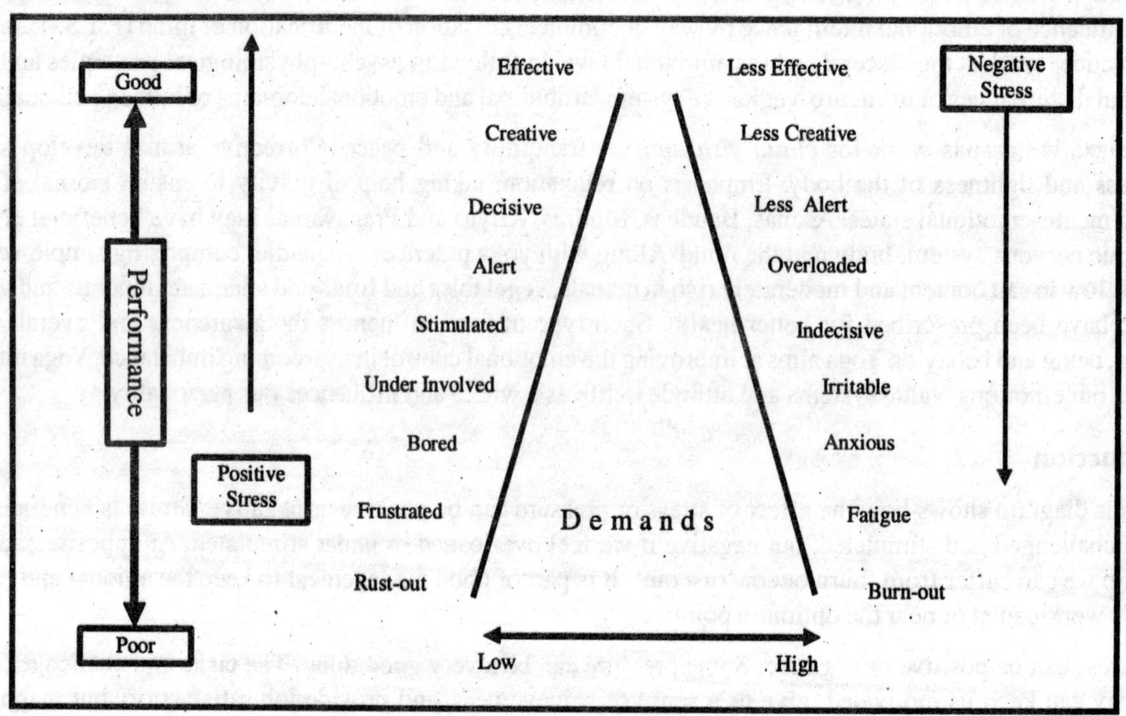


**Fig. 49 : Signs of Stress**

| *Physical Signs* | *Emotional Signs* | *Mental Signs* | *Relational Signs* | *Spiritual Signs* | *Behavioural Signs* |
|---|---|---|---|---|---|
| Appetite changes | Bad temper | Lacking humour | Isolation | A feeling of emptiness | Pacing |
| Headaches fatigue | Anxiety Nightmares | Dull senses Lethargy | Defensive Intolerance | Apathy Inability to forgive | Swearing Substance abuse |
| Insomnia Indigestion | Irritability Depression | Boredom Indecisiveness | Resentment Loneliness | Cynicism Loss of direction | Nail biting Slumped posture |
| Colds Weight change | Frustration oversensitivity | Forgetfulness Poor concentration | Nagging Lower sex drive | Doubt Need to prove self | Restlessness Risk aversion |
| Teeth grinding | Mood swings | Personality changes | Aggression | Negative outlook | Eating disorders |
| Tension | fearfulness | Stuck in past | Abuse | Gloom | Headaches |

**Psychologists classify the stress into 4 basic areas:**

1. **Future stress:** is caused by concern over the future i.e. worries.
2. **Situational stress:** is stress of the moment, it is an immediate treat, challenge or agitation.
3. **Chronic stress:** is stress over time, it may stem a tough experience over which we have no control except to endure(bear) or accept, such as the lost of a loved one, an illness, accident, etc.
4. **Residual stress:** is a stress of the past memories of bad incident or old hurts.

## Management through Yoga and others Holistic Approach

1. Yogic Hygiene
2. Sports and Recreational activities
3. Balanced Food
4. Positive attitude towards life
5. Good Company
6. Attracting divine grace

## Personality at different levels

What are common symptoms of stress?

Manifestation of stress are numerous and varied but fall into four categories

**Hurry, worry, and curry** are responsible for disturbance of health.

The study was conducted in Govt. Medical College, Nagpur in 2006 to know stress-induced medical problems in postgraduate students. Hypertension was seen in 4.6 per cent [service candidates], Ashama in 5.8 per cent, Backache in 15.2 per cent,Indigesion in 7 er cent, Insomnia 19.1 per cent, Allerigic Vrhinitis 17.5 per cent, Acidity 21.3 per cent, Bodyache 11 per cent, Anxiety 12 per cent, Changes in behaviour 7 per cent,Depression 5.8 per cent Stress-induced problems were 54 per cent in Post-graduates from different clinical Departments [Medicine, Surgery, gynaec & obstetrics, paediatrics, ophathalmology]. as against 70. % **in Department of Anesthesiology.** Study indicates that the stress factor is overall increased right from young age..

But we know that it is difficult to change the external factors which give us stress. It is beyond our capacity. What we can do is to change our inner equipment so that our response to stress is altered. It will not disturb our health.

We should know our inner equipment then we can adjust it in stressful situation.

Every human being is constituted of physical, mental and intellectual equipment and conscious principle i.e., spiritual core. Human personality is at four different levels.

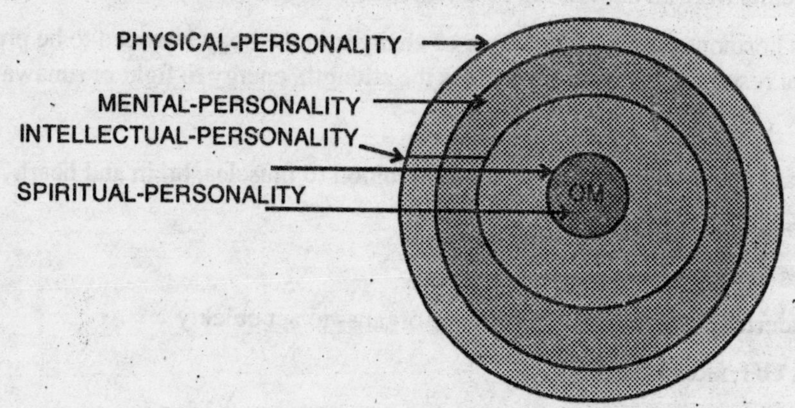

The physical personality is the grossest aspect of our personality. Which one can see and perceive,. Mind is psychological personality. It is the centre of emotions. Intellect is the subtlest of the three. This is the decision-making personality. You know what is good and what is bad. The three personalities at body, mind and intellect level together constitute matter which by itself is inert and insentient. The consciousness is the spirit in us which propels, motivates and causes these equipments to function. Spirit and matter together causes manifestation of life and activity.

For maintenance of good health there should be proper integration of personality at all the four levels. According to W.H.O., health is a state of the individual who is free from disease at physical, mental, intellectual and spiritual level. Doctors mainly deal with physical and mental level, but intellectual and spiritual well-being remains neglected.

## Role of Pranayam Yoga in Stress Management

Explanation of Stress?

Dr. Hans Selye - father of stress theory defines stress as:

"The nonspecific response of the body to any demand upon it. The demand can be threat, a change which requires the body to adapt." The response is automatic and immediate. Stress can be good when it helps us to perform better or it can be bad when it causes upset or make us sick.

Increased stress increases performance initially ie. Eustress.

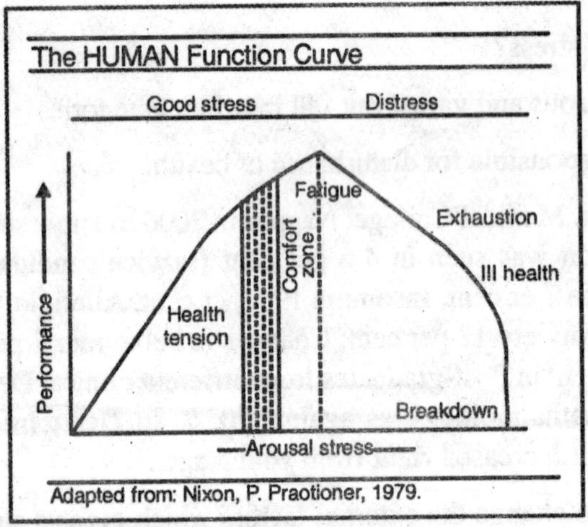


**Fig. 50**

After peak, more stress results in decreased performance, fatigue followed by exhaustion.

What does stress reaction consist of?

The stress reaction results from an outpouring of adrenaline,a stimulant hormone into blood stream.

This with other stress hormones produce a number of changes in the body intended to be protective The result is called "The flight or fight response" because it provides the strength, energy to fight or runaway from the danger.

Changes include

- Increase in heart rate and blood pressure to get more blood to muscles, brain and heart.
- Faster breathing to get more oxygen.
- Tensing of muscles to prepare for action.
- Increased mental alertness and sensitivity of sense organs- to act quickly
- Less blood to skin, GIT, kidney, liver.

- Increase in blood sugar, fats, cholesterol to get extra energy.
- Rise in platelets and blood clotting factors to prevent hemorrhage in case of injury.

So we should learn correct breathing. Rewards with correct breathing are incalculable.

Pranayam is control of Breath. On subtle level 'pran' represent the pranic energy responsible for life or life force and ayam means 'control'. One can control the rhythm of pranic energy with pranayam and achieve healthy body and mind. Pranayam brings more oxygen to blood. The pran is related to mind and mind is related to brain, the brain to soul and soul is ultimately related to that eternal divine force called God. Thus, objective of pranayam is to stimulate,/communicate, regulate and control life force that exists in the body.

In the words of C.L. Schleich "From the moment the umbilical cord is cut, the lungs are the placenta which binds man to the cosmic mother."

## To Be Alive is to Breathe

Few points to be remembered before starting Pranayam..

- Stomach should be empty.
- Wear loose cloths which are comfortable so that full chest expansion is possible.
- Slow and complete exhalation is important, unless receptacle is empty it can not be filled with fresh air.
- At the end of expiration abdominal muscles should contract so that residual air is exhaled completely.

Majority of us are not breathing correctly. Only part of the thorax moves. Diaphragmatic movements are not enough so alveoli at bases remain collapsed. During inspiration, diaphragm goes down and abdominal wall should come forward. During expiration diaphragm goes up and abdomen should go in.

1. Empty Lungs
2. Filled Lungs

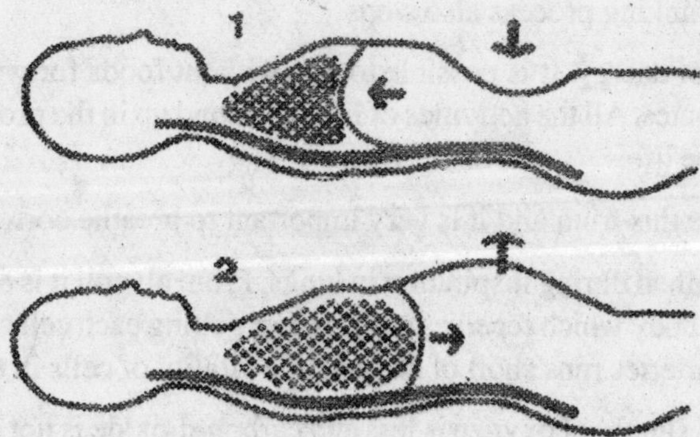


Hypertension, Coronary artery disease, Tension headache, Acidity, Indigeion, Asthma, Allergic Rhinitis, Diabetes, Backache.

Several Depts at AIIMS have been independently researching people who practice these breathing techniques.

The Neurology Dept. checked EEG and found out more beta waves which help to cure depression, in persons doing pranayam.

At Endocrinology Dept. blood cortisol [hormone related to stress]was less in those practicing pranayam.

The Immunology Dept. noted presence of high levels of natural killer cells to fight diseases. Andew Weil MD Say.

The core of human personality is the consciousness which is the life centre around which all activities of body, mind and intellect revolve. It remains ever changeless, immovable like an axel in the wheel but causes all changes and movement to occur. When person succeeds in identifying with this changeless immovable conscious principle within him he is no longer victimised by the changing phenomena of perception, emotions and thought.

If we start thinking who am I? Am I physical body which is constantly changing? As a child it was small and with many limitations. In young age one is conscious about looks and as one is growing old one is conscious about health. In old age one is afraid of diseases and death.

One can observe mind. Sometimes, it is happy or unhappy, disturbed or at peace. One can observe different ideas and thoughts in intellect. If simple logic is applied that subject and object can not be one, subject is pure consciousness and observing all changes in body, mind, and intellect which are objects and One is different from it. Concentrating on real self is meditation. When is my health disturbed? When mind is tense and agitated our stress hormones are secreted which affect our body. Now everybody is talking about meditation for mental peace. All western medical literature is advocating meditation for all medical problems. Meditation is not easy. If we sit for meditation, more and more thoughts come to our mind. If we decide not to think of certain unpleasant events, we start remembering them more. This mind is like a naughty child.

Arjun in Bhagwad Geeta tells Shreekrishna

Chanchalam hi manh Krishna pramathi balvadddhrudam

means O,Krishna mind is restless,turbulent,strong and unyielding

And Shreekrishna says

"Asanshayam maha baho manodurni graham chalam

Abhyasen tukauntey vairagye nacha gruhyate"

It is difficult to control mind but with practice it is possible. We can not control mind but we can control breathing so that automatically mind will be controlled. In 'Upadeshsaram' Raman Maharshi says " Vayurodhaya liyate manh".

If we stop breathing one's thinking process also stops.

Breathing is a great source of energy. It is possible to live without foods for weeks without water for days but without air, we die within few minutes. All the activities of life are bound up in the process of oxidation and reduction. Without 'Oxygen' there can not be life.

It is vital for us to appreciate this truth and it is very important to breathe correctly.

20 per cent of oxygen is breathed during inspiration in lungs. From alveoli it is absorbed in blood. From blood it is carried to billions of cells in the body which receives oxygen. For getting each cell oxygen, it is necessary to breathe correctly. When blood stream in arteries runs short of oxygen, the vitality of cells in the body is diminished.

When breathing is incorrect, supply of oxygen is less and carbon-dioxide is not eliminated properly. When cells receive less oxygen, organs will not be able to function properly .

"The simplest and most powerful technique for protecting your health is absolutely free and right under your nose".

Study was conducted in general population in 2006 in Nagpur for effect of pranayam and yoga on stress-induced medical problems. It was observed that more than 65 per cent patients had 75 per cent relief within one month.

Pranayam was taught to the post-graduate students from Department of Anaesthesia. Nagpur.They were told about relaxation techniques i.e., After 90 minutes of work or study they should take 10-20 minutes rest.

## Relaxation Technique

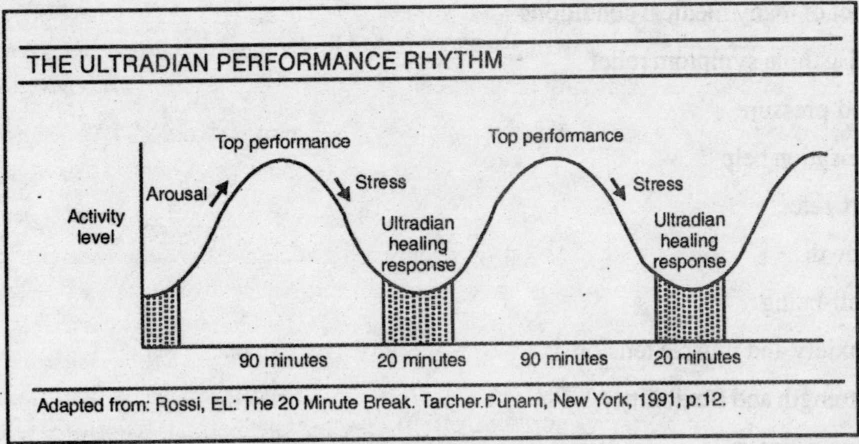


Fig. 51

After one month it was observed that Acidity was decreased in 90% students, Concentration was improved in 80%students, and Students with Asthma had no acute episode. Had more energy, less fatigue in 90% students..

## Health Conditions Benefited by Yoga

The following is a summary of the results of a survey conducted by Yoga Biomedical Trust in 1983-84. 3000 individuals with health ailments for which yoga was prescribed as an alternative therapy were surveyed. The results show that yoga is very effective for treating alcoholism, back pain, nerve or muscle disease, heart disease management, anxiety, arthritis, ulcers and managing cancer. The complete results are shown in the table below.

| Ailment | Number of Cases Reporting | Per cent Claiming Benefit |
|---|---|---|
| Back Pain | 1,142 | 98 |
| Arthritis or rheumatism | 589 | 90 |
| Anxiety | 838 | 94 |
| Migraine | 464 | 80 |
| Insomnia | 542 | 82 |
| Nerve or muscle disease | 112 | 96 |
| Menstrual problems | 317 | 68 |
| Premenstrual tension | 848 | 77 |
| Menopause disorders | 247 | 83 |
| Hypertension | 150 | 84 |
| Heart disease | 50 | 94 |
| Asthma or bronchitis | 226 | 88 |
| Duodenal ulcers | 40 | 90 |
| Hemorrhoids | 391 | 74 |
| Obesity | 140 | 74 |
| Diabetes | 10 | 80 |
| Cancer | 29 | 90 |
| Tobacco addiction | 219 | 74 |
| Alcoholism | 26 | 100 |

**Yoga's effects on the body:** the following is only a partial list of yoga's benefits:

- Reduced stress
- Sound sleep

- Reduced cortisol levels
- Improvement of many medical conditions
- Allergy and asthma symptom relief
- Lower blood pressure
- Smoking cessation help
- Lower heart rate
- Spiritual growth
- Sense of well-being
- Reduced anxiety and muscle tension
- Increased strength and flexibility
- Slowed aging process

## Relieving Stress

The diaphragm, according to yogic science, is the seat of the intelligence of the heart and the window to the soul. During stressful situations, however, when you inhale and exhale, the diaphragm becomes too taut to alter its shape. Yogic exercises address this problem by developing elasticity in the diaphragm, so that, when stretched, it can handle any amount of stress,, whether intellectual, emotional, or physical.

The practice of asanas and pranayama helps to integrate the body, breath, mind, and intellect. Slow, effortless exhalation during practice of an asana brings serenity to the body cells, relaxes the facial muscles, and releases all tension from the organs of perception: the eyes, ears, nose, tongue, and skin.

When this happens, the brain, which is in constant communication with the organs of action, becomes shunya, or void, and all thoughts are stilled. Then, invading fears and anxieties cannot penetrate to the brain. When you develop this ability, you perform your daily activities with efficiency and economy. You do not dissipate your valuable bio-energy. You enter the state of true clarity of intellect. Your mind is free of stress and is filled with calm and tranquillity.

## Asanas & Stress

The practice of asanas and pranayama is the most natural therapy for stress. Practicing asanas with props builds up your stamina and allows you to benefit from the pose without unnecessary strain.

Every individual has the power to discriminate between good habits and bad, and to develop his or her sense of ethical behaviour. By adopting good habits, such as regular yoga practice, you can check the stress that depletes the body's bio-energy. The practice of asanas and pranayama is not just the most effective, but also the most natural therapy for stress, and unlike many other therapies, there is no danger of harmful side effects. Mere relaxation is not sufficient in itself to counter the negative effects of stress, the regular practice of yoga, along with a healthy diet and lifestyle, helps to generate enormous amounts of energy in the body, stimulating the cells and relaxing tensed muscles.

While the effect of asanas and pranayama on the mind takes longer to be felt, with patience and dedication, you will soon discover a feeling of mental poise and well-being during and after your practice. While practicing asanas and pranayama, the five senses of perception that divert the mind to the external environment are drawn inward. When the restlessness of the mind is stilled, your entire being becomes calm and steady. The impact of negative stress are enhanced, building up the resilience and flexibility of the nerves, organs, senses, mind, and intelligence to create a healthy mind and body. Clarity, firmness of purpose, self-discipline, and ethical and moral sensibility follows naturally, enabling you to live a tranquil life, free of stress, and in harmony with your environment.

Yoga-based Remedial Solutions

Why Yoga?

Yoga is derived from the Sanskrit root "Yuj" meaning to unite, to integrate or to cohere and is thus taken to represent the highest state of union, integration or coherence between individual with his goal of life.

- Through Yoga Subject (Traveller) & Object (Goal) get merged leading to excellence. Yoga bestows inner strengths, sharpens intellect, teaches us to control our emotions and brings a rare concentration and efficiency into our actions and work, making one to do the right thing in the right way and at the right time.
- Yoga is a methodical effort towards self perfection by the development of the potentialities latent in the individual. It is a process by which the limitations and imperfections can be washed away.-Sri Aurobindo

**Yogabased Art of Success Model**

Yoga is the only total solution provider for the problems of achieving goal. Thus the basic 'Art of Success Model' has been encompassed into Saint Patanjali Yoga Sutras and Patanjali Ashtanga Yoga Path. So evolved 'Yoga based Art of Success Model' is very simple, universal and adaptable for all walks of life. It can be used by any one for achieving any type of goals may be materialistic or spiritual. It is applicable to every one like Doctors, Engineers, Sportsmen, Politicians and persons from Art and Culture etc

21st Century marked the era of globalisation. The biggest challenge of this century is to develop the human beings, who are competitive, effective, productive and capable of achieving excellence in the international arena. For the realisation of success and attain excellence in all walks of life the **'Yogabased Art of Success Model'** is developed. The Model is very simple, universal and adaptable for all walks of life .Model is having following three fundamental components:

| | | |
|---|---|---|
| The Goal | : | Should be clear and focused. |
| The Path | : | Should be right and holistic. |
| The Traveller | : | Should be able (competent +capable) |

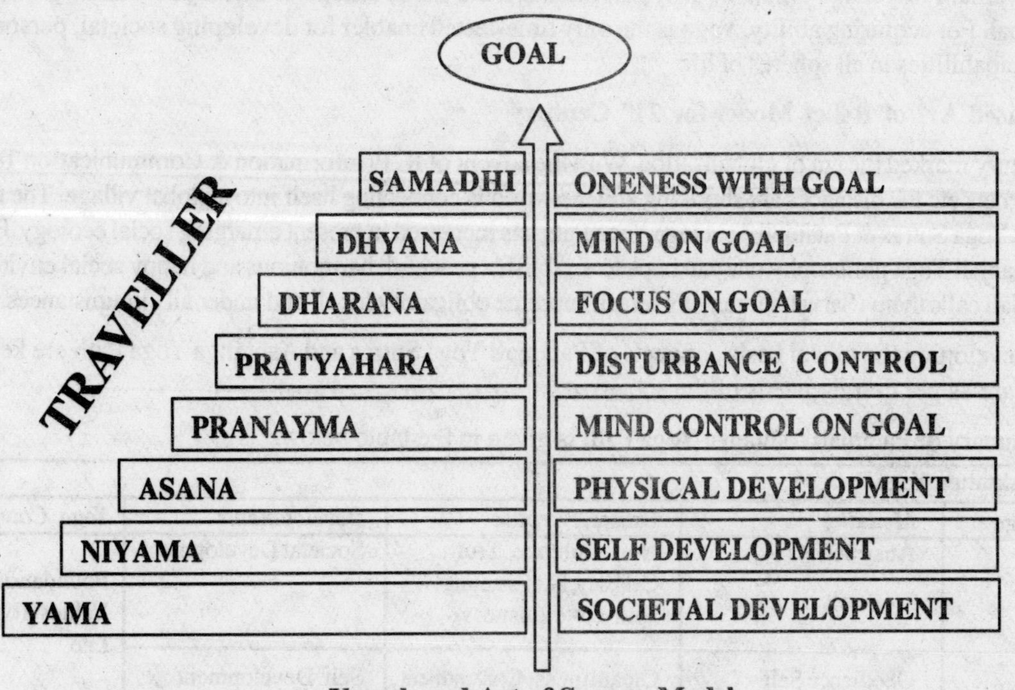


Yoga based Art of Success Model

ASHTANG YOGIC PATH

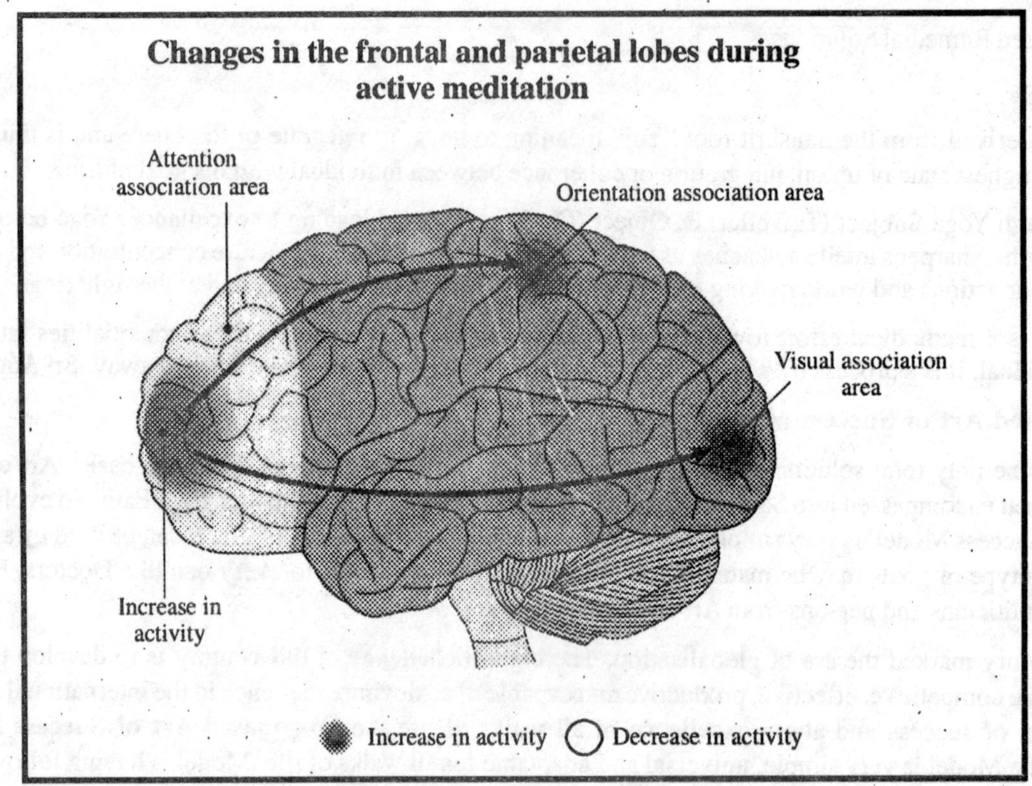


Fig. 52

Selection and achievement of the Goal is the main objective of life. It is the most difficult decision as the mind is always wavering due to environmental influences. However, it is the practice of Yoga that gives the techniques of Meditation to concentrate on the Goal. To achieve the Goal the Path should be right and holistic. Yama, Niyama, Asana, Pranayama, Pratyahara, Dharana, Dhyana, Samadhi are the footsteps of **Patanjali Ashtanga Yoga Path** to achieve the goal. For acquiring ability, **Yoga** is the only time-tested enabler for developing societal, personal, mental, and spiritual capabilities in all spheres of life.

**Yoga-based Art of Relief Model for 21st Century**

21st Century marked the era of globalisation. With the advent of ICT (Information & Communication Technology), TV, Web, Internets etc the distances are shrinking and the world is connecting itself into a global village. The relevance of Saint Patanjali Yoga Sutras & Patanjali Ashtanga Yoga Path has increased in present emerging social ecology. By sustained practice of Patanjali Yoga philosophy one can hope to establish a peaceful, harmonious and happy social environment. No wonder Patanjali calls them (Sarvabhauma) universal, supreme obligatory for all and under all circumstances.

While developing the model basic concepts of Patanjali Yoga Sutras and Ashtanga Yoga Path are kept same but explanations are as per current needs of the society

The summary of Patanjali Ashtanga Yoga Path is given in the table below.

| **Patanjali Ashtanga Yoga Path** | | | | |
|---|---|---|---|---|
| ***Limbs of Yoga*** | ***Meaning*** | ***Values/Purpose*** | ***Developments*** | ***Yoga Categories*** |
| **Yama** | Abstinences | Non-violence, Truth, Celibacy, Non-stealing, Non-covetousness | Societal Development | Foundation -Ethical Values Yogic Way of Life |
| **Niyama** | Obedience Self - Discipline | Cleanliness, Contentment, Self-Study, Dedication to God/Teacher | Self Development | |

| Asana | Body Postures | Physical development and Health | Physical Development and Good Health | Bahiranga Yoga External Yoga Practice and Development |
|---|---|---|---|---|
| Pranayama | Energy Control | Control of breath and vital functions of the body | Mind Control | |
| Pratyahara | Abstraction, Control of senses organs | Control of sense by restraining them from object. | Disturbance Control | |
| Dharana | Concentration | Focus on the Goal | Clear and Focused Goal | |
| Dhyana | Meditation | Total knowledge of the goal | Mind on Goal | Antaranga Yoga Internal Yoga Practice and Development |
| Samadhi | Absorption | Oneness with the Goal | Oneness with Goal and Detachment | |

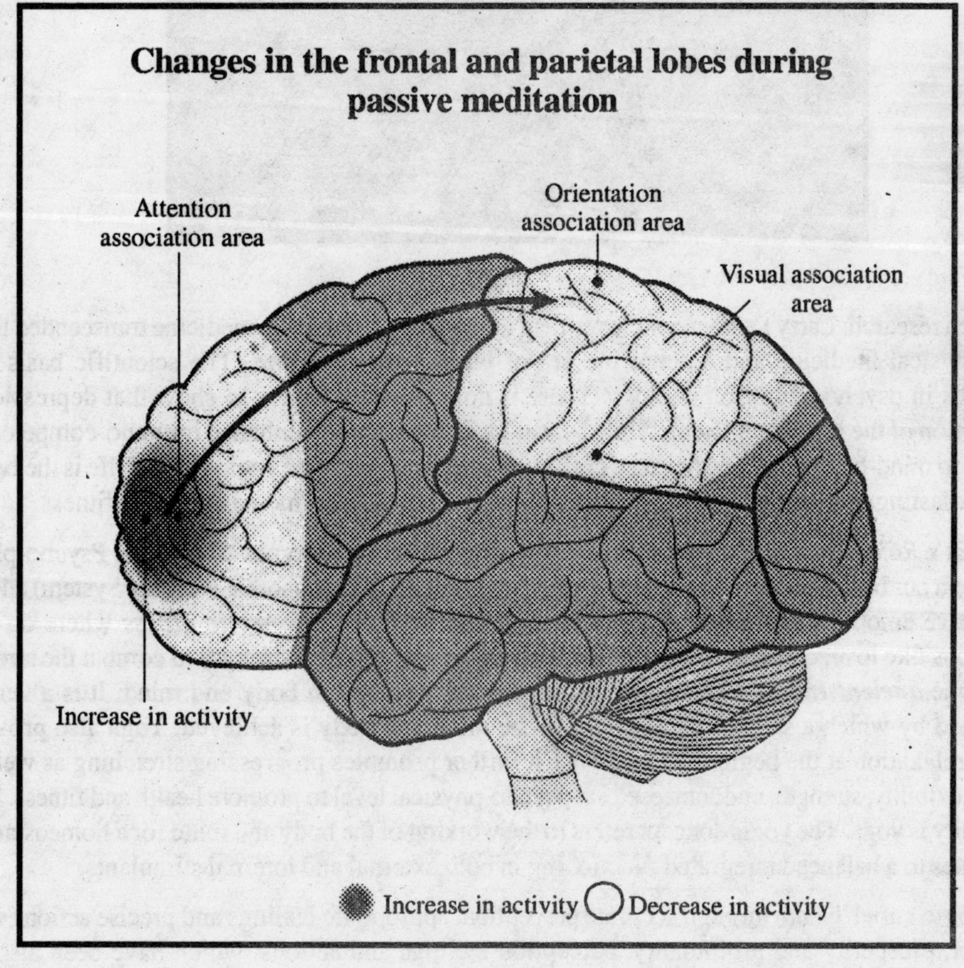


Fig. 53

Fig. 54

After much research, Larry Dossey concludes that, around 1950, scientific medicine transcended the mechanistic approach of physical medicine and entered the era of ***mind-body medicine.*** The scientific basis of mind-body medicine resides in psycho-neuroimmunology. There is now ample evidence to show that depression and despair impair the function of the immune system, while peace, love, hope and joy enhance immuno-competence. **Yoga** is of great relevance to mind-body medicine because of the way it looks at life. The yogic view of life is the best prescription ever written for lasting peace and joy, even at the cellular level, which promote health and fitness.

Emotion is a *Rajas guna of Prakriti,* which is responsible for many types of disease. Psycho-physiologically, emotions act upon our body through hypothalamus which controls ANS (Autonomic Nervous System) and the endocrine systems. Negative emotions like anger, fear, greed, jealousy give rise to ***somatic illness*** where on the other hard positive emotions like love, compassion, friendship, affection, etc. give the strength to combat the stress. Yoga plays a vital role as the ***ancient Indian healing art,*** which brings harmony in body and mind. It is a very rational and scientific method by which a state of equilibrium in the mind and body is achieved. Yoga also provides muscular stretching and relaxation at the beginning; however, it further promotes progressing stretching as well as relaxation that enhances flexibility, strength, endurance, etc. at psycho-physical level to promote health and fitness. Self-perfection or state of divinity is yoga. The yogic concept refers to the working of the body and mind for a homeostatic mechanism, which contributes to a balanced integrated functioning in both external and internal stimulants.

Yoga helps to enrich health through accurate perception, appropriate feelings and precise actions with increasing pleasure, power, prosperity and profoundity, perception feelings and actions, which have been also expressed by terms *Cognition, Affection and Conation* respectively. In traditional parlance, this is called fulfillment of four *Purusharthas,* viz., *Dharma, Artha, Kaama, and Moksha.*

Thus, Yoga works for better health in increasing an appropriate satisfaction of physical, instinctual, emotional, intellectual needs and fulfillment and happiness arising from it.

## Summary

### Asanas for Stress:

Tadasana Samasthithi Tadasana Urdhava Hastasana Tadasana Urdhva Baddha Hastasana Tadasana Paschima Baddha Namaskar Tadasana Paschima Namaskar

Tadasana Gomukhasana Utthita Trikonasana Utthita Parsvakonasana Ardha Chandrasana Uttanasana Prasarita Padottanasana Adhomukha Svanasana Dandasana Virasana Urdhavamukha Janu Sirsasana Baddhakonasana Swastikasana

Paripurna Navasana Upavista Konasana Paschimottanasana Adhomukha Swastikasana Bharadvajasana Marichyasana Utthita Marichyasana Parsva Virasana

Salamba Sarvangasna Halasana Viparita Karani Setubandha Sarvangasana Viparita Dandasana Ustrasana Supta Padangusthansana Supta Baddhakonasana

Suta Virasana Ujjayi Pranayama Viloma 2 Pranayama Savasana

"The body is your temple. Keep it pure and clean for the soul to reside in."

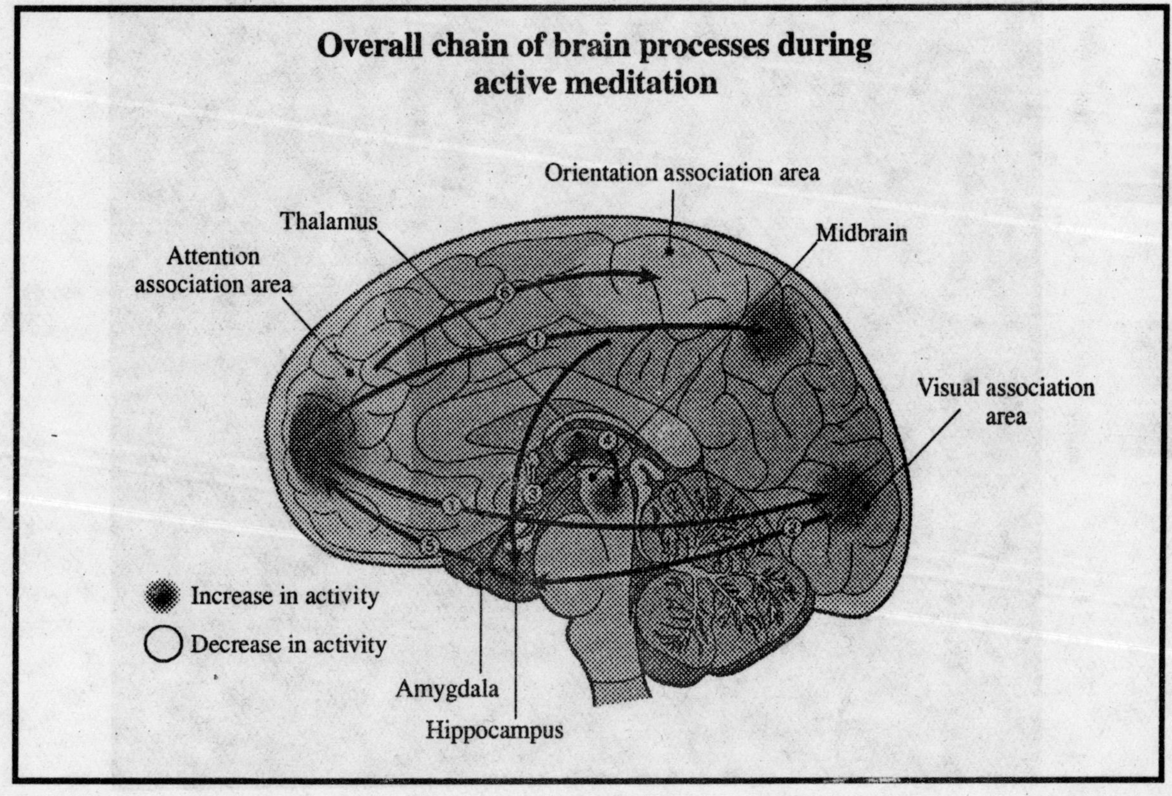


**Overall chain of brain processes during active meditation**

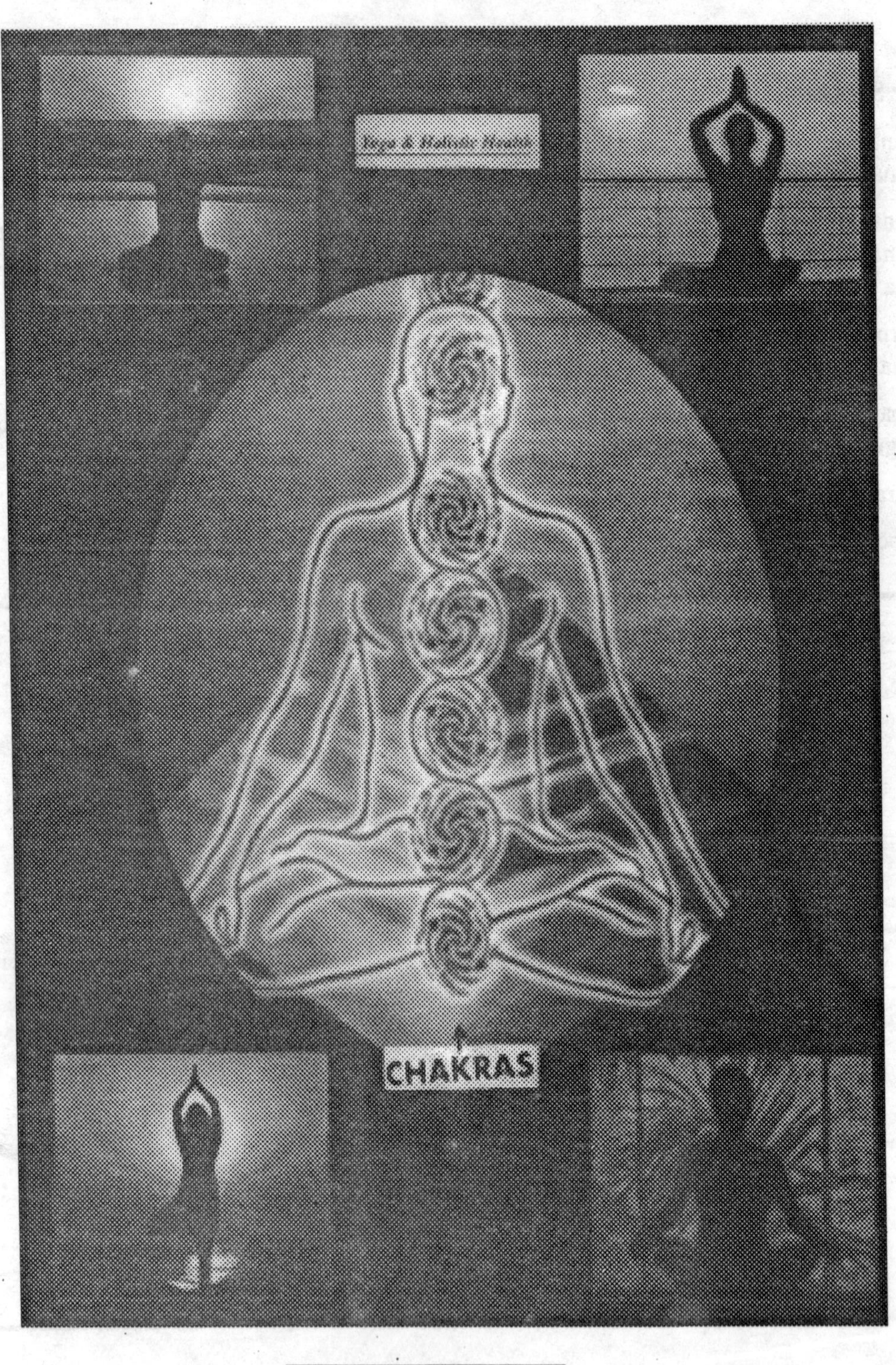


## CHAKARAS

### Understanding Imbalance

Everything that happens to us on an emotional level has an energetic impact on the subtle body (or aura), which in turn has an impact on the physical body. Chakras are thought to be non-physical energy centres located about an inch away from the physical body. The energy field of each extends beyond the visible body matter in the subtle body.

It is important to remember that chakras do not have a physical form and any illustration of the chakras is merely a visual aid to the imagination and not a literal, physical reality.

Chakras are a way of describing the flow of subtle energy and are said each to be related to an endocrine gland, which the chakra is thought to influence. The chakra exists in a state of synchrony and balance. However, with stress, the chakra can lose their ability to synchronise and they become unbalanced.

If negative energy accumulates in a chakra, the function of the chakra become impaired. Ultimately, this can lead to energy blocks. If one chakra ceases to function, this creates an imbalance as the other chakras attempt to compensate, creating additional strain on the energy system.

An accumulates of negative energy in one or more chakras can manifest as an emotional or physical condition. Often we are only aware of a change in the physical body as our attention is drawn to pain or disease; we do not usually link the symptom to a cause within the subtle body.

So chakras are the focal points for the subtle energies and are the key to restring balancing. By placing hands along the axis of the chakras, energy can be aligned and harmony restored. By working with the subtle energy, the chakras may be strengthened and energy may be increased, decreased or balanced as required by the body at the time of the treatment.

## The Base or Root Chakra

**Location** at the base of the spine

**Relevance** the foundation chakra; linked with nature and planet Earth; concerned with all issues of a physical nature – the body, the senses, sensuality, a person's sex, survival, aggression and self-defense; at a physical level, it is linked to the endocrine system through the adrenal glands; its energies also affect the lower parts of the pelvis, the hips, legs and feet.

**Imbalance** if this chakra is unbalanced it can make a person feel as if they are ungrounded and unfocused; they may feel weak, lack confidence and be unable to achieve their goals.

**Colour Association** Red

## The Sacral Chakra

**Location** at the level of the sacrum between the naval and the base chakra.

**Relevance** concerned with all issues of creativity and sexuality; at the physical level; it is linked to the testes in the male and the ovaries in the female; its energies also affect the urino – genital organs, the uterus, the kidneys, the lower digestive organs and the lower back.

**Imbalance** a person with an imbalance in this chakra may bury their emotions and be overly sensitive; an imbalance may also lead to sexual difficulties and energy blocks which affect creativity.

**Colour Association** Orange.

## The Solar Plexus Chakra

**Location** at approximately waist level.

**Relevance** relates to our emotions, self – worth; feelings such as fear, axiety, insecurity, jealousy and anger are generated here; at a physical level, it is linked to the Islets of Langerhans in the pancreas; its energy also affects the solar and splenic nerve plexuses, the digestive system, the pancreas, liver, gall bladder, diaphragm and middle back.

**Imbalance** people who are under stress will imbalance in this chakra; shock and stress have a greater impact on this chakra; it is in the solar plexus chakra that negative energies relating to thoughts and feeling are processed; people with an imbalance in this chakra may feel depressed, insecure, lacking in confidence and may worry what other things.

**Colour Association** Yellow.

## The Heart Chakra

**Location** In the centre of the chest

**Relevance** concerned with love and the heart; it deals with all issues concerned with love and affection; at a physical level it is linked to the thymus gland; its energies also affect the cardiac and pulmonary nerve plexuses, the heart, lungs, bronchial tubes, chest, upper back and arms; the point of connection between the upper and lower chakras.

**Imbalance** If the energy does not flow freely between the solar plexus and the heart, or between the heart and throat, it can lead to energy withdrawal into the body; a person with an imbalance in this chakra may feel sorry for themselves, be afraid of letting go, feel unworthy of love or feel terrified of rejection.

**Colour Association** Green

## The Throat Chakra

**Location** at the base of the neck

**Relevance** concerned with communication and expression, it also deals with the issue of truth and true expression of the soul; at a physical level, it is linked to the thyroid and parathyroid glands; its energies also affect the laryngeal nerve plexus, the organs of the throat, the neck, nose, mouth, teeth and ears.

**Imbalance** If this chakra is out of balance it may effect our ability to express our emotions, frustration and tension may result, a person with an imbalance in this chakra may feel unable to relax.

**Colour association** Blue.

## The Brow Chakra

**Location** In the middle of the forehead over the third eye area

**Relevance** Commonly know as the 'third eye' the brow chakra is the storehouse of memories and imagination and is associated with intellect, understanding and intuition; at a physical level, it is linked to the hypothalamus and pituitary gland; its energies also affect the nerves of the head, brain, eyes and face

**Imbalance** If this chakra is not functioning correctly, it can lead to headaches and nightmares; a person with an imbalance in this chakra may be oversensitive, be afraid of success, be non-assertive and undisciplined.

**Colour Association** Indigo

## The Crown Chakra

| | |
|---|---|
| Location | on top of the head |
| Relevance | the centre of our spirituality and is concerned with thinking and dicision-making , at a physical level it is linked to pineal gland; its energies also affect the brain and the rest of the body |
| Imbalance | an imbalance in this chakra may be reflected in an unwillingness to open up to our spiritual potential and imbalance, may also be in an ability to make decisions |
| Colour Association | Violet |

The Figure depicts the various Chakras and their placement on the body as explained above.

A WESTERNER IN SAMADHI – JAMES J. LYNN' (RAJASI JANAKANANDA)

On a private beach at Encinitas, Calif., in January 1937, after five years of daily practice of kriya Yoga, Mr. Lynn received in samadhi (superconsciousness) the Beatific Vision : the Infinite Lord as the Indwelling Glory.

## MEDITATION TOOLS

Meditation is best practised somewhere quiet and free distractions, and at a moderate temperature. This may be in your home or in a natureal setting. Aside from these basics, you need little more than the proper attitude and a keen desire to expand your inner horizons.

### SACRED SPACE

The place in which you meditate should be kept clean and tidy. Place fresh flowers in it daily. An altar, covered with a clean cloth, will act as a focus for your meditation. An oil lamp or candle may be kept burning to purify the environment, or lit when you sit for your practice. Add some uplifting pictures, statues, or symbols that have meaning for you.

## INCENSE

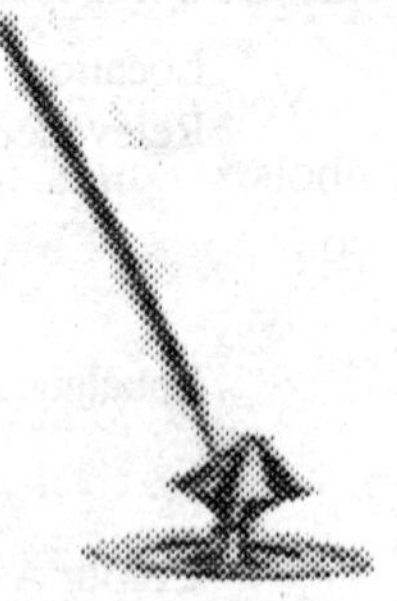

Burn soothing incense to help calm the mind when you sit for meditation. Sandalwood and frankincense have this effect.

## JAPA MALA

Repetitions of mantras, or Japa. May be counted using a string of 108 mala beads. Hold them in the right hand and count them between the thumb and middle fingers (not the index finger, as it symbolizes the ego)

## CANDLE OR OIL LAMP

By lighting an oil lamp or a candle, you are symbolizing your readiness to tune yourself to the inner light.

## FRESH FLOWERS

The meditation area should be kept clean and sattvic (pure). A bouquet of fresh flowers placed on the altar every day will inspire and uplift the mind.encouragng a mood that is conductive to meditation.

## COMFORTABLE SEAT

Arrange a place to sit facing the altar, using a low cushion or mat. A cushion under the buttocks will relieve any possible strain on the kness.

## MANTRAS AS MENTAL TOOLS

The word "Mantra" is derived from the Sanskrit words "manas", meaning mind, and "tra", meaning to take across or to go beyoud. A Mantra is a mystical symbol encased in a sound structure, a mental tool that, through repetition, helps the mind in its quest to transcend its normal limitations. Once you have chosen a Mantra, you should never change it. Eight Mantras are described here, and some are shown with images and models of the particular Hindu gods with which they are associated. All of these gods represent aspects of the One God that dwells in all.

## THE ALTAR

You may choose to place a combination of any of the elements shown here on your altar. If you don't like symbols, pictures, or statues at all, simple place a clean cloth and some flowers on a low table and use this simple altar as your point of focus.

## OM NAMO BHAGAVATE VASUDEVAYA

(Om Na-Mo Bha-Ga-Va-Tay Vaa-Soo-Dave-Aya) Krishna is seen as the supreme world teacher as he is the giver of the Bhagavad Gita. One of the great texts on Yoga.

## OM NAMAH SIVAYA

(Om Na-Mah She-Va-Ya)

As Nataraja. The Cosmic Dancer. Siva presides over the constant destruction and re-creation of the Universe the energy that destroys the lower self to allow positive personal growth.

## OM NAMO NARAYANAYA

(Om Na-Mo Naa-Raa-Ya-Na-Ya)

This mantra is associated with the god Vishnu, representing the preserving energy that keeps the universe in balance. It is seen as a 'Peace Mantra', of particular use at this time, when negative energies seem to be out of control.

## OM SRI MAHA LAKSHMYAI NAMAH

(Om Shree Ma-Ha Laksh-MeYay Na-Mah) Lakshmi is seen as God taking the form of the ever-giving Mother. She is the source and giver of all blessings and wealth, especially the blessings of inner peace and spiritual prosperity.

## OM GAM GANAPATAYE NAMAH

(Om Gam Ga-Na-Pa-Ta-Yay-Na-Mah) Ganapathi is another name for Ganesha, the elephant headed deity who is revered as the remover of obstacles and bestower of success.

## SOHAM

(So-Ham) This is a philosophical, or Velantic, Mantra. The words may be roughly translated as "I am that I am", meaning that no limitations can be put on the divine. Soham is the natural sound of the breath being inhaled and exhaled.

## OM

(A-U-M) Om is the highest and most abstract mantra of all. Om is the Shabdabrahman, or the sound by which the universe was created, the ancient name for the 'big bang' theory of modern scientists. Om is all sounds, all vibrations, and all Mantras together.

## OM SRI DURGAYAI NAMAH

(Om Shree Dur-Ga-Yay Na-Mah)

In Durga, we see God as Mother. She is the divine protector. In her arms. She holds all the powers of the Universe. She rides a lion. Symbolizing the forces of nature.

## (1) Zen Meditation

The word Zen, in fact, means meditation. It is a Japanese word, corresponding to the Chinese chan and the Hindi dhyana. It is the essential theme of a sect of Buddhism which flourished in China during the Sung period (between A.D. 1000 and 1300), and entered Japan in the twelfth century.

Zen meditation is difficult to describe in words in words. It means more like the words "intuition" and "realization". It means a way of life in which there is no division between thought and action no gulf between the unconscious and the conscious mind and no absolute distinction between the self and the external world, even between the various parts of the external world and the whole. For a student, Zen practice begins with his continuing the inhalations and exhalations of his breath while he is in the motionless Zen posture. Mind is concentrated on breathing-in and breathing-out, for-getting all other things, surroundings and environments. In continuing the in-and out-breaths in natural rhythm and without strain, the mind, as it were, has a scaffolding to support it. When concentration on the breathing becomes such that awareness of the counting is clear and the count is not lost, the next step, a slightly more difficult type of Zen, is following the inhalations and exhalations of the breath with the mind's eye only, again in natural rhythm. A blissful state of mind is said to flow from concentration on the breath in this manner. Next follows Zen with a Koan, a riddle, to meditate on. The aim is not for the student to find a solution of the riddle through rational processes, but to provide a more difficult exercise in concentration. Through intense self-inquiry, the mind gradually be-come denuded of its delusive ideas which in the beginning hamper its effort to become one with the koan. As these abstract notions fall away, concentration on the koan strengthens. Once the koan grips the heart and mind, the inquiry goes on ceaselessly in the sub-consciousness. So long as the mind is occupied with a particular task, the question fades from consciousness surfacing naturally as soon as the action is over. The highest form of Zen meditation is shikan taza, "just sitting". A person meditating is not supposed to do anything except to be sitting. During meditation, thinking and fantasy are treated as intruders or distracting influences, to be patient with until they go away. Sitting Zen and mobile Zen are two aspects equally dynamic and mutually reinforcing. One who sits devotedly in Zen everyday, his mind free of discriminating thoughts, finds it easier to relate himself wholeheartedly to his daily tasks, one who performs every act with total attention and clear awareness, finds it less difficult to achieve emptiness of mind during sitting periods.

To learn doing Zen meditation is not easy. One has to be thoroughly embued in its philosophy before One can approach it. The uniqueness of Zen lies in the fact that the mind is freed from bondage to all thought forms, visions, objects and images. In the broad sense, Zen means to enter fully into every action with total attention and clear awareness.

**Heart Beat:** In 1972, Goyeche and his colleagues compared the effect of Zen meditation with relaxation in eight subjects. They found that the heart rate decreased appreciably during Zen meditation.

**Respiration:** Japanese physiologists Sugi and Akutsu in 1968, observed a 20 per cent decrease in oxygen consumption and reduction in output of carbon dioxide during meditation in ten Zen monks. In 1960, Japanese neuro-psychiatrist Hirai noticed that the respiratory rate decreased during Zen. In 1968, Akishige showed both a decreased in oxygen consumption and rate of respiration during Zen meditation. In another study by Goyeche, Chihara and Shimizu in1972, rate of respiration associated with Zen meditation was found to be slower than during control periods.

In 1957, Japanese neuro-psychiatrist Kasamatsu reported substantial increase in alpha activity during Zen meditation by an experienced practitioner of Zen. Blocking of alpha activity by external stimuli was not observed. In another study by Kasamatsu and Hirai in 1966, 48 priests and disciples of Zen Buddhism were selected as subjects and their E.E.G.'s were continuously recorded before, during and after meditation. The appearance of alpha waves was observed, without regard to open eyes, within 50 seconds after the beginning of meditation. The alpha waves continued to appear and their amplitudes increased. As meditation progressed, a decrease from alpha frequency gradually manifested and a theta pattern with alpha background was observed in some of the priests. These E.E.G. Changes could be classified into four stages: the appearance of alpha waves (Stage I), an increase of alpha amplitude (Stage II), a decrease of alpha frequency (Stage III), and appearance of rhythmical theta pattern (Stage IV), These four stages of the .E.E.G. Changes ran parallel with the disciples' mental stages and years spent in Zen training. In 1969, Kasamatsu and Hirai observed that both alpha and theta activity were blocked by the presentation of auditory (sound) stimuli.

**Skin Resistance and Relaxation:** In 1968, in his study of experienced practitioners of Zen, Akishige reported an increase in galvanic skin resistance.

To sum up, the data obtained from experimental studies on Zen meditation show almost the same pattern of response as observed during yogic meditation. Exposure to sound stimuli, however, blocked alpha pattern of brain waves produced through Zen mediation: in yogic, meditation this blocking of alpha waves did not occur, showing thereby that through yogic meditation, one becomes more oblivious to external environments than is possible through Zen meditation.

## (2) Transcendenal Meditation (TM)

Transcendental meditation is a techniques for expanding conscious awareness and for reducing stress and tension. The word "transcendental" means "going beyond". The technique claims to take the practitioner beyond the familiar level of wakeful experience to a state of profound rest coupled with heightened awareness.

**Heart Beat:** Robert Keith Wallace, initially at the University of California, Los Angeles, and later at Harvard Medical School, and Herbert Benson, cardiologist and associate professor of medicine at Harvard Medical School, have made the maximum number of scientific observations in transcendental meditation. In Wallace's study of 1970, heart rate of each of the subjects decreased during meditation, with a mean decrease of five beats per minute. In 1972, Wallace and Benson, again reported a decease in heart rate during transcendental meditation.

**Respiration:** In 1970, Wallance found that during transcendental meditation, oxygen consumption decreased in all subjects within 5 minutes after beginning meditation. The mean decrease was about 45 cubic cms. Per minute or about 20 per cent decrease from control period. A mean decrease in total ventilation during meditation of about one litre per minute was observed. The observed decrease in total ventilation was caused by either decrease in frequency of breath or tidal volume, varying from subject to subject.

Wallace, Benson and Wilson in 1971, and Wallace and Benson in 1972, confirmed in precise detail what had been reported earlier about oxygen consumption and showed that carbon dioxide elimination decreased from 219 cubic cms per minute to 187 cubic cms, during meditation, and then returning to about the premeditation, level afterward. The relation of carbon dioxide elimination to oxygen consumption remained essentially unchanged throughout the three periods, which indicated that the controlling factor for both was the rate of metabolism. The reduction in metabolic rate (and hence in the need for oxygen) during meditation was reflected in decrease, essentially involuntary, in the rate of respiration (two breaths less per minute) and in the volume of air breathed (one litre less per minute).

The most interesting finding they reported was about blood lactate concentration. Measurements of lactate concentration in the blood (an indication of metabolism in the absence oxygen) showed that during meditation, the subject's lactate level declined precipitiously. During the first 10 minutes of meditation, the lactate level in the subject's arterial blood decreased at the rate of 10.26 mgs per 100 cubic cms. per hour, nearly four times faster than the rate of decrease in people normally resting in a supine position or in the subjects themselves during their pre-meditation period. After the subjects ceased meditating, the lactate level continued to fall for a few minutes and then began to rise, but at the end of the post-meditation period, it was still considerably below the pre-meditation level. The mean level during the pre-meditation period was 11.4 mg. per 100 cubic cms., during meditation 8 mg. and during post-meditation 7.3 mg.

Lactate level in the blood is said to be one of the indices of the state of mind of a person. It is diminished during sleep and in a relaxed state of mind; it is increased when the person is tense ans agitated.

**Brain-waves:** In 1970, Wallace reported E.E.G. Findings in fifteen normal colleage students whose practice of transcendental meditation had ranged from six months to 3 years. Each subject sat quietly with eyes open for 5 minutes and then with eyes closed for 15 minutes. He meditated for 30 minutes, continued to sit with eyes closed for 10 minutes, and then sat with eyes open for 5 minutes. Before meditation, with eyes closed all subjects showed alpha activity. During meditation, the regularity and amplitude of the alpha waves increased sed in all subjects. In four of the subjects, the alpha waves changed to a slower alpha wave frequency and in some cases stopped for 2 to 5 minute periods and low valtage theta waves predominated. In almost all subjects, alpha wave blockade appeared after sound or light stimuli. After meditation, regular alpha activity continued when eyes were closed, and irregular alpha activity developed when eyes were open. In 1971, Wallace Benson and Wilson substantiated these findings

Neurologist Banquet conducted very comprehensive investigations on the E.E.G. Patterns in subjects during transcendental meditation and in control subjects who relaxated for 30 minutes with eyes closed. He noted that alpha waves which were present in the resting state of all meditators incerased in amplitude during the first stage of meditation. Then occurred a shift to slower frequencies, mainly theta wave patterns, but unlike the theta and delta patterns of drowsiness. Four advanced meditators went into a third stage which they identified as either deep meditation or pure awareness. During this stage, synchronous beta waves of an almost constant frequency and amplitude appeared over the entire scalp. In all meditating subjects, the end of meditation repeated the stage one pattern, with an increase in alpha waves. In the advanced meditators, alpha waves. In the advanced meditators, alpha and some times theta waves persisted after meditation, even with eyes open.

A significant finding that emerged form Banquet's researches was that the brain wave patterns tend to synchronize during deep meditation. To this phenomena of marked uniformity of frequency and amplitude in electical activity from all areas of the brain, Banquet gave the name of 'hypersynchrony'. According to him,this may have something to do with the feeling of pure awareness or consciousness.

**Skin Resistance and Relaxation:** In 1970, Wallace reported a substantial increase in palmer G.S.R during meditation. This increase was, however, not sustained in the rest period following meditation. In 1971, Wallace and his colleagues observed a substantial increase of approximately 60 per cent G.S.R. during meditation. In 1973, Schwartz reported a very slight increase in G.S.R. During meditation.

To sum up, the data obtained from experiental studies on transcendental studies on transcendental meditation show a response akin to that found in yogic meditation and Zen meditation: pulse and respiration rate is decreased, oxygen utilization and carbon dioxided output is decreased, there is slowing and in some studies, increased synchronization of electrocortical rhythms and an increase in G.S.R. tested on 77 healthy subjects, 10 females and 7 males. The subjects taught themselves this relaxation technique from an instruction sheet provided to them. Each subject was observed for five consecutive periods of twelve minutes each. Three of the periods were control periods in which the subjects sat quietly and read material selected for its neutral emotional content; for one period the subjects were instructed only to close their eyes, and for another period, instructions for the relaxation technique were followed.

**Results:** During the practice of this relaxation, oxygen consumption decreased by 13 per cent, carbon dioxide production decreased by 12 per cent, and respiratoy rate decreased by 4.6 breaths per minute below control values(obtained while sitting quiently, reading). Respiratory quotient remained unchanged throughout the experiment. The precedure of simply sitting quietly and closing the eyes failed to produce a statistically significant drop in oxygen consumption, carbon diaxide production and respiratory rate below the mean control values.

The results of this study were closely parallel to the 1970 and 1971 findings of Wallance and others, in which these parameters were measured during the practice of transcendental meditation. These findings show that meditation as such without any esoteric ritual, as is inserted in other systematized forms, can be as effective in providing relaxation. This is a significant finding. If and when confirmed by other researchers, it can be made use of by more and more people without actually learning it from teachers or undergoing long-drawn preliminaries and precedures.

...✎...✎...✎

# CHAPTER 16

# Beating Stress With Alternative Therapies

## REDUCING STRESS

Stress in itself is not harmful, but it can seriously affect those who react badly to it. To improve your effectiveness as a manager, you must be able to recognise your limits and take action to reduce stress when it threatens your performance.

**A. Recognising the signs:** Everyone reacts to stress differently, but it may manifest itself in physical symptoms, such as skin complaints or digestive troubles. You may feel irritable and run-down. Work can become obsessive, and nervous problems can result in depression, anxiety or other psychological disorders. Look out for warning signs and tackle stress before it becomes debilitating.

**B. Coping with stress:** Deal with stress positively by seeking support from superiors, close friends, and colleagues, and prioritising your workload.

**C. Analysing Personality:** Research has shown that certain types of people are more prone to stress and its by-products, such as heart disease. If you are an ambitious manager who is extremely competitive, fast in thought, speech, and action, committed, impatient, and pressed for time, you are likely to be a Type A personality - at risk from stress. If you are more placid, you are less at risk and classed as Type B, Type A managers may also be tense egotists who lack self-control and are quick to anger. If you fit the Type A pattern, modify your behaviour to reduce the chances and incidence of stress.

**D. Handling Anxiety:** Being anxious is an unpleasant experience. It can have a perfectly understandable cause. A merger or re-organisation, for instance, may threaten your job or your powers. Threats produce anxiety. But what action can you take to remove the threat? In the above examples, almost certainly none. However, you should try to calm your anxiety. Avoid listening to rumours and think positively.

After all, the threat may not even materialise, in which case, you have made yourself feel awful for nothing. Whatever the cause of the anxiety, identify that cause, develop a plan for removing the cause, if possible, and/or form a contingency plan to cope. Occupying yourself with this three-part formula will lessen anxiety anyway, and could make it wholly unnecessary.

**E. Tackling Difficulties:** It is easy to procrastinate, but this habit (which is all but universal) can increase your stress in two ways. First, you may feel guilty about leaving the task undone. Second, you are building up stressful time pressure for the future. Procrastination is itself a symptom of stress. For example, a decision may involve taking a risk, or a necessary action (say, firing somebody) may loom ahead. Your reaction to these stresses may be to delay the evil hour. That is bad stress management. You will still have to grasp the nettle, and will pass more stressful hours, days, or months before you do so. Do it now.

## Tips for De-Stressing

1. Work more effectively, rather than for longer hours
2. Discuss personal problems with a wise listener
3. Defuse anxieties by listing possible future events, good and bad
4. Analyse reasons for procrastination and face them squarely. Then set yourself a deadline for action
5. Get excited about challenges in a positive manner
6. Find relaxation methods that suit you and use them

**Managers or employers efforts to reduce stress at work**

Stress on the job creates high costs for businesses and institutions, reducing morale, productivity, and earnings, Clearly, it is in every employer's best interest-fiscal and otherwise–to reduce workplace stress as much as possible, Businesses can lower and prevent job stress through two methods:

- Stress management programmes and training for employees.
- Organisational changes that improve working conditions

**Improve communication**

- Share information with employees to reduce uncertainty about their jobs and futures.
- Clearly define employees' roles and responsibilities.
- Make communication friendly and efficient, not mean-spirited

Consult your employees

- Give workers opportunities to participate in decisions that affect their jobs.
- Consult employees about scheduling and work rules.
- Be sure the workload is suitable to employees' abilities and resources; avoid unrealistic deadlines.
- Show that individual workers are valued.

Offer rewards and incentive.

- Praise good work performance verbally and institutionally
- Provide opportunities for career development
- Promote an "entrepreneurial" work climate

Cultivate a friendly social climate

- Provide opportunities for social interaction among employees
- Establish a zero-tolerance policy for harassment
- Make management actions consistent with organisational values.

**Employees efforts to reduce job stress**

While organisational change comes from management, there are still many things employees – individually or collectively——can do to reduce workplace stress.

**Stand Up for Yourself**

**Get a job description.** If your employer hasn't provided a specific, written description of your job, ask for one, or, better, ask to negotiate one. According to the American Psychological. Association, the act of negotiating a job description "does more to dispel a sense of powerlessness than anything else we know. You can object to what and insist on what you do want. If there is a compromise, it is because you agreed to it. With a clear job description, your expectations are spelled out, as are your boss's."

**Change your job.** If you like where you're working but your job is too stressful, ask if the company can tailor the job to your skills or move you to a less pressured slot.

**Get support.** Use the local, state and federal agencies created to support workers' interests and your union, if you belong to one to back you up in situations that expose you to unnecessary danger unsafe or unhealthful conditions, or undue harassment. While some locations and agencies are more sympathetic to employees' rights than others, sometimes simply mentioning that you know where to turn for help is enough to start an employer thinking about improvement.

**Get a new job.** If the level of stress at your job is harming your health and your relationships, and you don't see any prospect of real change, it may be time to move on.

Managing Occupational Stress – Suggestion

1. We bring our own particular situations to the job, so we are in part, responsible for our own job stress...what to do?
2. Search for an optimal level of occupational stress - not too much and not too little.
3. You, the job and other people in the job all contribute to occupational stress...have to tackle all of them to combat stress.
4. Business management is truly interested in doing whatever is financially/operationally reasonable to combat stress of employees.
5. Whenever possible 'ensure that jobs are clearly defined, responsibilities are given and ambiguity is minimised
6. Whenever possible minimise role fulfillment problems at work.
7. Note that workaholics have both good and not so good characteristics.
8. Be aware of possibilities of burnout.
9. Note the problems/challenges facing women who work outside of the home...try to help reduce their stressors.
10. Fix the established and unfair situations affecting women who work outside of the home.
11. Eliminate sexual harassment in the workplace.
12. Make a note of the stressors faced by homemakers...help them whenever possible.
13. Use a variety of techniques to combat occupational stressors.
14. Be especially aware of women's stressors...remove/reduce/fix them whenever possible life-situation intervention: change/quit the job.
15. Perception intervention: see the bright side (look up and see the stars, rather than down and see the mud.
16. Emotional arousal intervention: practice relaxation.
17. Physiological arousal intervention: exercise.

We all face different challenges and obstacles and sometimes the pressure is hard to handle. When we feel overwhelmed, under the gun, or unsure how to meet the demands placed on us, we experience stress. In small doses, stress can be a good thing. It can give you the push you need, motivating you to do your best and to stay focused and alert. Stress is what keeps you on your toes during a presentation at work or drives you to study for your midterm when you'd rather be watching TV. But when the going gets too tough and life's demands exceed your ability to cope, stress becomes a threat to both your physical and emotional well-being.

## DETOX YOUR WAY TO HEALTH

A well- planned detox diet help remove toxins from your system.

Detox regimen is the buzzzword today. And no, we are not referring to some treatment for substance or alcohol abuse. Short for detoxification, detox therapy has more to do with cleansing system and help eliminate potentially toxic substances from the body. This would entail a planned diet and other means to remove dietary toxins from the body. This might include fasting as in water or juice fasts, combining certain types of food in your diet, increased consumption of fish, restricting calories or a herbal detox (where herbs are used more for their dietary benefits, not for medicinal properties).

### Why do you need to detox

"Detox is not for everyone," stresses Sonal Wagle, dietician. "It has to be done under expert supervision. So please don't decide to do it on your own or follow some regimen or diet picked up from the net, as that will cause more harm than health benefit." she says. "Detox diet is generally recommended to those suffering from obesity, stress or having some food addictions such as caffeine, sweet, junk, etc," says Sonal.

### Detox diet

A detox diet plan incorporates all food that would help eliminate, cleanse, enhance circulation and clear toxic substances from the diet. At the same time one has to make sure that they provide adequate nutrients to support and protect the liver, the main organ involved in detoxification. Also, a detox diet must ensure that it does not affect or interfere with regular bowel movements—the body's primary method of getting rid of toxic substances.

**Duration**: "Not more than a week, under strict medical guidance," says Sonal. Some practitioners stretch it to two weeks, though.

### Food you must eat

**Fluids**: Water, lemon water, pure fruit and vegetable juices.

**Fresh fruits and vegetables**: Includes cauliflower, onions, garlic, beets, red and green veggies plus all fresh fruits.

Grains and beans like brown rice, millet. You can easily get them at the local health food or organic food stores. Add beans, split green peas and lentils that require least soaking time and are easy to digest. Have nuts and seeds like unsalted nuts, seeds like flaxseed, pumpkin seeds, sesame seeds, sunflower seeds, almonds and walnuts. Avoid peanuts. Use oils like olive oil, salts like vegetable salt, sea salt, vinegar, naturally fermented soy sauce, culinary herbs or spices, limited amounts of honey, herbal teas, green tea are fine.

### Things to remember

* Drinking plenty of water—at least 8 glasses of water per day, preferably warm or at room temperature.
* Water is a must to clear waste from the blood.
* Do not drink liquids around mealtime.

* Chew food well, especially grains.
* Go for fruits and veggies containing antioxidants (citrus fruits, strawberries), betacarotene (carrots, sweet potatoes, squash, green peppers), selenium (broccoli, sprouts, cabbage), zinc (kiwi, blackberries, peas, corn) and for fibres.

## Food you must avoid

Sugar especially refined sugar and mixtures containing refined sugar, including sucrose, dextrose, corn syrup, brown sugar and also avoid artificial sweeteners. Dairy products like milk, butter and other dairy products. Wheat and wheatbased products, gluten-containing grains, including barley, rye. Caffeine like coffee, both regular and decaffeinated, black tea, and other drinks containing caffeine should be reduced. Green tea is a great substitute to regular coffee. Steer clear of all additives and preservatives.

## Health Byte: Ginger

Ginger (also known as *adrak*) is a very useful kitchen herb. Very effective in arthritic conditions, ginger also relieves gas and menstrual cramps. Ginger paste also helps relieve headaches and pain.

* Pieces of ginger should be soaked in honey and a teaspoonful of the concoction should be consumed every morning.

This helps avert premature greying of hair and facial wrinkles and assists in rejuvenation.

* A mixture of ginger and onions, taken with honey, helps patients suffering from vomiting and nausea.
* A 35 ml concoction of the juices of ginger, pomegranate and honey (in equal quantities) helps cure cough and asthma.
* Half a teaspoon of ginger juice with 1 tsp each of fresh lime, mint juice and a tablespoon of honey, taken thrice a day, helps cure dyspepsia, nausea, indigestion and morning sickness.
* A 25 ml mixture of the juices of ginger, lemon and onion in equal quantities, taken twice a day for two days, helps cure whopping cough.
* A piece of fresh ginger should be powdered and boiled in a cup of water. This should then be sweetened and taken thrice a day. The resulting concoction helps those suffering from painful and irregular menstruation.
* Those suffering from headaches should rub dry ginger with a little water and apply it to the forehead.
* One teaspoon of the powder of dried ginger and pepper, mixed with honey, helps those suffering from bronchial asthma.
* Generally, it is important to remember that any plant substance, whether used as food or medicine, whether consumed or merely applied to the body, may adversely affect certain people. In order to guard against allergies, it might be a good idea to avoid self-diagnosis and rely on qualified medical practitioners alone.

## Did you know?

To treat digestive problems, Greeks would eat ginger wrapped in bread. Eventually ginger was added to the bread dough creating that wonderful treat many around the globe love today:gingerbread!

## COPING WITH COLD STRESS (HYPOTHERMIA) AND HEAT STRESS

**Temperature Sensation: Cold and Warmth:** Experiences of cold and warmth are elicited by changes in the normal gradient of skin temperature – that is, by changes in the difference between the temperature of the skin surface and the temperature of the blood circulating beneath it. In the case of the forearm, for example, this gradient is about 5⁰C. The temperature of the skin surface is usually about 32⁰C or 33⁰C and that of the blood beneath it is about 37⁰C. A stimulus of 34⁰C, which can be felt as warmth, decreases it a little. Thus it takes a change in skin temperature of only 1 to 2⁰C to be experienced as warmth or cold.

In skin maps, the cold spots and warm spots are found in different places. This has been taken to mean that there are two different sensory channels for the experiences of warmth and cold. You might therefore expect different receptors to lie under the cold and warmth spots, but this does not seem to be true. Instead, free nerve endings, physiologically specialised but not obviously anatomically specialised, appear to be responsible for signalling information about temperature. Increasing the temperature gradient by cooling the skin causes certain free-nerve-ending fibres to increase their rate of firing. These fibres might be called "cold fibres". And, up to a point,decreasing the temperature gradient by warming the skin causes an increase in the firing of certain fibres. These might be called "warm fibres". Thus the afferent code for the experiences of cold and warmth appears to be the rates of firing in cold and warm fibres.

**Cold Stress (Hypothermia):** Much like high blood pressure, hypothermia can be called a "silent killer" in the sense that many of its victims are not aware of the threat. In the case of hypothermia, elderly persons may not be aware they are becoming cold as readily as younger people, and their bodies may not adjust to changes in temperature.

Hypothermia, (literally "low-heat") is a condition marked by an abnormally low internal body temperature. It develops when body heat is lost to a cool or cold environment faster than it can be replaced. Temperatures do not have to be below freezing for hypothermia to occur, especially in vulnerable individuals. Many older adults can develop a low body temperature after exposure to conditions of mild cold, which would only produce discomfort in younger people.

**Who is At Risk:** Although older adults are more vulnerable to hypothermia than younger members of the population, infants under one year are also particularly susceptible. Among the elderly, those most like to develop hypothermia are the sick, the frail, the very old, the poor who can't afford enough heat, and those medically vulnerable individuals who do not know how to keep warm when exposed to the cold.

Others who are susceptible include individuals who (1) live alone or in isolated areas (particularly is they do not have access to nearby phones to reach help in case of accident or illness); (2) do not shiver or react to cold; and (3) take certain medications that prevent the body from regulating temperatures normally, such as anti-depressants, sedatives, tranquilizers, and cardiovascular drugs. Drugs deserve special mention because they are thought to be a major predisposing factor to hypothermia, in older adults, who, while comprising little more than 10 per cent of the population, consume 25 per cent of the nation's prescription drugs. Check with a doctor or pharmacist for information on other drugs that increase susceptibility to hypothermia.

Hypothermia can cause illness and death. Although there are no accurate data on the number of elderly persons dying of this condition, it is estimated that about 10 per cent of all persons over 65 have some sort of temperature-regulating defeat, and between three and four per cent of all hospital patients over 65 are hypothermic. The National Institute on Aging (NIA), estimates that over 2.5 million older Americans are especially vulnerable to hypothermia, and Dr. Richard Besdine of the Harvard Medical School estimates that 25,000 older adults may die from hypothermia each year in the United States.

**What You Can Do:** To avoid being harmed by hypothermia, during the cold reasons - some suggestions:

- If you live alone, arrange for a daily check-in call with a friend, neighbour, relative, etc.
- Insulate your home properly. Caulking is a particularly low-cost and effective technique.
- Wear warm clothing. Instead of tight clothing, wear several loose, warm layers. Wear a hat and scarf to avoid significant heat loss through your head and neck. Stay dry. Moisture from perspiration, rain, or melting snow can seriously reduce or destroy the insulating value of clothing because water conducts body heat over 25 times faster than air.
- Use extra blankets because hypothermia can develop during sleep.
- Eat nutritious foods and exercise moderately; proper diet and physical conditioning helps protect you against abnormal heat and cold.
- Get proper rest; fatigue makes you more vulnerable to subnormal heat and cold.
- Drink adequate amounts of liquids, such as water. Limit your alcohol intake because alcohol speeds up body heat loss.

**What To Look For:** Some people die of hypothermia because they or those around them do not recognize the symptoms. Here are some signs to watch for:

- **Muscles:** The muscles are often unusually stiff, particularly in the neck, arms and legs.

  This stiffness may be accompanied by a fine trembling, perhaps limited to only one side of the body or one arm or leg.
- **Shivering:** Shivering is a sign that the body is having trouble keeping warm. The shivering response is frequently diminished or absent in older adults, and the fact that an older person is not shivering in a cool or cold environment does not guarantee that the person is not cold.
- **Face:** The face is frequently puffy or swollen, and this can be an important sign, especially when found in combination with cold skin and signs of confusion.
- **Co-ordination:** The person often has difficulty walking and has problems with balance. Look for poor co-ordination and jerky movements.
- **Breathing and Heart Rate:** Both are slowed at low body temperatures, and may be very difficult to detect in severe hypothermia.

- **Skin:** The skin is cool or cold. Pay special attention to the stomach, lower back, arms, legs, hands, and feet. The skin color is usually very pale, but it may also have large, irregular blue or pink spots.
- **Consciousness:** As the body cools, consciousness is depressed. Some hypothermia victims will still be conscious when their body temperatures are as low as 80 degrees. Remember, though, that "conscious" and "mental clarity" are two different things. A person can be "conscious and reactive" and yet still be in a confused, disoriented, and hypothermic state, so the level of consciousness is not always a reliable indicator of the victim's condition.
- **Confusion:** One of the first changes brought on by hypothermia is a growing mental confusion, which becomes progressively worse as body temperature falls. Logical thinking becomes impossible and the person may become completely disoriented. Memory is affected and familiar things are often forgotten.
- **Attitude:** Apathy is common. Often the person doesn't care what happens and will do nothing to help reduce the danger; he or she may behave strangely, or become irritable, hostile, mean, and aggressive.

**What To Do:** If you believe someone may be a victim of hypothermia, call an ambulance or rescue squad immediately. Hypothermia is a dangerous, complicated medical problem and the victim needs professional attention. However, before help arrives, here are some suggestions:

- Be very careful in handling the person. Failure to do so can cause sudden death because the heart is very weak when the body is cold.
- Insulate the victim with available covering such as blankets, towels, pillows, scarves or newspapers.

Some steps can worsen a victim's condition:

- Do not give the victim any food or drink.
- If the victim is unconscious, do not raise the feet. This will cause cold blood from the legs to flow into the body "core" and further depress the body temperature.

**Heat Stress:** "Energy issues are truly life and death issues for the elderly. The ultimate risk is death from hypothermia or heat stress," Virginia H. Knauer.

According to the Centre for Environmental Physiology the body needs time to adjust to hot weather. A sudden increase in temperature, especially at this time of year, is particularly serious because it can place a dangerous strain on the heart and blood vessels before the body can acclimatise itself.

Heat stress, which can lead to heat exhaustion, heart failure, and strokes, may well be a life threatening problem for the elderly in summer.

The elderly are more vulnerable to heat stress than younger people because they do not adjust as well to heat. They perspire less. They are also more likely to have health problems requiring medicines that work against the body's natural defenses to adjust to heat. For example, diuretics (often prescribed for high blood pressure, a common disease of the elderly) prevent the body from storing fluids and restrict the opening of blood vessels near the skin's surface. Certain tranquilizers and drugs used to treat Parkinson's disease interfere with perspiring. These other chronic conditions (such as circulatory problems, diabetes, a previous stroke, overweight, and a weak or damage heart) often upset normal body responses.

**Warning Signals:** Early symptoms - feeling hot, uncomfortable, and listless - are mild and usually pose no threat unless they persist. However, because the serious signs of heat stress listed below *are* usually preceded by the milder ones, it is important that you get medical attention if you experience any of the following:

- Dizziness
- Rapid heartbeat
- Diarrhoea
- Nausea

- Cramps
- Throbbing headache
- Dry skin (no sweating)
- Chest pain
- Great weakness
- Mental changes
- Breathing problems
- Vomiting

(**Note:** These symptoms can also signal other major problems, such as heart failure. Again, if you experience any of them, call a doctor immediately).

**Keeping Cool:** The best advice for avoiding heat stress is to keep as cool as possible. So if you are up in years or have a loved one who faces a special risk from heat stress, this information may help you avoid problems:

- Air conditioning can provide lifesaving relief from heat stress, especially if you have heart disease. If you do not have air conditioning, spend as much time as possible in cool shopping malls, senior centres, libraries, movie theatres, or in the coolest room in your home.
- Fans can draw cool air into your home at night or help to circulate indoor air during the day. Air movement reduces heat stress by removing extra body heat.
- Cool baths or showers provide relief from the heat because water removes extra body heat 25 times faster than cool air. Placing ice bags or wet towels on the body is also helpful.
- Loose fitting lightweight, light coloured clothing is more comfortable in hot weather. Hats and umbrellas protect your head and neck when you are outdoors.
- Your body needs more water in hot weather. Don't wait until you are thirsty to have a drink. If you have a disease, a medical condition, or a problem with body water balance **CHECK WITH YOUR DOCTOR** for advice on how much water you should drink.

**Heat Fatigue.** Lack of acclimatisation is one factor that predisposes an individual to heat fatigue. Therefore, a programme of acclimatisation and training for work in hot environments is advisable. Signs and symptoms of heat fatigue include performance of skilled sensory motor, mental or vigilance jobs. The only treatment is to remove the heat stress before a more serious heat-related condition develops.

**Heat Rashes.** These are the most common problem in hot work environments. Prickly heat is manifested as red papules and usually appears in areas where the clothing is restrictive. As sweating increases, these papules give rise to a prickling sensation. Prickly heat occurs in skin that is persistently wetted by unevaporated sweat, and heat rash papules may become infected if they are not treated. In most cases, heat rashes will disappear when the affected individual returns to a cool environment.

**Heat Collapse (fainting).** In heat collapse, the brain does not receive enough oxygen because blood pools in the extremities. As a result, the exposed individual may lose consciousness. This reaction is similar to that of heat exhaustion and does not affect the body's beat balance.

However, the onset of heat collapse is rapid and unpredictable. To prevent heat collapse, the worker should gradually become acclimatised to the hot environment.

**Heat Cramps.** These are usually caused by performing hard physical labour in a hot environment. The cramps have been attributed to an electrolyte imbalance caused by sweating. It is important to understand that cramps can be caused by both too much and too little salt. Cramps appear to be caused by the lack of water replenishment. Because sweat is a hypotonic solution (+–0.3% NaCl), excess salt can built up in the body if the water lost through sweating is not replaced. Thirst cannot be relied on as a guide to the need for water; instead, water must be taken every 15 to 20 minutes in hot environments.

Under extreme conditions, such as working for six to eight hours in heavy protective gear, a loss of sodium may occur. Recent studies have shown that drinking commercially available carbohydrate-electrolyte replacement liquids is effective in minimising physiological disturbances during recovery.

**Heat Exhaustion.** Signs and symptoms include headache, nausea, vertigo, weakness, thirst and giddiness. This condition responds readily to prompt treatment. Heat exhaustion should not be dismissed lightly, however, for several reasons. One is that the fainting associated with heat exhaustion can be dangerous because the victim may be operating machinery or controlling an operation that should not be left unattended; in addition, the victim may be injured when she faints. Signs and symptoms seen in heat exhaustion are similar to those of heat stroke, a medical emergency. Workers suffering from heat exhaustion should be removed from the hot environment and given fluid replacement. They should also be encouraged to get adequate rest.

**Heat Stroke.** This condition occurs when the body's system of temperature regulation fails and body temperature rises to critical levels. It is caused by a combination of highly variable factors and its occurrence is difficult to predict.

Heat stroke is a medical emergency. Primary symptoms are confusion; irrational behavior; loss of consciousness; convulsions; lack of sweating; hot, dry skin; and an abnormally high body temperature (e.g., a rectal temperature of 41 degree C or 105.5 degree F). If body temperature is too high, it causes death. The elevated metabolic temperature caused by a combination of work load and environmental heat load, both of which contribute to heat stroke, are also highly variable and difficult to predict.

**Heat Index Chart**

| Description Zone | Heat Index | Possible Heat Disorders for People in Higher Risk Groups |
|---|---|---|
| Extreme danger | 130 degree F or higher | Heat stroke/sun stroke highly likely with continued exposure. |
| Danger | 105 degree F to 130 degree F | Sun stroke, heat cramps or heat exhaustion likely, and heat stroke possible with prolonged exposure and/or physical activity. |
| Extreme caution | 90 degree F to 105 degree F | Sun stroke, heat cramps and heat exhaustion possible with prolonged exposure and/or physical activity. |
| Caution | 80 degree F to 90 degree F | Fatigue possible with prolonged exposure and/or physical activity. |

Other personal factors that may negatively affect the body's ability to respond to heat stress include: .

- previous heat illness;
- heart disease, high blood pressure or diabetes;
- skin disease, sunburn or skin rash;
- liver, kidney or lung problems;
- pregnancy;
- fatigue;
- acclimatisation;
- diarrhoea or vomiting;
- infections, fever, recent illness or injury;
- recent inoculation or immunization; taking medications that limit sweating (e.g., sleeping pills);

- beta-blocker medications (used for heart rate control);
- vocative medications (control blood vessel size), which influence heat loss and blood supply;
- low-salt diets.

Below - A soothing fort bath will help everyday achesand stiffness.

Foot Bath

## Special Precautions

- Curtail physical activity during extremely hot weather. Activity adds to heart strain.
- Avoid hot foods and heavy meals. They add heat to your body.
- Watch salt use. Check with your doctor before increasing the amount of salt or potassium in your diet. Do not take salt tablets without your doctor's permission.
- Avoid alcohol. Alcohol acts as a diuretic, resulting in fast water loss. In addition, alcohol can promote a sense of well-being, making you less aware of the danger signs of heat stress.
- If you live alone, make sure a relative or neighbour checks on you regularly.
- Take the heat seriously, pay attention to the danger signs, and call your doctor at the first sign of trouble.

Following recommendations are made for carrying out future research investigations.

1. Separate stress management studies needed for individuals working under different work atmosphere since stress may vary from job to job, industry to industry, etc. Similar studies are necessary for women engaged in various fields viz. those doing social work, those working in the office since they are subjected to varying degrees of stress.
2. Various complementary medicines are available and it is needed that from each of these medicines e.g. homoeopathy, naturopathy, yogic exercises, meditation, etc., case studies should be carried out separately to ascertain their efficacies in managing stress and strain related health problems.

## Using Music for Transformation & Healing

Helpful free tips show how to listen to music for transformation and healing. This free information reveals secrets to support recovery, mediation spiritual growth through music healing. All music can be healing especially when it is played in sequence using the entrainment principle.

The following information gives you guidelines on creating your own healing music sequence, even if you do not play an instrument! However, for your convenience, you may wish to use music that has already been created for this purpose.

### 1. Select Appropriate Music.

Most of us choose music that we "like" but will this give us the best result? In fact, often the music we are least attracted to will have the greatest benefit (when played in the right sequence). Let's say you are very angry music. Does it really help, or does it kind of perpetuate how you feel? Yet, on the other hand if you play you some light and happy music, by comparison to how you are currently feeling, it will probably make you feel angrier! As you see, selecting music is not a simple one-short process.

**2. Consider Music Sequencing.**

Sometimes it is necessary to first choose music that totally matches your current mood rather than the mood you wish to acquire. Consider arranging a series of different musical compositions in sequence that are customize just for your needs. For example, if you are dealing with depression, select a position which represents depression in its extreme form, to you. Follow this with one that is only mildly depressing. Then select a neutral composition, end with a composition which is clearly uplifting and motivating. Listening to music in a sequence like this allows for your current stress level or mode to be first honoured and then to be gradually transformed.

**3. Speakers Are Ideal.**

It is ideal to listen to the music through speakers rather than headphones so that the call cells of the body, themselves may "listen" to the sound.

**4. Prepare yourself to Listen.**

Take off your shoes. Stand relaxed, sit or lie down and breathe.

**5. Listen All the way Through.**

It is preferable to listen to the musical composition all the way through, without interruption. This allows for the optimum response to the transformation proses.

**6. Foreground, Not Background.**

We all have the tendency to use music for the background of other activities. Try developing the technique of just listening to the music, not doing anything else this way, you will get the best benefit.

**7. Your Response is What is Important.**

It is through your response that the emotional/cellular memory may be released. Do not thing that you have to just stay still and concentrate on the music! In fact, if the music inspires you to get up and do something or your mind begins to wander allow, allow, allow! Allow all responses without judgement. On the other hands, do not begin listening to the music while you are already doing other unrelated activities. The important thing is to let the music embrace you totally.

**8. Listen Actively Not Passively**

Allow the music to reach your inner feeling and respond freely to it every one has a different manner of expression. You may experience visual images, thoughts, movement, an intensification of emotion, physical vibrations, sleep, or nothing at all.

**9. Observe Mind/Body Connection.**

A lot of research has been done recently showing that there is a definite connection between the mind and the body. (actually this refers to the emotions too but is sounds succinct to say "mind / body".) even through music healing is often related to relaxation and emotional issues, there is the likelihood that this indirectly could have a benefit on physical illnesses as well.

**10. Enjoy the Silence!**

When the music stops, it is suggested that you bask in the silence for many movements. This will help integrate the feelings.

# MUSIC THERAPY

Listening to music does wonders to alleviate stress. Please not that every one has different tastes. I music. Listen to the music that you feel comfortable. Sitting down and forcing yourself to listen to relaxation music that you don't like may create stress, not alleviate it.

Music has always been a great healer. In the bible, we learn about how David played the harp to help ease his severe depression of kind Saul.

Music is a significant mood-changer reliever of stress, working on many levels at once.

## Music/Singing

> Play a tune on the guitar and sing along. That works even in the worst of times. By the time I'm done with the song, I've breathed deep, I've controlled myself to sun degree to be able to sing on key:), and I've come back into myself, and more into the real time movements.
>
> Internet discussion forum

Many experts suggest that is the rhythm of the music or the beat that has the calming effect on us although we may not be very conscious about it. They point out the when we were a baby in our mother's womb, we probably were influenced by the heart beat of our mother. We response to the something music at lather stages in life, perhaps associating it with the safe, relaxing, protective environment provided by our mother.

Music can be one of the most soothing or never wracking experience available. Choosing what will work for any individual is difficult, most will chose something they 'like' instead what might be beneficial. In doing extensive research on what any given piece of music produces in the physiological response system many unexpected thing were found. Many of the so-called Meditation and Relaxation recording actually produced adverse EEG patterns, just as bad as hard Rock and Heavy Metal. The surprising thing was many selections of Celtic, Native American as well as various music containing loud drums or flute were extremely soothing. The most profound finding was any music performed live and even at moderately loud volumes even if it was somewhat discordant had very a beneficial response. Whenever the proper sound were experienced an amazing right/left drain hemisphere synchronization occurred. The normal voltage speaking pattern change to a smooth sinusoidal waveform and the usual voltage differential equalized. The entire human energetic system is extremely influenced by sound, the physical body and chakra centres respond specifically to certain tones and frequencies. Special Consideration should be given to the positive effect of one actually playing or creating music themselves.

Among the first stress-fighting changes the take place when we here a tune is increase in deep breathing. The body's production of serotonin also accelerates.

Music was found to reduce the pain during dental procedures.

Playing music in the back ground while we are working, seemingly unaware of the music itself, has been found to reduce the stress.

Music was found to reduce heart rates and to promote higher body temperature-an indication of the onset of relaxation. Combining music with relaxation therapy was more effective then doing relaxation therapy alone.

## Maximizing with Music Therapy

As we mentioned before, there is not a single music that good for everyone. People have different tastes. It is important that you like the music being played.

The following are general guidelines to maximize the effectiveness of the music.

1. To wash away stress, try taking a 20-nets "sound bath". Put some relaxing music on your stereo, them lie in a comfortable position on a couch or on the floor near the speakers. For a deeper experience, you can wear headphones to focus your attention and to avoid distraction.

2. Chose music with a slow rhythm-slower the natural heart beat which is about 72 beats per minute. Music that has repeating or cyclical pattern is found to be effective in most people.

3. As the music plays, allow it to wash over you, rinsing off the stress from the day. Focus on your breathing, letting it deepen, slow and become regular. Concentrate on the silence between the notes in the music; this keeps you from analysing the music and make relaxation more complete.

4. If you need a stimulation after a day of work, go for a faster music reader then slow calming music.

5. When going gets though, go for a music you are familiar with-such as a chilled hood favourite or favourite oldies. Familiarity often breeds calmness.

6. Take walks with favourite music playing on the walk man. Inhale and exhale in tune with the music. Late the music text you. This is a great stress reliever by combining exercise (brisk walks), imagery and music.

7. Listening to the sound of nature, such as ocean waves or the calm of a deep forest can reduce stress. Try taking a 15-to-20- minute walk if you're near the seashore or a quit patch of woods. If not, you can buy tapes of these sound in many stores.

## INDIAN MUSIC PICK A RAGA

The foundation of all healing music is its unde – tones (drones). Most drones are prolonged, contentions and undisturbed; the magic coming from the tone intervals. Most instrument like the jaw harp, bagpipe, didgeridoo, sitar, shimingbowl, mountain horn, various single or multiple – stringed instrument can be tuned to certain undertones. According to cardiologist, Dr. Neelam Verma, music was best when used with YOGA or meditation. For example a person suffering from arthritis should combine music with regular exercise and meditation, while those with cardiac problems a should opt for PRANAYAMA with music. Some RAGAS are also more effective during a certain pert of the day:

Bhairavi in the morning hours, Megh and Malhar in the day, Yaman and Bhopali in the evening. Take your pick!

## Human Condition, Stress Management and Music

The predominant role human conditioning plays in stressful environment. Perspective, reaction and remedy. How music can help.

Creating music for stress management can be rather completed process.

Due to the nature of stress, music must promote and sustain a therapeutic ambience and provide a calming influence that opens the door to refraction, corrective action and ultimately, inner place. Consequently, creative effort in this genre often leads to consideration that have more to do with psychology than music per se.

In its development stages a musical sequence may point to possibilities for music therapy. But to successfully complete the final sequence, one must consider the variables of human nature.

Weather or not these musical possibilities grow into some thing of benefit depends upon many factors, not the least of which is the creation of sound structure that are compatible with an beneficial to human organism.

Another extremely important issue that must be considered during the composition process is that all humans are conditioned science birth and there is little that human experience throughout there lives that is not filtered through previous layers of conditioning.

At first glance, human conditioning may appear to have little if any relationship to stress management, anxiety, burnout, or for that matter music. But a closer lock revels the connection.

To understand how this connection works, well need to big into some information that may seem a bit 'heavy'. The subject of conditioning is extensive and of necessity, comment here must be confined to only a few of its more prominent twists and tune.

Weather one a agrees or disagrees with the statements presented here the following is the result of years of observation, study and application. Its presentation here is indented to promote a better understanding of how and why we so often react in counter-productive ways when dealing with tress full conditions.

Admittedly, this information is but a small part of marks deeper subject. Nonetheless, it is my sincere hope that what is presented here will provide some insight for those who suffer from the unpleasant, debilitating and unhealthy conditions of stress. That said, please read on and it will become apparent that where human conditioning is concerned, almost everything is related.

## The Problem

When one studies the work of men such as Roger Sperry, Freud. Jung, Wilhem Reich and others, it becomes clear that (1) general reaction to stressful condition tends to be aberrant and (2) the manner in which humans perceive and react is, for the most part, a learned behaviour.

This learned behaviour has much to do with how we view our selfs and our place in society. The picture that we present to the out side world is our identity or image, of who we thing we are and that image is the direct result of everything we have been taught and everything that has ever happened to us. Consequently, is new encounter or situation we experience filtered thought previous conditioning and in this way, previous conditioning becomes the measurement we apply to all future experience. Unfortunately, this measurement is often flowed and when used to evaluate and respond to stressful condition, tends to produce reaction rather then remedy and this in turn can lead to errors in judgment that may actually make matters worse.

Why don't we recognize these reaction patterns when they occur?

Well, for most of us, the basic underlying causes of conditioned reaction have been lost to conscious memory. Yet, without realising why, we often continue to react in a sort of robotic way to the emotional stimuli of circumstances that occurred long ago and which contain little if any corrective value for resolving the here-and-now problems of today.

## How does this relate to press management?

The relevance to stress management lies in the fact conditioning is like a one-way street, paved with beliefs, opinions and prejudgements that often lead ask in very subtle ways to the wrong destination. In other words, when belief, the opinion and prejudgements are used as a measurement of stressful condition, the result of that measurement will most likely be erroneous due to a lack of facts.

Stated another way, one night say that in lieu of facts, we are more likely to create and/or contribute to the stressful condition that we seek to resolve.

### Truth or belief?

Belief, opinion and prejudgements indicate a lack of fact or truth. One reason this lack occurs is because of a widespread assumption that the word "believe" is synonymous with the word "truth". When we say we believe in something or believe or believe something to be true, what we are really saying is that we do not possess all the facts. Conversely, if we possessed all the facts we world no longer believe-we would know.

Thus the disparity between "belief" and "truth" becomes one of the main reasons we react to stress rather then take remedial or constructive action to minimize it. In other words, the tendency is to make judgement (based on belief or opinion) before obtaining all the facts in a given situation.

According to statistics, the sources below are most commonly mentioned as a cause of stress:

The boss not enough sleep family pressures the worked not enough societal pressures co-workers not enough time marital issues traffic criese Divorce.

When stress enters our lives, the tendency is to blame some one or something other then ourselves. In some cases we may be right. But many times successful conditions are of our own making. One example would be stress created as a result of maxed-out credit cards or a lack of financial discipline.

Another causes might originate with any one of the sources in the list above, but because our tendency to misunderstand and mishandle this experiences we often proceed to make the problem worse and thereby increase the level of stress, how we deal with these conditions is of paramount importance if we are to resolve them successfully.

Generally speaking, we react emotionally to stress when we have something to defend and when we allow defensive emotion to get out of hand, we're not being rational-we're merely reacting. By reacting we compound the problem because our reaction tends to produce a counter-reaction.

Why a counter-reaction? Well, if the object of our wrath happens to be another person, that person will most likely have something to deafened also and our emotional display may therefore be interpreted as a threat. Remember, that other person is conditioned too!

## The sky is falling!

Conditioned reaction also indicates a fear of something. Eugene Albright, the author of unichotometrics-A a new way of life, once said, "there is only one valid fear – a direct threat to survival of the organism. All the other can be traced to false concept of one sort or another".

If this statement is true, then another reason we have difficulty dealing with stress has been exposed. Excluding a direct threat to lives, it suggests that we allow stressful situation to provoke aberrant fears or of losing something, exposing something, or fear retribution for having done something. The oddity is our seeming inability to consciously recognize this when it is happening.

Conditioning influences our interpretation of everything we see, here and project to the out side would and yes, it even influences our choice of music. Generally, we are not aware hat we live out live according to the beliefs, opinions and prejudgements of others, (peer-pressure among teenagers is one example) nor do we realize that by accepting these viewpoints, we are perpetuating them.

Thus we place ourselves in a loop wherein we often repeat the same mistake over and over.

Now here is the good news : it is possible to break out of the lop when on realize that (a) over-reaction to stress does not work and (b) there must be a better way – and then takes action by proceeding to summon the courage, stamina and discipline to search out and reveal the truth according to fact. In this way one begins to take responsibility for one's own actions.

## Aw, do I have to do that?

Accepting responsibility is the first step we take on the road to a less stressful and more productive existence. By taking control of our lives, we'll sometimes move against the grain of the status quo and because of that, we'll most likely meet a measure of resistance along the way. But if we persist in our quest for fact and truth, and ability to deal constructively with stress with become much easier.

There will be times when we may sleep and fall back in to the old ways-meaning, when the pressure of stress becomes too much to handle, the general tendency will be to get in to someone's face, below of steam, antagonize imagined enemies, worse-meekly swallow the problem and risk a bigger stomach ache in the near future.

. Sure, that's quite a bumpy cumbersome and questionable way to move forward and a lot of people bear the scars to prove it. Nonetheless usually and up learning something from our stressful encounters and when you don't well, we're fallen back in to that look. If that happens, is not a disaster. It just means we haven't quite gotten a handle on how to responds to stress in constructive manner.

A friend once commented, "if you don't want to be crucified, don't hang around crosses". That simple logic may also be applied to stressful conditions. For example, we must learn to recognized and walk away from dead-end situations that are beyond our avility to improve next we must fully understand that resolution of stressful condition does not come about from trying to change others. Instead, we must change our selves.

We may stumble, bruise egos and make mistake but however inept our approach, if we persist in our such for the facts or truth in all situations we will eventually learn how to live our lives in a more efficient and productive manner.

## Helps is out there

Fortunately, there are tools methods that can help lighten the load as we optimize our chances for a less stressful tomorrow.

Among them are inspiring books by authors such as Deepak Chopra, Dr. Wayne Dyer and others that may provides better understanding of oneself. Employing of the various methods of meditations may also work. When the need is acute, seeking the guidance of a professional counsellor may be an appropriate choice.

Of course, music is one of those tools mentioned above. One of the nice things about music is its synergistic quality – it often work well as an adjunct to other stress management tools or methods. When we introduce music to the conditioning/stress management equation, some interesting and unexpected result may occur.

For example, when listening to properly crafted music, it is some time possible to by – pass one's conditioning temporarily. When this happens, the listen may experience strong feeling of freedom, inner peace, and a profound sense of well-being. In other words, the exact opposite of stress.

We're speaking here of major change in perspective. Consciousness may become altered to the extent that conditioned reaction becomes temporarily suspended. Some may describe their musical experience as 'spiritual'. Others may have meditated on a particular personal problem and see it in such clarity that the necessary corrective action become obvious.

At times, people may be moved to tears. Other may find it difficult to put their experience into word. In some cases, the combination of empathy, understanding and emotional release can be life-changing and yes, there will be a few times when a listen may be a so rigid and structured as to be unable to get in tough with their own feeling.

Whatever the response, the point to remember is this : it is the energy of music initially helps to unlock and open the door-the we might enter a place where peaceful reflection will allow us sort out thing and possibly develop a new, more positive and constructive perspective.

## You mean, it didn't come from outer space?

To be sure, music possesses many beneficial qualities but we should be mindful not to elements to music that it does not possess.

Of itself, music does not 'cure' anything. It does not 'solve' anything. And contrary to the more bizarre claims one may find on the internet, it certainly does not 'originate' from and "unknown composer who resides on a planet in a distant galaxy" … or other similar nonsense! As a point in fact, the composition "GROVE SUITE" (offered at http://www.channel11records.com) was pirated some years ago by a metaphysical organization that actually made that claim!

What properly created music DOES do, it does very well. It possesses the ability to put our hearts and minds at ease and in so doing, facilitates entrance to a clearer understanding of ourselves, reality and finally-inner peace. By any measurement, that is remarkable!

That music can be an effective tool for stress management is a given it has been known for centuries that music can be therapeutic and there are many references in art and literature that attest to its soothing qualities. The therapeutic capabilities of music have been proven many times over and its success as a stress management tool is well documented.

**Music Therapy**

## How to Get Rid of Your Anger The angry

Fillings occur to everyone. In fact, anger occurs in our mind so often that it may be properly regarded as our close friend. All of us regularly receive lot of pressures from the environment we live in on a daily basis. It seems people around us tend to get agitated and bad-tempered quite easily nowadays. Realistically, we cannot escape from anger. The point which really matters is show me can deal with the on increasing pressures around us which can trigger of angry feeling.

## The Impact from Pressures in your Face

When you get angry, your face will drive every guest away, no matter who he on she is, because of your brutal face. The feelings of anger which have been accumulated in your mind for a long time can also harm your physical, body tremendously. Anger is likened to fire; when it increasingly gets accumulated, it will turn destructive and will first bur your body and mind directly. In particular, it can cause physical illness to your body. The following diseases occur apparently when the mind is continuously burnt by anger.

1. Heart disease. The anger can cause you to have a higher maximum heart rate.
2. Mental depression which makes you feel exhausted an lack of energy.
3. High blood pressure.

It is various hormones in our body change by which our body cannot carry on our normal duty. In addition, a study show that a female who has increasingly accumulated her depression right after she starts to work, is inclined to suffer a heart disease during her middle age. The percentage is as high as 50% having known this, one should try to pacify one's one anger as soon as possible.

**Four Effective Ways to Get Rid of Your Anger**

1. Understanding you own need. You should express your anger in a proper way rather than let it take you away with aggressiveness. In this respect, you have to clearly understand what you really want. After understanding yourself, you can move on with your plan to achieve your goal in a peaceful way. Doing this, you can avoid destroying the good feelings of your self and other.
2. Stopping the feeling of anger. If your anger is getting more developed, you have to stop it immediately. Don't let the anger bother your feelings and try to look at thing positively in order to refresh your feelings. For example, when you have a problem with your colleagues, you should turn your interest towards your hot dating with a young lad in the evening instead to wipe out all the unpleasant memories and replace them with pleasant feelings.
3. Relaxing and pacifying your mind. As said earlier, anger is likened to fire. If you want to eliminate your anger totally, you have to pour down some water in it. Precisely, you need water to distinguish it. Water means peace. You should calm down your agitated mind by either meditating or following some other relaxing exercises such as the practice of YOGA to still your mind which get strained because of anger. If you concentrate your mind on a particular object and be mindful when you breathe in or out, your mind which is full of anger will be totally controlled in a peaceful state. You can also. Opt for turning your eyes at a beautiful scenery in a public beautiful park, full of various kinds of green trees and still water.
4. Leaving the stressful situations behind. If you cannot your anger by any means when you get angry, instead of staying in such a stressful atmosphere, you should try to avoid bursting out in anger by going away from the spot right away, because the anger which is without control can turns destructive.

**Control Angen**

# HYPNOSIS AND RELAXATION

Relaxation of the body and mind is an integral part of the multimodal approach to headache relief. It has long been known that anxiety expressed as muscular tension as a "busy mind" functions as part of what can be termed the "feedback loop of pain". In other words, pain that results from headache is a negative sensations that carries an increase in physiological (muscle) and cognitive (mental) arousal. For the purpose of this discussion, heightened physiological and cognitive arousal can be termed anxiety. Anxiety, in urn, causes an uncomfortable increase in muscular tension and mental distress which serves to increase the intensity of pain.

The feedback loop of pain is a natural involuntary response to the noxious perception of pain. To break this snowball effect, you must learn to relax. Sounds simple? Unfortunately, relaxation in general-and particularly in the face of pain is not so simple. Deep and effective relaxation is a skill that, like other skills, must be perfected through proper technique and practice. In this chapter we shall first study how to utilize effective relaxation to decrease the frequency and intensity of headaches and then examine the role of hypnosis, a special type of relaxation, in headache relief.

## Relaxation

For our purpose we can consider relaxation the opposite of tension. Most people readily assume that one flourishes in the absence of the other; that is, if you're not tense, you must be relaxed. Unfortunately, the human body does not function that simply. If you consider relaxation positioned on one end of a continuum and tension on the other, there is a huge grey area in between where we all exist most of the time. A typical day may have some moments of tension and some of relaxation, most of us in a kinds of psychic limbo. Yet it is often that tension is building within us. Stimuli too small to be consciously registered are tightening our muscles, aggravating our nerves and constricting our blood vessels. At the end of the day here will be a blinding headache, with no apparent cause.

Relaxation cannot be building quietly in our bodies as we go through a routine day because so much stress exists in our lives. To combat the negative, one must learn to relax. Simply defined, relaxation is the absence of mental and physical stress which is achieved when the body is in equilibrium and the mind is unhampered by anxiety. It is physiologically impossible and physiologically impractical for an individual to be always relaxed, since the mind thrives on a certain amount of controlled, creative turbulence. It is, however, feasible for each of us to be able to control bodily processes enough to regulate the energy and excitation flow of the system.

The ability to relax can have a dramatic effect on headaches. Amazing physiological changes occur in the relaxed body; heartbeat and respiration slow, and the quality of electrical waves in the brain changes. Alpha waves, which can be recorded from the brain during peaceful, tranquil mo ments when the eyes are closed, become more numerous. Research conducted at the Johns Hopkins Headache Clinic in Baltimore, Maryland, suggest that using biofeedback to teach subject to increase the percentage of Alpha waves from the brain could often reduce headache frequently. Muscles also loosen and lengthen during relaxation.

Physiological relaxation most often leads to cognitive or physiological relaxation. The emotions are tranquil, and a feeling of pace prevails. Western scientist have found that the simple process of medication, through by many to be a from relaxation, can have wide-reaching physiological effects. Studies conducted on Zen monks in Japan showed that during medication, the monks were able to decrease their consumption of oxygen and output of carbon dioxide by approximately twenty per cent. Slowdowns in heartbeat and respiration have also been observed in yoga practitioners. All of this leads to a declaration in metabolism, a tranquillizing of the emotional states, a reduction in tension and a decrees in the incidence of headaches.

## Learning to Relax

Relaxation is a skill that can be learned and perfected with practice. One particularly effective and popular relaxation technique is known as progressive muscular relaxation and involves practicing exercises that mechanically manipulate the skeletal muscles of the entire body into a more relaxed state. In the early 1900s, Dr. Edmond Jacobson first outlined the principles of progressive muscular relaxation, and the exercises have since been modified numerous times. Once the basic relaxation technique is learned, it is vital that the technique be practiced. With serious practice, less time is required to achieve the desired stage of deep relaxation. The technique can then be use to ward off headaches, reduce stress, assist in sleep and decrease the intensity of headache pain. The following producer and technique are recommended.

**Procedure:**

1. When first learning to relax, a quite, dimly lit place is an ideal one in which to practice.
2. Lie on your back on a carpeted floor or sit in a comfortable chair. Avid practicing relaxation exercise in bed since most mattresses do not provide sufficient support.
3. Try to eliminate all other competing thoughts from your mind. Relaxation exercises are intended to relax your body and your mind.
4. Focus all attention on the muscle group being tensed.
5. Tense muscle groups on cue. Get in a habit of following the same producer each time time you practice relaxation exercises.
6. Hold the tension and focus all attention on the buildup of tension in every muscle group for six to ten seconds.
7. Release the tension from each muscle group all at once. Do not gradually relax a muscle group at end of six to seconds, but instead let the muscle relax.
8. After relaxing a muscle group, focus all of your attention on relaxation for twenty to thirty seconds. Concentrate on the different sensation between tension and relaxation.
9. Repeat for each muscle group.
10. Practice relaxation exercises at least twice daily, but the more the better!

**Technique:**

1. Lie on your back on the floor. Make a tight fist and tense the muscle of the forearm of the right hand arm. Imagine you are holding a golf ball in the palm of the right hand and squeezing it. Relax.
2. Make a tight fist, bending the right arm at the elbow and tensing the muscle of the upper arm. Relax.
3. Make a tight fist and tense the muscle of the forearm of the left hand and arm. Imagine you are holding a golf ball in the palm of the left hand and squeezing it. Relax.
4. Make a tight fish, bending the left arm at the elbow and tensing the muscle of the upper arm. Relax.
5. Tense the muscles of the neck. Push your chin towards your chest, and pulling your head at the same time, lift your head off the floor. Relax.
6. Tense the muscles of your face. Clamp your jaw tightly shut and pull back on the corners of the month. Squint your eyes tightly shut and wrinkle your nose. Raise your eyebrows towards your hairline and wrinkle your forehead. Relax.
7. Tense the muscles of your shoulders, chest and back. Take a deep breath and hold it. Now pull the shoulders back and together much like the military attention posture. Relax.
8. Tense the muscle of the abdomen. Take a deep breath and bear down with the stomach muscles. Relax.
9. Tense the muscles of the buttocks and right thigh. Press the back of the right knee down into the floor. Relax.
10. Tense the muscles of the right calf and foot. Bend the foot at the ankle and stretch the toes towards the head. Relax.

11. Tense the muscles of the buttocks and left thigh. Press the back of the left knee down into the floor. Relax.
12. Tense the muscles of the left calf and foot. Bend the foot at the ankle and stretch the toes towards the head. Relax.

When you have completed this exercise, take two to three deep breaths and hold each one for a moment, deeply relaxing as you exhale. Enjoy this relaxed state, breathing regularly and slowly to enhance it. Imagery has been found to occur when and individual feels deeply relaxed; if you experience pleasant imagery, allow it to continue and focus on it. When you are ready to end the exercise, slowly count backwards from five to one. Move slowly until filly alert. The key to managing your headaches by achieving deep muscular relaxation is to practice continually.

Note : The above – described relaxation exercise is only one of many relaxation techniques designed to reduce muscle tension. While relaxation techniques are very useful, they should not serve as substitutes for professional health care. See your doctor if you have difficulty learning this technique, if it dose not seem to be reducing your tension levels or if your body feels relaxed but your mind continues to race.

## Hypnosis

Hypnosis has it recent years gradually gained more acceptance as a useful medical and psychological treatment technique. Perhaps the most effective use of hypnosis in the treatment of headaches and other pain states is physiological and psychological relaxation. Hypnosis has been found to facilitate decreased physiological arousal and is an excellent relaxation technique. Research has shown hypnosis to be effective in the treatment of pain associated with search disorders as burns, anxiety, cancer, tension, arthritis, leukemia, menstrual discomfort, ulcers, postoperative pain and nausea, childbirth, neck and lower back pain, dental procedures and headaches.

### The Hypnotic experience.

The hypnotic experience can best be thought of as a continuum, ranging from a very light state which we can drift into without even being aware of it, to the deepest stages which may appear similar to a sleepwalker's state of consciousness. The lightest stages of hypnosis seem almost like a game that the brain placed on us. Perhaps you can remember times when you gaze seemed drawn to sum blank wall or even into space and your mind seemed totally blank. May be your breathing become full and slow, your heart rate decreased and your muscles seemed unusually relaxed. You felt clam, tranquil and totally peace.

When you snapped back to reality you felt as if you had been a million miles earth, although you remembered exactly what you were thinking and feeling. The feeling is similar to the sensation experienced just before falling asleep, except that rather than feeling dulled and hazy, our concentration seems crystal clear!

The middle or intermediate stage of hypnosis is characterized by the increased intensity of those sensations experienced in the lightest stage. The body feels even more peaceful and relaxed, while the mind seems more alert and clearer than ever. During this stage we also become more susceptible to suggestion. The body and mind seem free from the limitations of everyday living, and we are more fully able to achieve our true physical and mental capabilities. Frequently, we find that an arm or leg can be extended for prolong periods of time without strain or fatigue. We may even sense that time has stopped, or is speeding rapidly by; that a stationary object is moving, or that a once painful area of the body is now less painful or pain-free.

Individuals susceptible to the intermediate stage of hypnosis will often report being completely aware of what they were doing and feeling unusually calm, relaxed and confident that they could achieve whatever the hypnotist suggested. These individuals frequently report a feeling of confidence that they could bring themselves out of the hypnotic state at will.

The deepest stage of hypnosis is sometimes termed somnambulism and is best described as similar to a sleepwalker's state of consciousness. This stage is characterised by an even more powerful intensity of those perceptual and physical sensations common in the light and intermediate stages of hypnosis. For example, in the deepest stage of hypnosis, mental acuity may be so concentrated as to enable the person to recall past events that have long been forgotten or suppressed. The technique of age regression, so popular in the somnambulistic stage. Needless to say, susceptibility to suggestion is greatly enhanced in the deepest stage, and individuals returning to normal consciousness from somnambulistic hypnosis occasionally report no memory of there thoughts or actions the session. It is generally agreed that only about one in ten individuals is susceptible to the somnambulistic stage.

It is important to understand that the stages of hypnosis are not as clearly defined as this presentation may appear. While in a light stage of hypnosis, some individuals experience the perceptual and physical sensations common in the deepest stage. Again, it is best that one thing of hypnosis as a flexible continuum rather than as three separate and distinct stages and realize that the therapeutic effects of hypnosis do not depend on the depth of the hypnotic state. Many individual are able to relax deeply while in alight hypnotic stage.

## How hypnosis works

As mentioned, no one knows exactly how hypnosis works, but we do know three general components that appear to be most important successful hypnosis : concentration, suggestibility and imagination. Successful hypnotic indication depends, to a great extend, on the voluntary cooperation of the patient who is asked to concentrate intently on the suggestions of the doctor. The ability to concentrate deeply varies among individuals, but it is most likely to be found I people who readily accept the fact that there are several states of consciousness. How well can you concentrate? Are you able to shut out the distractions of the day when you go to bed at night? Can you read a book in a noise dorm or when the television is blaring?

A second important component of hypnosis may be termed suggestibility – meaning that hypnosis tends to be most effective if you expect it to be. Some people feel that suggestibility is a negative trait. Perhaps they equate being suggestible with being naive or gullible. This is unfortunate, for suggestibility is a positive and important trait in hypnosis.

During hypnosis the patient may receive a suggestion from the doctor that he is engaged in some other mental or physical activity that is incompatible with the problem behavior. To illustrate, let's imagine a patient with (headaches described as tightness around the head with pain up the back neck). During hypnosis. The doctor may suggest that the patient is experiencing a warm, relaxed feeling through the neck and head rather than (tight, constricting pain). As the neck and head warm, the pain gradually subsides, and the experience of pain is replaced by an experience of relaxed warmth. Though the patient's central nervous system continues to receive pain impulses, his concentration has been diverted to the feelings of warm and muscle relaxation. Remember, pain exists only if it is perceived!

A third component of hypnosis is imagination. Do you have a vivid and strong imagination? If you were asked to site quietly, close your eyes, and imagine floating high above the ground on a giant, pillowy white cloud, could you do it? Would feel the texture of the could against your skin? Would look far below and see the green treetops and the colours of the landscape? Would you close eyes and feel a warm breeze gently blowing your cloud across the sky? The ability to create rich, vivid mental images may be more closely related to hypnotic susceptibility than any other characteristic.

In summary, research suggest that those who benefit most from hypnosis tend to be able to concentrate well and are suggestible, imaginative and truly motivated to seek relief from their pain. Is this an accurate description of you? If so, then the chances are excellent that you will be a good candidate for hypnotic pain control.

# PROPER RELAXATION

## REST AND RELAXATION POSTURES

Savasana.

Supta Vajrasana.

Apanasana.

When the mind, body, and senses are Continually bombarded with stimuli, they have no chance to rejuvenate themselves. In order to achieve radiant health and well-being, a time must be set aside each day to allow this rejuvenation to take place.

...✎ ...✎ ...✎

Homoeopathy dates back to the end of the eighteenth century, although it has much earlier antecedents. A German doctor, Samuel Hahnemann, gave up his medical practice in the 1780s, in protest at the violent measures then practiced, such as blood-letting and strong purging. He felt that such treatments often made patients weaker than their original illness, and for a time, he turned to making a living as a translator of medical works. While working on a herbal by a Scottish writer called Cullen, he came across the assertion that cinchona bark (from which quinine was later derived) was a helpful treatment for malaria because it was a good astringent.

Since there were plenty of better astringents available, Hahnemann decided to test cinchona bark on himself to see its effects. After a few days, he started to get all symptoms of malaria, although he did not have the disease. This led Hahnemann to the concept that symptoms were not a sign of disease but an indication of the body's attempts to fight illness, the cinchona strengthened this response. To test this theory further, he tried out many more medicines on himself, friends and others, and eventually came to the principle of similia similibus curantur – "like will cure like" : that is, a remedy which induces certain reactions in a healthy person will be a valuable remedy for treating an illness in which these same symptoms are seen.

Hahnemann also found that symptoms often seemed to get worse initially when people were given a remedy. In order to overcome this, he diluted his remedies in a special way until they became almost undetectable, and yet the therapeutic effect seemed to get stronger. He reasoned that the healing effect must be carried out on a subtle, energetic level. He termed his system homoeopathy, literally meaning "like disease".

## HOMEOPATHIC PRINCIPLES

- Homeopathic remedies act by stimulating our immune responses into greater action, to bring about a cure.
- The remedy itself does not bring about a cure, this comes from within us.
- The correct remedy for someone is the one that when given to a healthy person produces the same symptoms as the disease is producing in the ill person.
- To reduce or avoid aggravations of the symptoms, the remedy should be given in very small dosages.
- Dilution of the remedy, accompanied by a vigorous shaking, acts in such a way as to potentise its effects; the greater the dilution, the quicker and more effective the remedy.

Remedies are often diluted using the centesimal scale, that is one part of the original substance is diluted and successed with 99 parts of a liquid, usually alcohol or water. This would make a 1c potency. One part of this is then diluted with 99 parts of liquid for a 2c potency, and so on.

Homoeopathy has been widely used in some countries for a long time; in the last 20 years, its popularity has increased across the world and it has become much more accepted.

## NATUROPATHY

This section is intended to cover those areas of self-help and professional therapies that do not fit into the other categories of this book. More than that, however, they comprise those approaches that focus on our natural healing abilities and try simply to enhance them. Iridology has been included here since it aims to diagnose imbalances by "reading" our own natural body sings, and treatment is often along r aturopathic lines.

Naturopathy is itself a professional therapy, including diet, exercise, supplements and hydrotherapy within its field. Some traditions of naturopathic training also link with some of the hands-on professions such as osteopathy or chiropractic, and the practitioners of these latter disciplines may advocate other measures to help to restore full health. Hydrotherapy, or "water cure" has a strong tradition in Northern Europe, and is still carried out at centres in Germany, Austria, Switzerland and France. Increasingly it is also become more widerpread in the US.

Both diet and exercise are vital elements in achieving and maintaining optimal health, and most of us can make adjustments in these areas. Some ideas for improvement are presented here; a key factor is to include exercise and dietary changes that you will enjoy, as a part of really appreciating life.

Fig. 55

## DIET AND EXERECISE

Probably the two most obvious and successful ways in which we can affect our health are through nutrition and exercise. Most of the natural therapies will include an assessment of and advice about these areas; indeed naturopathy focuses largely on them as a means of treating illness. A healthy diet and adequate exercise are essential for health, and although many books and magazines are devoted to encouraging us to work on these factors, they provide so much advice and differing theories and methods that it seems difficult to fulfil these aims.

A healthy died involves eating foods that provide all the nourishment that our bodies need for growth, tissue repair, energy to carry out vital internal processes and to stay fit and active. In the last hundred years or so, the changes in eating habits in many countries have meant that large numbers of people have become overfed. Ironically, at the same time these dietary changes have left a lot of us undernourished, lacking in vitamins, minerals and trace elements that would help us to be in the peak of health.

Eating for health does not have to mean switching to a fussy, complicated diet, or adopting every new fad that comes along. In the first place, a healthy diet should be an enjoyable one. For conventional nutritionists, food intake is broken down into various essential ingredients, such as carbohydrates, protein, fats, vitamins and minerals; however, people generally do not think in this way but eat meals or snacks which are a mixture of various elements. What is useful is to have an understanding of which foods contain which of these ingredients, and then to look at the overall balance within the diet. Balance is probably the key word in nutrition, and it is the unbalanced nature of many Western diets that lowers vitality and may lead to ill-health. With a better understanding of the elements it is easier to create a healthy diet without too much thought and analysis.

## CARBOHYDRATES

Carbohydrates are out main source of energy, and need really to form the major bulk of our diet. They are broken down in the body into glucose, and used immediately for energy or else converted into glycogen for short-term strorage in the liver. An cxcess of carbohydrates over time will be changed and stored as fat. That is a particular danger with refined carbohydrates or sugars, which do not take much processing in the body and provide large amounts of instant energy. Since they have less starchy bulk, refined carbohydrates do not make you as full, and therefore it is easier to eat too much of them, leading to fat storage and obesity.

The main sources of unrefined carbohydrates, providing dietary fibre and trace elements, are flour and grains, beans, peas and lentils, and potatoes. With grains, this is especially true when they are unprocessed, like wholegrain bread, whole oat cereals, muesli, wholewheat pasta, bran rice and so on, which supply long-term energy supplies. For more immediate energy, fresh fruit, dried fruit or vegetables such as carrots or beetroot are high in fructose, or fruit sugar. This is easily broken down by the body for energy use, and since fructose metabolism does not require insulin, it can be an essential energy resource for diabetics.

There is almost complete accord among official governmental nutrition advisers and natural dietary therapists, that carbohydrates should be the chief element in our diet. In practical terms that means eating plenty of fresh vegetables and fruit, grains of all kinds (unless there are specific reasons for avoiding a particular grain, such as with a wheat allergy), potatoes, beans and lentils. A recent piece of advice from official organisations, for instance, has been to consume five portions of fruit or vegetable a day.

## FIBRE FACTS

Fibre is important to a healthy diet. Your body can not digest it, so, in rather basic terms, it goes in and comes out, taking other waste with it. Fibrous foods include bread, rice, cereals, vegetables, fruit, and nuts. We should aim for about 30g (just over l oz) of fibre a day. These are some examples of good fibre sources.

Table 109

| GOOD SOURCES | AVERAGE PORTION | GRAMS OF FIBRE |
|---|---|---|
| Wholemeal pasta | 75g/30z(uncooked) | 9 |
| Baked beans | 125g/40z | 8 |
| Frozen peas | 75g/30z | 8 |
| Bran flakes | 50g/20z | 7 |
| Muesli | 50g/20z | 4-5 |
| Raspberries | 100g/31/zoz | 6 |
| Blackberries | 100g/31/zoz | 6 |
| Banana | Average fruit | 3.5 |
| Baked jacket potato | 15g/50z | 3.5 |
| Brown rice | 50g/20z | 3 |
| Cabbage | 100g/31/zoz | 3 |
| Red kidney beans | 40g/11/zoz | 3 |
| Whole wheat bread | 1 large slice | 3 |
| High-fibre white bread | 1 large slice | 2 |
| Stewed prunes | 6 fruit | 2 |

## Proteins

Proteins are the essential body-builders, helping us to create muscles, bones, tendons, hair, skin and nails. They are also vital in most of our hormone and enzyme production. The first thing to say about protein is that in most developed countries people eat too much, so the problem is not so much increasing those foods that are high in protein but getting the balance right. An excess of high protein foods in the diet will be converted into glucose for energy use or else stored as fat.

Foods rich in protein include meat, fish, poultry, eggs, milk and other dairy products, nuts and seeds, beans and lentils, and grains (bread has a little under ten per cent protein). Human protein is made from a number of simple substances called amino-acids, and these needs to be present in certain amounts or combinations in the protein in our diet for us to make use of them. Animal sources do contain the right amounts of these amino-acids, but also contain relatively high levels of fat. Plant sources of proteins often need to be combined in order to give adequate levels of amino-acids, this can be something as simple as beans on toast, or a spicy bean dish with rice, and generally means having a more varied, or even a more adventurous diet.

## Fats

Fats are vital too, helping to form part of the cell structure and maintaining our inner organs and nerves. They also act to provide insulation and temperature regulation. It is, however, well-recognized that in the developed world much of our diet is too rich in fats, especially animal fats, and this is a major factor in heart disease, obesity and even some cancers, especially when we have such sedentary lives. Growing children, however, especially active ones, do need fats more than adults, and we should not reduce their intake so much.

Advice on fat-containing goods tends to be what to reduce rather than what to increase. Meat and dairy products can contain concentrated sources – a nice, juicy steak may have 30 per cent fact, for example. There are some differences between the effects of saturated fats( from animal products) and unsaturated fats such as are found in oily fish like salmon or plant oils like sunflower products. In general terms , more the emphasis towards the latter, using oils such as olive, sun flower, corn or safflower with salads or in cooking, but most people need to reduce all kinds of fats, they are the most concentrated sources of energy and anything over small amounts easily leads to obesity. There are plenty of reduced-fat items, particularly dairy products, which are now available and which can help in controlling fat intake.

**Easy ways to cut down fat and saturated fat**

| *Eat Less* | *Instead* |
|---|---|
| Butter and hard fats. | Spread butter more thinly, or replace it with a low fat spread or polyunsaturated margarine. |
| Fatty meats and high fat products, such as pies and sausages | Buy the leanest cuts of meat you can afford and choose low fat meats like skinless chicken or turkey. Look for reduced fat sausages and meat products. Eat fish more often, especially only fish. |
| Full-fat dairy products like cream, butterhard margarine, milk and hard cheeses. | Choose skimmed or semi-skimmed milk and milk products and try low-fat yogurt, low-fat fromage frais and lower fat cheeses such as skimmed milk, soft cheese, reduced – fat Cheddar, mozzarella or Brie. |
| Hard cooking fats such as lard or hard margarine. | Choose mono-unsaturated or polyunsaturated oils for cooking, such as olive, sunflower, corn or soya oil. |
| Rich salad dressing like mayonnaise or salad cream. | Make salad dressing with low fat yogurt or fromage frais, or use a healthy oil such as olive oil. |
| Fried foods | Grill, microwave, steam or bake when possible. Roast meats on a rack. Full up on starchy foods like pasta, rice and couscous. Choose jacket or boiled potatoes, not chips. |
| Added fat in cooking | Use heavy-based or non-stick pans so you can cook with little or no added, fat |
| High fat snacks such as crisps, chocolate, cake, pastries and biscuits | Choose fresh or dried fruit, breadsticks or vegetable sticks. Make your own low-fat cakes and bakes. |

## Vitamins and Minerals

Vitamins and minerals are needed for proper growth and development and body maintenance. They control the absorption of other nutrients and without them a series of complaints can develop, from headaches to sterility. There are 13 major vitamins which, apart from K and D, must be obtained from the food we eat. They fresher the food the higher its vitamin content. Food loses it vitamins through cooking, exposure to light or cold and storage, so buy small quantities of fresh and eat it as soon as possible.

**MINERAL AND VITAMIN VALUE**

| *Vitamin* | *Sources Include* | *Benefits* |
|---|---|---|
| Vitamin A | Liver (specially fish livers), egg yolk, fortified margarine, oily fish, oranges, apricots, carrots, tomatoes, melons, dark green leafy vegetables. | Eyesight ; skin; may protect against cancer. |
| Vitamin B1 | Most foods – including wheatgerm and pulses, wholegrains, brewer's yeast, nuts, fortified breakfast cereals. | Helps break down carbohydrates; nervous system', repairs body tissues. |
| Vitamin B3 | Wheatgerm , wholegrain cereals, meat, fish | Essential for tissue chemical reactions. |
| Vitamin B6 | Avocados, liver, wholegrains, egg yolk, lean meat, bananas, fish, potatoes. | Nervous system ; skin; red blood cells. |
| Vitamin B12 | Liver, kidney, some fish (including shellfish), eggs, milk, | Healthy blood and nerves. |
| Vitamin C | Citrus fruits, potatoes, tomatoes, leafy greens | Helps heal wounds, may fight colds, flu and infections, protects gums, keeps joints and ligaments in good working order. |
| Vitamin D | Fish liver oils, fatty fish, eggs, fortified margarine, also synthesised by ultraviolet light | Calcium deposits in bones. |
| Vitamin E | Vegetable oils, some vegetables, wheatgerm. | Cell growth; antioxidant. |
| Vitamin K | Most vegetables-especially leafy green ones, liver | Essential in production of some proteins. |

| *Minerals* | *Sources Include* | *Essential For* |
|---|---|---|
| Calcium | Cheese, milk, yogurt, eggs, bread, nuts, pulses, fish with soft bones such as whitebait and tinned sardines, leafy green vegetables. | Healthy bones , teeth and nails; muscle and nerve function; blood clotting; milk production in nursing mothers. |
| Iron | Liver, red meat, oily fish, wholegrain cereals, leafy green vegetables. | Makes haemoglobin, the pigment in red bloods cells that helps transport oxygen around the body. |

## HEALTHY EATING

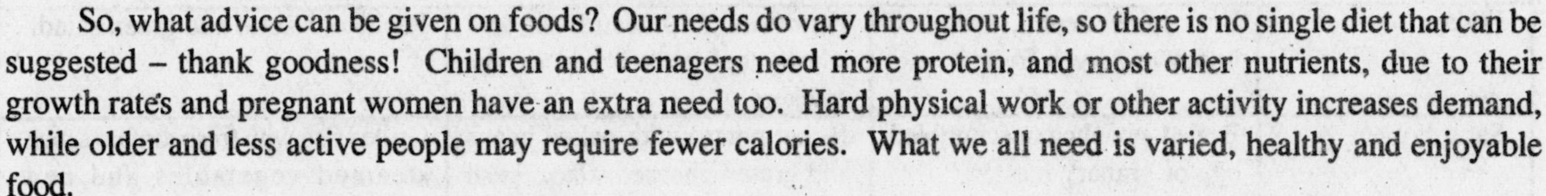

So, what advice can be given on foods? Our needs do vary throughout life, so there is no single diet that can be suggested – thank goodness! Children and teenagers need more protein, and most other nutrients, due to their growth rates and pregnant women have an extra need too. Hard physical work or other activity increases demand, while older and less active people may require fewer calories. What we all need is varied, healthy and enjoyable food.

Three key works are freshness, wholeness and variety. As far as possible make fresh foods the major part of your food intake – fresh fruit and vegetables, freshly cooked bread, pasta or other grains, and a little freshly prepared meat, poultry, fish or other protein – containing foods. Preparation of foods should aim to retain as much of the original goodness as possible, so grill or bake foods rather than frying them. Wholeness can be taken to indicate not just trying to use wholegrains but cutting back on proceeded foods as far as possible. Try to have fresh foods first, then frozen and only occasionally resort to packaged or canned food. Variety means exactly what; it is unhealthy to eat just oranges all days as it is to eat nothing but hamburgers all day.

### Some Ideas Might Include

- More fresh fruit and vegetables; they are high in vitamins and minerals and low in fats.
- Steadily increase fibre-rich foods, such as fruit, vegetables, wholegrains, beans and lentils.
- Eat fish, poultry and leaner cuts of meat and avoid frying them as far as possible. Cut down on meat products such as pies, sausages and so on, which generally have high levels of fat.
- Eat fewer dairy products and use low – fat versions of say, yogurt or milk.
- Keep pastries, caked, biscuits and chocolates for special occasions.
- Drink plenty of water, many of us get dehydrated.
- Ease up on stimulants such as coffee and tea, and also alcohol.
- Try to use less salt – this also means reducing intake of processed foods, since they can often be high in salt.
- Enjoy food ! There is a lot of pleasure to be gained from the taste and aroma of a varied diet.

## 7 DAYS HEALTHY EATING PLAN

This healthy eating plan gives suggestions for a balanced way of combining goods. Try to choose low, fat, low sugar foods aiming to include plenty of wholegrain high fibre foods and 5-6 portions of fruit and vegetables each day.

To the suggestions below, add your own choice of fruit juices and water and limited wine, tea and coffee. Try drinking some of them, many blends of herb teas which are now available and which are a delicious, healthy substitute for tea and coffee. For snacks and desserts, choose fresh fruit, and low fat fromage frais or yogurt with occasional high fibre bran muffins or carrot cake for treats.

| *Monday* | *Breakfast* | *Lunch* | *Dinner* |
|---|---|---|---|
| | Fruit juice, porridge, fresh fruit. | Sardines or pilchards on toast | Macaroni cauliflower and broccoli cheese |
| Tuesday | Grilled mushrooms or tomatoes on toast | Homemade coleslaw with cottage cheese and rye crispbreads. Fresh fruit and carbar or flapjack. | Salade Nicoise : lettuce, tomato, cucumber, new potatoes, tuna, olives, hard-boiled eggs, anchovies. |
| Wednesday | High energy drink, juice or milk and banana, yoglurt, honey and wheatgerm. | Onion soup with grilled cheese croutons. Fresh fruit and fruit cake. | Stir-fried vegetables and chicken or cashew nuts with rice or noodles. |
| Thursday | Muesli topped with low-fat live yoglurt and chooped apple. | Wholemeal sandwich of cream cheese, avocado and salad. Fruit. | Pasta with tomato, bacon and mushroom sauce and parmesan cheese and mixed salad. |
| Friday | Fruit juice, cereal, toast and honey and fresh fruit | Hummus with crudités and wholemeal pitta bread or rye crackers. | Paella or risotto and green salad. |
| Saturday | Boiled, poached or scrambled egg or granary toast. | Jacket potato with baked beans and grated cheese, salad. Fresh fruit. | Grilled fish with fresh tomato sauce, steamed vegetables and new potatoes. |
| Sunday | Fresh or soaked dried fruits with low – fat live yoglurt. Wholemeal or granary toast. | Roast chicken joint with roast Mediterranean vegetables, whole garlic, peppers, courgette, aubergine, etc. and potatoes or rice. Fruit and yogurt brulee. | Thick vegetable and lentil soup with wholemeal bread. Fresh fruit salad and cheese. |

## Move to Keep Alive

As far as exercise is concerned, the best phrase to sum up the importance of movement to your body and health is, "Use it or lose it". Inactivity, sedentary lifestyle, means that our bodies steadily deteriorate and various health problems star to develop. Equally importantly, exercise helps to reduce the effects of strees and worry and makes us feel better. The value of exercise is high at all times of life, for children growing up and developing strong bones and muscles, for adults to keep fit, active and healthy, and for older people to reduce problems like osteoporosis and simply to keep mobile and independent.

This is another area where official encouragement has occurred in recent years, with suggestions of a minimum of 20 minutes of brisk exercise three times a week as one example. Having activity goals can be very useful, but they should not act as a deterrent to getting started, any amount of exercise is better than none. It must be said, of course, that sudden, unaccustomed or inappropriate exercise can cause musculoskletal problems and people with certain conditions may need to seek medical advice before undertaking exercise. Nevertheless, steadily increasing exercise is likely to benefit the great majority of us. Improving the efficiency of our heart, lungs and muscles, improving our posture and making us feel fitter and look healthier.

The first advice is to take the kinds of exercise that you enjoy and that you can incorporate into your lifestyle. Walking up and down stairs rather than taking the lift can be a simple example of fitting more movement into your life. Weekend walks, gardening cycling or dancing are some leisure activities that can also help you go get fitter.

If you have not done much exercise for some time, do try to warm up and loosen the body before doing anything more strenuous, and don't exercise straight after meals. If you are ill or very tired, then limit physical exertion too. To allow easier movement, try to wear loose, comfortable clothing when exercising,. And use the correct shoes and clothing when playing a particular sport. A good idea may be to join a class with exercises like aerobics, low – impact exercises or weight training, a class is essential to make sure that you are doing the movements safely and correctly. Personal trainers provide detailed exercise programmes for you, with advice on the training zone, or optimal heart-rate, that you should aim for. Serious exercisers have access nowadays to all kinds of scientific back up on how to plan and carry out exercise, but for most people it is most important to get fun and enjoyment out of physical activity.

Another important aspect of physical fitness is the effect it has on the way we feel about ourselves. Without becoming neurotic about your size and weight, try to take an interest in the state your body is in. An enjoyable and invigorating fitness regime, at a level you can sustain without undue stress, can enhance your mental and physical well-being, when you are until you tend to feel more lethargic and uninterested in the world and the people around you. A straight back, a spring in your walk and an alert, energetic expression will create a better impression than bad posture, slumped shoulders and unco-ordinated movements. So improve your fitness and your self-esteem at the same time.

## Warming-up Exercises

Some suggestions for warming-up exercise are given here. If you haven't done much exercise for a long time, or are recovering from a long illness, initially they may be enough on their own to get you more mobile. They will also be helpful to prepare you for something more strenuous. If you are exercising for the first time in a long while, pay attention to how your body responds. If you become out of breath or your heart races, stop, and ask your doctor's advice on suitabled exercise. If you are more used to exercise, use this routine as a warm-up before moving on to something more strenuous. Try to breathe freely and comfortably when doing these and any other exercises, and remain aware of your body's responses to the movements.

## Hydrotherapy

Hydrotherapy, or the 'use of water for healing purposes', has an ancient pedigree, and different applications of using water can be found in many classical civilisations. Both the ancient Greeks and Romans used hot and cold – water baths extensively and many of the modern spas throughout Europe owe they origins to Roman bathing centres. Similarly, the Native Americans were familiar with the use of sweat – lodges, for physical and spiritual cleansing and were proficient in various hydrotherapeutic techniques.

In recent centuries, however, some of this knowledge and expertise was lost. The therapeutic uses of water were largely revived in Europe in the nineteenth century by a Bavarian Dominican monk, Sebastian Kneipp. He believed that people had considerable innate healing powers and that water applications were a medium for similating or occasionally, soothing our recuperative efforts. His ideas have continued to be influential to this day, and it is possible to experience one of 50 or so different water applications for a variety of ailments.

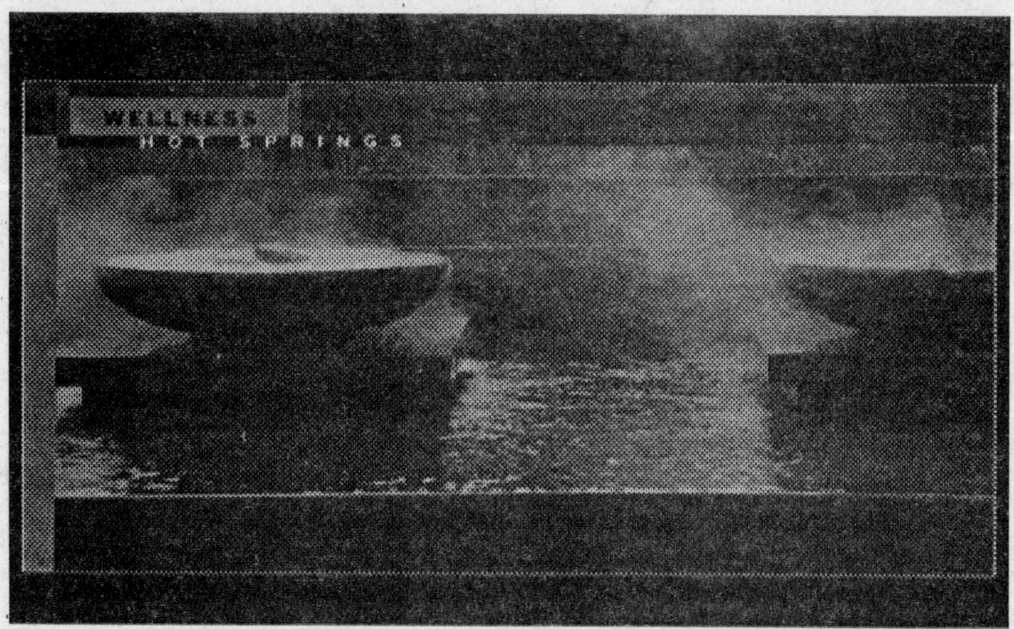


Fig. 56

Typical treatments may include contrast bathing, using alternating baths of hot and cold water, These are usually what are termed size baths, a kind of hip bath that immerses the lower trunk, while the feet may be placed in foot-baths of contrasting temperature in order to stimulate the circulation. Other forms of treatment many include high pressure hosing with cold water, hot or cold body wraps, friction, rubs, or baths with various ingredients added for extra elimination – for example, mud baths, Epsom salts baths or thalassotherapy (seawater baths).

Cold body wraps are made by soaking a sheet in cold water and wrapping it around the body, then covering this with a dry sheet and blanket. The initial cold is quite nicely replaced by warmth. These wraps are used for a number of conditions such as chronic muscle strains and backache. The sitz baths are often recommended for conditions such as chronic constipation, congestion in the pelvic area, recurrent cystitis and period pains. The sprays have similar effects to the baths, depending on their temperature, but are generally more stimulating to the circulation. A milder effect is achieved by whirlpool baths, which are increasingly popular in homes, gyms and spas.

Some recent medical research has shown the benefits of cool baths for reducing high blood pressure and improving peripheral circulation and the contrasting application of hot and cold water compresses and such like have a strong effect on the immune system, so hydrotherapy has very definite physiological effects. As a note of caution, prolonged exposure to water is not a good idea for pregnant women or anyone with hypertension or heart disease, so be careful with saunas. Turkish baths, whirlpools and so on. Regular shorter sessions are often more beneficial.

Home applications can be very simple, a sprained ankle or similar injury with swelling needs a cold application initially, such as an ice pack or cold compress. After a while, older injuries may respond to hot, then cold applications, while chronic areas of muscular stiffness often do better with just warm water treatments. Although largely neglected by orthodox medicine in the UK. Europeon countries and indeed the US, have been much more positive about hydrotherapy, and new research is confirming its potential.

## Mind-body Move

**TAI CHI :** A graceful marital arts form , tai chi is based, in large part, on an ancient Chinese martial art called Tai Chi Quan, which required tranquility and calmness while emphasising slow, soft movements. Research in countries around the world has demonstrated that tai chi can reduce stress and improve back health.

Tai chi also helps the back at the site of the back itself. Many tai chi movements, which strengthen the core of the body, uses the spine as a pivot. And that causes the spine and the muscles surrounding it to gently flex through tai chi post with names like. Spasma. In addition, some massage therapists encourage their clients to stretch and exercise, which could ameliorate back pain in themselves.

**MASSAGE :** In a study conducted at the University of Miami, it was found that massage therapy lessened lower back pain, not only by acting directly on the back but also by working on the brain. Specifically, it reduced depression and anxiety and improved sleep, all of which may have contributed to the beneficial effect.

Massage is thought to work directly on the back by improving blood circulation and relaxing muscles, leading to an improved range of motion, the soft tissue manipulation can also reduce pain and improve one's ability to move around. And it can loossen up tightened muscles or relieve muscle spasms. In addition, some massage therapists encourage their clients to stretch and exercise, which could ameliorate back in themselves.

As for the lessening of depression and other contributions to emotional stress, it is thought that massage may lead to increased levels of endorphins – "feel good chemicals" in the brain.

The type of massage said to be helpful for alleviating muscle aches that may be involved in back pain is not Swedish massage which is gentle and lulling. It is a more aggressive massage, either in the form of deep-tissue massage, fascial release, neuromuscular facilitation of Rolfing. The first three types are all meant to stretch muscles and connective tissue (known as fascia) with the application of steady, even and, at times, very pressure. Neuromuscular massage, in particular, applies strong pressure to painful knots or spasms in the muscles. Rolfing "re-educated" the body about posture by realigning the back and other areas through working the connective tissue surrounding muscles.

## Homoeopathy

There are many people who find the word homoeopathy quaint. They do not understand why the word is used and think its is something practiced generations ago before modern medicine began, vaguely to go with herbs.

Yet the word is easy. Homoeo, like so many words in our English language is Greek and translated is "like". Homoeopathy then us simply the medical practice of treating like with like, and who hasn't heard of the precept "the hair of the dog that bit you" let alone vaccination and inoculation.

The principal was known to Hippo crates and Paracelsus but the main debt of those who follow it is to Samuel hahnemann, a great doctor of the late 18th Century. He, appalled by the existing medical practices which so often did more harm than good, south for a method which would be safe, gentle and effective. He believed that human being have a capacity for healing themselves, and that the symptoms of disease reflect the individual's struggle to overcome the forces antagonistic to life. The physicians work must bee to discover, and if possible remove, the cause of the trouble, and to stimulate the vital healing force of nature.

Hahnemann and his followers were so convinced of their theories that they carried out experiments upon themselves (called Proving) in which over long periods they took small does of various reputedly poisonous or medical substances carefully noting similar symptoms were then treated with these substances with very encouraging results.

Having thus established the principle of similarity hahnemann worked to establish the smallest effective does. For he realised that this was the best way to avoid side effects. To his surprise he found that, using a special method of dilution, the more the similar remedy was diluted, the more active it became, whilst dissimilar remedies were ineffective. He therefore called his method potentisation and his serial dilutions potencies, to indicate the power that developed.

This paradox, that less of a substance could be more effective, was perhaps not unsurprisingly to the scientific through of the time, Hahnemann and his followers were ridiculed, but homoeopathy survived simply because it archived remarkable results, and today a changing outlook in science renders the concept of the infinitesimal does less incredible.

Homoeopathy consider it better to treat the sick person rather the disease, so the patient is treated rather than his disease. For this to be possible, a lot must to known about the patient, his past health and life circumstances, the pattern of health in his family, and his present condition. Together with those characteristics which go to make up his personality-whether he prefers hot or cold weather, the sea, or the mountains, whether he is musical or artistic, quick-tempered or sulky, dark fair or red-headed; his hopes, fears and aspirations.

The homoeopathy physician endeavours to build a multidimensional picture of his patient, which will be matched by one of the drug-picture derived from the proving of remedies. Infinitesimal does of that remedy will help that patient to heal himself.

Because the patient is treated and not his disease, patients suffering from the same "disease" will often require different remedies; whilst another group of patients with different "disease" may all benefit from the same remedy. Although this makes controlled trials problematical the basic principles of homoeopathy indicate clearly why this is so.

What are the remedies? they can be animal, venerable and mineral. Homoeopathy do use herbs and botanical medicines but usually only after potentisation. They also use drugs. Like morphine, cocaine and arsenic, but again in their potentised for, no longer poisonous but marvellously effective for good-for the right patient. Substances which in their natural state little or no obvious effect upon the human body –sand, charcoal, common salt, pencil lead-develop in potentised form powerful healing properties in the right patient.

Homoeopathy is essentially natural healing; the remedy assisting the patient to regain health by stimulating nature's vital faces of recovery. Adequate rest and appropriate diets in a satisfactory environmental will obviously support recovery, and those using homoeopathy medicines may have to require their patients to exercise patient, especially in the management of chronic illness.

Rapid results can be achieved in acute illness but if the patient's vitality is low the treatment will be of a long –term nature. Sometimes irreversible bodily changes are present in these cases other form of medical or surgical treatment may be necessary to give the patient a fresh start, after which homoeopath does not underrate the value of surgery in advanced cases but it argue that if homoeopathic treatment were started earlier, far fewer cases a world need the skill of the surgeon.

Some of the happiest results of homoeopathic treatment can be seen in babies and children. Here natural vitality is or should be at its highest and infrequent high potencies of the well-chosen remedy can set the small person's feet firmly on the way to health.

Homoeopathy, then is not a cure – all nor an elixir of life. Rather it is an idea, a way of looking at people in their surrounding, enabling them to increase their harmony and well-being. It dos not reject the great discoveries of modern medicine, it stands in the tradition that extends from the time of Aesculapius until the present day.

## Homoeopathic home remendies for common ailments Twelve tissue remedies in tablets in 3x, 6x, 12x, potencites

| | |
|---|---|
| **CALCFLOUR** | Varocose veins, piles, cataract, gumbolis, arteriosclerosis |
| **CALCPHOS** | Dentition. Growth supplement for children, puberty, pregnency, old age factures, poor nutrition, poor circulation. |
| **CALCSULPH** | Cystic tumors, fibroids, hastens suppuration, eczema, boils punpils. |
| **FERRUMPHOS** | Anamia, feverish condition, catarrhal condition of reapiratory tract. |
| **KALIMUR** | Controls affections of middle ear, throta, grandular inflamationsea |
| **KALIPHOS** | Prostration, weakness and exhaustion, mental and physical weakness, backpain, depression, sleeplessness, examination fear. |
| **KALISULPH** | Catarrh with yellow discharge (Bronchitis), itching of the skin and seasonal rashes, shifting pain in legs. |
| **MAGPHOS** | Muscular pains, cramps, convulsions, flatulent colic, mestral pains. |
| **NATRUMMUR** | Intermittent fever, sunstoke, headeche, toothache, somach ache, diabetes. |
| **NATRUMPHOS** | Sour eructation's and vomiting, heart burn, indigestion with acidity, noctumal enuresis, dizziness, dull feeling. |
| **NATRUMSULPH** | Gastric billousness, liver diseases, uric acid and diathesis. |
| **SILICEA** | Growth disturbánces of hair, nails, diseases of bones, caries, skin does not heal easily weeping eczema pyorrhoea. |

## HOMOEOPATHIC DILUTIONS IN PILLS FOR COMMON AILMENTS

| ABDOMINAL PAIN | Agonising, cutting pain in abdomen | COLOCYNTH |
|---|---|---|
| ACIDITY | Acute or chronic with or without foul eructation, flatulence. | CARBO VEG |
| ACNE & BOILS | Pustular & painful to touch. | HEPAR SULPH |
| BACKACHE | Pain and stiffness in small of back, better by moving, worse sitting and on beginning to move or walk. | RHUS TOX |
| BLEEDING | Various types of haemorrhages, after operations or knows bleeding. | MILLEFOLIUM |
| BODY PAIN | Body pain, coryza with headache, pains worse by motion, better on rest. | BROYONIA |
| | After prolonged exercise. | ARNICAMONT1 |
| | Painful joints & soreness of limbs. | RHUS TOX |
| BITES | Bites of insects. | LEDUMPAL |
| BONE INJURIES | Fractures slow to heal, bones refuse knit dislocation. | SYMPHYTUM |
| BRUSIES | For falls blows contusions, overuse or any muscle, strains. | ARINCAMONT |
| | Sprains injured bones of wrists or ankles. | COLOCYNTH |
| BURNS | All kinds of burns and scalds apply cantharis ointment externally, | CANTHARIS |
| COLIC | Colic several hours after eating. | NUX VOM |
| | Colic with diarrhoea. | COLOCYNTH |
| COMMONCOLD | Running noes with sneezing and burning nasal discharge. | ALLIUMCEPA |
| | After exposure to cold air. | ACONITE |
| | With blocked nose and yellow nasal discharge. | PULSATILLA |
| CONSTIPATION | Dry and hard stools | BRYONA |
| | With frequent, ineffectual urging, incomplete and unsatisfactory stool | NUXVOM |
| COUGH | Dry cough with plain in throat, worse at night | BELLADONA |
| | Dry cough with plain in chest while coughing | BRYONIA |
| | Whooping cough | DROSERA |
| | Rattling cough with nausea and wheezing | IPECAC |
| DIARRHOEA | During detention with irritability | CHAMMOMILLA |
| | Severe diarrhoea with white, watery stools & vomiting | VERATRAUMALB |
| | Painless, watery, profuse, offensive greenish stools. | PODOPHYLLUM |
| | Immediately after eating and drinking. | ALOESOC |
| DYSENTERY | Bloody and slimy stools with pain and tenesmus. | MERCSOL |
| EAE-ACHE | Pain in ears child cries out in sleep. | BELLADONA |
| | Pain in ears, eyes or teeth. | PLANTAGO |
| FLU | Body ache, head ache, fever, chill with coldness. | BRYONIA |
| FOOD POISONING | Pain in abdomen, vomiting and diarrhoea. | ARSENIC ALB |
| HAY FEVER | Burning in yes, lachrymation & sneezing. | ARSENIC ALB |
| INDIGESTEION | After heavy and fatty food. | PULSATILLA |
| | With nausea and vomiting. | IPECAC |

| | | |
|---|---|---|
| JOINTS | Swelling in joints worse by least movement. | BRYONIA |
| | Joints pain, worse on beginning to move and better by motion. | RHUS TOX |
| MENSTURAL PAIN | Spasmodic and severe pain. | CAULOPHYLLUM |
| NERVE INJURY | Nerve injure e.g. crushed fingers and toe. . | HYPERICUM |
| PILES | Protruding, sore, bleeding better by cold application. | ALOESOC |
| SCIATICA | Pain left side, better by pressure & head. | COLOCYNTH |
| TONSILLITIS | Tonsils red swollen, painful with difficulty in swallowing. | BELLADONA |
| TRAVEL SLCKNESS | Nausea, vomiting, giddiness, while traveling. | COCCULUSIND |
| URINARY | Burning and sourness, when urinating with | APISMEL |
| CONPLAINTS | Scanty urine | |
| URTICARIA | Allergic conditions with red eruptions, burning better by cold washing. | APISMEL |
| WORMS | | |
| WORMS | With grinding to teeth, variable appetite, child irritable itching in anus. | CINA |
| WOUNDS | As an antiseptic and healing agent, useful for open wounds. | CALENDULA |

** DOSAGE IN CASE OF PILLS 3 TO 5 globules 2 to 3 times a day for 2 to 3 days.

** IF THE PROBLEM STILL, PERSIST & IN CASE OF EMERGENCY CONSULT A DOCTOR OR HOSPITAL.

| | | |
|---|---|---|
| ARNICA MONT | : | Useful in conditions from injures blows and contusions |
| BERBERIS | : | Useful in skin eruptions & acne. |
| CALENDULA | : | Useful in cuts, wounds & ulcers. |
| PLANTAGOM | : | Locally applied in cases of toothache. |

## COLOUR THERAPY

For centuries, no one knew why the rainbow arched across the sky after a storm or why its colours always appeared in the same order. It was long believed that the colours were produced by differing mixtures of light and darkness. However. In 1666 the English scientist Sir Isaac Newton discovered that the colours of the spectrum were, in fact, all contained in white light. In a darkened room, he passed a ray of light through a prism. He found that the prism refracted the light and, because each colour has a different angle of refraction, a rainbow of colours emerged from the opposite side of the prism. The appearance of a rainbow is the result of raindrops acting like a prism, refracting the sunlight. The larger the rain-drops, the purer and brighter the refracted colours.

Each colour of the spectrum vibrates at its own frequency and has its own wavelength. Albert Einstein proved that the spectral colours are composed of small packets of energy, which he called photons. The longer the wavelength the more spaced out the photons. The colours blue, indigo and violet have short wavelengths and compacted photons, and so contain the most energy. The colours at the at the other end of the spectrum have longer wavelengths and less energy. In this chapter, we will look in more detail at colour energy, which lies at the heart of colour therapy.

## The Importance of Colour

The vibrational energies of colour contained in sunlight are essential for our health – indeed, no life form could survive without the light and warmth of the sun. In the summer, when we tend to spend more time outdoors, most of us feel happier and healthier.

One condition resulting from light deprivation is Seasonal Affective Disorder (SAD). This begins in autumn,when days become shorter and our exposure to sunlight is diminished, and disappears in spring as the days lengthen again. The symptoms of SAD are lethargy depression and a craving for carbohydrates.

Sunlight also helps to build strong healthy bones. When we spend time outdoors, we absorb through our eyes the middle waveband of ultraviolet light, which enables the body to produce vitamin D, essential for the metabolization of calcium. Researchers have shown that ultraviolet light cannot pass through glass, so wearing spectacles, sunglasses(particularly of the "wraparound" variety) or contact lenses inhibits its absorption.

## The History of Colour Therapy

In his books on the lost city of Atlantis, Frank Alper attributes to the Atlanteans the earliest use of color therapy. He describes circular temples containing healing rooms. Roofs of interlocking crystals refracted the sunlight, filling the rooms with the spectral colours. These chambers were used not only for treating ailments, but for aiding childbirth and helping the dying to make the transition from earthly to spiritual life.

Archaeologists have discovered that the Egyptians, too, had healing rooms built into their temples – rooms constructed so that when sunlight entered them its rays were separated into the colours of the spectrum. Patients were "colour diagnosed", then treated in the room that radiated the prescribed colour.

In ancient India medical treatment included the use of minerals and gemstones, which were believed to be a concentration of the seven cosmic rays – each stone relating to a certain ray (for example, onyx to ultraviolet, cat's eye to infrared). Healers viewed the gems through a prism to ascertain their true cosmic colour, which was not always the same as their manifested color.

Among the ancient Greeks, treatment by sunlight (heliotherapy) was a common practice, the city of Heliopolis being famous for its healing temples. The physician Hippocrates explained the basic mechanism of illness in terms of four humours or bodily fluids. Each of which was designated by a different colour. These were red blood, connected to the heart: yellow bile, associated with the spleen; black bile, arising in the brain: and white phlegm, deriving from the liver. Good health required these four humours to be kept in equilibrium – imbalances were remedied by administering the colour of the deficient humour in the form of food, flowers, plasters, ointments and minerals.

During the early Christian era, medical practices involving colour were deemed to be pagan, and many of the ancient writings on holistic medicine have been lost. Colour therapy was revived in the eleventh century CE by an outstanding Persian physician named Avicenna. His most famous book, *The Canon*, sets out his theories on the therapeutic use of colour – including the adverse effects that colour can produce. For example, he noted that red increased blood pressure and blue lowered it, while yellow seemed to reduce inflammation and pain.

In Renaissance Europe another notable physician named Paracelsus, medicated with colour which he administered in the form of light, herbs and minerals.

In the nineteenth century there were great advances in the understanding of anatomy, surgery and medication. This emphasis on the physical marginalized the spiritual emotional and psychological aspects of healing and the concept of treating the whole person was lost. With this loss the use of colour therapy declined.

However, heliotherapy was rediscovered in the mid-nineteenth century. The Danish physician Niels Ryberg Finsen was the first to use artificial light to treat skin tuberculosis. In Switzerland, Augustus Rollier used heliotherapy on a larger scale both to prevent and to treat tuberculosis.

Practitioners of heliotherapy now began to turn their attention to the colours that make up sunlight. Pioneers included the American physicians Seth Pancoast and Edwin Babbit. Pancoast worked mainly with red and blue, believing that the red ray accelerated the nervous system and the blue ray relaxed it. Babbit's work involved the red, yellow and blue primaries. He encouraged his patients to drink colour-solarized water, and also invented a cabinet, which he called the "Thermolume", to administer coloured sunlight.

In the early twentieth century, the philosopher, mystic and teacher Rudolf Steiner considered colour from a metaphysical point of view. He believed that colour was a living entity, each hue bearing a spiritual significance. He argued that illness was caused by the separation of earthly consciousness from higher perception, and that we could heal this rift through art.

Max Luscher, a professor of psychology from Basle University, contended that by measuring a person's preference for certain colours it was possible to diagnose and treat both physical and psychological conditions. Luscher's colour theories were supported by a Russian scientist S.V. Krakov, who later proved that red stimulates the sympathetic nervous system. Which accelerates autonomic (involuntary) body functions, such as breathing and heartbeat, while blue stimulates the parasympathetic system, which slows them down.

Two further twentieth-century colour therapy innovators were Dinshah P.Ghadiali and Harry Riley Spitler. Ghadilia, well versed in electricity, mathematics and physics, argued that sound, light, colour and heat were all the same energy, only differentiated from each other by their vibrational frequency. He formulated a scientific approach for the application of colour to the human body, investing two machines designed to apply through slides, the 12 colours with which he worked. Spitler a medical doctor and optometrist was responsible for a system of colour treatment which he called "Syntonics". He demonstrated that light entering the eyes plays an important role in the functioning of both the endocrine and autonomic nervous systems.

The colour therapy of today benefits from the influence of these enquiring minds and continues to develop, as we shall as see in this book.

## Colour and Light in Conventional Medicine

Although commonly seen as the tools of complementary therapy, colour and light are also used in modern allopathic medicine. For example, skin problems such as acne and psoriasis can be treated with ultraviolet light. In surgery, the argon laser, which produces the green wavelength, is used to stem bleeding tissues; the carbon dioxide laser, which produces an infrared beam, is used to make incisions. In ophthalmology, lasers are used to treat detached retinas and proliferative retinopathy.

Soft laser light, pioneered by Professor Endre Mester, alleviates burn pain, accelerates the healing of wounds and reduces scar tissue. Hungarian scientists have developed polarized light treatment to heal leg ulcers and bedsores, an to deal with varicose veins.

Two forms of treatment being carried out in Russia by Professor Kira Samoilova are Ultraviolet Irradiated Blood Retransfusions (UVIBR) and Intravenous Visible Light Irradiation of Blood (ILIB). These techniques were built upon research initially carried out by Emmit Knott and Virgil Hancock. Dr. Knott invented an instrument called the Haemo-Irradiation Machine, which irradiated with ultraviolet light a small sample of a patient's blood-blood which was then reinfused into the patient. The published findings of Knott and Hancock included accounts of the successful treatment, by this method, of viral infections, peritonitis and advanced toxaemia – treatment that worked were conventional drug therapy had failed. The treatment was used in Germany, the United States and the Soviet Union until the mid – 1950s. It was then abandoned until the mid – 1970s when it was reintroduced into medicine in the Soviet Union.

Another important treatment, pioneered in the United States in 1970 by Thomas Dougherty, is called Photodynamic Therapy (PDT). This technique uses red light in coujunction with a light-sensitive compound, to eliminate malignant tumours. Doctors have also used PDT to treat skin cancer and to reduce scarring at the site from which a malignant tumour has been removed.

# COLOUR AND GEM THERAPY

The seve ı hues of the rainbow are cosmic colours which are connected with the Tridoshas through their constituent elements and their associated senses. Colour can be used to feel the mind and emotions through the sensations we absorb – and these, of course, affect the bodily Doshas.

These colours, used for their therapeutic value, can be brought into your life through the clothes you wear, the walls of the rooms you spend time in, or, more specifically, by coloured light bulbs or filters such as paper stretched over windows, colouring all the incoming light. Similarly, water can be charged with the vibrations of particular colours by standing it in coloured glass vessels (or glass covered in coloured paper) in sunlight for several hours.

Vata is most positively affected by the colours red, orange and yellow, white and lighter shades of blue and green. Care should be taken with the frequency of use of red particularly, but also with any very strong, intense shades, because Vata is delicate. Paler shades are definitely recommended. Darker colours including grey, black and brown are to be avoided.

Pitta is benefited by the use of white, blue, green and purple, though again, avoid too strong or overly intense shades of these colours. Likewise, red and black are not recommended though grey and black are acceptable, but dark blue can lead to congestion. Also, avoid white and the pastel shades of blue, pink and green.

The most natural the source of colour, the more replenishing, balancing and strengthening the effect. Therefore, colour combined with the natural qualities of minerals imbued with that colour (gemstones) is going to be extremely potent. The effect of gemstones will often be similar to that of other sources of colour, but some stones have a *Prabhava*, which means that the expected effect of their colour will be over-ridden by the special effect of their individual nature.

Gemstones may be used in rings and necklaces, or steeped in a glass or water overnight, then removed next morning so the water can be drunk. Care must be taken to ensure that the stone are intact when they are to be worn, but pieces of gemstones can be used to make gem waters. If worn as jewellery, stones are most beneficial if set so that they touch the skin. Some of the more common gemstones are listed below, and the Doshas they beneficially affect are indicated.

- **Amethyst** – contains the elements Ether and Water. Aids in balancing the emotions and in protecting healers (in the widest sense). It increases clarity of perception and spirituality. It has associations with the endocrine system. Wear it in gold around the neck. Benefits Vata and Pitta.
- **Beryl** – contains the elements Fire and Ether. Increases power and social position. It is associated with the visual arts and music. Wear it in silver as a ring on the left ring finger or around the neck. Benefits Vata and Kapha.
- **Coral (Red)** – contains the elements Fire, Water and Earth. It is balancing to Pitta despite its colour, and soothes Pitta emotions. It has a slightly Kaphagenic effect as it increases body muscle and it improves stamina. Good for Pitta and Vata but best avoided by Kapha.
- **Diamond** – contains all five elements. The gem water is a heart tonic and is rejuvenating. Also good in pregnancy. The stone is spiritually uplifting, increases creativity and creates close bonds in relationships as well as bringing prosperity. Wear it set in white gold or white and yellow gold mixed on the right ring finger. Diamonds particularly benefit Pitta (specifically the blue and white gems) but all diamonds can be used for Vata, though may slightly increase Kapha.
- **Emerald** – contains Ether, Air and Water. It balances the nervous system, thereby affecting the mind (improving mental functioning) and the body (relieving pain). It is good for strengthening the pulmonary system, coronary circulation and the immune system. It restores balance and so is good for degenerative conditions. wear it on the middle or little finger in silver for Pitta, or gold for Vata and Kapha (which it may slightly increase).

- **Garnet** – contains the elements Fire and Earth (red, brown and yellow garnets) or Fire and Air (green) or Water (white). Red, brown and yellow stones warm Vata and Kapha (set in gold and worn around the neck), while green and white stones set in silver reduce the heat of Pitta.
- **Lapis lazuli** – contains the elements Ether, Fire and Water. It has a strengthening effect on the body (particularly the eyes) and mind, and increases spiritual awareness. Wear it in gold around the neck. Good for Vata and Kapha.
- **Moonstone** – contains the elements Ether, Air and Water. As with the moon herself, the moonstone is closely associated with water in the body and with the emotions. It benefits those who are suffering from the effects of stress. Wear it set in silver on the right ring finger. Best for Vata and Pitta.
- **Pearl** – contains the elements Air, Water and Earth. Useful for all Pitta afflictions as it is cooling and promotes the Rakta/blood qualities of vitality and vigour. As a gem water made overnight it can be used to treat inflammatory conditions and acidity. Pitta should wear it set in silver on the right ring finger.
- **Ruby** – contains the elements Ether, Air and Fire. Ruby is good for the circulation and heart. It stimulates positive Pitta characteristics like good digestion and mental functioning. It brings decisiveness and confidence. Good for Vata and Kapha for its heating effect. Wear it set in either gold or silver (depending on the degree of warming required) on the ring finger of the left hand.
- **Sapphire (Blue)** – contains the elements Ether and Air. This stone has a particular association with the Saturn (the god and the planet). It has an affinity with the nervous system and though it is a dark blue colour to the naked eye, is useful in the Vata conditions – from neuralgia, nervousness and anxiety to ME and MS. It decreases Kapha-type problems like fatty deposits and over-attachment. Set it in silver or platinum and wear it on the middle finger or round the neck.
- **Sapphire(Yellow)** – contains the elements Ether, Fire and Water. Good to promote all-round health and vitality. Increases the production of Ojas. Increases spirituality and God consciousness. Can be used by all Doshas but is of particular benefit to vitiated Vata as it increases centredness. Wear it set in gold on the index finger.

## RELIEF THROUGH MASSAGE

Throughout history we have used our hands to impact comfort and healing to one another. Touching is contact, warmth, reassurance that we are not alone, affirmation of our sense of being band self-worth. It is a simple way of communicating, something we can do naturally. And with a little willingness and commitment we can turn this natural talent into a creative healing skill, by learning the basic strokes and techniques of message and widening our vocabulary in the language of touch.

Our sense tough is registerd by our skin-our leargest and most sensitive organs. In the developing embryo, the skin arises from the same cell layer as the nervous system and can thus be seen as the external portion of the nervous system – able receive and register a vast quantity of varied signals, and to make a wide range of responses to them. Also, touch is the first sense to become functional in the embryo.

### The value of message

The intent that egos with touch makes all the difference to its effect. When we lay our hands on another with compassion and good-will many subtle change take place. Gentle holding and stroking, touching given with tenderness and care, cause transformations both physically and psychologically.

In the 1920s in Philadelphia the anatomist Frederick Hammett and other American researchers in the 1950s and 60s conducted experiments with groups of rats to investigate the effects of touch. Some were consistently handled and strc ked and others were not. The rats that were regularly touched showed faster growth rates, better immunity to disease and higher fertility and were less subject to stress than those that were not. Is is well known, too, that for infants, fondling and tender touch that go beyond the basis needs for food and cleaning are vital for in institutions were conducted by Dr. Chaplin and infancy and J. Brennemann. They found that many babies died in infancy and others showed clear sings of disturbance and poor physical and emotional development as a result of too title tactile stimulation.

Physiologically, caring touch and message help the flow of blood and lymph in our bodies. Touch can also decreases tension, producing relaxation and a state of well-being. It has been suggested that message may aid the production of endorphins balance the flow of vital energy.

Wholeness goes beyond the body, mind and emotions. In wholeness is health, and in any kind of healing touch technique you are treating's "subtle" body restoring balance to the flow of energy. This subtle body includes the energy field or "aura" in and around the body, and the major centres of subtle energy or vitally known as the chakras. The aura is composed of interpreting fields of subtle or vital energy that emanates from the body, out beyond the periphery of the skin, and is constantly in motion. Within the aura and along the mid line of the body are the seven main chakras, whose functions is to relay vital energy between the physical body and the subtle body. The word chakra is a Sanskrit word meaning wheel, which indicates the circling movements of energy in these centres. Five are situated on the spine and two in the head. They relate to different parts of the body – to glands, organs, and nerve plexii, and also to areas of our psychological and spiritual development. With practice you can learn to sense the energies of the aura and chakras with your hands.

## Using Shiatsu as a healing tool

In this book, we have chosen to teach not only massage but also Shiatsu to give you a wide range of effective techniques for the relief of everyday health problems.

Shiatsu has its origins in oriental medicine. The world literally means finger or thumbs pressure, although other parts of he hand and body are also used. In Japan Shiatsu has traditionally been practised as a simply remedy to promote health, alleviate pain and prevent sickness. Its techniques are based on the understanding that the body functions as a whole, linked by vital energy, or ki, which flows along channels, or meridians, which interlace as a network throughout the body, mostly on the ki energy surface. Discorporate, pain, stress and illness, making the internal organs either deficient in or overloaded by energy. By holding and applying pressure to points, or tsubos, on the meridians. You can stimulate the ki energy, helping it to rebalance itself. This affects the physical body and can help to relieve pain alleviate the cause and symptoms of illness.

Shiatsu should not be painful. Although some tsubos and meridians may be tender, pressure can be applied gently and slowly, so that it always feels comfortable. Shiatsu is a form of communication, and its effectiveness is dependent on a willingness to be open and receptive to your partner. (Meaning "morphine within"), the brain chemicals that functions as natural pain-killers. One of these, enkephalin, enkephalin, has the ability to reduce pain and produces a state of mind akin to euphoria.

The experience of being nourished and cared for and allowing ourselves to receives to receive healing touch affirms our self-esteem, creates trust and openness and can sometimes facilities the release of blocked emoting as tense muscles relax. Touch can make us feel values, peaceful and more aware of our whole body and being.

It is not only receiving touch that is beneficial, however. Giving massage is also highly rewarding. There is undulations of the body as you being to develop a sense of the muscles, bones and other tissues. There is enjoyment in knowing the body, in being alive to its different tensions and energies, and in realizing that you can care for and help another. There is also satisfaction in experiencing the results of your massage as you feel muscles relaxing and realised that your concern and your touch can help to stimulate the receiver's won on healing process. Often the interaction between the givers and receivers induces a similar state in both – a state that is very similar to meditation.

## Preventing and treating ill health with massage

When you already have the gift of health you need to maintain it. Touch does not just have to be used as a way of healing and hastening recovery-it can be a way of preventing sickness. In today's "civilized: it is only too easy to get caught up in striving accomplishing, and conforming to society's mores. In the process you can become overly head-oriented and touch with reality, however, for it is through your body that you receive sensory message, that let you know what you need, what you are feeling emotionally, and what is all vital information for self-regulation, in the sense of giving your body what is best for health and balance. In order to be truly healthy you need to stop thinking that ideas and concepts are the only reality and wake up to the information that your whole body can give you. As Fritz Pearls, the founder of Gestalt therapy, said "lose your head and come to your sense."

Massage is a way of getting back in touch with your body and finding trust in what it has to say. When you become more aware of yourself as a whole being, physical, mental, emotional and spiritual, you can start to respond more to fulfilling your real needs. Eating a healthy and balanced diet, exercising daily and breathing more freely can all be done with a sense of pleasure and rightness rather than as chores or acts of grim will-power.

Nevertheless, everyone gets sick from time to time, and illness is often a manifestation of the body's attempt to heal itself and to eliminate tins and clear the system. This book is about how to use touch to help the body's natural healing process when you or your family or friends do succumb to any of the common ailments. It is not about miracle cures, but about giving warmth and support to another by a variety of caring touch techniques, which can help to speed recovery. As many illnesses result from stress and strain calm and soothe tension and bring balance to your being. Both massage and Shiatsu work with and for the body's healing energies; in contrast to states of stress and effort they create the conditions for healing to take place. As well as learning how to do a whole body massage, which you can use when an ailment is more general and affects the whole body – such as insomnia or fatigue conditions, such as headaches, bachaches, constipation and cramp. Use the book wisely. Don't try to take over a doctor's role – give where you can and seek medical advice where you can't. Your hands have healing in them. Use them.

## The History of Shiatsu

A simple Japanese word meaning "finger pressure", SHIATSU is the coined earlier this century to describe an increasingly distinguished form of healing. Massage, along with acupuncture, moxibustion and herbalism, had for centuries been an integral part of traditional Chinese medicine. As it developed in Japan however, the practice of massage known by the old name of "Anma" became gradually divorced from medicine and more associated in people's minds only with relaxation and pleasure. Certain practitioners were concerned to preserve massage and related techniques as an accepted healing art; Shiatsu thus emerged as a form of manual therapy incorporating gentle manipulations and stretches derived from newer disciplines such as physiotherapy and chiropractic, with pressure techniques exerted through the fingers or thumbs. Shiatsu become recognised by the Japanese Government as a therapy in its own right, distinct from Anma and Western Massage, in the middle of this century.

In a Shiatsu session pressure is applied to various parts of the body which correspond with the points and energy lines (meridians) used in acupuncture, which is why Shiatsu become popularly known in the West by the rather inexact term "acupressure". The practitioner may use thumbs and fingers, elbows, and even knees and feet to apply pressure to points on the meridians. Physically this has the effect of stimulating circulation and the flow of lymphatic fluid, it works on both divisions of the autonomic nervous system, helps to release toxins and deep seated tension from the muscles and can stimulate the hormonal system. On a more subtle level Shiatsu allows the receiver to relax deeply and get in touch with his body's own healing abilities: treatment usually leaves a feeling of calmness and well being of being more in touch with one's body and Self.

For a complete perspective on the theories behind diagnosis and treatment in Shiatsu, we must look back to China. These theories relate directly to the ancient philosophical concepts regarding the nature of existence, which have formed the basis for scince, art, politics and religion in China for over two thousand years. All phenomena were understood in terms of the two primary archetypal forces represented symbolically as Yin and Yang. These are the positive and negative aspects of the all-pervading life energy of the Universe which the Chinese call "Ch'i" (the Japanese word is "Ki"). The cycles of the seasons, the influence of the Heavenly bodies on the Earth, and ultimately the intricate relationship between all natural events and their influence on human life were observed and studied. The theory of Yin and Yang as complementary but opposing dynamics was refined and developed producing subsidiary philosophical models such as the "Five Transformational phases" – Wood, fire, Earth, Metal and Water – representing more specifically the essential qualities of things, and the interaction of events. Inevitably these theories began to be applied in medicine.

## How Shiatsu Works

Although energy is present everywhere in the body, it was noted that there were many placed where it seemed to accumulate or flow near the surface. In illness, when the energy is disturbed, it will sometimes manifest in these areas as pain, swelling, irritation, redness etc. It was then found that such conditions, even internal ones, could be ameliorated were systesmatised as an understanding emerged which was the birth of the related therapies of acupuncture, moxibustion and massage. These make use of needles, heat and healing touch to adjust the energies of the body, for the cure of disease. Ch'i flows in the channels which in the West, have come to be known by the French word "meridian". These channels are considered to be either Yin or Yang according to position and direction of the energy flow. They correspond with the internal organs, each of which contributes uniquely to the harmony of the whole organism, and each is represented by one of the five "Phase", For example: the energy of the stomach is cinsidered to be Yang in nature. Its channel goes from the head downwards to the feet and it is associated with "Earth", the source of food; the kidneys, on the other hand, which regulate body fluids, are associated with "Water their energy is Yin and flows in the reverse direction, from the feet to the throat.

Because an imbalance of Ch'i or Ki in the body often precedes the overt symptoms of disease, all aspects of Oriental medicine have a preventative role. However, their suitability to treat specific diseases is of paramount importance and it is worth listing here the most common syndromes which may be amenable to treatment by Shiatsu. These include: headaches and migraine, respiratory illnesses including asthma and bronchitis, sinus trouble and catarrh, insomnia, tension, anxiety and depression, fatigue and weakness, digestive disorders and bowel trouble, painful menstruation and some other urogenital conditions, circulatory problems, rheumatic and arthritic complaints, back trouble, sciatica and conditions following sprains and injuries. Treatment of all these conditions will be given according to Oriental diagnosis, though it is always important that the modern Western diagnosis is confirmed and considered as well.

## Diagnosis

One of the real strengths of oriental medicine is the subtlety and precision of traditional diagnosis, which includes the four methods of asking, observation, listening and touching. These can all be used in Shiatsu, but of course the latter is especially applicable, and the Japanese have perfected the art of abdominal or "Hara" diagnosis, whereby the abdomen is palpated gently to determine the energetic quality and balance of the various internal organs. Like acupuncturists and herbalists, the Shiatsu practitioner may also diagnose from the pulse, but further refinement of the treatment is made according to the "feel" or response from each point as it is held or pressed. So, in skilled hands, Shiatsu can revitalise or restore health by promoting the circulation of energy in the meridians. Thus the functions of the organs, blood and body fluids are regulated, and increased nourishment to the muscles and joints aids flexibility and relaxation. Shiatsu is complementary to orthodox medicine and other natural therapies. Professional Practitioners will often give advice in exercise, diet and lifestyle. Most people can benefit from Shiatsu, from children to the elderly.

## Guidelines for Patients

In order to gain the most benefit from a Shiatsu treatment, here are simple guidelines to follow:

1. It is best not to eat or drink alcohol on the day of treatment; have a light meal at least one hour before your treatment.
2. Do not take a long, hot bath on the day of treatment.
3. For treatment wear loose clothing, preferably cotton, such as a track or jogging suit. You will usually remain fully clothed during Shiatsu treatment, which takes place on a padded surface at floor level.
4. If applicable, have details available of current medical diagnosis and of nay medication you may be taking.

## Response to treatment

After Shiatsu you will probably feel invigorated yet relaxed. Sometimes the first benefits to occur do not improve the main complaint, but rather overall health. For example, the body's eliminative functions may have to be improved before specific pain can be relieved. The duration and frequency of treatment will vary from person to person, as well the total number of sessions. Most people have two opposing tendencies; one; the wish to regain health and freedom; the other, to remain attached to old behaviour patterns which reinforce the sickness. While patients generally experience increased well-being, there may be temporary "healing reactions" as toxins and negative emotions are released; these may take the form of a headache or flu-like symptoms for 24 hours, in such cases contact your therapist so that he can reassure you.

Shiatsu affects all levels of our being, the physical, emotional, psychological and spiritual; treatment is attuned to the individual's personal development of total health and character. The practitioner may give advice on diet, exercise and lifestyle, encouraging self-understanding and greater independence in health matters. This in turn leads to improved self-confidence and lasting peace of mind for the patient.

## Shiatsu in the community

Shiatsu is now recognised by the Japanese government as a remedial therapy and there are several well known schools for training practitioners. But it should be remembered that, as in many other parts of the world, massage still forms an important part of the local folk medicine. There is a long tradition of massage practised among Japanese family members for mutual well-being and the relief of minor ailments. It was on this level that Shiatsu first became generally known outside Japan. Over the last fifteen to twenty years it has become established in America, Europe, and other parts of the world through the influence of a few dedicated teachers. Shiatsu classes have fulfilled an importance role in the new movement towards greater awareness of social and individual responsibility in Health. For the modern lay person, study of basic Shiatsu can be a relaxing, enjoyable activity through which people can reach out and touch one another, gain mutual understanding and give practical hel and support in times of stress. Traditional exercises are often tought, which not only improve the ability to perform Shiatsu, but which also serve as a valuable means towards self development.

## Styles of Shiatsu

Shiatsu, as many therapeutic disciplines, ahas a number of different styles, philosophical approaches and theoretical basis. Within the Shiatsu Society we encourage an electric outlook so that practitioners and students become familiarly with and respect the different forms and styles of Shiatsu. The approaches most commonly found in Britain are Zen Shiatsu, Macrobiotic Shiatsu, Healing-Shiatsu, Namikoshi Shiatsu and Hara Shiatsu. Different schools tend towards particular styles and prospective students should discuss this aspect with teachers before deciding upon which course to join.

## Sprains and Strains

A strain is an injury to muscle fibers or ligaments that have been forcibly stretched beyond their proper length. This can result in some local pain and perhaps swelling. A sprain is more severe and is caused by a violent wrench or twist, causing tearing of the muscle fibers or the ligaments or a joint, resulting in pain swelling and bruising. The most common areas to be affected are wrists, ankles and backs. These are both common injuries that can be helped by massage in the recovery stages, but you will need to follow the process outlined below. Having ascertained from a doctor that no bones are broken, the best initial treatment for sprains and strains is an ice pack or a cold-water compress if no ice is available. Then you should apply a bandage and support the joint, elevating it if possible. Rest for between 24 and 48 hours, or until tenderness has subsided. Remedial massage treatment can then begin.

Don't work directly on swollen areas, but start with gentle gliding strokes that push up toward the heart, above the injury. In the case of a sprained ankle, for example, work first from knee to thigh, and then from ankle to knee, to help disperse the fluid (see below). As the injury heals you can begin to work all around the areas with careful kneading and friction strokes. Finally, where possible, you can work with passive movements to help restore mobility. Always keep within the threshold of pain. You could use a moisture of lavender and rosemary essences.

## Ice and water compresses

For sprains and strains ice is useful for reducing internal bleeding, but you should never apply ice directly to the skin. Always wrap it in a cloth, or use a bag of frozen peas. Apply ice for five minutes in every hour, for several hours, during the first day or two. If you do not have any ice, a cloth wrung out in cold water is also effective. Where there is persistent aching from strained muscles, alternating hot and cold compresses can bring relief.

## Applying hot and cold compresses

You need two bowls, one containing iced water and the other very hot (not boiling) water, and two cotton cloths or small towels. It is useful to start with the hot compress, so wring out one cloth in the hot water, then fold it to shape and apply it to the area of pain for three minutes. Next wring out the cold cloth and apply it for one minute. Continue alternating these compresses for between ten and fifteen minutes.

## Arthritis

There are many different kinds of arthritis, all of them involving the joints. The most common are rheumatoid arthritis and osteoarthritis. Rheumatoid arthritis is a generalized disease that can start in childhood, usually in the small bones of the hands or feet. Joints become very painful, swollen and inflamed, and the condition can spread throughout the body. Osteoarthritis is a disease of later life, linked with wear and tear and mechanical deterioration of joints, bones and discs. It is often found first in the lower neck and lower back, and can occur in joints where there have been previous injuries. Massage can help to reduce pain in both these ailments. However if a joint is swollen or inflamed do not work on it. You may give it hand healing by just resting your hands lightly on the painful area for several minutes while remaining centred. Then work with light gliding strokes above the remaining centred. Then work with light gliding strokes about the swelling, in the direction of the heart. Where there is no swelling you can use whatever strokes feel good to your partner, from the section of the book that deals with that part of the body.

Before doing passive movements on arthritic joints check with a doctor to see if this is alright and then always go very sensitively and keep within the pain threshold. Never force movements beyond their range. General soothing, slow stroking and gentle kneading and thumb circling around the affected areas can be comforting and relaxing. Rosemary and lavender essences dissolved in oil will also help to alleviate pain.

## Supporting the Limb

As people with arthritis may feel to stiff climb on to a table or get down on to the floor you can improvise in a variety of way with chairs of different kinds and stools or foot stools to support the legs. Watch your own posture and avoid bending to much. Set on the floor or on stool or chair as you work.

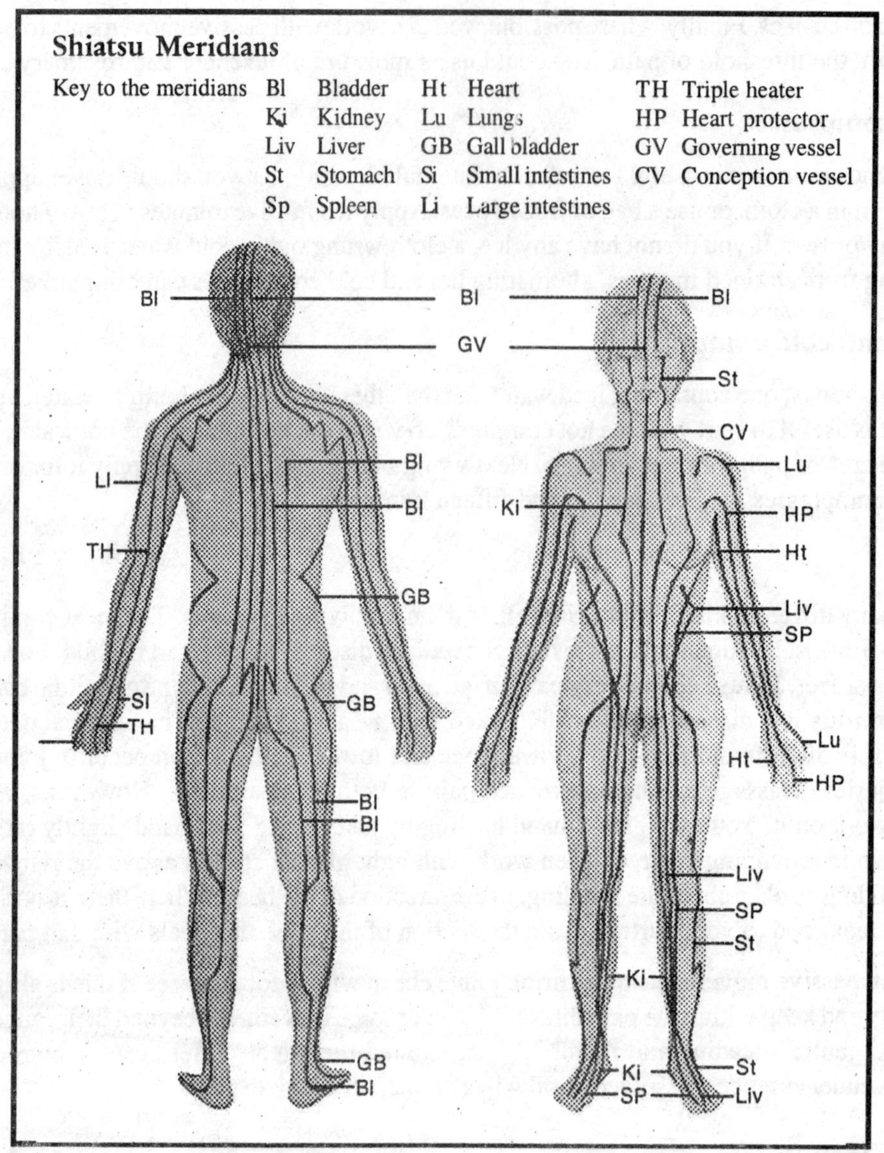


## When massage should not be used

There are certain conditions which should not be treated by massage or Shiatsu and these are listed below. It is very important to take note of these contraindication. However, the fact that a person is suffering from any of these ailments does not mean that he or she should be totally deprived of any healing touch. Touch is reassuring calming and comforting and can help to mobilize the body's own healing processes. So very gentle touching or light stroking on unaffected areas of the body can be soothing though never massage without first obtaining a doctor's consent. The warning "Don't massage means don't use any deep strokes on or near the affected areas.

## Hand healing

Hand healing is done by first centring and then very gently letting your hands come to rest on a part, or two parts, of the body and holding them lightly there for some minutes. Meanwhile you remain present and aware and visualize your hands as channels for healing energy.

## Contraindication

### Localized infections or inflammation

Don't massage where there is an infection or inflammation, as you may spread it.

**You may :** do very light hand healing through clothes or dressing. With a doctor's consent do gentle stroking massage on parts of the body that are not sites of infection.

### Swelling

**Don't :** massage on swollen areas.

**You may :** do light hand healing and work above swelling with upward strokes to disperse fluid.

Skin eruptions (ire. acne, eczema, heat rash)

**Don't :** massage over skin eruptions.

**You may :** do light hand healing through clothes and massage on parts that are clear, craning upward to drain wastes from tissue.

Bruising

**Don't :** massage on bruises.

**You may :** work upward about the bruse and stroke around it to disperse it.

### Varicose veins

**Don't :** massage on varicose veins and don't up from below toward them.

**You may :** do hand healing, apply cold-water compresses, elevate the leg and do gentle gliding strokes about the varicose veins, up toward the heart. If a doctor agrees you can also work with very light, slow upward strokes on either side of the veins, not directly on them. This can relieve the aching caused by swollen varicose veins.

**Fever**

**Don't :** massage a person with a fever.

**You may :** do hand healing The skin is often hypersensitive during a fever. Stroking or holding may give comfort.

### Thrombosis or phlebitis

**Don't :** massage a person with these conditions, which mean that blood clots are present and massage could dislodge them.

**You may :** do light hand healing or do very gentle massage of hands feet or face if a doctor agrees.

### Broken bones

**Don't :** massage if a bone is broken or suspected to be broken. Seek medical help.

**You may :** give hand healing and comforting touch to other parts of the body for reassurance in later healing stages consult a doctor, then massage as for sprains and strains.

### Tumours

**Don't :** Massage where there are tumours.

**You may :** do hand healing if a doctor agrees do gentle stroking of areas such as face, feet, hands and shoulders. Cancer patients can get great comfort from caring touch.

### Pregnancy

**Don't :** use Shiatsu pressure around ankles or massage with any heavy, deep or percussion strokes on lower back or abdominal areas.

**You may :** with the consent of a doctor of a doctor, give gentle massage throughout pregnancy, using light and gentle strokes but be particularly careful in the fist three months.

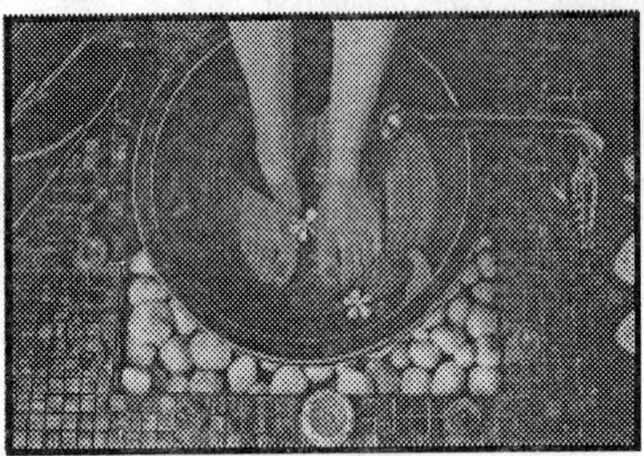

**Sawa Di or foot massage is a perfect treat to go for at Aroma Thai**

## DAILY DOS DAILY DONTS

You may go to the salon once a last night for a pedicure, but it is simple everyday rules of foot care that can keep the doctor away. Wash your feet in warm (not boiling) water every day. Pat them dry especially between the toes. Rub in some lotion to avoid dryness. If you have corns and calluses, file them gently with an emery board after your bath.

Cut your toenails at least once a week. If you have a problem of in-grown toenails, consult your podiatrist. Put your feet up when sitting for an extended period. Don't cross your legs for long stretches. Exercise your feet regularly.

Don't wear tight socks, elastic or rubber bands or garters around your legs. Wear seamless socks.

The American Orthopaedic Foot and Ankle Society recommends that women should not wear heels more than 2 $^{1}/_{4}$". Regular use of very high heels weakens the Achilles tendon and causes serious heel pain.

Several get insoles and scientifically designed footwear are available in the market. Dr. Scholl's range is a name to reckon with. Use them.

### Coping Stress with Massage Therapy

#### Stress

Stress is an unconscious and automatic reaction to anything we believe may be threatening to us. In the stress response, the body is primed for "fight" or 'flight', by messages carried by the sympathetic branch of the nervous system. Whether we are confronted by job pressure of find ourselves in a long line at the bank on a short lunch hour, the effects are the same, impacting all levels-physical, mental and emotional.

We are at full readiness as our body tenses and our breathing gets shallower and more rapid. There is an increase in heart rate, blood pressure and adrenaline production, with a corresponding decrease in blood flow to the extremities, digestive function, and immune system activity. Ideally, this defensive reaction will subside once the situation has resolved, allowing our body to return to its normal state. We often help this process with some rest, the right exercise, a massage or meditation.

A person, frequently under stressful influences, remains locked into a pattern of stress response, and is unable to relax or let go. This is damaging to the body. As it escalates, it ultimately leads to discomfort or pain, and is a contributing factor in most disease processes. Our pleasures and pains, the ups and downs of daily life affect the body profoundly, often in ways we are not aware of. Stress is more than a household word these days – it is something everyone feels to some degree more or less.

## Antidote to Stress

The antidote to stress is known as the "relaxation response". Which is triggered by the parasympathetic branch of the nervous system. This action sends messages to the body to relax; saying in effect, "It is time for rest and healing." There are a number of ways to promote this response, such as exercise, meditation, listening calming music, guided visualization, biofeedback, and therapeutic massage.

Massage takes place in a comfortable and safe environment, which is generally away from most stressors. As massage stimulates the relaxation response, muscle tension is released, blood circulation is increased and sensory receptors are activated. Also areas that have been "cut off" by accumulated stress can begin to feel once again. Massage teachers us to tune in to body signals and soothes us at the same time. They result in greater body awareness which help us to more carefully monitor our own body's response and needs. Then we can release tension before it becomes chronic and damaging. Living in a more relaxed and balanced body will enable us to better handle the stresses in our life, and noting can take us back to that state of well-being more quickly than massage.

### Types of Massage Therapies

(a) **SWEDISH MASSAGE :** uses a system of long strokes, kneading and friction techniques on the more superficial layers of the muscles, combined with active and passive movements of the joints. Used primarily for a full-body session it promotes general relaxation, improves circulation and range of motion and relieves muscle tension.

(b) **DEEP MUSCLE/CONNECTIVE TISSUE MASSAGE :** It releases the chronic tensions in the body through slow strokes and deep finger pressure on contracted areas, either following or going across the grain of muscles, tendons and fascia. Can be used for specific work or fullbody.

(c) **TRIGGER POINT THERAPY :** (a.k.a. Myotherapy or Neuromuscular Therapy) : It applies concentrated finger pressure to "trigger points" – painful irritated areas in muscles – in order to break the cycle of spasm and pain. Often used to deal with pain.

(d) **SHIATSU AND ACUPRESSURE :** A Oriental systems of finger-pressure massage which treat special points along acupuncture "meridians"–the invisible channels of energy flow in the body. Blocked energy along these meridians can cause physical discomforts. So the aim is to release the blocks and re-balance the energy flow. Full-body or specific work.

(e) **REFLEXOLOGY (Zone Therapy) :** It is organized around points on the hands and feet that thought to correspond (or "reflex") to all areas of the body and has full-body effects.

(f) **POLARITY THERAPY :** It is an energy-based system, created by the late Randolphg Stone, an American chiropractor naturopath and osteopath. It attempts to harmonize the body's energy flow and structural balance through both gentle and structural balance through both gentle and deeper contacts. A subtle and somewhat esoteric approach, but very powerful. Full-body or specific work.

(g) **HYDRO THERAPY :** It is traditionally used as an adjunct to massage. It includes modalities such as hot packs and ice applications, along with saunas, steam baths and whirlpools.

(h) **AROMA THERAPY :** It is a massage by rubbing therapeutic plant essences on the body. Oils via the skin and inhaling the scent counteract disharmony.

According to Vagbhata (Astanga Hrdaya : Sutra :2:7-8), a person, with a view to preserving his positive health and preventing the disease, should use massage therapy every day. It has the following specific attributes :

(i) It prevents and corrects ageing process (*jard*)

(ii) It helps a person to overcome fatigue because of routine hard work in life. (*Srama*)

(iii) It prevents and corrects disorders caused by the afflication of the nervous system. (*Vata*)

(iv) It promotes eye-sight (*drsti prasada*)

(v) It helps nourishment (Pusti) of the body

(vi) It promotes longevity (ayus) of an individual.

(vii) It helps the individual to get sleep (svapna)

(viii) It promotes sturdiness (dardhya) of the individual.

## Benefits of Massage

### A. Physical level

1. Deep relaxation and stress reduction.
2. Relief of muscle tension and stiffness.
3. Reduced muscle spasm and tension.
4. Greater joint flexibility and range of motion.
5. Increases ease and efficiency of movement.
6. Promotes deeper and easier breathing.
7. Better circulation of blood and lymph fluids.
8. Reduced blood pressure.
9. Relief of tension-related headaches and eye-strain.
10. Healthier and better nourished skin.
11. Improved posture.
12. Faster healing of pulled muscles and sprained ligments; reduced spasm, pain and swelling; reduced formation of scar tissue.
13. Strengthened immune system and disease prevention.
14. Health maintenance

### B. Mental Level

1. Relaxed state of alertness.
2. Reduced mental stress; a calmer mind.
3. Greater ability to monitor stress signals and respond appropriately.
4. Increased capacity for clear thinking.

### C. Emotional Level

1. Satisfying the need for caring and nurturing touch.
2. Feeling of well-being.
3. Greater ease of emotional expression.

4. Enhanced self-image.
5. Reduced levels of anxiety.
6. Increased awareness of the mind-body connection.
7. A sense of being unified and in harmony.

## Ancient Traditions and modern Methods

This healing art has a history which stretches back thousands of years. The first written records of massage go back 3,000 years to China, although it is certain that the use of touch to heal and soothe extends into the farthest reaches of human experience. To rub or stroke a sore muscle is a natural human instinct, and the "laying on of hands" has been valued among spiritual healing traditions. Greek and Roman physicians used massage, as did Egyptians, Islanders in the South Pacific, Persians and Hindus. Hippocrates (considered the father of modern medicine) wrote: "the physician must be experienced in many things, but most assuredly in rubbing."

The methods we utilize today come from two main traditions, Eastern and Western, Eastern traditions can be traced back to the systems of folknmedicine of China and Ayurvedic medicine of India. Shiatsu, aupressure and reflexology spring from these sources, as do other contemporary methods. Western massage can be traced back to Peter Heinrik Ling, an educator and athelete from nineteenth-century Sweden. His approach, which combined hands-on techniques with active movements, become known as Swedish massage one of the most commonly used methods in the Western world.

As the twenty-first century approaches massage continues as an integral part of the health systems of most cultures. In the Soviet Union, West Germany, China and Japan, the therapeutic effects of massage have been recognised for many years. Consequently, massage therapists there have been working along with doctors in the hospital setting as an important member of the health care team. In West Germany today, doctors write a prescription for 10 massage treatments as readily as for a bottle tranquilizer and massage is covered by their national health insurance plan.

In the past 40 years, a new wave of pioneers have brought forth innovative approaches to the field. People such as Janet Travell, M.D.(Trigger Point Work), Ida Rolf, Ph.D. (Stuctural Integration) and Randolph Stone, D.C.(Polarity Therapy) have made invaluable contributions to health management. Many of these new therapies synthesize informations from traditional approaches with modern-day scientific knowledge and the latest hands-on techniques, producing therapeutic models which are more precise and effective.

## Conclusion

Massage Therapy is utilized in a wide variety of ways both as an adjunct to medical treatment and in the promotion of health. According to Dr. Willibald Nagler, head of Rehabilitation medicine at New York hospital :– "massage is better than a good tranquilizer, and can serve as a very helpful adjunct to other therapies." In the words of the ancient philosopher Cicero, "Only the person who is relaxed can create and to that mind ideas flow like lightning." Massage relaxes. It frees the body and opens the mind; It sharpens the senses and clears the thinking – releasing the individual's innate creativity and allowing it to expand to new dimensions. In an overloaded, stressed society, in need of contact, strength and leadership, the healthy relief of a non-invasive massage "treatment", with no unhealthy side effects, could be a literal lifesaver – and a stroke of sanity.

Unfortunately all good things in life come after prolonged practice. So there are no quick fixes in naturopathy. Those coming for short sessions only can get an exposure to what they need to do. Normally all naturopathic practices which are mostly lifestyle changes can be practised at home also. So after getting the exposure, persons will have to continue when they go back.

## Hydrotherapy

Hydrotherapy, or the use of water for healing purposes, has an ancient pedigree, and different applications of using water can be found in many classical civilizations. Both the ancient Greeks and Romans used hot and cold-water baths extensively, and many of the modern spas throughout Europe owe their origins to Roman bathing centres. Similarly, the Native Americans were familiar with the use of sweat-lodges, for physical and spiritual cleansing, and were proficient in various hydrotherapeutic techniques.

In recent centuries, however, some of this knowledge and expertise was lost. The therapeutic uses of water were largely revived in Europe in the nineteenth century by a Bavarian Dominican monk, Sebastian Kneipp. He believed that people had considerable innate healing powers and that water applications were a medium for stimulating, or occasionally soothing, our recuperative efforts. His ideas have continued to be influential to this day, and in spas in Germany it is possible to experience one of 50 or so different water applications for a variety of ailments.

Typical treatments may include contrast bathing, using alternating baths of hot and cold water. These are usually what are termed sitz baths, a kind of hip bath that immerses the lower trunk, while the feet may be placed in foot-baths of contrasting temperature in order to stimulate the circulation. Other forms to treatment may include high-pressure hosing with cold water, hot or cold body wraps, friction rubs, or baths with various ingredients added for extra elimination – for example, mud baths, Epsom salts baths or thalassotherapy (seawater baths).

Cold body wraps are made by soaking a sheet in cold water and wrapping it around the body, then covering this with a dry sheet and blanket. The initial cold is quite quickly replaced by warmth. These wraps are used for a number of conditions such as chronic muscle strains and backache. The sitz baths are often recommended for conditions such as chronic constipation, congestion in the pelvic area, recurrent cystitis and period pains. The sprays have similar effects to the baths, depending on their temperature, but are generally more stimulating to the circulation. A milder effect is achieved by whirlpool baths, which are increasingly popular in homes, gyms and spas.

Some recent medical research has shown the benefits of cool baths for reducing high blood pressure and improving peripheral circulation, and the contrasting applications of hot and cold water compresses and such like have a strong effect on the immune system, so hydrotherapy has very definite physiological effects. As a note of caution, prolonged exposure to very hot water is not a good idea for pregnant woman or any one with hypertension or heart disease, so be careful with saunas, Turkish baths, whirlpools and so on. Regular shorter sessions are often more beneficial.

Home applications can be very simple; a sprained ankle or similar injury with swelling needs a cold application initially, such as an ice pack or cold compress. After a while, older injuries may respond to hot, then cold applications, while chronic areas of muscular stiffness often do better with just warm water treatments. Although largely neglected by orthodox medicine in the UK, European countries and indeed the US have been much more positive about hydrotherapy, and new research is confirming its potential.

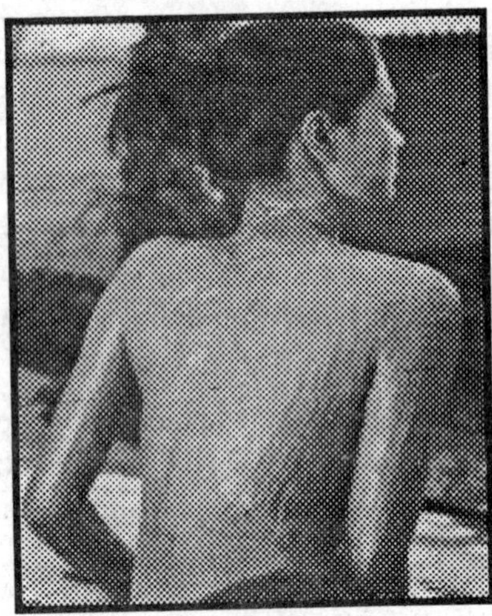

**Mud Therapy**

Though fasts upto 2 to 3 days can be observed, longer fasts should be undertaken under the supervision of a doctor only.

In normal fasts, one may take normal or lukewarm water with lemon juice and honey, lemon juice in warm water retards the formation of gas on empty stomach.

During fasting, however, full use should be made of enema mud and hydrotherapy to expedite elimination process.

## Fasting

Importance of fasting can be learnt from animals. When they fall sick, they stop eating, go and lie in sn and drink a lot of water. Almost all the religions prescribe fasting in one way or the other. During fasting the body recoups considerably the 'Aakash' element by fasting all body mechanisms which produce blood, flesh, bones or body juices are cleansed and overhauled. During fasts that body energy which was ordinarily employed for nutritional puposes also becomes available and that too is utilised for elimination of unwanted and toxic matter.

One must understand that the above treatments are not substitute to our food habits put are only as supplement to them.

Constipation, if untreated, if untreated, could cause havoc to our mental and physical health and cause a number of ailments like, general lethary, headache, indigestion, fissures, piles, fistula, insomnia, vomiting, belching, regurgitation, vertigo, pimples on the face, dark black spots below eyes and what not.

Isabgol Husk, one of therichest sources of dietary fibre

Keep to a routine

A hectic lifestyle isn't good for your health.

Just 2 spoonfuls

Provide as much as 1/3rd of daily fibre requirement

Help restore and maintain regularity of motions

Give relief in 24 hours

**And make a few lifestyle changes to help ease constipation**

Exercise regularly any aerobic exercise (running, jogging, swimming, etc) – even 10 to 15 minutes briskwalking several time a day will help drink upto 2 litres of fluid (6 to 10 glasses) everyday to keep your digestive system moving.

It doesn't have to be just water – fruit juices are just as good. Just try and avoid too much tea or coffee as they can de-hydrate you

## Summary

### What is the stress

Stress! What does it mean to you? Traffic jams, dedlines, eating on the run, bills to pay, job changes, endless chores and errands, and demands, demands, demands.

Stres is the body's response to any demand or pressure. These demands are called stressors. Stressors include major life events, such as divorce or the birth of a child. They also include chronic strains that last over a preiod of time, such living on unemployment. And stressors include daily or occasional strains, like taking care of a sick, child.

Whatever the stressors is, it requires the body to make physical and chemical adjustment in order to maintain the necessary physiological balance for survival. raching heart, a burst of energy, and muscle tension are the body's physical respone to demands. What faced with danger, some of the first stress reactions are a rise in blood pressure, quicker breathing and heart beat, and dilated pupils. Sight and hering become more alert.

This reaction is an instinctive response that protects us from threats to survival. Physiological changes are part of the "fight or flight" response, which prepares and energizes a person to confront or fle from danger. After the threat has passed or a change take place, the "alarm" signs disappear. The body is still aroused but is adapting to the change. However, if high levels of stress continue, the energy to adapt runs out. Exhustion occurs, causing damage to the person's physical and emotional well-being. Enier families may experience distress from tensions and pressures on the family to change.

Surprising as it seems, some stress has positive out comes. "Good Stress" can give an athlet the energy to excel in physical competition. It can stimulate a scientist's thinking or a composure's creative enargy. It can give many people the enargy to solve problem and to finish hard work.

Often, however, lives are filled with many demands that continue over a long period of time. Demands such as work overload may result in negative stress, which is called distress.

Unrelieved stress can take an emotional as well as physical toll, in the form of anxiety or depression, or high blood pressure and heart disease. If unattended, stress can seriously damage physical health; Psychological well-being; and relationship with friends, family, and coworkers.

### Am I Under Stress

Major problem can be avoided if symptoms of stress are identified early. Some of the signs of serious problems with stress are: persistent intense depression chronic sleeping and eating inability to concentrate outbursts of violence persistent family conflict and excessive drinking or drug use.

Simple checklists will give you a clue as to whether or not you are under stress. You probably know some of the symtomps of stress from experience headache tense muscles knitted stomach sweaty palms Symtomps may also be psychological and interpersonal such as feelings of insecurity or arguments with a spouse or child.

Think about a stress or you have experienced in the last week or so.

Take a look at the chart below and check off how you usually react to stress.

Look over the stress symptoms you've checked. Circle those that occur frequently Which of these concern you the most? What ideas do you have about how to stop these stress symptoms from happening?

Once you know some of your symtomps of stress and are aware of when Stress occurs, you can begin to use stress management strategies to deal with stress. In fact many stress experts believe that how a person deals with stress may be important than the number or type of demands he or she faces. Ideas for ways to prevent and cope with stress given in the book.

| Physical | Emotional | Mental | Social |
|---|---|---|---|
| Headaches | Anxiety | Forgetfulness | Isolation |
| Teeth grinding | Frustation | Poor concentration | Loneliness |
| Fatigue | Nervousness | Low productivity | Lashing out |
| Insomnia | Depression | Negative Attitude | Clamming up |
| Back aches | Worrying | Confusion | Lowered sex drive |
| Stomach problems | Tension | No new ideas | Nagging |
| Colds | Mood Swings | Lathargy | Fewer contacts with |
| Neck aches | Easily discouraged | Boredom | friends |
| Shoulder pains | Crying spells | | Using people |
| Increased use of | Irritability | | |
| Drugs | | | |

To avoid the problems associated with stress, people need to manage their stress. Before they can manage their stress, however, they need to decide whether they need ***professional help*** **or whether** ***self-help*** is enough. Once people decide on a source of help, regardless of the source of the help and the *stress management techniques* involved, a series of steps are involved in the *process of change*.

## Professional Help or Self-Help

When trying to manage stress, it is often difficult for people to decide whether self-help will be enough or whether they should seek professional help. In practice, people usually turn to self-help instead of professional help. The public appears to be very accepting of self-help resources. Self-help is not always the best way to manage stress, though. Sometimes professional help is necessary. Professional help is probably necessary if self-help fails or does not offer any worthwhile solution or if the problems associated with stress develop into mental disorders or physical illness.

A wide range of professionals is available to people with stress-related problems, ranging from medical doctors to mental health professionals. A medical doctor, such as a general practitioner or a specialist, is a good choice when stress leads to symptoms that may indicate physical illnesses. A mental health professional, such as ***clinical psychologist*** **or a** ***psychiatrist,*** is a good choice when stress leads to symptoms that may indicate a mental disorder. Clinical psychologists and psychiatrists along with other mental health professionals like *counselling psychologists* can also provide assistance with stress management in general, not just with mental disorders that may accompany stress. ***Other mental health professionals like marriage and family counsellors, social workers, nurses, clergyperson*** may also be able to provide some assistance with stress management.

## STRESS MANAGEMENT TECHNIQUES

Countless stress management techniques have been used for stress management. These techniques usually involve ***cognitive-behavioural approaches, relaxation, exercise, diet and nutrition,* and/or *medication.***

**1. Cognitive-Behavioural Approaches:** Cognitive-behavioural approaches to stress management attempt to change stress-related thoughts, feelings, and actions. Cognitive-behavioural techniques traditionally have been used within the context of three types of therapies: ***cognitive restructuring, coping skills therapies,* and *problem-solving therapies*** More recently, however, the same principles have been incorporated into self-help methods.

**a. Cognitive Restructuring:** The goal of cognitive restructuring is to establish patterns of thinking that are more adaptive and less stress provoking. Examples of cognitive restructuring are *rational-emotive therapy*', *rational behaviour therapy*, *cognitive therapy*, *self-instructional training*, and *structural psychotherapy*

A fundamental concept in rational-emotive therapy is the *ABC model.* According to this model, *consequences* (*C*; i.e., stress responses) occurs as a result of *beliefs* (*B*; i.e., appraisals) about *antecedents* (*A*; i.e., stressors). The main purpose of rational-emotive therapy is to identify irrational beliefs (i.e., stress-provoking appraisals) and reveal why they do not make sense. A unique feature of rational-emotive therapy is the philosophical emphasis of its major goals:

- Social interest
- Self-direction
- Tolerance of self and others
- Flexibility
- Acceptance of uncertainty
- Commitment to vital interests
- Self-acceptance
- Scientific thinking
- Realistic expectations in life
- Self-Interest

Rational behaviour therapy is essentially the same as rational-emotive therapy, but it lacks the obvious philosophical emphasis of rational-emotive therapy and focuses on *neuropsychophysiology* (psychological relevance of brain functioning) and learning theory.

**b. Coping Skills Therapies:** The goal of coping skills therapies is to develop a set of skills designed to help people cope with a variety of stressful situations. Examples of coping skills therapies are ***systematic, rational restructuring, anxiety-management training,* and *stress inoculation training***

**c. Problem-Solving Therapies:** The goal of problem-solving therapies is to develop general strategies for solving a wide range of problems. Problem-solving therapies are essentially a combination of cognitive restructuring and coping skills therapies.

**2. Relaxation:** The purpose of relaxation techniques is to reduce stress responses. Sometimes, it is easy to relax just by getting a massage, listening to calming music, or admiring peaceful works of art. Similarly, simple environmental or ergonomic changes in people's lives can be relaxing by allowing their interactions with specific objects and their surroundings in general to be less strenuous. Other times, however, people have trouble relaxing and need to learn relaxation techniques. Relaxation techniques include *progressive muscle relaxation*, *autogenic relaxation*, *meditation*, the *relaxation response*, *diaphragmatic breathing*.

**3. Exercise:** *Aerobic exercise*, *weight lifting*, *yoga*, and *tai chi* are examples of forms of exercise that can help with stress. Aerobic exercise uses the large muscle groups in continuous, repetitive motions and involves increased oxygen intake and increased breathing and heart rates. Aerobic exercises include the following types of exercise:

- Running
- Swimming
- Brisk walking
- Bicycling
- Jumping rope

An exercise programme aimed at improving physical fitness should include aerobic exercise 3 to 4 times a week for 20 to 30 minutes preceded and followed by a 5- to 10-minute warm-up and cool-down period, respectively .Yoga involves aspects of meditation and special physical and breathing techniques used to control bodily processes like heart rate and blood pressure. It is one of the six orthodox systems of Indian philosophy. Yoga is not a religion, though; it is a way of life, combining the body, mind and spirit.

**4. Diet and Nutrition:** Switching to a diet that is healthier can relieve stress for people who do not already have a healthy diet, especially for people who are overweight. No dietary secrets or miracle diets can lead to long-term stress reduction (or weight loss). People just need to eat right. The following recommendations may be helpful for people who want to improve their diet:

- Eat more fresh fruits and vegetables, enough so that fresh fruits and vegetables make up 50% to 75% of your diet.
- Avoid processed foods and all foods that are stressful for the body, such as artificial sweeteners, carbonated soft drinks, chocolate, eggs, fried foods, junk foods, meat, and chips and similar snack foods.
- Try getting rid of dairy products from your diet for 3 weeks. Then, slowly add them back into your diet and see if stress responses coincide with them.
- Avoid caffeine.
- Avoid alcohol, nicotine, and mood-altering drugs.

**5. Medication:** Over-the-counter pain relievers are used frequently by many people to relieve the pain of some problems associated with stress. Regarding prescription drugs for stress, *amitriptyline*, an antidepressant drug, has been used to treat tension headaches. Additionally, a wide variety of prescription drugs are used to treat mental disorders and physical illnesses associated with stress. Anxiety and depressive disorders, for instance, are often treated with *anti-anxiety agents* and *antidepressants*, respectively. Examples of anti-anxiety agents are as follows:

- Hydroxyzine
- Propranolol
- Other beta-blockers
- In conclusion, the study confirms that stress at work risks have been increasing year on year, but that high pace work seems to be levelling off.

**ASSESSING YOUR WORK-LIFE BALANCE-** Notice how people react to your positivity.

Find out how well you manage your work — life balance by responding to the following statements. Mark the options that are closest to your experience. Be as honest as you can: if your answer is "never", mark Option 1; if it is "always", mark Option 4, and so on. Add your scores together, and refer to the Analysis to see how you scored. Use your answers to identify areas that need improvement.

## Options

1. Never
2. Occasionally
3. Frequently
4. Always

| *Technique* | *Description* | *Assessment* |
|---|---|---|
| Muscle relaxation | Uses slow deep breathing, systematic muscle tension reduction, and an altered state of consciousness to reduce stress. | Inexpensive and easy to use, may require trained professionals to implement. |
| Biofeedback | A machine is used to train people to detect muscular tension; muscle relaxation is then used to alleviate this symptom of stress. | Expensive due to costs of equipment, however, equipment can be used to evaluate effectiveness of other stress reduction programmes. |
| Meditation | The relaxation response is activated by redirecting one's thoughts away from oneself, a four-step procedure is used. | Least expensive, simple to implement, and can be practiced almost anywhere. |
| Cognitive restructuring | Irrational maladaptive thoughts are identified and replaced with those that are rational or logical. | Expensive because it requires a trained psychologist or counsellor. |
| Holistic wellness | A broad, interdisciplinary approach that goes beyond stress reduction by advocating that people strive for personal wellness | Involves inexpensive but often behaviorally difficult lifestyle changes. |

**ANALYSIS:** Now you have completed the self-assessment, add up your total score and check your work—life balance by referring to the corresponding evaluation below. Identify your weakest areas, and refer to the relevant sections in this article to develop and hone those skills.

32-62: You are working too hard and need to examine your priorities. Implement the strategies in this article to try something new and improve your work-life balance.

65-95: To make changes for the belter you need to know how, and you must want to. You are doing well, but allow yourself the chance to enjoy even more balance.

96-128: You are focused, well-motivated, and have a clear direction. Remember: work—life balance is an ongoing process, so keep refining your skills.

## Summary

The words 'positive' and 'stress' may not often go together, But, there are innumerable instances of athletes rising to the challenge of stress and achieving the unachievable, scientists stressing themselves out over a point to bring into light the most unthinkable secrets of the phenomenal world, and likewise a painter, a composer or a writer producing the best paintings, the most lilting of tunes or the most appealing piece of writing by pushing themselves to the limit. Psychologists second the opinion that some 'stress' situations can actually boost our inner potential and can be creatively helpful. Sudha Chandran, an Indian danseuse, lost both of her legs in an accident. But, the physical and social inadequacies gave her more impetus to carry on with her dance performances with the help of prosthetic legs, rather than deter her spirits.

Experts tell us that stress, in moderate doses, are necessary in our life. Stress responses are one of our body's best defense systems against outer and inner dangers. In a risky situation (in case of accidents or a sudden attack on life et al.), body releases stress hormones that instantly make us more alert and our senses become more focused. The body is also prepared to act with increased strength and speed in a pressure situation. It is supposed to keep us sharp and ready for action.

Research suggests that stress can actually increase our performance. Instead of wilting under stress, one can use it as an impetus to achieve success. Stress can stimulate one's faculties to delve deep into and discover one's true potential. Under stress the brain is emotionally and biochemically stimulated to sharpen its performance.

Finally, excessive teacher stress, left undiagnosed and untreated, can have long-term negative consequences not only for individual teachers, but ultimately for the entire institution. A caring work environment, however, is highly effective in reducing teacher stress and making it easier to treat. This paper has presented ways in which administrations can work to create caring work environments, and also ways for teachers to care for themselves and each other while waiting for institutions to undergo the slow process of change. When put into practice, these ideas can not only make teachers' lives more bearable, but at the same time, help them to work more efficiently, and thereby improve the quality of education as a whole.

## The Future of Culture Change Approaches

As the field of health promotion matures, it is likely that companies will begin to adopt approaches that focus simultaneously on individual change processes and culture change processes. Benchmark studies are presenting compelling evidence concerning the need to create supportive cultural environments (O'Donnell, Bishop and Kaplan 1997). Working with cultural values, norms, peer support, organisational support and work climate will greatly enhance the likelihood of sustained positive results.

The future and spirit of the culture-based approach is summarised in the words of the late Robert F. Allen: "We must transform our cultures so that our need for one another is not an obstacle to overcome, but rather a virtue to be celebrated."

## Conclusion

Technological advances have inadvertently extended our working hours as we can now communicate across time zones in a matter of seconds at all hours of the day or night. However, this has turned us into a nation of workaholics who regularly suffer from stress.

- UK employees are the most overworked in Europe.
- UK workers average 44 hours a week, compared to 39 in Holland, Belgium and Denmark and 40 in France and Germany
- The Health & Safety Executive claims 6.5 million sick days are being taken every year as a result of stress

Businesses in the entertainment and leisure sectors have extended their opening hours to cater for those living in this 24-hour society. We now have restaurants and supermarkets open 24-hours, bars and nightclubs open till the early morning, and transport services working day and night. But, to keep these support services going requires the help of others, many of whom do shift work and irregular hours, which can create stress through irregular sleeping patterns and lack of proper sleep like in a BPO.

Stress is not just confined to the workplace however. We also experience stress in our private lives be it planning a holiday, moving house, getting married, etc.

Stress is not just a state of mind, but has physical manifestations - irritability, loss of appetite, sleeping disorders and headaches are all signs that stress is getting to us. People choose to deal with stress in different ways...some talk it over with friends and family, some go to the gym to thrash it out, others have a couple of drinks in the pub to relax, but an increasing number of people are now looking for a natural way to manage everyday stress. Finally SUCCESS = INDIVIDUAL INITIATIVE + CULTURAL SUPPORT. Companies have a long history of offering a single solution to complex behavioural problems. Companies turn to the usual solutions: conduct a survey; create a new department; write a new policy. Unless organisations modify their approach, it is easy to see how one failure could be followed by an endless series of failures that might lead a company to abandon health promotion entirely.

"Lifestyle change can be facilitated through a combination of efforts to enhance awareness, change behaviour and create environments that support good health practices. Of the three, supportive environments will probably have the greatest impact in producing lasting change." (O'Donnell 1989)

A more systematic culture-based approach will enhance individual lifestyle improvement efforts. State-of-the-art individual change programmes now embrace a process approach to change. For example, James Prochaska and his colleagues have identified six stages of individual change that are necessary to lasting self-improvement (Prochaska, Norcross and DiClemente 1994). Unfortunately, it is not a cultural norm to approach personal or organisational change as a process. It is normal to see change as a question of personal revelation or a function of picking the right goals. To improve success rates, health promotion practitioners will need to change this "quick fix" culture to one that embraces systematic ongoing change.

## References

**Allen, J.R.** (1998) "Lifestyle Change attempt and success rate findings from Lifegain Health Culture Audit surveys conducted at over 50 companies," Research Report from the Human Resources Institute, Burlington, Vermont.

**Allen, J.R.** (1998) "Wellness mentoring can help rebuild the corporate culture," *Worksite Health*, Summer, pp. 27-30.

## Remedial Measures- Undoing Stress

***Exercise:*** Physically inactive individuals have a higher incidence of heart attacks and death than do active individuals. Exercise, as most of the studies indicate, reduces depression, anxiety and phobias. When you do the exercise regularly, the day-long tension on the job is given a decent burial. You focus more on your body than on your mind. It may be useful to recount the benefits of exercise here (See Table).

Not surprisingly, many organisations nowadays encourage their executives to be physically fit and active. Companies like Infosys Technologies, Escorts, NIIT, Tata Group companies have created in-house physical fitness facilities for the benefit of the employees.

**Meditation and relaxation:** Mind gets the needed relaxation when we engage in a creative hobby like painting, reading, gardening, etc. The wonderful effects of prayer as a relaxation measure have been well-documented in our ancient scriptures. Meditation also helps in putting our nagging thoughts to rest. Meditation is a way of focussing on something in a relaxed state in a serene and quiet environment. You can focus on muscular relaxation, an image, an object, a symbol, a point or anything you like. The advocates of Transcendental Meditation™ have scientifically proved the beneficial impact of the technique on human brain in recent times. The practice of TM involves the use of a meaningless sound called a 'mantra'. A trained instructor individually assigns the mantra to the meditator, and proper use of the mantra is said to automatically reduce the level of excitation and disorderly activity of the nervous system and to quiet the mind while maintaining its alertness. One sits comfortably with closed eyes and repeats the mantra for about 20 minutes twice a day.

**Benefits of Regular Exercise**

| *Benefits to overall health* | *Specific benefits to the heart* |
|---|---|
| • Increased strength and endurance | 1. Resting heart rate is lowered, meaning that the heart does not have to work as hard as to circulate blood to the body. |
| • More efficient use of energy even in mental tasks | 2. Cardiac output is increased, meaning that under stress, the heart is better able to distribute blood. |
| • Proper circulation is maintained | 3. Number of red blood cells is increased, meaning that more oxygen can be carried per pint of blood. |
| • Improved grace, poise and appearance | 4. Elasticity of arteries is increased. |
| • Improved posture and muscle tone | 5. Blood cholesterol level and triglyceride levels are lowered. |

| | |
|---|---|
| • Reduction of chronic tiredness and tension | 6. Adrenal secretions in response to emotional stress are lowered. |
| • Improved weight control | 7. Lactic acid causing fatigue is more efficiently eliminated. |
| • Reduced ulcers, pains, and stiffness | 8. Heart muscle is strengthened and additional blood vessels within it are formed. |
| • Reduction in degenerative risk factors. | |

*Biofeedback* is another popular relaxation technique. This technique uses sophisticated equipment to observe some of the internal body processes and to report this in observable ways. The equipment is used to measure skin temperature, muscular tension, heartbeat and blood pressure. This information is given to the person in the form of sounds, lights or wavy lines on a graph. When you look at your brain waves or blood pressure, you can begin to control them by observing the internal and external conditions that caused them to change. Once you are aware that your internal body responses are in a state of stress, you can begin to make adjustments by altering the environment or your own frame of mind to reduce your anxiety, tension, stress levels, etc.

An article published in the Hindustan Times, dated 31.1.1998 catalogues other individual coping strategies thus:

1. **Keep a Pet:** There is nothing funny about keeping a pet. Research has indicated that keeping a pet can be a very effective stress killer. Families that have a dog or a cat or for that matter any kind of pet suffer from fewer stress related afflictions than families without pets. And you do not require a pedigreed pet to fight stress, even a mongrel is capable of giving you the love and companionship you need to destress yourself. People living in small houses can even settle for a parrot or a goldfish.

2. **Say Your Prayers:** Being religious helps in controlling stress. Prayers and meditation done in private often provide cathartic release. Research has proved that faith and religion do wonders for individuals under stress. It could be the comfort, hope and spirituality that comes with religious feelings that alleviate tension. 'Do not believe it?' Try singing hymns or bhajans in a group. Not only will you forget your worries, you will come out feeling 'cleansed', refreshed and rejuvenated.

3. **Sing Aloud:** It doesn't matter if you do not sound too good or the neighbours object. Singing gives that release of emotions (and power to the lungs) which helps you live with fewer frowns. Shy? Well, one can always start in the bathroom and then graduate to the living room. Singing is an acknowledgement of the wonders of creation, the joy of living and a vocalisation of inner feelings.

4. **Laughter, The Elixir:** Break into laughter and see the tensions dissolve around you. A good laugh relaxes the mind, exercises facial muscles, reduces blood pressure and improves circulation. Laughing heartily is one of the best ways of getting rid of the frustration and tensions of modern existence. Develop a sense of humour: it will work wonders for you as well as your family.

5. **Sleep Right:** A sleeping beauty is less likely to be prone to stress than a workaholic. Napping 'and dozing can refresh and relax. Catching those 40 winks is a sure way to peace and tranquility. People with chronic sleep problems tend to get tired and stressed more often than those who manage to grab adequate sleep.

6. **Be Good at Loving:** A good lover definitely means leading a good and healthy sex life. Fulfilling and satisfying sex is the key to many problems and is one of the most effective stress busters ever invented. Aerobics, workouts and other forms of exercise can not bring the same amount of benefit and happiness as a good sex life. It can drive away the tensions, relax and soothe as well as exercise the heart too.

7. **Spend Time with Children:** Children have a therapeutic effect on people who spend time playing with them. Their innocence, joie de vivre and capacity for happiness can be infectious. An hour spent with children can bring loads of relaxation and happiness. Parents should spend more time with their children. You will see stress thinning out once you start interacting with kids. And it doesn't cost too much either.

8. **Take a Walk:** Walk in the mornings, walk in the evenings, walk just about anytime. Walk with friends or walk alone but do try long walks for cutting down on stress. Walking is one exercise which doesn't have a cut-off age. It has no side-effects, doesn't need any special equipment and can be done anytime. It is also a refreshing exercise which works on almost all major muscle groups.

9. **Make Friends:** Friends are for all times, especially when you are down in the dumps and need a shoulder to cry on. They are great sounding boards for your worries and tensions. But one must take care to have a few reliable and good friends instead of several fair weather ones. So go all out and make friends who can help you just as you can help them.

10. **Enjoy the Idiot Box:** Watching one's favourite sitcom on TV can be a great relaxant. No matter what people say about the idiot box, it does have some good effects. And one of them is helping you unwind. Put your feet up on a stool, your favourite drink in hand and let the magic of the small screen take over and cast a spell over you. It will make you forget all the worries and tensions of a long day.

11. **Cultivate Interests:** An interesting pastime is one of the greatest anxiety busters. It could be gardening, playing an instrument, reading, writing, cooking, just about anything that interests you. Plants have a very relaxing effect on most people. Music too. Some people swear by their books and yet others dabble with paints and brushes. Take up any hobby, let it be one that pleases you most. It need not be a compulsion but an outlet for your creative instincts and energies.

12. **Dare to Dream:** Everyone has secret dreams and ambitions. They may be simple or complex but they are closest to our hearts. Most of us don't want to share our dreams with people lest they laugh at us. But the truth is that it is these dreams that keep us going. They add colour to our lives, give us hope and the drive to carry on. And if you find someone to share your dreams with, nothing like it.

## Organisational Coping Strategies

Stress management includes stress prevention also. This is best achieved through certain organisational coping strategies. These include:

1. **Role clarity:** Define employee roles clearly. Employees must have a clear understanding of the job. They must know what the company expects and be confident that they can meet these expectations. Stress, most often, occurs when employees are not very sure about their work roles or fear they cannot do their jobs. When excessive stress is present in a role, management can initiate steps such as:
   - Redefining the person's role
   - Reduce overload by redistributing the work
   - Set up procedures to prevent hindrances to work
   - Arrange for a meeting of all those involved in a messy situation and try to find a way out
   - Make the job intrinsically meaningful, challenging and rewarding.
2. **Supportive climate:** Factors such as freedom to think and act independently, a certain amount of informality with key employees, clear communications, participative decision making, friendly conversations - all help in reducing stress levels in an organisation. If practiced regularly, they also reveal a supportive organisational climate where everybody is willing to contribute his best and share the rewards thereafter. There is very little room for disruptive political games, and conflicts to occur, vitiating the whole atmosphere. A friendly, supportive climate builds trust and confidence among employees and they will be quite happy to extend a helping hand to management, whenever required.
3. **Clear career paths:** To reduce uncertainty, each employee must be sure of where he is heading for, say after 5 years within the same organisation. A clear career path and the job rewards and benefits that follow committed service would go a long way in preventing or reducing stress levels greatly.
4. **Company-wide programmes:** A variety of programmes can be used to manage work stress. These include:

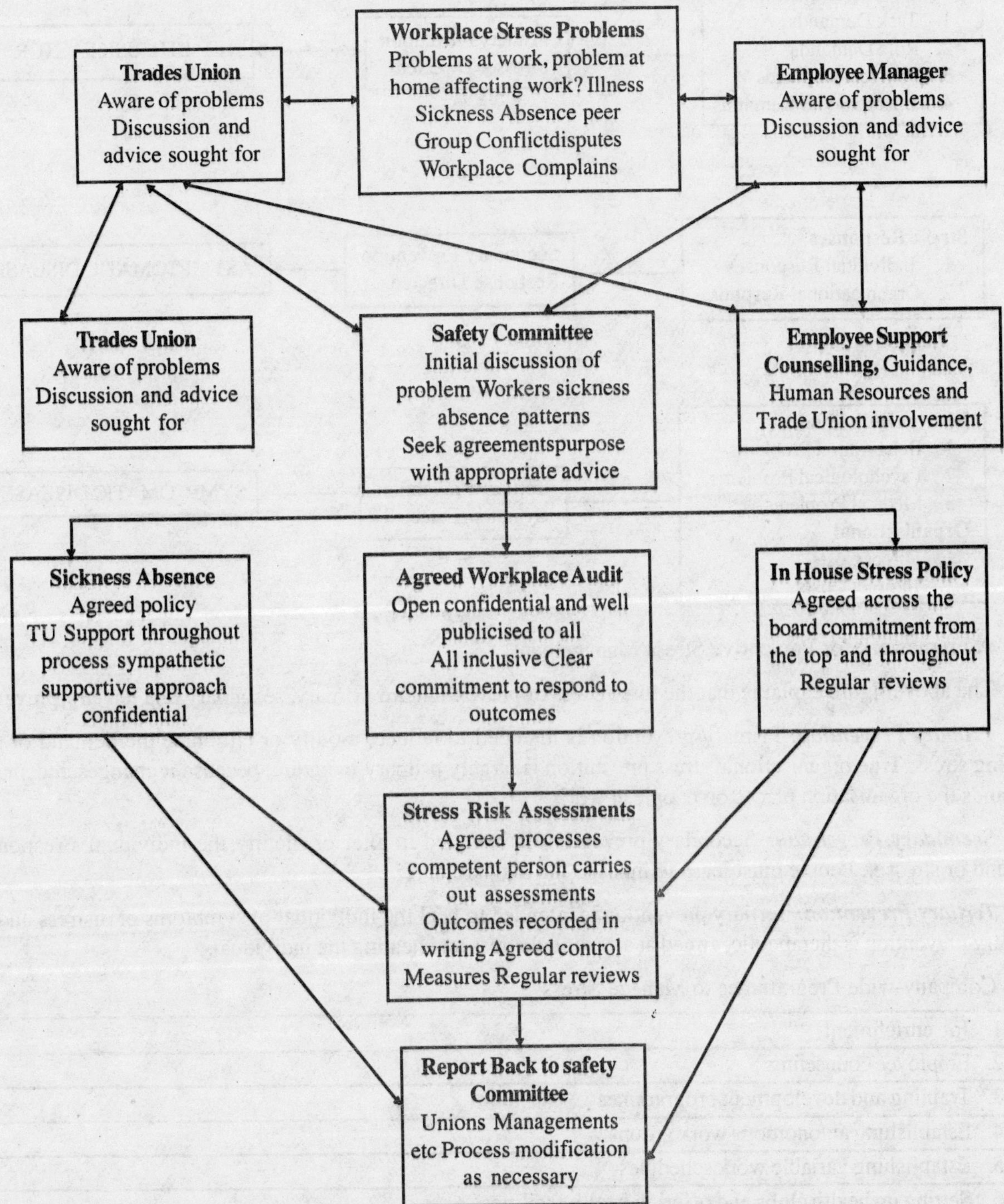


## Framework For Preventive Stress Management

Stress is an inevitable feature of work and personal life. Individual and organizational distresses are not inevitable. A framework for understanding preventive stress management is presented in the figure below.

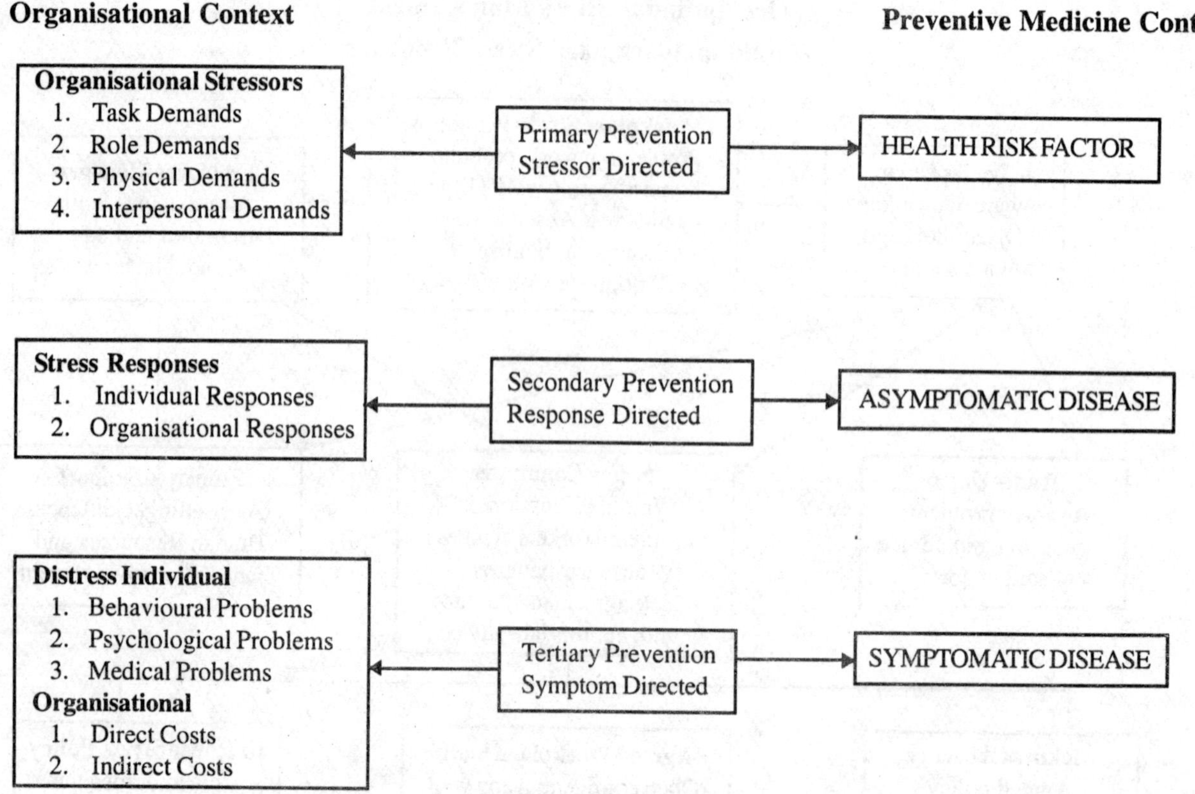


A Framework for Preventive Stress Management

The above figure explains that the three stage of prevention are primary, secondary and terriary prevention.

***Primary Prevention:*** Primary prevention is intended to reduce, modify or eliminate the demand or stressor causing stress. True organisational stress prevention is largely primary in nature, because it changes and shapes the demands the organisation places on people at work.

***Secondary Prevention:*** Secondary prevention is intended to alter or modify the individual's response to a demand or stressor. People must learn to manage the inevitable.

***Tertiary Prevention:*** Tertiary prevention is intended to heal the individual of symptoms of distress and strain. Tertiary prevention is therapeutic, aimed at arresting distress and healing the individual.

Company-wide Programmes to Manage Stress

| Company-wide Programmes to Manage Stress |
|---|
| 1. Job enrichment |
| 2. Employee counseling |
| 3. Training and development programmes |
| 4. Establishing autonomous work groups |
| 5. Establishing variable work schedules |
| 6. Setting up health clubs and offering health facilities |
| 7. Service benefits including marriage gifts, birthday bonus, transport subsidy, long service bonus (NIIT for example, offers this to those employees who stay with the company for more than 5 years. Infosys Technologies offers the stock option plan to all employees who remain committed and loyal etc.) family planning gifts, health club memberships, credit cards, housing/car loans etc. |

Management can help reduce stress in the work environment by holding team meetings, using proper management techniques, employing effective communication system, and reducing uncertainty among employees.

## MANAGERIAL IMPLICATION OF STRESS

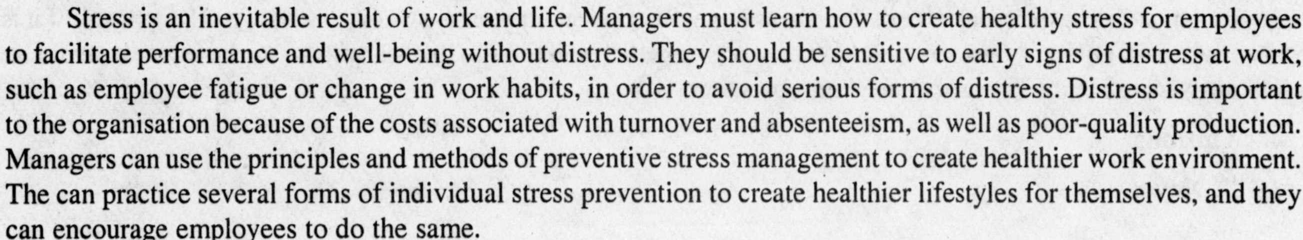

Stress is an inevitable result of work and life. Managers must learn how to create healthy stress for employees to facilitate performance and well-being without distress. They should be sensitive to early signs of distress at work, such as employee fatigue or change in work habits, in order to avoid serious forms of distress. Distress is important to the organisation because of the costs associated with turnover and absenteeism, as well as poor-quality production. Managers can use the principles and methods of preventive stress management to create healthier work environment. The can practice several forms of individual stress prevention to create healthier lifestyles for themselves, and they can encourage employees to do the same.

### Stress in IT Industry

Sensing the high stress levels among employees that lead to lower productivity and higher attrition rates, Information Technology and Business Process Outsourcing (BPO) firms are resorting to unconventional methods, including teaching dancing and music, to tackle and beat the stress.

**Top 10 Software Companies in India**

| Rank | Company |
|---|---|
| 1. | Tata Consultancy Services Ltd. |
| 2. | Infosys Technologies Ltd. |
| 3. | Wipro Technologies Ltd. |
| 4. | Satyam Computer Services Ltd. |
| 5. | HCL Technologies Ltd. |
| 6. | Patni Computer Systems Ltd. |
| 7. | I-flex Solutions Ltd. |
| 8. | Tech Mahindra Ltd. (formerly Mahindra-British Telecom Ltd.) |
| 9. | Perot Systems TSI (I) Ltd. |
| 10. | L&T Infotech Ltd. |

Some of the leading Indian IT firms have lined up their resources so as to tackle this acute problem persisting in their organisation. India's largest IT services firm, **Tata Consultancy Services** for instance, creates a balance between work and fun which is facilitated through different clubs like Theatre Club, Bibliophile Club, Adventure & Trekking Club, Fitness Club, Sanctuary Club, Music Club and Community Services Club, among others.

At **Infosys** a unique Health, Safety and Environmental Management System (HSEMS), called the 'Ozone Initiative' is equipped to make the employees happy and willing to work. **Infosys** ,on its part, has a custom-designed instrument, which assists in increasing self-awareness. Based on the response, further guidance is provided to identify ways of effectively coping with the stress. The company also conducts a series of workshops by experts. Even smaller companies like **Nucleus** and **Tulip** practise their innovative ways to keep the stress levels among employees under check. What they believe is that there is a high amount of stress among employees these days, and this is largely due to lack of interpersonal interaction among the members of the company. To counter such problems, they have a system of mentors and an 'open door' policy, where all employees are free to talk to their superiors.

Tulip has also gone the extra mile by conducting salsa and jazz classes, besides the stress management workshops.The BPO sector, with its irregular hours and strenuous working conditions, are badly hit with the stress syndrome contributing to approximately **25 to 30** per cent attrition rate among the BPOs. The BPOs have also adopted innovative methods of reducing the high attrition rates, besides the normal facilities of taxi services, and subsidised cafeterias. Gurgaon-based BPO **Convergys**; to reduce the stress of its young employees, helps them continue their education even while working. Convergys also has a Special Education Assistance Programme that allows one to get up to Rs. 24,000 of the course fee reimbursed.

## Assessing your work-life balance

Find out how well you manage your work—life balance by responding to the following statements. Mark the options that are closest to your experience. Be as honest as you can: if your answer is "never", mark Option 1; if it is "always", mark Option 4, and so on. Add your scores together, and refer to the Analysis to see how you scored. Use your answers to identify areas that need improvement.

### Options

1. Never
2. Occasionally
3. Frequently
4. Always

Every matter animate or inanimate, in existence in space or planet is under stress at one time or other. But stress is the price which a living being has to pay for existence. Stress is significant for human beings because he can perceive it, feel it and express it. Man is prone to stress, since times immemorial, because of his struggle to live within the environment to which he is not fully evolved or suited, unlike the animals, who are in a very advanced stage of compatability living on Earth, because of higher adaptability to the changes on the Earth. Stress is peculiar to human beings of all ages from childhood to old age. Stress is stimulus to growth, progress; development and creativity to some extent, which can reach a breakpoint beyond certain limits of capability and capacity.

Human beings are unique because of their superior intellect, thoughts, configuration to translate ideas and thoughts, for transformation of matter to creativeness, and formation of newer objects. This transformation has been added from generation to generation, which has resulted in materialism and ethical and value-based civilisation. Man has been engaged relentlessly in pursuit of creativity through hard work, without the impact of stress or slow down. The hard work itself is the stimulus to work more and destress. A sincere hard work with dedication is impetus to long life, which is useful to society as a whole. One works most of the times for others as well. But at times, a situation comes when a person gives way, and feels unable to cope up with his responsibilities , either due to limitations of capability or due to anxiety, fear and uncertainty. Thus stress basically means inability to achieve what is expected out of one, due to physical or mental inadequacy. Thus stress is peculiar to a individual with compromised physical, mental and spiritual well-being. One individual can cope up with huge multiple responsibilities throughout his life, whereas the second individual finds it difficult to do even smaller commitments. Therefore, stress is an individuals inability to stand to a commitment successfully, and the factors responsible to this may be environmental or genetic. Stress is of diverse nature; it may be due to physical stress where an individual is incapacitated due to illness or bodily weakness, or it may be due to mental outlook, anxiety, worries, domestic and social conflicts, or due to personality traits like jealousy, competition, hostile surroundings, lack of physical and social support, lack of amenities and services, or due to swallowing or accepting much more than is possible to digest. A student is under stress due to exams or studies, youth is under stress due to personal problems, habits, or due to uncertain future. An elderly is under stress due to responsibilities towards families. These situations affect the duties of an individual. A stressed individual becomes a liability to himself and the society. Therefore, persons who are unreasonably or genuinely under stress require guidelines to help them out to cope up with stress.

Stress does not mean that one should not undertake the work or responsibilities entrusted to him. One should not avoid the responsibilities. One must strike a balance between body, mind and thoughts. For any person the stress lies in the mind. But one thing is certain; that one should realise one's capacity and capability to undertake the task, otherwise result will be stress, confusion, irritation and demoralisation. To perform successfully, one must have a suitable and friendly environment. One can't work in hostile surroundings. It is better to come out of such a situation and set one self free from tension and stress, rather than to be with unfriendly people and choose better and good human beings to work with.

One gets into stress and tension because of ones own deeds and works. So control your tongue, lest harm may come to you. Always speak firmly, but in gentle and polite tone. One must prioritise his work in a perfect order. Select the work and finish it meticulously, preferably case by case. Jumping to multiple tasks at the same time will lead not only to confusion, but also to imperfection, delays and ultimately loss of trust, dissatisfaction and stress. To execute tasks successfully one should choose a trusted and competent team. One should be humane to his colleagues and friends. One must help others genuinely. One should relax de-stress himself by walking, exercises, praying, meditation, humour and by accommodative nature. One should not get drowned in one's own pent up feelings and emotions. Let your emotions and feelings be out and thus, keep your heart and mind light. Be frank, forthright and clear in your actions and speech. Keep your time well, work within a time-frame, regulate your life as per the time calls for it. Fix a time table for your work and routine, pleasure and leisure. Trust your subordinates and delegate responsibility. Do not be overbearing. Do not be over corrective. Learn from mistakes and never loose temper. Always receive the problems and solve them. Do not pass on responsibilities to others just to avoid them. One should de-stress by developing a hobby. One may pick up and choose a game, take interest in nature. Love for it can do wonders. Never get entangled with anything which may steal your energy, thoughts and efforts and divert your creativity towards turmoil and nothinglessness.

One must eat healthy food. One should de-stress by walking, sleeping and talking moderately. One must live a life full of ethics, which includes truthfulness, non-violence in action, thoughts and speech. One should be above jealousy. One must respect others, especially the elders and lead life by example. Stress, to a large extent, is the result of mental incompetence and incomplete personality development. Let us work silently for the sake of justification for existence of life given to us by Nature and God, and out of the bossom of Mother Earth. Let this precious life, before it dissolves back into trth, be returned to it only after accomplishments for others. May it be family or society, with the aim of repaying the debt of bounty of life given to us by God. Let us lead a useful happy life by serving Mother Earth and the nature.

Let each and every living being on this Earth live like family. This is the key to peace in this world and beyond. An individual with higher goals passes through the turbulence of life with happiness and contentment, and knows not what the stress is.

Finally- Any Living Being Who is Stable In Body And Mind Can withstand Any Storm till It Lives.

Is workplace stress always negative— Under normal circumstances, people should be able to find new balances and responses in their reactions to new situations. Stress is not necessarily a negative phenomenon and it would therefore be a mistake to concentrate only on its pathological effects. A moderate level of stress can be an important motivational factor and can be instrumental in achieving a dynamic adaptation to new situations. If health is considered as a dynamic equilibrium, stress is part of it. There is no health without interaction with other people and with the environment. Only excesses of stress are pathological. Some stress is therefore normal and necessary, at work and outside it. But if stress is intense, continuous or repeated, if a person is unable to cope, or if support is lacking, stress then becomes a negative phenomenon which can lead to physical illness and psychological disorders. In a work context, it often results in inadequate adaptation to situations and people and failure to perform at an optimal level.

Learn to develop a sense of humor about yourself and your problems.

**"Stress is not all bad".** Bear in mind that an appropriate stress response is a healthy and necessary part of life. One of the things it does is to release norepinephrine, one of the principal excitatory neurotransmitters. Norepinephrine is needed to create new memories. It improves mood. Problems feel more like challenges, which encourages creative thinking that stimulates your brain to grows new connections within it. Stress management is the key, not stress elimination. The challenge in this day and age is to not let the sympathetic nervous system stay chronically aroused. This may require knowledge of techniques that work to activate your relaxation response.

**"It's not what happens to you that matters, but how you take it".**

-Hans Selye

**Physical Fitness**

Fig. 57

Competition is the spice of SPORTS; but if you make spice the whole meal you'll be sick.

Tactics, fitness, stroke ability, adaptability, experience and SPORTSmanship are all necessary for winning.

Management can help reduce stress in the work environment by holding team meetings, using proper management techniques, employing effective communication system, and reducing uncertainty among employees.

Managment competencies for preventing and reducing stress at work : Thereby Improved performance

| Competency | Sub-competency | Do (✓) Don't(×) | Examples of Manager behaviour |
|---|---|---|---|
| Respectful and responsible: managing emotions and having integrity | Integrity | Π | • is a good role model<br>• treats team members with respect<br>• is honest |
| | | × | • says one thing, then does something different<br>• speaks about team members behind their backs |
| | Managing emotions | ✓ | • acts calmly in pressured situations<br>• takes a consistent approach to managing |
| | | × | • is unpredictable in mood<br>• passes on stress to employees<br>• panics about deadlines<br>• takes suggestions for improvement as a personal criticism |
| | Considerate approach | ✓ | • makes short-term demands rather than allowing planning<br>• creates unrealistic deadlines<br>• gives more negative than positive feedback<br>• relies on others to deal with problems<br>• imposes 'my way is the only way'<br>• shows a lack of consideration for work–life balance |
| Managing and communicating existing and future work | Proactive work management | ✓ | • clearly communicates employee job objectives<br>• develops action plans<br>• monitors teams workload on an ongoing basis<br>• encourages team to review how they organise work<br>• stops additional work being taken on when necessary<br>• works proactively<br>• sees projects/tasks through to delivery<br>• reviews processes to see if work can be improved<br>• prioritises future workloads |
| | Problem-solving | ✓ | • deals rationally with problems<br>• follows up problems on team's behalf<br>• deals with problems as soon as they arise |

| Group | Competency | | Behaviour |
|---|---|---|---|
| | Participative/ empowering | × | • is indecisive at decision-making |
| | | ✓ | • gives employees the right level of responsibility |
| | | | • correctly judges when to consult and when to make a decision |
| | | | • keeps employees informed of what is happening in the organisation |
| | | | • acts as a mentor |
| | | | • delegates work equally |
| | | | • helps team members develop in their role |
| | | | • encourages team participation |
| | | | • provides regular team meetings |
| | | × | • gives too little direction to employees |
| Reasoning/managing difficult situations | Managing conflict | ✓ | • acts as mediator in conflict situations |
| | | | • deals with squabbles before they become arguments |
| | | | • deals objectively with conflicts |
| | | | • deals with conflicts head on |
| | | × | • acts to keep the peace rather than resolve issues |
| | Use of organisation resources | ✓ | • seeks advice from other managers when necessary |
| | | | • uses HR as a resource to help deal with problems |
| | | | • seeks help from occupational health when necessary |
| | Taking responsibility for resolving issues | ✓ | • follows up conflicts after resolution |
| | | | • supports employees through incidents of abuse |
| | | | • makes it clear they will take ultimate responsibility if things go wrong |
| | | × | • doesn't address bullying |
| Managing the individual within the team | Personally accessible | ✓ | • speaks personally rather than uses email |
| | | | • provides regular opportunities to speak one to one |
| | | | • returns calls/emails promptly |
| | | | • is available to talk to when needed |
| | Sociable | ✓ | • brings in treats |
| | | | • socialises with the team |
| | | | • is willing to have a laugh at work |
| | Empathetic engagement | ✓ | • encourages employee input in discussions |
| | | | • listens when employees ask for help |
| | | | • makes an effort to find out what motivates employees at work |
| | | | • tries to see team member's point of view |
| | | | • takes an interest in team's life outside work |
| | | | • regularly asks 'how are you? |
| | | | • treats all team members with equal importance |
| | | × | • assumes rather than checks that employees are okay |

*Source:* CIPD/HSE (UK)

## Competencies of line managers in reducing stress levels among staff

Given the key role of line managers in this area, the CIPD has been involved in a four-year research project exploring the management behaviour needed to prevent and manage stress at work. Funded by the CIPD, the HSE and Investors in People, the research has identified the following four broad groups of competencies that managers need to demonstrate to reduce stress levels among staff.

1. **Respect and responsibility:** This is about treating staff with respect, and also includes acting with integrity, managing emotions and being considerate. It means, for example, that managers must act calmly when the going gets tough and behave with consistency, rather than panicking or exhibiting mood swings. Setting realistic deadlines, giving more positive than negative feedback and showing consideration for employees' work-life balance are other key elements so, too, are honesty and integrity, which become all the more important during an economic downturn, when people tend to be suspicious of their employer's motives.

2. **Managing and communicating existing and future work:** This includes proactive work management- for example, communicating job objectives clearly, monitoring workloads, developing action plans and prioritising tasks. It's equally crucial for managers to deal rationally with problems and act decisively. They also need to keep staff informed of what is happening to the business and encourage their participation when this is appropriate, for example, through team meetings and individual discussions. Effective communication and work management are especially important when the pressure is on to hit targets and many people feel uncertain.

3. **Managing the individual in the team:** This can be as simple as being willing to have a laugh and socialise with staff. It is about speaking to people personally, rather than using email, and being available to talk to them on a one-to-one basis when necessary. Again, these skills become even more important than usual in tough financial conditions, when individual employees are likely to need different types of support.

4. **Reasoning and managing difficult situations:** This involves dealing objectively with conflicts, mediating between the parties, seeking advice from others where necessary and following up conflicts once they've been resolved. Managers must make it clear that they will take ultimate responsibility when things go wrong. Conflict and bullying tend to increase during financial downturns, and therefore managers need to be ready to address incidents early so as not to let them damage well-being or performance.

The research findings so far suggest that the relative importance of each group of competencies will vary in each situation. The research also reveals that one of the main barriers to managers behaving in ways that prevent and reduce stress for their staff is the pressure that they themselves are under. In current economic conditions, many managers are facing extra challenges, not least having to make staff redundant- a task that they may not have the confidence or skills to perform effectively. It is vital, therefore, that they receive support and coaching from their own line managers or HR to help them deal with these difficult issues.

For this reason, the research team from Goldsmiths, University of London and the consultancy Affinity Health at Work is currently exploring how best to help managers develop the positive behaviours outlined above. This isn't about asking managers to undertake additional activities on top of their usual responsibilities, but about the way they behave towards their staff on a day-to-day basis. Giving managers clear feedback on how their current hehaviour is perceived seems to be among the most effective ways of helping them make changes.

Of course, some people will suffer from stress regardless of how their organisation manages the issue, so it is important to help them access appropriate support. CIPD research consistently identifies access to occupational health services and rehabilitation programmes as the most effective ways of managing long-term absence. Employee assistance programmes, which often offer counselling and confidential helplines, can provide further help.

Even though budgets are becoming increasingly tight, employers can't afford to ignore the issue of stress. Apart from other considerations, they have a legal obligation under a health and safety law to conduct a risk assessment for work-related stress and take action to remedy any risks identified. The HSE's management standards on stress provide stepby-step guidance on conducting a stress risk assessment. This can be done in a number of ways, including through staff attitude surveys and focus groups to determine whether employees are under excessive pressure at work.

Assessing the risks and taking action to reduce stress levels-especially by changing line managers' behaviour- can make a real difference to employees' well-being. It could even help organisations take advantage of the opportunities that will no doubt arise when economic recovery eventually comes.

## Reducing Stress

Stress in itself is not harmful, but it can seriously affect those who react badly to it. To improve your effectiveness as a manager, you must be able to recognise your limits and take action to reduce stress when it threatens your performance.

**(a) Recognising the signs:** Everyone reacts to stress differently, but it may manifest itself in physical symptoms, such as skin complaints or digestive troubles. You may feel irritable and run-down. Work can become obsessive, and nervous problems can result in depression, anxiety or other psychological disorders. Look out for warning signs and tackle stress before it becomes debilitating.

**(b) Coping With Stress:** Deal with stress positively by seeking support from superiors, close friends, and colleagues, and prioritising your workload.

**(c) Analysing Personality:** Research has shown that certain types of people are more prone to stress and its by-products, such as heart disease. If you are an ambitious manager who is extremely competitive, fast in thought, speech, and action, committed, impatient, and pressed for time, you are likely to be a Type A personality - at risk from stress. If you are more placid, you are less at risk and classed as Type B, Type A managers may also be tense, egotists who lack self-control and are quick to anger. If you fit the Type A pattern, modify your behaviour to reduce the chances and incidence of stress.

**(d) Handling Anxiety:** Being anxious is an unpleasant experience. It can have a perfectly understandable cause. A merger or re-organisation, for instance, may threaten your job or your powers. Threats produce anxiety. But what action can you take to remove the threat? In the above examples, almost certainly none. However, you should try to calm your anxiety. Avoid listening to rumour and think positively.

After all, the threat may not even materialise, in which case, you have made yourself feel awful for nothing. Whatever the cause of the anxiety, identify that cause, develop a plan for removing the cause, if possible, and/or form a contingency plan to cope. Occupying yourself with this three-part formula will lessen anxiety anyway, and could make it wholly unnecessary.

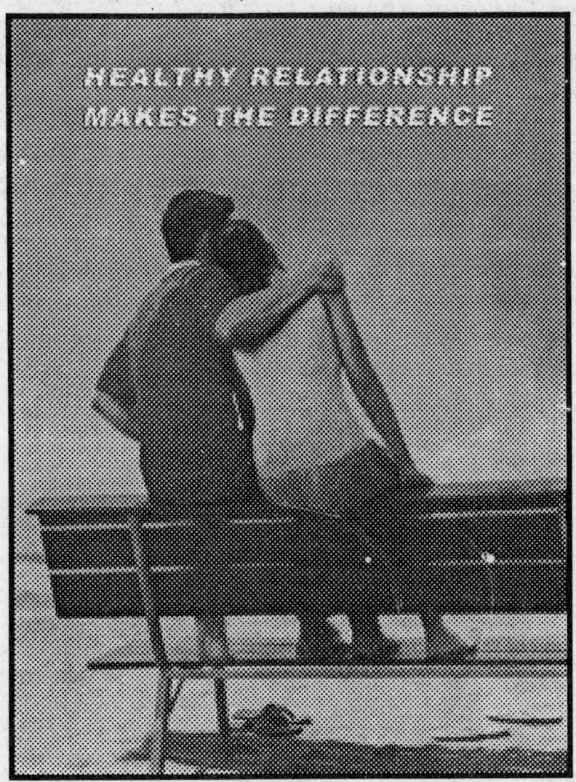


**Fig. 58**

**(e) Tackling Difficulties:** It is easy to procrastinate, but this habit (which is all but universal) can increase your stress in two ways. First, you may feel guilty about leaving the task undone. Second, you are building up stressful time pressure for the future. Procrastination is itself a symptom of stress. For example, a decision may involve taking a risk, or a necessary action (say, firing somebody) may loom ahead. Your reaction to these stresses may be to delay the evil hour. That is bad stress management. You will still have to grasp the nettle, and will pass more stressful hours, days, or months before you do so. Do it now.

**(f) Using Stress Positively:** A crisis can descend out of the blue, or build up over months. It can affect everyone in an organisation, or may be entirely personal, but it is important not to allow yourself to slump into despair. In fact, you can turn the stress of a crisis to your advantage. Because stress raises your levels of adrenaline, you can harness that extra energy to resolve the emergency successfully, if that is feasible. Begin by assessing what can actually be done and whether the crisis can be cured. Then start on a no-holds-barred effort to recover from the disaster. You will benefit from the healthy stress of constructive achievement under pressure.

**(g) Learning to Relax:** The more effectively you rest, the better you use your energies. Few people, however, make positive use of daytime rests, even though that is one of the best means of controlling stress. Make time during the day to get rid of superfluous and stressful emotions, and to substitute relaxed calm. Many techniques are available, from deep breathing to yoga. What they have in common is mental concentration on non-stressful thoughts, and assertion of self-control over your emotions and body. The most useful tecknniques are those that can be applied any time and anywhere, such as the relaxation exercise shown right.

**(h) Relaxing at Home:** Relaxation is a technique that can easily be learned. Take time out to enjoy a regular period of relaxation in your busy daily routine. Find a quiet spot in the house, place a rug or mat on the floor, with a cushion, then lie down and

1. After having a good stretch, sit or lie in a comfortable position, eyes closed.
2. Concentrate your inner attention on a fixed image or point - try the point between and above your eyebrows.
3. Deeply relax your muscles one by one. Start with the feet and work up the legs to the abdomen, chest, shoulders, neck, and face; let your jaw muscles hang loose.
4. Concentrate on your breath passing deeply, easily, and naturally through the "one" (or a mantra if you have one) every time you breathe out.
5. Allow yourself to relax completely.
6. If music helps, have it playing softly. Conjure up images of warm climates, and try to imagine your body becoming warmer and heavier.
7. Continue for 10 to 20 minutes; if you fall asleep or doze, it doesn't matter, you are still relaxing.

**Tips for De-Stressing**

1. Work more effectively, rather than for longer hours
2. Discuss personal problems with a wise listener
3. Defuse anxieties by listing possible future events, good and bad
4. Analyse reasons for procrastination and face them squarely. Then set yourself a deadline for action
5. Get excited about challenges in a positive manner
6. Find relaxation methods that suit you and use them
7. Enjoining a hobby eg. gardening/reading, etc.

Fig. 59

## New Ways to Cope-suggestions

Even though the need for mental health and substance abuse services has increased because of the recession, that doesn't mean all providers are seeing more patients. Financial difficulties are forcing many clients to choose cheaper, less-intensive forms of treatment.

Mental health providers in Minnesota have seen more people asking about free medications and sliding scale fees, says Sue Abderholden, MPH, executive director of the state's chapter of the National Alliance on Mental Illness (NAMI). Abderholden says she expects many people to forgo traditional treatment and seek less-expensive alternatives, such as support groups, fitness classes, yoga, and meditation. Kallal says parents served by the centre have formed informal support networks to help each other out during tough times.

Some people are turning to the Internet for help. A few months ago, the Ruth Rales Jewish Family Service in Boca Raton, FL, launched several web sites where people can go to receive counseling via e-mail. The organization decided to start the service to cater to the increasing number of people using the Internet to look for jobs and employment advice, says Mark Cherny, LCSW, the organisation's supervisor of outreach and community services.

The online counselling has attracted e-mails from people throughout the United States and Canada who are struggling with financial problems. Cherny says his responses to these messages are designed to help people realise that they are not alone in their struggles and to remind them that they have strengths they can tap into to respond to crises. He also refers people to support services in their local areas.

"When you do [counselling] on the Internet, it brings more people to the process," Cherny says. "That doesn't get someone a job, but it allows them to know that they are reacting in a very normal way to a very difficult situation." As clients look for less-expensive services, social work practitioners who offer traditional in-person psychotherapy are trying to find ways to make their services more accessible to clients. Charles Rizzuto, MSW, a faculty member of the Smith College School for Social Work in Northampton, MA, who also has a private practice, says he has had to become more flexible with how he charges and collects fees, even if that means he has less income.

Similar trends are emerging in the substance abuse field. Conway says many of her patients are spacing out their appointments and relying more on 12-step programmes. Wiedemann-West says her organisation's outpatient business has picked up in recent months while demand for its residential services has declined. Insurers are more likely to pay for outpatient treatment, and people are increasingly averse to leaving their workplaces for inpatient treatment, she says.

"I think people are afraid to leave their jobs for an extended period of time," Wiedemann-West says. "They are afraid to disappear and don't want their employers to consider them 'out of sight, out of mind."

Handley believes economic trends mean bad news for inpatient treatment centres that rely on self-paying clientele. Many of those providers may go out of business if economic trends continue, he says.

## Communication Can Ease Anxiety

Many employees are stuck in an anticipatory phase, unsure of when and if the announcement or dreaded "pink slip" will arrive. During this time, anxiety levels are low-level but consistently in the person's life and affect not just their work performance but their other social interactions. Regular communication from management in order to inform employees of the company's current position can allay employee's anxiety and potentially stop self-medication with alcohol, tobacco or other drugs.

## Employee Assistance Programmes

Although businesses are looking to reduce expenses in order to remain profitable during this tough economic period, it is not the time to remove your employee assistance program. In fact, the opposite is true, with the ongoing stresses associated with the economic slowdown, a review of the Employee Assistance Program may be warranted, including increasing the number of sessions provided with counsellors or providing new forms of assistance for employees who have been made redundant as part of scaling back operations.

## Career Counselling

For employees that have to be made redundant, provide them with an opportunity to undertake career counselling with an external provider. Career counselling will provide the employee with the chance to review his/her working life and have support while making the next step. Many people have turned redundancy into an opportunity rather than a death sentence.

## Company Newsletters

The company newsletter can be used to communicate to staff about the organisation's current position, the likelihood of redundancies and what programmes the company offers to assist staff during tough times. An organisation can also use their newsletter to educate staff about dealing with mental health issues, the impact of stress and what services are available in the local area to assist them, whether that is financial counselling, personal counselling, life coaching or low cost physical activity or food suppliers.

The global credit crunch is not going to go away quickly and every business is going to be affected. In turn, this economic slowdown will affect physical and mental health of human beings, particularly through the work environment. Employers should routinely communicate with employees to allay anticipatory stress and provide practical assistance through counselling and skills assessment to assist employees cope.

## Concern for the Future

A prolonged economic slowdown could have disastrous consequences for people struggling with mental health problems and addictions. Many people who cannot afford to access the services they need will eventually enter the system when they are much sicker or even suicidal, says Sita Diehl, MSSW, executive director of NAMI's Tennessee chapter. And it is unlikely that states—many of which are facing multi-billion-dollar deficits—will be able or willing to provide more funding for services, Diehl says.

"So, many people will end up in emergency rooms or jails," she says. "We're really rolling back the clock a couple hundred years before Dorothea Dix."

"I think most people feel that it looks pretty dismal out there," she says. "I think people are still wondering if one person can turn it around so quickly."

No matter what happens, the downturn has at least raised the public's awareness of the importance of social workers' role in helping people struggling with mental illness and addiction, says Dennis Derr, EdD, Director of EAP products for Aetna Behavioral Health.

"The need for social workers is incredibly important right now," he says. "It's a great time for social workers to come to the forefront."

— *Christina Reardon.*

## A Loving Relationship

With consciousness we have created very beautiful concepts, and one of them is the idea of relationships. Whatever we create, whatever we discover is to make life more comfortable, beautiful, peaceful and happy. We invest our mental, spiritual and psychic energies in building relationships.

The first relationship has to be with you. You must have a very clear relationship with yourself, knowing why you feel the way you do , why you think in a particular way and so on. The first step is to aware of your own self.

Second, why do we want a relationship? Is it for happiness, for security? If that is so, the best source of what we call happiness and security is the Divine. So establish, a relationship with the Divine. What is Divinity? Divine is present everywhere, also in those you consider close to you. And your psyche can give you everything you need.

In daily life, how do you find divinity in your spouse or companion, for instance? Be sincere and faithful. The key is to give without expectation. These things are possible if your understanding is healthy, if your consciousness is full of light and brightness.

How are relationships established? Even huger can create relationships: you enter into relationships with food, don't you? Grow with relationships, and at the same time remember that all possibilities are inside, they are not coming from the outside, what you are looking for outside you is inside you.

Your body is like a television set. It displays visuals all the time. So when you display negative things it is your hands to change the channel.

When we do meditation we are feeding the soul, and when you feel the hunger of your soul then constant meditation begins, and it becomes effortless. When your stomach is empty, all you think of is food, all your being is looking for food, but when you are full you don't think about food at all.

The food for the soul is the Divine. Right now we are making an effort to remember the Divine, but when we start feeling the hunger we will not have to make any effort; It will come naturally.

Aurobindo gives this concept of Divine life: he didn't say that the life is an illusion, that we have to run away from life, or go to the Himalayas. He just said that life is beautiful, and the future of life is life Divine, sooner or later, when the psychic hunger starts. And life diving means that here, in this world, with these situations we have to awaken to the hunger of our being, listen and find that hunger. When we do that we will start seeing the Divine everywhere. Then there will be no ego.

Relationships sour primarily due to ego Use your ego. But do not allow your ego to use you. It is a tool, if you know how to use it, it will build you and give you many wonderful things.

If the ego is using you, you will see ego everywhere. Only ego sees ego. Ego is without substance: a lack of knowledge, a lack of light. Hate is too much love. You never hate someone you don't know. We call it hate but hate has also substance of love there. It is too much connection.

Swami Brahmdev lives in Aurovalley Ashram, Raiwalla.

## DE-STRESSING

Here are six top tips for getting active and staying motivated throughout the day – and the year:

**1. Kick-start your exercise regime and beat the afternoon slumps for good:** Regular exercisers enjoy increased energy throughout the day. This is because exercise helps to increase your blood flow and regulate your exercise three or four times a week, you will therefore help increase your energy levels and general well being. It doesn't have to be a hard slog at the gym either. It can be anything from going for a swim to doing a workout DVD – or simply going for a jog or a brisk walk. The best thing about going for a walk. The best thing about going for a walk is that it can be accomplished in a lunch break. Getting active at lunchtime can also help blow off stress which may cause slumps and nervous exhaustion in the afternoon. By exercising and working tense muscles you will relax and feel more stimulated. So make sure you have regular breaks from sitting at your desk or in your car. Regular exercise has also been shown, in some cases, to lead to a subconscious choice of healthy foods and snacks, which in turn will also combat those dreaded energy slumps.

**2. Enjoy a hearty breakfast and a balanced lunch:** The first thing to do is make sure you have a good healthy breakfast such as wholemeal toast and banana or an omelette, porridges or some chopped fruit. Try to avoid cereals if you can, as they tend to be full of sugar.

The ideal lunchtime meal is small and balanced, such as a combination of a protein source (meat, fish etc.) and fibrous vegetables. Examples include chicken and vegetables or a tuna salad. If you do include a starchy carbohydrate source (pasta, rise etc.) then ensure it is a small amount and keep it wholemeal. And try and avoid the temptation of stopping of at the garage to pick up a sandwich that is high in salt or, worse, nipping to the canteen for a plate of chips.

Eating smaller meals more frequently will ensure your blood sugar levels remain stable all day. It will also prevent the rapid rise and fall that causes energy drain to kick in. Ideally, four or five small meals a day should be eaten – this pattern also prevents sugar cravings. Ensuring that each meal contains protein will also help, as this stabilises your blood sugar and can stimulate brain cells, which keeps you feeling more alert and is a big aid in fat burning and eight loss.

Meals laden with carbohydrates should be avoided, however, as these raise blood sugar to a high level, which then plummets, causing major energy slumps and fat storage. In particular, refined and processed carbohydrates will cause this, so if you do feel the need for 'carbs' go for the wholemeal or natural variety.

**3. Stay hydrated:** Water is by far the best drink. Being gully hydrated throughout the day will help significantly increase, your mental performance and alertness, and also boosts your metabolism. A common cause of lethargy and energy slump is simply dehydration, so drinking more water can prevent this. Six to eight large glasses of water is best, but avoid sugary flavoured water as this will only have the opposite effect.

Caffeine should be avoided if possible. Try a peppermint tea instead-or a green tea, which, although containing caffeine, also contains many an oxidants so is better for you than coffee.

**4. Eat smart snacks:** If you are peckish mid-morning or again after lunch there don't deprive yourself – just be smart with your choice of snacks. Good snacks as the low sugar options such as yogurt, any type of fruit, or certain cereals such as muesli, with milk. Alternatively, have a smaller version of a meal, such as a sandwich or small pasts or salad. As above, snacks should also contain some sort of protein source to keep blood sugar levels stable.

You should avoid sugar mainly carbohydrate snacks like sweets and chocolate, crisps or corn snacks, and certain cereal bers, as well as plain toast or toast and jam. All these will cause a very sharp rise and fall in blood sugar. This fall is what causes us to nod off at our desk in mid-afternoon, and also leads to weight gain. This rise and fall in blood sugar can also influence food cravings. Blood sugar is the only nutrient (energy source) that the brain can run or. If the brain detects a fall in blood sugar, it will protect its energy source by causting extreme cravings for high-sugar snacks. This is why many people pig out on junk foods just a couple of hours after dinner.

**5. Get some fresh air:** Get away from your desk at lunchtime – even if it's only to stretch your legs by walking around the block. This is the perfect time to refresh yourself to help you remain focused throughout the afternoon. It could also be an opportunity for some bonding with your colleagues if you decide to make it a group activity. Likewise, get out of the car and have a brisk walk when you can – opening the window is no enough.

**6. Try a desk workout:** Common complaints from those seated all day for work are stiffness in the neck and shoulders or lower back. There are some simple things you can do to relieve the aches:

Neck stretches – lift your arm up over your head and place on your left ear. Then let your head fall to the right side, while applying a little pressure to create a nice stretch along the left side of your neck. Repeat on the other side.

Head rotations – let your head drop and rotate it to the left and right. Then tilt it backwards and rotate it again. Do not roll in a full circle.

Shoulder rolls – lift your shoulders and rotate them ten times clockwise, then anti-clockwise.

Ankle rotations – lift your left foot and move your ankle in clockwise and anti-clockwise movements. Repeat with the right foot.

**Mineral and vitamin valuesVitamin**

| Vitamin | Sources Include | Benefits |
|---|---|---|
| Vitamin A | Live (especially fish livers), egg yolk, fortified margine, Oily fish, oranges, aprisots, carrots, tomatoes, melons, dark Green leafy vegatable. | Eyesight, skin |
| Vitamin B1 | Most foods-including wheatgerm and pulses, wholegrains Brewer's yeat, nuts, fortifed breackfast cereals. | Helps break down Carbohydrates, nervous system |
| Vitamin B2 | Brewer's yeast, liver, kindney, dairy produce, wheat brain Wheargerm, eggs. | rapairs body tissues |
| Vitamin B3 | Wheatgrem, wholegrains, egg, yolk, cerals, meat, fish | essentail for tissue chemical Reactions. |
| Vitamin B6 | Avocados, live · Wholograins, egg yolk, lean meat, banana Fish, potatos. | Nervous system skin Red blood cells. |
| Vitamin B12 | Liver, kidney some fish (including shellfish), eggs, milk | Healthy blood and nerves |
| Vitamin C | Citrus fruits, potatos, leafy greesn. | Help heal wounds, may fight Colds, flu and infections protects Gums, kwwps joints and ligaments in good working order. |
| Vitamin D | Fish liver oils, fatty fish, eggs fortified margarine, also Synthesized by ultraviolet light. | Calcium deposits in bones. |
| Vitamin E | Vegetable oils, some vegetables, wheatgerm. | Cell growth; antioxidant |
| Vitamin K | Most vegetables – especially leafy green ones, liver. | Essential in production of some proteins. |
| Mineral | Source Inclade | Essential for |
| Calcium | Cheese, milk, yogurt, eggs, bread, nuts, pulses, fish with soft bone such as whitebait and tinned sardines, leafy green vegetables. | Healthy bones, teeth and nails muscle and nerve function; Blood clotting; milk production in nursing mothers. |
| Iron | Liver, red meat, oily fish, wholegrain cereals, leafy green Vegetables | Makes haemoglobin, the pigmnt in red bloods cells. That helps transport oxygen Around the body. |

## Carbohydrares

Carbohydrates are our main source of energy and need really to form the major bulk of our dirt. They are broken down in the body into glucose and used immediately fore energy or else converted into glycogen for short term storage in the liver. An excess of carbohydrates over time will be changed and stored as fat. This is a particular danger with refined carbohydrates or sugars, which do not take much processing in the body and provide large amounts of instant energy. Since they have less starchy bulk, refined carbohydrates do not make you as full, and therefore it is easier to eat too much of them, leading to fat storage and obesity.

**LEAF VEGETABLES**

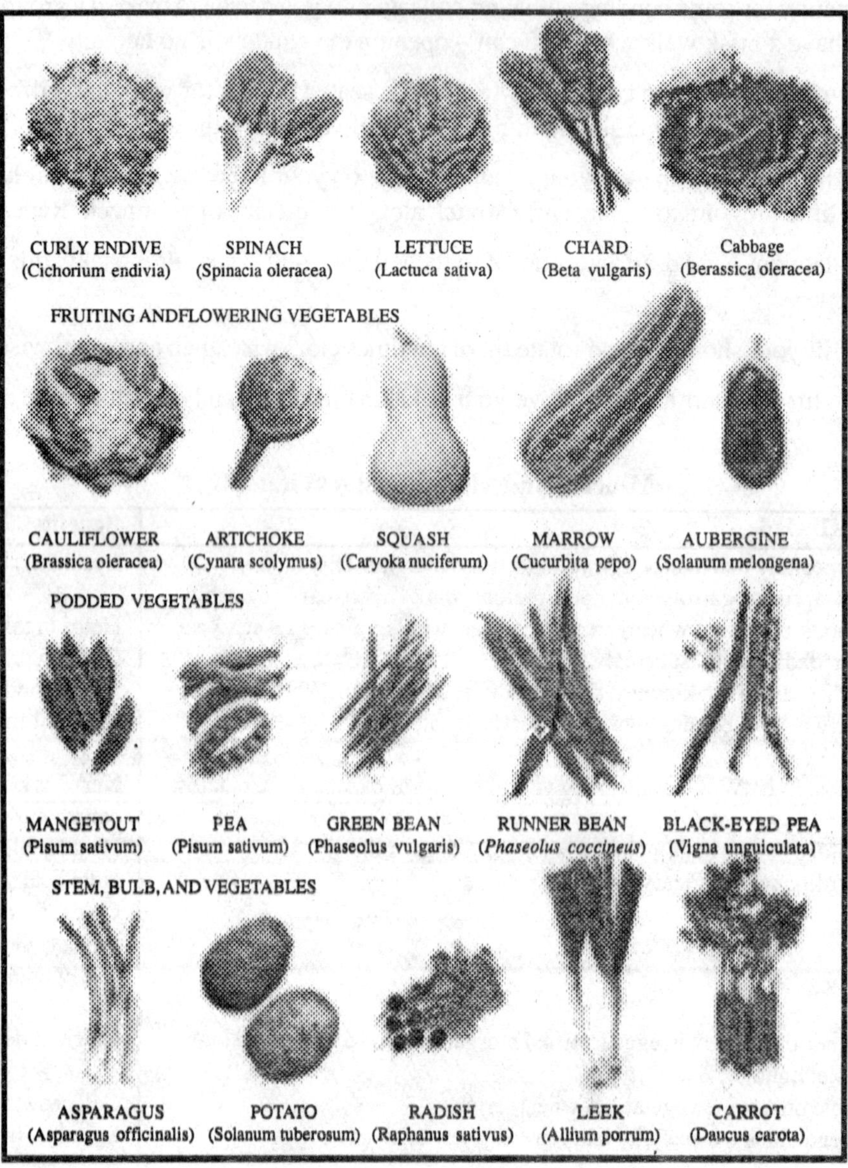


The main Sources of unrefined carbohydrates, providing dietary fibre and trace elements are flour and grains, beans, peas and lentils and potatoes. With grains this is especially true when the re unprocessed, like wholegrain bread, whole oat cereals, muesli, whole wheat pasta, brown rice and so on which supply long term energy supplies. For more immediate energy, fresh fruit, dried fruit or vegetables such as carrots or beetroot are high in fructose, or fruit sugar. This is easily broken down by the body for energy use, and since fructose metabolism does not require insulin, it can be an essential energy resource for diabetics.

There is almost complete accord among official governmental nutrition advisers and natural dietary therapists, that carbohydrates should be the chief element in our diet. In practical terms that means earthing plenty of fresh vegetables and fruit, grains of all kinds (unless there are specific reasons for avoiding a particular grain, such as with a wheat allergy), potatoes, beans and lentils. A recent piece of advice from official organizations, for instance, has been to consume five portions of fruit or vegetables a day.

## Fibre Facts

Fibre is important to a healthy diet. Your body cannot digest it, so in rather basic terms, it goes in and comes out, taking other waste with it. Fibrous foods include bread, rice, cereals, vegetables, fruit and nuts. We should aim a for about 30g (just over loz) of fibre a day. These are some examples of good fibre sources.

| Good Source | Average Portion | Grams of Fibre |
|---|---|---|
| Wholemeal Pasta | 75g/30z (uncooked) | 9 |
| Baked Beans | 125g/40z | 8 |
| Frozen Peas | 75g/30z | 8 |
| Bran Flakes | 50g/20z | 7 |
| Muesli | 50g/20z | 4-5 |
| Raspberries | 100g/3$_{1/20}$z | 6 |
| Black Berries | 100g/3$_{1/20}$z | 6 |
| Banana | average fruit | 3.5 |
| Baked jacket potato | 150g/50z | 3.5 |
| Brown rice | 50g/20z | 3 |
| Cabbage | 100g/3$_{1/20}$z | 3 |
| Red kidney beans | 40g/1$_{1/20}$z | 3 |
| Whole meal bread | 1 large Slice | 3 |
| High Fibre White bread | 1 Large Slice | 2 |
| Stewed Prune | 6 Fruit | 2 |

## Vitamins and minerals

Vitamins and minerals are needed for proper growth and development and body maintenance. They control the absorption of other nutrients and without them a series of complaints can develop, from headaches to sterility. There are 13 major vitamins which, apart from K and D must be obtained vitamins control from the food we eat. The fresher the food the higher its vitamin control. Food loses its vitamin through cooking, exposure to light or cold and strong, so buy small quantities of fresh and eat can it as soon as possible.

## Fats

Fats are vital too, helping to form part of the cell structure and maintaining our inner organs and nerves. They also act to provide insulation and temperature regulation. It is, however, well recognized that in the developed world much of our diet is too rich in fats, especially animal fats and this is a major factor in heart disease obesity and even some cancers, especially when we have such sedentary lives. Growing children, however, especially active ones do need fats more than adults and we should not reduce their intake so much.

Advice on fat containing foods tends to be what to reduce rather than what to increase. Meat and dairy products can contain concentrated source – a nice, juicy steak may have 30 per cent fat, for example. There are some differences between the effects of saturated fats (from animal products) and unsaturated fats such as are found in oily fish like salmon or plant oils like sunflower products. In general terms, move the emphasis towards the later, using oils such as olive, sunflower, corn or safflower with salads or in cooking, but most people need to reduce all kinds of fats, they are the most concentrated sources of energy and anything over small amounts easily leads to obesity. There are plenty of reduced fat items, particularly dairy products, which are now available and which can help in controlling fat intake.

**Easy ways to cut down fat and saturated fat**

| *EAT LESS* | *INSTEAD* |
|---|---|
| Butter and bard fats | Spread butter more thinly or replace it with a low fat spread or polyunsaturated margarine. |
| Fatty meats and high fat products such as pies and sausages | But the leanest cuts of meat you can afford and choose low fat means like skinless chichen or turkey. Look for reduced fat sausages and meat products. Eat fish more often, especially oily fish. |
| Full-fat dairy products like cream, butter, hard margarine, milk and hard cheeses. | Choose skimmed or semi-skimmed milk and milk products and try low-fat yogurt, low-fat fromage frais and lower fat cheeses such as skimmed milk soft cheese, reduced-fat Cheddar, mozzarella or Brie. |
| Hard cooking fats such as lard or hard margine. | Choose monounsaturated or polyunsaturated oils for cooking, such as olive. Sunflower, corn or soya oil. |
| Rich salad dressinfs like mayonnaise or salad cream. | Make salad dressings with low-fat yogurt or fromage frais, or use a healthy oil such as olive oil. |
| Fried foods | Grill, microwave, steam or bake when possible. Roadt meats on a rack. Fill up on starchy foods like pasta, rice and couscous. Choose jacket or boiled potatoes, not chips. |
| Added fat in cooking | Use heavy-based or non-stick pans so you can cook with little or no added fat. |
| High-fat snacks such as crisps, chocolate, cakes, pastries and biscuits. | Choose fresh or dired fruit, breadsticks or vegetable sticks. Make your own low-fat cakes and bakes. |

## Healthy Eating

So, what advice can be given in foods? Our needs do very throughout life, so there is no single diet that can be suggested – thank goodness? Children and teenagers need more protein, and most other nutrients, due to their growth rates, and pregnant women have an extra need too. While older and less active other activity increases demand, while older and less active people may require fewer calories. What we all need is varies, healthy and enjoyable food.

Three key word are freshness, wholeness and variety. As far as possible make fresh foods the major part of your food intake-fresh fruit and vegetable, freshly cocked bread, pasta or other protein containing foods. Preparation of foods should aim gill or bake foods rather than frying to use wholes gains but cutting back on processed foods as far as possible resort to packaged or canned food. Variety means exactly that, it is as unhealthy to eat just oranges all day it is to nothing but hamburgers all days.

Some ideas Might Include

- More fresh fruit and vegetables: they are high in vitamins and minerals and low in fats.
- Steadily increase fibre-rich foods, such as fruit vegetables, whole grains, beans and lentils.
- Eat fish, poultry and leaner cuts of meat, and avoid frying them as far pies, sausage and so on meat generally have high levels of fat.
- Eat fewer dairy products and use low-fat versions of, say yogurt or milk.
- Keep pastries, cakes, biscuits and chocolates for special occasions.
- Drink plenty, of water many of us get dehydrates.
- Ease up on stimulants such as coffee and tea, and also alcohol.
- Try to use less salt-this also means reducing intake of processed foods, since they can often be high in salt.
- Enjoy food there is a lot is pleasure to be gained from the taste and aroma of a varied diet.

**Sports helps De-Stressing**

**Don't get defeated by obesity. Just fight it away!**

Obesity is an excess proportion of total body fat. A person is considered obese when his or her weight is 20 per cent or more above normal weight. By preventing obesity you are preventing medical conditions such as diabetes, high cholesterol, high blood pressure, heart disease.

## Practical Tips

- Recognise that obesity is a disease. While most epidemics can be defeated with a pill or vaccine, obesity requires people to change the way they eat and live.
- Eat healthy. Include fruits, green vegetables, cereals and whole grain foods in your daily diet. Avoid sweets, fried, junk, pack-aged and refined foods. Eat small meals.
- Set aside at least 30 minutes every day for cardiovascular exercise. Walking, jogging, running, cycling and swimming are great for weight loss.
- Ignore popular quick-fix weight loss methods unless they are medically supervised. This category includes fad diets, weight loss pills and powders and fat burning machines.
- Become a non-smoker.
- Avoid drinking. Most forms of alcohol contain a high percentage of fat.
- Reverse the clock. Discouraging as this state of health might be, remember that you are not a lost cause. Give life a second chance. There are effective solutions; from lifestyle modification, diet and exercise on one end of the spectrum to bariatric surgery on the others.

### What does physically fit mean?

Physical fitness is defined as "a set of attributes that people have or achieve that relates to the ability to perform physical activity" (USDHHS, 1996). However, it is more than being able to run a long distance or life a lot of weights at the gym. Being fit is not defined only by what kind of activity you do how long you do it, or at what level of intensity. While these are important measures of fitness, they only address single areas.

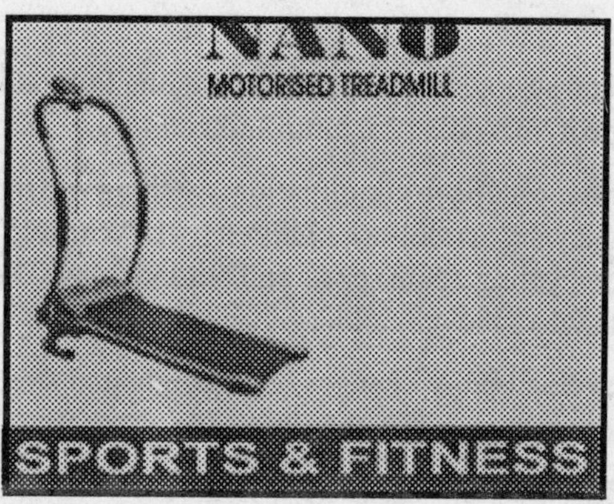


## Fit and Happy Kids – Not Fat

It is important that you encourage him to pursue some form of physical exercise to put him on the road to fitness. Instilling an activity habit in children when they are young is vital.

Play has taken on a different garb with many children. Activity is more with the hands and minds watching television, the computer or even on the mobile for more than two to three hours a day on an average. A sedentary lifestyle at a young age leads to an inactive adult life with its attendant health problems. Curb this and usher them on to a path of fitness.

## Give unto them their daily exercise!

Exercise should be as much a part of a child's daily routine as eating and sleeping. Start young to stay young. The benefits of exercise grow with the years. Physical activity increases cardiovascular endurance, builds muscle strength, improves flexibility, coordination and balance. This reduces chances of developing cardiovascular diseases, high blood pressure, diabetes and other obesity and stress-related problems. Exercise also helps manage weight, improve alertness, builds team spirit and a sense of well being and enhances self-image.

## Introduce a lifetime of health

Play in any form is exercise, be it running, chasing, catching, bouncing a ball or even turning somersaults. Informal play can be moulded into regular exercise as the child grows. While the school has physical training as part of its timetable, parents and the family too should encourage their children to be fit. Proper diet and exercise nurture good health. Exercise builds the three vital elements of fitness-endurance, strength and flexibility.

## Fitness can be fun

Exercise need not be imposed and structured but can be made fun. For toddlers, (1-3 years) it can be simple and enjoyable. They can play at the jungle gym, walk, run, jump and kick.

Preschoolers (3-5 years old) develop skills in coordination, catching and throwing a ball, hopping and balancing on one foot, pedalling a tricycle or a bicycle. School-age children (6-12 years old) develop hand eye coordination, and understands can include swimming, bicycling, team sports and outdoor play. They should start with non-competitive sports and opt for competitive sports when they are older.

Adolescents (13+years old) develop bodily changes, gain height and strength as they grow into young adults. The choice and form of exercise is their own, but it should be age appropriate. Whether it is jogging and running, competitive sports, fitness classes, gymnastics, bicycling, or exercise videos, it has to be vigorous, and at least three days a week.

Specific Exercises that enhance muscular strength and bone health include skipping, climbing, jumping and gymnastics.

Aerobic Activity develops endurance, strengthens the heart and improves the body's ability to deliver oxygen to the cells. Aerobic activities include basketball, bicycling, skating, tennis, swimming, walking, jogging and running.

Flexibility Exercises help improve suppleness, allowing the body to bend and move easily through their full range of motion. Flexibility exercises include simple stretches, yoga asanas.

## Problems kids face today

How much is too much? With reports of students taking their own lives trickling in at an alarming rate, do parents need to hit the alarm button? Thanks to the increased rate of awareness, several institutions and families are waking up to this problem. There are several reasons why a child takes this extreme step.

## Play therapy

According to Clinical Psychologist Seema Hingorrany, Play Therapy (PT) is a mode of therapy that helps children explore their feelings and helps them make sense of their lives' experiences. "Play is children's natural medium to learn to communicate. Recovery from a difficult experience can be facilitated by play therapists allowing a child freedom of expression in a safe environment. A PT room is stocked with therapeutic toys for children to ply," says Seema.

## Behavioural workshops

Being a child counsellor, Chandni Mehta holds regular workshops that deal with children and their behavioural issues related to academics, family issues as well as teenage infatuations and heart breaks. "My workshops cover issues related to studying and stress as well as family and peer pressures and also involves an interaction with parents in the last hour," informs Mehat. The increase in the number of child suicide cases indicates that somewhere in our interactions with these young impressionable minds, we're goofing up, says Clinical Psychologist Dr. kanan Khatau Chikhal.

## Being a friend

Psychiatrist Dr. Jyoti Sangle says that parents should try to be friends with their children. Kids have to feel that their home is their comfort zone. A child needs appreciation for every effort he/she makes. The child's self-respect has to be preserved. If hurt, this could be a stepping stone towards developing discontent, which could finally lead to the undesirable.

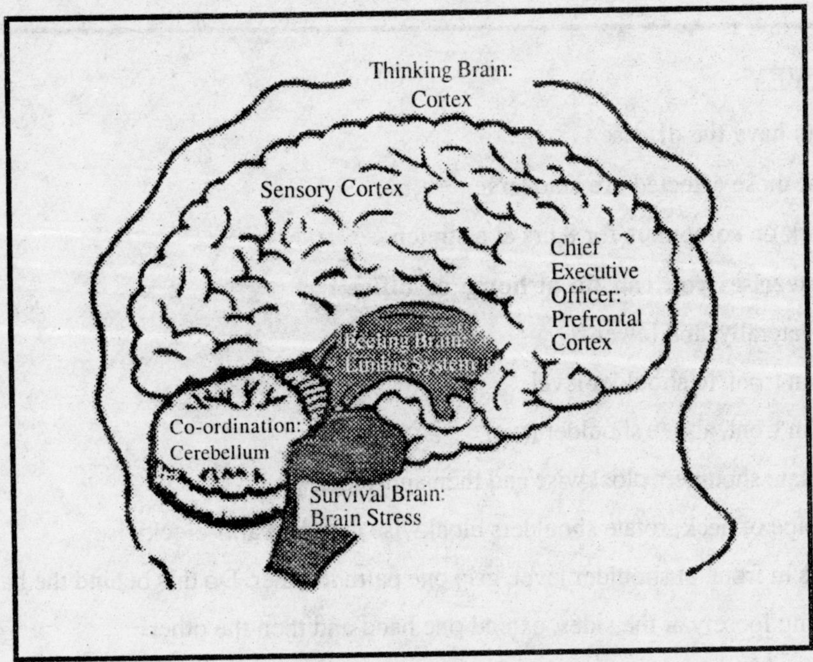


When Calm, a child is Better Equipped to Behave in Positive Ways

**WHY YOUR KID IS DRIVING YOU CRAZY**

Emotional outbursts, reckless risk-taking and rule-breaking occur in children because their brains lack the facilities for mature, responsible behaviour, shows a new research.

**Prefrontal Cortex:** The CEO of the brain, also called the area of sober second thought, is the last part of the brain to mature-which may be why teens get into trouble.

**Corpus Callosum:** A bundle of nerve fibres involved in problem solving and creativity. Slow maturation in children lead to emotional imbalance.

**Basal Ganglia:** Matures over the years. It acts like a secretary to the prefrontal cortex by helping it prioritise information.

**Amygdala:** A Developing Amygdala leads teens to react explosively to situations. This is the emotional centre of the brain, home to feelings like fear and rage.

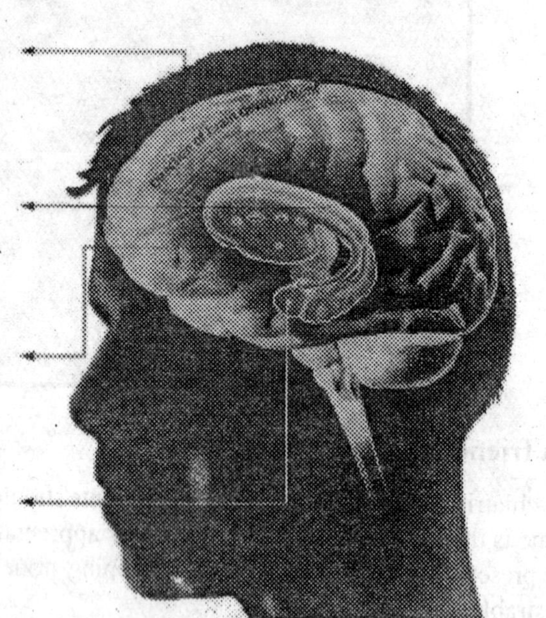

KOLKATA SURVEY

10% IT workers have the disease

At least 60% of those affected are smokers

All of them work on computers for 8 hrs at a stretch

**Two-minute exercises you can do at home or office**

1. Raise hands laterally, and lower
2. Raise hands in front, to shoulder level
3. Raise hands in front, above shoulder level
4. Arms out, rotate shoulders clockwise and then anti-clockwise
5. Fingers on nape of neck, rotate shoulders clockwise and then anti-clockwise
6. Stretch hands in front, at shoulder level, grip one palm in other. Do this behind the back as well
7. Let hands hang loosely at the sides, extend one hand and then the other
8. Rotate your neck clockwise and then anti-clockwise, slowly
9. Shrug. Shrug away those blues

Do these exercises standing or sitting on a chair

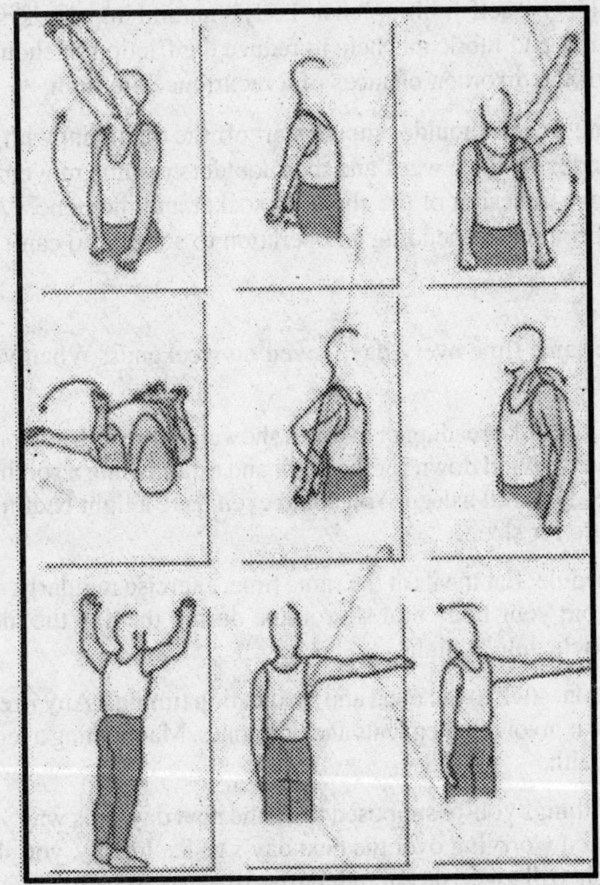

Frozen shoulders exercises

## TAKE A WALK

**Start exercising & quite smoking: Docs**

Watch your diet, move your joints and kick the butt. That is the simple recipe to avoid disaster. Regular exercise not only helps you to keep in shape but also keeps your limbs and joints moving, say experts.

And if you are the type that has to sit before a computer for hours to earn a living, you can do without limb movements and yoga. A frozen shoulder is not only excruciatingly painful, it also puts your livelihood at risk.

"Working 4-5 hours at a stretch causes fatigue. When people take a break, the tendency is to slouch on a chair and remain immobile. But that doesn't helps. Rather, get up and move your shoulders, legs and hips for two minutes. Then relax on a chair, without slouching or taking a wrong posture," advises Debashish Basu, preventive medicine specialist. Breaks should be taken every hour and if the work gets stressful, even every 30 minutes, he advises.

Diet and lifestyle also matter a lot. At first glance, burgers, colas and cigarettes may not seem to have any link with the condition of your joints, but they do. Avoid junk food and cigarettes to keep your shoulders flexible, say doctors. In case you have a stiffness or feel pain in the shoulders or joint as soon as you get up in the morning, start taking measures immediately.

"It should start with a regular lifestyle. But nothing can replace exercise. You needn't go to a gym. Brisk walks around the apartment complex will do. But those who already have the symptoms would do well to do some yoga," says Kalyan Mukherjee, orthopaedic specialist. He suggests par batasana and bhujangasana, among a host of others.

In 80% of the cases, IT shoulder is "self-limiting". The body's natural immune system repairs the damage to the affected tissues around the shoulders and lubricants help to reduce the friction of shoulder joint with the bones. But unless you can avoid the causes of the disorder, chances of a recurrence are high.

Those suffering from an acute frozen shoulder should start off the treatment with exercises, physiotherapy and ultrasound. Usually, the pain subsides within a week and the shoulders resume movement. In less than 5% of cases, victims require injections to remove adhesion of the shoulder socket and the bone. "Arthoscopy or surgery is rare among youngsters. But we have been recommending an operation to some who can't be treated otherwise,"

## DOS

1. Wake up and sleep at the same time every day – even on weekends. When your sleep cycle has a regular rhythm, you will feel better.
2. Develop a pre-bedtime routine, like reading or taking a shower before retiring for bed, and follow it religiously every night. A sleeper needs to wind down for the night and establishing a soothing ritual will give your body the clues it needs to get ready to fall asleep. You could even have a light bedtime snack, like warm milk or a banana, to help you prepare for sleep.
3. Follow a regular daily schedule. Eat meals at the same time, exercise regularly, do your daily chores as usual. The more you can accustom your body to a set routine during the day the more likely your body will be prepared to fall asleep on schedule at night.
4. If you are kind of medication, stick to the meal and medication timings. Any irregularity in either of these can lead to sleep disorders since it involves chemicals and hormones. Maintaining a regular diet while on medication of also as important for health.
5. Every day prepare a list of things you're supposed to do the next day This way you will have planned the day and will not lie awake in bed worrying over the next day's tasks. Ideally, you should plan at least two hours before your sleep time. This will give you enough buffer time to reschedule things, if required.
6. Is your bedroom sleep friendly and comfortable? If it is too bright, hot, loud or uncomfortable, it will make it hard for you to fall and stay asleep. Make sure your bed and bedroom are quiet and comfortable. A hot room can be uncomfortable. A cooler room along with enough blankets to stay warm is recommended. If noise bothers you, wear earplugs. Even a little bit of light in the room can affect your sleep, since light leads to the secretion of hormones that regular your sleep cycle. If you can't install heavy blinds on your windows or get your bed partner to read in another room at night, wearing a sleep mask might help you sleep better.
7. Do make sure you have a comfortable mattress and pillows. If you suffer from back problems or stiffness, there are many bed products available to support your body and help make you more comfortable. If you sleep on your side, a wedge between your knees can make a word of difference. If you sleep on your back, a wedge under your knees can relieve lower back tension.

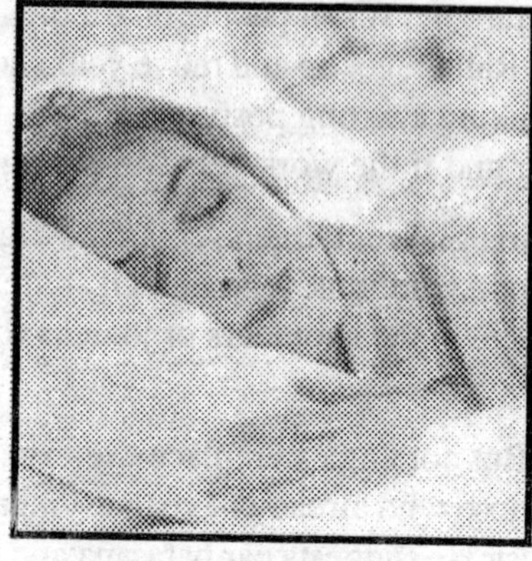

**Sleep well**

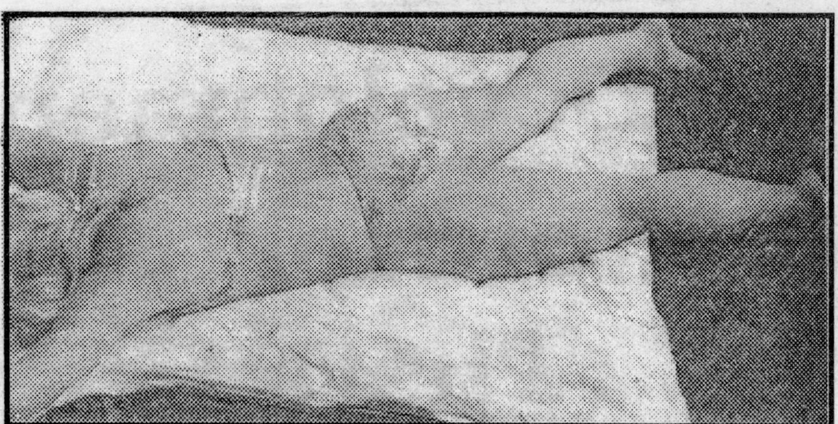

Relax

## DONT'S

1. Don't go to bed if you are not drowsy. This reduces the times you spend awake in bed.
2. Don't stay in bed if you have not fallen asleep within 20 minutes and don't feel tired. Go to another room and engage in a quit, relaxing activity. Just don't fall asleep there. Once you are feeling drowsy return to your bed. Of you still don't fall asleep. Repeat the process.
3. Don't use your bed for anything other than sleeping (of course there are exceptions to this rule, like sex and recovering from illness). If you read, eat, work and do everything else sitting in your bed, your brain might confuse your sleep time.
4. Don't nap during the day. If you must nap, do it at the same time every day, and don't let it last for more than an hour and make sure you're up and awake by 3 pm. Otherwise, the nap may affect your ability to fall asleep that night.
5. Don't have big meals right before bedtime. They can affect your digestive system and make you feel sick.
6. Don't do intensive exercise any later than early afternoon or mild exercise any later than late afternoon. Yes, even though many of us hit the gym only after work, those with sleep disorders need to strictly adhere to this rule. Doing stretches before bedtime, however, may aid sleep.
7. Don't have caffeine, nicotine and alcohol in the evening. That means steer clear of coffee, tea, soft drinks and chocolate. Nicotine is a stimulant, so it pushes your body to say awake. If you are used to smoking every few hours or more during the day, your body may experience withdrawal symptoms in the middle of the night, which can interfere with good sleep.
8. Don't consume too much liquid before bedtime – chances are that you'll be woken up by nature's call.
9. Don't use alcohol to help you fall asleep. It can disturb your sleep after just a few hours. Even if it doesn't prompt you to wake up in the middle of the night, you are more likely to awaken the next morning not feeling refreshed, because alcohol also keeps you from getting quality sleep. Also avoid alcohol when on medication.
10. Don't let a pet interfere with your sleep. It can be delightful sleeping with a pet, unless your animal companion is keeping you awake.
11. Don't let a partner interfere with your sleep. If your bedmate tosses and turns while sleeping or gets up at night, you might consider twin beds, so that you are less likely to feel the disturbance.

CHAPTER 19

# Development of Holistic Therapies

With the increase in the growth and development of holistic therapies in the 1990s and into the new millennium, it has become apparent that we are moving towards a profound structural change in our healthcare system.

The terms 'alternative' and 'unconventional' medicine have become outdated, as there has been a growing recognition of the value of holistic and complementary therapies in healthcare. With this, there is a greater need for therapists to become more professional and accountable for their individual therapies.

This chapter explores the concept of holistic therapies and presents a perspective on how and why they have grown in popularity. More importantly, we look at how they can be used to subtly enhance core conventional methods of treating illness.

The term 'holistic therapies' is used loosely to describe a unique approach to treatment through a range of different therapies, rather than a medical concept or system.

Although, the application of the word 'holistic' is relatively new, the concept of holistic healthcare goes back at least 2500 years to when Hippocrates, the father of holistic medicine believed health was restored by facilitating a state of equilibrium within the fluid essences of the body. He stressed the importance of holistic therapies and placed great emphasis on proper diet and lifestyle. He used drugs to support healing, rather than to cure disease.

The opposing school of thought to Hippocrates, the father, held that a disease could be overcome with a specific cure. Later the scientific revolution of the nineteenth century, brought with it the development of new drugs such as aspirin. The holistic concept of restoring balance and self-healing was abandoned in favour of drugs which appeared to have spectacular results by relieving symptoms.

During the first half of the nineteenth century, the holistic concept of treatment was shunned and all but 'out lowed; some therapies were even branded witchcraft! However, the 1990s in particular have witnessed a happy convergence of medical and complementary, or holistic therapies towards what on› may term 'medical pluralism'.

The unique feature of holistic or complementary therapies, despite the diversity of the individual therapies, is that they all aim to activate the self-healing capacity of the body and each has a theoretical base, linked by nature.

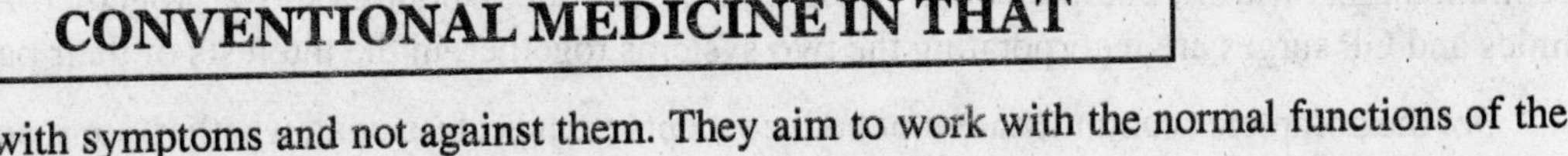

## HOLISTIC THERAPIES DIFFER FROM CONVENTIONAL MEDICINE IN THAT

- Therapies work with symptoms and not against them. They aim to work with the normal functions of the body.
- The persons individuality is taken into account – each person's condition is different and, therefore, requires a different approach. In holistic healthcare no standard treatment can be appropriate for all individuals, or for individuals with the same condition.
- The treatment strategy aims to work towards physical and emotional well-being and not towards the absence of symptoms, as in conventional medicine. There is, therefore, no fixed beginnings or end to the treatment as the approach is one of preventive healthcare and maintenance of a state of well-being.
- The patient or client is an integral part of the process, with the emphasis on selfhealing and the patient taking responsibility for their own health. The concept of holistic health care is not about an individual being the passive recipient of a cure.
- Holistic practitioners help clients to examine their lifestyle patterns as well as their bodily symptoms and work towards a long-term approach of restoring balance, rather than a short –term response to each incidence of disease.

The expansion in holistic and complementary therapies relates to the growing need to address the vast numbers of people suffering with stress-related illness, such as skin problems, digestive problems, heart disease and high blood pressure. There is a proliferation of media coverage of health – related problems as patients become more and more interested in how they can become an active part of restoring their physical and emotional well-being. Magazines and newspaper articles are full of testimonials from individuals who verify that holistic therapies such as massage, aromatherapy and reflexology, have helped them with musculo-skeletal problems such as backache and arthritis, cronic pain as in headaches and migraines, allergies, cardiovascular problems, chronic immune-related problems such as ME, chronic infections like cystitis, and the non-specific conditions which are hard to diagnose by conventional medical techniques.

It would seem that, in the past, the principle school of thought in medicine has been blind to anything but disease. However, medicine is now starting to integrate some of the holistic concepts into healthcare such as stressing the importance of changes in diet and lifestyle and reducing stress levels in cases of cardiovascular diseases.

However, it should not be denied that in the process of accommodating both complementary and conventional medicine in healthcare services, both in our health care service, both systems will have areas of failure as well as success. For instance, no amount of development in the field of complementary medicine could replace the excellence of traditional treatment, can help patients to cope with their condition and effect the restoration of physical and emotional balance.

Patients should receive traditional medicine for acute, life-threatening conditions in order to help sustain life. However, complementary forms of treatment, which may be used simultaneously with traditional treatment, can help patients to cope with their condition and effect the restoration of physical and emotional balance.

Complementary health practitioners are now starting to be acknowledged as professionals in their own right, as more and more doctors admit that, although they wish to learn more about complementary therapies, it is a diverse field which requires specific skills, knowledge and training.

It is interesting to note that the British Medical Association's educational requirement is for doctors to become sufficiently familiar with the forms of treatment available in complementary medicine to know what to expect from the related system and to decide who may benefit, as well as being aware of how and to whom to refer. Referral from a medical practitioner to a complementary practitioner has inherent difficulties in that, as certain therapies that is most effective for a specific disease or condition.

Although the medical profession has accepted the development of complementary therapies and seeks accommodation with it, complementary medicine forges these brances closer, together. Already many hospitals, clinics and GP surges are incorporating the two systems together, in the interests of their patients.

For the complete accommodation of both concepts each professional, whether approaching the patient's health from a conventional or holistic point of view, must grow to appreciate the limitations of their own system in order to create a truly holistic healthcare system.

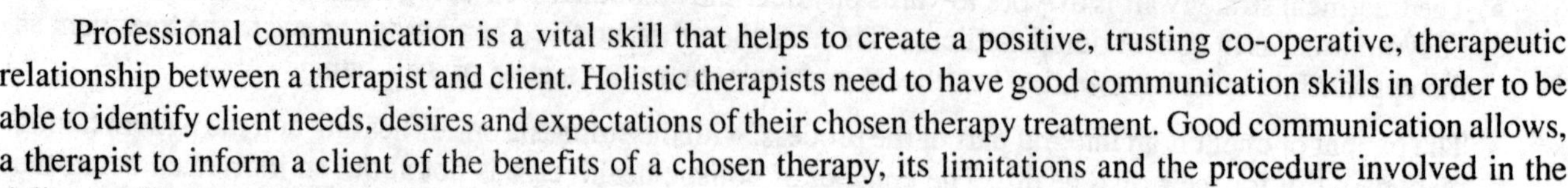

## CLIENT MANAGEMENT THE HOLISTIC APPROACH

Professional communication is a vital skill that helps to create a positive, trusting co-operative, therapeutic relationship between a therapist and client. Holistic therapists need to have good communication skills in order to be able to identify client needs, desires and expectations of their chosen therapy treatment. Good communication allows, a therapist to inform a client of the benefits of a chosen therapy, its limitations and the procedure involved in the delivery of the treatment service.

Professional communication involves the collection, recording and transmission of information of theraputic benefit and will include assessing the client's health, their needs, treatment, objectives and anticipated response. This chapter examines the importance of good client communication skills in order to establish a positive professional relationship with clients and to establish professional standards for the holistic therapy profession.

## CLIENT COMMUNICATION SKILLS

When exchanging information during a consultation, therapists use four types of communication skills.

Speaking

Listening

Assessing non- verbal message

Writing

### Verbal Communication

Holistic therapy treatments involve one – to – one communication. The arts of successful communication lies in listening to what the client is saying. Interpreting the information being conveyed and giving feedback to verify the message has been received correctly.

Clients like to feel that their therapist is able to identify with their needs and that they have been listened to. When speaking to a client, it is important to choose words which convey intent clearly, concisely and tactfully and to avoid using language that the client may not understand, such as medical terminology.

Verbal communication involves co-operation from both the client and the therapist. When exchanging information, there should be periodic reflective pauses in the conversation. This provides opportunities to verify the message intended, and enables any corrections or alterations to be made.

### Listening Skills

One of the most important skills in verbal communication is in the art of listening. Through effective listening, a therapist can identify with client needs and customise a treatment plan.

KEY NOTE – Therapists should be aware that clients may not find it easy to make themselves understood. Depending on their condition, they may be speaking through a screen of emotionally- charged feelings. Effective listening will, therefore, involve understanding not only what the client is trying to say, but the tone and the emotion with which the information is imparted.

One of the main responsibilities of a therapist during a client consultation, is to help facilitate the client's communication and to concentrate on the focus of their message. Active listening should always be undertaken in a non- judgmental way. This will help the client feel safe to disclose sensitive and personal information in an honest and open way. To be non-judgmental, a therapist must withhold their own personal evaluation on the client's situation and respect the client's right to reveal their feelings in a supported environment.

It is important for the therapist to realise that clients may be guarded about disclosing personal feeling until there is an established measure to trust. Therapist need to take care to consider their attitude and body language when carrying out a consultation, and should be aware of the importance of maintaining eye contact. Good listening skills require empathy and reflection. In other words, consider the client's feelings but also take time to reflect in order to avoid making incorrect assumptions, which would lead to inappropriate treatment, planning and, ultimately client dissatisfaction.

## BARRIERS OF EFFECTIVE COMMUNICATION

During a client consultation, it is useful to use a combination of open – ended and closed questions. Open- ended questions allow a client to reflect on their own feelings (e.g., 'what be the trigger for your migraine attacks? How do they make you feel? whilst closed question are more focused on the specific client details (e.g., 'Are you taking any medication at this moment?) Open – ended questions allow the client to give in their own words questions simply demanded a yes or no response.

Therapist, must take care not to suggest a client's response or to finish sentences, both of which may block effective communication. In addition, it is important to keep the focus of the questions limited to the benefit of the treatment therapy session. Communication can be non- productive if the therapist is unable to set their own personal issues aside or if they make biased generalisations about their client's condition, assuming that they understand the problem.

If the therapist is obsessed with their own problems and they bring this into the therapy session, they will be unable to facilitate positive communication to the benefit of the client.

### Non- verbal Communication

In order to enhance communication with clients, therapists need to consider the implications of non-verbal communication: messages that are projected by the body without the speaker's awareness. Non-verbal messages are an important part of communication as they often convey information about the emotional state of the client.

### Non- verbal signs may include

Facial expressions — lack of eye contact, frowning, grimacing.

Gestures — gripping the sides of the chair or couch, fidgeting, noddings making fists

Sounds — signs, grunts and groans, changes in breath, yawning

Posture — hunched shoulders

Sudden movements — looking down, tightening buttocks, toes lifting off the couch, lifting the head.

Therapist need to be aware of body language as a form of inner communication, and all non-verbal signs exhibited by a client should be observed throughout a consultation and treatment, and responded to in a positive way.

Therapist should also realise that, consciously or unconsciously, clients will be reading their body language. If the therapist behaves in an open and caring way, this will give the client a sense of security and show that the therapist has sincerity in the professional relationship.

## Writer Communication

Written documentation is an important of what establish a holistic therapist as a professional practitioner. It confirms their educated assessment, choice of treatment and ongoing evaluation of the clients progress towards health and well-being.

Through written records, therapists can gain respect from others for their professional findings within the scope of their therapy. This can serve to increase the status and professionalism of the holistic therapy profession as a whole. Written records include the client consultation form, treatment plans, along with any referral data and correspondence from healthcare practitioners. Accurate records are important to help a therapist to recall specific details from previous treatments and to facilitate accurate, ongoing assessment and treatment planning. The systematic recording of specific information ensures the highest quality of therapeutic continuity and can protect a therapist from malpractice claims.

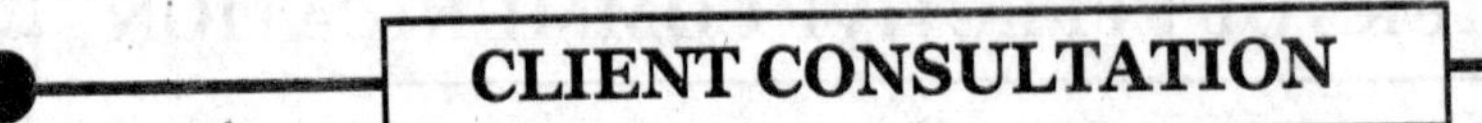

# CLIENT CONSULTATION

Establishing trust during an initial consultation often results in client satisfaction and a continued therapeutic relationship, so it is important that sufficient time is allowed and the consultation is not rushed. It is important to ensure that the environment in which the consultation is to take place is as comfortable, private and warm as possible. If clients feel relaxed they are more likely to communicate openly, making it easier for the therapist to establish a rapport and identify their needs. It is also important to consider seating; side by side may be less threatening and intimidating than sitting opposite.

A client consultation provides the foundation from which a suitable treatment plan may be formulated.

Consultations are necessary to:

- Establish the parameters of a therapeutic and professional relationship.
- Gain the client trust, respect and co-operation.
- Help put the client at ease, answer any queries and allay their fears about treatment.
- Help establish a client's medical history and to discuss their current state of health.
- Determine whether the client is suitable for treatment and whether they need to be referred to their GP or to other healthcare professionals.
- Determine the need for special care or adaptation of treatment, such as in the case of a pregnant client.
- Identify a client's needs, desires and expectations.
- Provide an opportunity for an explanation of the benefits, costs and limitations of the proposed treatment.

It is important when carrying out a consultation, that a client is assessed from a holistic point of view. Medical information is necessary for safety reasons, but it is equally important for the client's lifestyle exercise, occupation, stress levels and sleep patterns to be taken into consideration. This information will give a holistic view of a client's situation and may help to identify others factors which are relevant to the treatment plan and therapy proposed.

When asking personal questions, it is important for the therapist to maintain a polite and sensitive, but professional, manner. It should be stressed to clients that personal and medical questions are necessary in order for the therapist to establish how they can help.

## Holistic Therapies

If the consultation is carried out in a relaxed, rather than a formal, manner, clients generally are more co-operative with their answers. Forms are necessary as they form a structure for the consultation and may be used as a guide to ensure nothing is overlooked.

### Visual Assessment

This aspect of the consultation begins when the therapist greets the client, observations may be made of the client's mood, their gaits posture and breathing pattern. Visual assessment may direct the therapist to any problems or any lifestyle enhancements which may benefit the client. It is important when making a visual assessments the therapist avoid diagnosing a condition although they may recognise the signs and symptoms, only a medical practitioner may make a diagnosis. Within the limitations of their chosen therapy, therapists may observe and note specific signs, but should avoid labelling the condition.

If, upon assessing a client for treatment, a therapist suspects that the client may have a serious health problem, they should seek further clarification from the client's doctor before proceeding with the treatment.

### Manual or Placatory Assessment

This assessment is carried out through touch and is used to determine the condition of the tissue, (Skin, muscles, tendons, ligaments). Whatever modality of holistic therapy is being practiced, therapist must be proficient in placatory skills. By massaging, a therapist may be able to feel abnormalities in the tissue such as constrictions and adhesions, temperature changes and areas of excess fluid. Each holistic therapy requires a slightly different approach to palpation and abnormalities in the tissues or imbalances in energy flow may be determined by their characteristics feel within that discipline.

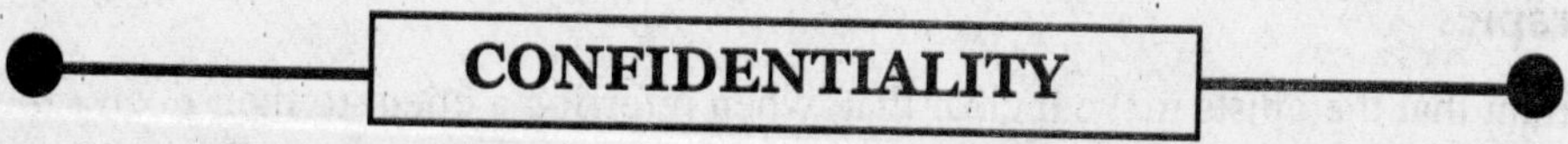

## CONFIDENTIALITY

Confidentiality is an important part of their therapeutic relationships between a client and a therapist. Whilst carrying out a consultation, it is important for a therapist to stress that all personal information relating to the client will remain completely confidential, and that the information will not be disclosed to a third party without the client's written consent. Maintaining confidentiality projects a high degree of professionalism and prevents embarrassment and loss of client loyalty. It will also help to establish a good rapport with the client and encourage their confidence.

Client management – the holistic approach

Therapists can maintain client confidentiality by:

Carrying out the consultation in private, or as privately as possible

Ensuring that all consultation and treatment records are stored in a secure place.

Ensuring that client records and personal details are never left lying around.

Never discussing a client's personal details or their treatment with another person, unless it is to liaise with another professional concerned with the client's progress, and the client's permission has been granted.

Checking whether, if the client has to be contacted by phone, it is convenient to ring home or work, and when speaking to other parties that all details of their treatment remain private.

### Liaising with other healthcare professionals

As the effectiveness of holistic therapies is increasingly proven, there are more and more opportunities for holistic therapists to work alongside healthcare professionals. Therapists must apply professional etiquette when liaising with other healthcare professionals and, if a client has been referred to them by another healthcare professional, they need to be able to write a status report on the client's progress.

### Status Reports

Writing report is an essential part of networking with other healthcare professionals, status reports do not just report on an individual's progress, they also raise awareness of the benefits of holistic therapies and demonstrate their value in healthcare generally.

A status report should include the following information:-

- A general introduction explaining how the client was referred.
- A summary of the client's main present problem or problems.
- The therapist's findings.
- The therapeutic modalities used and their results.
- The therapist's evaluation of client progress.
- Recommendation as to which therapy, or combination of therapy treatments, would be required to maintain progress.

## Referral

It is also necessary for the therapists to be able to refer a client to a medical or other healthcare professional, if they present with a contra – indication or medical condition requiring medical care. It is best for the therapist to have a prepared form for this purpose. Use headed note paper, and a form layout which states clearly and concisely what information is required. This may either be taken by the client to their doctor or may be posted with a stamped addressed envelop. It is advisable to include with the referral form, literature on the therapy proposed, in order to raise the doctor's awareness of its methodology and potential benefits.

## Holistic Therapies

It is important that therapists make it clear that, when referring a client to their doctor they are not asking the doctor to take responsibility for the therapeutic treatment. They are seeking more information or advice regarding the client's medical state in order to decide the client's suitability for treatment.

## Example of Referral form

Therapist's Name
Clinical Address
Date

Doctor's Name_ - - - - - - - - - - - - - - - - - - - - - - - - - - - - - - - - - - - - - - - -

Surgery Address_ - - - - - - - - - - - - - - - - - - - - - - - - - - - - - - - - - - - - - - -

Holistic therapy treatment for which medical referral is required

- - - - - - - - - - - - - - - - - - - - - - - - - - - - - - - - - - - - - - - - - - - - - - - -

Dear Doctor - - - - - - - - - - - - - - - - - - - - - - - - - - - - - - - - - - - - - - - - - -

I am writing with regard to one of your patients (Patient's name) of

(Patient's address)

- - - - - - - - - - - - - - - - - - - - - - - - - - - - - - - - - - - - - - - - - - - - - - - -

Who has requested (Type of treatment) treatment_ - - - - - - - - - - - - - - - - - - - - - - - -

(Enter explanation of treatment and its benefits_ - - - - - - - - - - - - - - - - - - - - - - -

- - - - - - - - - - - - - - - - - - - - - - - - - - - - - - - - - - - - - - - - - - - - - - - -

- - - - - - - - - - - - - - - - - - - - - - - - - - - - - - - - - - - - - - - - - - - - - - - -

I have carried out a detailed consultation with patient and would be grateful if you could outline any recommendations or restrictions that you would advise regarding their medical suitability to the proposed treatment by completing the consent form below.

Should you require any further information regarding the proposed treatment, please do not hesitate to contact me.

Thank you for your assistance in this matter.
(Therapist's name and signature)_ _ _ _ _ _ _ _ _ _ _ _ _ _ _ _ _ _ _ _ _ _ _ _ _ _ _ _ _ _ _

Doctor's consent

I agree/disagree that the proposed treatment of_ _ _ _ _ _ _ _ _ _ _ _ _ _ _ _ _ _ _ _ _ _ _ _ _ _ _ _

Would be suitable/unsuitable for this patient.

I recommended the following restrictions.

_ _ _ _ _ _ _ _ _ _ _ _ _ _ _ _ _ _ _ _ _ _ _ _ _ _ _ _ _ _ _ _ _ _ _ _ _ _ _ _ _ _ _ _ _ _ _ _ _ _

_ _ _ _ _ _ _ _ _ _ _ _ _ _ _ _ _ _ _ _ _ _ _ _ _ _ _ _ _ _ _ _ _ _ _ _ _ _ _ _ _ _ _ _ _ _ _ _ _ _

_ _ _ _ _ _ _ _ _ _ _ _ _ _ _ _ _ _ _ _ _ _ _ _ _ _ _ _ _ _ _ _ _ _ _ _ _ _ _ _ _ _ _ _ _ _ _ _ _ _

Signed_ _ _ _ _ _ _ _ _ _ _ _ _ _ _ _ _ _ _ _ _ _ Name_ _ _ _ _ _ _ _ _ _ _ _ _ _ _ _ _ _ _ _

Date_ _ _ _ _ _ _ _ _ _ _ _ _ _ _ _

## PROFESSIONALISM

Professional standards are the guidelines set in order to promote the integrity, scope of practice and professionalism of holistic therapies. They reflect current educational standards and are determined by professional associations. As the holistic therapy profession experiences growing demand, there is greater need for distinct borders and standards to be defined as these will help to distinguish it from other healthcare professions and to establish it as a profession in its own right.

### Professional Ethics

Professional ethics reflect the professional standards and moral principles that govern an individual or group's course of action and behaviour. All professional associations in this field publish their own that their members are required to follow.

### Typical ethics guidelines for holistic therapists are as follows:

- Acknowledge contra-indications for holistic therapies, and refer to the appropriate health professional before any treatment is given.
- Accurately inform clients, members of the public and other healthcare professionals of the scope and limitations of the therapies practiced.
- Have commitment to the industry by providing the highest quality of services to clients at all times.
- Represent the industry honestly by only providing services in which you are qualified to practice.
- Have respect for the religious, spiritual, social or political views of the clients, irrespective of creed, race, colour or sex.
- Never discriminate against other clients, therapists or other healthcare professionals.
- Act in a cooperative manner with other healthcare professionals and refer cases which are out of the sphere of the therapy field in which you practice.
- Always present a professional image by practicing the highest standards of personal and slon or clinic hygiene.
- Conduct yourselves in a professional manners at all times, with honesty and integrity.
- Be courteous to clients and treat them with dignity and respect.

- Keep accurate, up-to-date records of client treatment including advice given and the outcome or outcomes.
- Safeguard the confidentiality of all client information, unless disclosure is required by law. If liaison is required with a health care professional, the client's written permission must be sought.
- Only provide treatment when there is reasonable expectations that it will be advantageous to the client.
- Ensure that working premises comply with all current health, safety and hygiene legislation.
- Never give unqualified advice
- Never diagnose a medical condition or injury.
- Never prescribe or advice on the use of medication.
- Maintain and improve professional development through continuing education and personal development.
- Never abuse the client-therapist relationship.
- Explain the treatment accurately to the client and discuss the fees involved before any treatment commences.
- Ensure that any advertising is accurate, reflects the professionalism of the industry and that it does not contravene any consumer legislation.
- Be adequately insured to practice the therapy or therapies in which you are qualified.

## SETTING PROFESSIONAL BOUNDARIES

In order to have a healthy and professional relationship with clients there should be a balance between care, compassion for each client, and maintaining a distance. The setting of boundaries provides an important foundation upon which to build a professional relationship, with the client. Clients need to give space to facilitate healing in a therapeutic relationship, and it is therefore, important that a therapist avoids bringing items on their own agenda in the treatment room.

## TRANSFERENCE AND COUNTER-TRANSFERENCE

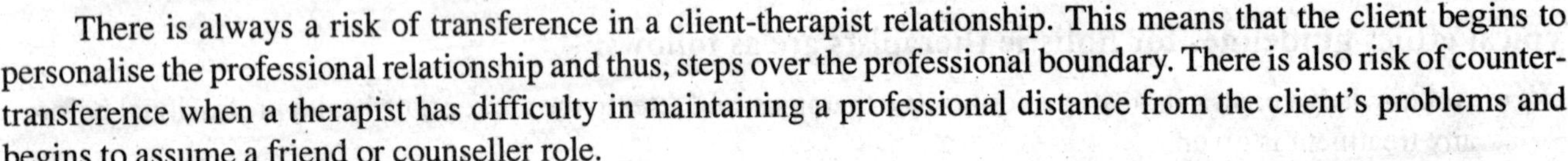

There is always a risk of transference in a client-therapist relationship. This means that the client begins to personalise the professional relationship and thus, steps over the professional boundary. There is also risk of counter-transference when a therapist has difficulty in maintaining a professional distance from the client's problems and begins to assume a friend or counseller role.

If either of these situations occur, it is important for the therapist to realise how potentially damaging this can be for the client and how it detracts from their healing process. If therapists are unable to keep a distance from a client and their problems, they need to consider whether the drive to help the client beyond their professional boundary may be fulfilling a need in them that is not being met elsewhere. If this need is not met and the problem continues to go unaddressed, it may also affect the future therapeutic relationships.

## CLIENT RECORD CARD

Client's Name ______________________ Date ______________________

Address ______________________ Sex: Male Female

______________________ Date of Birth ______________________

______________________ Height ______________________

Tel No. Day __________ Eve. __________ Weight ______________________

GP Address ______________________ Profession ______________________

Marital Status : Single Married Separated Divorced Sidowed

No. and Age of Children : ______________________

Preganant No. Yes. How many months. ______________________

Parental History ______________________

______________________

Medical History Operations ______________________

______________________

Medication/Present Health ______________________

Reason for Treatment ______________________

* Muscular/sekletel problems: Neck ☐ Back ☐ Rheumastism ☐ Aches & Pains ☐

Stiff joints ☐ Headadches ☐

*Digestive problems: Constipation ☐ Bloating ☐ Live/gall bladder ☐ stomach ☐

*Circulation : Heart ☐ Blood pressure ☐ Fluid retention ☐ Tied legs ☐

Varicosr veins ☐ Cellulite. ☐

*Kidney problems ☐ cold hands and feet ☐

*Gynacelogical : irregular period ☐ P.M.T ☐ Menosauce ☐ H.R.T. ☐ Pill ☐ Coil Other

Nervous system : Sensitive ☐ Migaine ☐ Tension ☐ Headaches ☐ stres ☐ Depression ☐

*Immune system Prone to infection ☐ sore throats ☐ clods ☐ chest ☐ sinuses ☐

*Regular antibiotic taken ☐

*Professional life (job details) : ______________________

*Ability to relalx : Good ☐ Poor ☐ Average ☐

*Time for : Hobbies or creative interests: ______________________

*Sleep patterens : Good ☐ Poor ☐ Average no. Of hours. ☐

*Do you see daylight in your workplace? Yes ☐ No. ☐

*Do you suffer from: Nervous tension ☐ depression ☐ anxiety ☐

*Do you eat regulars measl? Yes ☐ No. ☐

*Do you eat in a hurry? Yes ☐ No. ☐

*Do you take food/vitamin supplements? Yes ☐ No. ☐

*Do you exercise? Yes ☐ No. ☐

*Is your diet well balanced? Yes ☐ No. ☐

*How much of each of these items does your diest contain.

*Fresh fruit ____________________

*Fresh Vegetables: ____________________

*Protein (source): ____________________

*Dairy produce: ____________________

*Sweet things: ____________________

*Added salt: ____________________ Added sugar: ____________________

*How many daily drinks tea. ____________________ Coffee. ____________________

*Fruit juices ____________________ Water ____________________

*Soft Drinks ____________________ Others ____________________

*Do you suffer from food allergies? Yes ☐ No ☐ Bingeing: Yes ☐ No. ☐

*Overating: Yes ☐ No. ☐

*Do you smoke? Yes ☐ No. ☐ How many per day?

*Do you drink? No ☐ Light ☐ Medium ☐ heavy units per weeks ____________________

*Do you exercise? None ☐ Occesional ☐ Irregular ☐ Regular ☐ Types ____________________

*What is your skin type Dry ☐ Oily ☐ combination ☐ sensitive ☐ Dehydrated

*Do you suffer from : Dermatities: Yes ☐ No ☐ Acne : Yes ☐ No ☐

*Eczema: Yes ☐ No ☐

*Psoriasis : Yes ☐ No ☐ Allergies: Yes ☐ No ☐ Hay fever: Yes ☐ No. ☐

*Asthma: Yes ☐ No ☐

Client's Signature ____________________

Treatment result

Overall conclusion

# CHAPTER 20 Conclusion

The experience of feeling stressed is a fact of modern life. The frayed nerves, the short temper, the anxiety, depression and fatigue that makes up the emotional experience of stress are all too familiar in our day-to-day lives.

In our cave-dweller past, our bodily responses to severely stressful situations — increased blood pressure and pulse, respiratory rate, energy requirements, muscle tone and perspiration, all triggered by the release of stress hormones – kept us safe when under attack from wild animals or warring tribes. These 'fight-or-flight' responses have been exquisitely honed over the lengthy course of human evolution. Their purpose was to preserve life by providing a keener perception of potential dangers, greater strength in combat or other physical challenges, and greater speed, enabling escape from potentially dangerous situations.

Because of the flood of stress hormones that gets released when we are under stress, a body under stress is a chemically altered body. It is a body awash in hormones and other substances that are normally kept under tight control. In the right proportions hormones such as catecholamines (including dopamine, epinephrine and norepinephrine), glucocortoids such as cortisol, and androgens such as dehydro-epiandosterone (DHEA) keep our bodies healthy.

But get too much or too little of them and they become a form of slow poison, leading to a simply staggering list of stress-related disorders. This list now includes fatigue, indigestion, infections, irritability, diarrhoae, eczema, headaches, constipation, psoriasis, muscle tension, peptic ulcers, allergies, neck and back pain, irritable bowel syndrome, asthma, atherosclerosis, nutritional deficiencies, high blood pressure, anorexia nervosa, premenstrual symptoms, diabetes, sexual problems, arthritis, insomnia, psychological problems, cancer, depression and weight changes. Indeed, no part of our lives remains untouched by stress.

The human body is a vastly complex organism. It is finely tuned and adaptable. Indeed, it is this ability to adapt that helps us maintain our normal physiological state of balance. Our fight-or-fight responses are part of an inbuilt survival mechanism. Through a process referred to by doctors as 'allostasis' — the ability to achieve harmony and balance through change and adaption — your body is constantly adjusting itself to the prevailing conditions. The problem is that a body that is constantly adjusting itself to stressors is subject to a great deal of wear and tear. With all this overactivity, the adaptive mechanisms become worn out, leading to an inability to either adapt or shut themselves off (thereby reducing the levels of circulating stress hormones) once the stressful event has been resolved.

The complex relationship between physical and psychological health is still not well understood. But we do know that the major body systems — nervous, endocrine and immune — are intricately linked. They share hormones, neurotransmitters and cytokines (substances that promote cell growth and division), a relationship that helps maintain the equilibrium necessary for a healthy body. However, in times of stress, one or more of these systems may be affected, and what disrupts the balance in one system can disrupt the others. The interactions between these systems have been given rise to an entirely new branch of medicine: psychoneuroimmuno-endocrinology. Study in this field has greatly enhanced our understanding of the intricate workings of the body.

Through allostasis two adaptive pathways — the hypothalamic-pituitary-adrenel (HPA) axis and the sympatho-adrenal-medullary (SAM) axis, which controls the sympathetic nervous system — are initiated. Activation of these pathways leads to many neuro-endocrine changes, such as an elevation in hormones and proteins — for example, cortisol, epinephrine, norepinephrine, calcitonin, gastrin and insulin — which can result in common fight-or-flight responses like elevated blood pressure, heart and seat rate, coagulation (blood-clotting) time and blood-glucose levels.

During episodes of acute stress, hormones such as cortisol at first protect us by activating the body's defences through a complex chain of biochemical events. But when these same protective hormones are released repeatedly or in excess, as in the case of chronic stress, they can cause a gradual and steady cascade of harmful physiological changes. As levels of cortisol rise in response to chronic stress, so levels of another hormone, DHEA, drop. The result can be hypothyroidism (underactive thyroid), heart disease, prostate and breast cancer, menstrual irregularities, osteoporosis and autoimmune disorders such as systemic lupus erythematosus (SLE) and rheumatoid arthritis.

What is more, as part of what is known asa 'general adaptive syndrome', we become less and less sensitive first to whatever is stressing us, and second to the chemicals that our body released in order to help us cope. So in the same way that diabetics can become insensitive to the high levels of insulin released into the bloodstream to cope with excess glucose, and the bodies of people who are continually subject to toxic chemicals and allergens adapt to a chronic poison so the bodies of people under stress become less and less sensitive to the increasing amounts of cortisol released into their systems.

Stress, whatever its origin, can also become a circular path, For instance, physical stress can lead to emotional stress, and vice-versa. In addition, it is not just major stressors that cause problems. Evidence shows that high numbers of small daily hassles can take their toll. But whatever the source and intensity, the body responds if it is under attack by releasing a flood of stress hormones to help it maintain balance. When this happens the usual recommendations, such as relaxation and exercise, may no longer be enough to counteract the effects of stress.

## Stressed-out pets

Our pets can suffer from all the same disorders that we suffer from, including, it seems, the effects of stress. A recent survey for UK pet insurer More Than showed that obesity and behavioural symptoms are significantly on the increase as the health of the nation's pets is decline.

The survey, comprising 100 vets and 2,500 owners, found that almost 80 per cent of vets were seeing more obese pets, and blamed the animals' obsesity on a lack of exercise, overfeeding and poor diet. A quarter of pets suffer from stress, hyperactivity and depression, while three-fifths of vets claim that even more are suffering from diabetes and arthritis. Even when faced with an obviously overweight pet, the study claims, around 90 per cent of owners still refuse to believe that their pets are overweight.

A body awash in stress hormones for years at a time is most likely to develop a range of diseases and declines in mental and physical functioning, all of which modern physicians consider common with advancing age.

For instance, a lifetime of job stress (which usually involves high psychological demands and a perceived lack of control) can accelerate the progression of atherosclerosis and heart failure. Caring for a spouse or relative who is ill, for example with Alzheimer's disease, can also lead to a greater risk of coronary heart disease.

Higher cortisol levels have been recorded in patients with heart disease. Stress can also raise blood pressure, create harmful free-radicals (rogue molecules that attack body tissues and cause degeneration) and raise levels of homocysteine (an amino acid that damages cell linings and artery walls).

An eight-year study of 73,000 people in Japan recently showed that women who reported high mental stress were more than twice as likely to have a fatal stroke than those reporting low stress, and about three times as likely to have a deadly heart attack. Men who reported high mental stress were about one-and-a-half times more likely to die from a heart attack, though they did not show significantly increased deaths overall from strokes.

Although the women who reported high stress are more sedentary, more likely to have a history of hypertension or diabetes, smoked more and were more likely to work full time, the researchers concluded that, even after adjusting for these factors, the association between stress and heart attacks in both women and men, and an association between stress and strokes in women, remain.

## Stress and weight gain

In developed countries where life tends to be competitive, fast-paced, demanding and stressful, new links are continually being drawn between so-called modern life and increasing rates of overeating, overweight and obesity.

Chronic stress appears to feed both indirectly and directly into weight gain, through the way it alters our moods as well as the way it disrupts levels of key hormones. Stress alters the levels of several key brain hormones and may therefore lead to a lack of impulse control and thus, control of overeating habits. It is also associated with bad nutritional habits, like unpredictable eating times and eating much more rapidly than normal, or eating until you feel uncomfortably full. Given all this, it is hardly surprising that stress has been shown to lead to poor eating habits, poor glucose control and eventually obesity — cornerstones of many diseases later in life.

Two hormones, epinephrine and norepinephrine, released when you are under stress, trigger the fight-or-flight response. A third hormone cortisol, provides the energy for this response by stimulating insulin release and rapid fat and carbohydrate metabolism. This increases a person's appetite for high-starch and high-fat foods. If you are under constant stress, your cortisol levels will remain elevated. With elevated cortisol, people often turn to 'comfort food' - such as breads, pastas, sweets and high-fat snacks — for relief. Indulging in such foods is not just a psychological response; it is also a response to high levels of fight-or-flight chemicals circulating in the body.

Stress also inhibits the release of serotonin, a neurotransmitter that affects appetite, mood, learning and memory. Carbohydrates help increase serotonin levels, producing a calming affect.

The way in which stress stimulates an appetite for comfort foods was highlighted recently in an animal research from the University of California at San Francisco, published in the *Proceedings of the National Academy of Sciences.* In order to investigate the biological link between stress and the drive to eat, Professor Mary Dallman and her colleagues simulated chronic stress by increasing the brain concentration of a rodent version of cortisol. As concentrations of this stress hormone rose, the rats responded by drinking increasingly more sugar water, eating increasingly more lard — and gaining abdominal girth. The researchers noted that comfort foods that were high in sugar, fat and calories appeared to calm the body's response to chronic stress.

## Stress, memory and mood

Stress does more than poison the physical body. It also has a profound effect on our minds and moods. The same hypothalamicpituitary-adrenal (HPA) activity that causes physical disorders in some people can cause mental and emotional disorders in others.

Long-term stress may also affect memory by destroying neurons in the hippocampus, the area of the brain that contributes to visual memory and context.

The poor dietary habits associated with stress may also contribute to a range of psychological problems, including mild depression and anxiety. Depressed individuals often have significantly higher morning and midnight salivary cortisol levels and disrupted circadian rhythms — that is to say, the natural 24-hour rhythms of sleep and waking. At the extreme end of the scale, about some 60 per cent of chronic schizophrenia patients also show abnormal cortisol levels.

Women in particular are more prone to a depression/obesity cycle. Depression can both cause and result from stress, which may in turn cause women to change their eating and activity habits. In one study, obesity in women was associated with a 37 per cent increase in major depression. Another study of obese people with bing eating problems found that 51 per cent also had a history of major depression.

The link with stress and depression is important because depressed individuals may be less inclined to take care of themselves and to make positive nutritional choices. They may also fall prey to compulsive eating habits.

In addition, hormones such as cortisol also encourage the formation of fat cells. And to add insult to injury, research has found that high cortisol levels are linked to a tendency to store excess fat in the abdomen (rather than in the hips, thighs and buttocks). Excess abdominal fat is particularly dangerous as it places a greater strain on the heart and is associated with an increased risk of cancer and diabetes. Even healthy-weight individuals who are 'high-stress responders' have been found to store extra abdominal fat.

Indeed, a theory known as the 'stress cascade' suggests an interconnection between stress, glucose metabolism, obesity, hypertension and altered fat metabolism — all of which are aspects of the Metabolic syndrome.

The stress cascade results in the release of increasingly large amounts of catecholamines and corticosteroids, which in turn affect insulin regulation, glucose metabolism and fat storage. Sustained cortisol output caused by stress increases insulin insensitivity, tending to lead to decreased tissue glucose uptake. When this happens, insulin levels rise to counteract the increasing insensitivity to insulin.

Long-term elevations of cortisol along with the increase in insulin also increases the accumulation of visceral fatty tissue — for instance, around the abdomen — creating a much higher risk of heart disease and diabetes as we age.

Sadly, children are not immune to the stress/weight-gain cycle. A good example of this effect has recently come from doctors at Bristol University in the UK. Girls in the UK are reaching puberty one and a half years before their mothers did, and two years before their grandmothers did. The onset of puberty in the UK now starts when a girl is ten years and three months old, and it seems that the trend towards earlier puberty is advancing.

The Bristol scientists found a possible explanation in the appetite-controlling hormone, leptin, which is produced exclusively by fat cells. Girls in the UK are heavier than they used to be. Because they are carrying more fat, they are also producing more leptin. This overproduction of leptin may be interfereing with their levels of reproductive hormones, specifically progresterone and oestrogen. This, combined with an increasingly stressful life, which further alters hormone levels, may be triggering earlier and earlier menstruation.

## Can stress be good for you?

The right kind of stress may actually be beneficial.

Investigators now distinguish between passive stress (for instance, watching a scary movie) and active stress (such as trying to meet a deadline). According to one report, active stress can boost the immune system, increasing one's ability to fight off infection.

The researchers evaluated 30 male volunteers who were exposed to two different types of stressful situations: an 'active' stressful event, where volunteers were asked to memorise information and take a 12-minute test; and a 'passive' event, where volunteers watched a 12-minute video of 'gruesome' surgical procedures.

During the experiments, each person gave saliva samples that were analysed for immune-system components known as secretory proteins. These proteins help protect the lining of organs such as the lungs and stomach, guarding against the invasion of bacteria and viruses. While levels of secretory proteins increased during active stress, the immune response actually dropped during passive stress.

Most acute stressors boost the immune system, at least initially. It is only when stress is unusually prolonged or repetitive that it becomes a potential threat to health. An exception to this rule appears to be when we experience stressors for which the only response is to endure passively. These types of stressors, over which we feel we have no control, have a rapid and strong suppressive effect on some aspects of immune function.

Bungee-jumpers, parachutists and other thrill-seekers will be delighted to heart that the authors of this study recommend these kinds of challenges as being active and beneficial to the immune system and thus, to your overall health.

## Environmental stress

Most of us continue to equate stress with the physical and emotional experiences of everyday life, although today these are more likely to concern bereavement, marriage, divorce, long working days, a new baby and unemployment rather than encounters with wild animals. But as humans have evolved, other sorts of stressors — physical, chemical, electromagnetic, nutritional, traumatic and even psychospiritual — have come into play. On a chemical level, the body does not differentiate between emotional stress and environmental stress. Anything that threatens to unbalance or harm the body can trigger its primitive fight-or-flight responses and cause the release of a flood of stress harmones.

Most of us are unaware of the contribution of environmental factors — for instance, exposure to pollutants, pharmaceutical drugs and noise pollution — to our stress levels. And yet, because they tend to bypass our conscious awareness, environmental and other stressors that are not emotional or psychological in nature are arguably the most harmful to our health.

When speaking of toxic exposures, the effects of stress should not be underestimated. A stressed-out body is a body less able to deal with poisons in the environment. It is one that may, ultimately, become overwhelmed and less efficient at metabolising and excreting toxins. When your internal systems are not working to excrete to toxins, the body tends to limit the damage by 'diluting' toxins. It does this in one of two ways: by retaining water or, if the toxins are fat-soluble, by storing them in fat. Not surprisingly, puffiness and weight gain, which are in themselves physically and emotionally stressful, are also associated with a body that is overwhelmed by toxic pollutants.

Certainly, in the face of the insidious poison of environmental hormones and indoor air infused with harmful gases, which surrounds us each day, the usual behavioural solutions for managing stress — such as reframing your perceptions of that stress to make them more positive or sharpening your coping skills — aren't really effective. After all, there isn't anything inherently positive about being poisoned. In a body overwhelmed by environmental poisons, usually effective recommendations such as relaxation and exercise (see below) may no longer be enough to counteract completely the effects of stress.

Few of us have the choice of living in an unpolluted environment. City dwellers are often obliged to travel and live in places where pollution from cars and factories is a fact of life. Many of us work and live in buildings so full of chemicals that they have come to be known as 'sick buildings'. Good evidence shows that many of the substances that we come into contact with each day are causing a health crisis in our bodies, and it behoves us to do what we can to reduce our exposure, whenever and wherever we can.

## How to beat stress

At some point in their lives virtually everyone will experience stressful events or situations that overwhelm their natural coping mechanisms. People response to stress differently depending on different factors, such as early nurturing, personality traits, genetic factors, immune-regulated diseases and the length and intensity of stressors.

Nevertheless, studies indicate that the following people are more vulnerable to the effects of stress than others. The very young and the very old, for instance, can be prone to stress-related illness, though stress often goes unnoticed in these age groups. Others at risk include:

- Women in general, but particularly working mothers
- Less-educated individuals
- Divorced or widowed individuals
- The unemployed

- Isolated individuals
- People who are targets of racial or sexual discrimination
- City-dwellers.

How we perceive and manage stress is important to our overall health. When stress becomes too great, the damage may be irreversible. So to maintain and even improve your level of health, start taking action now.

- Exercise. Of all the things we can do to lower stress levels and counteract the allostatic load, exercise — along with a prudent diet — seems to be the most effective. Moderate exercise (defined by the National Institute of Health as roughly equivalent to physical activity that uses about 150 calories of energy per day, or 1,000 calories per week) helps improve sugar metabolism through the more efficient use of insulin, and assists in ending the vicious cycles of stress-eating, overindulging in alcohol, cigarette smoking and other unhealthy habits.
- Consider adaptogenic herbs. Adaptogens work on a cellular level to normalise the function of every cell, thereby stimulating the healing process to enhance the body's natural defences and helping the body to function normally. Adaptogens have been found to provide temporary relief from the symptoms of many conditions that are brought on by stress. The major ones include schizandra berries, astragalus, ashwaganda, reishi mushrooms, gotu kola, holy basil, Angelica sinensis (dong quai), Echinacea, royal jelly and perhaps the most well-known-ginseng (Korean and Siberian). If you are at all unsure what to take, consult a qualified herbalist.
- Consider better nutrition. Nutrients commonly depleted by stress include the antioxidant vitamins A, E and C, as well as vitamin B-complex and the minerals zinc, selenium, calcium, magnesium, iron, potassium, sulphur and molybdenum. Along with a whole food diet and a high potency multivitamin and mineral supplement, ensure that you get adequate levels of B-complex and vitamin C. B vitamins are necessary to protect the brain and nervous system; B6 (20-50 mg daily) can alleviate depression, and B12 (1,000 mg daily) is necessary to maintain a healthy nervous system. Similarly, vitamin C is a valuable antistress antioxidant — aim for 500-1,000 mg daily. Among the minerals, calcium (500-750 mg daily) and magnesium (350-500 mg daily) should be considered. Many of these nutrients are also necessary for an efficient metabolism.
- Avoid alcohol. A high intake of alcohol may blunt the body's ability to respond appropriately to stress. People who abuse alcohol have all kinds of health-related problems and often find adapting to stress difficult — a problem related to worn-out adaptive pathways.
- Try stress management — it can make a difference. Stress management techniques address the behavioural aspect of 'handling' stress. People with heart disease can lower their risk of subsequent cardiac events by more than 70 per cent if they learn how to manage stress. Similarly, stress management techniques have been shown to improve glucose control in diabetics. Stress management can take the form of formal behavioural modification or of new/old practices such as yoga and tai chi.
- Quite smoking. Habitual smokers have higher cortisol levels following cigarette smoking compared to non-smokers. Ironically, smokers can exhibit lower cortisol levels than non-smokers when challenged by a psychological stress, though this is probably due to lowered HPA response.
- Stay optimistic. Two recent studies have found that optimists live longer and better. Optimists tend to develop better coping skills and a more supportive social network than those with a darker outlook, and this may shelter them from stress, illness and depression.
- Hug your children and teach them to cope better than you have. Experts have found that being touched and held during the first few years of childhood may set up positive stress-response patterns that last a lifetime.

To cope with personal, social and environmental stress, you need to be aware of your lifestyle and your environment, and understand how these things can affect you, even when you are not immediately aware of these effects. Once you know the sources of your environmental stress, the only way to 'cope' is to remove as much of it as possible from your life. Doing so will pave the way for the dietary changes suggested in the next chapter, which can help your body burn calories more efficiently.

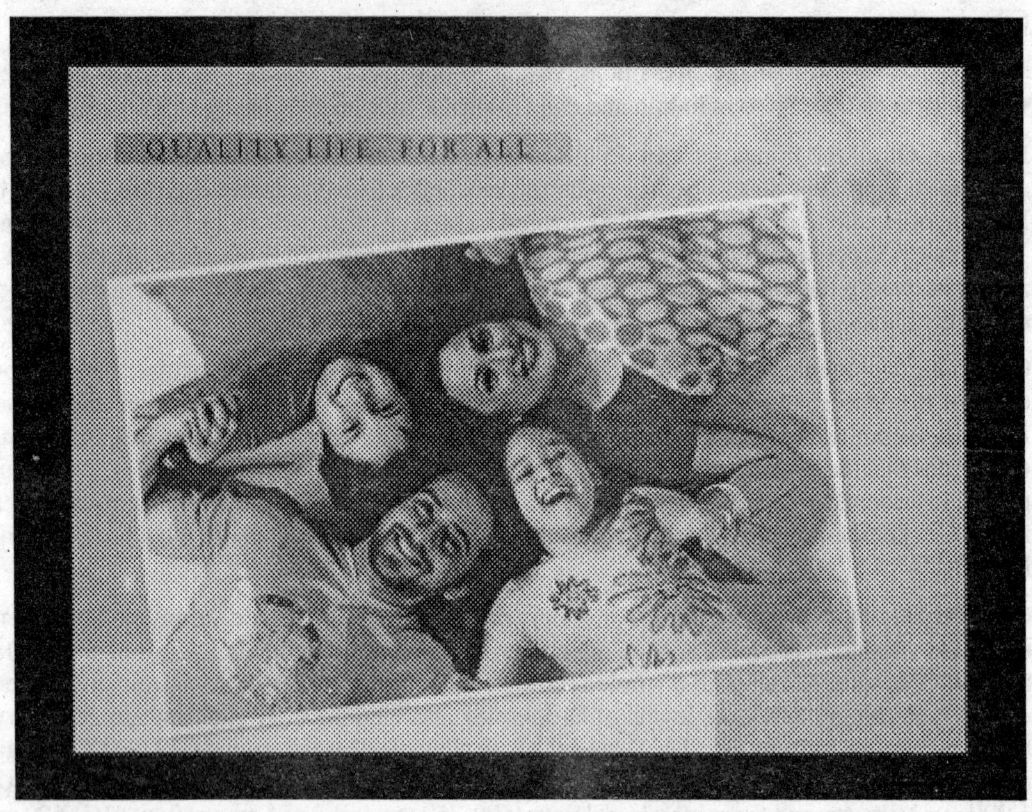


**Enlightenment**

'Buddhism is derived from the word 'Buddha'. It is aneasily accessible and practical way of life shown by Buddhas. By overcoming of all kinds of negative ideas a Buddha develops positive virtues in him and rises to the stature of world's mentor.'

## INSTANT RELIEF, EVERY DAY

Small movement done frequently help prevent muscular tensions from creeping up on you. Here is an easy way of making some relaxing and stretching movements an integrated part of your lief. The trick is to associate certain movements with certain places, such as the head turn with every elevator you enter. Remember Pavlov's famous experiment with dogs? Every time Pavlov fed the dog he rang bell. After many petitions of the routine, the dogs salivated at the sound of the bell, even when no food was given. Pavlov had induced a conditioned reflex; the sound of the bell 'reminded' the dogs of food. Similarly, you can induce a 'conditioned reflex' in your mind so that you automatically associate elevator with the head turn.

The following pages more places and situations to like with the tension-releasing movements of the previous chapters. But there are many possibilities, so pair the relaxing movements you need most, the stretches you like best, with the places you frequent. The important thing is to always use the same movement at the same places.

### Here are some suggestion

At the office: the Neck and Chest Liberator is a good choice. If you are alone in the office for a couple of minutes add the rag doll and the hanging Side pull.

**At the movies:** Shrug your shoulder three or four times, pull the shoulders high up to your ears and drop them. This is also a good place to do the Ear to Shoulder Stretch.

**At a party:** After an hour of party fun, find the bathroom. Wipe that arty smile from our face. Look into the mirror and practice the jaw and tongue relaxers from chapter 5. alternate them at least three time at you will feel refreshed and rejuvenated. Now you can really smile when you return to the party.

**At the beach:** Build cushions of sand under you neck and under you knees. Put your beach towel over the "pillows" and lie in the relaxing position. Hearing soothing sound of the ocean enhance total muscle relaxation. Be sure to cover your eyes and use a protective sunscreen.

**In the shower:** Aim the water flow at your shoulder blades and do the Elbow Cross. The Backup Crawl is another own to try.

**In the elevator:** I have suggested the Headturn for the elevator. Facial relaxes are also easy to do.

**In bed:** Before getting up each morning, concentrate on relaxing your thigh muscles by tensing the quadriceps and letting them go loose. Your legs work a lot for you all day; why not be good to them each morning? Here is a quick neck loosener for people who are comfortable lying on their stomachs. If feels delicious. Why on your stomach, extended your arms out at shoulder level. Rest your head on one cheek. Slowly raise your head and turn it, bringing it beck word as far as possible. Rest on the other cheek. Do three times, side to side.

**On a bus:** you cant do too much on a bus without attracting a lot of attention. Yet I use every bus ride to relax my eyes and forehead. I lower my chin to my chest and close my eyes lightly. Them I frown, wringing my forehead, and hold it for a count of five. Next I late loose of the frontalis muscles and picture a smooth forehead. I lift my head, open my eyes and start over again.

**On a plane:** the shoulder and neck loosener and the arms overhead stretch are easily done on an air plane. Whenever I get up to go to the wash room I also do the hang and reach stretch, but I admit that one does attract attention. Since I feel a strong need for that stretch after setting for a couple of hours, I just ignore the stares.

**At the end of the day:** at the end of some hectic days the tension headache threatens, and it also seems that most of my blood supply is stuck in my legs and feet, making every step an effort and a chore. An evening appointment looms, so theirs no time and/or peace of mind for "reversing the blood flow." standing on ones head or resting on a slant board are age-old, effective yoga remedies. But a headstand can hurt the neck and a slant board takes up a lot of room. This is a simpler "picker upper" I have devised. Lie diagonally on a bed and raise your legs, resting feet against the wall. Then inch your body toward the edge of the bed and slowly lower your head over the side. Eyes lightly closed, start relaxing all facial muscles. While hair and scalp benefit from an increased blood flow, the usual constant downward pull of gravity on legs and face is reversed. Facial relaxes also have a cosmetic benefit. Practiced frequently, they can help ward off unwanted lines and wrinkles the position may not be comfortable for everyone. Start with one minute and work up to five.

Most of us have a daily routine we follow. I leave it to your imagination to find other times and which lend-themselves to doing your favourite stretch and relaxation exercises.

**Even Exercising Won't Help If You Spend Hrs At Office Desk Or Watching TV**

Here's a new warning from health experts: Sitting is deadly. Scientists are increasingly warning that sitting for prolonged periods even if you exercise regularly — could be bad for your health. And it doesn't matter where the sitting takes place — at office, at school, in the car or before a computer or TV — Just the number of hours it occurs.

Research is preliminary, but several studies suggest people who spend most of their days sitting are more likely to be fat, have a heart attack or even die.

In an editorial published in the British Journal of Sports Medicine, Elin Ekblom-Bak of the the Swedish School of Sport and Health Sciences suggested that authorities rethink how they define physical activity to highlight the dangers of sitting.

"After four hours of sitting, the body starts to send harmful signals, "Ekblom-Bak said. She explained that genes regulating the amount of glucose and fat in the body start to shut down.

Even for people who exercise, spending long stretches of time sitting at a desk is still harmful. Tim Armstrong, a physical activity expert at the World Health Organization, said people who exercise every day — but still spend a lot of time sitting — might get more benefit if that exercise, were spread across the day rather than in a single bout,

That wasn't welcome news for Aytekin Can, 31, who works at a London financial company, and spends most of his days sitting in front of a computer. Several evenings a week, Can also teaches jiu jitsu, a Japanese martial art involving wrestling, and also does Thai boxing. "I'm sure there are some detrimental effects of staying still for too long. But I hope that being active when I can helps," he said.

Still, in a study published last yeur that tracked more than 17,000 Canadians for about a dozen years, researchers found people who sat more had a higher death risk, independently of whether or not they exercised.

## Conclusion

**74 Way to Manage Stress and Leading a Hassel Free Successful Life**

1. Try to remain neutral in every situation- means in happy situation don't be over excited and in sad situation don't be so much sad. Accept both situations as a part of life and two side of coin I found above philosophy is killer blow for stress or any kind of mental illness and of course seems hard to applied at first glance but let me assure you that it can be possible with some practice.
2. Say good bye to anger you feel for anyone to mange stress effectively. Let my tell you one more thing that anger will destroy your hundred virtues. All your virtues become invisible because of anger.
3. Accept principle of high thinking and simple living. You must try your best to achieve your goal but never blame yourself or situations around you. If you fail then accept it a part and parcel of life.
4. Don't be a cry baby and never ever blame yourself or situation or people around you for failure and accept it in good spirit and of course never stop trying.
5. Money is one of most important factors in life and try your best to earn it as much as possible but never be mad for it.
6. To manage stress you must remove every bit of jealousy you have for your friends, colleagues or anyone because it doesn't harm anyone but yourself. It will eat you. Like the 1st rule this rule is also a golden one.

7. To cope with stress you must accept that you are a unique individual and like everyone you have some good and some bod points. Search you inner self and find out what is unique in you and let me tell you that you will find something unique in your self among thousands if not millions.

8. Try to help others who are in need of it, whenever possible. This will help you to manage stress

9. To cope with stress you must give up your addictions. Keep in mind that these addictions are part of the problem not solutions.

10. To manage stress, you must start yourself. Never expect the world to change for you, rather you must change for the better.

11. The best habit one can develop to live a stress — free life is to plan things before hand and this will decrease the no of surprises in life. Surprises are one of major factors for stress. Fewer surprises are best factor to manage stress.

12. Develop a habit of prioritizing things and work everything as per priorities. Do one thing at a time it will manage your stress.

13. Limit your expectations from others because over expectation from others or life are a major source of stress. This habit will reduce your stress to a great extent.

14. Develop a habit of meeting new people and developing new relationships and kick out every bit of shyness or fear of meeting people. If you are a victim of shyness then make a habit of talking with at least one stranger a day for 30 to 40 minutes and your shyness will run away.

15. Try to be financially as secure as possible. In the modern world financial insecurity is one of the major causes of stress. Develop a habit of savings at least 20% of your income and manage stress by feeling financially secure.

16. If you are a victim of anxiety disorder or panic attacks then always keep in mind that Fear of anxiety is always bigger then fear itself. Always hope for the best and remain prepared for the worst.

17. Face the problems like a lion instead of running away like a rabbit.

18. The secret of success is how you use your pain and your pleasure instead of them using you, so be in control of your life and do not let your life control you.

19. Control your emotions when you take a decision. Take decision by mind instead of heart. Don't make emotions be part of your decisions.

20. Don't be impatient for the result of your action and don't change goals and actions hastily.

21. Kick out habit of comparing someone's wealth with that of yours. In the modern world this is one of the major sources of stress.

22. Relieve your self from every bit of jealousy or grudge you feel for anyone. Try to make your line bigger instead of erase line of other. This habit will even destroy every bit stress from your life.

23. Decrease level of your big ego. Ego is main source of anger and anger is major source of stress or bad decisions. Ego may become major factor to strain your relations with someone.

24. Apply one eastern proverb in your life. The proverb is "Everything is good in limit" so don't cross limit of anything. This golden rule may change one's life.

25. If you are a victim of anxiety disorder then find out the reason behind it, consider it and define it in two groups. One group will be you can do something about and other you can't do anything about it. For example if you constantly worry about your financial position then instead of worrying about your financial position, start work in that direction to make money and be financially secure.

26. If your worry about second group like what will happen if terrorists attack your city with nuclear bomb then you should treat your worry by facing it and tell your worry that there is nothing I can do about it so let's wait and see.

27. Don't let go any of your worry in third cycle. For example you worry about your stomach pain. First cycle is you worry about your stomach pain, second cycle is you worry that you may have gas in stomach because you overeaten yesterday. Now cut here third cycle like you may have stone in kidney or tumor in liver and forth cycle like you may have liver cancer. Let it be decided by your able physician.
28. When you feel alone and require a helping hand then never forget that you will find somehow who can lend a helping hand.
29. Use the term "we" in conversation instead of me and you don't feel alone and you will get a team to work with you.
30. Never forget that your are not alone with problems or critical problems in the world. There are more like you or in worst condition then you and live life. Just accept good and bad conditions as a part and parcel of the life and that's why the world keeps going.
31. Avoid company of negative people means people who think negative, talking negative and if you are one of them then you must rectify yourself because the world of today is the work of people of positive thinking. Because every major invention you will find one positive thought of someone.
32. To manage stress search for company of positive people means people who think positive, don't be cry baby in every situation but remain optimistic in worst situations.
33. This is not a sin to do mistakes but it is a sin not to rectify it and repeat the same again. And worst mistake one can do is to live life without mistakes and this is greatest sin, just think about it.
34. Develop the habit of saying no very kindly and firmly when you think that things may go against your will. This habit you must develop to manage stress.
35. Develop your personal constitution and follow it in letter and spirit and review it every week and you will know difference.
36. Every Sunday review your week and think about good things you have done and mistakes you have made and rectify mistakes and be determined to never make them again.
37. Plan your next week in advance and try to follow it in the best possible way.
38. Don't make decisions too fast (This is no way to make decisions) but ones you make a decision follow it and don't let your mind get confused in any situation. It should be always known to you where you stand. So even harsh condition never put decision-making on hold. Ones you know where you stand you will be relieved from the stress you feel.
39. Make the habit of inserting positive words in your vacabulary and don't use negative words.
40. Think high but go always move step by step and avoid short cuts.
41. Take care of body and always control your bad eating habits. Healthy mind can reside in healthy body as general principle.
42. Control your weight to be out of vicious cycle of over weight and over stress.
43. Use kind words in vocabulary instead of sarcastic ones. You must always know that use of sarcastic words may give you some satisfaction for some time but not going to help to solve problem but complicate it. It may strain your relations with other.
44. You should know where you stand and what your goal is. Life without a goal is a waste. So define your goal clearly and don't stop until you achieve it.
45. Do not confine your self in age, system or anything like that. Some people jail them in age factor like now I am forty so I can't do anything to make difference. This worst kind of lie you will tell yourself unconsciously. There is nothing like as age factor as obstacle to improve yourself or manage your stress or achieve success.
46. Read autobiography of great people and you will know that there is no such thing as good luck but just fruition of sheer determination. There is nothing like easy money or easy success.

47. Make habit of taking risk and challenges in life. Without risk there is no great success.
48. Don't fear failure because it may be your biggest mistake of life. Accept failure without blaming anyone because if you can fail one time you may succeed the second time. You just have to amend your mistakes and change your ways. We will either find a way or make one.
49. Don't change your goal after a failure because some people change their goal instead of changing their way to achieve the goal. Changing your goal may be big a mistake.
50. Be soft on the outer and tough from inner.
51. Be optimistic and never forget that after a black night there will be a dawn of hope (But don't give up without a try).
52. Be confident and courageous and note that every virtue of yours will follow your courage.
53. Don't take in mind what people say about you and be indifferent to it and if you find valid criticism then amend you mistake but no way should you upset yourself because of someone saying something about yourself. Just give a damn. This will help you to mange stress greatly.
54. Make habit of breaking a big task into smaller number of tasks and then make a timetable for each task and then you will feel difference and manage stress at job.
55. Make habit of doing tomorrow's work today and tody's work now. Don't waste time anymore. Value your time and use it like money because once gone time never returns.
56. Never hesitate to express your thoughts. Don't make a habit of keeping stressful thoughts a secret from family or loved once. Share with them and this will help manage stress.
57. Make a habit of minding your own business and don't advise someone if not asked to.
58. If you don't like someone's doings or anything then tell him straight but kindly and firmly and only if it is your business. But don't keep it to yourself and think about it for days. Just express yourself when and where required.
59. Keep harmonious environment in your family and accept principle of "let go" for at least your family members. Always keep in mind that it is easy to fight and win stranger but not with loved one. Charity must be begin from home.
60. Take a vacation with family for 7 to 10 days every year from your work and switch off your mobile if possible for that time. These will be best for manage job stress and it will rejuvenate you completely.
61. Always spend some time with family and children at least on Sundays and it will help great to manage stress.
62. Always be loyal to your life partner.
63. Start your day after offering a prayer to the Almighty.
64. Develop new hobby and give some time to it, like reading learning new language or some new unknown sport or collecting something.
65. Develop habit of daily meditation and follow it. This is one of few things to kick out stress successfully and help you know yourself better. If possible do meditation in yoga mudra Padmasana.
66. Do daily yoga and pranayama and it will improve your body and mind co- ordination and you will feel more comfortable with yourself. It will boost your immune system and filtered out toxins from your body.
67. Live like a bird and wake up early in the morning and sleep early at night and stay relieved from stress.
68. Walk every day at least 30 to 40 minutes or do exercise in the morning.
69. Make a habit of breathing as deeply as possible, this hard to develop habit will help manage stress.
70. Get enough sleep to rest your body and mind and please note that enough sleep is a must to manage stress.

71. Don't forget to apply at least 10 to 15 golden rules mentioned above, in life.

72. – HA-HA-HA laughter is the best medicine try it.

73. – Read – Comics

74. Watch movies (Human)

**Butler and the brinjal**

COMICS - e.g., -

CALVIN AND HOBBES BY WATTERSON

GARFIELD BY JIM DAVIS

BLONDIE BY DEAN YOUNG AND DENIS LEBRUN

74. Watch movies

(1) Tom and Jerry

(2) Charlie Chaplin

(3) Pogo

(4) Humor Films

**Set your Goals**

**What really matters**

**Stress Management Goal-Setting Plan**

**Practice**

**Take Control**

Helping People Grow

**Happiness doesn't come from doing what we like to do but from liking what we have to do.**

- Wilfred Peterson

# SPIRITUAL NAL HEALING

## Quest & Conquest

*Mukto Sango, naaham baadidhrutyut Saaha Samanwitah,*

*Siddhya Siddhyour Nibikarrah Kartaa Saatwika Uchyate. // 26 //*

*Raagi Karmaphala Prepsur Lubdho Himsatmako' Shuchih.*

*Harsa Shokaanwitah Kartaa Raajasah Pareekirtitah. // 27 //*

*Ayuktah Praakrutah Stabdhah Shatho Naiskrutiko' Lasah.*

*Bisadee Deerghasutri Cha Kartaa Taamasa Uchyate. //28// Ch.18: Gita*

(The doer who is free from attachment, does not speak of 'I'. has steadiness and zeal, unmoved by success and failure, is saatwika. One seeking fruits of works, passionate greedy, harmful, impure, touched by delight and grief, is a Raajasika doer. A doer being unbalanced, vulgar, stubborn, treacherous, malicious, indolent, frustrated and dilatory, is called taamasika).

Accustomed with the day-to-day activities of worldly life one rarely gets a little thinking time for the above established and seasoned truths-the never-shaking and non-controversial wisdoms for elevating the profile of meaningful existence of human race. Unlike the animals, man has been confered powers to discriminate between permanent and temporary, truth and false, and good and bad etc. By transcending the lower tendencies one becomes virtuously human by realising the inherent Divinity within. Schlolarly achievemnets with scriptures cann't reach this level alone, and so a doer with saatwika temperament who sees all beings as one's self is the "Realised" (Aatmabat Sarba Bhuteshu Ya Pashyati Sah Panditah). Self-interest, selfishness, greed, possessiveness and anger etc. are attributes of animals. In the irony of the modern days they have been over-powering the mass, and humanness with kindness, compassion and sympathy has gone awry, and such a plight is a a fair indicator of the prevailing mess. One can scrupulosly avoid becoming theatrical by determined transformation through saatwik Yogic life, concurrent with the guiding principles of Nature.

To be born as a human being is a prospective privilege and is the greatest gift of God. In the present era one has acquired knowledge and wealth but still there is a feeling of lacking is some thing, and these are the divine qualities. Being slave of matters and machiness only man has taken to corruption taste, tongue and tradition. Diversion from kindness and compassion has divested many of mercy and benevolence. One is neither born good nor bad. Obviously in the process of growth one turns virtuous or wicked by the circumstances, the company, the foods and many such factors. By associating with evil characters one trods the path of vices and by resorting to Godly activities he develops a worthy code of conduct and turns fragrant to show lights to others. Shri Sathya Sai Baba said once that every one should feel that God resides in each of his creations, and they must be treated as equals. Thoughts, words and actions should be similar and parallel, even in a very hostile atmosphere,to categorically uphold the validity of moral laws for fruitful existence of mankind. When they are cumbersome and inconvenient people promptly denounce and circumvent them, but the sages and yogis follow the rigorous paths without any submissions to the exceptions in these laws. Once sage Apasthambar saw a man killing a cow. On coming back home he saw same killer infront of his house washing hands and asking for food by ruminating the scrip that a guest should not be turned out as per law. Though perplexe the sage hesitatingly asked him to sit. Listening to further quotations by the criminal about the procedures of respecting a guest the host washed the feet of the visitor and after completing other formalities spread the utensils at a distance. Mentioning other provisions of law he said that they should sit closed to each other and the sage sat drawing only a line of water between them to record his anger Now the evil doer showed his original figure i.e., the lord of Righteousness (*Dharma Devta*), who was pleased to see the proper observations of moral laws.

In the ancient days kings were keen to uphold the laws of virtue and they were conscious of their moral responsibilities. They were aware that by doing wrong they would be disregarded and thrown out. Thus the then administrators followed the principle of handing over responsibilities to succeding younger generations, well in advance, and trained them to run the affairs of the state in a better manner because they had fair perception of the never ending possessive desires of human nature. Such ideologies are frowned upon now because all are after the materialistic pleasures till death. Multiple desires penetrate them incessantly, it is a crying questing as to how to avoid them. It is impossible to relinquish all the needs totally, but they can be kept to a bare minimum only, and thus the singular path for this is to imbibe spiritual knowledge. Great men do not lay emphasis on wealth, and they always work for the welfare of the people. Bees collect the nectar from various flowers to produce honey which is benificially used by man and this is a brilliant lesson for mankind for getting engaged benevolent activities. Nearly five centuries back the great saint poet Purandaredase, considered as the divine ministrel Narada, appealingly sang that the basis of stable happiness was in a life lived in or for God, after he renounced his vast wealth wondering at the hollowness of these worldly possessions. Giving a dip in sacred river can not make on holy. Which is essentially obtainable by inner purity. Another famous saint. Haridasa, outpoured that devotion, knowledge and charity constitute the true 'Bath' which cleanses anyone. Feeding the hungry mass, service to elders and pious persons are highest amongst all virtueous deeds. Therefore duties with ethical values must be performed by all with proper cultural and aesthetic temper to culminate in social good.

Spirituality and morality are formidable necessities for healthy development of human race on this earth. They are the tochstones and best available instruments for efficient blossoming of humanity. Inspite of this brutal truth all are in a rat race for consumerism in the present time aspiring for the high standards of living of developed (so called, materially ?) nations and so with confounded confusions worries are mounting leaps and bounds. Being slave of matter and machines it is becoming impossible to get rid of mental tensions. Many from one spiritual teacher to another, treating their hearts as misical chairs, for some solace and they are performing various kinds of rituals. Instead of such a merry-go-round the wise sees one God whether calling Vishnu, Shiva, Rama, Jesus, Allah, Krisna, Budha, Jina, Zoroaster, or Guru Nanak-it is all the same. The Divine is omnipresent and one must have a Yogic acumen to achieve a steady state of mind versus acquisition of knowledge alone. By simply getting informations the life becomes wasted instead of being purposeful. By practising atleast a fraction of what is learnt from good knowledge one can at self-examination and inner purity. To seek this truth it is not necessary to run to a cost, temple, church or a masjid. What all one has to do is to renounce the earthly luxuries simple living and High thinking) and explore the inner beauty of life. This is the surest way or attaining immortality as revealed by the various scriptures and the hightened souls.

Wealth is not confined to money. Gold or other physical collections. Proper knowledge and skills acquired are also wealths, rather better. A good health, power to think and mental abilities, and utilising time properly are superior wealths. Paving the way towards Satyam-Shivam-Sundaram (Truth, Auspiciousness, Beauty) will roll out the red carpet instantaneously to find the wealthiest fulfillment. A rich crop can be collected when the piece of land is well-ploughed, weeded, manured and good seeds are used. Similarly the field of everybody's heart must be cleared of the weeds of bad thoughts and habits, fertilised by manure of good virtues and feelings, sprayed with seeds of love to harvest the rich crops of wisdom in reality. Or a practitioner of Yoga this is not difficult. In the traditional terms 'Yoga' means joining of 'Jivaatma' with 'Paramaatmaa' — "Yujyate anena Iti Yogah" (Yoga is that which joins). With it there is an expansion of the narrow and constricted ego-ladden personality to an eternal, all-prevasive and blissful (Ananda) state. While making a proliferative contribution about Yoga earlier than 2000 B.C., Patanjali voiced it as a conscious process of gaining irreversible and concrete mastery over the mind through credible practices of 8-fold (Astaanga) combinations of activities, ranging from Yama to Samadhi. Bhagbat Gita (ch.2:53) clearly states:

*"Sruti Viprati Panna Te Yadaa' Sthasyati Nischalaah,*

*Samaadhaa Vachalaa Buddhih Tadaa Yoga Mabapsyasi".*

(On hearing confusing and conflicting words when the mind still remains cool, unpertubed from Samadhi, you reach Yoga.)

Such sacred feeling does not come due to the blockades set by attachment, fear and hatred (Raaga, Bhaya, Dwesha) etc. Sense of attachment appears when one considers that something from outside can give happiness, and not able to look for the joy within, wandering like the dear having the scented kasturi in the navel and never to discover it. From attachment emanates fear-the fear of loosing the external object, landing finally into the realm of hatred (Dwesha). For everybody Yoga can easily throwout these measly gimmicks to hit the target of the target of the sphere of non-attachment (Vairagya). Hence the 3 enemies-Raaga. Be should Dwesha-have to be brought under control by heralding a command over the sense thoughts, the mind, as prefered in Kathopanisada:

*"Taam Yoga Miti Manyate Sthiraam Indriya Dhaarnaam" 2.5.4.*

(Beholding the senses firmly is called Yoga).

Personally development can never be acieved by unidirectional approach. Scores of agencies must be switched on simultaneously for putting the physical, mental, emotional, intellectual and spiritual faculties in to gravitated actions, and all of them are streamined the balanced life-style of Yoga without any controversy, "Will Power" is the biggest attributes to make a dig into this to churn out the perfected human being, encompassing two factors, i.e., 'Creativity' and 'Steadfastness', in its folds. This power is the driving force for mobilising the dyanamics of any task, great or small. "Niti Satakam" Speaks about various types of personal as :

*"Praarabhyate na Bighna Bhayena Nichei.*
*Praarabhya Bighna Bihata Biramanti Madhyaah.*
*Muhurmuhu Rapi Prati Hanyamaanaah,*
*Praarabdha Muttama Janaah Na Parityajanti."*

(The lowest does not start a work fearing obstacles; the middle group starts but leaves in the middle facing obstacles; and the best ones reach the goal despite repeated crushings and tortures).

Thus for the best mind, resulting from Yoga, a hurdle is simply a challange to arouse enormous strength to tackle the situation. Being steady in confrontations such a person braves with composure and transtorms them into golden opportunities. Without a sound spiritual growth i.e. oneness of God, not shabbily differentiating religious rituals, strong physique, highest intellectual calibre cantrolled emotion and supreme creativity are of no avil. Continous meditational experiences provide an introspective inner awarness unfolding the subtle layers of the mind by making an upward move towards the causal state of mind. The sub-stratum of the intellect and the spring of emotions. Notwithstanding the glamors of the external world, flashes of looking into one's inner dimensions come at times to all and many can not trap them due to lack of determination. Given trial one can find the astounding hidden treasure of the magnanimous personally within.

Intellectuality has various hues and so there is always an inherent place for doubts in it. All knowledge are totally useless if one is devoid of the knowledge of the self. Such a person can belabelled as intellectually clever, but can not truly called intellgent. Therefore while having the pursuits for knowledge one must feel the 'Self' in all living creatures, like one's self, though spirituality. So good qualities must be promoted in the learners during the academic basses. In the last few decades science has produced many marvells, but many out of them are in the process of mobilisation for destroying the world. All are now thinking about the dreaded inventions. Never before was it so very assential, as is today, to encourage a responding development of discrimination (Viveka), with a bit of Divine wisdom (Pragnyana), right use of science (Vignyana). A giant spirtual teacher of this centry, Shri P.R.Sarkar hamed as Ananamurti), advocates that spirituality is the absolute goal for human race and to search for it is genuine inellectuality. In his "Progressive Utilisation Theory" (PROUT) he laid down five fundamental principles for universal yogic state for making the world a single happy and divine family They are:

1. No individual should be allowed to accumulate any physical wealth without the clear permission or approval of the collective body.
2. There should be maximum utilisation and rational distribution of all mundane, supra-mundane and spiritual potentialities of the universe.

3. There should be maximum utilisation of physical, metaphysical and spiritual potentialities of unit and collective bodies of human society.
4. There should be proper adjustment amongst these physical, metaphysical,mundane, supra-mundane and spiritual utilisation.
5. There method of utilisation should vary in accordance with changes in time, space and person, and the utilisation should be of progressive nature.

By giving a little attention to these cardinal rules every intellectual can metamorphose to offer perpetual progress by dramatically changing the ridiculous scenario of the present times.

Experimenting with matter only without taking into account the inner consciousness (self) is prodigious technological march leading to annihilation, and so man is away from peace, It can come only by harmonising the body, mind and the spirit which is the corner stone of and therefore everybody has the basic right to perceive and practice it fully. No amount of costly and externeous equipments are needed to justify the benefits accrued because can be subjectively felt. In the progress of practice itself the results can be monitors and follows :

*"Laghutwa Marrogya Muloluptwam Bamaprassdam Swara Sosthabam*

*Gandhah Subho Mutra Purisa Malpam Yoga Prabruttim Prathamaam Badanti.*

*Swetaswatara Upanishada:*

(Light feel, health, thirstless mind, clear complexion, fine voice, agreeable body modest urine and stools, are first signs of entry to Yoga.

In the Hatha Yoga Pradipika (2.78) identical measurement have been elaborates as:

*"Bapur Krushatwam Badane prasannataa Naada Sphutatwam Nayane Sunirmale,*

*Arogota Bindu Jayo' Gnidhi Panam Naadibhih Suddhih Hath Yoga Lakshyanam".*

(Lean body, glowing face, Divine voice, brilliant eyes, diseaseless, sex discharge under control, increased appetite purification of Naadies and fruits of Yoga.)

God is the preceptor of Nature (Prakrit) and hence man should have proper unity (Yoga) with her. Five elements (Panch Tattwa) like Vayu (Air), Aap (Water), Marut (Air), Prithwi (Soil). Tej (Fire) – VAMPT, have been affected by pollution, and they must be purified with priority for seeing the Divine smiles with all. Let all embrace Yogic way of life, irrespective of caste creed, religion and sex, better late than never, with a determination of conquest for preserving and continuing a Godly life for posterity, free from unhappiness and miseries.

"Aano Bhadrah Kratawo Yantu Bishwatah"

(Let nobte thoughts come to all from all sides)

*Om Shanti ! Om Shanti ! Om Shanti !*

*(Let peace pervade everywhere)*

## A word of caution

All the therapies discussed in the book are scientific in nature. Do consult the Doctor, therapist, experts or specialist, on the subject before practising the therapies, are also for medical guidance. Some of the therapies mentioned in the book may not suit your needs.

For any help consult your family physician always.

# CHAPTER 21

# Self Assessment – Stress Audit

## QUESTIONS TO ASK YOURSELF

Q. 1. What aspects of my work am I passionate about?

Q. 2. What is my purpose at work, and what do I hope to achieve in my career?

Q. 3. How could I make work more enjoyable, rather than viewing it as a chore?

Q. 4. How could I be more creative at work?

Q. 5. How could I make more of a difference at work?

Q. 6. Is there a better attitude I could approach my work with?

Q. 7. Why am I feeling anxious and what can I do to alleviate the feeling?

Q. 8. What is the root cause of this anxiety?

Q. 9. Would it help to talk to someone about this?

It is useful to divide stress inducers into three broad categories. First, there are setbacks which are significant life-events about which there is often little we can do. Examples of setbacks include serious illness to ourselves or those close to us, or redundancy.

Second, there are hassles. Theses are situations which we have not been proactive in bringing about and in many cases are ones we most definitely wish were not happening. These cover a wide range of situations from the hard disk on our computer 'crashing ' to the organisation announcing a far-reaching change programme.

Third, there are what we shall describe as challenges which are largely sought after or welcomed. An example might be an interview for a new, exciting and well-paid job. It is something we have actively wanted but it is nevertheless going out put us into a situation which is full of pressure.

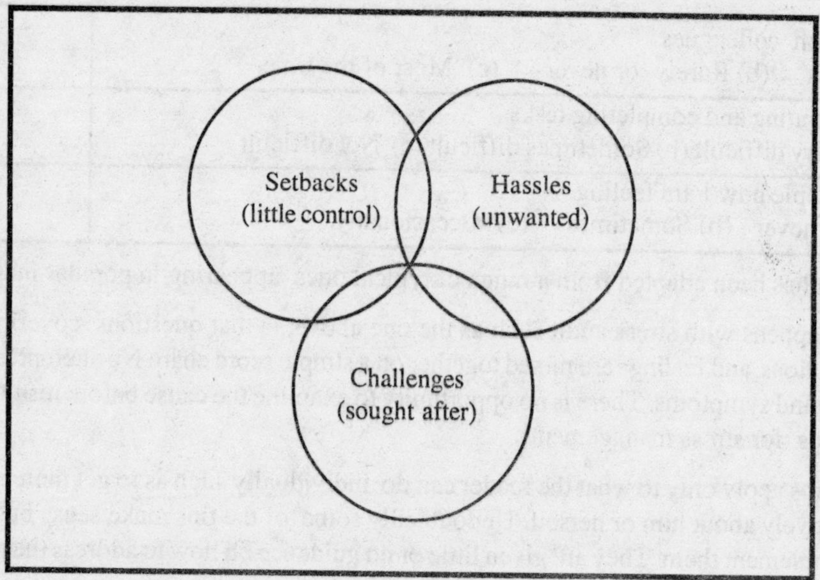


The diagram above is a helpful analytical tool bearing in mind.

The differences between individuals mentioned in Part I of this Workbook. When someone is feeling under pressure from a number of sources and therefore less able to cope. The challenge of that job interview may feel more like a severe hassle. The hassle of the announced change programme may be perceived as a major setback.

It can work the other way too. If you are feeling on top of things then the setback of sudden redundancy may become an exciting challenge of trying something new, especially if there is a good financial package with the new job.

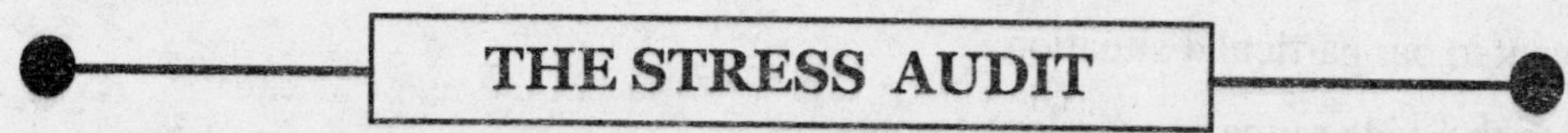

## THE STRESS AUDIT

The important first step in dealing with stress is to understand what is causing it in the first place. The process s is called a stress audit. You will find popular stress audits in the pages of many magazines.

### Are you pushing yourself too hard?

The children were late for school, the computer won't print out the vital document and you haven't had time for lunch or to prepare for your performance review in ten minutes.

No wonder we get stressed out ! But are you the type who soldiers on always putting everyone else first ?

James Pilkington, our resident psychologist, invites you to slow down for a moment and think about yourselves. His practical stress audit will tell you whether you are simply 'Pushing Yourself Too Hard.'

| | a | b | c |
|---|---|---|---|
| 1. I get headaches<br>(a) Often (b) Rarely (c) Occasionally. | | | |
| 2. As a worker I feel I am a failure<br>(a) Rarely or never (b) Sometimes (c) Often. | | | |
| 3. I get to sleep quickly and have a good night's rest.<br>(a) Rarely or never (b) Usually (c) Always | | | |
| 4. I get attacks of giddiness and sickness<br>(a) Hardly ever (b) Occasionally (c) Frequently | | | |
| 5. I have recently changed jobs, moved house, got married, got divorced<br>(a) All of the above (b) One or two of these (c) None | | | |

| | | | |
|---|---|---|---|
| 6. I am angry with colleagues<br>(a) Sometimes (b) Rarely or never (c) Most of the time | | | |
| 7. I find concentrating and completing tasks<br>(a) Usually very difficult (b) Sometimes difficult (c) Not difficult | | | |
| 8. I tell other people how I am feeling<br>(a) Rarely or never (b) Sometimes (c) Occasionally. | | | |

This stress audit has been adapted from a range of typical ones appearing in popular magazines and journals.

What usually happens with stress audit such as the one above, is that questions covering symptoms, events, stress inducers, perceptions and feelings are mixed together on a simple score chart. No attempt is made to differentiate between or to understand symptoms. There is no opportunity to examine the cause before results are givens followed by a list of 'handy tips for stress management'.

Inevitably, the tips apply only to what the reader can do individually such as to get more sleep, take up jogging or start thinking positively about him or herself. Undoubtedly some of the tips make sense but people reading them may feel unable to implement them. They are given little or no guidance on how to address the pressures arising from their working situation or how to prevent stress in the future.

Such approaches are simplistic. Minimal learning takes place and acting is rare. They may also increase anxiety or feeling or helplessness.

## CREATING A USEFUL STRESS AUDIT

If a stress audit is to have real value it should:

1. carefully separate and analyse stress inducers and symptoms
2. be relevant to our particular situation
3. recognise the wide range of reactions to pressure
4. be based on self-knowledge
5. acknowledge our changing life circumstances
6. identify existing good habits
7. generate clear action plans
8. emphasise the importance of helping each other

*The authors of this book cannot write a stress audit applicable to the situation of every reader. However, what we will do is invite you to create your own audit after reading this book.*

*Please remember all the therapies discussed in the boook are tested world-wide. But you must consult a specialist (doctor) or your physician before starting you treatment and de-stressing.*

### Analysing Personality

Research has shown that certain types of people are more prone to stress and its by-products, such as heart disease. If you are an ambitious manager who is extremely competitive, fast in thought, speech, and action, committed, impatient, and pressed for time you are likely to be a Type A personality – at risk from stress. If you are more placid, you are less at risk and classed as Type B. Type A managers may also be tense egotists who lack self-control and are quick to anger. If you fit the type A pattern, modify your behaviour to reduce the chances and incidence of stress.

Characteristics of Type A Personality

- Always moves, walks and eats rapidly
- Feels impatient with the pace of things, hurries others, dislikes waiting
- Does several things at once
- Feels guilty when relaxing
- Tries to schedule more and more in less and less time
- Uses nervous gestures such as clenched fist, banging hand on table
- Does not have time to enjoy life

Type B's, on the other hand, work at a steadier pace. They do not work against the clock. They set reasonable targets for themselves and do not feel the pressure. They are likely to 'let things roll off their backs' rather than fight every issue. Some, of the typical characteristics of Type B ipersonalities may be stated thus:

Characteristics of Type B Personality

- Is not concerned about time
- Is patient
- Does not brag
- Plays for fun, not to win
- Relaxes without guilt
- Has no pressing deadlines
- Is mild mannered
- Is never in a hurry

The Type A could be compared to a racehorse and the type B to a turtle. Though the recent studies question the relationship between Type A behaviour pattern and stress, it has been generally agreed that Type A's are more prone to stress than Type B's.

## Identifying your personality type

Read through the following questions. The more "yes" answers you give, the closer you are to the Type A personality. You can reduce your stress levels by adopting the opposite, or Type B behaviour. For example, if you walk and eat rapidly, make a conscious effort to slow down. Do you:

1. Feel a constant pressure to get things done?
2. Often compete against the clock?
3. Always hurry?
4. Make decisions quickly?
5. Get restless and impatient with being idle?
6. Speak fast?
7. Always arrive on time?
8. Think about and do several things at the same time?
9. Move, walk, and eat rapidly?
10. Often get impatient?

11. See yourself as very ambitious?
12. In conversation, display brisk and impatient body movements; taut facial muscles; fist-clenching; explosive and hurried speech patterns; or a lack of bodily relaxation?

## Using stress positively

A crisis can descend out of the blue, or build up over months. It can affect everyone in an organisation, or may be entirely personal, but it is important not to allow yourself to slump into despair. In fact, you can turn the stress of a crisis to your advantage. Because stress raises your levels of adrenaline, you can harness that extra energy to resolve the emergency successfully, if that is feasible. Begin by assessing what can actually be done and whether the crisis can be cured. Then start on a no-holds-barred effort to recover from the disaster. You will benefit from the healthy stress of constructive achievement under pressure.

The following is a complete stress audit based on the three separate sections developed in the Workbook.

## STRESS AUDIT – Part One : Inducers

### Section one: Setbacks

Make a list of the setbacks you are currently facing or have faced in the last 1 year.

**1 - 6 months -**

______________________________

______________________________

______________________________

______________________________

**7 - 12 months -**

______________________________

______________________________

______________________________

### Section two: Hassels

Environmental hassles:

List the hassles you regularly face in relation to your working environment under the given headings.

Unfriendly Physical features ______________________________

______________________________

Internal physiological states ______________________________

______________________________

Social contact ______________________________

______________________________

Travel ______________________________

______________________________

Information flow ______________________________

______________________________

Work pattern ______________________________

______________________________

## Section three: Challenges

Challenges ____________________ ____________________

____________________ ____________________

____________________ ____________________

Overall pressure level

Position yourself on the continuum line below taking into account all the setbacks, hassles and challenges you are facing. We suggest you return to this three or four times over a couple of days to produce an average estimate.

Too Low — Low — Optimal — High — Too high

Now record the level pf pressure created by the cultural hassles you face. Mark the level (high, medium or low)- for each issue and create your own graph by linking the points.

## Cultural hassles

Record level of pressure created by the cultural hassles you face.

| | Low | Medium | High |
|---|---|---|---|
| Change | | | |
| Conflict | | | |
| Confusion | | | |
| Constraints | | | |
| Constant demand | | | |
| Contractual Worries | | | |
| Control | | | |
| Career development | | | |
| Others | | | |

## Stress Audit – Part Two : symptoms

| Physiological Symptoms (Audit Questions) | | | | |
|---|---|---|---|---|
| Nail biting | Yes | No | Comments | Remarks |
| Dry mouth | | | | |
| Weight loss or gain | | | | |
| Heart-pounding | | | | |
| Dry skin | | | | |
| Bruxism (teeth – grinding) | | | | |
| Headache | | | | |

| | Yes | No | Comments | Remarks |
|---|---|---|---|---|
| Clenched fists | | | | |
| Increase or decrease in appetite | | | | |
| Tight shoulders | | | | |
| Frequent urination | | | | |
| Diarrhoea or constipation | | | | |
| Neck pain | | | | |
| Back pain | | | | |
| Nervous twitch | | | | |
| **Emotional Symptoms (Audit Questions)** | | | | |
| Mood swings | | | | |
| Hostility | | | | |
| Anxiety | | | | |
| Insomnia | | | | |
| Crying easily | | | | |
| Apathy | | | | |
| Depression | | | | |
| Decreased sex drive | | | | |
| Anger | | | | |
| Hopelessness | | | | |
| Fear | | | | |
| Withdrawn | | | | |
| **Cognitive Symptoms (Audit Questions)** | | | | |
| **Over alertness** | | | | |
| Anxious | | | | |
| Unable to focus | | | | |
| Intrusive thoughts | | | | |
| **Under - alertness** | | | | |
| Foggy thinking | | | | |
| Day-dreaming | | | | |
| Prone to errors | | | | |
| Disorganized | | | | |
| Forgetfulness | | | | |
| Decreased alertness | | | | |
| **Distorted thinking** | | | | |
| Hostility | | | | |

| Polarized thinking | | | | |
|---|---|---|---|---|
| Personalisation | | | | |
| Minimization and magnification | | | | |
| **Behavioural Symptoms (Audit Questions)** | | | | |
| **Over alertness** | | | | |
| Easily started | | | | |
| Sleeplessness | | | | |
| Increased speed of talking | | | | |
| **Under – alertness** | | | | |
| Decreased exercise | | | | |
| Lack of social interest | | | | |
| Withdrawal | | | | |
| **Escapes** | | | | |
| Increased smoking | | | | |
| Increased sugar or fat intake | | | | |
| Increased alcohol and drug use | | | | |

**Note -** Use seperate sheets where required for self analysis work.

**KEEP/CHANGE AUDIT – Part A: Physical and Mental Well – being**

| Keep | Change |
|---|---|
| 1. | |
| 2. | |
| 3. | |
| 4. | |

**KEEP/CHANGE AUDIT – Part B: Obtaining and Giving Support**

| Keep | Change |
|---|---|
| 1. | |
| 2. | |
| 3. | |
| 4. | |

**KEEP/CHANGE AUDIT – Part C: Being Assertive**

| Keep | Change |
|---|---|
| 1. | |
| 2. | |
| 3. | |
| 4. | |

**KEEP/CHANGE AUDIT – Part D: Learning to Relax**

| Keep | Change |
|---|---|
| 1. | |
| 2. | |
| 3. | |
| 4. | |

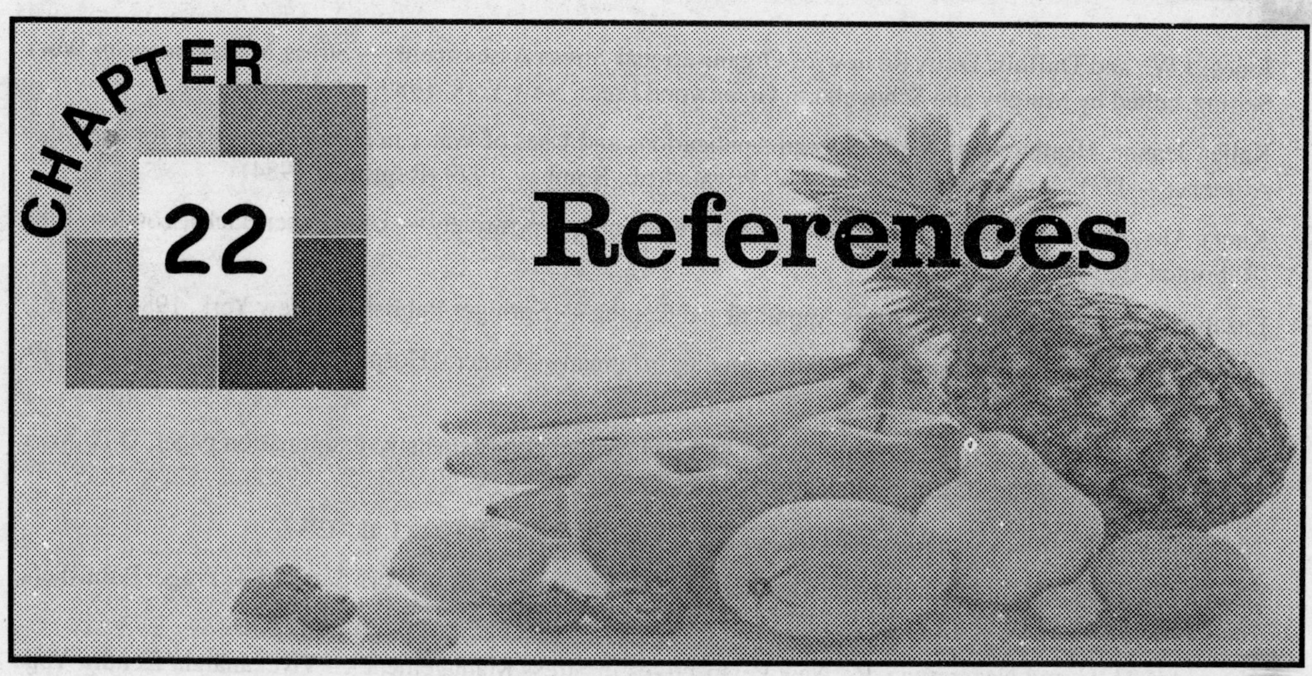


# References

Ashton, David, Corporate Health Care Revolution, Strategies for Preventive Medicine at Work — Institute of Personnel Management — Kogan Page Ltd., London, 1989.

Ashton, D. and Davies, B., Why Exercise — Basil Blackwell Ltd., Oxford, UK, 1986.

Bhole, M.V., Psycho-Physiological importance of some yoga practices — Paper presented at the International Seminar on Stress in Health and Diseases. Banaras Hindu University, Varanasi, Feb. 1977.

Caplan, R.D., Cobb, S., French, J.R.P., Van Harrison, R., and Pinneau, S.R., Job Demands and Worker Health — US Department of Health, Education and Welfare Publication, No. (NIOSH) 1975, pp. 75-160.

Cerney, J.V., Acupuncture without Needles — D.B. Taraporewala Sons & Co. Private Ltd., Bombay, 1977 (Reprinted 1985).

Cohen, A., and Margolis, B., Initial psychological related to Occupational Safety and Health Act of 1970 — American Psychologist 28, 1973, pp. 600-606.

Coleman, V., Life Without Tranquillizers — Judy Piatkus (Publishers) Ltd., London, 1985.

Cooper, C.L., Psychosocial Stress and Cancer — John Wiley & Sons, UK, 1984.

Cooper, C.L., and Marshall, J., Occupational Sources of Stress: A review of the literature relating to coronary heart disease and mental ill-health — *Journal of Occupational Psychology* 49, 1976, pp. 11-28.

Dash, Bhagwan, Massage Therapy in Ayurveda — Concept Publishing Co., Delhi, 1992.

Fontana, David, Managing Stress — BPS Books, Routledge, London, 1989.

Fulder, Stephen, The Handbook of Complementary Medicine — Coronet Books, UK, 1989.

Hales, D., Psycho-immunity — Science Digest, November, 1981, pp. 12-18.

House, J., Occupational Stress and Coronary Heart Diseases: A review and theoretical integration — *Journal of Health and Social Behaviour*, 15, 1974, pp. 12-27.

Jaggi, Dr. O.P., Mental Tension and its Cure — Orient Paper Backs, Bombay, 1974, (Reprinted 1990).

Jones, J.W., and DuBois, D., A Review of Organisational Stress Assessment — Stress Management in Work Setting, edited by Murphy and Schoenborn, Greenwood Press, New York, 1989, pp. 45-61.

Keller, Jeanne, Healing with Water: Special Applications and Uses of Water in Home Remedials for everyday Ailments — D.B. Taraporewala Sons & Co., Private Ltd., Bombay, 1979 (Reprinted 1984).

Kirsta, Alix, The Book of Stress Survival — How to relax and live positively — Unix Paper Backs, London, 1986 (Reprinted 1989).

Lazarus, R.S., and Folkman, S., Stress Appraisal and Coping — Springer Publishing, New York, 1984.

Locke, S.E., Stress, Adaptation and immunity: Studies in human — General Hospital, Psychiatry, 1982, 4, pp. 49-58.

Mathew, V.J., Job stress of a creative manager — FPM written comprehensive examination paper, O.B. Area, Indian Institute of Management, Ahmedabad.

Montgomery, Dr. Bob, Coping with Stress, — A.H. Wheeler & Co., Private Ltd., 1987.

Murphy, Lawrence R., and Schoenbore, Theodore F., Stress Management in Work Settings — Prager Publishers, New York, 1989.

Nagendra, H.R., and Nagarathna, R., New Perspectives in Stress Management — Vivekananda Kendra Yoga Research Foundation, Bangalore, 1988.

Naidu, R.K., and Pande, N., On Quantifying a Spiritual Concept: An Interim research report about Non-attachment and Health — Paper presented at the National Seminar on Mental Health and Stress, Bhopal, March, 1988.

Poddar, P.P., Gangwal, K.M., Vinod, S.D., and Palsane, M.N., Psychological Management of Essential Hypertension — Poona University, Pune, 1984.

Palsanem, M.N., Bhavsar, S.N., Goswami, R.P., Evans, G.W., The concept of stress in the Indian tradition — *Journal of Indian Psychology*, 5(1), 1986.

Pelletiar, Kenneth, R., Healthy people in unhealthy places — Stress and Fitness at work — Dell Publishing Company, New York, 1984.

Pestonjee, D.M., Executive Stress: Should it always be avoided — Vikalpa 12(1), 1987a, pp. 23-30.

Pestonjee, D.M., Stress and Coping: The Indian Experience — Saga Publications, New Delhi, 1992.

Pestonjee, D.M., and Singh, G.P., Organisational Behaviour Issue for Managers and Systems Analysis — Indian Institute of Management, Ahmedabad, Working Paper No. 650, 1987.

Poppen, Roger, Behavioural Relaxation Training and Assessment — Pergamon Press, UK, 1988.

Rai, S.D., Deshpande, P.J., and Udupa, K.N., Neurohumoral Response to Traumatic Stress and its management by an Indian indigenous drug — Paper presented at the International Seminar on Stress in Health and Diseases, Banaras Hindu University, Varanasi, 1977.

Sahasi, G.D., and Kacker, C., Effectiveness of yogic techniques in the management of Anxiety — Journal of Personality and Clinical Studies, 5(1), 1989, pp. 51-55.

Saks, Mike, Alternative Medicine in Britain, — 1991.

Sahoo, Dr. Bhabani, Prasad, Handbook of Recent Acupuncture treatment and research — Deep Prakashan, Kolkata, 1992.

Santwani, Dr. M.T., Magnet Therapy for common diseases — Hind Pocket Books, Delhi, 1982.

Saraswati, Dr. Swami, Karmananda, Yoga and Cardiovascular Management — Bihar School of Yoga, Munger, India, 1984.

Saraswati, Swami Satyananda, Meditations from the Tantras — Bihar School of Yoga, Munger, India, 1983.

Saraswati, Dr., Swami, Shankardevananda, The effects of Yoga on Hypertension — Bihar School of Yoga, Munger, India, 1984.

Seligman, M.E., Helplessness: On depression development and Death — San Francisco: W.H. Freeman, 1975.

Selye, H., A syndrome produced by diversenoxious agents — Nature 138, 1936, p. 32.

Selye, H., The general adaptation syndrome and diseases of adaptation — *Journal of Clinical Endocrinolgoy*, 6, 1946, pp. 217-230.

Selye, H., The Stress of Life — McGraw-Hill, New York, 1956.

Selye, H., Selye's Guide to Stress — Research Vol. I, Van Nostrand Reinhold, London, 1980.

Singh, R.H., Sinha, B.N., Mehta, A.K., Malaviya, P.C., Singh, L., Sarkar, F.H., and Udupa, K.N., Studies on Psychotropic effect of some indigenous drugs — Paper presented at the International Seminar on stress in Health and Diseases, Banaras Hindu University, Varanasi February, 1977.

Singh, R.H., and Udupa, K.N., Psychobiological studies on certain Hatha Yogic Practices — Paper presented at the International Seminar on Stress in Health and Diseases, Banaras Hindu University, Varanasi, February, 1977.

Thompson, Jane, H., Spiritual Consideration in the Prevention, Treatment and Cure of Diseases — Oriel Press, London, 1984.

Tollison, David, C., and Tollison, Joseph, W., Headache: A Multimodel Programme for Relief — Sterling Publishing Co. Inc., New York, 1982.

Toon, Dr., Peter, Brown, Hedley and Jarrett, Paul, Your Heart and Lungs — Galgotia Publications Pvt. Ltd., New Delhi, 1991.

Toon, Dr., Peter, Tripp, Penny and Evans, Mark, Your Mind — Galgotia Publications Pvt. Ltd., New Delhi, 1991.

Turner, Roger Newman, Naturopathic Medicine (Treating the whole person the principles and practices of Naturopathy) — Thomsons Publishing Group, UK, 1990.

Udupa, K.N., Singh, R.H., and Dwivedi, K.N., Biochemical studies on Meditation — Paper presented at the International Seminar on Stress in Health and Diseases, Banaras Hindu University, Varanasi, February, 1977.

Varma, M.D., Singh, R.H., Gupta, J.P. and Udupa, K.N., A study on stress factors in Peptic ulcers and its treatment with an Indian indigenous drug — Paper presented at the International Seminar on Stress in Health and Diseases, Banaras Hindu University, Varanasi, February, 1977.

Visintainer, M.A., Volpicelli, J.R., and Seligam, M.E., Tumour rejection in rats after inescapabile or escapable shock — Science, April 23, 1982, pp. 216, pp. 437-439.

Weikang, FU, The story of Chinese Acupuncture and Moxibustion — Foreign Languages Press, Beijing, 1986.

Whiteside, Good nutrition for long life, 1991.

Adams, J.D. (1986) : *Understanding and Managing Stress,* San Diego, University Associates.

Ahmad, B. (1990) : *Black Perspectives in Social Work*, Birmingham, Venture Press.

Allan, M., Bhavnani, R. and French, K. (1992) : : *Promoting Women*, London, HMSO.

Andrisani, P.J. and Nestel, G. (1976) : 'Internal-External Control as a Contributor to, and Outcome of Work Experience, *Journal of Applied Psychology*, 61.

Argyle, M. (1989) : *The Social Psychology of Work*, Harmondsworth, Penguin.

Arnold, H.J. and Feldman, D.C. (1982) : 'A Multi-Variant Analysis of the Determinants of Job Turnover', *Journal of Applied Psychology*, 67(3).

Aroba, T. and James, K. (1987) : *Pressure at Work*: A Survival Guide, London, McGraw-Hill.

Atkinson, R.L., Atkinson, R.C. and Hilgard, E. R. (1983) : *Introduction to Psychology*, New York, Harcourt Brace Jovanovich.

Audit Commission (1985) : *Good Management in Local Government*, London, HMSO.

Back, K. and Back, K. (1982) : *Assertiveness at Work : A Practical Guide to Handling Awkward Situations,* London, McGraw-Hill.

Bandura, A. (1977) : *A Social Learning Theory,* Englewood Cliffs, N.J., Prentice-Hall.

Barclay Committee, (1982) : *Social Workers : Their Role and Tasks*, London, Bedford Square Press.

Barker, P. (1986) : *Basic Family Therapy*, Oxford, Basil Blackwell.

Bate, P. (1992) : 'The Impact of Organisational Culture on Approaches to Organisational Problem-Solving', in Salaman, (1992).

Berge, P. (1996) : *Invitation to Sociology*, Harmondsworth, Penguin.

Berkowitz, A.D.and Perkins, H.W. (1984) : 'Stress among Farm Women : Work and Family as interacting Systems', *Journal of Marriage and Family,* 46.

Braike, H.B. (1986) : *'The Stress of Success', Working Woman*, August, 1986.

Bramhall, M. and Ezell, S. (1981) : *'How Burned out are You?', Public Welfare*, Winter, 1981.

Breakwell, G. (1989) : *Facing Physical Violence*, London, Rutledge.

Brown, A. (1984) : *Consultation*, London, Heinemann.

Buck, V. (1972) : *Working under Pressure,* London, Staples Press.

Burnard, P. (1991) : *Coping with Stress in the Health Professions*, London, Chapman & Hall.

Burnout Study and Support Group (1986) : 'Less Sympathy for Women', *Social Work Today, 17.*

Cabinet Office (1987) : *Understanding Stress, Part One: A Line Manager's Guide,* London, HMSO.

Cade, B. (1983) : 'Snuffed Out Fire Within', *Social Work Today,* 11 January, 1983.

Caplan, G. (1961) : *A Community Approach to Mental Health,* London, Tavistock.

Caplan, G. (1967) : 'The Family as a Support System', in Caplan and Killea (1967).

Caplan, G. and Killea, M. (eds) (1967) : *Support Systems and Mutual Help,* New York, Grune & Stratton.

Carkhuff, R.R. and Berenson, B.C. (1977) : *Beyond Counselling and Therapy,* 2nd edn, New York, Holt, Rinehart & Winston.

CCETSW, (1991) : *One Small Step Towards Racial Justice,* London, CCETSW.

CD Project Steering Group (eds) (1991) : *Setting the Context for Change,* London, CCETSW.

Centre for Occupational Studies (1991) : 'Code of Practice for Staff-care in the Health and Social Services', Keele University of Keele/LGTB.

Cherniss, C., (1980) : *Staff Burnout; Job Stress in the Human Services,* London, Sage.

Cherniss, C., Egnatios, E., Wacker, S. and O'Dowd, W. (1979) : 'The Professional Mystique and Burnout in Public Sector Professionals', unpublished paper, University of Michigan, Ann Arbor.

Clark J., (1988) : *Social Work: The Personal and the Political*, Open University, Unit 13 of D 211, Social Problems and Social Welfare.

Clarke, M and Stewart, J., (1988) : *Managing Tomorrow,* Luton, LGTB.

Cohen, S. and Willis, T.A., (1985) : 'Stress Social Support and the Buffering Hypothesis', *Psychological Bulletin, 98.*

Colman, V. (1988) : *Stress Management Techniques*, London, Mercury Business Paperbacks.

Cooper, C.L. and Davidson, M., (1982) : *High Pressure : Working Lives of Women Managers,* London, Fontana.

Cooper, C.L. and Makin, P. (eds.), (1984) : *Psychology for Managers,* London, Macmillan.

Cooper, C.L. and Marshall, J., (1976) : 'Occupational Sources of Stress: A Review of the Literature Relating to Coronary Heart Disease and Mental Health', *Journal of Occupational Psychology, 49.*

Cooper, C.L. and Payne, R., (1980) : *Current Concerns in Occupational Stress,* London, Wiley.

Cooper, C.L. and Payne, R. (eds.), (1988) : *Causes, Coping and Consequences of Stress at Work*, London, Wiley.

Cooper, C.L. Cooper, R.D. and Baker, L. (eds.), (1988) : *Living with Stress,* Harmondsworth, Penguin.

Corby, B., (1989) : *Working with Child Abuse*, Buckingham, Open University Press.

Cousins, J., (1991) : 'Take Charge', *Social Work Today*, 31 October, 1991.

Coulshed, V., (1990) : *Management in Social Work,* London, Macmillan.

Cox, T. (1987) : 'Stress, Coping and Problem-solving', *Work and stress,* 1 (1).

Crouter, A.C. (1984) : 'Spill Over from Family to Work: The Neglected Side of the Work-Family Interface', *Human Relations, 37.*

Dale, P., Davies, M., Morrison, T. and Waters, J. (1986) : *Dangerous Families,* London, Routledge.

Devison, G.C. and Neale, J.H., (1986) : *Abnormal Psychology*, New York, Wiley.

DOH (Department of Health) (1991a) : *Child Abuse: A Study of Inquiry Reports,* 1980-1989, London, HMSO.

DOH (Department of Health) : (1991b) : *The Children Act, 1989 Guidance and Regulation, Volume 4: Residential Care*, London, HMSO.

DOH (Department of Health) (1991c) : *Working Together under the Children Act, 1989,* London, HMSO.

Dominelli, L. (1989) : 'An Uncaring Profession? An Examination of Racism in Social Work', *New Community, 15(3).*

Dunham, J. (1988) : 'Review of the Stress Research Literature in Three Helping Occupations', in Mcdermetan (1988).

Edelwich, J. and Brodsky, A. (1980) : *Burn-out : Stage of Disillusionment in the Helping* Professions, New York, Human Sciences Press.

Etzioni, E. (ed.) (1969) : *The Semi-professions and their Organisation,* New York, Free Press.

Ferns, P. (1987) : 'The Dangerous Delusion', *Community Care,* 8 January 1987.

Fielder, F.E. (1967) : *A Theory of Leadership Effectiveness,* New York, McGraw-Hill.

Fineman, S. (1985) : *Social Work Stress and Intervention*, Aldershot, Gower.

Fogarty, M. (1987) : 'Women Social Workers Talking…', *Social Work Today,* 26 October 187.

Folkman, S. (1984) : 'Personal Control and Stress and Coping Processes: A Theoretical Analysis', *Journal of Personality and Social Psychology, 46.*

Folkman. S. and Lazarus, R.S. (1980) : 'An Analysis of Coping in a Middle-aged Community Sample', *Journal of Health and Social Behaviour, 21.*

Folkman, S., Lazarus, R.S., Dunkel-Schetter, C., Delonigis, A. and Gruen, R.J. (1986) : 'Dynamics of a Stressful Encounter: Cognitive Appraisal, Coping, and Encounter Outcomes', *Journal of Personality and Social Psychology*, 50.

Frankl, V.E. (1973) : *Psychotherapy and Existentialism*, Harmondsworth, Penguin.

Freud, S. (1973) : *New Introductory Lectures on Psycho-analysis*, Standard Edition 22, London, Hogarth Press.

Freudenberger, H. (1975) : 'Staff Burnout', *Journal of Social Issues*, 30(1).

Gale, H. de (1991) : '*Black Students' Views of Existing CQSW Courses and CSS Schemes: 2*', in CD project Steering Group (1991).

George, L.K. (1989) : '*Stress, Social Support and Depression over the Life-Course*', in Markides and Cooper (1989).

Gibson, F., McGrath, A. and Reid, N. (1989) : '*Occupational Stress in Social Work*', British Journal of Social Work, 19.

Girdano, D.A., Everly, G.S. and Dusk, D. (1990) : *Controlling Stress and Tension*, New York, Prentice-Hall.

Goldstein, H. (1973) : *Social Work Practice; A Unitary Approach*, Carolina, University of South Carolina Press.

Gore, S. (1978) : "The Effect of Social Support in Moderating the Health Consequences of Unemployment', Journal *of Health and Social Behaviour, 19.*

Guteck, B., Repetti, R. and Silver, D. (1988) : 'Non–work Roles and Stress at work', in Cooper and Payne (1988).

Hackman, J.K. and Oldham, G.R. (1980) : *Work Design,* Reading, Mass., Addison-Wesley.

Hall, S. (1980) : 'Race, Articulation and Societies Structured in Dominance', in UNESCO, (1980).

Handy, C. (1985) : *Understanding Organisations,* Harmondsworth, Penguin.

Hanmer, J and Statham D. (1988) : *Women and Social Work*, London, Macmillan.

Harper, J. and Murphy, M. (1993) : 'Child Protection Work : A Case for Multi-Disciplinary Staff Care', unpublished paper.

Haynes, S. and Feinleib, M. (1982) : 'Women, Work and Cornary Heart Disease: Prospective Findings from the Framingham Heart Study', *American Journal of Public Health, 70.*

Heather, N. (1976) : *Radical Perspectives in Psychology,* London, Methuen.

Hemsley, J. (1986) : 'Slow to Come Forward', *Community Care,* 5 June, 1986.

Hickson, D.J., Butler, R.J., Cray, D., Mallory, G.R. and Wilson, D.C. (1986) : *Top Decisions; Strategic Decision-Making in Organisations, Oxford, Basil Blackwell.*

Hobfall S.E. (1988) : *The Ecology of Stress*, New York, Hemisphere

Holmes, T.H. and Rahe, R.H. (1967) : 'The Social Readjustment Rating Scale', *Journal of Psychosomatic Research, II.*

Hopkins, J. (1987a) : 'Meeting the Care and Needs of Staff in the PSS', *Social Work Today,* 16 November, 1987.

Hopson, B. (1984) : 'Transition: Understanding and Managing Personal Change', in Cooper and Makin, (1984).

House, J.S. (1981) : *Social Support and Stress,* Reading, Mass., Addison-Wesley.

Howe, D. (1986a) : *Social Workers and their Practice in Welfare Bureaucracies, Aldershot, Gower.*

Howe, D. (1986b) : 'The Segregation of Women and Their Task in the Personal Social Services', *Critical Social Policy, 15.*

Hugman, R. (1991) : *Power in Caring Professions,* London, Macmillan.

Hutchinson-Reis, M. (1989) : "And for Those of Us who are Black ?" Black Politics in Social Work', in Langan and Lee (1989).

John, G. (1991) : "Taking Sides" Objectives and Strategies in the Development of Anti-Racist Work in Britain', in CD Project Steering Group (1991).

Johnstone, J.H. and Sarason, I.G. (1978) : 'Lifestress, Depression and Anxiety: Internal-External Locus of Control as a Moderator Variable', *Journal of Psychosomatic Research, 22.*

Jones, F., Fletcher, B.C. and Ibbetson, K. (1991) : 'Stressors and Strains amongst Social Workers : Demands, Supports, Constraints and Psychological Health', *British Journal of Social Work, 21.*

Judd, D. (1992) : 'Psychic Trauma in Response to Life-threatening illness', paper presented at the Second International Conference on Children and Death, Edinburgh.

Kadushin, A. (1974) : *Child Welfare Services,* New York, Macmillan.

Kahn, R.L., Wolfe D.M. Quinn, R.P., Snoek, J.D. and Rosenthal, R.A. (1964) : *Organisational Stress: Studies in Role Conflict and Ambiguity,* New York, Wiley.

Kanter.R.M. (1983) : *The Change Masters,* London Unwin.

Kearns, J. (1986) : *Stress at Work : The Challenge Master*, London, Unwin.

Kearns, J. (1986) : Stress at Wok : The Challenge of Change, London, BUPA.

Kendall, P.C. (ed.) (1986) : *Advances in Cognitive-Behavioural Research and Therapy: Vol. 5,* New York, Academic Press.

Kirschner, D.A. and Kirschner, S. (1986) : *Comprehensive Family Therapy: An integration of Systematic and Psychodynamic Models, New York, Bruner.*

Kline, P. (1972) : *Fact and Fiction in Freudian Theory,* London, Methuen.

Kobasa, S.C. (1979) : 'Stressful Life-Events, Personality, Health : An Enquiry into Hardiness', *Journal of Personality and Social Psychology, 37.*

Kobasa, S.C. Maddi, S.R. and Kahn, S. (1982) : 'Hardiness and Health: A Prospective Study' *Journal of Personality and Social Psychology,* 42.

Kobasa, S.C. and Puccetti, M.C. (1983) : 'Personality and Social Resources in Stress Resistance, *Journal of Personality and Social Psychology,* 45.

Laing, R.D. (1971) : *The Politics of the Family,* Hardiness Penguin.

Langan, M. (1992) : 'Introduction', in Langan and Day, (1992).

Langan, M. and Day, L. (eds.) (1992) *: Women, Oppression and Social Work*, London Routledge.

Langan, M. and Lee, P. (eds.) (1989) : Radical Social Work Today, London, Unwin Hyman.

Lawrence, M. (1992) : 'Women's Psychology and Feminist Social Work Practice', in Langan and Day (1992) :.

Lazarus, R.S. (1996) : *Psychological Stress and the Coping Process,* New York, Springer.

Lazarus, R.S. and Folkman, S. (1986) *: Stress, Appraisal and Coping,* New York, Springer.

Levy, P. and Kahan, B. (1991) *: The Pindown Experience*, Staffordshire County Council.

LGTB (1988) *: Going for Better Management*, London, Local Government Training Board.

Looker, T. and Gregson, O. (1989) *: Stresswise,* Seven Oaks, Hodder & Stoughton.

Lupton, C. (1992) : ' Feminism, Managerialism and Performance Measurement', in Langan and Day (1992).

Maddi, S.R. and Kobasa, S.C. (1984) *: The Hardy Executive : Health under Stress,* Homewood III, Dow Jones Irwin.

Markides, K. and Cooper, C.L. (eds.) : (1989) : *Ageing, Stress and Health*, New York, Wiley.

Martin, R.A. and Lefcourt, H.M. (1983) : ' Sense of Humour as a Moderator of the Relation between Stressors and Moods', *Journal of Personality and Social Psychology, 45.*

Maslach, C. and Jackson, S. (1981) *: The Maslach Burnout Inventory*, Palo Alto, Cal,. Counsulting Psychology Press.

Masson, H. and Morrison, T. (1991) : 'A 24-Hour Duty System: Using Practitioner Research to Manage the Stress', *British Journal of Social work, 21.*

Mathews, K.A. and Haynes, S.G (1986) : 'Type A Behaviour Pattern and Coronary Disease Risk : Update and Critical Evaluation', *American Journal of Epidemiology. 123.*

McDerment, L. (ed.) (1988) *: Stress Care, Surbition, Social Care Association.*

McDerment, L. (1992) : 'Present Tense, Future Perfect', *Care Weekly,* 13 August, 1992.

McGee, R.A. (1989) : Burnout and Professional Decision-Making, *Journal of Counselling Psychology, July, 1989.*

Megranahan, M. (1983) : Counselling : *A Practical Guide for Employers*, London, IPM.

Meichenbaum, D. (1985) *: Stress Inoculation Training,* Oxford, Pergamon.

Melhuish, A. (1978) *: Executive Stress*, London, Business Boooks.

Mills, A.J. and Murgatroyd, S.J. (1991) : *Organisational Rules*, Buckingham, Open University Press.

Minizberg. H. (1988) : 'Crafting Strategy', *Mckinsey Quarterly Seminar, Summer,* 1988.

Morgan, G (1986) : *Images of Organisation,* California, Sage.

Morrison, T. (1990) : 'The Emotional Effects of Child Protection Work on the Worker', *Practice, 4 (4).*

Morrison, T. (1993) : *Supervision in Social Care: An Action-Learning. Approach,* London, Longman.

Morrison T., Waters, J., Roberts, W., Craig E., Steane, E. and Erooga, M. (1987 ) : *Surviving in teens*, Rochdae Child Protecton Training Sub-Committee.

Murphy, M. (1991) : 'Pressure Points', *Social Work Today,* 13 June, 1991.

NALGO (1989) : 'Social Work in Crisis', London, National and Local Government Officers' Association.

New, C. and David, M. (1985) : *For the Children's Sake: Making Child-Care More than Women's Business, Harmondsworth, Penguin.*

Newman, J.E. and Beehr, T.A. (1979) : 'Personal and Organisational Strategies for Handling Job Stress: A Review of Research and Opinion', Personal Psychology, 32.

Newton, T. and Keena, A. (1985) : 'Coping with Work–related Stress', Human Relations, 38 (2).

Paine, W. (ed).(1982) : *Job Stress and Burnout,* London, Sage.

Pyne, M. (1991) : *Modern Social Work Theory: A Critical Introduction.* London, Macmillan.

Payne, R. (1980) : 'Organisational Stress and Support', in Cooper and Payne (1980).

Peck, D. and Whitlow, D. (1975) : *Approaches To Personality Theory,* London Methuen.

Phillipson, J. (1992) : *Practising Equality: Women, Men and Social Work,* London, CCETSW.

PIncus, G. (ed) (1959) : Hormones and Atherosclerosis, New York, Academic Press.

Pines, A. and Kafry, D. (1978) : 'Occupational Tedium in the Social Services', *National Association of Social Workers, November, 1978.*

Pink, D. (1991) : 'Black Students', 'Views of Existing CQSW Courses and CSS Schemes: I', in CD Project Steering Group (1991).

Pottage, D. and Evens M. (1992) : *Work-based Stress: Prescription is not the Cure*, London, NISW.

Preston-Shoot, M and Braye, S. (1991) : 'Managing the Personal Experience of Work', *Practice, 5(1).*

Pynoos. R. and Eth, S. (1984) : 'The Child as Witness to Homicide', *Journal of Social Issues, 40(2).*

Quick, J.C. and Quick, J.d. (1984) : *Organisational Stress and Preventative Management, New York, McGraw Hill.*

Ramdin, R. (1987) : *The Making of the Black Working Class in Britain*, Aldershot, Gower.

Randell, G, Packard, P. and Slater, J. (1984) : *Staff Appraisal,* London, IPM.

Raphael, B. (1990) : *When Disaster Strikes,* 2nd Edn, London, Unwin Hyman.

Rees, S. and Grahm, R.S. (1991) : *Assertion Training,* London, Rutledge.

Richards, M. and Payne, C, with Sheppard, A. (1990) : Staff Supervision in Child Protection, London, NISW.

Rickford, F. (1992) : 'Monster of Job'., *Social Work Today*, 30 January, 1992.

Rojek, C., Peacock, G. and Collins, S. (1988) : *Social Work and Received Ideas*, London, Rutledge.

Rosenman, R.H. and Friedman, N.I. (1959) : 'The Possible Relationship of the Emotions to Coronary Heart Disease', in Rincus (1959).

Rosenman, T.H., Friedman, N.I. and Strauss, R. (1966) : 'Coronary Heart Disease in the Western Collaborative Group Study' Journal of American Medical Association, 195.

Rotter, J.B. (1954) : *Social Learning and Clinical Psychology*, Englewood Cliffs, N.J., Prentice-Hall.

Rotter, J.B. (1966) : 'Generalised Expectancies for Internal Versus External Control of Reinforcement', *Psychological Monographs* 30(1).

Rotter, J.B. and Hochreich, D.J. (1975) : *Personality*, Glenview, III., Scott, Foresman.

Rychnam, R.M. (1978) : *Theories of Personality*, New York, Van No strand.

Salaman, G. (ed.) : (1992) : *Human Resource Strategies*, London, Sage.

Sancler, I. N. and Lakey, E. (1982) : 'Locus of Control as a Stress Moderator: The Role of Control, Perceptions and Social Support', *American Journal Of Community Psychology*, 10.

Sanders, G. and Julss, J. (eds) : (1982) : *The Social Psychology of Health ad Illness*, Hillside, N.J,. Erilbaum.

Satir, V. (1975) : *Self-Esteem*, Milbrae, Cal., Celestial Arts.

Satyamurti, C. (1981) : *Occupational Survival*, Oxford, Ergamon.

Schulz R. and Decker, S. (1985) : 'Long-Term Adjustment to Physical'. Disability : The Role of Social Support, Perceived Control and Self Blame', *Journal of Personality and Social Psychology, 48.*

Schwartz, R. M. and Garamoni, G.L. (1986) : 'A Structural Model of Positive and Vegetative States of Mind: Asymmetry in the Internal Dialogue', in Kendall (1986).

Scott, M.J. and Stradling, S.G. (1992) : *Counselling for Post-Traumatic Stress Disorder*, London, Sage.

Scott, M.J. and Stradling, S.G. (1993) : 'Post-Traumatic Stress Without the Trauma', *British Journal of Clinical Psychology*, 32(3) :.

Seligman, M.E.P. (1975) : *Helplessness*, San Francisco. Freeman.

Selye, H. (1974) : *Stress Without Distress*, Sevenoaks, Hodder & Stoughton.

Skinner, B.F. (1974) : *About Behaviourism*, New York, Knopf.

Smith, M. (1992) : 'Utility and Human Resource Management', Unit 13, Supplementary Readings for the Open University Course : B884 Human Resource Strategies.

Smith, M. Beck, J., Cooper, C.L. Cox, C., Ottoway, D. and Talbot, R. (1982) : *Introducing Organisational Behaviour, London, Macmillan.*

SSI (Social Services Inspectorate) (1991) : *Women in Social Services: A Neglected Resource, London, HMSO.*

Suaza, PL. De (1991) : 'A Review of the Experiences of Black Students in Social Work Training', In CCETSW (1991).

Spielberger, C. (1979) : *Understanidng Stress and Anxiety*, London, Harper & Row.

Spielberger, C. and Sarason I.G. (eds) : (1978) : *Stress and Anxiety*, Vol. 5, New York, Hemisphere.

Stevenson, O. (1991) : 'Social Work Intervention: Aspects of Research and Practice', paper presented at the BASPCAN Conference, Leicester.

Stevenson, O. and Parsloe P. (1978) : *Social Services Teams*: The Practitioner's View, London, HMSO.

Stone. M. (1990) : *Child Protection Work: A Professional Guide*, Birmingham, Venture Press.

Storey, J. (1992) : 'Human Resource Management in the Public Sector', in Salaman (1992).

Sutherland, V. and Cooper, G.L. (1991) : *Understanding Stress : A Perspective for Health Professionals, London, Chapman & Hall.*

Tache, J. and Selye, H. (1978) : 'On Stress and Coping Mechanisms, in Spielberger and Sarason (1978).

Taylor, S. (1983) : 'Adjustment to Life-Events: A Theory of Cognitive Adaptation', *American Psychologist*, 38.

Taylor, S. and Brown, J.D. (1980) : 'Illusion and Well-being; A Social Psychological Perspective on Mental Health', *Psychological Bulletin,* 103.

Thompson, N. (1990) : 'The Uncertainty Principle in Teaching Social Work and Social Science', *Social Science Teacher,* 19(2).

Thompson, N. (1991a) : 'Breaking Cycles', *Community Care,* 31 January, 1991.

Thompson, N. (1991b) *: Crisis Intervention Revisited,* Birmingham, paper.

Thompson, N. (1991c) : 'The Legacy of Laing: A Critique of the Medical Model in Social Work and Social Care', *Social Science Teacher,* 20 (2).

Thompson, N. (1992a) *: Child Abuse: the Existential Dimension,* University of East Angia Social Work Monographs.

Thompson, N. (1993) *: Anti-Discriminatory Practice,* London, Macmillan.

Thompson, N., Osada, M. and Anderson, B. (1990) *: Practice Teaching in Social Work: A Handbook, Birmingham, Paper.*

Thompson, S.C. (1981) : 'Will It Hurt Less If I can Control It? A Complex Answer to Simple Question', *Psychological Bulletin, 90.*

Toffler, A. (1970) *: Future Shock,* Londo, Bodley Hread.

Torrington, D. and Hall. L. (1988) *: Personnel Management,* New York, Prentice Hall.

Torrington, D., Weightman, J and Johns, K. (1985) *: Management Methods,* London, IPM.

Totman, R. (1990) *: Mind, Stress and Health,* London, Souvenir Press.

Tubesing, N.L. and Tubesing, D.A. (1982) : 'The Treatment of Choice: Selecting Stress Skills to Suit the Individual and the Situation', in Paine (1982).

UNESCO (1980) : Sociological Theories: *Race and Colonialisnm,* Paris, UNESCO.

Wade, C. (1970) *: Natural Ways To Health Through Controlled Fasting,* New York, Arch Books.

Wade C. and Tavris, C. (1990) *: Psychology,* London, Harper & Row.

Walsh, J.A. (1987) : 'Burnout and Values in the Social Service Profession', *The Journal of Contemporary Social Work, May, 1987.*

Warr, P. and Payne, R. (1982) : 'Experience of Strain and Pleasure among British Adults', *Social and Medicine, 16.*

Webb, A. (1989) : 'Organisational responses to Occupational Stress and Stressful Incidents in Residential Child Care, unpublished Dissertation, University of Manchester.

Webb, R. and Tossell, D. (1991) *: Social Issues for Careers,* London, Edward Arnold.

Weinstein, H.M. and Zappert, L.T. (1985) : 'Six Differences in the Impact of Work on Physical and Psychological Health ', *American Journal of Psychiatry,* October (1985).

Weintraub, J.K., Caver, C. Scheier, M. (1989) : 'Assessing Coping Strategies: A Theoretically-based Approach', *Journal of Personality and Social Psychology,* 56 (2).

Wiener, R. (1989) : 'Stress Within the Team', *Social Work Today,* 11 May, 1989.

Wilkinson, R. and Wilson, G. (1992) : 'Pressure Points', *Social Work Today,* 11 June, 1992.

Williams, F. (1989) *: Social Policy :A Critical Introduction,* London, Polity.

## Further Reading

Allen, Jeffrey & Klein, Roger. *Ready Set R.E.L.A.X., A Research-Based Programme of Relaxation, Learning and Self-Esteem for Children,* Inner Coaching, 1996.

Amen, Daniel. *Healing the Hardware of the Soul,* the Free Press, 2002.

Armstrong, Thomas. *The Myth of the A.D.D. Child,* Plume, 1997.

Bailey, Becky. *Conscious Discipline Brain Smart Classrom Management,* Loving Guidance, 2001.

Benson, Herbert. *The Relaxation Response, Updated and Expanded Edition,* Harper Torch, revised, 2000.

Chidre, Doc & Martin, Howard. *The HeartMath Solution, Herper,* San Faranciso, 1999.

Craig, Gary. *Emotional Freedom Techniques Manual,* 2004, emofree.com.

*Calories and Carbohydrates,* B. Kraus and M. Reilly-Pardo (Signet Books, 2001)

Dennison, Paul & Gail. *Brain Gym,* Revised Teacher's Edition, Edu-Kinesthetics, Inc., 1994.800-388-9898, www.braingym.org.

Feinstein, Sheryl. *Secrets of the Teenage Brain,* The Bran Store, 2004.

Geiedd, Jay & Colleagues, National Institute of Mental Health. *Nature Neuroscience,* 2 (10), 1999.

Goleman, Daniel. Emotional Intelligence, Bantam books, 1997.

Gottman, John. *Raising An Emotionally Intelligent Child,* Simon and Schuster, 1997.

Hannaford, Carla. *Awakening the Child Heart,* Jamilla Nurr Publishing, 2002.

Hannaford, Carla. *Smart Moves, Why Learning Is Not All In Your Head,* Great River Books, Revised Edition, 2005.

Humphrey, James. *Helping Children Manage Stress, A Guide for Adults,* Child and Family Press 1998.

Lewis, Sheldon & Sheila. *Stress-proofing Your Child,* Bantam Books, 1996.

Tennant, Victoria. *Calming Ourselves in Stressful Moments,* Comprehensive Health Education Foundation, 2003, www.chef.org.

Witkin, Georgia. Kidstress : *What It Is, How It Feels, How To Help,* Viking Penguin, 1999.

Arden, J. B. (2000) : *Surviving Job Stress.* Franklin Lakes NJ: Career Press.

Cassidy, T. (1999) : *Stress Cognition and Health,* London: Routledge.

Cooper, C. I. And Palmer, S. (2000) : *Conquer your Stress,* London: CIPD Books.

Crandall, R. and Perrewe, P. L. (eds.) : (1995) : *Occupational Stress: A Handbook,* Washington: Taylor and Francis.

Harns, C. (2003) : *Minimise Stress, Maximum Success,* London: Duncan Baird Publishers.

Kets de Vries, M. F. R. (1995) : *Life and Death in the Executive Fast Lane,* San Francisco: Jossey-Bass.

Lazarus, R. S. and Folkman, S. (1984) : *Stress Appraisal and Coping,* New York: Springer.

Leiter, M. and Masiach, C. (2000) : *Preventing Burnout and Building Engagement,* Chichester: Wiley.

Meichenbaum, D. (1997) : *Treating Post-Training Stress Disorder: A Handbook and Practice Manual for Therapy,* Chichester: Wiley.

Schabraig, M. J. Winnubst, A. M., and Cooper, C. L. (eds.) : (1996) : *Handbook of Work and Health Psychology,* Chichester: Wiley.

Williams, S. and Cooper, L. (2002) : *Managing Workplace Stress,* Chichester: Wiley.

## Recommended Reading


*Treating Type A Behaviour and your Heart,* Dr Meyer Friedman and Dianne Ulmer (Alfred A. Knopf, 1984).

*Type A Behaviour and your Heart,* Dr Meyer Friedman and Dr Ray Rosenman (Wildwood House Ltd/ Fawcett, 1974).

*Type A Behaviour : its diagnosis and treatment,* Dr Meyer Friedman (Plenum Press 1996)

*The Which Guide to Managing Stress,* Mark Greener (Which Books, Consumer Association, 1996)

*Diet and Nutrition,* Brenda Piper (Chapman and Hall, 1996)

*Stress Management and Counselling: theory, practice, research and methodology,* edited by Stephen Palmer and Windy Dryden (Cassell, 1996)

*Relaxation Techniques,* Rosemary Payne (Churchill Livingstone, 1995)

*Why Zebras Don't get Ulcers: a Guide to stress-related diseases and coping,* Robert Sapolsky (W.H. Freeman and Company, 1994)

*Who Can I talk to? The User's guide to Therapy and Counselling,* Judy Cooper and Jenny Lewis (Hodder and Stoughton, 1995)

The Optimum Nutrition Bible, P. Holford (Piatkus 1997)

*Feeding the Body, Nourishing the Soul,* D. Kesten (Conari Press, 1997)

*Why Geese Don't Get Obese and We Do,* E.P. Widmaier (W.H. Freeman, 1998)

*The Molecules Within Us: Our Body in Health and Disease,* C.A. Pasternak (Plenum, 1998)

*Molecules of Emotion: Why you feel the way you feel,* C.B. Pert (Simon and Schuster, 1997)

*The New Couple. Why the old rules don't work and what does,* M.T. Taylor and S. McGee (Harper, 2000)

*The Endorphin Effect: A Breakthrough Strategy for Holistic Health and Spiritual Wellbeing,* W. Bloom (Piatkus, 2000)


...✎...✎...✎

## APPENDIX - I

**STRESS AND STRAIN PROBLEMS OF WORKING EXECUTIVES AND THEIR HEALTH CARE MANAGEMENT THROUGH COMPLIMENTARY MEDICINES**

**QUESTIONNAIRE FOR EXECUTIVES/MANAGERS/PROFESSIONALS**

### A. IDENTIFICATION

Region: North__________, South__________, East__________,

West__________

1. Name of the Respondent :______________________________
2. Address :______________________________

   ______________________________

   ______________________________
3. Pin Code :______________________________
4. Phone No. : Office_______ Res__________
5. Nationality :______________________________

### B. PERSONAL INFORMATION

1. Sex : Male________ Female__________
2. Age in Years : ______________________________
3. Marital Status : Single_______ Married________

   Widow_______ Divorcee_______

   Separated________________________

4. Age at Marriage : ____________________

5. Birth Place : ____________ State________

6. Language : Hindi__________ Urdu__________

Punjabi__________ Bangla__________

Tamil__________

Others, specify__________

____________________

7. Religion : Hindu__________ Muslim__________

Sikh__________ Christian__________

Others, specify__________

____________________

8. Husband/Wife Both working : Yes__________ No.__________

9. Education : E1. Secondary Education__________

E2. Graduate__________

E3. Post-Graduate__________

E4. Professional__________

E5. Specialised Qualification Diploma/Certificate__________

____________________

10. Profession : Husband__________

Wife__________

11. Type of Organisation :____________________

Name of Organisation :____________________

Type of Organisation : Private______ Pubic/Limited______

Government __________

Government Undertaking__________

Own Business__________

Autonomous Body__________

____________________

12. Designation : ____________________

## C. INCOME GROUP

| (Basic salary) | (Please tick) |
|---|---|
| 1. Upto Rs. 1000/- | 3000/- (L)__________ |
| 2. Rs. 3001/- | 5000/- (M)__________ |
| 3. Rs. 5001/- | 7000/- (H)__________ |
| 4. Above Rs. 7001/- | (Very High)__________ |

## D. ENVIRONMENT/LIVING CONDITION

(a) Housing facility : Own house_______, Rented__________

(b) Size of family : Number of Adults______________
Number of Children_____________

(c) Dependents : Nos.______________(Parents/etc.)

(d) Occupation : Husband__________________________
Wife_____________________________

(e) Nature of your job/ Responsibilities : ______________________________
______________________________

(f) Are you happy with your present job : Yes____________ No. ___________
If no, why ___________________
___________________

(g) Are you looking for a change (Present position/ location) : Yes____________ No. __________
: Why _____________________________
(e.g. wife working in another place/housing problems, etc.) : _____________________________
_____________________________

(h) Work place and its distance from home : _____________________________
_____________________________

(i) How do you go to : Bus / Car / Auto / Cycle / on foot, Other specify _________
_____________________________

(j) Do you perceive any health problem due to transporation system - give reasons : Yes ___________ No. ___________

(k) Does it create - Worry - Fatigue - Anxiety - Stress - Tension (Please tick)

(l) Does your job Involve touring/ Travelling : Yes _____________ No. _________

(a) Does it relate To Stress/Strain - Problems : Yes _____________ No. _________

## E. HEALTH SERVICES

1. Whom do you consult for your usual health problems - especially stress and strain problems?

   (a) Local Healer ________ (b) Traditional Medicine ________
   (c) Ayurveda ________ (d) Unani ________
   (e) Homoeopathy ________ (f) Allopathy ________
   (g) Naturopathy ________ (i) Modern Medicines ________
   (j) Physical fitness experts ________
   (k) Acupuncturist ________
   (l) Psychotherapist ________
   (m) Yoga Therapist ________
   (n) Any other, pls specify ________
   ________

2. Health Services provided by: (to you and your family)]
   Employer ________ Govt. ________ Voluntary agencies ________
   Others, pls specify ________
3. What expenditure is incurred by the family per month on medical / health care?
   Certain proportion of the monthly income ________(Rs.)
4. Is that amoung reimbursed by your employer?
   Fully ________, Partially ________, Nil ________
5. Are you covered under any Medical Insurance Scheme?
   Yes ________ No. ________
6. Do you get any medical assistance from your employer?
   Yes ________ No. ________

| **If Yes** | **Periodicity** |
|---|---|
| Check up only________ | Monthly ________ |
| Treat & Medicines ________ | Quarterly ________ |
| Tonics ________ | Six monthly ________ |
| Financial aid ________ | Medical leave ________<br>No. of days |
| Clinical tests ________ | Maternity leave ________ |
| Hospital expenses ________ | |

## F. NUTRITION

1. Do you feel natural food is related to good health?
   Yes ________ No. ________
2. Which food causes you discomfort? ________
   Vegetarian: ________ Non-vegetarian: ________

3. Did you even control stress and strain problems by changing your food habits?

   Yes ________________ No. ________________

   If yes, please explain ________________________________________

4. Would you like to lose weight?

   How much ____________________ Why ____________________

   Gain weight ____________________ How much ____________________

   Why ________________________________________

   Stay same ____________________ Why ____________________

## G: FOOD INTAKE**

| | DAILY | OCCASIONALLY | MONTHLY | SEASONAL* | NEVER |
|---|---|---|---|---|---|
| 1. Milk | | | | | |
| 2. Cheese | | | | | |
| 3. Yoghurt | | | | | |
| 4. Ice-cream | | | | | |
| 5. Bread | | | | | |
| 6. Rice | | | | | |
| 7. Cereal | | | | | |
| 8. Potatoes | | | | | |
| 9. Eggs | | | | | |
| 10. Fruit | | | | | |
| 11. Fruit Juice | | | | | |
| 12. Fried Beans | | | | | |
| 13. Peas | | | | | |
| 14. Peanut | | | | | |
| 15. Green Vegetables | | | | | |
| 16. Salads | | | | | |
| 17. Red meat | | | | | |
| 18. Fish | | | | | |
| 19. Poultry | | | | | |
| 20. Candy/Sweets | | | | | |
| 21. Soda | | | | | |
| 22. Cookies | | | | | |
| 23. Cake | | | | | |
| 24. Pulses | | | | | |
| 25. Ghee | | | | | |
| 26. Others | | | | | |

* Seasonal: Summer (S), Monsoon (M), and Winter (W)

** Please tick appropriate columns / appropriate places

## H. OTHERS

1. How much of the following do you drink in a day?

   Coffee _______ Cups, Tea _______ Cups, Soda_______ Glasses

2. Are you on a Special Diet? Yes __________, No.

   If Yes, Why: ______________________________________________

3. Do you frequently add salt to your food? Yes ___, No. ___

   If Yes, Why: ______________________________________________

   If No. Why: ______________________________________________

4. Do you take iron, vitamins, etc. or other diet supplement?

   Yes ___________, No. ___________ Which type ___________

   If Yes, Why: ______________________________________________

5. Do you take fast foods? Yes ___________ No. ___________

6. Do you take snacks from outside i.e. restaurant/hotels, etc.?

   Yes ___________________________, No. ___________________________

7. **SMOKING**

   Which of the following do you smoke?

   Cigarettes ______________________, Packs a day ______________

   Ciger ___________________________, Nos. a day ______________

   Chewing tobacco (pan masala) ______________________________

   (a) If you have smoked in the past but have now stopped, please complete:
   How much you smoked ______ per day
   For how many years ______________
   When you stopped ______________

   **If increased:** No. of cigarettes per day ______________

   (b) Smoking / Chewing due to:

   Tension ___________, Worry ___________ Relaxation ___________

   Anxiety ___________________, Stress ___________________

8. **ALCOHOL AND DRUG USE**

   On the average how much

   Of the following do you drink?

| | **In a day** | **In a week** | **Reducing** | **Increasing** |
|---|---|---|---|---|
| Beer | ________ | ________ | ________ | ________ |
| Wine | ________ | ________ | ________ | ________ |
| Others | ________ | ________ | ________ | ________ |

9. Do you use any drug/pills or tranquillisers? Yes__, No. __

Does drug use cause any problems?

(a) With your job - Yes __________, No. __________

(b) With your friends - Yes __________, No. __________

(c) With your family - Yes __________, No. __________

Reasons for taking drugs: ____________________

What type

I. Please read the following statements in the questionnaire and put a tick in the appropriate space which you feel matches your own view most accurately i.e. in your day-to-day operations as a - working executive/manager/ professional

**Level of Stress**

| Statements | Always Stress | Frequent Stress | Occasional Stress | Rarely any Stress | No Stress at all |
|---|---|---|---|---|---|
| 1. Planning your Career | ____ | ____ | ____ | ____ | ____ |
| 2. Getting on in your job | ____ | ____ | ____ | ____ | ____ |
| 3. Managing Boss | ____ | ____ | ____ | ____ | ____ |
| 4. Keeping upto date (knowledge) | ____ | ____ | ____ | ____ | ____ |
| 5. Maintaining your integrity | ____ | ____ | ____ | ____ | ____ |
| 6. Your monthly check-up (Medical) | ____ | ____ | ____ | ____ | ____ |
| 7. Analaysing your job | ____ | ____ | ____ | ____ | ____ |
| 8. Managing operations (all types) | ____ | ____ | ____ | ____ | ____ |
| 9. Planning | ____ | ____ | ____ | ____ | ____ |
| 10. Managing with objectives | ____ | ____ | ____ | ____ | ____ |
| 11. Controlling Staff | ____ | ____ | ____ | ____ | ____ |
| 12. Decision-Making | ____ | ____ | ____ | ____ | ____ |
| 13. Communicating at all levels | ____ | ____ | ____ | ____ | ____ |
| 14. Managing your time | ____ | ____ | ____ | ____ | ____ |
| 15. Co-ordinating with various departments | ____ | ____ | ____ | ____ | ____ |
| 16. Working with your team | ____ | ____ | ____ | ____ | ____ |

| | | | | | |
|---|---|---|---|---|---|
| 17. Human Resources Development | ______ | ______ | ______ | ______ | ______ |
| 18. Selection/ Inter-Viewing | ______ | ______ | ______ | ______ | ______ |
| 19. Training | ______ | ______ | ______ | ______ | ______ |
| 20. Delegating | ______ | ______ | ______ | ______ | ______ |
| 21. Motivating your staff | ______ | ______ | ______ | ______ | ______ |
| 22. Improving people's jobs | ______ | ______ | ______ | ______ | ______ |
| 23. Developing leadership | ______ | ______ | ______ | ______ | ______ |
| 24. Counselling your Staff | ______ | ______ | ______ | ______ | ______ |
| 25. Running a staff appraisal System | ______ | ______ | ______ | ______ | ______ |
| 26. Discipling Staff | ______ | ______ | ______ | ______ | ______ |
| 27. Controlling your organisation | ______ | ______ | ______ | ______ | ______ |
| 28. Handling your Organisation | ______ | ______ | ______ | ______ | ______ |
| 29. Managing Meeting | ______ | ______ | ______ | ______ | ______ |
| 30. Writing/ Reports, etc. | ______ | ______ | ______ | ______ | ______ |
| 31. Reading Research Findings, etc. | ______ | ______ | ______ | ______ | ______ |
| 32. Listening to employees | ______ | ______ | ______ | ______ | ______ |
| 33. Speaking in Public/ Seminar | ______ | ______ | ______ | ______ | ______ |
| 34. Telephoning | ______ | ______ | ______ | ______ | ______ |
| 35. Negotiating /Labour | ______ | ______ | ______ | ______ | ______ |
| 36. Managing Conflict | ______ | ______ | ______ | ______ | ______ |
| 37. Managing Change | ______ | ______ | ______ | ______ | ______ |

## J. HEALTH PROBLEM FACED BY YOU IN THE PAST ONE YEAR:

| | Circle One | If yes, Give Reason |
|---|---|---|
| **CONSTITUTIONAL** | | |
| Do you have trouble With your appetite | YES | NO |
| Have you had more than a 10 kg. Change in weight in the last Year | YES | NO |
| Do you have (a) Fevers | YES | NO |
| (b) Sweats | YES | NO. |
| (Regularly/Occasionally) | | |
| **CONSTITUTIONAL** | | |
| **SKIN/ALLERGIES** | | |
| Do you have any (a) Skin rashes | YES | NO |
| (b) Sores | YES | NO |
| (c) Itching | YES | NO |
| Do you have allergies to Pencillin ______, Other drugs ________ | | |
| Any of the following things: Any food ___________, Other _______ | | |
| **EYE, EAR, TOOTH, ETC.** | | |
| Do you have eye problem or trouble with your vision? | YES | NO |
| Do you have any problem with your ears or with your hearing? | YES | NO |
| Do you have any trouble with your teeth, gums? | YES | NO |
| Do you have any trouble with throat/speech problem? | YES | NO |
| Do you have any sinus trouble? | YES | NO |
| **RESPIRATORY** | | |
| Do you have a persistent cough or phlegm production? | YES | NO |
| Do you have any wheezing? | YES | NO |
| Did you ever cough up blood? | YES | NO |

| | | | |
|---|---|---|---|
| **CONSTITUTIONAL** | | | |
| **CARDIAC** | | | |
| Do you have trouble with breathing? | YES | NO | |
| Do you ever have a pain or tightness in your chest? | YES | NO | |
| Do your ankles swell? | YES | NO | |
| **GASTRO-INTESTINAL** | | | |
| Do you have any difficulty in swallowing? | YES | NO | |
| Do you have any | | | |
| (a) Stomach pains | YES | NO | |
| (b) Heartburn | YES | NO | |
| (c) Vomitting Symptoms | YES | NO | |
| Do you have constipation? | YES | NO | |
| Do you use a laxative often? | YES | NO | |
| Do you have frequent diarrhoea? | YES | NO | |
| Have you had any tarry, black, or bloody bowel movements? | YES | NO | |
| **CONSTITUTIONAL** | | | |
| Has there been any change in the colour, size, or consistency of your bowel movements recently? | YES | NO | |
| Do you have rectal hemorrhoids? | YES | NO | |
| **GENITO-URINARY** | | | |
| Do you get up more than once at night? | YES | NO | |
| Do you urinate at night? | YES | NO | |
| Do you have any burning sensation with urination? | YES | NO | |
| Have you passed any red or dark urine? | YES | NO | |

| | | | |
|---|---|---|---|
| Do you have trouble in starting or stopping your urine? | YES | NO | |
| Do you ever lose your urine accidentally when you cough or sneeze? | YES | NO | |
| **CONSTITUTIONAL** | | | |
| **MUSCULOSKELETAL** | | | |
| Are you bothered by pains in | | | |
| (a) your back | YES | NO | |
| (b) arms | YES | NO | |
| (c) legs or joints | YES | NO | |
| (d) slipped discs | YES | NO | |
| **NEUROLOGIC HEMATOLOGIC** | | | |
| Are you bothered by frequent headaches? | YES | NO | |
| Do you have fainting or falling out spells? | YES | NO | |
| Do you bleed easily? | YES | NO | |
| **EMOTIONAL** | | | |
| Do you often feel depressed or sad? | YES | NO | |
| Do you have trouble in sleeping? | YES | NO | |
| Have you had any serious trouble with your money matters? | YES | NO | |
| **CONSTITUTIONAL** | | | |
| **MALE SEXUAL** | | | |
| Do you have any discharge or drip from your penis? | YES | NO | |
| Do you have a sore or lump on or near penis? | YES | NO | |

**WOMEN WITH MENSTRUAL PERIODS**

First day of last menstrual period:

Length of usual menstrual period: ........................... Days.

Heavy bleeding or spotting: ........................... Days.

Lighter bleeding or spotting: ........................... Days.

Usual time between periods: ........................... Days.

Do you have any severe symptoms at or near the time of your menstrual periods? YES NO

What kind ..........................................................................................................

Do you have any change in your monthly cycle? YES NO

Do you have any vaginal bleeding between periods or after intercourse? YES NO

**CONSTITUTIONAL**

**WOMEN WITHOUT MENSTRUAL PERIODS**

| | | | |
|---|---|---|---|
| Age at last menses | ________ | | |
| Are you bothered by hot flashes? | YES | NO | |
| Do you ever have vaginal bleeding or spotting? | YES | NO | |
| **ALL WOMEN** | | | |
| Are you bothered by a vaginal discharge or vaginal itching? | YES | NO | |
| Do you have any breast lumps, discharge, or pain? | YES | NO | |
| Do you examine your Breasts monthly? | YES | NO | |

**MEDICATION**

Please list all prescription drugs you have currently taken:

| **Health Problem** ** | **Medication** | **Dose** | **How often** |
|---|---|---|---|
| 1. ____________ | ____________ | ____________ | |
| 2. ____________ | ____________ | ____________ | ____________ |
| 3. ____________ | ____________ | ____________ | ____________ |
| 4. ____________ | ____________ | ____________ | ____________ |

**(Such as diabetes, High blood pressure, Allergies, Eye problems, Thyroid, Angina, Pain management (etc.)

## K. SPECIAL FUNCTIONING

How satisfied are you with your present sexual activity?

Very satisfied ____________, Dissatisfied ____________

### HOBBIES/RECREATION

1. What things do you do to occupy your leisure time?

   ..........................................................................................................

2. Are you involved in any community/social activities? If so, which one:

   ..........................................................................................................

3. How many weeks vacation do you take each year? ..............................

4. How do you spend your holidays? ..........................................................................

   ..........................................................................

### EXERCISE

1. Do you engage regularly in any type of exercise?

   YES .............. NO ...........

   If yes, please give details ..........................................................................

   Type of exercise (Swimming, Walking, Jogging, Tennis, Golf, etc.)

### LEISURE

1. What kind of leisure activities do you and your family enjoy doing? (Music/Clubs/Reading, etc.)

   ..........................................................................................................

   ..........................................................................................................

Please indicate any complementary medicine/Therapy tried to solve your health/medical problems including stress/strain problems:

..........................................................................................................

..........................................................................................................

| Medicine/Therpay | Please put a tick mark | |
|---|---|---|
| **A. TRADITIONAL MEDICINES** | | |
| Ayurveda | YES | NO |
| Unani | YES | NO |
| Folk/Primitive | YES | NO |
| Siddha | YES | NO |
| Indigenous/Herbal | YES | NO |
| **B. ORIENTAL/CHINESE MEDICINES** | | |
| Acupuncture/Ear Acupuncture | YES | NO |
| Acupressure (Shiatzu) | YES | NO |
| Electro - Acupuncture | YES | NO |
| Moxibustion | YES | NO |
| **C. HOMOEOPATHY** | | |
| Homoeopathic Remedies | YES | NO |
| Biochemic Remedies | YES | NO |

**D. NATURAL REMEDIES**

| | | |
|---|---|---|
| Hydropathy | YES | NO |
| Massage | YES | NO |
| Reflexology | YES | NO |
| Naturopathy (Nature Cure) | YES | NO |
| Psychosomatic | YES | NO |
| Mud Therapy | YES | NO |
| Colour Therapy | YES | NO |

**E. NUTRITIONAL THERAPIES**

| | | |
|---|---|---|
| Nutritional Therapy | YES | NO |
| Dieting | YES | NO |
| Fasting | YES | NO |
| Vegetarianism | YES | NO |

**F. YOGA**

| | | |
|---|---|---|
| Yogic Asanas | YES | NO |
| Breathing Exercises | YES | NO |
| Pranayama | YES | NO |

**G. SPIRITUAL THERAPIES**

| | | |
|---|---|---|
| Faith Healing | YES | NO |
| Spiritual Healing | YES | NO |
| Mantras | YES | NO |
| Meditation | YES | NO |
| Tantras | YES | NO |

**H. MANIPULATIVE THERAPIES**

| | | |
|---|---|---|
| Manipulative Therapy | YES | NO |
| Chiropractic | YES | NO |
| Osteopathy | YES | NO |
| Bone Setting | YES | NO |
| Postural Therapy/ Postural Integration | YES | NO |

**I. BEHAVIOURAL THERAPIES**

| | | |
|---|---|---|
| Bio feed back | YES | NO |
| Relaxation Techniques | YES | NO |

**J. OTHER THERAPIES**

| | | |
|---|---|---|
| Physical Exercises | YES | NO |
| Electrical Therapy | YES | NO |
| Magnetic Therapy | YES | NO |
| Bach Flower Remedies | YES | NO |
| Hypnotherapy (Hypnosis) | YES | NO |
| Physiotherapy | YES | NO |
| Art Therapy | YES | NO |
| Organic Remedies | YES | NO |
| Music Therapy | YES | NO |
| Speech Therapy | YES | NO |

L. In your opinion, which of the above mentioned therapies, gave you the best results in controlling stress and strain problems?

1.......................................................................2.................................................................................

M. Kindly state any other method tried to manage stress - from your experience - (Any unusual/uncommon method adopted).

N. What is your present health problems which is of major concern to you?

.......................................................................................................................................

O. Express your views on who should be responsible for healthcare.
Management (a) Individuals ...........(b) Society ........ (c) Government ........... (d) Corporate Office ............
(e) Voluntary Organisations ................ (f) Any other ..................

**Below mentioned questions are only for women/ladies/mothers:**

1. Did you visit any ante-natal clinic during pregnancy?

   YES ................................ NO .................................

2. If, yes, how often did you visit the clinic?

   Regularly ..........................., Irregularly ..........................

   Occasionally ...................., Once Only ..............................

3. If not, what was the source of your information about pregnancy, mother care and child birth?

   Elder lady .............., Dai .............., Doctor .............., Other specify ..............

4. Who attended you at the time of your child birth?

   Trained Dai .............., Untrained Dai .............., Nurse ..............

   Doctor .............., Relative .............., Other specify ..............

5. Where did the child birth take place? (last issue)

   At home .............., Nursing Home .............., Govt. Hospital .............., Private Hospital ..............

6. (a) Do you have any problems related to stress, and strains, worry/anxiety/tension, others please specify, during confinement of child birth:

   .........................................................................................

   .........................................................................................

   .........................................................................................

   (b) Source of problems (such as Stress/Strain/Tension, etc.)

   (i) Working place, please specify ..........................................

   (ii) Family conditions, please specify .............................

   (iii) Any other ..........................................................................................................

7. Do you try any of the complementary system of medicine?

   YES ................................................., NO ..................................................

   (a) If yes, please give details (e.g., Ayurved/Unani/Homoeopathy, Naturopathy, Folk medicine, therapies, etc.)

   .........................................................................................................................................

8. What is your concept of an ideal family?

(i) Number of children

Male ................................................................

Female ................................................................

Total ................................................................

(ii) Spacing (in years) ................................................................

Stress/Strain problem in bringing up the children:

................................................................................................................................

9. Did you (women) experience any sort of complication during pregnancies?

YES ........................................................, NO ........................................................

If yes, specify the type of complication (Anaemia, Vomiting)

................................................................................................................................

10. When you are an expectant mother, do you take extra diet?

YES ........................................................, NO ..............

If yes, what special additions/deletions are made to her diet

................................................................................................................................

11. Kindly mention any of the Complementary Therapies adopted by you or your family members for personal healthcare management.

| **Sl. No.** | **Medical problems/ disorder** | **Therapies used** | **Benefits obtained** |
|---|---|---|---|
| 1. | ........................................ | ........................................ | ........................................ |
| 2. | ........................................ | ........................................ | ........................................ |
| 3. | ........................................ | ........................................ | ........................................ |
| 4. | ........................................ | ........................................ | ........................................ |

12. What methods have you tried for pain management (different types of pain you had)

(a) Types of Pain experienced ................................................................

(b) Remedies tried ................................................................

(c) Result obtained ................................................................

THANK YOU VERY MUCH

# APPENDIX - II

## STRESS AND STRAIN PROBLEMS OF WORKING EXECUTIVES AND THEIR HEALTH CARE MANAGEMENT THROUGH COMPLEMENTARY MEDICINES

## QUESTIONAIRE FOR HEALTH PROFESSIONALS/DOCTORS/SPECIALISTS

### A. IDENTIFICATION

Region: North ................., South ................., East ................., West .................

1. Name of the Respondent : ................................................................
2. Address : ................................................................
   : ................................................................
   : ................................................................
3. Pin Code : ................................................................
4. Phone No. : ................................................................
5. Nationality : ................................................................

### B. PERSONAL INFORMATION

1. Sex : Male ........................., Female .........................
2. Age in Years : ................................................................
3. Marital Status : Single ....................., Married ..................
   : Widow ..........................., Married ..................
   Separated ..............................
4. Age at Marriage : ................................................................
5. Birth Place : ................................................................
6. Language : Hindi ..................., Urde .......................
   Punjabi ............., Bangla .................
   Tamil .....................
   Others, Specify ....................................
   : ................................................................
7. Religion : Hindu ......................, Muslim ....................
   Sikh ........................., Christian ...........
   Others, Specify ....................................
8. Husband/wife both working : Yes .............................. No .........................

### C. EDUCATION

1. Professional/Qualification : ................................................................
2. Specialists, if any : ................................................................
3. Research Experience, if any : ................................................................

4. Registered : YES .............................. NO ..........................
5. Registration No. : ..........................................................................

Kindly mention the name of the

(a) Board : ..........................................................................
(b) Association : ..........................................................................
(c) Institutions : ..........................................................................
(d) Professional bodies : ..........................................................................
(e) Others : ..........................................................................

## D. HEALTH-PROFESSIONAL EXPERIENCE

1. Professional/Qualification : ..........................................................................
2. Attached to : ..........................................................................
(Give name and address) : ..........................................................................
..........................................................................
3. Clinics : Government ......, Private .........
4. Polyclinics : Government ......, Private .........
5. Health Centres : Government ......, Private .........
6. Hospitals : Government ......, Private .........
7. Others (Please specicy) : ..........................................................................
8. Health Consultant to : ..........................................................................
9. Any training received in complementary medicine in India and abroad
: YES ........................., NO ..........................
If yes, give details : ..........................................................................
: ..........................................................................

## E. IN YOUR OPINION - COMPLEMENTARY MEDICINES ARE:

(a) Expensive : YES ........................., NO ..........................
(b) Cheaper : YES ........................., NO ..........................
(c) Safer : YES ........................., NO ..........................
(d) No side-effect : YES ........................., NO ..........................
(e) Avoiding drugs : YES ........................., NO ..........................
(f) For the masses : YES ........................., NO ..........................
(g) Easily administered : YES ........................., NO ..........................
(h) Less time consuming : YES ........................., NO ..........................
(i) Less Technicalities : YES ........................., NO ..........................
(j) Curative in Nature : YES ........................., NO ..........................
(k) Preventive in Nature : YES ........................., NO ..........................

(l) More time consuming for recovery : YES ......................, NO ........................

(m) Any other, please specify : YES ......................, NO ........................

## F. TO WHAT EXTENT DO YOU AGREE (FROM YOUR EXPERIENCE) THAT THE FOLLOWING ISSUES ARE CAUSES OF STRESS FOR WORKING EXECUTIVES/ MANAGERS/PROFESSIONALS (OCCUPATIONAL STRESS)

| Statement | Level of Agreement | | | | |
|---|---|---|---|---|---|
| | Strongly Agree | Agree | Neither Agree nor Disagree | Disagree | Strongly disagree |
| 1. Socioeconomic Changes | ............... | ............... | ............... | ............... | ............... |
| 2. Political Changes | ............... | ............... | ............... | ............... | ............... |
| 3. Military Crisis | ............... | ............... | ............... | ............... | ............... |
| 4. Environmental Threats | ............... | ............... | ............... | ............... | ............... |
| 5. New Government Legislations | ............... | ............... | ............... | ............... | ............... |
| 6. Racing Violence | ............... | ............... | ............... | ............... | ............... |
| 7. Threat of Unemployment | ............... | ............... | ............... | ............... | ............... |
| 8. Hiring Policies | ............... | ............... | ............... | ............... | ............... |
| 9. Plant Closings | ............... | ............... | ............... | ............... | ............... |
| 10. Layoffs | ............... | ............... | ............... | ............... | ............... |
| 11. Relocation | ............... | ............... | ............... | ............... | ............... |
| 12. Automation | ............... | ............... | ............... | ............... | ............... |
| 13. Market Shifts | ............... | ............... | ............... | ............... | ............... |
| 14. Changes in Technology | ............... | ............... | ............... | ............... | ............... |
| 15. Mergers/Takeovers | ............... | ............... | ............... | ............... | ............... |
| 16. Task/Target | ............... | ............... | ............... | ............... | ............... |
| 17. Supervision | ............... | ............... | ............... | ............... | ............... |
| 18. Co-workers Participation | ............... | ............... | ............... | ............... | ............... |
| 19. Decision-Making | ............... | ............... | ............... | ............... | ............... |
| 20. Divorce | ............... | ............... | ............... | ............... | ............... |
| 21. Separation | ............... | ............... | ............... | ............... | ............... |
| 22. Maritial discord | ............... | ............... | ............... | ............... | ............... |
| 23. Conflict with Family | ............... | ............... | ............... | ............... | ............... |
| 24. Conflict with Friends | ............... | ............... | ............... | ............... | ............... |
| 25. Children Education | ............... | ............... | ............... | ............... | ............... |
| 26. Financial Problems | ............... | ............... | ............... | ............... | ............... |
| 27. Illness | ............... | ............... | ............... | ............... | ............... |

28. Housing ……………… ……………… ……………… ……………… ………………
29. Neurosis ……………… ……………… ……………… ……………… ………………
30. Mental Illness ……………… ……………… ……………… ……………… ………………
31. Ineffective Coping Skills ……………… ……………… ……………… ……………… ………………
32. Poor Communication ……………… ……………… ……………… ……………… ………………
33. Addictive Behaviour ……………… ……………… ……………… ……………… ………………
34. Disease ……………… ……………… ……………… ……………… ………………
35. Disability ……………… ……………… ……………… ……………… ………………
36. Appetite Disturbance ……………… ……………… ……………… ……………… ………………
37. Chemical Dependency ……………… ……………… ……………… ……………… ………………
38. Biochemical Imbalance ……………… ……………… ……………… ……………… ………………
39. Pregnancy ……………… ……………… ……………… ……………… ………………
40. Poor Air ……………… ……………… ……………… ……………… ………………
41. Climatic Conditions ……………… ……………… ……………… ……………… ………………
42. Noise Exposure ……………… ……………… ……………… ……………… ………………
43. Toxic Subtance ……………… ……………… ……………… ……………… ………………
44. Poor Lighting ……………… ……………… ……………… ……………… ………………
45. Radition Exposure ……………… ……………… ……………… ……………… ………………
46. Poor Equipment Design ……………… ……………… ……………… ……………… ………………
47. Change Sleep Wake Habits ……………… ……………… ……………… ……………… ………………
48. Lack of Managerial Support ……………… ……………… ……………… ……………… ………………
49. Poorly Defined Goals /Responsibilities ……………… ……………… ……………… ……………… ………………

## G. WHAT TYPE OF COMPLEMENTARY MEDICINE/THERAPY IS USED BY YOU FOR CURING THE PROBLEM FACED BY EXECUTIVES/PATIENTS SPECIALLY RELATED TO STRESS/STRAIN.

| Medical Problem | Type of Medicine/Therapy Used | Results obtained |
|---|---|---|
| 1. Alcoholism | | |
| 2. Anaemia | | |
| 3. Asthma | | |
| 4. Allergies | | |
| 5. Cancer | | |
| 6. Diabetes | | |
| 7. High Blood Pressure | | |
| 8. Epilepsy | | |
| 9. Angina | | |
| 10. Hepatitis | | |

11. Intestinal Disease
12. Migraine
13. Mental Illness
14. Obesity
15. Smoking
16. Drug Abuse
17. Stroke
18. Kidney Stones/Disease
19. Thyroid Disease
20. Glaucoma/Blindness
21. Gallstone/Gallbladder
22. AIDS
23. Rheumatic Fever
24. Urinary Infection
25. Colitis
26. Bronchitis
27. Ulcers
28. Skin Disease
29. Arthritis or gout
30. Heart murmur

---

In your view, leisure activities are essential for working executives?

YES .............................................................. NO ..............................................................

Which activities are most helpful? ..............................................................

..............................................................

What benefits will be derived by them? ..............................................................

In your opinion, physical exercises needed for working executives?

YES .............................................................. NO ..............................................................

Which exercises are most effective in controlling stress and strain problems?

Please tick ( ):-

| | | |
|---|---|---|
| 1. Swimming ..................... | 2. Cycling ..................... | 3. Running ..................... |
| 4. Squash ..................... | 5. Karate ..................... | 6. Steam bath ..................... |
| 7. Archery ..................... | 8. Cricket ..................... | 9. Fishing ..................... |
| 10. Skiing ..................... | 11. Tennis ..................... | 12. Slimming Exercises ..................... |
| 13. Badminton..................... | 14. Rowing ..................... Sauna Baths..................... | 15. Turkish/ |
| 16. Gardening..................... | 17. Walking ..................... | 18. Dancing (Aerobics) ..................... |
| 19. Mountain Climbing ..................... | 20. Skating ..................... | 21. Jogging ..................... |

## H. DO YOU FEEL BEHAVIOURAL CHANGES/CHANGES IN ATTITUDES OF EXECUTIVES ARE ESSENTIAL TO REDUCE STRESS AND STRAIN.

Yes .................................. No ...........................

If **Yes,** please mention the changes required **such** as:

Behaving decently ......................................Walking Straight ......................................

Working sincerely ......................................Breathing deeply ......................................

Sleeping sufficiently ..................................Planning orderly ......................................

Earning honestly ....................................... Sitting properly ......................................

Learning from their mistakes ..........................Believing in hard work .................

Doing good to others ..........................................................................................................

**WATCHING** their words ........................ actions ........................ thoughts ...................... character ........................ health ........................

**AVOIDING**........................ Irregular habits ........................ Animosity ........................ Bossism ........................ Cunningness ........................ Hot headedness ........................ Jealously ........................ Malice ........................ Quarrelsomeness .................................. Rashness ........................ Selfishness ........................ Yaffling .......................................... Zoilism ........................

Please read the following Therapies in terms of importance in coping with Stress/Strain problems of Executives.

| Therapy | Most important<br>1 | Degree of Importance<br>Important<br>2 | Neither important nor unimportant<br>3 | Unimpor-tant<br>4 | Most important<br>5 |
|---|---|---|---|---|---|
| **A. TRADITIONAL** | | | | | |
| Ayurveda | | | | | |
| Unani | | | | | |
| Siddha | | | | | |
| Tribal | | | | | |
| Home Made (Indigenous) | | | | | |
| Herbal | | | | | |
| **B. ORIENTAL/ CHINESES** | | | | | |
| Acupuncture | | | | | |
| Acupressure (Shiatzu) | | | | | |
| Electro-Acupuncture | | | | | |
| Ear Acupressure | | | | | |
| Moxibustion | | | | | |

| C. HOMOEOPATHY | | | | | |
|---|---|---|---|---|---|
| Homoeopathic Remedies | | | | | |
| Biochemical Remedies | | | | | |
| **D. NATURAL REMEDIES** | | | | | |
| Hydrotherapy | | | | | |
| Massage | | | | | |
| Reflexology | | | | | |
| Nature Cure | | | | | |
| Psychosomatic Therapy | | | | | |
| Mud Therapy | | | | | |
| Colour | | | | | |
| Therapy | | | | | |
| **E. NUTRITION** | | | | | |
| Nutritional | | | | | |
| Therapy | | | | | |
| Dietetics Fasting | | | | | |
| Vegetarianism | | | | | |
| Veganism | | | | | |
| **F. YOGA** | | | | | |
| Yogic Exercises | | | | | |
| Breathing Exercises | | | | | |
| Pranayama | | | | | |
| **G SPIRITUAL** | | | | | |
| Faith Healing | | | | | |
| Spiritual Healing | | | | | |
| Mantras Meditation | | | | | |
| Tantras | | | | | |
| **H. MANIPULATIVE** | | | | | |
| Manipulative Therapies | | | | | |
| Chiropractic | | | | | |
| Osteopathy | | | | | |
| Bone Setting | | | | | |

| | | | | | |
|---|---|---|---|---|---|
| Postural Integration | | | | | |
| Postural Remedies | | | | | |
| **I. BEHAVIOURAL** | | | | | |
| Bio feed Back | | | | | |
| Relaxation Techniques | | | | | |
| **J. OTHERS** | | | | | |
| Physical Exercises | | | | | |
| Electrical Therapy | | | | | |
| Magnetic Therapy | | | | | |
| Bach Flower Remedies | | | | | |
| Hypno-therapy (Hypnosis) | | | | | |
| Physio-therapy | | | | | |
| Art Therapy | | | | | |
| Organic Remedies | | | | | |
| Music Therapy | | | | | |
| Speech Therapy | | | | | |

**"Thank you for your cooperation"**

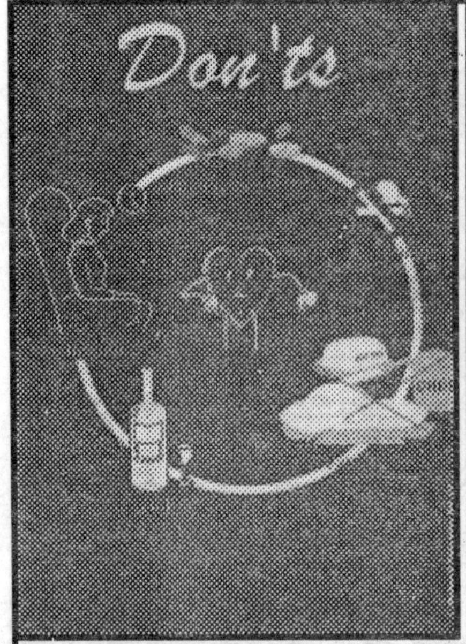


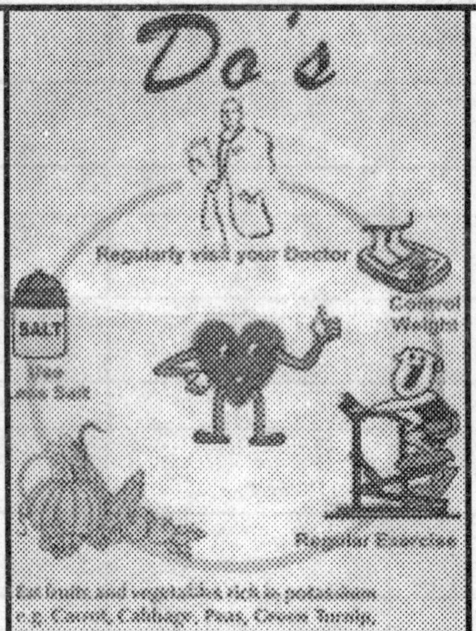


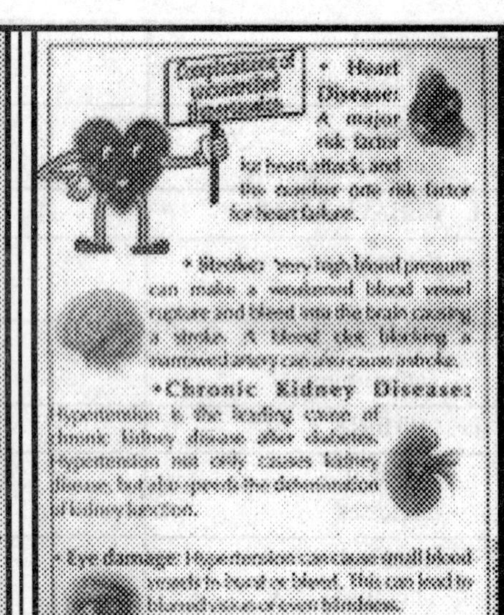


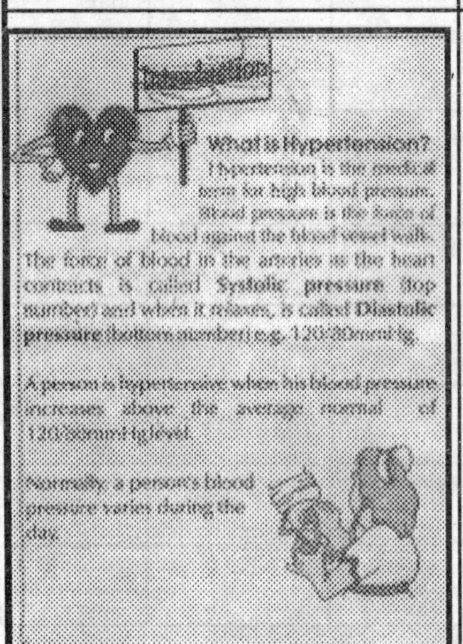


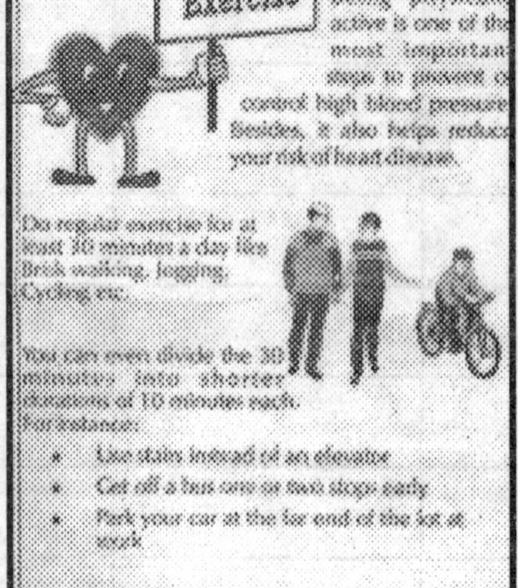


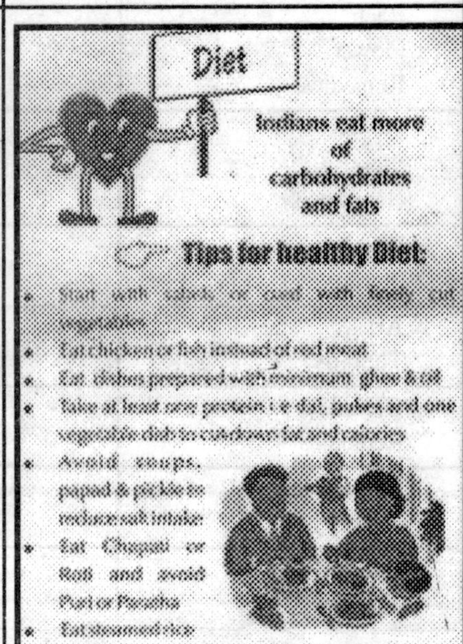

**Dancing** – Symbolizes the emotion of celebration.
Celebrate the beauty of healthy living

## HEALTH PROTECTION PLAN

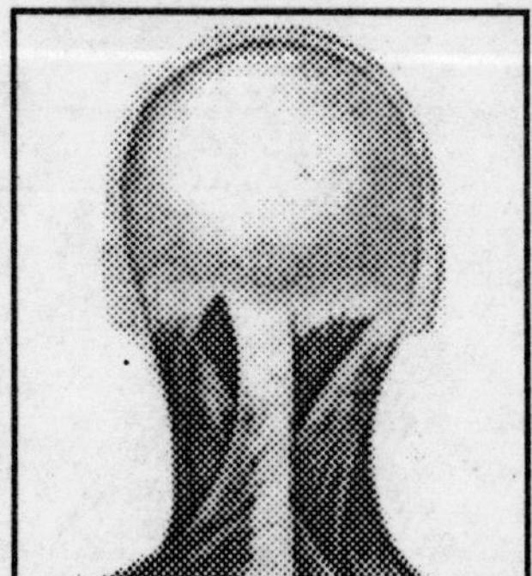
1. Head and Neck

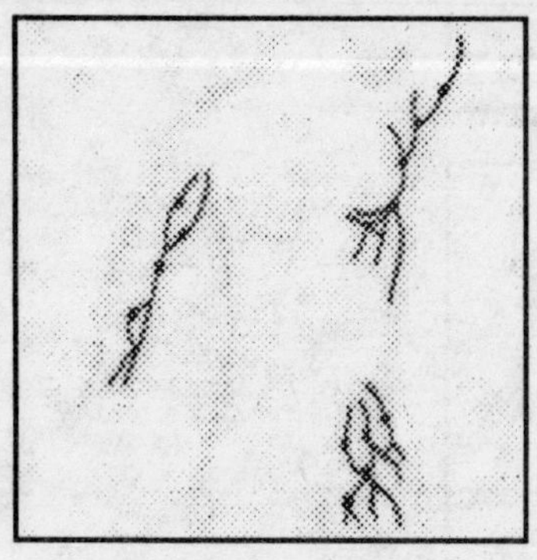
2. Skin and Lymph Nodes

This *HEALTH PROTECTION PLAN* consists of 9 topics

**A CATEGORY** refers to symptoms which may indicate some thing is wrong. A "yes" answer in this category does not necessarily mean there is a problem, but that these symptoms should be brought to the attention of a physician as soon as possible. You can be alert to the symptoms, but only a trained person can evaluate them.

**B CATEGORY** is a family history your physician should have. If you are not sure about some of these, check with other family members.

**C CATEGORY** is important medical history your physician should have.

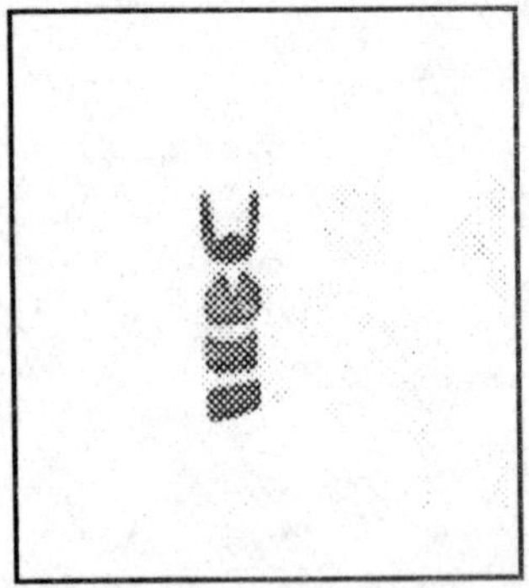

3. Head and Neck

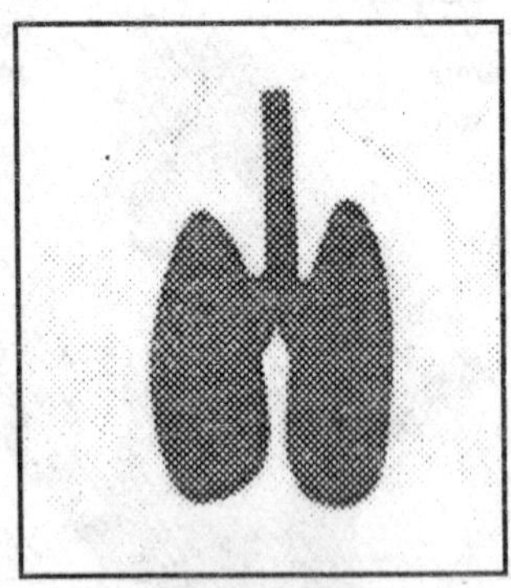

4. Respiratory System

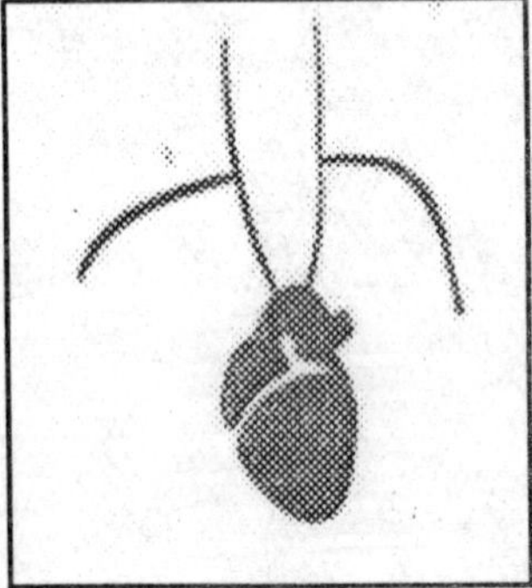

5. Cardiovascular System

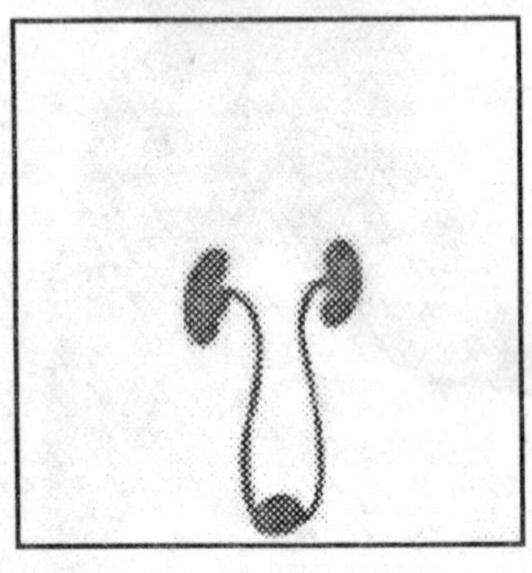

6. Urinary Tract

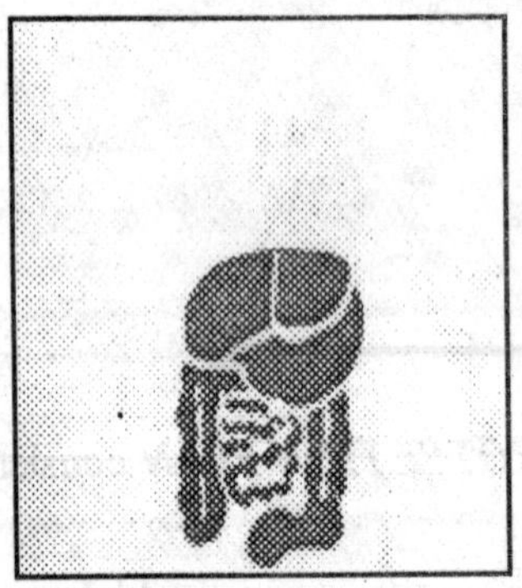

7. Gastrointestinal Tract

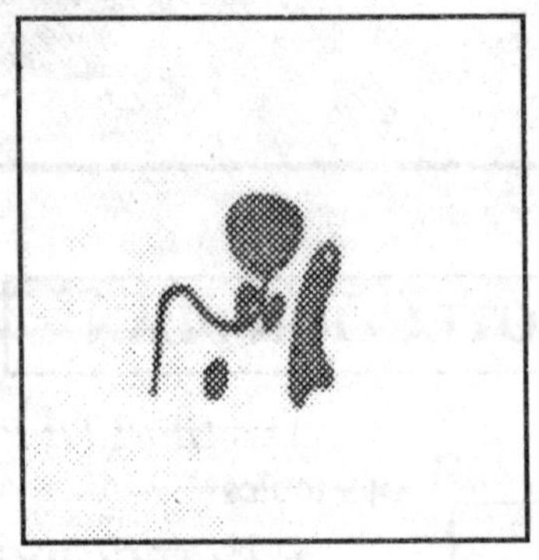

8. Male Reproductive System

9. Female Reproductive System

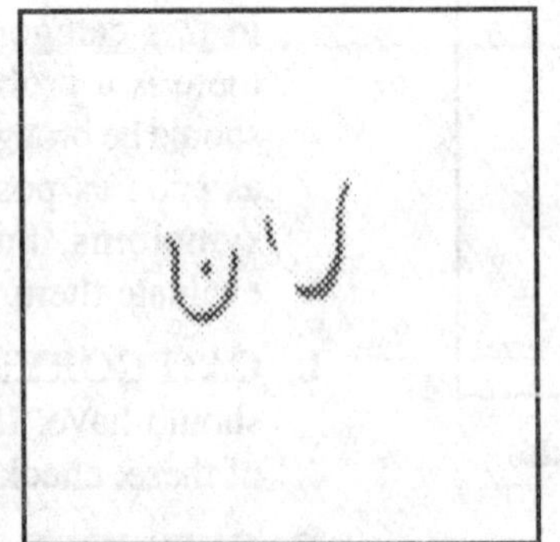

10. Cancer of the Breast (For Women)

D **CATEGORY** is to alert you to preventive measures which can help you to protect yourself from certain health hazards. There is additional information available from the Preventive Medicine Institute to help you control some of these health hazards.

**Drawings:**

The drawings illustrate those areas of the body that relate to the diseases we are discussing. They are to assist you to place the organs and sites in the body.

**Risk Factors:**

A risk factor indicates whether you are more likely to get a particular disease than some-one who does not have that risk factor. Having any of the risk factors does NOT mean that you will get the disease. Even though some risk factors cannot be changed, such as family history, some are up to you. Controlling smoking. drinking, and weight can reduce some risks.

## 1. Skin and Lymph Nodes

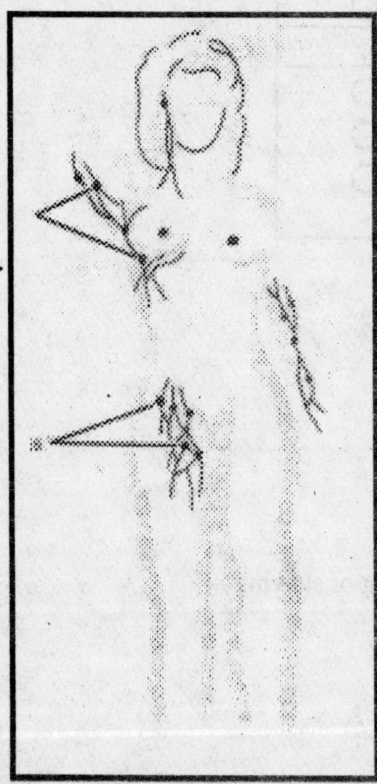

Both skin and lymph nodes cover the entire body. Lymph nodes are located at strategic points int he body to fight infection.

An enlarged lymph node will appear as a single firm swelling under the skin. It is often confused with a hernia, infection or cyst.

| A. Do you now have...? | YES | NO |
|---|---|---|
| . . . Any unexplained itching | O | O |
| . . . Unexplained sweating or fever during the night which has lasted for more than two weeks | O | O |
| . . . Swelling or enlargement (painful or not) of lymph glands | O | O |
| . . . Non-healing ulcers, sores, or growths which have lasted for more than a month | O | O |
| . . . Red scaling patches of skin which do not heal | O | O |
| . . . Any moles which have changed color, changed size, become ulcerated (sore) or bleed | O | O |
| **B. Has a member of your family ever had. . . ?** | | |
| . . . Cancer of the skin | O | O |
| . . . Leukemia | O | O |
| . . . Lymphosarcoma | O | O |
| . . . Hodgkin's disease | O | O |
| **C. Have you ever had...?** | | |
| . . . Cancer of the skin | O | O |
| . . . A mole removed | O | O |
| . . . A skin growth removed | O | O |

| | | |
|---|---|---|
| ... Treatment with X-rays (radiation therapy)<br>... A burn with scarring | O<br>O | O<br>O |
| **D. Doyou...?** | | |
| ... Have frequent boils or other skin infections<br>... Have skin that sunburns more easily than others<br>... Have an outdoor occupation<br>(example: farmer, fisherman, etc.) | O<br>O<br>O | O<br>O<br>O |

## CANCER OF THE SKIN

### Risk Factors:

- Extremely fair skin
- Prolonged exposure to the sun
  (more than 4 hours a day for 4 months out of the year)
- A history of skin cancer or malignant moles
- Moles on the soles of your feet or in areas irritated by tight clothing or shaving
- Scars from severe burns
- A non-healing scaling sore on your skin

### Awareness Counts:

You can reduce your risks for skin cancer by wearing protective clothing, such as sun hats, or by lightly covering the over-exposed parts of your body when out in the sun for long periods.

Avoid excess sun-bathing if you are fair-skinned; apply *sun-screening ointment* (different from regular suntan lotion) to filter out harmful rays.

Avoid contact with arsenic (found in some insecticides) and coal tar derivatives since these agents play a role in the development of skin cancer.

## 2. Head and Neck

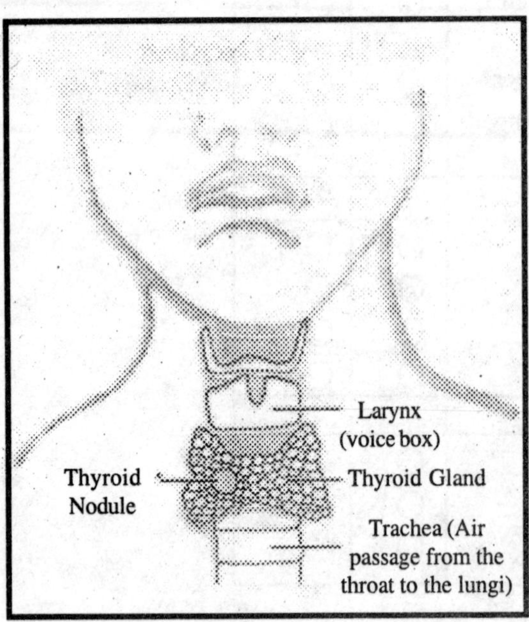


*Lumpiness or swelling of the thyroid are most often benign goiters (enlargement of the thyroid gland), while a single solid swelling (nodule) is more likely to be serious.

| A. Do you now have...? | YES | NO |
|---|---|---|
| . . . Sores or white spots in the mouth or lip lasting for one month or more | ○ | ○ |
| . . . Fullness, soreness, or swelling in the lower front of the neck | ○ | ○ |
| . . . Hoarseness or changes in the voice | | |
| . . . Difficulty or pain in swallowing lasting one month or more | | |
| . . . Any irritation in the mouth due to poor-fitting dentures or sharp teeth | ○ | ○ |
| . . . Any small solid lump in the neck area | ○ | ○ |
| **B. Has a member of your family ever had. . . ?** | | |
| . . . Cancer of the head and neck | ○ | ○ |
| **C. Have you ever had. . . ?** | | |
| . . . A tumor in the throat or neck | ○ | ○ |
| . . . A thyroid disorder | ○ | ○ |
| . . . X-ray treatments to the head or neck in youth | ○ | ○ |
| **D. Doyou...?** | | |
| . . . Smoke cigarettes, cigars or a pipe | ○ | ○ |
| . . . Drink beer, wine, or hard liquor daily | ○ | ○ |
| . . . If yes, is it more than 5 beers, 5 glasses of wine, or 3 hard liquor drinks per day? | ○ | ○ |
| . . . Fail to check inside your mouth and cheek monthly for signs of oral cancer ( spots or irritations) | ○ | ○ |
| . . . Fail to have regular dental checkups | ○ | ○ |

## Cancer of the Larynx

### Risk Factors:

- Heavy smoking
- Heavy drinking
- Cancer of the oral cavity or lung

### Awareness Counts:

*WHEN DETECTED EARL Y, CANCER OF THE LARYNX CAN BE CURED.* The preventive measure you can take is to cut down on your drinking and smoking. Alcohol and smoke are irritants to the lining of your mouth and throat. Any reduction of this kind of irritation to your mouth and throat decreases your risk.

## Cancer of the Mouth and Throat

### Risk Factors:

- A broken tooth which irritates the inside of your mouth
- Broken or ill-fitting dentures
- Heavy smoking or drinking
- A non-healing sore or white patch in your mouth

### Awareness Counts:

Any sores of the mouth, throat or gums which do not heal properly should be brought to the attention of a physician or dentist. Cutting down on alcohol consumption and smoking is an important preventive measure and can reduce your risk.

## 3. Respiratory System

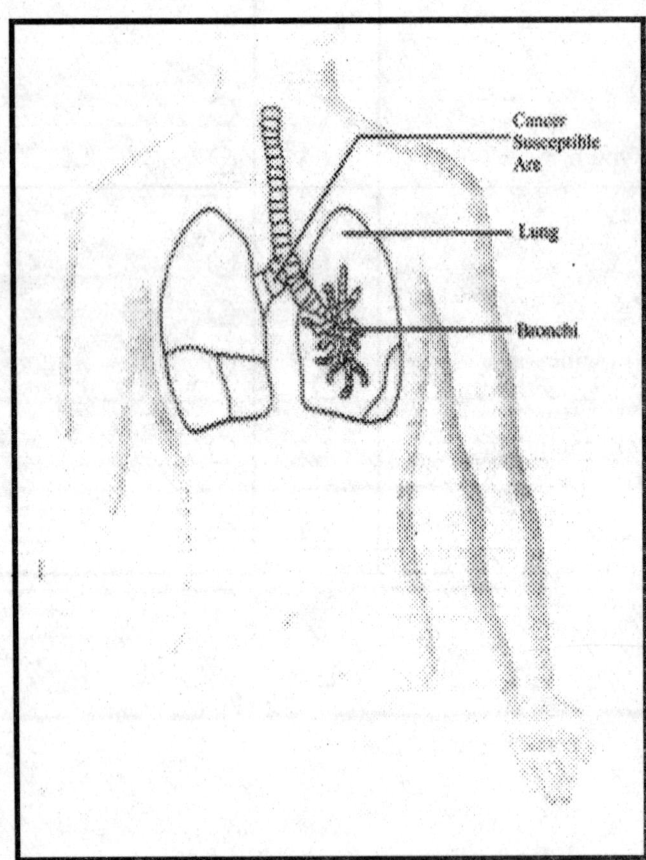


*Cancer of the ling most often starts in this area, which is continuously bathed in cigarette smoke.

| A. Do you now have....? | YES | NO |
|---|---|---|
| . . . A cough, producing sputum (mucus from the lungs), which has lasted more than one month | O | O |
| . . . Sputum which is streaked with blood | | |
| . . . Chest colds more than 3 times a year | | |
| . . . Chest pain in the same area which has lasted more than one month | O | O |

| B. Has a member of your family ever had....? | | |
|---|---|---|
| ... Tuberculosis (TB) | O | O |
| **C. Have you ever had....?** | | |
| ... Tuberculosis | O | O |
| ... Chronic bronchitis | O | O |
| ... Asthma | | |
| ... Emphysema | O | O |
| ... Pneumonia, more than once | | |
| **D. Do you....?** | | |
| ... Smoke cigarettes, cigars or a pipe | O | O |
| ... Smoke more than one pack of cigarettes a day | O | O |
| ... Work with or have you ever worked with: radio active materials, asbestos, dust of coal, stone or other mineral, nickel or chromates | O | O |

## Cancer of the Lung

### Risk factors:

- **Cigarette smoking – the smoker's risk of developing lung cancer is proportional to the number of cigarettes smoked, number of years smoking, age at which smoking started, and how deeply smoke is inhaled.**
- **Working in an occupation which brings you into contact with asbestos, nickel, chromates or radioactive material**
- A history of tuberculosis
- A chronic cough

### Awareness counts:

Your risk for lung cancer can be reduced if you avoid cigarette smoking. This is an effective preventive measure. Cigarette smoking can not only lead to death from lung cancer, but can also increase the chances of dying from other lung diseases (asthma, emphysema, pneumonia) or heart disease. Occupational exposure to the cancer causing agents mentioned should be avoided or carefully controlled. Be aware of the materials you work with.

### 4. Cardiovascular System

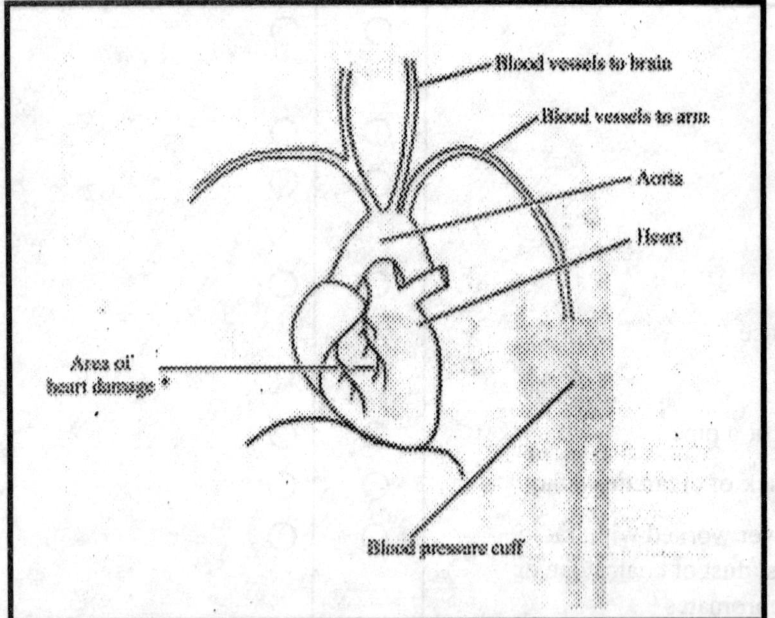


*A myocardial infarction, or heart attack, cuts off the supply of blood and causes damage to the muscle of the heart. This weakens the ability of the heart to circulate the blood.

| | YES | NO |
|---|---|---|
| **A. Do you now have. . . ?** | | |
| . . . Shortness of breath for no apparent reason | O | O |
| . . . Palpitations of the heart | O | O |
| . . . A squeezing or pressing feeling in the mid portion of your chest | | |
| . . . Swelling of both ankles | O | O |
| . . . Phlebitis (inflammation of the veins) more than once | O | O |
| . . . Unexplained dizzy spells | | |
| **B. Has a member of your family ever had. . . ?** | | |
| . . . Hypertension (high blood pressure) | O | O |
| . . . Heart disease under age 60 | O | O |
| . . . Stroke | O | O |
| **C. Have you ever had. . . ?** | | |
| . . . Rheumatic fever, scarlet fever, heart murmur | | |
| . . . Hypertension (high blood pressure) | O | O |
| . . . Stroke | O | O |
| . . . An abnormal electrocardiogram (EKG) | O | O |
| . . . Abnormal blood cholesterol | O | O |
| . . . Diabetes | O | O |
| **D. Are you. . . ?** | | |
| . . . A cigarette smoker | O | O |
| . . . Obese? (20% more than maximum for your height) | O | O |
| . . . Eating eggs, butter and red meat daily | O | O |
| . . . A person who does not exercise regularly (at least 20 minutes a day, 3 days a week) | O | O |

## Heart Disease and Stroke

### Risk factors

- A history of cardiovascular disease
- Hypertension (high blood pressure)
- Phlebitis (inflammation of the veins)
- Heavy smoking
- Overweight
- An elevated level of cholesterol in your blood
- Diabetes
- Any of the symptoms listed under A

### Awareness Counts:

You can reduce your risk for hypertension by weight control, low fat diet, avoiding cigarettes, and reduction of tension. If you already have cardiovascular disease, you must have regular examinations by your physician.

**WEIGHT CHART FOR PERSONS 20 YEARS AND OLDER**

| WEIGHT FOR MEN | | | WEIGHT FOR WOMEN | | |
|---|---|---|---|---|---|
| Height | Normal | Obese* | Height | Normal | Obese* |
| 5'3" | 118-141 | 169 | 5'0" | 100-118 | 142 |
| 5'4" | 122-145 | 174 | 5'1" | 104-121 | 145 |
| 5'5" | 126-149 | 179 | 5'2" | 107-125 | 150 |
| 5'6" | 130-155 | 186 | 5'3" | 110-128 | 154 |
| 5'7" | 134-161 | 193 | 5'4" | 113-132 | 158 |
| 5'8" | 139-166 | 199 | 5'5" | 116-135 | 162 |
| 5'9" | 143-170 | 204 | 5'6" | 120-139 | 167 |
| 5'10" | 147-174 | 209 | 5'7" | 123-142 | 170 |
| 5'11" | 150-178 | 214 | 5'8" | 126-146 | 175 |
| 6'0" | 154-183 | 220 | 5'9" | 130-151 | 181 |
| 6'1" | 158-188 | 226 | 5'10" | 133-156 | 187 |
| 6'2" | 162-192 | 230 | 5'11" | 137-161 | 193 |
| 6'3" | 165-195 | 234 | 6'0" | 141-166 | 199 |

Mens and women over forty years of age may weigh more than the above maximum for their height. This is not usually considered a health problem unless it exceeds 20% of the maximum, at which point it is regarded as obesity, and a weight control program should be instituted.

## 5. Urinary Tract

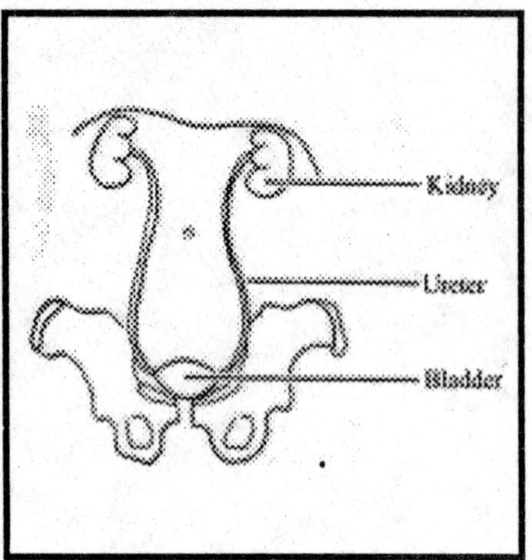


> Kidney stones or urinary infections will cause bleeding and pain, but tumors in the kidney or bladder usually cause painless bleeding.

| | YES | NO |
|---|---|---|
| **A. Do you now have. . . ?** | | |
| . . . An urge to urinate more frequently than usual | ○ | ○ |
| . . . Pain or burning upon urination | ○ | ○ |
| . . . Narrowing stream of urine | ○ | ○ |
| . . . Blood in the urine | ○ | ○ |
| **B. Has a member of your family ever had. . . ?** | | |
| . . . Cancer of the kidney or bladder | ○ | ○ |
| . . . Any congenital (present from birth) urinary tract disease | ○ | ○ |
| **C. Have you ever had. . . ?** | | |
| . . . A urinary tract infection | ○ | ○ |
| . . . Blood in the urine | ○ | ○ |
| . . . Kidney stones | ○ | ○ |
| . . . Any chronic (long-lasting) kidney disease | ○ | ○ |
| **D. Do you. . . ?** | | |
| . . . Work daily with cleaning fluids, paints. dyes or in factories which manufacture these substances | ○ | ○ |
| . . . Smoke cigarettes | ○ | ○ |

## Cancer of the Kidney and Bladder

### Risk Factors

- Congenital abnormalities of the kidney or bladder (your physician should have informed you if these conditions exist)
- Exposure to certain chemicals such as naphthalines, aniline dyes, or benzidines (be sure to read labels)
- Blood in the urine

- Frequent urinary tract infections, especially after age 50
- A history of schistosomiasis (a tropical disease)
- Heavy cigarette smoking – smoking leads to the presence of chemicals in the urine which may contribute to the development of cancer of the urinary tract

## Awareness counts:

You can prevent urinary tract cancer by avoiding occupational exposure to cancer-causing chemicals and by seeking medical attention when any symptoms exist.

Blood in the urine is always an important sign and requires *immediate* medical evaluation.

These symptoms are not specific for cancer; more commonly, they are found with bladder infection. However, a physician should be consulted. Frequent urinary tract infections may be due to underlying cancer.

## 6. Gastrointestinal Tract

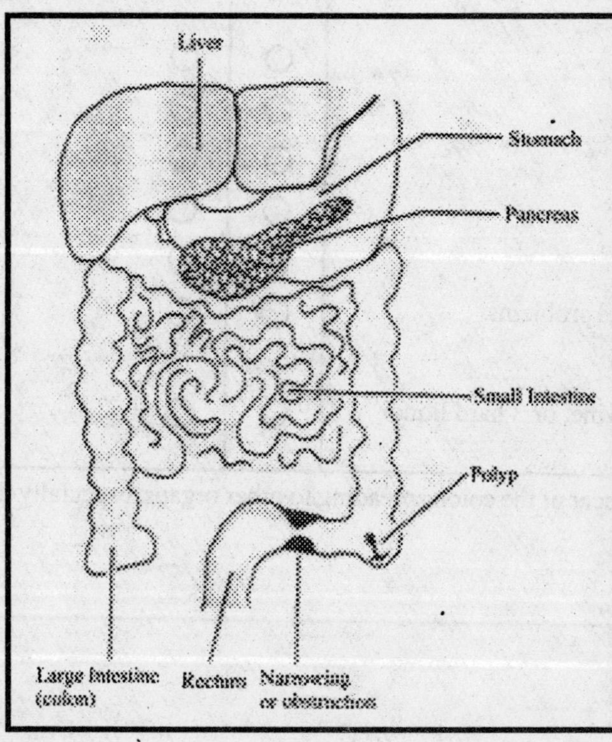


If the growth is removed early the chances of cancer of the colon spreading to other organs, especially the liver, is reduced.

| A. Do you now have. . . ? | YES | NO |
|---|---|---|
| . . . Heartburn, indigestion or abdominal pain which has lasted for more than one month | O | O |
| . . . Nausea or vomiting which has lasted more than one week | O | O |
| . . . Fullness after eating small amounts | O | O |
| . . . Unexplained weight loss, more than 10 lbs. in three months or less | O | O |
| . . . Any vomiting of blood | O | O |
| . . . Bowel movements more frequently or less frequently than usual | O | O |

| | | |
|---|---|---|
| ... Increasing narrowness of stool (ribbon-like) | O | O |
| ... Pain in rectum with bowel movements | O | O |
| ... Blood in stool, or tarry-black stool | O | O |
| ... Passage of mucus alone or with stool | O | O |
| **B. Has a member of your family ever had. . . ?** | | |
| ... Cancer of the stomach | O | O |
| ... Stomach or duodenal ulcer | O | O |
| ... Pernicious anemia | O | O |
| ... Polyps of the colon | O | O |
| ... Cancer of the colon or rectum | O | O |
| **C. Have you ever had. . . ?** | | |
| ... Gall bladder disorder | O | O |
| ... Stomach or duodenal ulcer | O | O |
| ... Pernicious anemia | O | O |
| ... Jaundice, hepatitis, cirrhosis of the liver | O | O |
| ... Polyps of the stomach or colon | O | O |
| ... Ulcerative colitis or other chronic bowel problems | O | O |
| **D. Do you. . . ?** | | |
| ... Have more than 5 beers, 5 glasses of wine, or 3 hard liquor drinks a day | O | O |

In the growth is removed early the chances of cancer of the colon spreading to other organs, especially the liver, is reduced.

## Cancer of the Stomach

### Risk Factors:

- A lack of normal stomach acid
- Pernicious anemia (a special kind of anemia treated by vitamin $B_{12}$ injections)
- Chronic gastritis or stomach polyps

### Awareness Counts:

Ulcers and ulcer symptoms may be mistaken for stomach cancer and vice versa. If any symptoms listed above last for more than one month, consult a physician.

## Cancer of the Colon

### Risk factors

- Polyps in the colon
- A family history of cancer of the colon or rectum

### Awareness counts

Any changes in your regular bowel habits should be reported to your physician promptly. Cancer of the colon is infrequent in countries where the diet is high in fruits, vegetables and fish and low in meat.

## 7. Male Reproductive System

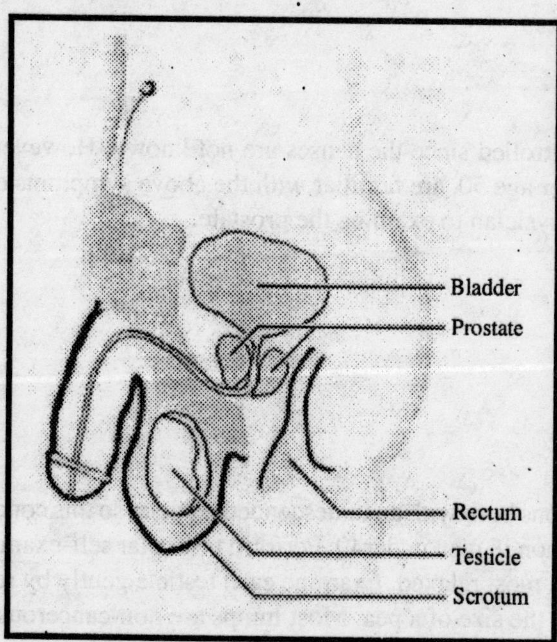


Cancer of the prostate changes the way the prostate feels when it is examined rectally. The usual rubbery firm consistency hardens to a wood-like firmness.

| | YES | NO |
|---|---|---|
| **A. Do you now have. . . ?** | | |
| . . . A lump in the testicle or pain that has lasted for more than two weeks | O | O |
| . . . Swelling of either testicle | O | O |
| . . . Difficulty in starting to urinate | O | O |
| . . . Pain or uncomfortable pressure deep in the pelvis or between the legs | O | O |
| . . . Recent problems with sexual function, such as difficulty or pain with ejaculation | O | O |
| **B. Does not apply. . . ?** | | |
| **C. Have you ever had. . . ?** | | |
| . . . Undescended testicle (only one testicle in the scrotum) | O | O |
| . . . Inflammation of the prostate | O | O |
| . . . Cancer of the prostate or testicles | O | O |
| .. Venereal disease | O | O |

| D. Do you. . . ? | | |
|---|---|---|
| . . . Forget to have your prostate examined every three years, or every year if you are over 45 | O | O |
| . . . Forget to examine your testicles for lumps or tenderness, especially if you are under 40 | O | O |

## Cancer of the Prostate

### Risk Factors:

- A history of venereal disease
- A history of prostate infections (more than 2)
- Risk increases after the age of 50

### Awareness Counts:

The occurrence of cancer of the prostate cannot be controlled since the causes are not known. However, the death rate can be greatly lowered if men, especially those over age 50, are familiar with the above symptoms of the disease and if the prostate is examined regularly. Ask your physician to examine the prostate.

## Cancer of the tests

### Risk Factors:

- Undescended testicle not corrected before age 6

### Awareness Counts:

There is a high incidence of cancer of the testicle in persons born with an undescended testicle, so this condition should be corrected early. Cancer of the testicle is most common in men under40. Perform testicular self-exam once a month after a warm bath or shower, when the scrotal skin is most relaxed. Examine each testicle gently by rolling it between the thumb and fingers. Feel for a firm lump about the size of a pea. Most lumps are non-cancerous.

Cancer of the prostate changes the way the prostate feels when it is examined rectally. The usual rubbery firm consistency hard-ens to a wood-like firmness.

## 8. Female Reproductive System

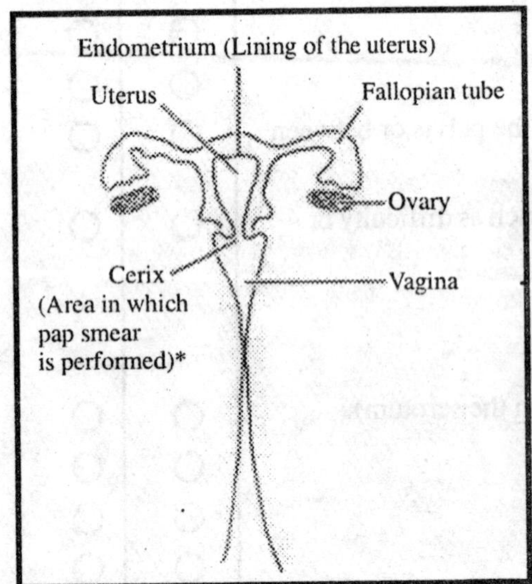


* A Pap smear is done by placing a cotton swab in the vagina and wiping cells off the surface of the cervix. The cells are then examined under a microscope for evidence of cancer. Having a Pap smear is a painless procedure.

| A. Do you now have... ? | YES | NO |
|---|---|---|
| ... Bleeding between menstrual periods | O | O |
| ... Bloody discharge unrelated to menstrual periods | O | O |
| ... Bleeding after sexual intercourse | O | O |
| ... Having completed the menopause, any bleeding or spotting | O | O |
| **B. Has a member of your mother's side of the family ever had... ?** | | |
| ... Cancer of the cervix, vagina, uterus (womb), or ovary | O | O |
| Did your mother take female hormones when she was pregnant with you? | O | O |
| **C. Have you ever had... ?** | | |
| ... Abnormal cervical (Pap) smear | O | O |
| ... Ovarian cyst or tumor | O | O |
| ... Fibroid tumor of the uterus | O | O |
| ... A Dilatation and Curettage operation ("D & C") or scraping) | O | O |
| ... Cauterization of the cervix | O | O |
| ... Other surgery of female organs | O | O |
| Do you use birth control pills? | O | O |
| Do you use female hormones (estrogens)? | O | O |
| **D. Do you...?** | | |
| ... Forget to have a Pap smear. . . | O | O |
| ... Every 3 years (if between 25-35 years of age) | O | O |
| ... Every 2 years (if between 35-45 years of age) | O | O |
| ... Every year (if over age 45) | O | O |

## Cancer of the Cervix

### Risk Factors:

- Completed pregnancies (more than 5)
- Marriage at an early age (intercourse before age 18)
- A history of syphilis or gonorrhea
- Any of the symptoms listed under A

### Awareness Countless:

Cancer of the cervix is usually slow-growing and can be detected early by the Pap smear and cured. Exam ination of any adult female should include a Pap smear, and pelvic examination as well as an examination of the breasts.

## Cancer of the endometrium

### Risk factors

- Having completed the menopause.
- Never having been pregnant
- A family history of cancer of the endometrium (lining of the uterus)
- Being a diabetic
- Having hypertension
- Being obese
- Any of the symptoms listed under A

## Cancer of the Ovary

### Awareness countless

In most cases, a woman is unaware of the presence of tumors in the ovaries. There are seldom early symptoms. The ovaries are examined at the time of a Pap and pelvic examination. These examinations should be done on a regular basis (see D. above).

## 9. Cancer of the Breast (For Women)

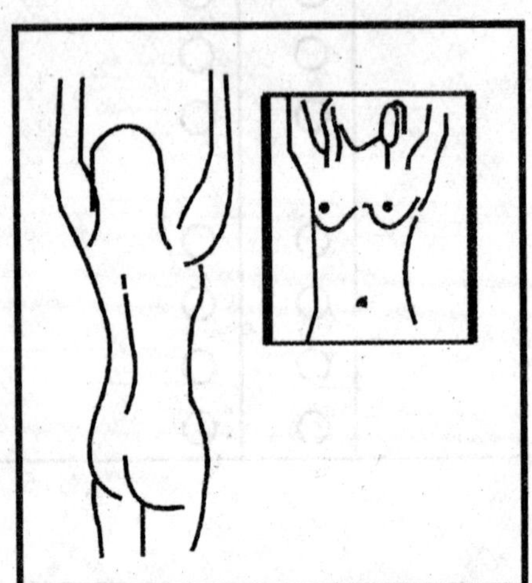

Look for any changes in size, shape, or contour of the breasts. Look for skin changes such as puckering or dimpling. Squeeze nipples gently for discharge. *(Remember it is perfectly normal to have one breast which is larger than the other.)*

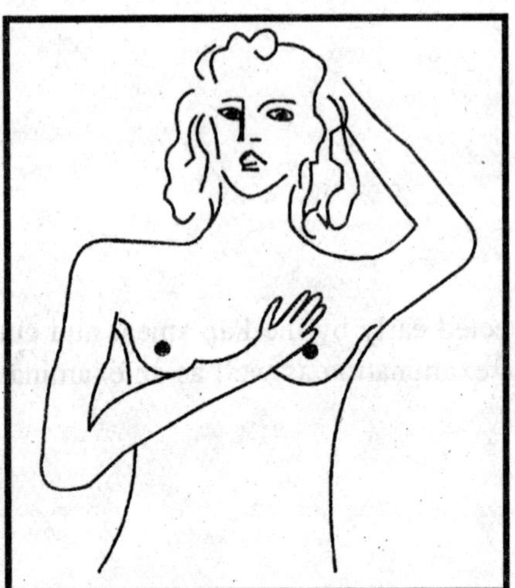

Lying down, examine the breasts one at a time with one hand behind your head and the other hand crossed over to examine the opposite breast.

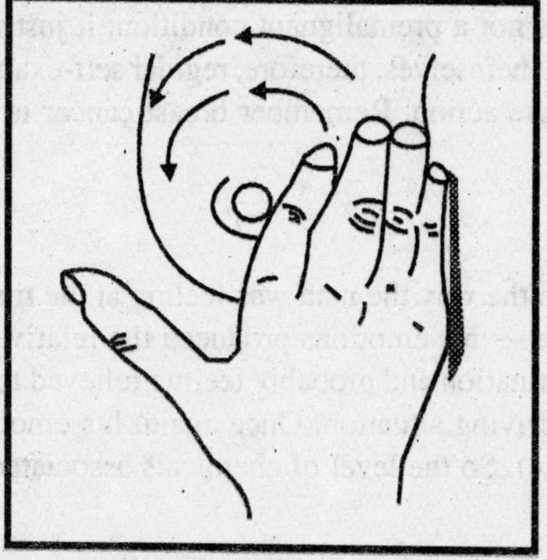

Still lying down, hold your fingers closely together; use gentle pressure and small circular motions. Start at the outer margins proceed in the same way in smaller circles until you have covered the entire breast.

| | YES | NO |
|---|---|---|
| **A. Do you now have... ?** | | |
| ... Breast pain not related to menstrual periods | O | O |
| ... A lump in either breast | O | O |
| ... Any discharge from the nipples | O | O |
| ... Ulceration (sores), puckering or scaling of breast or any unusual color change of skin or scaling or peeling of nipples | O | O |
| **B. Has a member of your mother's side of the family ever had... ?** | | |
| ... Cancer of the breast | O | O |
| ... Cysts or tumors of the breast (which were not cancer) | O | O |
| ... Any surgery of the breast | O | O |
| **C. Have you ever had... ?** | | |
| ... Cancer of the breast | O | O |
| **D. Do you... ?** | | |
| ... Forget to examine your breasts each month after your period? | O | O |

## Cancer of the Breast

### Risk Factors:

- A family or personal history of breast cancer
- Never having had a baby, if you are over age 50
- Having a first pregnancy after age 35
- Any of the symptoms under A

If you have any of the above risks and are ( ination of the breasts (a mammography) is

### Awareness Counts:

Breast cancer is curable if detected early. Breast examinations should be performed regularly and each time a Pap smear is done. Ask the doctor or nurse to teach you to do breast self-examination. Practice this yourself once a month 2 or 3 days after your menstrual period is over. Many women have cystic breasts. When cysts are present it is advisable to have breast examinations more frequently. This is not a premalignant condition, it just makes the breasts more difficult to examine. Most lumps are found by women themselves; therefore, regular self-examination is necessary. If you find any of the above symptoms, take immediate action. Remember breast cancer is curable if identified at any early stage.

## Your emotions are revealed in your blood chemistry

The levels of moradrenaline and adrenaline can be related to the way the man was feeling at the time. Where he was not in control of the situation — a passenger on the plane — his emotions produced the relative levels of adrenaline (high) and noradrenaline (low). Having reached his destination and probably feeling relieved to be on the ground, he got into his car, drove off and felt in control of the driving situation. Once again, his emotions were reflected in the levels of noradrenaline (high) and adrenaline (low). So the level of chemicals associated with the stress responce is very much determined by our emotions.

**Actions of cortisol**

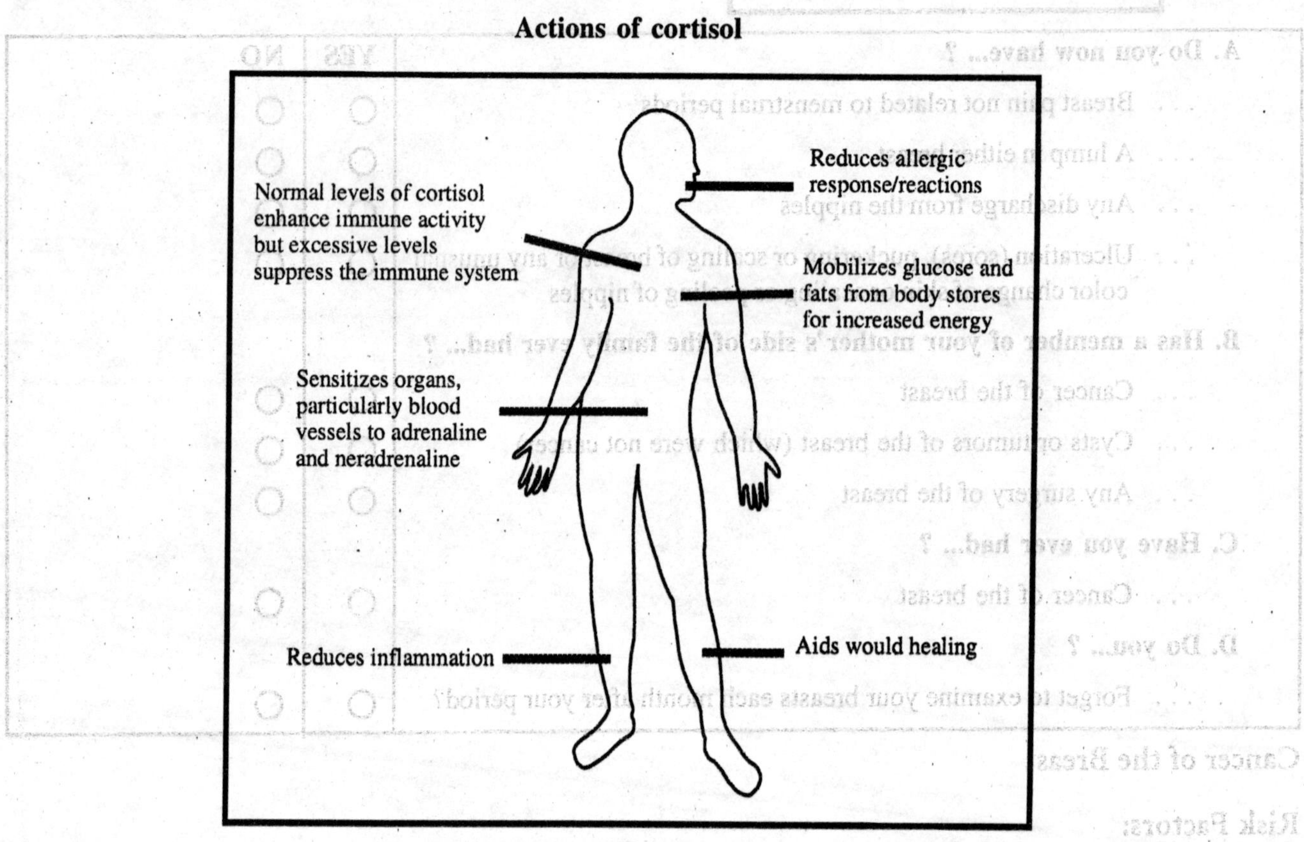

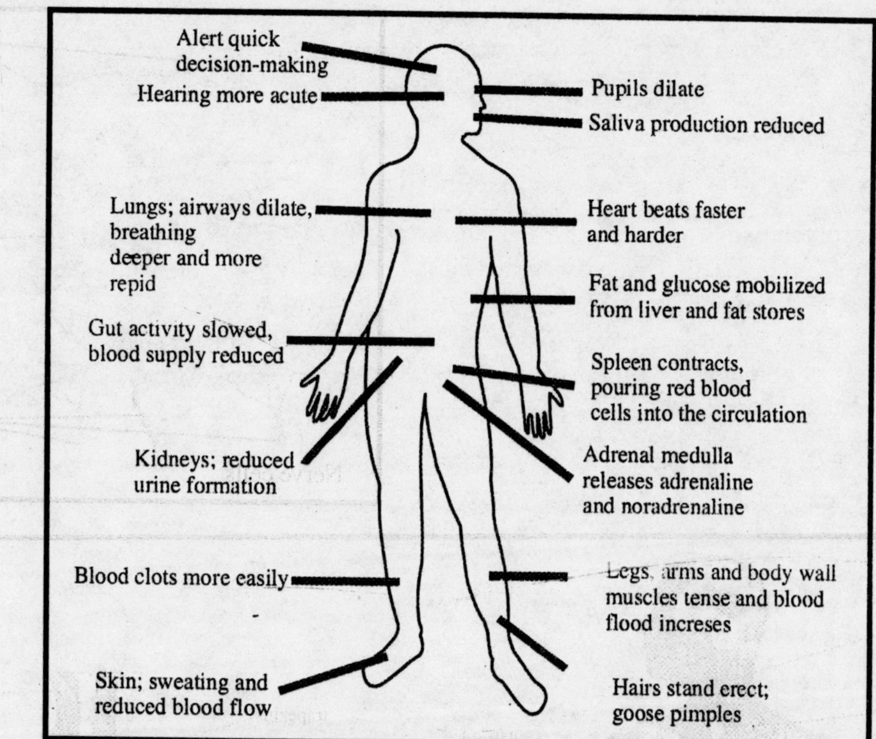


## Nervous System

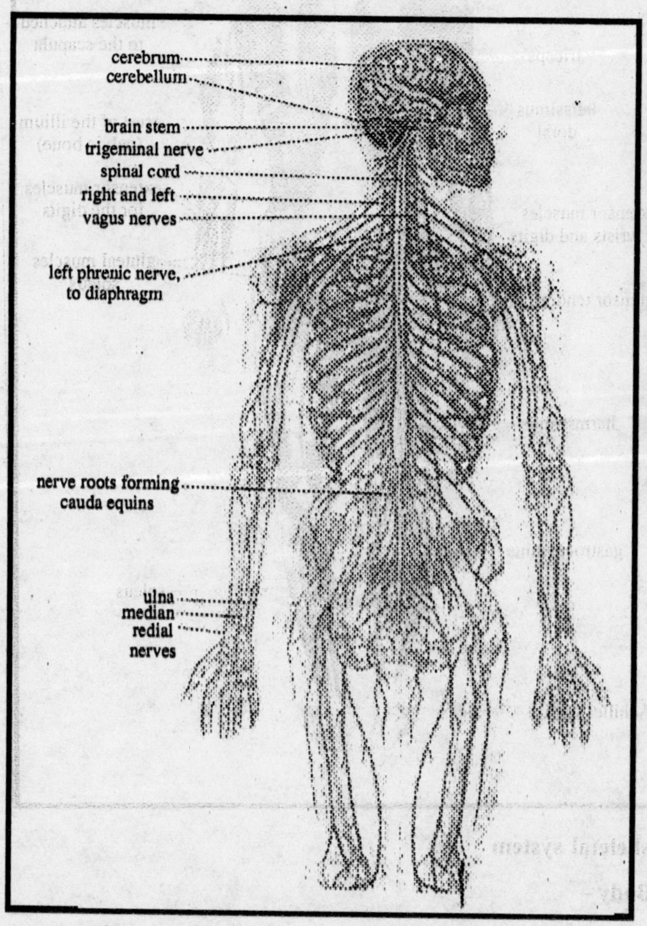

cerebrum
cerebellum
brain stem
trigeminal nerve
spinal cord
right and left vagus nerves
left phrenic nerve, to diaphragm
nerve roots forming cauda equins
ulna
median
redial
nerves

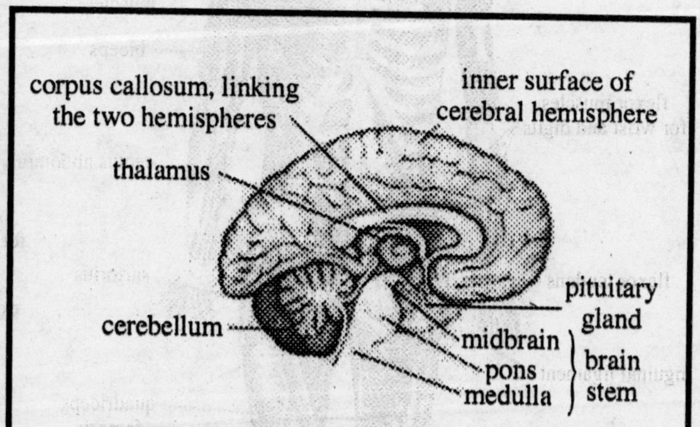

corpus callosum, linking the two hemispheres
inner surface of cerebral hemisphere
thalamus
pituitary gland
cerebellum
midbrain
pons
medulla
brain stem

Midline section of the brain

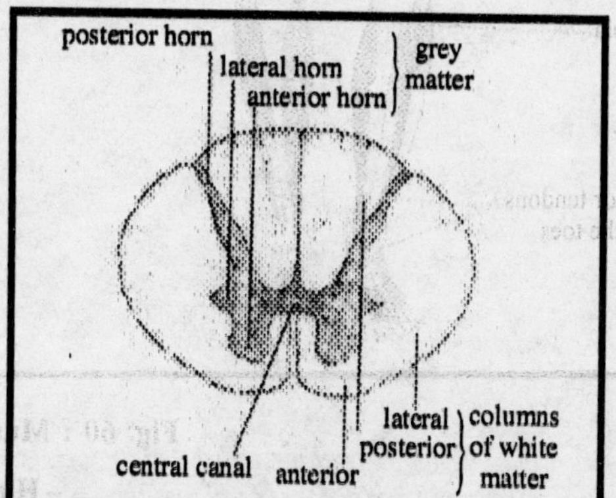

posterior horn
lateral horn
anterior horn
grey matter
lateral
posterior
anterior
columns of white matter
central canal

Section of the spinal cord in the thoracic region

The brain and spinal cord (central nervous system) and nerves connected to them (peripheral nervous system).

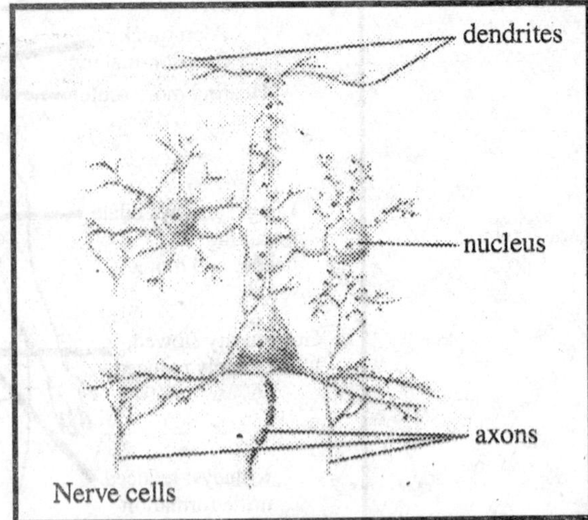

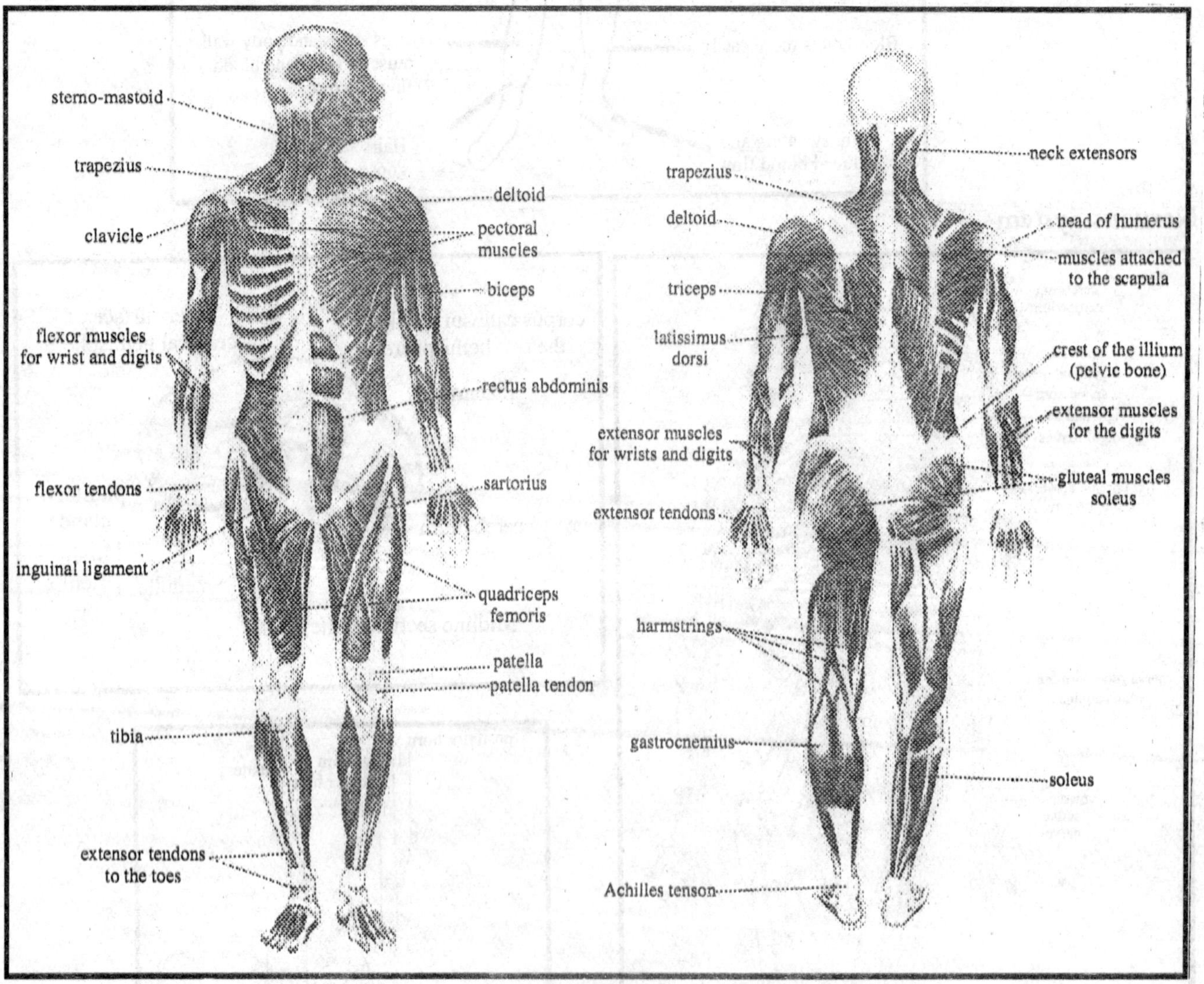

**Fig. 60 : Muscles sheletal system**

**– Human Body –**

The main skeletal muscles, from the front and back. On the right side of the body in each case the most superficial layer has been removed to show the deeper muscles

## LIFE IS A JOURNEY

"IN THE END, EACH OF US WILL BE JUDGED BY OUR STANDARD OF LIFE, NOT BY OUR STANDARD OF LIVING; BY OUR MEASURE OF GIVING, NOT BY OUR MEASURE OF WEALTH; BY OUR SIMPLE GOODNESS, NOT BY OUR SEEMING GREATNESS."

## SUCCESS

"SUCCESSFUL IS THE PERSON WHO HAS LIVED WELL, LAUGHED OFTEN AND LOVED MUCH, WHO HAS GAINED THE RESPECT OF CHILDREN, WHO LEAVES THE WORLD BETTER THAN THEY FOUND IT, WHO HAS NEVER LACKED APPRECIATION FOR THE EARTH'S BEAUTY, WHO NEVER FAILS TO LOOK FOR THE BEST IN OTHER OR GIVE THE BEST OF THEMSELVES."

**Actions of adrenaline and Noradrenaline**

# SUBJECT INDEX

## A



## B



## C

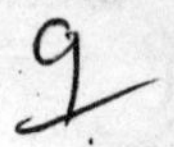



## U



## V



## W



## Y



## Z